A CLASSICAL DICTIONARY OF INDIA

A
CLASSICAL DICTIONARY OF INDIA

ILLUSTRATIVE OF THE

MYTHOLOGY PHILOSOPHY
LITERATURE ANTIQUITIES ARTS
MANNERS CUSTOMS &C.

OF

THE HINDUS

JOHN GARRETT

GYAN

Published by

Gyan Publishing House
5, Ansari Road
Daryaganj, New Delhi-110002
Phone: 011-47034999, 9811692060
E-mail: books@gyanbooks.com

Distribution Network
gyanbooks.com
India, USA, Canada, UK, Australia, France

ISBN: 978-81-212-9362-4 (PB)
First Published, 1871

2nd Impression 2023

Printed at: Gyan Press, Delhi.

A CLASSICAL DICTIONARY OF INDIA

AUTHOR: JOHN GARRETT

A

CLASSICAL DICTIONARY OF INDIA

ILLUSTRATIVE OF THE

MYTHOLOGY PHILOSOPHY

LITERATURE ANTIQUITIES ARTS

MANNERS CUSTOMS &c.

OF

THE HINDUS

BY JOHN GARRETT

DIRECTOR OF PUBLIC INSTRUCTION IN MYSORE

EDITOR OF THE BHAGAVAT GITA, IN SANSKRIT AND CANARESE

PANCHA TANTRA, KATHA MANJARI, SHABDA MANI DARPANA, ETC.

MADRAS

HIGGINBOTHAM AND CO

1871

PREFACE.

No Student of Indian Literature, whether he has studied it in its ancient classic tongue, the Sanskrit, in which its earliest and most original works are written; or has derived his acquaintance with it from the scantier range of some modern Indian vernacular, but has felt the difficulties that arise from the frequent mention of mythical personages, places, and objects, whose very names are so utterly unknown to him that he often even fails to recognise that they *are* proper names (oriental characters having no capital letters to indicate this) while of the facts concerning them he has little or no means of information. Hence he has to trust to such information as he can obtain from his Múnshi —information mostly very imperfect and often quite incorrect. The course of many years' reading gives the desired knowledge, but it is acquired at the cost of much time, labour, and research—nearly all of which might be saved did any such work exist for the Indian student, as the classical learner has long had in his "Lempriere," and now has in the well-known and far superior Dictionaries of Dr. William Smith.

The Universities in India have placed the Sanskrit and some of the vernacular languages, in the same position as the Universities of Europe have assigned to the languages of ancient Greece and Rome. A knowledge of ancient Hindu Literature is therefore now necessary to the attainment of University honours. At present there is no work in existence in the form of a Classical Dictionary, designed to afford direct aid to a student in acquiring a knowledge of the Mythology and Antiquities of India.

To supply in some measure these wants is the object of the present work. It contains an account of all the Hindu deities, and all the mythical personages and objects, that are likely to be met with in the study of Hindu Literature, whether Sanskrit or vernacular. The various terms of Brahmanical and Buddhistical theology and ritual, and of the schools of Indian philosophy, will be found briefly explained. Such information as can be obtained on the subject of ancient Indian Geography has been given. It may be thought that many names of comparatively obscure persons and places have been included. But the Hindus attach great importance to their genealogical lists, and the present work was intended to contain *every name* occurring in their ancient books, though nothing is recorded of them but the line or family to which they belonged. No doubt many names, some probably of importance, have been omitted; but this is only what might be expected in the first edition of a book of this nature.

The work was commenced about twenty years ago, and most of the legends were at first taken from the vernacular writings current in Southern India; but when the valuable work of Dr. JOHN MUIR,* came under the writer's notice, he felt it his duty to exclude all the traditionary and imperfect accounts previously collected, and to substitute for them extracts from the authentic writings of the Hindus, which alone can furnish a reliable knowledge of their religion, mythology, and historical traditions. As however the materials of the work have been picked up at intervals, and put together as opportunities occurred, it is possible that the critical reader will discover many defects; though it is doubtless very much more trustworthy than it could have been had it been published before the appearance of Dr. MUIR'S volumes.

The writer has also been greatly indebted to Professor WILSON'S Translation of the Vishṇu Purána, as well as to the Essays on Sanskrit Literature, and on the Religion of the Hindus, of the same distinguished scholar. The editions of the Mahábhárata and Rámáyana published by Mr. TALBOYS WHEELER, have also been laid under contribution. The Poetical Translation of the Rámáyana by Mr. GRIFFITH, Professor of Sanskrit at the Benares College, the 'Idylls from the Sanskrit,' and 'Scenes from the Rámáyan' by the same author, have served to enrich and enliven the volume with many passages of great beauty; while Mr. GRIFFITH'S own Notes, and others selected by him from SCHLEGEL, GORRESIO, and others, have thrown light on several difficult points.

* "Original Sanskrit Texts, on the Origin and History of the People of India, their Religion and Institutions."

Professor MAX MULLER'S History of Ancient Sanskrit Literature, and his Chips from a German Workshop, have supplied much information, and many extracts of great value have been taken from those works. The articles on Hinduism contributed by Professor GOLDSTUCKER to the English Cyclopædia, and more especially to CHAMBERS' Encyclopædia, and the few parts of the Sanskrit Dictionary issued by the same learned author, have given to the world the fruits of great research, and the writer has availed himself of much new matter in the above publications.

Many other works might be specified which have added to the interest and utility of the present volume. Among others the following should not be omitted. Ancient and Mediæval India, by Mrs. MANNING. Indian Epic Poetry, by Professor MONIER WILLIAMS. Handbook of Sanskrit Literature, by G. SMALL, M. A. ZIEGENBALG'S Manual of the Mythology of Southern India. TOD'S Annals and Antiquities of Rajasthan. COLEBROOKE'S Essays, &c., &c. A complete list of the editions used will be found on another page.

In the Prospectus of this work published a year ago, the writer, in acknowledging that the Mythological legends of India had never commanded the attention accorded to those of Greece and Rome, expressed an opinion that this has arisen not only from the extravagant oriental imagination by which they are characterized, but chiefly from the fact that they have never yet been studied by Europeans in youth. There is no doubt that much of the charm of early Greek and Roman story belongs to the associations in the midst of which a knowledge of it was first acquired. The interest that educated Europeans feel in the classic tales of Greece and Rome may be traced to the familiarity acquired with them in the enthusiasm of youth, amid scenes and circumstances which stand out through life as bright phases of their existence.

The beauty, however, as well as the value, of the two great Epics of India, is now acknowledged. They are no longer regarded as worthless fictions or mere idle flights of imagination.* It is now admitted that these two heroic poems, the Rámáyana and the Mahábhárata, contain "all that we can ever know of India's early history;" and that notwithstanding their exaggerations, they bring before us a state of society, and a condition of thought and feeling, through which mankind has had to pass in pre-historic times. The people who figured in these early tales were men and women 'of like passions with ourselves'—animated by the same joys and hopes—depressed by the same sorrows and disappointments. It is consequently interesting to observe the traces they have left behind them—"their foot-

* "In the Rámayana all is pure measureless raving. An imagination which seems to combine the advantages of mania, superstition, and drunkenness, is put a-going, makes a set of what it names worlds, of its own, and fills them with all sorts of agents; gods, sages, demi-gods, monkeys, and a numberless diversity of fantastic entities, at once magnified and distorted to the last transcendent madness of extravagance,—some additional monster still striding and bellowing into the hurly-burly, whenever the poet thinks it not sufficiently turbulent and chaotic."—JOHN FOSTER, *Eclectic Review, Sept.* 1810.

prints on the sands of time"—to glean all we can from the records they have left us of what people used to think and say and do at a period so remote as to take our thoughts to the very infancy of the human race.

" Greatly as our times are distinguished by discovery and progress, we are yet continually reminded, amidst its changes, of that world of the Past out of which the Present is born. The century which has witnessed such onward strides of physical and political science, has also unlocked the secrets of the hieroglyphics of Egypt. Major RAWLINSON is now giving a voice to dumb inscriptions upon Persian rocks; and in the same way, in India's mythic poetry, we become contemporaries with Greece's earliest history. The heroic times and youth of the race thus rise up in earth's later days, in startling contrast with our science and commerce, as if nature would expressly teach us that there lies a romance in the past which can never grow obsolete to man; and howsoever our civilization may change us, and under all the new developments of the human race, the memories of old ages will still survive and come back to us, like the stories of childhood among the sterner realities of manhood."*

BANGALORE,
August 15, 1871.

J. GARRETT.

* Westminster Review, Vol. L, p. 62.

LIST OF BOOKS QUOTED OR REFERRED TO IN THE FOLLOWING PAGES.

Adelung's Historical Sketch of Sanskrit Literature, Oxford, 1832.

Asiatic Researches, 11 vols., London, 1812.

Ainslie's Materia Indica, 2 vols., London, 1826.

Balfour's Cyclopædia of India, Madras, 1862.

Ballantyne's Aphorisms of the Sankya Philosophy.

Ballantyne's Aphorisms of the Nyáya Philosophy.

Ballantyne's Lecture on the Vedánta.

Ballantyne's Tarka Sangraha.

} Benares and Allahabad, 1849 to 1852.

Ballantyne's Christianity and Hindu Philosophy, London, 1859.

Benares Magazine, 1851.

Buchanan's (F.) Journey through Mysore, &c., 3 vols., London, 1807.

Brande's Dictionary of Science, Literature and Art, 3 vols., London, 1 867

Bernier's Travels in India, 2 vols., 8vo., London, 1826.

Bower's Chintámani, Madras, 1868.

Colebrooke's (H. T.) Miscellaneous Essays, 2 vols., 8vo., London, 1837.

Carey's Rámáyana, Serampore, 1806.

Cox's Mythology of the Aryan Nations, 2 vols., 8vo., London, 1870.

Calcutta Review, 35 volumes.

Cudworth's Intellectual System of the Universe, 3 vols., 8vo., London.

Chambers' Encyclopædia, 10 vols.

Dubois' Manners and Customs of People of India, quarto, London, 1817.

Duff's India and Indian Missions, Edinburgh, 1841.

Elliot's (H. M.) Memoir of the History, &c., of the Races of N. W. P. of India, by Beames, 2 vols., 1869.

Elphinstone's History of India, 2 vols., London, 1843.

Erskine's History of India, 2 vols., 1854.

Elphinstone's Caubul, Account of, quarto, London, 1815.

English Cyclopædia.

Forbes' Oriental Memoirs, 2 vols., 8vo., London, 1834.

Frere's Old Deccan Days, London, 1870.

Goldstucker's Sanskrit Dictionary, 6 parts.

Grote's History of Greece, 12 vols., 8vo., London, 1846-56.

Griffith's Idylls from the Sanskrit, London, 1866.

Griffith's Scenes from the Rámáyan, Benares, 1870.

Griffith's Rámáyan of Valmíki, vols. I and II, Benares, 1870-71.

Haug's, Dr. Aitareya Brahmanam of the Rig Veda, 2 vols., Bombay, 1863.
Halhed's Code of Gentoo Laws, London, 1777.
Hardy's (Spence) Eastern Monachism, London, 1850.
Hardy's (Spence) Manual of Buddhism.
Heber's Journey through the Upper Provinces of India, 3 vols., 8vo., London, 1828.
Hunter's Comparative Dictionary of the Non-Aryan Languages of India, quarto, 1869.
Hunter's Annals of Rural Bengal, London, 1868.
Jones', (Sir W.) Works, 13 vols., 8vo., London, 1807.
Journal of the Asiatic Society of Bengal, Calcutta, 1835-45.
Kennedy, Vans, Col., Researches into the Nature and Affinity of Ancient and Hindu Mythology, London, 1831.
Marshman's History of India, 3 vols., London, 1867.
Mill's History of India, by Wilson, 9 vols., London, 1858.
Manning's, Mrs., Ancient and Mediæval India, 2 vols., London, 1869.
Moor's Hindu Pantheon, London, 1810.
Muir's Original Sanskrit Texts on the Origin and History of the People of India, their Religion and Institutions, London, 1868, vol. i, 2d edition, vol. iii, 2d edition, 1868, vol. iv, 1863, vol. v, 1870.
Muller's (Max) History of Ancient Sanskrit Literature, 1859.
Muller's (Max) Chips from a German Workshop, 3 vols., 1868-70.
Muller's (Max) Lectures on the Science of Language, 2 vols., 1866.
Muller's (Max) Rig Veda Sanhita, London, 1869.
Oriental Astronomer, a complete System of Hindu Astronomy, Jaffna, 1848.
Sherring's Sacred City of the Hindus, London, 1868.
Small's Handbook of Sanskrit Literature, London, 1866.
Thomson's Translation of the Bhagavad-Gita, Hertford, 1855.
Ward's View of the History, Literature and Mythology of the Hindus, 3 vols., London, 1822.
Wheeler's History of India from the Earliest Times, 2 vols., London, 1867-69.
Wilson's (H. H.) Vishnu Purána, quarto, London, 1840.
Wilson's Works, by Dr. Rost and others, 10 vols., London, 1862-70.
Wilson's Select Specimens of the Theatre of the Hindus, 2 vols., London, 1835.
Wilson's Sanskrit and English Dictionary, Calcutta, 1840.
Williams' Indian Epic Poetry, London, 1863.
Williams' English and Sanskrit Dictionary, London, 1851.

ABBREVIATIONS.

A. S. L.	Muller's Ancient Sanskrit Literature.
A. & M. I.	Mrs. Manning's Ancient and Mediæval India.
H. P.	Moor's Hindu Pantheon.
H. S. L.	Handbook of Sanskrit Literature.
I. E. P.	Williams' Indian Epic Poetry.
O. S. T.	Muir's Original Sanskrit Texts.
V. P.	Wilson's Vishnu Purána, the quarto edition unless where the 8vo. edition is specified.

ERRATA.

At page 218, line 19, for *Glendoveer's* read *Glendoveers.*

At page 688, line 13, for *assist* read *assert.*

At page 518, line ' 6, for *Griffiths'*, read *Griffith's.*

☞ This mistake has occurred several times in connection with this name.

A

CLASSICAL DICTIONARY OF INDIA.

अ **Akara**—The first letter in the Sanskrit and all Indian Alphabets. A name claimed by Krishna as the Supreme Being, (Bhagavat Gíta, Chapter X, verse 33) similar to the name Alpha given in the Book of Revelation to the Lord Jesus Christ.

Abhasara—The name of the thirteenth heaven of Buddhism.

Abhaya—(Fearlessness) one of the sons of Dharma, see Vishnu Purána, p. 55.

Abhidhana Chintamani—A vocabulary of the Jain doctrines written by Hemachandra, and described by Professor Wilson as one of great utility that may be relied on.

Abhidharmma.—The third class of the sacred books of the Buddhists, which are called in Páli, the language in which they are written, Pittakattyan, from Pittakan, a basket or chest, and táyo, three, the text being divided into three great classes. The Abhidarmma contain instructions which the Buddhists imagine to be addressed to the inhabitants of the celestial worlds. This is accordingly accounted the highest class of sacred books, and the expounders of it are to be held in the highest honor, for it contains *pre-eminent truths*, as the word itself implies. The books of which it consists are not in the form of sermons, but specify terms and doctrines, with definitions and explanations. The work contains seven sections.—*Gardiner*.

Abhijit—A Yádava Chief, V. P., p. 436.

Abhimani—The eldest son of Brahma: he was an Agni, and by his wife Swábá had three sons of surpassing brilliancy, Pávaka, Pavamana, and Súchi. They had forty-five sons, who, with themselves and Abhimáni, constitute the forty-nine fires. V. P.

Abhimana—In Hindu philosophy means 'selfish conviction.' See Colebrooke's Essays, Vol. I, p. 242.

Abhimanyu—1, A son of Arjúna and Subhadra, renowned for his strength and valour. He was married to Uttara, the daughter of Rája Viráta. He fought with distinguished valour on the first day of the great war; cutting down the ensign in Bhíshma's chariot. On the second day he slew a son of Duryódhana, and when attacked by the latter was rescued by Arjúna. On the thirteenth day of the war, he was commanded by Yudhishthira to charge the Kauravas who were drawn up in the form of a spider's web; he drove his chariot into the enemy's ranks and performed prodigies of valour, but was finally overpowered by six warriors and slain. His posterity through the line of his son *Paríkshit*, were the royal race of the lunar line at Hastinápura, (old Delhi); 2, A son of Chákshusha. V. P., 98.

Abhiras—1, An ancient race of people inhabiting the North-West of India: they are mentioned in the Mahá Bhárata, the Rámáyana, and in the V. P., but nothing is known of their history; 2, The name of a dynasty referred to in the V. P. supposed to have reigned in Magadha, B. C. 200.

Abhutarajasas—A class of gods of the fifth Manwantara.

Abhyudaya—Offerings to the progenitors of an individual and of mankind, which form part of a religious ceremony on an occasion of rejoicing or an accession of prosperity. See Vriddi Srádda.

Abja—The father of Vísala who became incarnate as Nárâyana.

Aborigines—In all the large jungles and hilly tracts of country throughout India there exist thousands of human beings in a state not very different from that of the Germans as described by Tacitus nearly two thousand years ago. These primitive races are the ancient heritors of the whole soil, from all the rich and open parts of which they were expelled by the Hindu.

These non-Aryan races have always been misrepresented and oppressed. The early Sanscrit writers depicted "the forest tribes as black noseless demons, of small stature and inarticulate speech." In the two great epics and in the Puránas they are termed Rákshakas.

"During the struggle between the worn-out Sanscrit civilization and the impetuous prime of Islam, the Hindus discovered the value of the aboriginal races. Many chiefs of noble Áryan blood maintained their independence by such alliances; others founded new kingdoms amongst the forest peoples. To this day some of the tribes exhibit a black original section living side by side with a fair-skinned composite kindred, sprung from the refugees; and the most exalted Hindu princes have to submit to a curious aboriginal rite on their accession to the throne. It was stated before the Royal Asiatic Society in 1852 that the investiture of the Rájput Rájah of Nerwar is not complete till one of his purely aboriginal subjects, a Mina, paints a round spot on his forehead with blood freshly drawn from the toe of another Mina. Without this formal recognition his non-Áryan subjects could not be depended upon; when once it has been performed their fidelity has never been known to waver. They form the treasury and palace guards, hold the personal safety of the prince entirely in their hands, and supply the sole escort to whom he entrusts the honor of his daughters when they go abroad. The Ranah of Udayapur, cited by General Briggs as the highest in rank of all the sovereigns in India, renders the same homage, however ill it may comport with his caste and personal dignity, to the traditions of his aboriginal subjects. Before he ascends the throne his forehead must first be marked with the blood of a Bhíl. The Hinduized chieftains of Central India, receive investiture by the blood of a pure Kol; and so strong a hold has this ceremony on the minds of the people, that amongst the Cheris—once a great tribe, who defended themselves with honor against Shere Shah and the imperial army, now reduced to five or six families,—the head of the little community is still installed under the title of Rájah, with the token of the round spot of warm aboriginal blood.

"But it is not the Hindus alone that have proved the loyalty of these neglected races. Scarcely a single administrator has ruled over them for any length of time, without finding his prejudices conquered, and his heart softened, and leaving on record his sorrow for their present condition, and his belief in their capabilities for good. * * * * 'They are faithful, truthful and attached to their superiors, writes General Briggs, ready at all times to lay down their lives for those they serve, and remarkable for their indomitable courage. These qualities have been always displayed in our service. The aborigines of the Carnatic were the sepoys of Clive and of Coote. A few companies of the same stock joined the former great Captain from Bombay, fought the battle of Plassey in Bengal, and laid the foundation of our Indian empire. They have since distinguished themselves in the corps of Pioneers and Engineers, not only in India, but in Ava and Afghanistan, and in the celebrated defence of Jelalabad. An unjust prejudice has grown up against them in the armies of Madras and Bombay, where they have done best service, produced by the feelings of contempt for them, existing among the Hindu and Mahomedan troops. They have no prejudices themselves, are always ready to serve abroad, and embark on board ship, and I believe no instance of mutiny has ever occurred among them." '* Other testimonies are quoted by the same writer from equally high authorities all showing that the truthfulness and fidelity of these despised races are most satisfactorily established.

Their condition, after many centuries of suffering, is now likely to be improved. Their character and claims are beginning to be understood. It is seen too how they may be utilized by being made to take the place of English soldiers. "In interest, in race, in religion, in habits of life, they are cut off from the Hindus and Mussulmans by a gulf of whose breadth the people of Christian States can form no idea ; and their ethnical repugnance is kept in a constant glow by the remembrance of ancient wars and recent wrongs." By extensively employing these tribes as a military police and as soldiers, we should not only relieve the English population of a burden, but we should offer a livelihood to brave predatory peoples whom the stern order of British rule has deprived of an important source of subsistence."* See Bhíls, Bhúteeas, Gonds, Ghúrkas, etc.

* W. W. Hunter, Preface to Non-Aryan Dictionary.

Achara—A name of Siva. A name of Vishnu. BRAHM, the Supreme BEING, (in this sense it is sometimes *Mas.*) The word also means eternal beatitude, or exemption from further transmigration. Also religious austerity or moral merit.

Acharas—Observances of caste and order. The V. P. contains a complete and systematic description of the Ácháras, or personal and social customs and obligations of the Hindus. See Chapter VIII *et seq*.

Acharya—The term Achárya sometimes means a priest; but its most usual meaning is a spiritual guide or preceptor, one who invests the student with the sacred thread, and who instructs him in the law of sacrifices, and the mysteries of religion.

Achyuta—A common name of Vishnu: meaning "the imperishable."

Achyuta—Krishnánanda Níthi, author of a commentary on the Siddhánta Kalpataru, called Krishnalankára.

Adbhuta—The Indra of the ninth Manwantara.

Adharma—A son of Brahma—the husband of Falsehood (Mrisha) and the father of Hypocrisy and Deceit; (Dambha and Máyá). From them descended Covetousness, Wrath, Slander, Fear, &c.

Adharma—1. Unrighteousness; all behaviour contrary to the Sruti and Smriti, or religious and legal institutions.

2. In philosophy, according to the Nyáya and Vaiṣeshika: moral demerit, the result of doing what is forbidden, the peculiar cause of pain, one of the twenty-four qualities united with substance. According to the Sánkhya, one of the changeable dispositions of the mind, which being the efficient cause, makes the soul migrate into an animal, a deer, a bird, a reptile, a vegetable, a mineral. According to the Buddhistic doctrine it is the consequence of upádána or exertion of body or speech. According to the Jains it is that which causes the soul in general to continue embarrassed with body, notwithstanding its capacity for ascent and natural tendency to soar.

3. As a personification, Adharma occurs in the Puránas as one of the Prajápatis or mind-born sons of Brahmá; his wife is

Hinsá (mischief) on whom he begot Anrita (falsehood) and Nikriti (immorality) or according to others, Mrishá (falsehood) and his children Dambha (hypocrisy) and Máyá (deceit) who were adopted by Nirriti (misfortune). Adharma is also mentioned as one of the eighteen servants of the sun. V. P.

1. **Adhidaiwata**—"The Supreme Being in his personality, considered as a deity, and therefore the Supreme Being in his relation to the gods. This includes the two parts, the essence of spirit, and matter, called

(*a*) *Adhyátma*, the essence of spirit, the origin of souls, and the Supreme Being in his relation to man or individual soul;

(*b*) *Adhibhuta*, the material essence, or the Supreme Being in his relation to matter.

2. The one indivisible (*akshara*); that is, the universal energy called indivisible, as contrasted with individual souls (*kshara*).

3. *Adhiyajna*, the Supreme Being as Vishnu or Krishna, a manifest object of worship, and therefore the Supreme Being in his relation to religion."—*J. C. Thomson.*

Adhipurusha—The presiding spirit of the Universe—descended from Vishnu.

Adhiratha—A son of Satyakarman, one of the kings of Anga. He found Karna in a basket on the banks of the Ganges, where he had been exposed by his mother Pritha.

Adhogati—The Jains believe that below this world there is a world called *Adhogati*, the Abyss, the nethermost hell, above which there are seven infernal worlds; and above these again are ten *Pavanalokas*, purifying worlds, (Purgatories) above which is this world of earth.

Adhosiras—One of the divisions of the Hindu Hell (or Naraka) in which persons are punished for bribery. V. P.

Adhyaropa—A technical term used in the *Vedánta* system of Hindu Philosophy, meaning "erroneous imputation"—an allegation that the Unreal is the Real. One of the four Requisites to the study of the Vedánta is, "the discrimination of the eternal substance from the transient." This is the discerning that God is the eternal substance, and that all else is non-eternal. To understand this fully the Adhyáropa or erroneous imputation must be refuted.

Adhyatma—The ministers of the Soul. A technical phrase in the Sánkhya philosophy. Thirteen instruments or ministers of the soul are enumerated, each of which has a "province" and "presiding deity," viz :—

1—Intellect is a minister of the soul,
" Whatever is to be understood" is its province ;
Brahma is its presiding deity.

2—Self-consciousness is a minister of soul ;
Whatever is to be believed is its province,
Rudra is its presiding deity.

3—Mind is a minister of soul ;
Whatever is to be resolved on is its province,
The moon is its presiding deity.

4—The hearing is a minister of soul,
Whatever is to be heard is its province ;
The Ether is its supernatural presiding power.

5—The touch is a minister of soul,
Whatever is to be touched is its province ;
The air is its supernatural presiding power.

6—The sight is a minister of soul,
Whatever is to be seen is its province ;
The sun is its presiding deity.

7—The taste is a minister of soul,
Whatever is to be tasted is its province ;
Varuna (the god of waters) is its presiding deity.

8—The smell is a minister of soul,
Whatever is to be smelled is its province ;
The earth is its supernatural presiding power.

9—The voice is a minister of soul,
Whatever is to be uttered is its province ;
Saraswati (or Fire) is its presiding deity.

10—The hands are ministers of soul,
Whatever is to be grasped is their province ;
Indra is their presiding deity.

11—The feet are ministers of soul,
Whatever is to be gone over is their province ;
Vishnu is their presiding deity.

12—The organ of excretion is a minister of soul,
Whatever is to be excreted is its province ;
Mitra is its presiding deity.

13—The organ of generation is a minister of soul,
What is to be enjoyed is its province ;
Prajápati is its presiding deity.—*Ballantyne.*

Adhyatma Ramayana—A spiritualized version of the Rámáyana, being an abridgment of the story, the authorship of which is attributed to the mythical Vyása, in which the whole has been spiritualized, and every conflicting incident either explained or omitted, whilst the greatest stress has been laid upon the character of Ráma as a—" saviour and deliverer."—*Wheeler.*

Adhyatmika—In the Sánkhya philosophy. The pain which arises from any of the *Adhyátma* or instruments of soul.

Adhvarya priests—The third class of priests at sacrifices, who had to prepare the sacrificial ground, to adjust the vessels, to procure the animals, and other sacrificial oblations, to light the fire, to kill the animal, and do all the manual labor.

Adi—The first. A name given to the Bramha Purána, containing ten thousand stanzas.

Adina—The son of Sahadeva, celebrated in the wars between the demons and the gods.

Aditi—A daughter of Daksha, wife of Kásyapa, and mother of the gods. At the churning of the ocean, Adití received the ear-rings then produced, which were given her by Krishna. Her history, with that of the other daughters of Daksha, is regarded by Professor Wilson as an allegorical personification of Astronomical phenomena. " The thoughts of primitive humanity were not only different from our thoughts, but different also from what we think their thoughts ought to have been. The poets of the Veda indulged freely in theogonic speculations without being frightened by any contradictions. They knew of Indra as the greatest of gods, they knew of Agni as the god of gods, they knew of Varuna as the ruler of all; but they were by no means startled at the idea that their Indra had a mother, or that their Agni was born like a babe from the friction of two fire-sticks, or that Varuna and his brother Mitra were nursed in the lap of Adití." (*Max Müller*). "Adití is an object of frequent celebration in the Rig-veda, where she is supplicated for blessings on children and cattle, for protection and for forgiveness." (*Muir.*) "Adití, an ancient god or goddess, is in reality the earliest name invented to express the Infinite; not the Infinite as the result of a long process of abstract reasoning, but the visible Infinite, visible by the naked eye, the endless expanse, beyond the earth, beyond the clouds, beyond the sky. If we keep this original conception of Adití clearly before us, the various forms which Adití assumes, even in the hymns of the Véda, will not seem incoherent."—(*Müller.*)

Dr. Muir, in an elaborate article, discusses the following points: "Adití as the mother of the Ádityas." "Is Adití ever identified with the sky?" "Adití seems to be distinguished from the earth." "Adití may be a personification of universal nature." "Adití as a forgiver of sin." "Adití's position sometimes subordinate."

In the two epics, and in the Bhágavata Purána, Adití is described as the wife of Kásyapa, and the mother of Vishnu in his dwarf incarnation: "An older authority however, the Vaj-sanhitá, gives quite a different account of the relation of Adití to Vishnu, as it represents her to be his wife. In the following passage of the Tattiríya-sanhitá also she is similarly described. "Supporter of the sky, sustainer of the earth, sovereign of this world, wife of Vishnu, may the all-embracing and powerful Adití, filling us with vigour, be auspicious to us (abiding) in her lap."—*Muir, O. S. T., Vol. V, p. 53.*

Aditya—The Sun, called also Súrya, (and Vivaswat) the chief of the gods at a very early period. The twelve solar dynasties, or personifications of the sun under a different name and sign of the zodiac in each month of the year, are called Ádityas. They belong to a period before the time of the Vedas, when the worship of the elements, particularly of the sun, was first enriched and extended by fancy. The name, Ádityas, is a matronymic from Aditi. The various stories related of the sun, or of the Ádityas, will be given in connection with the histories of the demi-gods to which they refer. Vishnu is called chief of the Ádityas.—See Appendix.

Adoption—If a married brahman is without male issue he is required to procure a son by means of adoption. He must have a son to perform his obsequies, or believes he would be excluded from happiness after death. So prevalent is this notion amongst the Hindus that women who have only daughters will themselves find their husbands a second wife, notwithstanding all the inconveniences involved. "The adopted son wholly renounces all claim on the property of his natural father, and acquires an unlimited right of succession to all that belongs to his adopted father. From him he is entitled to maintenance and education, as if he were his own son ; and to receive, through his means, the advantages of the Triple cord, and of being settled in marriage. The adopted son is obliged, on his part, to take care of his acquired parents in their old age, and attend to their funeral when they die. He farther enters into the *Gótra* or lineage of him by whom he is adopted ; and is considered as descended from the same ancient stock. When the ceremonies of adoption commence the new parents perform one which is held to be the most important and essential of any, by tying round the loins of the youth that little string which every male child in India (not an outcast) is ceremoniously invested with at the age of two or three years. If the ceremony has been previously performed by the natural parents, the adopting ones break the cord, in token of dissolving the Gótra from which the child descended ; and put in a new one in sign of being called to theirs. On this, as in all other solemn occasions, their first care is to select an auspicious day, by the help of astrology. The child adopted may be a relative or not, but must be of the same caste."—*Dubois.*

Adrika—The mother of *Vyása.* "The *muni Parásara,* having occasion to cross over from one side of the Ganges to the other bank, employed a ferry boat, rowed by a fisherman's daughter, towards whom he felt an attraction ; the consequence of which was the birth of a son. A Tamil version of the *Bháratam* enigmatizes the matter, by stating that *Vyása* was born from a fish ; but the Sanskrit original, not remarkable for fastidiousness, states the case with all simplicity."—*Taylor*.

Adrisyanti—The wife of Sakti, and mother of Parásara, which see.

Advaita—The name of a school of philosophy and theology, established by Sankaráchárya, founder of the monasterium of Sringéri, near the Túmbúdra river. The system regards the Supreme spirit and the human spirit as one ; in degradation through ignorance, and re-absorbed on obtaining true wisdom. It regards the world as an illusion ; all external objects as different forms of the one deity, besides whom there exists nothing else. As gold is one, though in various forms, as money, ear-rings and other ornaments, so the one sole existent deity is found in all the various forms that appear to exist around us. "The *Vedánta* of *Vyása*, which considered all existing beings and things to be an evolution of deity, and the deity in and throughout all beings and things, was, by *Sankaráchárya*, drawn out to the full consequence ; which is, that the soul of man is a part of deity, not different ; the body is a temporary prison ; on its decease the soul flows into deity, as air in a closed earthen vessel, when this is broken, flows into the common atmosphere. It does not, however, appear that the idea of deity, on this system, philosophically includes personality ; but means the supreme universe. It leans towards the female energy system ; of matter (or nature) being the great spontaneous mother. *Sankaráchárya* discoursed freely of *Siva* and *Párvati*, and wrote hymns to both ; maintaining, besides, the oneness of *Bramha*, *Vishnu* and *Siva*." There are many treatises in Tamil, Telugu and Canarese, on the Adwaita philosophy, which seems to have been made a special study in the south more than the north of India.

Advaitananda—The author of a commentary on the Védánta; and preceptor of Sadánanda who wrote the Védánta Sára. Nothing certain is known as to the time when he lived.

Adyas—One of the five classes of gods prevailing in the sixth Manwantara, of which period Chákshusha was the Manu.

Agada—One of the eight branches into which medical science is divided by the Hindus. Agada treats of the best antidotes to Poisons.

Agama—A divine system of doctrine.

Agastya—A great sage whose hermitage was situated in a beautiful locality, on the borders of a forest near the Vindhya mountains. Ráma, with his wife Síta and brother Lakshmana, paid the sage a visit, which is thus narrated in the Rámáyana ; " As they went they beheld the trees of the forest in full flower, surrounded by climbing plants, broken by the trunks of sportive elephants, enlivened with playful monkeys, and vocal with joyous birds. Ráma, as he viewed the beautiful wilderness, said to his brother Lakshmana :—" The hermitage of Agastya appears in view ; this is the abode of that sage who freed the southern quarter from the Rákshasas ; at whose command the Vindhya mountain forbore to rise higher in the sky ; who drank up the sea abounding in crocodiles and great fishes ; who was entreated by the gods, with Indra at their head, to destroy the Dánavas : O Lakshmana, here will I spend the remainder of my exile : Here the perfect men, the great sages, cast off their old bodies, and ascend in new bodies to heaven on chariots as resplendent as the sun."

Agastya presented Ráma with the bow of Vishnu, the arrow of Brahma, two inexhaustible quivers and a scimitar ; also with a superb coat of mail which had been given to the sage by Indra.

The Rámáyana gives the following legend of Vátápi and Ilwala who were destroyed by Agastya :—" In former times, two cruel Rákshasas, the devourers of Bráhmans, resided here, and their names were Vátápi and Ilwala, and Ilwala was accustomed to assume the form of a Bráhman, and speak the sacred tongue, and invite the Bráhmans under pretence of solemnizing a Śraddha : Then his brother Vátápi assumed the form of a ram, and was consecrated for the sacrifice by Ilwala ; and when the Brahmans had eaten the ram, Ilwala called to his brother to come forth, and Vátápi came forth out of the stomachs of the Bráhmans, bleating like a sheep, and tearing his way through their bodies. Thousands of Bráhmans were thus destroyed, when Agastya came to this spot, and accepted the invitation to a Śráddha ; and Agastya had not eaten for many years, and he devoured the whole of Vátápi in the form of a ram, and then prayed to Ganga ; and the goddess appeared in his alms dish, and he touched the water, and pronounced her divine name : Then when Ilwala called on his brother to come forth, Agastya laughed and said :—'Your brother has been eaten by me in the form of a ram and has now gone to the abode of Yama, and for him there is no coming forth :' Ilwala in a rage began to assail Agastya, but was immediately consumed by the fire which flashed from the eyes of the sage : This hermitage, which formerly belonged to the two Rákshasas, is now inhabited by the brother of Agastya." Goldstucker writes, "Agastya was the reputed author of several hymns of the Rig Veda. He is represented as of short stature, and is said by some to have been born in a water jar. He is also mentioned as one of the oldest medical authors, considered as the civilizer of the south and as the regent of the star Canopus."

Agastya—A celebrated Tamil author, who is considered by Dr. Caldwell to have lived in the 6th century, B. C., but the Tamulians assign a much earlier date.

Agathamma—One of the tutelary goddesses of Madras.

Aghorahanta—The Priest of *Chámundá*, a terrific goddess in the drama of Málati and Mádhava.

Aghori, or Aghorapanthi—The original *Aghorí* worship seems to have been that of *Deví* in some of her terrific forms, and to have required even human victims for its performance. In imitation of the formidable aspect under which the goddess was worshipped, the appearance of her votary was rendered as hideous as possible, and his wand and water-pot were a staff set with bones and the upper half of a skull : the practices were of a similar nature, and flesh and spirituous liquors constituted, at will, the diet of the adept.

"The regular worship of this sect has long since been suppressed, and the only traces of it now left are presented by a few disgusting wretches, who, whilst they profess to have adopted its tenets, make them a mere plea for extorting alms. In proof of their indifference to worldly objects, they eat and drink whatever is given to them, even ordure and carrion. They smear their bodies also with excrement, and carry it about with them in a wooden cup, or skull, either to swallow it, if by so doing they can get a few pice ; or to throw it upon the persons, or into the houses of those who refuse to comply with their demands. They also for the same purpose inflict gashes on their limbs, that the crime of blood may rest upon the head of the recusants ; and they have a variety of similar disgusting devices to extort money from the timid and credulous Hindu. They are fortunately not numerous, and are universally detested and feared."—*Wilson, Vol. I, p.* 234.

Agneya—The name of one of the eighteen Purános. [See Agni Purána.]

Agneyastram—The name of the fiery weapon given by Aurva to Sagara, and with which he conquered the barbarians who had invaded his patrimonial possessions.

Agneyi—The wife of Uru, a descendant of Dhruva, and mother of six excellent sons, Anga, Sumanas, Swati, Kratu, Angiras and Śiva.

Agni—"The deity of Fire, one of the most ancient and most sacred objects of Hindu worship. As such, Agni is considered as the mediator between men and gods, as protector of mankind and their home, and as witness of their actions ; hence his invocation in all solemn occasions, at the nuptial ceremony, &c. He is one of the eight Lókapálas, or guardians of the world, and especially the Lord of the south-east quarter. He appears in the progress of mythological personification as a son of Angiras, as a king of the Pitris or Manes, as a Marut, as a grandson of Sandila, as one of the seven sages during the reign of Tamasa, or the fourth Manu, as a star, and as a Rishi or inspired author of several Vaidic hymns."*

* Goldstücker.

He is generally described as having two faces, three legs and seven arms, of a red or flame color, and riding on a ram. Before him is a swallow-tailed banner on which a ram is also represented. He is described by others as a corpulent man of a red complexion, with eyes, eyebrows, head and hair, of a tawny color, riding on a goat. From his body issue seven streams of glory, and in his right hand he holds a spear. Agni is the son of Kásyapa and Adití. His consort or Sakti is Swaha, a daughter of Kásyapa. Brahman priests are ordered to maintain a perpetual fire ; and in the numerous religious ceremonies of the Hindus Agni is commonly invoked. The god is sometimes figured with a forked representation of fire issuing from his mouth ; and sometimes with seven tongues of fire. (See Colebrooke's Essays.)

Agni, like Indra, is sometimes addressed as the one great god who makes all things, sometimes as the light which fills the heavens, sometimes as the blazing lightning, or as the clear flame of earthly fire. The poets pass from one application of the word to another with perfect ease, as conscious that in each case they are using a mere name which may denote similar qualities in many objects. There is no rivalry or antagonism between these deities. Agni is greatest, Varuna is greatest, and Indra is greatest : but when the one is so described, the others are for the time unnoticed, or else are placed in a subordinate position. Thus Agni is said to comprehend all other gods within himself, as the circumference of a wheel embraces its spokes ;* and not unfrequently Indra is said to be Agni, and Agni is said to be Indra ; while both alike are Skambha, the supporter of the world.

Hence the character of the god is almost wholly physical. The blessings which his worshippers pray for are commonly temporal. In the earlier hymns he is generally addressed as the fire, which to mortal men is an indispensable boon ; in the more developed ceremonialism of later times he is chiefly concerned with the ordering of the sacrifice.

* * * * * "As the special guardian and regulator of sacrifices Agni assumes the character of the Hellenic Hestra, and almost

* Muir.

attains the majesty of the Latin Vesta. He is the lord and protector of every house, and the father, mother, brother and son of every one of the worshippers. During life he shields men from harm, and at death he becomes the *Psycho pompos*, as conveying the 'unborn part' of the dead to the unseen world."*

2. Agni is also the name of a star in the tail of the planetary porpoise.

Agni Purana—This Purána derives its name from its having been communicated originally by Agni, the god of Fire, to the Muni Vasishtha, for the purpose of instructing him in the two-fold knowledge of Brahma. By him it was taught to Vyása, who imparted it to Súta ; and the latter is represented as repeating it to the Rishis at Naimisháranya. The contents of different copies vary from fourteen to sixteen thousand stanzas. The early chapters of the work describe the Avatáras, and in those of Ráma and Krishna avowedly follow the Ramáyana and Mahábhárata. Other portions contain instructions for the performance of religious ceremonies—chiefly mystical forms of Saiva worship. There are also chapters descriptive of the earth and the universe, the duties of kings, &c., much of which has obviously been taken from the Vishnu and other Puránas. On these accounts Professor Wilson regards it as a comparatively modern work, without "legitimate claims to be regarded as a Purána," and only "valuable as embodying and preserving relics of antiquity."

Agnibahu—One of the ten sons of Príyavrata and Kamya, famous for strength and prowess. It is said of him in the V. P., that when he adopted a religious life, he remembered the occurrences of a prior existence, and did not covet dominion, but diligently practised the rites of devotion, wholly disinterested, and looking for no reward.

Agnidhra—The brother of the above, was made by his father king of Jambudwipa, and had nine sons who are enumerated and more or less celebrated in the Puránas.

Agnihotra—A burnt offering, or libation of clarified butter on sacred fire.

* Cox, Mythology of Aryan Nations.

Agnishtoma—1, A son of the Manu Chakshusha; 2, the name of a sacrifice produced from the eastern mouth of Brahma, along with the Gáyatri, and the Rig Véda. V. P., 42.

Agnishwattas—A class of Pitris, a divine race inhabiting celestial regions of their own. This class consists of those householders who when alive did not maintain their domestic fires, nor offer burnt sacrifices. Some of the Puránas identify the Agnishwattas with the seasons. V. P., p. 239.

Agnivarchas—One of Súta's scholars, who became a celebrated teacher of the Puránas.

Agnivarna—A prince whose name occurs in various Puránas; but little more is known of him beyond his being a descendant of Ráma.

Agrahara—A village granted to brahmans by government free, or at a favorable assessment; there are three kinds, viz :—

1. Sarvamánya—rent free.
2. Jódi—partially rent free.
3. Trishvéga—one-third part of the produce is given for rent.

Agrahayana—The name of one of the lunar months.

Agrasya—The first day of the Hindu year which falls on the new moon in March. A feast goes on for three days at this period —the new year's day festival.

Ahalya—The wife of the rishi Gautama, of whom the following legend is related: One day when the sage was absent from his dwelling, the mighty Indra passed by, and burned with an impure passion for the wife of Gautama; he entered the hut in the disguise of the sage, and began to entreat Ahalyá; and Ahalyá, knowing him to be the Rája of the celestials, in the wantonness of her heart yielded to his desires. Then the sovereign of the gods left the hermitage, but at that moment Gautama entered, and he was invincible even to the gods, through the power of his austerities. Perceiving him, Indra was overwhelmed with sadness; and the sage, beholding the profligate lord of gods in his disguise, thus addressed him in words of dreadful anger :—'O depraved wretch, assuming my form you have perpetrated this great crime! Therefore from this moment do you become a eunuch !' The great sage then pronounced this curse upon his wife Ahalyá :—'O sinful wretch, for thousands of years shall you remain in the forest, abandoned by all and invisible to all, until Ráma, the son of Dasaratha, shall enter here, and you from beholding him shall be cleansed from all sin, and again approach me without fear.' With these words the illustrious Gautama abandoned this hermitage, and performed religious austerities on the summit of the Himálaya mountains.

Having heard this holy legend, Ráma entered the hermitage, preceded by Viswámitra ; and at that moment, Ahalyá was released from her curse, and became visible to all ; and a shower of flowers fell from heaven, and divine music was heard in the sky. Then the illustrious Gautama, beholding with divine eye that his consort was cleansed from all sin, repaired again to his hermitage ; and having paid due honors to Ráma, he engaged in sacred austerities with his purified spouse. And Ráma proceeded to Mithilá with his brother and Viswámitra.—It is said that Indra means the sun, and Ahalyá, the night ; and as the night is seduced and ruined by the sun of the morning therefore is Indra called the paramour of Ahalyá.

Ahankara—Consciousness, or Egotism. The sense of Ahankára, says Professor Wilson, cannot be very well rendered by any European term. It means the principle of individual existence, that which appropriates perceptions, and on which depend the notions, I think, I feel, I am. It might be expressed by the proposition of Descartes reversed. 'Sum, ergo cotigo, sentio,' &c. The equivalent employed by Mr. Colebrooke, egotism, has the advantage of an analogous etymology. In the Sánkya Kárika three varieties of Ahankára are described. From the first kind proceed the senses; from the third the unconscious elements ; both kinds being equally inert of themselves, are rendered productive by the co-operation of the second, the energetic modification of Ahankára, which is therefore said to be the origin both of the senses and the elements. Colloquially "Ahankára" is still in common use throughout India in the sense of pride, or great conceit.

Ahar—Day. One of the forms of Bramha during the work of Creation. V. P., p. 40.

Ahikshetra—The capital of the northern portion of Pánchála, supposed to be the same as Adisathrus in Ptolemy.

Airavata—The king of elephants, produced from the churning of the ocean, and taken by Indra, who subsequently used it as his vehicle. The name has been derived from Iravat "watery," and supposed to allude to the north, as the quarter whence rain comes, or to the original idea of a cloud, in which Indra as the king of clouds, is mounted, and therefore called his elephant. Professor Wilson refers it to the fact of his being produced from the watery ocean ; 2, Airávata is also the name of the north portion of the sun's path among the lunar asterisms ; 3, The name of a celebrated serpent with many heads, one of the progeny of Kadru.

Aitareya Brahmanam of the Rig Veda : this work contains the earliest speculations of the Brahmans on the meaning of the Sacrificial Prayers, and on the origin, performance, and meaning of the Rites of the Vedic Religion. It consists of forty Adyhayas. Translated and edited by Dr. Martin Haug, 2 vols. 12 mo., Bombay, 1863.

Aitareya-aranyaka—A commentary on the beginning of the Rig Veda. It is ascribed to Mahidasu the son of Itará.

Aja—The unborn. A name of Bramha ; of Siva ; of Vishnu ; also of Káma, or Cupid. Aja is also the proper name of a mythical prince, the son of Raghu, and father of Dasaratha. This prince forms the subject of the first and longest of Mr. Griffiths' beautiful Idylls from the Sanscrit. The story is taken from the Raghuvansa of Kálidása. (See Raghu.) The childhood and youth of Aja are described in glowing terms, and in due course he was sent by his father to the Swayamvara of the princess Indumati Dévi, daughter of the Rája of Vidarbha. On his way thither while resting in the heat of the day, the encampment was disturbed by a wild elephant which Aja ordered to be shot. On being pierced by an arrow a figure of great splendour issued from the body of the elephant ; and standing in mid-air thus spoke : "Aja Mahárávya, I was formerly a gandharva, but for mocking a holy rishi was cursed to be born in an insane elephant; but on my begging for mercy was told I should be released by the son of Raghu Mahárája, called Aja, when on his way to be married." He then gave Aja the arrows used by the gandharvas and instructed him in the use of them.

On arriving at the capital of Vidarbharáya he was treated with great respect, and was selected from amongst all the assembled princes by the fair Indumati Dévi, who intimated her choice by herself placing the garland on the neck of Aja. In the contests that ensued with the other disappointed suitors Aja obtained a complete victory by means of the arrows received from the gandharva. He then returned to his father's kingdom, with his lovely bride; succeeded to the throne, and reigned wisely and well for many years.

After the birth of his distinguished son Dasaratha (father of Ráma) his beloved wife Indumati Dévi was killed by the fall of Nárada's garland, when asleep in an arbor of the summer palace. On Dasaratha's attaining his majority Aja is said to have ascended to Indra's paradise, leaving his body between the rivers Ganges and Sarayu.

Ajagava—The bow of Mahádéva which fell from the sky, at the birth of Prithu, with celestial arrows and panoply from heaven.

Ajaka—1, A descendant of Purúravas, the son of Sumanta (or according to others of Sunaha) and grandson of Jahnu; 2, A king of Magadha of the line of Pradyota.

Ajamadha—1, A son of Suhotra and author of vaidic hymns; 2, The twenty-sixth king of the lunar dynasty; 3, A surname of Yudhishthira, the friend of Aja.

Ajamidha—A son of Hastin, the founder of the celebrated city of Hastinápura, finally ruined by the encroachments of the Ganges, but vestiges of which were lately to be traced along the river nearly in a line with Delhi, about 60 miles to the east.

Ajanta—A river in the hills below the river Tapti, to the north of Bombay. "In this ravine, somewhere about the first century of our era, Buddhists began to excavate architectural caves. There are twenty-six in all, and of these twenty-two are conventual abodes, whilst the remaining four are Chaitya halls or places of worship." A. and M. I., p. 401. A full description of these caves is given in Fergusson's History of Architecture. It is seen from the costume carefully represented in the pictures at Ajanta, that the Hindus still dress in the fashion that then prevailed; and which was described by the Greeks who accompanied Alexander the Great to India, as consisting of two cloths, one reaching to the middle of the leg, whilst another is folded around the shoulders. The cloth is described as being made from wool which grows in trees.

Ajapas—Sons of Kardama, Pitris of the Vaisyas, called also Kávyas and Suswadhas.

Ajapashya—A surname of Rájíválóchana, the son of Swétakarna; his sides were black like the skin of certain goats, when he was drawn out of the water, after having been found exposed by his mother and purified by two sons of Sravishta.

Ajavithi—A division of the lunar mansions.

Ajigarta—A Rishi mentioned in the Aitareya Brahmana. He lived in the forests with his three sons Sunapuchha, Sunahṣepha and Śunolángúla. He sold his son Sunahṣepha to be offered as a sacrifice, showing that the Brahmans at that early period were familiar with the idea of human sacrifices. "If we accept the Áryan origin of Ajigarta, the seller and butcher of his own son, it is important to remark how great a difference there must have been between the various Áryan settlers in India * * * *. Yet there remains the fact that, with all the vaunted civilization of the higher Áryan classes, there were Áryan people in India to whom not only a young prince could make the offer of buying their children, but where the father offered himself to bind and kill the son whom he had sold for a hundred cows."*

Ajita—A form of Vishnu. "The unequalled energy of Vishnu combining with the quality of goodness, and effecting the preservation of created things, presides over all the Manwantaras, in the form of a divinity." V. P., p. 264.

* Max Müller, A. S. L., p. 415.

Ajita—Unconquered ; unexcelled.—1, The proper name of several gods and persons, viz., Vishnu, Siva ; 2, One of the seven Rishis who preside during the reign of the fourteenth Manu ; 3, A name of Maitreya or a future Buddha ; 4, The second of the Arhats or Jaina saints of the present Avasarpini ; 5, The attendant of the ninth Jaina Arhat ; 6, A descendant of Ikshwáku and a son of Jitasatru by Vijaya.

Ajitas—A class of deities whose history is thus given. In the beginning of the Kalpa twelve gods named Jayas were created by Brahma, as his deputies and assistants in the creation. They, lost in meditation, neglected his commands ; on which he cursed them to be repeatedly born in each Manwantara till the seventh. In the first they became Ajitas.

Ajnana—A technical term used in the *Védánta* system, meaning "ignorance," which the Vedántists declare is a somewhat that is not to be called positively either entity or non-entity—not a mere negation but the opponent of knowledge, consisting of the three fetters. According to the Naiyáyikas *ajnána* is merely the non-existence, or negation, (*abháva*) of jnána. To deny this the writer calls it *bháva*, implying that it is not *abháva*.

Akali—(Immortals). Zealots of the Sikh religion, soldiers of God, who with their blue dress and bracelets of steel, claimed for themselves a direct institution by Govindh Singh. They combined warlike activity with the relinquishment of the world, and became the armed guardians of Amritsir. It cost Ranjit Singh much time and trouble to reduce them to order.

Akanithaka—The name of the twenty-second heaven of Buddhism.

Akasa—Ether, the medium of sound. A very important 'element' in the philosophy of the Puránas. See V. P., p. 16, 17.

Akasavani—A divine manifestation, in which the deity is heard but not seen.

Akrura—The son of Swaphalka and Gandíní who took charge of the celebrated Syamantaka jewel from Satadhanwan, when he was pursued by Krishna ; and through the virtue of that gem there was no dearth nor pestilence in the whole country. When Krishna discovered that the precious jewel was in Akrúra's possession he desired him to retain it ; Akrúra, thus urged, afterwards wore it publicly round his neck, where it shone with dazzling brightness ; and he moved about like the sun, wearing a garland of light. Akrúra conveyed Krishna and Rama, when youths, to Mathura, where Krishna performed some of his great exploits.

Aksha—A son of the great giant Rávana, who was slain by Hanuman.

Akshata—Grains of rice tinged with a reddish hue, placed by the husband on the head of the infant after the ceremony of Arati, and after the women have retired.

Akshohini—An Army consisting of 109,350 infantry ; 65,610 cavalry ; 21,870 chariots ; and 21,870 elephants.

Akuli—The name of one of the priests of the Asuras. It was he who with another priest of the same class called Kiláta, obtained permission from Manu to sacrifice for him, and took for the victim first a bull of Manu's into which an Asura-slaying voice had entered. When it had been slaughtered the voice departed out of it and entered into Manu's wife Manávi. "Wherever they hear her speaking, the Asuras and Rákshasas continue to be destroyed in consequence of her voice. The Asuras said : 'She does us yet more mischief ; for the human voice speaks more.' Kiláta and Akuli said, 'Manu is a devout believer : let us make trial of him !' They came and said to him 'Manu, let us sacrifice for thee !' 'With what (victim) ?' he asked. 'With this (thy) wife,' they replied. 'Be it so,' he answered. When she had been slaughtered the voice departed out of her and entered into the sacrifice and the sacrificial vessels. Thence they were unable to expel it. This is the Asura-slaying voice which speaks out (when the two stones are struck with the *śamyá*, as a part of the ceremonial). Wretched become the enemies of that man for whom, when he knows this, they cause this voice here to reverberate."*

* Muir's O. S. T., vol. 1, p. 189.

Akuti—1, The second daughter of Sváyámbhuva Manu and his wife Saturúpa, the first pair. She was 'graced with loveliness and exalted merit.' She was married to Rúchi, and had twins. Yajna and Dakshiná, who afterwards became husband and wife, and had twelve sons, the deities called Yamas. Dr. Muir remarks that the word is found in the Rig Veda with the signification of "will" or "design;" but appears to be personified in a passage of the Taittiríya Bráhmana, where it is said. "Ira was the wife of the creators. Akúti kneaded the oblation." O. S. T., Vol. 1, p. 73. 2, Also the name of the wife of Chakshush.

Alaka—King over the earth for sixty thousand and sixty hundred years; this protracted existence was enjoyed through the favor of Lópamudra, and having lived till the period at which the curse on Kási terminated, he killed the Rákshasa Kshemaka by whom the city had been occupied after it was abandoned by Divodásu, and caused the city to be re-inhabited.

Alaka—The Himalayan residence of Kuvera the god of riches. It is termed in the "Cloud Messenger" the City of the Blessed; and is described as unmatched for lovely girls, who learn to choose the flowers that suit them best.

"The amaranth, bright glory of the spring;
The lotus gathered from the summer flood;
Acacias taught around their brows to cling;
The jasmine's fragrant white their locks to stud;
And bursting at thy rain the young Kadamba bud."*

Alakananda—One of the four great branches of the river Ganges, which was carried by Siva upon his head for a hundred years; and was the river which raised to heaven the sinful sons of Sagara, by washing their ashes.

Alambana—The exercise of the Yógi while endeavouring to bring before his thoughts the gross form of the Supreme Being. It also means the silent repetition of prayer.

Allama Prabhu—Among the *Víra Saivas* a lesser incarna-

* Griffiths' Translation.

tion, or form of ***Siva.*** He appears to have been a Brahman, who acted in close concert with the elder ***Basava***; whether as a primary instigator, or subsequent accomplice, is not clear. But he became ***Basava's guru*** or spiritual adviser, and, as such, was concerned in the revolution at Kalyánapuri, in which the king ***Bijala*** was slain, and a new religion established. The ***Prabhu linga líla*** is a popular poem, in Telugu, and composed expressly in order to magnify the great excellencies of ***Allamá prabhu*** as a form of *Siva*, and especially his chastity, that resisted all the fascinations of the *támasa guna* or evil portion of *Párvati*; which became incarnate as a woman, Máya or Frans, in order to tempt him. "In the *Basava puránam*, *Allamá prabhu* is stated to have travelled about, and especially to *Sri Sailam* in Telingana, performing various wonders, and possessed of a body invulnerable. No record of the manner of his death has been observed."—(*Taylor.*) There is a good abstract of Prabhu-linga líla, by C. P. Brown, in the Catalogue Raisonné, vol. 2, p. 838.

Alloo—A raw hide used by the Rájputs to cover themselves when they assert their claim to a disputed piece of land.

Aluvar—*Rulers*; twelve heads and original leaders of the *Vaishnava* faith in the Peninsula only. They were born in various places, and lived in different times. To understand their office and importance the reader must be apprized that the *Saiva* system first obtained a hold and influence in the Peninsula; and, in some instances, by exterminating the Buddhists or Jains who preceded them. The Vaishnavas, on their coming, had not only to deal with a rude and savage people, following superstitious customs, some of which continue to the present day, but also had to contend with the astute and powerful Saivas already in possession; and sometimes in the way of public disputation—as at Villiputtúr in the Pandya kingdom, at Uriyur in the Chola kingdom, and at Srí Permattúr in the Tondamandalam. These, or others, were engaged in translating portions of the Vedas into Tamil poetry, now known as the ***Tiru-morhi*** or sacred word. Different books exist, containing in all many thousand stanzas, said to indicate the idiom of foreigners. Twelve individuals, distinguished in these or other ways in the first establishment of Vaishnavism, were named Aluvar; and are regarded with high veneration by modern votaries. An approximation towards deification has been assigned, by metaphorically viewing them as incarnations of Vishnú's arms, ornaments, or attendants. Their names in order are—1, Poyálvār ; 2, Puthatálvār ; 3, Péyálvár ; 4, Tirumal Péyálvár ; 5, Namálvár ; 6, Kulasec'harálvár ; 7, Periyálvar ; 8, Tirupanálvár ; 9, Tirumangayalvár ; 10, Tondamálvár ; 11, Yempramanár, or Yetirája, or Rāmánujácbárya ; 12, Kurattálvár.—*Taylor.*

Amara Kosha—A celebrated Sanscrit Vocabulary which is found in a more or less perfect state in all Indian languages. Like most other Sanscrit Dictionaries it is arranged in verse to aid the memory. Synonymous words are collected into one or more verses, and placed in fifteen different chapters, which treat of as many different subjects. The sixteenth contains a few homonymous terms arranged alphabetically, in the Indian manner, by the final consonants. The seventeenth chapter is a pretty full catalogue of indeclinables, which European philologists would call adverbs, prepositions, conjunctions, and interjections, but which Sanscrit grammarians consider as indeclinable nouns. The last chapter of the Amara Kósha is a treatise on the gender of nouns. See Colebrooke's Essay on the Sanscrit and Prácrit Languages.

Amara Sinha—The author of the Amara Kósha. He was also an eminent poet, and one of the nine gems, as these poets were termed, who were the ornaments of Vicramáditya's court. Unfortunately he held the tenets of a heterodox sect, and his poems perished in the persecutions fomented by intolerant philosophers against the persons and writings of both Jainas and Buddhists.

Amaravati—The capital of Indra, built by Visvakarma, the architect of the gods. It is described as 800 miles in circumference, and 40 miles high. Its pillars are composed of diamonds ; its thrones of pure gold ; it is surrounded with gardens and fountains, while music and dancing entertain the celestial inhabitants. There is a ruined town called Amarávati on the banks of the river Kistna containing numerous antiquities in the form of sculptures, all of

Buddhist origin. Sir Walter Elliot and Mr. Fergusson made considerable explorations there. The ruined Dágoba whence the relics were taken was on a mound of 150 feet diameter, now converted into a tank. It is called Dípaldinna, the Mound of Light.

Amavasya—The day of 'conjunction,' just before new-moon —a fast day for all brahmans.

Amba—The eldest daughter of the Rája of Kási. She was taken with her two sisters by Bhíshma, when he conveyed them away from the Swayamvara to be the wives of Rája Vichitravírya. But on the day when the marriage was to be performed, Amba said that her father had already betrothed her to the Rája of Salwa, and prayed that she might be sent to him. Bhíshma accordingly sent her under a safe conduct, to the Rája of Salwa, and Ambá related how she had been carried away, and had now come to fulfil her betrothal ; but the Rája of Salwa said, "You have entered the dwelling of a strange man and I will not take you to be my wife ;" and ordered his servants to drive her from the city : she went into the jungle and perished miserably. (Mahá bhárata) Another legend says she was born again as a man named Sikhandin and slew Bhíshma the author of all her misfortunes.

Amba and Ambika—Names of *Párvati,* the *Sakti* of *Siva.*

Ambi and Ambalika—The sisters of Ambá, who became the two widowed wives of Vichitravírya, on whom the Muni Vyása begot *Dritaráshtra* and *Pándu.* See Vyása.

Ambarisha—1, The son of the great monarch Mándhatri. He had fifty sisters, all of whom were married to the sage Saubhari ; 2, The name of several other princes mentioned in the Puránic histories.

Ambhansi—A mystic term for the four classes of beings, gods, demons, men, and pitris. It means literally 'waters.'

Ambha Matha, a Jaina goddess, still worshipped in various parts of India. The ruins of many beautiful temples erected to her may be seen in the high hills of Marwar.

Ambea—The mother of the Kurus,—a race of heroes or demigods related to the Pándus.

Amitabha—The Lord of the Munis, a deity in the Buddhist Pantheon.

Amogavarsha—The Jain king of Kánchi, or Tondamandalam, at the end of the ninth century of the Christian era. The principal Jain Puránas are supposed to have been written in his reign, by the king's spiritual preceptor Jina Séna Achárya.

Amogha Siddha—The remover of the ills of the Kali age; a deity in the Buddhist Pantheon to whom prayers are made and offerings addressed.—*Wilson.*

Amrita—Ambrosia. The beverage of immortality. It was produced at the churning of the ocean, a legend with which all Hindus are familiar, and is said to have occurred in the following way; When the gods were overcome by the Dánavas, they fled for refuge to Vishnu and sought his protection and advice. Hari, the creator of the universe, being thus prayed to by the prostrate divinities, smiled, and thus spake with renovated energy, "Oh gods, I will restore your strength. Do you act as I enjoin? Let all the gods, associated with the Asuras, cast all sorts of medicinal herbs into the sea of milk; and then taking the mountain Mandara for the churning-stick, the serpent Vásuki for the rope, churn the ocean together for Ambrosia; depending upon my aid. To secure the assistance of the Daityas, you must be at peace with them, and engage to give them an equal portion of the fruit of your associated toil; promising them that by drinking the Amrita that shall be produced from the agitated ocean, they shall become mighty and immortal. I will take care that the enemies of the gods shall not partake of the precious draught; that they shall share in the labor alone."

"Being thus instructed by the god of gods, the divinities entered into alliance with the demons, and they jointly undertook the acquirement of the beverage of immortality. They collected various kinds of medicinal herbs, and cast them into the sea of milk, the waters of which were radiant as the shining clouds of autumn. They then took the mountain Mandara for the staff; the serpent Vásuki [see Ananta] for the cord; and commenced to churn the ocean for the Amrita. The assembled gods were stationed by Vishnu at the tail of the serpent; the Daityas and Dánavas at its head and neck. Scorched by the flames emitted from his inflated hood, the demons were shorn of their glory; whilst the clouds driven towards his tail by the breath of his mouth, refreshed the gods with revivifying showers. In the midst of the milky sea, Hari himself, in the form of a tortoise; served as a pivot for the mountain, as it was whirled around. The holder of the mace and discus was present in other forms amongst the gods and demons, and assisted to drag the monarch of the serpent race: and in another vast body he sat upon the summit of the mountain. With one portion of his energy, unseen by gods or demons, he sustained the serpent king; and with another infused vigour into the gods.

"From the ocean, thus churned by the gods and dánavas, first uprose the cow Surabha, the fountain of milk, and curds, worshipped by the divinities, and beheld by them and their associates with minds disturbed, and eyes glistening with delight. Then, as the holy Siddhas in the sky wondered what this could be, appeared the goddess Váruní [the deity of wine,] her eyes rolling with intoxication. Next, from the whirlpool of the deep, sprang the celestial Párijáta tree, the delight of the nymphs of heaven, perfuming the world with its blossoms. The troop of Apsarasas, the nymphs of heaven, were then produced, of surprising loveliness, endowed with beauty and with taste. The cool-rayed moon next rose, and was seized by Mahádéva: and then poison was engendered from the sea, of which the snake gods (Nágas) took possession. Dhanwantari, robed in white, and bearing in his hand the cup of Amrita, next came forth; beholding which, the sons of Diti and of Danu, as well as the Munis, were filled with satisfaction and delight. Then, seated on a full-blown lotus, and holding a waterlily in her hand, the goddess Srí, radiant with beauty, rose from the waves. The great sages, enraptured, hymned her with the song dedicated to her praise. Viswavasu and other heavenly quiristers sang, and Ghirtáchí and other celestial nymphs danced before her. Gangá and other holy streams attended for her ablutions; and the elephants of the skies, taking up their pure waters in vases of gold, poured them over the goddess, the queen of the universal world. The sea of milk in person presented her with a wreath of never-fading flowers ; and the artist of the gods (Viswakarmá) decorated her person with heavenly ornaments. Thus bathed, attired, and adorned, the goddess, in the view of the celestials, cast herself upon the breast of Hari, and there reclining, turned her eyes upon the deities, who were inspired with rapture by her gaze. Not so the Daityas, who, with Viprachitti at their head, were filled with indignation, as Vishnu turned away from them, and they were abandoned by the goddess of prosperity (Lakshmí).

"The powerful and indignant Daityas then forcibly seized the Amrita-cup that was in the hand of Dhanwantarí : but Vishnu, assuming a female form, fascinated and deluded them ; and recovering the Amrita from them, delivered it to the gods. Sakra and the other deities quaffed the Ambrosia. The incensed demons, grasping their weapons, fell upon them ; but the gods, into whom the Ambrosial draught had infused new vigour, defeated and put their host to flight, and they fled through the regions of space, and plunged into the subterraneous realms of Pátála. The gods thereat greatly rejoiced, did homage to the holder of the discus and mace, and resumed their reign in heaven. The sun shone with renovated splendour, and again discharged his appointed task ; and the celestial luminaries again circled, in their respective orbits. Fire once more blazed aloft, beautiful in splendour ; and the minds of all beings were animated by devotion. The three worlds again were rendered happy by prosperity ; and Indra the chief of the gods, was restored to power." (V. P., p. 77.) The legend as given in the Rámáyana may be found in Carey's Translation, Vol. I, p. 410— and that of the Mahá Bhárata in Sir C. Wilkins' Bhagavat Gíta— Bangalore edit., p. 105.

Anabhitra—A proper name of ; 1, A prince of the solar race, a descendant of Sagara, son of Nighna and brother of Raghu, the fifty-second king of Ayodhyá ; 2, a son of the king Kroshtu or Kroshtri by Gándhári and father of Sini or, according to others, a grandson of Vrishni, son of Sumitra by Mádri and brother to Sini ; or, again, a grandson of Dhrishta, son of Sumitra, &c.

Anadi-chitta-para-meshti—Eternal intellectual heavenly dweller ; the Jain name of the Supreme Being, the Lord of all, who dwells in *Móksha-lóka*, the world of bliss.

Ananganu—A name of Cupid, the Hindu god of love.

Ananta—Infinite. Called also Sésha or Vásuki. The king of the Nágas, a race of serpents which inhabit Pátála. He belongs purely to the Puránic period, and is described as having a thousand hooded-heads, on the foreheads of which was inscribed the sign called Swastika, the mystic cross which betokens good fortune. He is clothed in purple and wears a white necklace. In one hand he holds a plough, in the other a pestle. At the end of each kalpa he vomits a venomous fire which destroys all creation. He bears the universe on his head and produces earthquakes whenever he yawns. On his body Vishnu reposes, during the intervals of creation, and is sheltered by his hoods which stretch out above him like a canopy. He proved a very useful personage at the churning of the ocean ; the gods seizing his tail and the demons his head, they twisted him round Mount Meru, and thus formed a churn on a large scale.—*J. C. Thomson.*

Ananta—1, A name of Vishnu or Krishna ; 2, a name of Baladeva, the elder brother of Krishna ; 3, a name of Siva ; 4, a name of Rudra, in an Upanishad of the Atharvana veda ; 5, a name of Sésha, the chief of the Nágas or serpent race as described above : the couch and constant attendant of Vishnu ; 6, a name of Vásuki, another king of the serpents, the brother of the former ; 7, a name of one of the Viswadevas ; 8, the name of the fourteenth of the twenty-four Arhats or Jaina deified saints of the present Avasarpini ; 9, the name of a king of Kashmír ; 10, a proper name common to several authors, &c.

Ananda Giri—A Sanscrit author who lived about the 10th century and wrote several works which are still extant and of some value : among them are the Sankara Dig Vijaya, the Life of Sankarácharya, &c.

Anaranya—A venerable patriarch whose daughter Pushkarani, was mother of the Manu Chakshusa.

Anasuya—Charity. The daughter of Daksha and wife of Atri, celebrated for her piety and virtue. Atri introduced her to Síta, to whom she gave an ointment to render her "beautiful for ever."

Andakataha—The shell of the mundane egg. Beyond the sea of fresh water is a region of twice its extent, where the land is of gold, and where no living beings reside. Thence extends the Lóká-lóka mountain, which is 10,000 yojanas in breadth, and as many in height; and beyond it perpetual darkness invests the mountain all around; which darkness is again encompassed by the shell of the egg.

Andhaka—A proper name of: 1, a demon, a son of Kásyapa and Diti with a thousand arms and heads, two thousand eyes and feet, and called Andhaka, because he walked like a blind man although he saw very well; in his attempt to take away the Párijáta tree of Swarga he was slain by Siva; 2, a grandson of Kroshtri, and son of Yuddhájita, who together with his brother Vrishni is the ancestor of the celebrated family of the Andhaka-Vrishnis; 3, a grandson of Vrishni (the brother of Andhaka), and son of Swaphalka by Gándiní; 4, a son of Sattwat, belonging to the same family, by Kausalyá; 5, a son of Bhima (of the same family) and father of Revata. [The foregoing lineage, 2–5, is taken from the Harivansa. In the Linga Purána an Andhaka is a son of Nahusha who, according to other Puránas, is the ancestor of Kroshtri; in the Kúrma Purána an Andhaka is a son of Ansa and father of Sáttwata, while in the Vishnu P. a prince of that name is mentioned as the son of Sáttwata who is apparently the same as the Sáttwat of the Hariv.]; 6, The name of a Muni (in the Padma Purána.)

Andhra kings, dynasty of, celebrated in the south of India from a very early period. Professor Wilson makes it commence about 20 years B.C., though they might not have established their authority in Magadhá until the first centuries of the Christian era. They are noticed by Pliny.

Andhra Dipaca—An old and very good Dictionary of the Telugu language, by Mámidi Vencaya.

Andhra—The Sanscrit name for the Telugu language. Andhra is the ancient name of Telingana, the Telugu country.

Andrajatias—The same as Andhras, the Telugu people, or inhabitants of Telingana, formerly called Gentoos.

Anga—1, A name of a minor Dwipa, peopled by Mlechchhas who worship Hindu divinities ; 2, A country in the neighbourhood of Bhagulpur. It is the scene of several of the legends of the Rámáyana. A dynasty of Buddhist Rajas reigned at Anga about the second century of the Christian era under the name of Karnas; and it is thought that the Brahmanical compilers of the Mahábhárata wished to establish a mythical connection between the Karna who fought in the great war, and the Karna Rajas of Anga who flourished at a much later period.

Anga—The eldest of the six sons of Uru, a descendant of Dhruva, of the famlly of Atri. Anga who had by his wife Sunítha, only one son named Vena, whose right arm was rubbed by the Rishis for the purpose of producing from it progeny. (See Prithu.)

Angada—A son of Lackshmaṇa, king of Angadí, and brother of Ráma ; 2, the son of Vali, who was installed Yuvarája of Kishkindha ; 3, a son of Gada by Vrihati.

Anganyasa karanyasa—The *mantras* used in the early morning by Brahmans, with certain motions of their fingers, and touching various parts of their bodies.

Angaja—(Lust). A son of Brahma. The virtues and vices are represented as the progeny of Bramha.

Angaraka—A Rudra. There are eleven well-known Rudras, lords of the three worlds ; but each one of the eleven has many appellations in the different Puranas.

Angaras—One of the peoples enumerated in the V. P.

Angas—There are six Angas, or subsidiary portions of the Vedas, viz :—Śiksha, rules for reciting the prayers, the accents and tones to be observed ; Kalpa, ritual; Vyákarana, grammar; Nirukta, glossarial comment ; Chhandas, metre ; and Jyotish, astronomy. The four Vedas, the six Angas, with Mimánsa, theology ; Nyáya, logic ; Dharma, the institutes of law, and the Puránas, constitute the fourteen principal branches of knowledge.

Angiras—A Prajápati who married Smriti (memory) one of the daughters of Daksha. He is the reputed author of many vaidik hymns, but is mentioned also in a subsequent period as one of the inspired legislators of India, and as the author of an astronomical work. " The various legends connected with his life seem to have been occasioned by the word Angiras coming from the same radical as, and its sound recalling that of Agni, fire (q. v.) Hence we find Angiras sometimes either as an epithet or as the father of Agni, and the saint himself connected chiefly with such hymns as are addressed to Agni, to Indra or to deities of a kindred description: a portion of the fourth Veda, the Atharvan, reports him also as an expounder of the Bramhavidyá (q. v.) or the sacred knowledge that had been imparted to him by Satyavaha, a descendant of Bharadvaja. Though Angiras, as may be concluded from his name being connected with the authorship of a great portion of the sacred Hindu literature, appears to have been one of the oldest civilizers of India, no historical date is to be obtained from the epic or puránic literature where the vaidik legends of his life are merely amplified; there he is named as one of the Prajápatis or progenitors of mankind, engendered, according to some by Manu, according to others by Brahmá himself, either with the female half of his body or from his mouth, or from the space between his eyebrows. As such he is considered also as one of the seven Rishis who preside over the reign of the first Manu, or Svayambhuva. He is called, besides, the priest of the Gods, the Lord of the Sacrifice, &c. Sometimes he is considered as a son of Uru by Agnéyí, the daughter of Agni. His daughters are the Richas (or vaidik hymns) and also Sasvati, Sinívali, Kuhú, Raka, Anumati; his sons are Samvarta, the manes called Havishmats, Utathaya, Brihaspati, Markandeya; his wives, Smriti (traditional science), two daughters of Daksha, Swadha and Satí, and Sraddha, the daughter of the sage Kardama. As an astronomical personification he is Brihaspati himself, or the regent of the planet Jupiter and presides over the sixth year of the cycle of sixty years."—*Goldstücker.*

Angirasas—Warrior priests. These who were kshatryas by birth, the heads of the family of Rathinara, were called Angirasas (sons of Angiras) and were brahmans as well as kshatryas. " This affords an instance of a mixture of character, of which several similar cases occur. Kshatryas by birth become brahmans by profession, and such persons are usually considered as Angirasas, descendants or followers of Angiras, who may have founded a school of warrior priests."—*Wilson.*

Anila—(Wind) Vasu. The deities called Vasus, because, preceded by fire, they abound in splendour and might, are severally named Apa, Dhruva, Soma, Dhava (fire), Anila (wind), Anala (fire), Pratúsha (daybreak) and Prabhása, (eight) ; 2, The son of Tansu and father of Dushyanta ; 3, A Rákshasa.

Anima—A superhuman faculty, or the possession of a divine influence to be attained by austere devotion ; or the faculty of assuming an atomic, subtle, invisible, supreme condition of existence, supposed to be attainable by men through a course of austerities, attended with magical rites, in honor of Śiva and Párvati.

Aniruddha—The son of Pradyumna. He is described as "a powerful and gallant prince, who was fierce in fight, an ocean of prowess, and the tamer of his foes." He was beloved by Usha, daughter of Bána. Her companion Chitralékha, being endowed with magic power, set off through the air to Dwáraká, and returned bringing Aniruddha along with her to the palace of Bána. The guards discovering him there with Usha reported it to the king, who sent a body of his followers to seize the prince ; but the valiant youth slew his assailants, on which Bána advanced against him and endeavoured to kill him. Finding however that Aniruddha was not to be subdued by prowess, he brought his magical faculties into the conflict, by which he succeeded in capturing the Yadu prince and binding him in serpent bonds. When Aniruddha was missed from Dwáraka, and the Yádavas were enquiring of one another whither he had gone, Nárada came to them and told them he was the prisoner of Bána. Krishna immediately summoned Garuda, who came with a wish, and mounting upon him, along with Bala and Pradyumna, he set off for the city of Bána. A great battle then took place in which Krishna with his discuss lopped away the thousand arms of Bána, and would have killed him but for the interference of Śiva on his behalf. Krishna then went to the place where Aniruddha was confined. The fetters that bound him were destroyed, being blasted by the breath of Garuda; and Krishna, placing him, along with his wife Usha, on the celestial bird, returned with Pradyumna and Ráma to Dwáraka." V. P. Professor Wilson thinks that the legend describes a serious struggle between the Saivas and Vaishnavas in which the latter were victorious.

Anjaka—One of the Dánavas, a son of Viprachitti, of the families of the Daityas.

Anjan—The second elephant of Indra.

Anjana—A serpent with many heads, one of the progeny of Kadru, V. P., V. I., c. 21.

Anrita.—Falsehood, son of Adharma, (vice) married to Nikriti, they had two sons, Bhaya (fear) and Naraka (hell), and twins to them two daughters, Máya (deceit) and Vedanú (torture), who became their wives. In the Rámáyana, Anrita is the name of one of the mystical weapons delivered by Ráma to Viswámitra.

Ansa—One of the twelve Ádityás. V. P., p. 122.

Ansuman—A mythical rája of the solar race, the son of Asamanj, and father of Dilípa. He was the grandson of Sagara, who was sent by him to recover the sacrificial steed. Ansumat having arrived at the place of the great Rishi, Kapila, prayed to him and so propitiated him, that the saint gave up the horse and predicted his future greatness. Sagara on recovering the steed completed his sacrifice.

"Prince Anṣumán, the strong and brave
Followed the rede Suparna gave,
The glorious hero took the horse,
And homeward quickly bent his course."—*Griffiths.*

Ansaumti—A river mentioned in the Rig Veda, on the banks of which Krishna the Dasyu was conquered by Rája Rigiswan.

Antacharas—A class of Border tribes, mentioned in the V. P.

Antariksha—A Vyasa, son of Kinnara, the arranger of the Védas in the thirteenth Dwápara. The great Rishis are said in the

V. P. to have arranged the Védas twenty-eight times, a list is given of the twenty-eight Vyásas of the present Manwantara ; 2, A king of the family of Ikshwáku, a son of Kinnara and father of Suvarna.

Anu—A son of Yayáti who was made by his father king of the North to govern as viceroy under his younger brother Puru, whom he appointed supreme monarch of the earth.

Anubhavamrita—A *vairágya* treatise, which exists only in the Dravidian languages, and appears to be entirely unknown in other parts of India. Dr. Ballantyne informed the writer in 1852 that none of the pandits in the Benares College knew of the work : it contains a treatise on the Upanishads,—a sort of exposition of Pantheism—shows that the existence of a material world cannot be proved—that all is Máya—recommends retirement from domestic life and meditation, in order to the soul's purification and final beatitude.

Anugraha—The eighth creation, which possesses both the qualities of goodness and darkness. This seems to have been taken from the Sánkya philosophy, and is described in the Padma, Linga, and Matsya Puránas. It is the creation of which we have a notion, or to which we give assent (anugraha) in contradiction to organic creation, or that existence of which we have sensible perception.

Anugraha-sarga—A technical phrase meaning "Benevolent Nature," one of the Aphorisms of the Sánkhya Philosophy as stated in the Compendium of Principles. "Benevolent creation" it is said consists of the production of external objects from the five subtile elements, viz., of sound, tangibility, colour, savour, odour. Bramha perceiving these (the senses) to be destitute of a sphere of action, created external objects, or "benevolent nature."

Anuhlada—Son of Hiranyakasipu, and brother of the wise Práhlada, the augmenter of the Daitya race [Práhlada.]

Anukramanis—Systematic indices to various portions of the ancient Vaidic literature. The most perfect Anukramaṇí is that of the Sanhita of the Rig Véda. It is ascribed to Kátyáyaná, an author chiefly known by his works in the Yajur Veda and Sáma Veda. Its name is Sarvanukramani, *i. e.*, the index of all things.

It gives the first words of each hymn, the number of verses, the name and family of the poets, the names of the deities and the metres of every verse. Max Müller fixes the date of Kátyáyaná's writing in the latter half of the fourth century, B. C.

Anula—A female Buddhistic Arhat or saint who is renowned for having introduced the Buddhistic religion into Lanká or Ceylon in the time of the king Asóka; she was the wife of Mahánága, the younger brother of Mahéndra and received the dignity of a female Arhat from Sanghamitrá, the sister of Mahéndra; 2, A queen of Ceylon renowned for her profligacy. She was the wife of Koránga, the brother of Mahákúla-mahátishya, whom she killed by poison as well as his son Tishya and four paramours whom she married in succession. A second son of Mahákúla, Kálakanatishya, revolted at last against her and caused her death in the year 41 B. C.—*Goldstücker*.

Anumati—One of the four daughters of Angiras; the first day of the moon's wane. The four daughters are the four phases of the moon, V. P., p. 83. The goddess of the day when the moon is in the third and fourth quarters.

Anuradha—A lunar mansion in Járadgaví. For an explanation of the divisions of the celestial sphere, see V. P., p. 226.

Anushtubh—1, A metre from the northern mouth of Brahma, along with the Sáma Véda, &c., V. P., p. 42; 2, A name of Saraswati.

Anuvatsara—Fourth cyclic year. Fifteen days of thirty Muhúrttas, each is called a Paksha (a lunar fortnight); two of these make a month, two months a solar season, three seasons a northern or southern declination (Ayana); and these two compose a year. Years, made up of four kinds of months, are distinguished into five kinds; and an aggregate of all the varieties of time is termed a Yuga or cycle. The years are severally called Samvatsara, Parivatsara, Idvatsara, Anuvatsara and Vatsara. This is the time called a yuga.

Anyadesya—The name given to words derived from foreign languages.

Apa—One of the deities called Vasus. (See Anila.)

Apamurtti—One of the sinless sons of Atri.

Apana—One of the ten winds which brahmans believe to be lodged in the body ; this one resides in the region of the navel, and forces out the solid and liquid secretions.

Apara—A technical term in the Sánkhya philosophy, denoting that kind of mental acquiescence or indifference which arises from the reflection that sensual objects perish in consequence of enjoyment, and that there is a feeling of pain or trouble when they perish.

Aparagodana—(In Buddhistic Cosmogony.) One of the four dwípas or continents, in shape like a round mirror, and seven thousand Yojanas in breadth, to the west of the Mahámeru which is in the centre of the earth.

Aparajita—1, One of the eleven Rudras ; 2, A name of Siva and of Vishnu ; 3, A name of Dúrgá.

Aparna—A name of Uma, a daughter of Himavat and Mena, so called because she did not even eat a leaf during her performance of religious austerities.

Apaspati—A son of Uttanapada, and brother of Dhruva, q. v.

Apastamba—A celebrated writer, author of the Sámayáchárica sutras. The precise period at which he lived is not known, but his writings are much valued.—A. S. L., p. 206.

Apava—A name of the Prajápati Vasishtha. "As" says Professor Wilson, "he performs the office of Brahma, he should be regarded as that divinity, but this is not exactly the case. Apava becomes two-fold, and in the capacity of his male half begets offspring by the female." V. P., p. 52.

Appamanabha—The name of the twelfth heaven of Buddhism.

Appamana Subha—The fifteenth heaven of Buddhism.

Apratisht'ha—One of the Narakas or hells, of which twenty-eight are enumerated. They are called the awful provinces of the kingdom of Yama, terrible with instruments of torture.

Apsarasas—The name given to the nymphs of heaven created by Brahma in the commencement of the Kalpa. They are also said to have been produced from the whirlpool of the deep, of surprising loveliness. In some of the Purános they are called the daughters of Kaṣyapa and Muni. The Apsarasas are of two kinds: Laukíka, "worldly," of whom thirty-four are specified; and Daivika or divine, ten in number; the latter furnish the individuals most frequently engaged in the interruption of the penances of holy sages. There are also fourteen Ganas—or troops of Apsarasas, bearing peculiar designations as Ahutas, &c. "Originally these deities seem to have been personifications of the vapours which are attracted by the sun, and form into mist or clouds: their character may be thus interpreted in the few hymns of the Rig Veda where mention is made of them. At a subsequent period when the Gandharva of the Rig Veda, who personifies there especially the fire of the Sun, expanded into the Fire of Lightning, the rays of the moon and other attributes of the elementary life of heaven, as well as into pious acts referring to it, the Apsarasas become divinities which represent phenomena or objects both of a physical and ethical kind, closely associated with that life; thus in the Yajurveda sunbeams are called the Apsarasas, associated with the Gandharva who is the sun; Planets are termed the Apsarasas connected with the Gandharva Fire; Constellations are the Apsarasas of the Gandharva Wind, &c., &c. In the last Mythological epoch when the Gandharvas have saved from their elementary nature merely so much as to be musicians in the paradise of Indra, the Apsarasas appear among other subordinate deities which share in the merry life of Indra's heaven, as the wives of the Gandharvas, but more especially as wives of a licentious sort, and they are promised therefore, too, as a reward to heroes fallen in battle when they are received in the paradise of Indra; and while, in the Rig Veda, they assist Soma to pour down his floods, they descend in the epic literature on earth merely to shake the virtue of penitent sages, and to deprive them of the power they would otherwise have acquired through unbroken austerities."—*Goldstücker, Sans. Dict.*

Aptoryama—A sacrificial rite produced from Bramha's northern mouth, V. P. "The *Aptoryam* is the seventh or last part of the Jyotishtoma, for the performance of which it is not essentially necessary, but a voluntary sacrifice instituted for the attainment of a specific desire. The literal meaning of the word would be in conformity with the *Praudhamanoramá* 'a sacrifice which procures the attainment of the desired object." '—*Goldstücker.*

Aradhya—The name of a class of Brahmans who recede somewhat from the extreme tenets of the *Vira Saivas*, and tend somewhat towards the Vaishnavas. Basava was originally an Aradhya brahman, though in the Purana bearing his name the sect is spoken of very contemptuously.

Araga—A Sun. When Vishnu assumes the character of Rudra, the destroyer, and descends to reunite all creatures with himself, he enters into the seven solar rays which dilate into seven suns—the name of the first is Araga.

Aranyakas—" The Treatises of the Forest." So named, as Sáyana informs us, because they had to be read in the Forest. "It might almost seem," says Max Müller, "as if they were intended for the Vanaprasthas only, people who, after having performed all the duties of students and householders, retire from the world to the forest, to end their days in the contemplation of the deity." In some instances the Aranyakas form part of the Brahmanas and thus share the authority of Sruti or revelation. Part of one however is ascribed to a human author Asvalanyaka. Another part is quoted by Sáyana as being a Sútra work of Saunakas. The Aranyakas pre-suppose the existence of the Brahmanas, and may be regarded as an enlargement upon them. The chief interest which they possess at the present moment consists in their philosophy. The philosophical chapters, termed Upanishads, are almost the only portion of Vedic literature extensively read to this day. The Vedánta, the Sánkya, the Vaiséshika, the Nyáya and Yoga philosophers, all appeal to the Upanishads in support of their tenets. "Traces of modern ideas are not wanting in the Aranyakas, and the very fact that they are destined for a class of men who had retired from the world in order to give themselves up to the highest problems, shows an advanced, and an already declining and decaying society, not unlike the monastic age of the Christian world."—*Max Müller*, A. S. L., Chap. II.

Arati, Alati—A ceremony on the birth of a brahman child. The Abbé DuBois thus describes it: "Upon a plate of copper they place a lamp, made of a paste from rice-flour. It is supplied with oil and lighted. The married women, but not widows, for their presence would be unlucky, take hold of the plate with both hands, and raising it as high as the head of the person for whom the ceremony is performed, describe in that position a number of circles with the plate and the burning lamp.

Sometimes, in place of the rice lamp, they fill the plate with water, colored red with a mixture of saffron and other ingredients; and with this describe their circle, raising it as high as the head of the person who is the object of the ceremony.

The intention of this ceremony is to avert fascination by the eye, and to prevent the accidents which arise out of I know not what evil impression occasioned by the jealous looks of certain persons. The credulity of the Hindus respecting this sort of injury is carried to excess: and it is for that reason that the ceremony of the *árati*, which is considered to have the virtue of preventing the effect of those glances, is so common and so universal among the Hindus, and especially among persons of high rank, who, being more observed and having more enemies than private individuals, are more exposed to the evil influence of malevolent or jealous looks. When such persons therefore appear in public, the first thing that is done on their return home, is to perform this ceremony of the árati over them, as an antidote to the ill-designed looks which may have been cast upon them. For the same reason princes have the ceremony repeated several times in a day.

This sort of superstition or idle observance is by no means peculiar to the Hindus. I have seen cantons in France, (and I suppose it is not different in many other countries,) where the people were scarcely less infatuated. I have known decent villagers who would not have dared to show their young children to people they did not know, or to persons of bad appearance, lest their invidious or ill-boding look should occasion some mischief to befall them."—*Manners and Customs of the Hindus.*

Arbudas—The people about Mount Abu in Guzerat—called Arbuda in the Purānas.

Archish—(Flame). The wife of Krisáswa, and mother of Dhúmaketu (comet).

Ardra—A lunar mansion in Gajavithi. The path of the sun and other planets amongst the lunar asterisms is divided into three portions or Avasthánas, northern, southern and central, called severally Airávata, Jaradgava and Vaiswánara. Each of these again is divided into three parts or Vithis. Each of these Vithis contains three asterisms.

Argha—A gift indicating great respect, such as fruit and flowers, or milk and honey, which are offered to an idol, or to a brahman, or to a bridegroom on his wedding day.

Ahrat—1, A king of southern Karnataka who was converted by Rishabha ; 2, A name of a deified sage among the Jainas.

Arhatas—A name applied to the Jains, q. v.

Arishta—1, A demon who in the form of a savage bull came one evening to the spot where Krishna and the Gopís were dancing together. His color was that of a cloud charged with rain, he had vast horns ; and his eyes were like two fiery suns, his tail was erect, his dewlap hung low, and he was a terror to the herds. The herdsmen and their women were exceedingly frightened, and called aloud on Krishna, who came to their succour, without any fear. He waited the near approach of the bull, when he seized him by the horns and pressed his sides with his knees. Tearing off one of the horns he beat the fierce demon with it till he died, vomiting blood from his mouth. The herdsmen then praised Krishna ; 2, A daughter of Daksha, and wife of Kaṣyapa. V. P.

Arishtanemi—1, A Prájapati, who married four daughters of Daksha ; 2, A name of Kaṣyapa. His daughter Kesini became the wife of Sagara.

Arjuna—The third of the five sons of Pándu by his wife Kunti or Pritha, who, however, received amatory visits from the gods Dharma, Váyu and Indra, who are therefore put forward as the real fathers of Yudhishthira, Bhíma and Arjuna, in order to give these heroes a divine origin. Arjuna is therefore called the son of Indra. He was taught the use of the bow by Dróna, and was his best loved pupil : this excited the jealousy of his cousin Duryódhana, and ultimately led to the banishment of the Pándavas from Court. Arjuna appeared at the exhibition of arms at Hastinápura, where he performed marvellous feats in archery, sword-playing, whirling the chakra, and throwing the noose. At the Swayamvara of Draupadí, Arjuna was disguised as a brahman, and succeeded in hitting the golden fish after all the Rájas had failed ; he was at once acknowledged by Draupadí as the victor ; she threw the garland round his neck, and permitted him to lead her away according to the rule of the Swayamvara. Draupadí became the wife of the five brothers ; each had a house and garden of his own, and Draupadí dwelt with each of them in turn for two days at a time ; and it was a law amongst them that if a brother entered the house of another brother, whilst Draupadí was dwelling there, he should depart out of the city and go into exile for twelve years. It happened that this rule was inadvertently violated by Arjuna, who went into exile in consequence. He was accompanied by many brahmans, and visited many sacred places. At Hurdwar a damsel named Ulúpi, the daughter of Vásukí, the Rája of the Nágás, saw Arjuna and besought him to espouse her, and he abode with her many days.

After this he visited the countries of the south, and in the Mahéndra mountain saw Parasu Ráma from whom he obtained some excellent weapons. In the city of Manipura, Chitrangada the daughter of the Rája, saw Arjuna and desired him for her husband. They were married on the condition that any son she might have should remain to succeed to the Ráj of Manipura. She gave birth to a son who was named Babhru-váhana. After a residence there of three years Arjuna took leave of his wife and son and proceeded on his travels.

The next place to which he went was Prabhása near Dwáraka. Here he was met by Krishna, who gave orders that the city of Dwáraka should be dressed out with flowers and banners and every sign of rejoicing. Krishna gave a great entertainment to all the chieftains and their ladies, on the beautiful hill of Raivataka,

Arjuna was smitten with the charms of Subhadra, the sister of Krishna. In a few days they were married by the contrivance of Krishna, and when the twelve years of exile were accomplished Arjuna departed with his wife Subhadra for the city of Indraprastha. His brothers received him with gladness and Draupadí was soon reconciled to Subhadra.

Arjuna's elder brother, the Rája Yudhishthira, determined to perform the great sacrifice called the Rájasúya. This was successfully accomplished, but it revived the old feud between the Kauravas and Pándavas. Duryódhana invited his kinsmen to a gambling match, seeking by under-hand means to deprive Yudhishthira of his Ráj.—[See Yudhishthira.]

In the course of the second exile of the Pándavas, Arjuna "by the advice of his mythical grandfather Vyása, for the sake of performing such penances as should propitiate the gods, and induce them to grant him celestial weapons which would ensure him the victory over Duryódhana and the Kauravas. On reaching the Mandara mountain he heard a voice in the sky calling upon him to stop; and Indra appeared in all his glory, and promised to give him the divine weapons provided he succeeded in propitiating the god Śiva. Arjuna then entered upon a course of austerities so severe that Śiva was perfectly gratified, but proved the valour of his worshipper by taking upon himself the form of a mountaineer and engaging Arjuna in single combat. Arjuna, unable to make any impression upon his enemy, at length discovered the deity, and prostrated himself at the feet of Śiva; upon which Śiva gave him one of his most powerful weapons. Subsequently the gods of the four quarters of the universe—Indra, Yama, Varuna, and Kuvéra—presented themselves to Arjuna, and respectively furnished him with their own peculiar weapons. Arjuna was then carried away in Indra's chariot to the city of Amarávatí, which is the heaven of Indra. There he spent many years in practising the use of arms; and at length was sent by Indra to make war against the Daityas of the sea.

The mythic account of Arjuna's wars against the Daityas of the sea, is also worthy of notice if only as a creation of the imagination. On approaching the coast in a chariot which flew through the air, Arjuna beheld the sea rising in vast heaps, and saw ships laden with rubies, and fishes and tortoises as large as mountains. He blew his war shell and the Daityas trembled with fear, but in return they sounded their drums and trumpets so loudly that the monsters of the deep leaped above the waves. Thousands of Daityas rushed upon him, but he uttered powerful mantras as he discharged his arrows, and kept them all at bay. They rained fire, water, and mountains upon him, but he triumphed in the end and slew them all. Then the women came out screaming like. cranes, but Arjuna passed them by and entered the city, where he saw chariots with ten thousand horses of the colour of peacocks. Meantime the women were terrified at the rolling of his chariot, and fled to their houses, whilst the noise of their ornaments resembled the falling of stones upon a mountain. After this victory Arjuna returned to Indra, and was rewarded with great praises ; and the sovereign of the gods presented him with a chain of gold and a diadem, and with a war-shell which sounded like thunder."

After these extravagant myths Arjuna is said to have been in the service of Rája Viráta, as teacher of music and dancing, until the expiration of the thirteen years of exile. When negotiations took place for the restoration of the Pándavas, Arjuna exerted himself to win over Krishna to their side ; and Krishna promised to drive his chariot in the war which ensued. It was then that the celebrated dialogue known as the Bhagavat Gíta, took place. On the first day of the war Arjuna fought with Bhíshma : on the following day he rallied the Pándavas after they had been repulsed by Bhíshma, and the latter reluctantly engaged in a second combat with him. He also rescued his son Abhimanyu from Duryódhana. In another terrible conflict with Bhíshma the latter was mortally wounded. Arjuna was afterwards challenged by Susarma and his four brethren : contrary to the advice of Yudhishthira he accepted the challenge, defeated Susarma and his brethren; fought Susarma a second time in another locality ; and during his absence his son Abhimanyu was slain by six of the Kaurava chieftains. Arjuna was overpowered with grief when he heard this, and vowed to take the life of Jayadratha before the setting of the morrow's sun. This he accomplished, and not long after killed

Karna with a crescent-shaped arrow. The armies stopped fighting, and the gods descended from heaven to witness the battle between Arjuna and Karna.

The Mahábhárata next relates Arjuna's adventures with the horse that was captured and then let loose for a year, previous to the great Asvamédha which Yudhishthira had resolved to perform. These adventures constitute twelve legends connected with the countries into which the horse is said to have wandered. In the seventh of them Arjuna is slain and beheaded by his own son Babhru-váhana in the city of Manipura, but restored to life by the application of a jewel brought from the city of serpents in the under world. After the massacre at Prabhása, Arjuna was summoned to Dwáraka by Krishna, and on his arrival he directed the residue of the people to leave the city. His strength now departed from him ; he was advised by Vyása to abandon worldly concerns, and died with the other Pándavas on the Himálaya mountains. His grandson Paríkshit (son of Abhimanyu) succeeded to the Ráj of Hastinápura.

Arshabhu—The first division of the central portion of the lunar mansions.

Arsha marriage—One of the eight modes of marriage described by Manu ; in which a father receives from a bridegroom one pair of kine, (a bull and a cow) or two pairs, for religious purposes, and then gives away his daughter in due form. This is the ceremony of the Rishis and probably prevailed amongst all the Vedic Aryans. It furnishes proof of the distinction between the marriage rite of the Rishis and that of the Brahmans. No religious qualification was required in the bridegroom, and the young man simply obtained a damsel by presenting her father with a pair or two of kine.—*Wheeler.*

Art'ha Brahmans—According to the *Kerala Ulpatti*, when *Parasu Ráma* had recovered a large strip of territory from the ocean, on the Malayalam coast, he set apart certain fishermen to officiate as *Brahmans* to the rest of the people, and promised to come at their call. They, however, acted so as to displease him ; whereupon he disfranchised them, and called in a colony of pure

Brahmans from *Hai Kshétram*, to whom he delivered charge of the people, in matters of rites and ceremonies. The fishermen had the title of "half-brahmans."—*Taylor.*

Art'hanesvari—A form of *Siva*, and, on the left-hand half, is *Párvati*. This is doubtless an early hieroglyphic to convey a chaste notion of the union of the active deity, with passive matter; whence creation.

Arthasadhak—The finance minister of Rája Dasaratha.

Arthasastra—One of the eighteen principal branches of knowledge, viz., the science of Government as laid down first by Vrihaspati.

Arugan—The name given by the Jains to the Supreme Being. The popular name of God is Jinan, or Jainau; hence the appellation Jains. To this God one thousand and eight sacred names are ascribed. The attributes of omnipotence and omniscience, of omnipresence and infinite benevolence, are given to this deity. See Jains.

Aruna—A celebrated son of Kaṣyapa and Vinata: and brother of Garuda the destroyer of serpents.

Arundhati—Daughter of Kardama, wife of Vasistha, evidently an allegorical personification of a religious rite. "One of the Pleiades and generally regarded as the model of wifely excellence;" it is a small star close to the middle one in the tail of *Ursa Major*: and is said to have been the wife of *Vasistha*. A newly-married couple, amongst brahmans, have this star pointed out to them by the Puróhita, or Astrologer, and are directed to pay it obeisance.

Arvarivat—One of the seven Rishis of the second Manwantara. By the seven Rishis we may often understand the constellation, *Ursa Major*.

Arvavasu—One of the seven principal solar rays, that which supplies heat to the planet Jupiter.

Aryabhatta—A celebrated ancient Hindu astronomer. It is difficult to determine with accuracy when he lived, but Mr. Colebrooke thinks he flourished soon after the commencement of the Christian era, or not later than the third or fourth century.

Aryaka—A cowherd in the Sanscrit drama of the Toy-cart. He conspired against the weak and unpopular king then upon the throne at Ananti or Ougein. Aryaka is described as a man with 'arms like elephants, vast tusks, his breast and shoulders brawny as the lion's, his eyes a coppery red.' He succeeded in obtaining possession of the throne.

Aryayhichita—A celebrated Dravida Brahman who lived at Agrahára in the 16th century of Sáliváhana ; his contemporaries considered him as an emanation of Śiva, on account of his devotion for this god, and his great learning. He is said to be the author of 84 books on theology, rhetoric and philosophy ; he died at Chillumbrum at the age of ninety.

Aryaman—One of the twelve Ádityas in the Manwantara of Vaivaswata.

Aryan Race, Aryan Languages—Aryavarta was the holy land of the brahmans, the country lying between the Himálaya and the Vindhya mountains, which was the ancient abode of the Hindus. In the north-western part of that region, in countries watered by the Saraswati, the earliest traditions of the brahmans place the ancestors of the Indian race. The name Aryan is now generally used to designate that ethnological division of mankind otherwise called Indo-European or Indo-Germanic. No one now doubts that the brahmans of India belong to the same family, the Aryan or Indo-European family, which civilized the whole of Europe. The Aryan race consists of two branches, an eastern and a western. The western branch comprehends the inhabitants of Europe, with the exception of the Turks, Magyars, and Finns : the eastern comprehends the inhabitants of Armenia, of Persia, of Afghanistan and Hindustan. The evidence on which a family relation has been established among these nations is that of language.

"At the first dawn of traditional history," says Max Müller, "we see these Aryan tribes migrating across the snow of the Himálaya southward toward the 'Seven Rivers' (the Indus, the five rivers of the Punjâb and the Sarasvatî), and ever since India has been called their home. That before that time they had been living in more northern regions, within the same precincts with the ancestors of the Greeks, the Italians, Slavonians, Germans and Celts, is a fact as firmly established as that the Normans of William the Conqueror were the northmen of Scandinavia. The evidence of language is irrefragable, and it is the only evidence worth listening to with regard to ante-historical periods. It would have been next to impossible to discover any traces of relationship between the swarthy natives of India and their conquerors, whether Alexander or Clive, but for the testimony borne by language. What other evidence could have reached back to times when Greece was not peopled by Greeks, nor India by Hindus ? Yet these are the times of which we are speaking. What authority would have been strong enough to persuade the Grecian army, that their gods and their hero ancestors were the same as those of King Porus, or to convince the English soldier that the same blood was running in his veins and in the veins of the dark Bengalese ? And yet there is not an English jury now-a-days, which, after examining the hoary documents of language, would reject the claim of a common descent and a legitimate relationship between Hindu, Greek and Teuton. Many words still live in India and in England, that have witnessed the first separation of the northern and southern Aryans, and these are witnesses not to be shaken by cross-examination. The terms for God, for house, for father, mother, son, daughter, for dog and cow, for heart and tears, for axe and tree, identical in all the Indo-European idioms, are like the watchwords of soldiers. We challenge the seeming stranger ; and whether he answer with the lips of a Greek, or German, or an Indian, we recognise him as one of ourselves. Though the historian may shake his head, though the physiologist may doubt, and the poet scorn the idea, all must yield before the facts furnished by language. There *was* a time when the ancestors of the Celts, the Germans, the Slavonians, the Greeks and Italians, the Persians and Hindus, were living together within the same fences, separate from the ancestors of the Semitic and Turanian races.

It is more difficult to prove that the Hindu was the last to leave this common home, that he saw his brothers all depart towards the setting sun, and that then, turning towards the south and the east, he started alone in search of a new world. But as in his language and in his grammar he has preserved something of what seems peculiar to each of the northern dialects singly, as he agrees with the Greek and the German where the Greek and the German seem to differ from all the rest, and as no other language has carried off so large a share of the common Aryan heirloom—whether roots, grammar, words, myths, or legends—it is natural to suppose that, though perhaps the eldest brother, the Hindu was the last to leave the central home of the Aryan family.

The Aryan nations who pursued a north-westerly direction, stand before us in history as the principal nations of north-western Asia and Europe. They have been the prominent actors in the great drama of history, and have carried to their fullest growth all the elements of active life with which our nature is endowed. They have perfected society and morals, and we learn from their literature and works of art the elements of science, the laws of art, and the principles of philosophy. In continual struggle with each other and with Semitic and Turanian races, these Aryan nations have become the rulers of history, and it seems to be their mission to link all parts of the world together by the chains of civilization, commerce and religion. In a word, they represent the Aryan man in his historical character.

But while most of the members of the Aryan family followed this glorious path, the southern tribes were slowly migrating towards the mountains which gird the north of India. After crossing the narrow passes of the Hindu kush or the Himâlaya, they conquered or drove before them, as it seems without much effort, the aboriginal inhabitants of the Trans-Himâlayan countries. They took for their guides the principal rivers of northern India, and were led by them to new homes in their beautiful and fertile valleys. It seems as if the great mountains in the north had afterwards closed for centuries their Cyclopean gates against new immigrations, while, at the same time, the waves of the Indian Ocean kept watch over the southern borders of the peninsula. None of the great conquerors of antiquity—Sesostris, Semiramis, Nebuchadnezzar, or Cyrus, who waged a kind of half-nomadic warfare over Asia, Africa and Europe, and whose names, traced in characters of blood, are still legible on the threshold of history, disturbed the peaceful seats of these Aryan settlers. Left to themselves in a world of their own, without a past, and without a future before them, they had nothing but themselves to ponder on. Struggles there must have been in India also. Old dynasties were destroyed, whole families annihilated, and new empires founded. Yet the inward life of the Hindu was not changed by these convulsions. His mind was like the lotus leaf after a shower of rain has passed over it; his character remained the same, passive, meditative, quiet and full of faith."—*A Sanscrit Lit, p.* 16.

Asamanj—The son and successor of Sagara; he is thus described in the Rámáyana:

"Prince Asamanj brought up with care,
Scourge of his foes was made the heir.
But liegemen's boys he used to cast,
To Sarju's waves that hurried past,
Laughing the while in cruel glee
Their dying agonies to see.
This wicked prince who aye withstood
The counsel of the wise and good,
Who plagued the people in his hate,
His father banished from the State;
His son, kind-spoken, brave and tall,
Was Ansumán, beloved of all."—*Griffiths.*

Asampricshana—The title of the fifth section of the Pancha Tantra; meaning Inconsiderateness.

Asamprajnata—Contemplation, in which reason is lost sight of; a complete restraint of the action of thought; the last stage of mental abstraction; in which even the reflection of his individual existence is lost sight of, and he is mentally one with the Supreme Being.

Asana—The third stage of Yoga. There are various postures in which the Yogi is directed to sit when he engages in meditation, Asana is that in which he crosses his legs underneath him, and lays hold of his feet on each side with his hands.

Ashadha—The name of a constellation.

Ashahra—The name of one of the lunar months in the Vedas.

Ashtavakra—A brahman, who by a long course of religious penance, standing in water, and meditating on the eternal spirit, became a celebrated sage or Muni. He was deformed from his birth, and on one occasion he was laughed at by the Apsarasas, or divine nymphs, on whom in consequence he denounced imprecations. The nymphs then endeavoured to appease him, and so far succeeded that he promised they should finally return to the sphere of the gods.

Asikni—The daughter of the patriarch Vírana, wife of Daksha, the great father of mankind.

Asipatravana—Sins punished in one of the Narakas or hells, of which twenty-eight are enumerated.

Asit—The son of Rája Dhruvasandhi, of the solar race; his career is thus described in the Rámáyana:

> " Asit had warfare, fierce and hot,
> With rival kings in many a spot,
> Haihayas, Talajanghas styled,
> And Sasivaindhus, strong and wild,
> Long time he strove, but forced to yield,
> Fled from his kingdom and the field.
> With his two wives away he fled
> Where high Himálaya lifts his head,
> And, all his wealth and glory past,
> He paid the dues of Fate at last."—*Griffiths.*

Asitanga—The name of one of the eight Bhairavas, or inferior manifestations of some portion of Siva.

Aslesha—A lunar mansion in Airávati, the third vithí of the northern Avashtana.

Asmita—Selfishness, one of the five afflictions of the Pátanjulu philosophy.

Asoka—A king of Magadha, patron of Buddhism. Th is king, is the most celebrated of any in the annals of the Buddhists. In the commencement of his reign he followed the Brahmanical faith, but became a convert to that of Buddha, and a zealous encourager of it. "He is said to have maintained in his palace 64,000 Buddhist priests, and to have erected 84,000 columns or topes throughout India. A great convocation of Buddhist priests was held in the eighteenth year of his reign which was followed by missions to Ceylon and other places. According to Buddhist chronology he ascended the throne 218 years after the death of Buddha, B. C., 325. As the grandson of Chandragupta, however, he must have been sometime subsequent to this. The duration of his reign was 36 years, bringing it down to B. C. 230. A number of very curious inscriptions in columns and rocks, by a Buddhist prince, in an ancient form of letter, and the Páli language, exist in India, and some of them refer to Greek princes, who can be no other than members of the Seleucidan and Ptolemaic dynasties, and are probably Antiochus the Great, and Ptolemy Energetes, Kings of Syria and Egypt in the latter part of the third century before Christ."—*Professor Wilson.*

Asokavarddhana—Another name for Asóka.

Asramas—A condition of life; "orders;" when the youth has been invested with the sacred thread, he is diligently to prosecute the study of the Vedas in the house of his preceptor, with an attentive spirit and leading a life of continence.

Asti—The wife of Kansa, and daughter of Jarásandha, king of Magadha.

Astika—A brahman whose father had practised great austerities, bathed in all the holy tanks, and abstained from matrimony, with his body dried up by fasting, he wandered hither and thither, till he accidentally came to a hollow place in which he perceived men hanging over an abyss. Their heads were downwards and suspended by a straw at which a rat was gnawing. Inquiring who they were he discovered that they were his own ancestors. These wretched men tell him that they are thus suspended because their posterity, who should have been the means of ensuring their bliss, had perished; and the one living descendant, whose son might have done so, was entirely given up to austerities, and did not marry. The ascetic tells them that *he* is that one descendant. The ancestors entreat him to marry and have a son who would release them. He promises to do what they desire, but will only marry a girl whose parents give her to him willingly. At length in the forest, Vásuki, king of serpents, offered him his sister, a young girl of lovely form. To her he was married, and the child born to them was Astíka. Of him we are told that he had a noble spirit, was well read in the Vedas, and became powerful through austerities.*

Asuras—Demons, born from the thigh of Brahma while the quality of darkness pervaded his body. Asura is a general name for all the giants and demons who composed the enemies of the gods, and the inhabitants of Pátála ; and a special designation for a class of these of the first order. They belong, in the wider sense, to the Epic ; in the more special sense, to the Puránic period. In the latter they are fabled to be sprung from Brahmá's thigh (Vishnu, P., p. 40), and to be the sons of Kaṣyapa, by Diti and Danáyu. As in the earliest period the Suras were personifications of light, so the Asuras were probably those of darkness ; and the original idea of the existence of malignant and terrible beings may thus be traced to the fear that man experiences in darkness, from the conviction that he is surrounded by creatures which he cannot see, in short, ghosts or goblins. "(The word is derived from *a*, privative, or rather negative, and *sura*, 'a deity.') XI, 22."—*J. C. Thompson*. In the Puránas the aborigines are described under the names of Asuras and Rákshasas ; as being giants and cannibals, and of course very repulsive. "The word Asura has a very interesting history. In classical Sanscrit it only means a demon ; and this meaning occurs occasionally even in the early books of the Rig Veda, and often in the later tenth. In the Atharva Veda it occurs very often in this sense, and the Brahmanas are never tired of beginning their legends with the phrase '*devásurá va eshu lokeshu samayatanta*,' 'the gods and asuras contended in these worlds.' But generally in the 'Rig Veda' the word has no such evil meaning, and it appears to have been originally derived from *as* 'to be' with

* Mrs. Manning, from Fragments du Mahábhárata, Par. T. Pavie.

the affix *ura* (a-sura), and to have meant ‘living,’ ‘spiritual.’ But in later times *asura* acquired a malevolent meaning, just as the Greek *δαίμων*; and even in the great epics, the Rámáyana and the Mahábharata, we find a new word *sura*, coined to express the good deities. Henceforth *sura* and *asura* play the same parts in the legends which had once been played by *deva* and *asura*; and a new legend is invented for an etymology, the *suras* being those heavenly beings who shared the liquor of immortality, (*sura*) while those who were excluded became the *asuras*."—*Quarterly Review, July* 1870, *p*. 202.

Asura-marriage—The fifth mode of marriage mentioned by Manu, in which the bridegroom gives as much wealth as he can afford to the damsel and her kinsmen, and then takes her according to his own pleasure.

Asvalayana—A distinguished author, who lived about 350 B. C. He was the pupil of Saunaka and the predecessor of Kátyáyana. He was one of the writers of the Kalpa-sutras which teach the mode of performance of sacrifices enjoined by the Vedas: and the author of the Grihya Sutras, or rules for household rites.

Asvamedha—The Sacrifice of a Horse. This forms the subject of the Bhárata of Jaimini. The sacrifice was an affair of great importance. It was of a politico-religious character. Any one claiming to be a supreme ruler, announced his intention of celebrating a horse sacrifice. A horse was selected and then turned loose to go whither it pleased: only being followed by armed men. If any other potentate contested the claim, he endeavoured to seize the horse; and there is much of Romance on this topic. If the armed men came back unconquered, and the horse with them, the sacrifice was conducted on a great, and most expensive scale. The flesh of the sacrifice was eaten, or burnt: the latter is the usual statement. The Aswamedha, performed a hundred times, raised the sacrificer to a level with Indra.

Asvapati—(Lord of Horses). 1, The Rája of Kekaya, and father of Maharája Dasaratha's wife Kaikeyi; 2, An ancient rája, the father of Sávitrí, q. v.

Asvini—A lunar asterism in Nagavithi, the first vithi in the northern Avastháṇa.

Asvins—" The Aṣvins seem to have been a puzzle even to the oldest Indian commentators." (*Muir.*) Professor Roth says " they are the earliest bringers of light in the morning sky, who in their chariot hasten onward before the dawn, and prepare the way for her."

" It may seem unaccountable that two deities of a character so little defined, and so difficult to identify, as the Aṣvins, should have been the objects of so enthusiastic a worship as appears from the numerous hymns dedicated to them in the Rig Veda, to have been paid to them in ancient times. The reason may have been that they were hailed as the precursors of returning day, after the darkness and dangers of the night. In some passages they are represented as being, like Agni, the chasers away of evil spirits.

" The Aṣvins are said to be young ancient, beautiful, honey-hued, lords of lustre, bright, of a golden brilliancy, agile, fleet as thought, swift as young falcons, possessing many forms, wearing lotus garlands, strong, mighty, terrible, possessed of wondrous powers, and profound in wisdom."—*Muir, O. S. T., vol.* v., *p.* 240.

" The following are a few of the modes in which the divine power of the Aṣvins is declared in different hymns to have been manifested for the deliverance of their votaries.

" When the sage Chyaváṇa had grown old and had been forsaken, they divested him of his decrepit body, prolonged his life and restored him to youth.

" In the same way they renewed the youth of Kali after he had grown old ; and when Viṣpalá's leg had been cut off in battle like the wing of a bird, the Aṣvins are said to have given her an iron one instead.

" They restored Parávjiṛ (or an outcast), who was blind and lame, to sight and the power of walking.

" Finally to say nothing of the succours rendered to numerous other persons, the Aṣvins did not confine their benevolence to human beings, but are also celebrated as having rescued from the jaws of a wolf a quail by which they were invoked.

"The Aṣvins are worshipped with uplifted hands, and supplicated for a variety of blessings, for long life, and for deliverance from calamities, for offspring, wealth, victory, destruction of enemies, preservation of the worshippers themselves, of their houses and cattle. No calamity or alarm from any quarter can touch the man whose chariot they place in the van."—*Ibid, p.* 249.

Professor Goldstücker writes, "The myth of the Aṣvins is, in my opinion, one of that class of myths in which two distinct elements, the cosmical and the human or historical, have gradually become blended into one. It seems necessary, therefore, to separate these two elements in order to arrive at an understanding of the myth. The historical or human element in it, I believe, is represented by those legends which refer to the wonderful cures effected by the Aṣvins, and to their performances of a kindred sort; the cosmical element is, that relating to their luminous nature. The link which connects both seems to be the mysteriousness of the nature and effects of the phenomena of light, and of the healing art at a remote antiquity. That there might have been some horsemen or warriors of great renown who inspired their contemporaries with awe by their wonderful deeds, and more especially by their medical skill, appears to have been also the opinion of some old commentators mentioned by Yāska, for some 'legendary writers,' he says, took them for 'two kings, performers of holy acts;' and this view seems likewise borne out by the legend in which it is narrated that the gods refused the Aṣvins admittance to a sacrifice on the ground that they had been on too familiar terms with men. It would appear then that these Aṣvins, like the Ribhus, were originally renowned mortals, who, in the course of time, were translated into the companionship of the gods; and it may be a matter of importance to investigate whether, besides this *a priori* view, there are further grounds of a linguistic or grammatical character for assuming that the hymns containing the legends relating to these human Aṣvins are posterior or otherwise to those descriptive of the cosmical gods of the same name.

"The luminous character of the latter can scarcely be matter of doubt, for the view of some commentators—recorded by Yáska,—

according to which they were identified with 'heaven and earth,' appears not to be countenanced by any of the passages known to us. Their very name, it would seem, settles this point, since *asva*, the horse, literally, 'the pervader,' is always the symbol of the luminous deities, especially of the sun. The difficulty, however, is to determine their position amongst these deities and to harmonize with it the other myths connected with them. I may here, however, first observe that, though Yáska records opinions which identify the Aṣvins with 'day and night,' and 'sun and moon,' the passage relied upon by Professor Roth to prove that Yáska himself identified them with Indra and Áditya (the sun), does not bear out any such conclusion. For the passage in question, as I understand it, means: 'their time is after the (latter) half of the night when the (spaces) becoming light is resisted (by darkness); for the middlemost Aṣvin (between darkness and light) shares in darkness, whilst (the other), who is of a solar nature (Áditya), shares in light.' There is this verse relating to them: 'In nights,' etc. Nor does Durga, the commentator on Yáska, attribute to the latter the view which Professor Roth ascribes to him. His words, as I interpret them, are: 'their time is after the (latter) half of the night when the (spaces) becoming light is resisted,' (means) when, after the (latter) half of the night, darkness intersected by light makes an effort against light, that is the time of the Aṣvins......Then the nature of the middlemost (between them) is a share in that darkness which penetrates into light; and the solar one (āditya) assumes that nature which is a share in the light penetrating into darkness. These two are the middlemost and the uppermost: this is the teacher's (*i. e.*, Yāska's) own opinion, for, in order to substantiate it, he gives as an instance the verse '*Vasātishu sma*,' " etc.

" To judge, therefore, from these words, it is the opinion of Yāska that the Aṣvins represent the transition from darkness to light, when the intermingling of both produces that inseparable duality expressed by the twin nature of these deities. And this interpretation, I hold, is the best that can be given of the character of the *cosmical* Aṣvins. It agrees with the epithets by which they are invoked, and with the relationship in which they are placed. They are young, yet also ancient, beautiful, bright, swift, etc.; and their negative character—the result of the alliance of light with darkness—is, I believe, expressed by *dasra*, the destroyer, and also by the two negatives in the compound *nasatya* (na+*a-satya*), though their positive character is again redeemed by the ellipsis of "enemies, or diseases, to *dasra*, and by the sense of *nasatya*, not un-true, *i. e.*, truthful. They are the parents of Púshan, the sun; for they precede the rise of the sun; they are the sons of the sky, and again the sons of Vivasvat and Saraṇyū. Vivasvat, I believe, here implies the firmament 'expanding' to the sight through the approaching light; and though Saraṇyū is to Professor Müller one of the deities which are forced by him to support his dawn-theory, it seems to me that the etymology of the word, and the character of the myths relating to it, rather point to the moving air, or the dark and cool air, heated, and therefore set in motion, by the approach of the rising sun. The Aṣvins are also the husbands or the friends of Sūryā, whom I take for the representative of the weakest manifestation of the sun; and I believe that Sāyaṇa is right when, by the sister of the Aṣvins, he understands Ushas, the dawn. The mysterious phenomenon of the intermingling of darkness—which is no longer complete night—and of light—which is not yet dawn—seems to agree with all these conceptions, and with the further details of a cosmical nature, which are so fully given in the preceding paper."—*Ibid, p.* 255-7.

Atala—The first of the seven regions of Pátála,—below the earth—ten thousand yojanas in extent—the soil of Atala is white, and the place is embellished with magnificent palaces.

Atarva—One of the fifteen teachers of the school of Vajasaneyi or white Yajush.

Atharva Veda—The name of the fourth of the four Vedas, created from the northern mouth of Brahma. It was arranged by Vyása. The illustrious sage Sumanta taught this Veda to his pupil Kabandha, who made it two-fold. The principal subjects of difference in the Sanhitas of the Atharva Veda, are the five Kalpas or ceremonials. "As to the internal character of the Atharva hymns, it may be said of them, as of the tenth book of the

Rík, that they are the productions of another and a later period, and the expressions of a different spirit, from that of the earlier hymns in the other Veda. In the latter, the gods are approached with reverential awe, indeed, but with love and confidence also; a worship is paid them that exalts the offerer of it; the demons, embraced under the general name *Rákshasas*, are objects of horror, whom the gods ward off and destroy; the divinities of the Atharva are regarded rather with a kind of cringing fear, as powers whose wrath is to be deprecated and whose favour curried, for it knows a whole host of imps and hobgoblins, in ranks and classes, and addresses itself to them directly, offering them homage to induce them to abstain from doing harm. The *mantra*, prayer, which in the older Veda is the instrument of devotion, is here rather the tool of superstition; it wrings from the unwilling hands of the gods the favours which of old their good-will to men induced them to grant, or by simple magical power obtains the fulfilment of the utterer's wishes. The most prominent characteristic feature of the Atharva is the multitude of incantations which it contains; these are pronounced either by the person who is himself to be benefited, or, more often, by the sorcerer for him, and are directed to the procuring of the greatest variety of desirable ends; most frequently, perhaps, long life, or recovery from grievous sickness, is the object sought; then a talisman, such as a necklace, is sometimes given, or in very numerous cases some plant endowed with marvellous virtues is to be the immediate external means of the cure; farther, the attainment of wealth or power is aimed at, the downfall of enemies, success in love or in play, the removal of petty pests, and so on, even down to the growth of hair on a bald pate. There are hymns, too, in which a single rite or ceremony is taken up and exalted, somewhat in the same strain as the Soma in the Pávámanya hymns of the Rík. Others of a speculative mystical character are not wanting; yet their number is not so great as might naturally be expected, considering the development which the Hindu religion received in the periods following after that of the primitive Veda. It seems in the main that the Atharva is of popular rather than of priestly origin; that in making the transition from the Vedic to modern times, it forms an intermediate step, rather to the gross idolatries and superstitions of the ignorant mass, than to the sublimated pantheism of the Brahmans."—*Whitney*.

"It has been surmised (Müller's *Ancient Sanscrit Literature*, p. 447, ff.) that the hymns of the Atharva Veda 'formed an additional part of the sacrifice from a very early time, and that they were chiefly intended to counteract the influence of any untoward event that might happen during the sacrifice.' This is possible; but the great importance which the adherents of this Veda themselves attach to it, is founded on other considerations than these. They argue, as appears from the treatise *Atharvanarahasya*, mentioned above, that the three other Vedas enable a man to fulfil the *dharma*, or religious law, but that the Atharva helps him to attain *móksha*, or eternal bliss. This doctrine is laid down, for instance, in the *Chúlika Upanishad* of this Veda, when it says: 'Those Brâhmans and others who know the science of the (neuter) Brâhman continued in the *Brahma Veda*, became merged in Brâhman;' and it is likewise inferred from other passages in the *Sáunaka Brâhmaná*. The name of *Brahma Veda* itself, by which this Veda is also frequently called, is therefore explained by them, not as implying the Veda which belongs to the province of the priest Brahman, but the Veda which contains the mysterious doctrine of Brahman, the supreme spirit, into which the human soul becomes finally absorbed. It is probable, therefore, that the very uselessness of the Atharva Veda for sacrificial purposes, and the reluctance which was felt to base its sanctity merely on its incantations and spells, invested it, in the mind of its followers, with a spiritual character, which was then fully developed in the numerous Upanishads (q. v.) now connected with it."—*Muir*.

Professor Müller, in his Ancient Sanscrit Literature, has given the following hymn from the Atharva Veda, of which the *Quarterly Review* says, "we know of no passage in Vedic literature which approaches its simple sublimity:"—

"The Great one who rules over these worlds beholds all as if he were close by. When any one thinks that he cloaks a thing, the Gods know it all.

'They know every one who stands or walks or glides along secretly or withdraws into his house or into any hiding place. Whatever two persons sitting together devise, Varuna the king knows it as the third.

'This earth too is Varuna the king's, and that vast sky whose ends are far off. The two oceans are Varuna's loins ; he resides too in this little pool.

'He who should flee far beyond the sky, would not there escape from Varuna the king ; his messengers from heaven traverse this world, thousand-eyed they look beyond this earth.

'King Varuna sees all,—what is within and beyond heaven and earth ; the winkings of men's eyes are all numbered by him ; he moves all these things as a gamester his dice.

'May all thy destructive nooses, O Varuna, which are cast sevenfold and threefold, bind him who speaks falsehood, and pass by him who speaks truth.' "

Atharvan—A priest who is considered to have obtained the fire from heaven, and who in the course of Mythological personification appears as a Prajápati or father of all beings, as the inspired author of the fourth or Atharva Veda, as the eldest son of Brahma to whom Brahma revealed the Brahma vidya, or knowledge of God ; and at a later period as the same as Angiras.

Atharvan—A distinguished sage, the generator of fire, and producer of Agni. Atharvan is mentioned as the earliest institutor of sacrifice. Atharvan was the first who by sacrifices opened up paths ; then the friendly Sun, the upholder of ordinances, was produced.*

Atharvas—A class or even caste of priests, who had secrets which they were prohibited from divulging ; they were the spiritual guides of their nation, and none but the son of a priest could become a priest—a rule which the Parsís still maintain.†

Atiratra—A form of sacrifice created from the western mouth of Brahma, along with the Sáma Veda. It is a division of the

* Muir, O. S. T., vol. 1, p. 169.
† Muir, O. S. T., vol. 1, p. 293.

service of the Jyotishtoma, the fifth part, or Somasamtha, and means literally, lasting through the night.

Atiratra—One of the ten noble sons of Chakshusha. V. P., p. 98.

Atma—A name of Vishnu, who has many appellations.

Atma—Soul, living soul, animating nature and existing before : "the highest object of their religion was to restore that bond by which their own self, (átma) was linked to the eternal self (paramátman) ; to recover that unity which had been clouded and obscured by the magical illusions of reality ; by the so called Máya of creation."—*Max Müller.*

Atri—A prajápati, one of the mind-engendered progeny of Brahma, with a form and faculties derived from his corporeal nature. One of the nine brahmans celebrated in the Puránas. He was married to Anusúya (charity), one of the twenty-four daughters of Daksha. When Atri was plunged, by the malice and arts of evil spirits, into a gloomy and burning abyss, the Aṣvins "speedily came to his assistance, mitigated the heat with cold, and supplied him with nutriment, so that his situation became tolerable, if not agreeable, till they eventually extricated him from his perilous position." (O. S. T., vol. v, p. 247.) The son of Atri was Soma (the moon), whom Brahma installed as the sovereign of plants, of brahmans, and of the stars.

Attapa—The name of the nineteenth heaven of Buddhism.

Aurva—A sage, the grandson of Bhrigu. When the sons of king Kritavírya persecuted and slew the children of Bhrigu, to recover the wealth which their father had lavished upon them, they destroyed even the children in the womb. One of the women, of the race of Bhrigu, in order to preserve her embryo, secreted it in her thigh (uru), whence the child in his birth was named Aurva ; from his wrath proceeded a flame that threatened to destroy the world ; but at the persuasion of his ancestors he cast it into the ocean, where it abode with the face of a horse. Aurva was afterwards religious preceptor to Sagara, and bestowed upon him the Agneyástram, or fiery weapon with which he conquered the tribes of barbarians, who had invaded his patrimonial possessions. The duties and ceremonies of various castes and classes were explained by Aurva to Sagara and may be seen in the V. P., Book III, Chapters VIII to XVI inclusive. It is said that Aurva earnestly longed for a son, and that Atri gave his children to him, but afterwards felt very lonely and weak.

Avanti—The ancient name of Ujein in Central India, where the scene is laid of the popular domestic drama named Mrichchhakato, or Toy Cart.

Auttama, or Attumi—The name of the third Manu, a descendant from Priyavrata.

Avalokita—A disciple of Kamandaki in the drama of the Toy Cart.

Avantyas—One of the five great divisions of the Haikaya tribe. The Avantyas were in Ujein, and preceded the Rajput tribes by whom that country is now occupied. There are still vestiges of them.—*Tod's Rajasthan, I*, 39.

Avarant—From *Avarana*, screening or surrounding; the name of a division of the sect of *Rámánujas* who prepare their own meals and eat in the strictest privacy : "they must not eat in cotton garments, but having bathed must put on woollen or silk ; all the Rámánujas cook for themselves, and should the meal during this process, or whilst they are eating, attract even the looks of a stranger, the operation is instantly stopped and the viands buried in the ground."—*H. H. Wilson, Vol. I, p.* 39. In the Jain system the five Avaranas mean the difficulties in acquiring as many gradations of holy or divine wisdom.

Avasarpini—The Jains divide time into two cycles or ages, viz., the Utasarpini and the Avasarpini time. The Avasarpini time, has six stages, viz., super-good time, good time, good-bad time, bad-good time, bad-time, and super-bad time. The stage in which we now live is the fifth, the bad time. Avasarpini means the age of decrease.

Avasthanas—The name of the divisions of the sun's course, which are three, viz., Airavata (northern), Jaradgavu (southern), and Vaiswanara (central).

Avatar—A descent, especially of a deity from heaven ; an incarnation, or birth. Professor Wilson states that the Vedas allude occasionally to the avatars of Vishnu. The story of the Rámáyana and Mahábhárata turns wholly upon the doctrine of incarnations. All the chief *dramatis personœ* of the poems being impersonations of gods and demi-gods and celestial spirits. In the Puránas, Siva and Vishnu, under one or other form, are almost the sole objects that claim the homage of the Hindus. In native books the most frequent references are to the ten avatars of Vishnu, viz :—

1.—The Matsya, or Fish avatar, under which form Vishnu preserved Manu the ancestor of the present human race, during a universal deluge.

2.—The Kúrma or Tortoise avatar.

3.—The Varáhu or Boar avatar.

4.—The Nara Simha or Man-lion avatar.

5.—The Vámana or Dwarf avatar.

6.—The Bhárgava or Parasu Ráma.

7.—The Ráma Chendra or Kódanda Ráma.

8.—As Krishna ; this is the most celebrated of his avatars, in which he is supposed to have been completely incarnate.

9.—As Buddha. The brahmans consider Buddha to have been a delusive incarnation of Vishnu, assumed by him to induce the Asuras to abandon the Vedas, by which they lost their supremacy.

10.—The White Horse, (yet future) an account of each will be found under the separate heads.

Avichi—One of the twenty-eight Narakas or hells enumerated in the V. P. They are all said to be situated beneath the earth and beneath the waters.

Avidya—Ignorance. One of the five afflictions of the Pátanjalu philosophy.

Avveyar—In former times, there existed among the Tamil people seven distinguished sages, of whom four were women and three men. Among them Avveyar and Tiruvalluvar were the most celebrated. Respecting the other five, but little is known either of their lives or their writings.

"The particulars given respecting Avveyar too, are so fabulous and so variously related in different books, that it is quite impossible to come to any true and satisfactory results. I shall attempt to state such results as far as I can, and refer the reader for specimens of the native biography to the history of Kabilar, and to the extract translated from the Scanda Puránam as given in the *Asiatic Researches.*

"Avveyar most probably flourished in the reigns of the three celebrated kings, Ukkiraperuvarithi Pándian and the monarchs of the Seran and Sorhan kingdoms who were his contemporaries. In her history as still transmitted by oral tradition, there are many references to these kings, and to the fabulous miracles she performed before them. Her father seems to have been a Brahman and her mother an outcast, who were united to each other without being aware of the wide difference in their cast. Afterwards however, on finding it out, the Brahman determined as the only condition on which they should live together, that any children who might be born to them should be deserted immediately on their birth. Avveyar was their second female child, and was born, reared, and educated at a village inhabited by Panars. (The business of the Panars was to attend on kings and celebrate their praises. But the race is now almost extinct.)

"If we may judge from her character and writings, Avveyar was educated by a Panar with great care and talent. One thing is very evident, she must have possessed eminent natural abilities. From the numerous fables respecting her, we may gather that she was not only clever but that she exerted herself to do good. The excellent moral maxims she has left, tend for the most part to the promotion of good sentiments and good conduct.

"Her principal productions now extant are as follows: Átthichuvaḍi Kondre-Vénthan, Muthuré (or Vakkundán), Nal-Vaḷi, Kalvi-Orḷuk-kam, Avvé-Kérao, Avvé-Kovḷ, Pilaiyar-Agaval, Ganapathi-Ásiria-Virutham, and a number of detached verses : but probably some of her productions have been lost : she is reputed to have been very clever in chemistry and medicine, and to have discovered the fabled panacea (or *Kalpa*) by eating which she lived to the age of 240 years.

"Her fame became widely spread abroad, and wherever she went, kings and nobles, the learned and the ignorant, alike showed her the highest respect.

"Her productions are universally read. Some of them are not only among the very first reading books put into the hands of children in almost every Tamil school, but are also greatly and deservedly esteemed."—*Sugden.*

Avyaya—A name of Purusha or spirit, it means inconsumable.

Awiha—The name of the eighteenth heaven of Buddhism.

Ayana—A period of six months, two Ayanas compose a year. The southern Ayana is a night and the northern a day of the gods. Twelve thousand divine years, each composed of such days, constitute the period of four Yugas, or ages. The word is also used in the sense of hemisphere ; the uttara-ayana is the apparent course of the sun through the northern signs, and the dakshaṇayana is the southerly course ; hence the northern and southern hemispheres appear to correspond with the two ayanas.

Ayatayama—Texts of the Yajur-veda, revealed to Yajnawalkya by the sun in the form of a horse : the Texts thus imparted were unknown to Vaisampayana.

Ayati—One of the descendants of the daughters of Daksha who were married to the Rishis. Lakshmi the bride of Vishnu was the daughter of Bhrigu by Káyati. They had also two sons, Dhátri and Vidhátri, who married the two daughters of the illustrious Meru, *Ayati* and Niryati ; and had by them each a son named Prana and Mrikanda.

Ayodhya—"The modern Oude, which is situated on the river Sarayu, the modern Gogra, about three hundred and fifty miles to the south-east of Delhi. In the present day the city of Ayodhyá has disappeared, and little is to be seen of the ancient site beyond a shapeless heap of ruins, a mass of rubbish and jungle which stretches along the southern bank of the Gogra river. But in olden time this city was one of the largest and most magnificent in Hindustan, and its memory is still preserved in every quarter of the Indian peninsula. Its geographical position is highly significant of the progress of Aryan invasion between two great epochs, namely, that of the war of Bhárata, and that of the birth of Ráma. In the Mahá Bhárata the Aryans had apparently advanced no further towards the south-east than the neighbourhood of Delhi; but in the Rámáyana they seem to have established a large and substantial Ráj in the very centre of Hindustan, and to have founded a metropolis which must ever be famous in the ancient History of India."—*Wheeler*.

The Rámáyana gives the following description of Ayodhyá: "The city of Ayodhyá was full of people, and every one was healthy and happy, and every one was well fed upon the best of rice; and every merchant in that city had storehouses filled with jewels from every quarter of the earth. The Brahmans constantly kept alive the sacrificial fire, and were deeply read in the Vedas and Vedángas, and were endowed with every excellent quality; they were profusely generous, and were filled with truth, zeal and compassion, equal to the great sages, and their minds and passions were under perfect control. All these Brahman sages had three classes of disciples; first, the youths who served them as servants serve their masters; then the students who were receiving instruction; and then the Brahmácháris who maintained themselves and their preceptors by collecting alms. Next to the Brahmans were the Kshatriyas, who were all warriors, and were constantly exercised in the practice of arms in the presence of the Maháràja. After these were the Vaisyas, or merchants, who sold goods of every description, and who came from every corner of the earth. Last of all were the Súdras, who were ever engaged in devotion to the gods, and in the service of the Brahmans. Besides these there were jewellers and artificers, singing men and dancing women, charioteers and footmen, potters and smiths, painters and oilmen, sellers of flowers, and sellers of betelnut. In all that city of well-fed and happy people, no man was without learning, or practised a calling that did not belong to his family or caste, or dwelt in a mean habitation, or was without kinsmen. There were no misers, nor liars, nor thieves, nor tale-bearers, nor swindlers, nor boasters; none that were arrogant, malevolent, mean, or who lived at another's expense; and no man who had not abundance of children, or who lived less than a thousand years."

Ayomukha—One of the sons of Kaṣyapa by Danu, hence termed a Dánava.

Ayuaveda—Medical science, as taught by Dhanwantari.

Ayus—The eldest son of Vikrama and Urvasi; Vikramorvasi, or the Hero and the Nymphs, is the title of a second drama attributed to Kálidása. Urvasi was one of the nymphs of heaven, and when love for the king induced her to dwell on earth, she had been warned that so soon as the king should see a son of hers she must return. From fear of this she kept her infant's birth concealed. Ayus was not seen by his father until he had grown up and was brought from the hermitage of the Rishi Chyavana. His inauguration as vice king then took place in circumstances of great splendour. The rite being concluded a chorus was heard without, invoking blessings upon Ayus—

" Son of the monarch the universe filling,
Son of the god of the mist-shedding night,
Son of the sage, whom the great Brahma; willing,
Called, with creation, to life and to light."

A. and M. I., p. 205.

Ayutayus—A descendant of the Kuru princes: also a king of Magadha, the name of one of the future kings of Magadha as enumerated in the V. P., p. 465.

B

Babhru-vahana—The son of Arjuna by his wife Chitrángada, daughter of the Rája of Manipura. Arjuna dwelt at Manipura for three years, and then according to previous arrangements took leave of his wife and son. When Babhru-váhana came of age and ascended the throne he is described as without an equal in prowess and manhood. His country was rich and prosperous ; his subjects virtuous, contented and happy. In the seventh adventure of the horse of Arjuna it is said that the horse was seized by Babhru-váhana when it approached the city of Manipura, but on discovering that it belonged to his father Arjuna he restored the horse with many demonstrations of affection and respect. Arjuna however considered that his son should not have restored the horse without a battle, and attributed it to cowardice, which led to a contest in which Arjuna was slain : when the tidings reached Chitrángada she wished to ascend a funeral pile. Arjuna was however restored to life again.

Badari—An extensive forest near Benares, celebrated as the scene of many mythical austerities. Krishna is said to have stood "on the spacious Badari a hundred years with his arms aloft, on one foot, subsisting on air." (O. S. T., Vol. IV). Of Arjuna it is said, "Thou wast Nara in a former body, and with Náráyana for thy companion didst perform dreadful austerity at Badari for many myriads of years." (O. S. T., Vol. IV, p. 196).

Badravati—A city about fifty miles from Hastinápúr, from which Bhíma forcibly brought away the horse for the great Aswamedha sacrifice performed by Yudhishthira, after the great war.

Badhas—There are twenty-eight kinds of badhas, which in the Sánkya system mean imperfections or disabilities, as defects of the senses, blindness, deafness, &c., defects of intellect, as incapacity, ignorance, &c., and moral defects, as stubbornness, discontent, &c.

Bahkali, Bahkala, Bashkali—One of the arrangers of the Vedas. Paila divided the Rig Veda, and gave the two Sanhitas, or collections of hymns, to Indrapramati and to Bashkali. Bashkali sub-divided his Sanhita into four, which he gave to his disciples Baudha, Agnimáthara, Yajnawalka and Parásara; and they taught these secondary shoots from the primitive branch.

Bahugara—A descendant of Puru, son of Sudyumna: called Bahuvidha in the Agni and Matsya Puránas.

Bahula—1, The name of one of the Prajápatis, V. P., p. 50; 2, the name of a Prince killed by Abhimanyu, (Linga. Purana); and 3, the name of one of the rivers enumerated in the V. P., p. 183.

Bahulaswa—The last but one of the kings of Mithilá. His son was Kriti, with whom terminated the family of Janaka.

Bahuputra—A Prajápati who married two daughters of Daksha, their children were the four lightnings, enumerated in Astrological works as brown, red, yellow and white; portending severally, wind, heat, rain, famine.

Bahurupa—One of the eleven Rudras, or lords of the three worlds.

Bahwaswa—Son of Mudgala, and father of Divodasa and Ahalya.

Bajiarana—One of the eight branches of Medical Science which treats of the use of aphrodisiacs.

Balabhadra—See Balaráma.

Balakhilyas—Pigmy sages, no bigger than a joint of the thumb, chaste, pious, resplendent as the sun, whose chariot they constantly surround. The wife of the sage Kratu Sannati, brought forth the sixty thousand Bálakhilyas; another account says they were produced from the hair of Brahma. V. P.

Balarama—An incarnation of a white hair of Brahma, born as the son of Vasudeva; by Devaki, but was transferred from the latter to the womb of Rohiṇi, the other wife of Vasudeva; hence he was the half-brother of Krishna. He was brought up by Nanda, and is the patron of Agriculture; the Yádavas, his tribe, being properly herdsmen and shepherds. He is often represented as armed with a ploughshare, and sometimes as carrying a pestle-like club. By some he is regarded as the eighth avatar of Vishṇu; by others as an incarnation of the great serpent Ananta. He was of great strength and irascible temper. He diverted the course of the river Yamuna, and compelled it to attend him. The fierce and malignant demon Dhenuka, in the form of an ass, attacked Bala Ráma when he was a mere boy playing with Krishṇa; Ráma seized him by both hind legs and whirled him round till he expired. On another occasion the Asura Pralamba came to the boys and attempted to carry off Ráma, who however, so squeezed and beat the powerful demon that he fell upon the ground and expired. Many other exploits are related of him. Bala Ráma was married to Révati, to whom he was attached and faithful. When Arjuna, by the connivance and help of Krishṇa, stole away his sister *Subadhra,* Ráma collected his retainers and set out in pursuit; but the matter was made up by the intervention of Krishṇa. One of the last feats of his prowess was the destruction of the dreadful Àsura Dwivida, in the form of an ape. Shortly aftewards Bala Ráma resumed the form of Sésha. V. P.

Bali—A celebrated Daitya, the son of Virochana, who rose to such an eminence in power that Indra and the other gods had to apply for the interference of Vishṇu to protect them from the destructive effects of Bali's rule. The Mahábhárata gives the following legend respecting Bali, as related by Viswámitra to the two young princes, Ráma and Lakshmana, when they visited his hermitage:—

"In ancient days, before the glorious Vishṇu became incarnate as the Dwarf, this was his holy hermitage, and here he practised sacred austerities as an example to all others. And it came to pass that Bali, the mighty Rája of the Asuras, conquered Indra and the gods; and the gods came to this hermitage and prayed to Vishṇu for succour: And Vishṇu was born on earth in the form of a Dwarf, and he assumed the dress of a mendicant, and went to the abode of Bali, and prayed Bali to give him as much earth as he could step over in three steps: And Bali granted his request:

then Vishnu took upon himself a mighty form, and took three steps ; and the first step covered the earth, and the second covered the heavens, and the third was on the head of Bali : And Vishṇu bound Bali, and sent him and all his legions to the realms below the earth, and once more restored the universe to the rule of Indra."

The meaning of this myth is not very obvious. It is said to have originated in an obscure Vedic idea that Vishṇu as the Sun took three steps ; viz., first, on the earth at his rising ; secondly, in the heavens at noonday ; and thirdly, on the under-world at his setting. (See Wilson's Rig Veda, Vol. I, p. 53, *note.)* The legend however is exceedingly popular, probably on account of the successful trick played against the giant ; and a festival is still celebrated in memory of the so-called event.

Bali then became the Sovereign of Pátála. He is said to have had a hundred sons.

Bali—The monkey chieftain of Kishkindyá ; he had treated his brother Sugríva with great cruelty, and on the latter securing the friendship of Ráma they both proceeded to Kishkindyá, where Báli was killed by Ráma, and Sugríva installed as sovereign of Kishkindyá.

Bana—The eldest of the hundred sons of Báli. He had a thousand arms. His daughter Usha having seen Párvati sporting with her lord Śambhu, was inspired with a wish for similar dalliance. Párvati promised her a husband, who should appear to her in a dream on a certain night. This came to pass, and by the magic power of her companion Chitralekka, the person she had beheld in her dream, Aniruddha, (q. v.) was conveyed from Dwáraka to her apartments in the palace. This led to the contest narrated in the article Aniruddha, when Báṇa wounded Krishṇa, but afterwards lost his thousand arms and was nearly killed by Krishṇa.

Banddhas—Those who take nothing upon authority and admit nothing that cannot be proved ; or it is explained, those who by argument cast a doubt upon the efficacy of acts of devotion.

Bandhayanas—Followers of a branch of the Vajasaneiyi, or white Yajush.

Bandhya—A disciple of Bashkala, who made him a teacher of a portion of the Sanhita of the Rig Véda.

Basava—The name of a bull in the Canarese and Telugu languages, and applied to Nandi the vehicle of Śiva.

Basava—The founder of the Lingait sect. He was originally an Aradhya brahman, and evidently a man of great independency of mind and possessed of great moral courage. He was born about the middle of the eleventh century, in a village to the east of Bijápúr in the Collectorate of Kalladighee. "Having become prime minister at the Court of Kaláyana, the capital of a great empire, which then stretched from ocean to ocean, he succeeded gradually in founding a new sect, called the Lingait, from its votaries wearing the Linga, which they consider to be the true symbol of the Creative divine power. This great success may be attributed to two, perhaps three causes, Basava had great power, popularity and influence, from his high station in life. Converts from Jainism to Lingaitism were unduly favored, though Basava's master, king Bajal, still remained a Jain. Basava is said to have connived at the intercourse the king had with a beautiful sister, and had great power over him. Pecuniary assistance was largely given to itinerant priests of the sect who went about preaching to the people. The second cause of Basava's success was that he addressed himself chiefly to the lower classes. These were flattered by the prospect of their social position being improved if they embraced the new religion. And indeed taking the Linga and becoming a Lingait, was according to the ideas of the Hindus, a step in advance. For the great privilege of wearing this sacred symbol on the body had been to that time confined exclusively to the brahmans. In fact Basava at first merely introduced the peculiar Linga worship, as it was performed by the Aradhya brahmans, to whom he himself belonged, among the different classes of Śudras.

"The spread of the sect was wide and rapid, so that even in the neighbouring *Telugu* and *Tamil* countries, many became the worshippers of Basava ; and books regarded as sacred, still extant, were written in those tongues in honor of him. The king however disapproved of this great change. He hated and persecuted the Lingaits. This led to his assassination in his own palace, by two fanatic Lingaits, who it is said were encouraged by Basava. A civil war then broke out, and the empire of Kalyána fell to pieces. Basava was thus the cause of great revolutions in the Deccan. It was to be expected that such a man would, after the lapse of sometime, be deified by credulous men, and the real facts of his history obscured by a mass of legendary lore."—*Wöerth*.

Basava Purana—The Purána that narrates the life of Basava, the founder or restorer of the Jangama sect. Professor H. H. Wilson places the date of the events it records in the early part of the eleventh century.

Basava's parents were both devout worshippers of Śiva. In recompense of their piety, *Nandi*, the bull of Śiva, was born on earth as their son, becoming incarnate by command of Śiva, on his learning from Narada the decline of the *Saiva* faith and prevalence of other less orthodox systems of religion. The child was denominated after the *Basva* or *Basava*, the bull of the deity. On his arriving at the age of investiture he refused to assume the thread ordinarily worn by brahmans, or to acknowledge any *Guru* except Iswara or Śiva. He then departed to the town of *Kalyán*, the capital of *Bijala* or *Vijala Ráya*, and obtained in marriage *Gangámbá*, the daughter of the *Dandanáyak*, or minister of police. From thence he repaired to *Sangameśvara*, where he received from *Sangameśvara Svámí* initiation in the tenets of the *Víra Saiva* faith. He was invited back from this place to succeed his father-in-law upon his decease in the office he had held.

After his return to Kalyán, his sister, who was one of his first disciples, was delivered of a son, *Chenna Basava*, who is not unfrequently confounded with his uncle, and regarded, perhaps more correctly, as the founder of the sect.

After recording these events the work enumerates various marvellous actions performed by Basava and several of his disciples, such as converting grains of corn to pearls—discovering hidden treasures—feeding multitudes—healing the sick and restoring the dead to life. The following are some of the anecdotes narrated in the *Purána* :—

Basava having made himself remarkable for the profuse bounties he bestowed upon the *Jangamas*, helping himself from the Royal Treasury for that purpose, the other ministers reported his conduct to *Bijala*, who called upon him to account for the money in his charge. Basava smiled, and giving the keys of the Treasury to the king, requested him to examine it, which being done, the amount was found wholly undiminished. Bijala thereupon caused it to be proclaimed, that whoever calumniated Basava should have his tongue cut out.

A *Jangama*, who cohabited with a dancing girl, sent a slave for his allowance of rice to the house of Basava, where the messenger saw the wife of the latter, and on his return reported to the dancing girl the magnificence of her attire. The mistress of the Jangama was filled with a longing for a similar dress, and the Jangama having no other means of gratifying her, repaired to Basava, to beg of him his wife's garment. Basava immediately stripped Gangámbá, his wife, and other dresses springing from her body, he gave them all to the Jangama.

A person of the name of *Kanapa*, who regularly worshipped the image of EKAMRESVARA, imagining the eyes of the deity were affected, plucked out his own, and placed them in the sockets of the figure. ŚIVA, pleased with his devotion, restored his worshipper his eyes.

A devout *Saiva* named *Mahădevala Macháya*, who engaged to wash for all the *Jangamas*, having killed a child, the Rája ordered Basava to have him secured and punished; but Basava declined undertaking the duty, as it would be unavailing to offer any harm to the worshippers of ŚIVA. *Bijala* persisting, sent his servants to seize and tie him to the legs of an elephant, but *Macháya* caught the elephant by the trunk, and dashed him and his attendants to pieces. He then proceeded to attack the Rája, who being alarmed applied to Basava, and by his advice humbled himself before the offended Jangama. Basava also deprecated his wrath, and *Macháya* being appeased, forgave the king and restored the elephant and the guards to life.

A poor Jangama having solicited alms of *Kinnaráyu*, one of

Basava's chief disciples, the latter touched the stones about them with his staff, and converting them into gold, told the Jangama to help himself.

The work is also in many places addressed to the Jainas in the shape of a dialogue between some of the Jangama saints, and the members of that faith, in which the former narrate to the latter instances of the superiority of the *Saiva* religion, and the falsehood of the *Jain* faith, which appears to have been that of *Bijala Ráya* and the great part of the population of *Kalyána.* In order to convert them, *Ekánta Ramáya,* one of Basava's disciples, cut off his head in their presence, and then marched five days in solemn procession through and round the city, and on the fifth day replaced his head upon his shoulders. The Jain Pagodas were thereupon, it is said, destroyed by the Jangamas. It does not appear, however, that the king was made a convert, or that he approved of the principles and conduct of his minister. He seems, on the contrary, to have incurred his death by attempting to repress the extension of the *Víra Saiva* belief. Different authorities, although they disagree as to the manner in which Bijala was destroyed, concur in stating the fact : the following account of the transaction is from the Basava Purána :—

"In the city of *Kalyána* were two devout worshippers of Śiva, named *Allaya* and *Madhuvaya.* They fixed their faith firmly on the divinity they adored, and assiduously reverenced their spiritual preceptor, attending upon *Basava* whithersoever he went. The king, *Bijala,* well knew their merits, but closed his eyes to their superiority, and listening to the calumnious accusations of their enemies, commanded the eyes of *Allaya* and *Madhuvaya* to be plucked out. The disciples of Basava, as well as himself, were highly indignant at the cruel treatment of these holy men, and leaving to *Jagaddeva* the task of putting *Bijala* to death, and denouncing imprecations upon the city, they departed from *Kalyána.* Basava fixed his residence at *Sangamesvara.*

Macháya, Bommidevaya, Kinnara, Kannatha, Bommadeva, Kakaya, Masanaya, Kolakila Bommadeva, Kesirajaya, Mathirajaya, and others, announced to the people that the fortunes of *Bijala* had passed away, as indicated by portentous signs ; and accordingly the crows crowed in the night, jackals howled by day; the sun was eclipsed, storms of wind and rain came on, the earth shook, and darkness overspread the heavens. The inhabitants of *Kalyána* were filled with terror.

When *Jagaddeva* repaired home, his mother met him, and told him that when any injury had been done to a disciple of the *Saiva* faith, his fellow should avenge him or die. When *Duksha* treated Śiva with contumely, Párvatí threw herself into the flames, and so, under the wrong offered to the saints, he should not sit down contented: thus saying, she gave him food at the door of his mansion. Thither also came *Mallaya* and *Bommaya*, two others of the saints, and they partook of *Jagaddeva's* meal. Then smearing their bodies with holy ashes, they took up the spear, and sword, and shield, and marched together against *Bijala*. On their way a bull appeared, whom they knew to be a form of *Basava*, came to their aid, and the bull went first even to the court of the king, goring any one that came in their way, and opening a clear path for them. Thus they reached the court, and put *Bijala* to death in the midst of all his courtiers, and then they danced, and proclaimed the cause why they had put the king to death. *Jagaddeva* on his way back, recalling the words of his mother, stabbed himself. Then arose dissension in the city, and the people fought amongst themselves, and horses with horses, and elephants with elephants, until, agreeably to the curse denounced upon it by Basava and his disciples, *Kalyána* was utterly destroyed.

Basava continued to reside at *Sangamesvara*, conversing with his disciples, and communing with the divine Essence, and he expostulated with Śiva saying: 'By thy command have I, and thy attendant train, come upon earth, and thou hast promised to recall us to thy presence when our task was accomplished.' Then Śiva and Párvatí came forth from the *Sangamesvara Lingam*, and were visible to *Basava*, who fell on the ground before them. They raised him, and led him to the sanctuary, and all three disappeared in the presence of the disciples, and they praised their master, and flowers fell from the sky, and then the disciples spread themselves abroad, and made known the absorption of Basava into the emblem of Śiva."—*Mackenzie's Collect., Vol. 2nd;* Hálakanara MSS. [pp. 3-12.]; *Wilson's Works, Vol. I, p.* 225.

Beerbhoom—Properly *Vír-bhúmi,* the hero-land. On the frontier of Lower Bengal, between the lofty plateau of Central India, and the valley of the Ganges. This country was the theatre of one of the primitive struggles of Indian history. It stood as the outpost of the Sanscrit race, on the west of Lower Bengal, and had to bear the sharp collisions of Aryan civilization, with the ruder types prevailing among the aborigines. On its inhabitants devolved, during three thousand years, the duty of holding the passes between the highlands and the valley of the Ganges. To this day they are a manlier race than their kinsmen of the plains, and from the beginning of history, one of the two kingdoms has borne the name of Mala-bhúmi, the country of the Wrestlers,—the other the appellation of Vir-bhúmi, the Hero-land.—*Hunter, Rural Bengal.*

Benares—The sacred city of the Hindus. It is called Kási, Váranási, Atimukta. It was once destroyed by the discus of Krishṇa. "The whole of a city that was inaccessible to gods, was wrapped in flames by the discus of Hari, and was totally destroyed." V. P., Chap. xxxiv. "The term Kási, denominating, if not a city, a people and its chieftains, occurs repeatedly in Sanscrit works of all but the highest antiquity.....................The kingdom of the Kásis and its rulers, as is evinced by the frequency of reference to them, enjoyed from distant ages, more or less of notoriety; and this is substantially all that the Hindu memorials teach us. The Puránas specify but one dynasty of Kási kings; a goodly catalogue, beginning in the most authoritative of those works, with the son of Kása. To Kása, by a lapse of perhaps two centuries, succeeded Divodása, in whose reign Buddhism seems still to have been acting on the aggressive. In this synchronism there is no discernible improbability; and with some likelihood it embodies an historic fact. A reflection of actual events may likewise be afforded in the story of the burning of Váránasí by the discus of Vishnu."—*Hall.*

Bhadra—The name of one of the many wives of Vasudeva.

Bhadrabahu—A son of Vasudeva by his wife Róhiní.

Bhadrabahu—The author of the Kalpa Sútra, the most sacred religious work of the Jainas. He lived in the early part of the fifth century of the Christian era, but nothing is known of his personal history, though his work is held in such reverence.

Bhadrachara—A son of Krishṇa by his wife Rukmini.

Bhadradeah—A son of Vasudeva by his wife Devaki. He and his five brothers were killed by Kansa.

Bhadrakali—A Rudra sprung from the anger of Deví, and sent by Śiva to destroy the sacrifice of Daksha, V. P., Chap. viii.

Bhadrasana—The posture in which the Yógi is directed to sit when engaged in meditation : viz., to cross his legs underneath him and to lay hold of his feet on each side with his hands.

Bhadrasena—One of the six sons of Vasudeva, who were killed by Kansa.

Bhadrasrenya—A Yádava prince, the son of Mahishmat. He is said to have had a hundred sons, all of whom but one, Durdama, were slain by Divodása, the Rája of Benares. Durdama was spared, being an infant ; and he lived to recover his patrimonial possessions.

Bhadraswa—A country to the east of Meru, and Ketumala on the west ; and between these two is the region of Ilavrita. Four great lakes are near, the waters of which are partaken of by the gods. Bhadraswas is one of the eight varshas or countries described as places of perfect enjoyment, where happiness is spontaneous and uninterrupted. In them there is no vicissitude, no dread of decrepitude or death, there is no distinction of virtue or vice, no difference of degree as better or worse, nor any of the effects produced in this region by the revolutions of ages.

Bhadravinda—A son of Krishṇa, who is said to have had in all one hundred and eighty thousand.

Bhaga—One of the twelve Ádityas ; in the Manwantara of Vaivaswata.

Bhaga—An Áditya ; the fifth of the eight sons of Aditi. His eyes were knocked out by Rudra (Śiva). " Rudra of dreadful power then ran up to the gods, and in his rage knocked out the eyes of Bhaga with a blow, and incensed, assaulted Púshan with his foot, and knocked out his teeth as he was eating the purodáṣa offering."* See Savitṛi.

Bhagavat—Vishṇu. The Supreme Being. The letter *Bh* implies the cherisher and supporter of the universe. By *ga* is understood the leader, impeller, or creator. The dissyllable Bhaga indicates the six properties, dominion, might, glory, splendour, wisdom and dispassion. The purport of the letter *va* is, that elemental spirit in which all beings exist, and which exists in all beings. And thus this great word Bhagavat is the name of Vasudeva, who is one with the Supreme Brahma, and of no one else. V. P., Book vi, Chapter 5.

Bhagavata—The name of a Purána, generally placed the fifth in all the lists, but the Padma Purána ranks it as the eighteenth, as the extracted substance of all the rest. According to the usual specification it consists of eighteen thousand slókas distributed amongst three hundred and thirty-two chapters, divided into twelve skandas or books. The Bhágavata is a work of great celebrity in India, and exercises a more direct and powerful influence on the opinions and feelings of the people than perhaps any other of the Puránas. For an analysis of its contents, see Professor Wilson's Preface to the V. P.

Bhagavat Gita—The Bhagavat Gíta is an episode of the Mahábhárata, the great epic poem of India, which, from its popularity and extent, corresponds with the Iliad among the Greeks. The leading story occupies only about a fourth part of the entire work ; numerous episodes and legends, chiefly didactic, and believed to be interpolations of a later date, make up the other three-fourths of the poem. The whole forms a collection of the traditions of the early history of the Aryan people during their first settlement in India.

According to the legendary history of India two dynasties were originally dominant in the north, called Solar and Lunar, under

* Muir, O. S. T., Vol. iv, p. 168.

whom numerous petty princes held authority, and to whom they acknowledged fealty. The most famous Rája of the Lunar race, who reigned in Hastinápura or ancient Delhi, was Bharata, who is designated a Mahá Rája, and whose Ráj is said to have included all the kingdoms of the earth. To this day the whole continent of India is known to the Hindus by the name of Bharata-varsha, or the country of Bharata.

The Kauravas and Pándavas were descendants of Bharata. Duryódhana and his brothers were the leaders of the Kauravas or elder branch of the tribe ; and the five Pándava princes, Yudhishthira, Bhíma, Arjuna, Nakula and Sahadéva, those of the Pándava or younger branch. The latter had been banished from their country, and after long wanderings and many hardships, they collected their friends around them, and with the help of the neighbouring Rájas mustered a great army, and prepared to attack their oppressors, who had also assembled their forces.

The hostile armies met on the plain of Kurukshetra. Bhíshma had the command of the Kaurava faction ; Bhíma was the General of the other party. The scene of the Bhagavat Gíta now opens, and remains throughout the same—the field of battle. The poem is in the form of a discourse between the Avatár Krishṇa, and his friend and pupil Arjuna. The fight began with a volley of arrows from both sides ; when Arjuna desired Krishṇa to draw up the chariot in the space between the two armies, while he examined the lines of the enemy. Krishṇa, who acted as charioteer, did so, and pointed out in those lines the numerous relatives of his friend. Arjuna, seeing his relatives drawn up in battle array, was suddenly struck with compunction at the idea of fighting his way to a kingdom through the blood of his kindred, and declared that he would rather be killed himself than continue to fight them. Krishṇa replied in a long metaphysical dialogue, full of fine passages, the moral of which is that as Arjuna belongs to the military caste, his duty is to fight. He said that the renunciation of the world ought not to involve the avoidance of action, or the neglect of professional duties. He then gave a full and most curious exposition of the half-mythological, half-philosophical pantheism of the Brahmans, and a general view of the mystic theology of the Hindus; following with some modification the theories of what is termed the Sánkhya School of Philosophy.

A. W. Schlegel calls this episode "the most beautiful, and perhaps the only truly philosophical poem that the whole range of literature known to us has produced." Dean Milman says, "It reads like a noble fragment of Empedocles or Lucretius, introduced into the midst of an Homeric epic." "In point of poetical conception," he adds, "there is something singularly striking and magnificent in the introduction of this solemn discussion on the nature of the godhead and the destiny of man in the midst of the fury and tumult in which it occurs."

Arjuna is overruled, if not convinced, by the arguments of the god; the fight goes on, and the Pándavas gain a complete victory over their opponents.

The Bhagavat Gíta was first translated into English by Sir Charles Wilkins, and published by the East India Company, with an Introduction by the then Governor-General of India, Warren Hastings. It was eagerly received in Europe, and translated into the French, German and Russian languages. Schlegel published an excellent Latin version.* More recently a new English translation has been published by Mr. J. Cockburn Thompson, with valuable notes.

Bhagiratha—The son of Rája Dilípa, who spent a thousand years in severe austerities upon a mountain, by which he propitiated Brahma and Śiva, and brought the Ganges to the earth; and with it watered the ashes of the sixty thousand sons of Sagara, who were at once restored to life, purified by the sacred water from all their sins, and ascended to heaven.

> " Soon as the flood their dust bedewed,
> Their spirits gained beatitude,
> And all in heavenly bodies dressed,
> Rose to the skies' eternal rest.

* The Bhagavat Gíta in Sanscrit, Canarese and English, with Schlegel's Latin version, and Humboldt's Essay on the Philosophy of the Gíta, was published in 1847 by the Editor of this Volume.

"Then thus to king Bhagírath said,
Brahma, when, coming at the head
Of all his bright celestial train,
He saw those spirits freed from stain:
'Well done! great Prince of men, well done!
Thy kinsmen bliss and heaven have won.'
The sons of Sagar mighty-souled,
Are with the Blest, as Gods, enrolled."

—*Griffiths' Rámáyan.*

Bhagirathi—A name of the Ganges in consequence of having been brought to the earth by Bhagíratha.

Bhaimyekadasi—The eleventh lunar day of the light half of Mágha (10th February.) This is also a festival of traditional origin, said to have been first observed by Bhíma, one of the Pańdu princes, in honor of Vishṇu, according to the instructions of Vasudeva. Every eleventh lunar day, it may be observed, is held in extravagant veneration by the Hindus, but more particularly by the Vaishńavas. Fasting on the eleventh is declared to be equally efficacious with a thousand aśwamedhas, and eating during its continuance as heinous a sin as parricide, or the murder of a spiritual teacher. This extravagance demonstrates its sectarian character, and consequently its more modern origin. The notion may have grown, however, out of particular appropriations of the lunar day, when the eleventh was set apart, as in the present case, to the adoration of Vishṇu.—*Wilson.*

Bhairava—An inferior manifestation of some portion of Śiva, with the idea of severity or cruelty. A Bhairava has the head of a dog. There are eight Bhairavas named respectively, Asitanga, Ruru, Chanda, Krodha, Unmatta, Kupati, Bhishana, Sanhara, all indicative of something fearful.

Bhajamana—A son of Andhaka, according to all the best authorities; the Agni makes him the son of Babhru.

Bhajina—A son of Satwata.

Bhalandana—A son of Nábhága, who had carried off and married the daughter of a Vaisya, in consequence of which he was degraded to the same caste, and deprived of his share of the patrimonial sovereignty, which his son and successor, Bhalandana, afterwards recovered.

Bhallada, Bhallaka, Bhallatta—A king of Hastinápura, the last of the race of Hastin, who had founded the city; which was destroyed by the encroachments of the Ganges.

Bhanu—A son of Krishṇa and Satyabháma.

Bhanu—The daughter of Daksha, wife of Kaṣyapa, who became one of the ten wives of Dharma.

Bhanus—The sons of Bhanu, who became suns, and deities presiding over moments of Muhúrtta.

Bhanumat—A prince, the son of Kusadhwaja, king of Kási or Benares; or according to the Rámáyana of Sankasya.

Bharadwaja—A sage, the son of Vrihaspati, who being abandoned by his natural parent was brought by the Maruts or winds to Bharata, who called the child Vitatha (unprofitable) in allusion to the birth and loss of his previous nine sons. Bharata had by different wives nine sons who were put to death by their own mothers, because Bharata remarked that they bore no resemblance to him, and the women were afraid that he would therefore desert them. From Bharadwája, a Brahman by birth and king by adoption, descended Brahmans and Kshatriyas, the children of two fathers.

Bharadwaja—One of the eight celebrated Rishis, the reputed father of Dróna. His hermitage was at Prayága, the modern Allahabad; he is said to have dwelt there surrounded by a band of Brahman disciples, 'who lead the ideal life of austerity, sacrifice, and devotion, which is so frequently described and lauded by Brahmanical bards.' He received Ráma and Síta when they set forth on their exile, and recommended the hill Chitra-kúta as a residence. The Rámáyana says, 'the great Bharadwája commanded Bharata to bring his whole army to the hermitage that he might feast them.'

> 'Bring all thy host,' the hermit cried,
> And Bharat, to his joy, complied.

Then to the chapel went the sire,
Where ever burnt the sacred fire,
And first, in order due, with sips
Of water purified his lips :
To Viṣvakarmá then he prayed,
His hospitable feast to aid:
'Let Viṣvakarmá hear my call,
The God who forms and fashions all:
A mighty banquet I provide,
Be all my wants this day supplied.
Lord Indra at their head, the three
Who guard the worlds I call to me :
A mighty host this day I feed,
Be now supplied me every need.
Let all the streams that eastward go,
And those whose waters westering flow,
Both on the earth and in the sky,
Flow hither and my wants supply.
Be some with ardent liquor filled,
And some with wine from flowers distilled,
While some their fresh cool streams retain
Sweet as the juice of sugar-cane.
I call the Gods, I call the band
Of minstrels that around them stand :
I call the Háhá and Huhú,
I call the sweet Viṣvávasu.
I call the heavenly wives of these
With all the bright Apsarases,
Alambushá of beauty rare,
The charmer of the tangled hair,
Ghritáchí and Viṣváchí fair,
Hemá and Bhímá sweet to view,
And lovely Nágadantá too,
And all the sweetest nymphs who stand
By Indra or by Brahmá's hand—
I summon these with all their train
And Tumburu to lead the strain.

* * * * * * * * *

The troops of Bharat saw amazed
What Viṣvakarmá's art had raised.
On every side, five leagues around,
All smooth and level lay the ground,
With fresh green grass that charmed the sight
Like sapphires blent with lazulite.
There the Wood-apple hung its load,
The Mango and the Citron glowed,
The Bel and scented Jak were there,
And Aonlá with fruitage fair.
There, brought from Northern Kuru, stood,
Rich in delights, the glorious wood,
And many a stream was seen to glide
With flowering trees along its side.
There mansions rose with four wide halls,
And elephants and chargers' stalls,
And many a house of royal state,
Triumphal arc and bannered gate.
With noble doorways, sought the sky,
Like a pale cloud, a palace high,
Which far and wide rare fragrance shed,
With wreaths of white en-garlanded.
Square was its shape, its halls were wide,
With many a seat and couch supplied,
Drink of all kinds, and every meat
Such as celestial Gods might eat.—*Griffiths' Rámáyan.*

In some of the vernacular versions of the Rámáyana the sage is represented as having provided a similar entertainment for the great army of monkeys and bears.

Bharadwajas—Inhabitants of the northern regions according to the Váyu, but Professor Wilson says they might be thought to be religious fraternities from the sages Atri and Bharadwája.

Bharadwaji—A deep river in Malwa, included in the V. P. list.

Bharani—A lunar asterism in Nagavithi, the first Vithi in Airávatha, or the northern Avasthána.

Bharata—See Mahábhárata.

Bharata—The eldest of the hundred sons of Rishabha, prince of Himahwa. Rishabha having ruled with equity and wisdom, and celebrated many sacrificial rites, resigned the sovereignty of the earth to the heroic Bharata. Bharata having religiously discharged the duties of his station, resigned the kingdom to his son Samati, a most virtuous prince; and abandoned his life at the holy place Sálagráma to become an ascetic. His thoughts were now wholly on God; his conduct was distinguished by kindness, and he effected in the highest degree the entire control over his mind.

On one occasion while bathing, a doe, being frightened by a lion, suddenly brought forth a fawn, and fell into the river. Bharata took the fawn to his hermitage and tended it with great care. His affection for it became so strong that it distracted his mind and interrupted his devotions. He at last died watched by the deer, with tears in its eyes. He was afterwards born again as a deer with the faculty of recollecting his former life; this gave him a distaste for the world and he again repassed to the holy place Sálagráma. Upon his death he was next born as a brahman, still retaining the memory of his prior existence. Possessed of all true wisdom he beheld soul as contra-distinguished from matter, (Prakriti) he beheld the gods and all other beings as the same in reality. This led him to disregard all castes and distinctions, and his conduct was so extraordinary that he was thought to be idiotic, and was treated with neglect or contempt: he worked in the fields, and on one occasion was pressed as a palankeen bearer for the Rája of Sauvira: being rebuked for his awkwardness, he replied and entered into a dialogue with the king, who soon discovered his merits. Bharata then expounded the nature of existence, the aim and object of life, and the identification of individual with universal spirit. The king then opened his eyes to truth and abandoned the notion of distinct existence. Bharata also obtained exemption from future birth. V. P.

Bharata—One of the four sons of Dasaratha and Kaikeyí. In youth he was sent to Girivraja, with his uncle Yudhájit. He was there educated in the house of his grandfather Rája Aswapati.

During his absence from Ayódhya, his brother Ráma was installed as Yuvarája (heir apparent). On the death of the Mahá Rája he returned to Ayódhya and was deeply grieved when he ascertained that his mother, in order to secure the kingdom to him, had effected the exile of Ráma whose right to the Ráj he loudly proclaimed. He then went to Chitrakúta, where Ráma resided, and offered to go into exile himself if Ráma would take the kingdom. It was at length decided that Ráma should ascend the throne after the fourteen years of exile had expired, and Bharata determined to govern Kósala in the name of Ráma. This he did by carrying away a pair of shoes which had been worn by Ráma, and which he treated as symbolical of Ráma's presence.

Bharata—In the Bhagavat Gíta a patronymic from Bharata, applied to Arjuna as his descendant. Arjuna is also called Prince of the Bharatas, and best of the Bharatas.

Bharata—" The son of Rája Dushyanta and Sakuntala. The legend of his birth forms the ground-work of Kalidása's drama of Sakuntala, or the Lost Ring. The Rája was hunting in the forest when he saw Sakuntala, a brahman's daughter, and fell in love with her. He induced her to accept him as her husband by a Gandharva marriage, and giving her his ring as a pledge of his troth. She afterwards gave birth to a son who was named Bharata, but having lost the ring, the Rája in the absence of such evidence, conveniently forgot his engagement to marry the daughter of a priest. Ultimately when the ring was found, and he either saw or heard of the exploits of Bharata in taming lions, he acknowledged the young hero to be his son and made the mother his chief Rání."

" There is no reliable information as to the extent of the kingdom of Bharata, but his wonderful doings and the greatness of his empire, have been set forth in the most extravagant terms. To this day India is known to the Hindus by the name of Bharatavarsha, or the country of Bharata. The Kshatriya bards declared that the Rájas of Bharata were descended from the moon, and that one of their number conquered Indra, the ruler of the gods." All that is really known is that an Aryan empire was established by Bharata amidst an aboriginal population. The original seat of the empire was at the site now occupied by the ruins of Takh-i-Bahi, in the country of the Yusufzais to the northward of Pesháwar.

Bharata-varsha—An ancient name for northern India, which was divided into nine portions.

Bharga—A prince, the son of Vainahótra, descended from Alarka.

Bhargas, Bhargavas—A people of the east subdued by Bhíma.

Bhargabhumi—The son of Bharga, the prince who is said to have promulgated the four rules of caste.

Bharika—A son of Krishṇa and Satyabháma.

Bhartri-hari—A Sanskrit grammarian who lived in the century preceding the Christian era. He was the brother of VICRAMADITYA. He wrote a grammatical treatise, but his Vákya Pradípa or Metrical Maxims on the philosophy of Syntax, are the best known. They are often cited under the name of Harikarica, and have almost equal authority wilh the precepts of *Panini*. His Satakas or centuries of verses, are also much admired.

Bhasi—One of the six illustrious daughters of Támra, the wife of Kaṣyapa. Bhasi gave birth to kites.

Bhatta—Bhaṭṭa. An honorary title given to learned brahmans who commit one of the Vedas to memory so as to be able to recite the whole without book.

Bhatta Murti—A distinguished Telugu poet, one of "the eight elephants," so styled of *Krishna-raya's* Court. He wrote the *Narasa* Bhúpāliyam during his patron's life ; but his chief poem, the *Vasu Charitramu*, after that patron's death. It contains florid descriptions of scenery and love affairs, in recondite versification, much esteemed. Bhaṭṭa Múrti ranks high as a poet.—*Taylor*.

Bhattacharyas—The name of those Hindu scholars who not only learn, as the Bhaṭṭas do, one of the vedas completely by heart, but who study the meaning of each verse and word, so as to be able to give orally the explanation of any passage required. The number of this class of scholars, who represent the doctors of

Hindu theology, is now very small. There are three or four, it is said at Benares. They are highly respected, and as incarnations of Vrihaspati (the Pandit of the gods,) at certain occasions regularly worshipped.—*Haug.*

Bhattoji Dikshita—A grammarian, the son of a Brahman, and born in the Mahratta country. He applied to study ; but, his own country ranking low in literature, he went to Benares studying Sanscrit and philosophy. He is now chiefly known by his celebrated work on grammar, entitled *Siddhánta Kaumudi* (moonlight of accuracy). *Pánini's* old sutras obtained three commentators, *Vara ruchi*, *Bhattoji*, and *Patanjali ;* the latter is the most diffuse and perfect ; but the *Siddhánta Kaumudi*, holding a medium place, has always been in wide and approved use. The author lived a studious and contemplative life ; and died at Benares, aged fifty-six—*Taylor.*

Bhaskaracharya—" A celebrated Brahman astronomer who resided at Beder, one of the four ancient Mahomedan principalities. He applied his mind chiefly to numerical science. His *Bíja ganita* was a work on arithmetic. He dedicated it to his only child, a daughter named *Lílávati*, under date S. S. 1036 (A. D. 1114). Singularly enough for such a work, it came to be called by her name ; *Bhaskara* was also an astronomer, in which science his calculations are not to be confounded with Pauranical fables. His *Siddhánta Sirômani*, (head jewel of accuracy) is an astrological work. It was published S. S. 1050 (A. D. 1128). He soon after died, aged sixty-five, at Beder. The authors of the *Siddhánta* and *Vákya* systems are no longer known ; but Bhaskara has no Indian rival of mediæval, or modern times." It has been said by some that Bhaskara was fully acquainted with the principle of the differential calculus, which was only discovered in Europe during the last century. In 1859 Professor Wilson wrote to Mr. Spottiswoode on this subject, and that gentleman replied to the inquiry in the following terms :—

" I have read Bâpû Deva Sâstrin's letter on Bhâskarâchârya's mode of determining the instantaneous motion of a planet, with great interest, and think that we are much indebted to him for calling our attention to so important an element in the old Indian methods of calculation. It still, however, seems to me, that he has over-stated the case, in saying that "Bhâskarâchârya was fully acquainted with the principle of the differential calculus." He has undoubtedly conceived the idea of comparing the successive positions of a planet in its path, and of regarding its motion as constant during the interval; and he may be said to have had some rudimentary notion of representing the arc of a curve by means of auxiliary straight lines. But on the other hand, in the method here given, he makes no allusion to one of the most essential features of the differential calculus, viz., the infinitesimal magnitude of the intervals of time and space therein employed. Nor, indeed, in anything specifically said about the fact, that the method is an approximate one.

Nevertheless, with these reservations it must be admitted, that the penetration shown by Bhâskara in his analysis, is in the highest degree remarkable; that the formula which he establishes,......and his methods of establishing it, bear more than a mere resemblance,—they bear a strong analogy,—to the corresponding process in modern mathematical astronomy; and that the majority of scientific persons will learn with surprise, the existence of such a method in the writings of so distant a period and so remote a region."—*Wilson*.

Bhautya—The son of Bhuti, the Manu of the fourteenth Manwantara.

Bhauma—' Mars,' whose splendid car is of gold, drawn by eight horses of a ruby-red, sprung from fire.

Bhava—1, Śiva, a Muni or Rudra, the husband of Sati, (Truth) who abandoned her corporeal existence in consequence of the displeasure of Daksha. She was afterwards the daughter of Himavat, (the snowy mountains) by Mena; and in that character, as the only Umá, the mighty Bhava again married her. V. P., p. 59; 2, The name of a son of Pratiharttá, one of the descendants of Bharata; also 3, of a son of Viloman.

Bhavabhuti—A celebrated Sanscrit author, some of whose dramas have been so well translated into English by Professor

Wilson. He was also named Śríkanta, or he in whose throat eloquence resides, was the son of a native of the South of India, a brahman of Berar or Beder, and a member of the tribe of brahmans who pretend to trace their descent from the sage Kaṣyapa. The site of Bhavabhuti's birthplace is fully corroborated by the peculiar talent he displays in describing nature in her magnificence, a talent very unusual in Hindu bards, and one which he no doubt derived from his early familiarity with the grand mountains and forests of Telingâna.—*Mrs. Manning, A. & M. I., Vol. II, p.* 208.

Bhavana—The mental impression or apprehension following upon knowledge. The formation of a fixed idea of the object of contemplation. It is also termed Bháva-bhávaná, apprehension of the being, the existence or substantiality of the object ; the thing contemplated.

Bhavaumanya—The son of Vithatha, and grandson of Bharata.

Bhavishya—One of the eighteen Puránas. "The Purána in which Brahma, having described the greatness of the sun, explained to Manu the existence of the world and the characters of all created beings in the course of the Aghóra Kalpa." This Purána as its name implies should be a book of prophecies. Dr. Wilson says : "It should be rather regarded as a manual of religious rites and ceremonies, in which a few legends enliven the series of precepts."

Bhavishyottara Purana—This is also a sort of manual of religious offices, the greater portion being appropriated to vratas, and the remainder to the forms with which gifts are to be presented.

Bhavya—One of the ten sons of Priyavrata, who became king of Sakadwipa. Also the name of one of the sons of Dhruva, by his wife Sámbha.

Bhavya—A king mentioned in the Rig Veda, who dwelt on the banks of the Sindhu or Indus.

Bhavyas—One of the five classes of demi-gods of the sixth Manwantara, when Chakshusha was the Manu of the period, and Manojava was the Indra.

Bhaya—(Fear). Son of Anriti (falsehood), and Nikriti (immorality).

Bhayada—A prince, the son of Manasya, one of the descendants of Puru.

Bhikshuka—A mendicant, the fourth order of men described in the V. P. He is to forego the three objects of human existence (pleasure, wealth and virtue)—to be constantly occupied with devotion, and abstain from all wrong-doing. He is to reside but for one night in a village, and not more than five nights at a time in a city: for the support of existence he is to apply for alms at the houses of the three first castes, when the fires have been extinguished and people have eaten. The mendicant is to call nothing his own, and to suppress desire, anger, pride and covetousness.

Bhils—A tribe of Aborigines who still occupy the hill tracts of Rájputána and Central India, and in ancient times seem to have dwelt in nearly the same localities; having Rájas or Chieftains of their own, but acknowledging or dreading the supremacy of the Kshatriyas. In the Mahábhárata they appear to the south of the Jumna, and in the immediate neighbourhood of the Ráj of Bharata; whilst in the Rámáyana they make their appearance further to the east, near the junction of the Jumna and Ganges. They have preserved their rude habits to the present day, and are known as cattle-lifters, robbers, hunters like Nimrod and Esau, capable of almost any outrage, yet imbued with a sense of truth and honour strangely contrasting with their external character. At the same time they are perceptibly yielding to the personal influence of British administrators and the advancing tide of British civilization.—*Wheeler, Vol. I, p.* 83.

Bhima—"Terrible." The second of the five sons of Pándu, but mystically begotten by Váyu, the god of the wind or air, through his mother Kunti, or Pritha. He is the principal General of the Pándava army, and is renowned for his strength and swiftness. Duryódhana attempted to take his life by poison when a youth, but he escaped through the agency of the Nagas; he was instructed in the use of the club by Dróna, and at the exhibition of arms at Hastinápur fought Duryódhana with the club. His wars with the Asuras are referred to the old wars between the Aryans and Aborigines. The myth of his marrying Hidimbi, the sister of the Asura Hidimba, whom he slew in the forest, is regarded as a later addition to the original tradition. The Mahábhárata also relates his slaughter of Vaka the Asura, his conquest of Jarásandha, the Rája of Magadha, his attempt at interference in behalf of Draupadi in the gambling pavilion; the fearful vow he uttered against Duryódhana and Dushásanas; his interview with his mythical brother Hanuman, the son of Váyu; his pursuit and treatment of Jayadratha after the abduction of Draupadi; his appearance in the council hall of Rája Viráta with a ladle in one hand and a scimitar in the other; his engagement as head cook; the enormous quantity of provisions he daily eat himself; his battle with Jimuta whom he killed, and the favour he consequently obtained from the Rája; his contest with the prime minister Kíchaka, whom he killed and rolled into a ball, because of his ill-treatment of Draupadi; how he rescued Rája Viráta from Susarman who was carrying him into captivity; his battle with Bhíshma in the first day of the great war; his slaughter of the Rája of Magadha and his sons; his conflicts with Dróna, with Dushásana, with Duryódhana; his return to the Mahárája Dhritarashtra at Hastinapur; his slaughter of the horse at the Aswamedha of Yudhishthira; his disputes with the Mahárája, and his death, along with his four brothers, in the Himálayás. It will thus be seen that Bhíma belongs to the epic period.—*Wheeler, Vol. I.*

Bhima—The Rája of Vidarbha (Berar), and father of Damayanti.

Bhima—The fifth of the eight Rudras, to whom was assigned the charge of fire: also the name of a son of Amávasa.

Bhimaratha—Son of Ketumat and grandson of Dhanwantari, the author of Medical Science. He was the father of Divodasa, of whom many curious legends are narrated.

Bhimarathi—The ancient name of the river Bhíma.

Bhimasena—One of the four sons of Paríkshit, son of Kuru.

Bhishma—Originally named Sántanavu, the son of Sántanu, the

Rája of Hastinápur ; the legend in the Mahábhárata is that when Rája Sántanu was very old he desired to marry a young and beautiful damsel, but the parents of the girl were unwilling to give her to the Rája, saying, "If our daughter have sons they will not succeed to the Ráj ; for when Sántanu dies, his son Sántanavu will become Rája." Then Sántanavu determined to sacrifice himself in order to gratify his father ; and he made a vow to the parents of the damsel, saying, "If you will give your daughter in marriage to my father, I will never accept the kingdom or marry a wife, or become the father of children by any woman ; so that if your daughter bear a son to the Rája, that son shall succeed him in the kingdom." And the vow of Sántanavu was noised abroad, and from that day he was called Bhíshma, or "the dreadful," because of his dreadful vow. Henceforth Bhíshma became the patriarch of the family, "and is represented as a model of faithfulness and loyalty, and indeed stands forth as one of the leading characters in the Mahábhárata."

He educated Dhritaráshtra, Pándu and Vidura ; and afterwards made Dróna the preceptor of the Pándavas and Kauravas ; and at a meeting of council proposed that the kingdom should be divided between the two parties. In the great war he became the generalissimo of the Kauravas and their allies. On the tenth day he was mortally wounded in a terrible conflict with Arjuna.

Bhishmaka—The king of Vidarbha (now Berar) who resided at Kundina. He had a son named Rukmin, and a beautiful daughter named Rukminí. Krishṇa fell in love with the latter and solicited her in marriage ; but her brother would not assent to the espousals. At the suggestion of Jarásandha, the powerful sovereign, Bhíshmaka affianced Rukminí to Siṣupála. Krishṇa went to witness the wedding and contrived to carry off the princess. Rukmin, with a large force, pursued and overtook Krishṇa, who with his discus destroyed the host of Rukmin, and would have slain him, but was withheld by the entreaties of Rukminí.

Bhishmashtami—The twenty-third of Mágha, and eighth lunar day of the light half (7th February). This is a festival which, at first sight, appears to be of special and traditional origin, but which has, probably, its source in the primitive institutes of the Hindus, of which the worship of the Pitris, the patriarchs or progenitors, the Dii Manes, constituted an important element. According to the Tithi Tattwa, this day is dedicated to Bhíshma, the son of Gangá, and great uncle of the Pándava and Kaurava princes ; who was killed in the course of the great war, and dying childless left no descendant in the direct line, on whom it was incumbent to offer him obsequial honors. In order to supply this defect, persons in general are enjoined to make libations of water on this day to his spirit, and to offer him sesamum seeds and boiled rice. The act expiates the sins of a whole year : one of its peculiarities is, that it is to be observed by persons of all the four original castes, according to a text of Dhavala, an ancient lawgiver, quoted by Raghunandana, " Oh twice-born ! persons of all the Varnas should on the eighth lunar day offer water, sesamum seeds and rice, to Bhíshma. If a Brahman, or man of any other caste, omit to make such offerings, the merit of his good deeds during the preceding year is annulled." According to a different reading of the text, however, it should be rendered : " Let all the twice-born castes make the oblations." This excludes Súdras, but extends the duty to the Kshatriyas and Vaisyas as well as Brahmans. The intention of the rite, as now understood, is expressed in the formulæ uttered at the time of presenting the offerings : " I present this water to the childless hero Bhíshma, of the race of Vyághrapada, the chief of the house of Sankṛiti. May Bhíshma, the son of Sántanu, the speaker of truth and subjugator of his passions, obtain by this water the oblations due by sons and grandsons." The simple nature of the offerings which are sufficient on such occasions, water and sesamum seeds, justifies the remark made by Ovid on the Feralia, that the manes are easily satisfied,—Parva petunt manes.

Bhiras—The people about Surat ; called Phauni or Phryni, by Strabo.

Bhogavati—The capital of Vásuki in Rasátala, one of the seven regions of Pátáḷa.

Bhojakata—The city near the Narmada, founded by Rukmin, after his defeat by Krishṇa, as he had vowed never to return to Kundani but as victor.

Bhojas—Inhabitants of the country near the Vindhya range of mountains ; a branch of the Yadavas. A Bhoja Rája is amongst the warriors of the Mahábhárata.

Bhoja Raja—A prince of Dhára ; or Dhar, in Malwa ; supposed to be the same as Vikrama. There is some uncertainty as to the exact time of Bhoja's reign; the "nine gems" are said to have flourished during his reign and that of Vikrama. The period is designated the golden age of Hindu literature. Dr. E. F. Hall says it is high time to give up speaking of this prince as a great patron of literature. His pretensions to be so considered rest on the frailest foundation possible.—*H. H. Wilson's Works, Vol. V, p.* 171.

Bhraja—The name of one of the seven suns into which the seven solar rays dilate at the consummation of all things when their radiance is to set the three worlds and Pátāḷa on fire.

Bhrajiras—One of the five classes of demi-gods on the fourteenth Manwantara.

Bhrami—(Revolving.) The daughter of Sisumara (the sphere) wife of Dhruva, according to the Bhágavata, which converts the family of Dhruva into personifications of divisions of time and of day and night.

Bhrigu—A Prajápati, or Rishi, chief of the Maharshis (see *Rishi.*) Also one of the ten Prajápatis, sons of Brahma and progenitors of mankind, and teacher of the *Dhanurveda,* or science of war, one of the Upavedas. As such he belongs to the Vedic period. In the Puránic period he is called the husband of Khyáti, or fame, the daughter of Daksha, by Prasúti.—*Vishnu Purána, pp.* 49, 284. In Muir's Original Sanscrit Texts there are many incidents related of Bhṛigu which illustrate the celebrity he had attained and the great influence he had acquired. When king Nahusha tyrannised over the brahmans and compelled even the Rishis to carry him from place to place, it once came Agastya's turn to perform the servile office. Bhṛigu then said to Agastya "Why do we submit to the insults of this king of the gods ?" Agastya answered that none of the Rishis had ventured to curse

Nahusha because he had obtained the power of subduing to his service every one upon whom he fixed his eyes ; and that he had nectar for his beverage. However Agastya said he was prepared to do anything that Bhṛigu might suggest. Bhṛigu said he had been sent by Brahma to take vengeance on Nahusha, who was that day about to attach Agastya to his car, and would spurn him with his foot ; and that he (Bhṛigu) incensed at this insult, would by a curse condemn Nahusha to become a serpent. All this accordingly happened. Bhṛigu however on Nahusha's solicitation, and the intercession of Agastya, placed a period to the effects of the curse, which Yudhishṭhira was to be the instrument of terminating. Vol. 1, p. 315.

Bhrihaspati—See Vṛihaspati. This is not only the name of the puróhita of the gods, but is also used in the ancient Sanscrit hymns as the name of the One Eternal.

Bhurishena—The third son of the holy sage Chyavána, according to the Bhágavata ; the V. P. only mentions one son Anartta.

Bhudevi—A name of the earth, and fabled to be married to *Prithu;* the first king who taught the mode of cultivating the ground. Hence the earth is named *Prit'hivi.* One of the *Puránas* was delivered to *Bhu-dévi,* by *Vishnu,* as *Varáha Swámi.* Bhū-devi, or *Bhumi-devi,* is the secondary wife of Vishnu.

Bhumimitra—A Kanwa prince, whose father Devabhuti, the last Sunga king, was murdered by his minister.

Bhuri—A son of Sómadatta, one of the descendants of Kuru.

Bhurloka—The sphere of the earth comprehending its oceans, mountains and rivers, and extending as far as it is illuminated by the rays of the sun and moon.

Bhuta—A son of Vasudeva by his wife Róhiṇi.

Bhutadi—The third variety of Ahankara, q. v.

Bhutas—Evil spirits, said to proceed from Brahma. Children of Kródha. Malignant spirits, goblins or ghosts, haunting cemeteries, lurking in trees, animating dead bodies, and deluding and devouring human beings. They are generally coupled with the

Pretas, and in this character belong to the Epic period. In the Puránic period they are personified as demi-gods of a particular class, produced by Brahma when incensed; and their mother is therefore considered in the Padma-purána as Krodhá, or 'Anger,' and their father, Kaṣyapa.—*Thompson.*

Bhutasantapana—A powerful Daitya, the son of Hiranyáksha. The descendants of Hiranyaksha are said in the Padma-purána to have extended to seventy-seven crores, or seven hundred and seventy millions.

Bhutatma—An appellation of Vishṇu, meaning one with created things.

Bhutavidya—The fourth branch of Medical Science, treating of maladies referred to demoniac possession.

Bhutesa—A name of Vishṇu, meaning lord of the elements, or of created things.

Bhuti—A sage, the son of Angiras, whose pupil Santi, having suffered the holy fire to go out in his master's absence, prayed to Agni, and so propitiated him, that he not only re-lighted the flame, but desired Santi to demand a further boon. Santi accordingly solicited a son for his Guru, which son was Bhúti, the father of the Manu Bhautya. Also the name of a goddess, wife of Kavi.

Bhuvana—The name of one of the eleven Rudras, according to the Váyu Purána list.

Bhuvar-loka—The sphere of the sky, both in diameter and circumference, as far upwards as to the planetary sphere, or Swar-lóka.

Bijala Raja—A Jaina king of *Kalyánapura,* otherwise *Silpagiri,* who had the celebrated *Basava,* for his minister of state. He was charged with wasting the state funds, in gathering around himself adherents to a new form of the *Saiva* religion. When called to account, he made up the deficiency in appearance; but soon after caused the king to be assassinated by three men, in his own palace. Thereupon, the *Jainas* were massacred. The exact date is not known; but Professor Wilson places it in the early part of the eleventh century. See *Basava.*

Bikya—The daughter of the minister of the Rája of Kutuwal in the Dekhan, who was married to Chandrahása, the fortunate boy, q. v.

Bodha—(Understanding). A son of Dharma, by one of Daksha's daughters, Buddhi.

Bodhana—A mountain to the east of Ramghur.

Bodhas—One of the tribes of Central India, according to the Váyu Purána ; it is also read Bahyas.

Brahma—The first deity of the Hindu triad ; the creator of the world ; the great father and lord of all ; the supporter of all : yet described as born in the lotus which sprung from the navel of Vishṇu ; and as born from the golden egg. The Vishṇu Purána says, the one only god Janárdana, takes the designation of Brahma, Vishṇu and Śiva, accordingly as he creates, preserves or destroys. Mr. Cockburn Thompson says : "In the ante-mythological age this was probably nothing but a name for the sun, considered as producer, vivifier and pervader. He afterwards replaced Súrya in the triad of elementary gods, and was coupled with Vishṇu and Śiva, who were substituted for Varuna and Váyu, the other components of that triad. In the earliest mythological period, Brahma (always masculine) is then first person of the triad, Brahma, Vishṇu and Śiva ; and when later the unity of these personages was established by referring them to one Supreme Being, Brahma was that being in his character of creator and enlivener, Vishṇu in that of preserver, and Śiva in that of destroyer. Thus in the Puránas (Vishṇu P., p. 22,) Brahma is said to live 100 of his own years, each of which consists of 360 days and nights. The days are called Kalpas, and consist of 4,320,000,000 years of mortals, during which the universe exists. During his nights the universe ceases to exist, and is reproduced at the commencement of the next day or Kalpa. He is described in the Puránas as having four faces, and as being produced from the cup of a lotus, which sprang from the navel of Vishṇu. In this mythological character of creator of the universe, he is mentioned in the Bhagavat Gíta and Vishṇu Purána. When, after the period of superstitious mythology, the idea of one Supreme Being was again brought forward, Brahma was considered the chief of the existing trinity, and was at first identified with that idea of an unknown god; and though afterwards Śiva and Vishṇu were each in turn identified with the Supreme Being by their respective followers, the Śaivas and Vaishnavas, the name Brahma, *in the neuter*, was still retained in the language of philosophy to designate the universal Supreme One. In this sense the word occurs throughout the Bhagavat Gíta with the exception of a few places where it is masculine; and once where it occurs in the neuter, but no longer signifies the Supreme Being in his complete character of the essence of both spirit and matter; but merely that portion of him which is the essence of all matter, the universal vital energy. We have thus:—' 1st, Brahma, *masculine,* the mythological personage, first person of the mythological triad, and personification of the creative power, considered as a mortal and material deity; 2nd, Brahma, *neuter*, a name used to designate the Supreme Being in philosophic language; and 3rd, Brahma, neuter, the personification, in later philosophical language, of the material portion of the Supreme Being. (The word has never been satisfactorily derived, though commonly supposed to come from the root *vrih*, to grow or increase."'—*Thompson.* Dr. Muir in the 5th Vol. of his *Original Sanscrit Texts,* translates a text which he says 'is interesting not merely as introducing Brahma but as containing what is probably one of the oldest extant expositions of the conceptions of nāma and rūpa (name and form) as comprehending the whole of the phenominal universe.'

"1. In the beginning Brahma was this [universe.] He created gods. Having created gods, he placed them in these worlds, viz., in this world Agni, in the atmosphere Vāyu, and in the sky Sūrya; (2) And in the worlds which were yet higher he placed the gods who are still higher. Such as are these visible worlds and these gods,—even such were those (higher) visible worlds in which he placed those (higher) gods, and such were those gods themselves; (3) Then Brahma proceeded to the higher sphere (parārddha—explained by the commentator to mean the Satyaloka, the most excellent, and the limit of all the worlds.) Having gone to that higher sphere, he considered 'how now can I pervade all these worlds?' He then pervaded them with two things—with form and with name. Whatever has a name, that is name. And then that which has no name—that which he knows by its form, that 'such is its form'—that is form. This [universe] is so much as is (*i. e.*, is co-extensive with) form and name ; (4) These are the two great magnitudes *(abhve)* of Brahma. He who knows these two great magnitudes of Brahma becomes himself a great magnitude ; (5) These are the two great manifestations of Brahma. He who knows these two great manifestations of Brahma becomes himself a great manifestation. Of these two, one is the greater, viz., form ; for whatever is name is also form. He who knows the greater of these two, becomes greater than him than whom he wishes to become greater ; (6) The gods were originally mortal, but when they were pervaded by Brahma they became immortal. By that which he sends forth from his mind (mind is form ; for by mind he knows, 'This is form')—by that, I say, he obtains form. And by that which he sends out from his voice (voice is name ; for by voice he seizes name)—by that, I say, he obtains name. This universe is so much as is (*i. e.*, is co-extensive with) form and name. All that he obtains. Now that all is undecaying. Hence he obtains undecaying merit, and an undecaying world."

"The deity who is described in the later hymns of the Rig Veda, and in the Atharva Veda, under the different titles of Viṣva-karman, Hiranyagarbha and Prajápati, appears to correspond with the Brahma of the more modern legendary books. Though this god was originally unconnected with Vishṇu and Rudra, while at a subsequent period he came to be regarded in systematic mythology as the first person in the triad of which they formed the second and third members, yet the general idea entertained of his character has been less modified in the course of his history than is the case in regard to the other two deities."

"Brahma was from the beginning considered as the Creator, and he continued to be regarded as fulfilling the same function even after he had sunk into a subordinate position, and had come to be represented by the votaries of Vishṇu and Mahádeva respectively, as the mere creature and agent of one or other of these two gods. In later times Brahma has had few special worshippers ; the only spot where he is periodically adored being at

Pushkara in Rajputana. Two of the acts which the earlier legends ascribe to him, the assumption of the forms of a tortoise and of a boar are in later works transferred to Vishṇu."

In the fourth Volume of ***Muir's Original Sanscrit Texts***, from which the above extract has been taken, the reader will find the life, character and attributes of Brahma fully illustrated. In some of the Texts translated it is maintained that Brahma, Vishṇu and Śiva, are three manifestations of the same divinity. "I shall declare to thee that form composed of Hari and Hara (Vishṇu and Mahádeva) combined, which is without beginning, middle, or end, imperishable, undecaying. He who is Vishṇu is Rudra ; he who is Rudra is Pitámaha (Brahma) ; the substance is one, the gods are three, Rudra, Vishṇu and Pitámaha." (O. S. T., Vol. IV, p. 237.)

Brahma-Purana—The, gives a description of the creation, an account of the Manwantaras, and the history of the solar and lunar dynasties to the time of Krishṇa. It also sets forth the sanctity of Orissa, with its temples and sacred groves, dedicated to the sun, to Śiva and Jagganath. Its object seems to be the promotion of the worship of Krishṇa as Jagganath.

Brahmabali—A disciple of Devaderṣa and teacher of the Sámaveda.

Brahmabhuta—To become identified with the Supreme Spirit : to have the conviction that spirit is one, universal, and the same.

Brahma bodhya—A river mentioned in the Vishṇu Puráṇa, but not identified.

Brahmachari—A religious student who has been invested with the sacred thread ; he is to prosecute the study of the Vedas in the house of his preceptor : and to wait on him constantly ; in the morning he is to salute the sun, in the evening fire ; and then to address his preceptor with respect. He must stand when his preceptor is standing ; move when he is walking, and sit beneath him when he is seated : he must never sit, nor walk, nor stand, when his teacher does the reverse. He is to read the Veda attentively, placed before his preceptor ; and to eat the food he has collected as alms, when permitted by his teacher. He is to bathe in water which has first been used for his preceptor's ablutions; and every morning bring fuel and water, and whatever else may be required. V. P.

One of the hymns translated by Dr. Muir in his Original Sanscrit Texts ascribes "very astonishing powers to the Brahmachārin or religious student." Dr. Muir says: "Some parts of it are obscure, but the translation I give, though imperfect, will convey some idea of the contents."

"The Brahmachārin works, quickening both worlds. The gods are joyful in him. He has established the earth and the sky. He satisfies his āchārya (religious teacher) by tapas; 2, The Fathers, the heavenly hosts, all the gods separately, follow after him, with the 6,333 Gandharvas. He satisfies all the gods by tapas; 3, The āchārya, adopting him as a disciple, makes him a Brahmachārin even in the womb, and supports him in the belly for three nights. When he is born the gods assemble to see him; 4, This piece of fuel is the earth (compare verse 9), the second is the sky, and he satisfies the air with fuel. The Brahmachārin satisfies the worlds with fuel, with a girdle, with exertion, with tapas; 5, Born before Brahma, the Brahmachārin arose through tapas, clothed with heat. From him was produced divine knowledge (brāmaṇa), the highest Brahma, and all the gods, together with immortality; 6, The Brahmachārin advances, lighted up by fuel, clothed in a black antelope's skin, consecrated, long-bearded. He moves straightway from the eastern to the northern ocean, compressing the worlds, and again expanding them; 7, The Brahmachārin, generating divine science, the waters, the world, Prajāpati, Parameshṭhin, Virāj, having become an embryo in the womb of immortality, having become Indra, crushed the Asuras; 8, The Áchārya has constructed both these spheres, broad and deep, the earth and the sky. The Brahmachārin preserves them by tapas. In him the gods are joyful; 9, It was the Brahmachārin who first produced this broad earth and the sky as an alms. Making them two pieces of fuel (compare verse 4) he worships. In them all creatures are contained; 10, The two receptacles of divine knowledge are secretly deposited, the one on this side, the other beyond the surface of the sky. The Brahmachārin guards them by tapas. Wise, he appropriates that divine knowledge as his exclusive portion... ; 16, The Brahmachārin is the Ácharya, the Brahmachārin is Prajāpati ; Prajāpati shines *(virājati)* ; the shining (*Viráj*) became Indra, the powerful ; 17, Through self-restraint and tapas a king protects his dominions. Through self-restraint an Ácharya seeks after a Brahmachārin ; 18, By self-restraint a damsel obtains a young man as her husband. By self-restraint an ox and a horse seek to gain fodder ; 19, By self-restraint and tapas the gods destroyed death. By self-restraint Indra acquired heaven from [or for] the gods ; 20, Plants, whatever has been, whatever shall be, day and night, trees, the year, with the seasons, have been produced from the Brahmachārin ; 21, Terrestrial and celestial beings, beasts, both wild and tame, creatures without wings and winged, have been produced from the Brahmachārin ; 22, All creatures which have sprung from Prajāpati have breath separately in themselves ; all of these are preserved by divine knowledge (Brahma), which is produced in the Brahmachārin ...; 26, These things the Brahmachārin formed ; on the surface of the water he stood performing tapas in the sea."

Brahmadatta—A sage, the son of Anuha. In the Hari Vamsam is a curious legend of the different transmigrations of Brahmadatta and his six companions, who were successively as many brahmans, then forests, then deer, then water fowl, then swans, and finally, brahmans again, when with the king they obtained liberation. According to the Bhágavat, Brahmadatta composed a treatise on the Yôga, a yóga tantra.

Brahmaloka—The highest heaven, the world of infinite wisdom and truth, the inhabitants of which never again know death.

Brahman—The name of the sacerdotal class ; though a priestly tribe, all brahmins are not priests. The true origin of the brahmans is not distinctly known. The fabulous tradition current amongst them derives them from the head of Brahma. A brahman is in a very different situation from a Kshatriya, a Vaisya or a Śudra. These are born in the condition in which they continue to live. But a Brahman becomes such only by the ceremony of the cord with which he is invested at an early age. (See Upanayana). They are after this rite designated Dwija, twice-born.

The seven castes of the brahmans have for their special origin the seven famous *Rishis* or penitents. These seven Rishis are highly celebrated in the annals of the country. They are the holiest and most venerated personages the Hindus acknowledge. Their names are held sacred and invoked by all the people. (See Rishis).

"If the fabulous stories which are told of the origin of certain great families in Europe, shed a lustre upon them by proving their antiquity, how much more reason has the brahman to vaunt his noble pedigree? and if the honor of being sprung from an illustrious family sometimes leads its descendants to look down with contempt upon the lower ranks, we cannot wonder at the haughtiness of the brahman, and the high disdain which he shows to every caste but his own."*

Every brahman professes to know from which of the seven Rishis he has descended. There is another and more general division which separates them into four distinct classes, each of which appertains to one of the four Vedas. But in the ordinary intercourse of life little attention is paid to this distinction. There are several sectarian divisions which are practically more operative. These are Vishṇuvite, Smárta or Saiva brahmans; and in different parts of India other sub-divisions are found.

Brahmanas—The portions of the Vedas which comprise precepts inculcating religious duties, maxims which explain these precepts, and arguments which relate to theology. "The Brâhmanas represent no doubt a most interesting phrase in the history of the Indian mind, but judged by themselves, as literary productions, they are most disappointing. No one would have supposed that at so early a period, and in so primitive a state of society, there could have risen up a literature which for pedantry and downright absurdity can hardly be matched anywhere. There is no lack of striking thoughts, of bold expressions, of sound reason-

* Abbe Dubois.

ing and curious traditions in these collections. But these are only like the fragments of a *torso,* like precious gems set in brass and lead. The general character of these works is marked by shallow and insipid grandiloquence, by priestly conceit and antiquarian pedantry. It is most important to the historian that he should know how soon the fresh and healthy growth of a nation can be blighted by priestcraft and superstition. It is most important that we should know that nations are liable to those epidemics in their youth as well as in their dotage. These works deserve to be studied as the physician studies the twaddle of idiots, and the raving of madmen. They will disclose to a thoughtful eye the ruins of faded grandeur, the memories of noble aspirations. But let us only try to translate these works into our own language, and we shall feel astonished that human language and human thought should ever have been used for such purposes."*

Brahmanda Purana—That which has declared in twelve thousand two hundred verses, the magnificence of the egg of Brahma, and in which an account of the future Kalpas is contained, is called the Brahmânda Purâna, and was revealed by Brahma. V. P.

Brahmas or Brahmarishis—According to the V. P. the names of the nine Brahmans, or Brahmarishis, are Brighu, Pulastya, Pulaha, Kratu, Angiras, Marichi, Daksha, Atri and Vasishta. They are also called Prajâpatis and Brahmaputras. Considerable variety prevails in the lists of them in the different books : but the variations are of the nature of additions made to an apparently original enumeration of but seven, whose names generally recur. In the V. P. they are termed the mind-engendered progeny of Brahma : born from his continued meditations. In the South of India they are usually termed the Seven Penitents. Two it is said were not originally brahmans, but they practised so long and severe a penance that they obtained the remarkable favor of being raised to that rank by the ceremony of the cord. From penitent Râjas they became penitent brahmans : their rise was from a still lower rank accord-

* Max Müller.

ing to the philosophical poet Vernana. These Rishis existed prior to the Vedas, in which they are often mentioned. The Abbe Dubois thinks they were the seven sons of Japhet.

Brahma-savarni—The Manu of the tenth Manwantara.

Brahmavaivartta-Purana—"That Purána which is related by Sávarne to Nárada, and contains the account of the greatness of Krishṇa, with the occurrences of the Rathantantara Kalpa, where also the story of Brahma Varáha is repeatedly told, is called the Brahma vaivartta and contains eighteen thousand stanzas." V. P.

Brahmajna—Sacred Study, that which communicates to soul the knowledge of good and evil: one of the five great sacrifices or obligations of the Brahmachári.

Bramharshis—Descendants of the five patriarchs who were the founders of races or Gotras of brahmans, or Kaṣyapa, Vasishtha, Angiras, Atri and Brighu. The Brahmarshis dwell in the sphere of Brahma.

Brammedhya—The name of a river in the Vishṇu Purána not yet identified.

Buddha—" Buddha, or more correctly, the Buddha,—for Buddha is an appellative meaning Enlightened,—was born at Kapilavastu, the capital of a kingdom of the same name, situated at the foot of the mountains of Nepal, north of the present Oude. His father, the king of Kapilavastu, was of the family of the Sâkyas, and belonged to the clan of the Gautamas. His mother was Mâyâdêvî, daughter of king Suprabuddha, and need we say that she was as beautiful as he was powerful and just ? Buddha was therefore by birth of the Kshatrya, or warrior caste, and he took the name of Sâkya from his family, and that of Gautama from his clan, claiming a kind of spiritual relationship with the honoured race of Gautama. The name of Buddha, or the Buddha, dates from a later period of his life, and so probably does the name Siddhârtha (he whose objects have been accomplished), though we are told that it was given him in his childhood. His mother died seven days after his birth, and the father confided the child to the care of his deccased wife's sister, who, however, had been his wife even before the mother's death. The child grew up a most beautiful and most accomplished boy, who soon knew more than his masters could teach him. He refused to take part in the games of his playmates, and never felt so happy as when he could sit alone, lost in meditation in the deep shadows of the forest. It was there that his father found him when he had thought him lost, and in order to prevent the young prince from becoming a dreamer, the king determined to marry him at once. When the subject was mentioned by the aged ministers to the future heir to the throne, he demanded seven days for reflection, and convinced at last that not even marriage could disturb the calm of his mind, he allowed the ministers to look out for a princess. The princess selected was the beautiful Gopâ, the daughter of Daṇḍapâṇi. Though her father objected at first to her marrying a young prince who was represented to him as deficient in manliness and intellect, he gladly gave his consent when he saw the royal suitor distancing all his rivals both in feats of arms and power of mind. Their marriage proved one of the happiest, but the prince remained as he had been before, absorbed in meditation on the problems of life and death. 'Nothing is stable on earth,' he used to say, 'nothing is real. Life is like the spark produced by the friction of wood. It is lighted and is extinguished—we know not whence it came or whither it goes. It is like the sound of a lyre, and the wise man asks in vain from whence it came and whither it goes. There must be some supreme intelligence where we could find rest. If I attained it, I could bring light to man; if I were free myself, I could deliver the world.' The king, who perceived the melancholy mood of the young prince, tried everything to divert him from his speculations: but all was in vain. Three of the most ordinary events that could happen to any man, proved of the utmost importance in the career of Buddha. We quote the description of these occurrences from M. Barthélemy Saint Hilaire:

'One day when the prince with a large retinue was driving through the eastern gate of the city on the way to one of his parks, he met on the road an old man, broken and decrepit. One could see the veins and muscles over the whole of his body, his teeth chattered, he was covered with wrinkles, bald, and hardly able to utter hollow and unmelodious sounds. He was bent on his stick, and all his limbs and joints trembled. "Who is that man?" said the prince to his coachman. "He is small and weak, his flesh and his blood are dried up, his muscles stick to his skin, his head is white, his teeth chatter, his body is wasted away; leaning on his stick he is hardly able to walk, stumbling at every step. Is there something peculiar in his family, or is this the common lot of all created beings?"

'"Sir," replied the coachman, "that man is sinking under old age, his senses have become obtuse, suffering has destroyed his strength, and he is despised by his relations. He is without support and useless, and people have abandoned him, like a dead tree in a forest. But this is not peculiar to his family. In every creature, youth is defeated by old age. Your father, your mother, all your relations, all your friends, will come to the same state; this is the appointed end of all creatures.'"

'"Alas!" replied the prince, "are creatures so ignorant, so weak and foolish, as to be proud of the youth by which they are intoxicated, not seeing the old age which awaits them! As for me, I go away. Coachman, turn my chariot quickly. What have I, the future prey of old age,—what have I to do with pleasure?'" And the young prince returned to the city without going to his park.

'Another time the prince was driving through the southern gate to his pleasure garden, when he perceived on the road a man suffering from illness, parched with fever, his body wasted, covered with mud, without a friend, without a home, hardly able to breathe, and frightened at the sight of himself and the approach of death. Having questioned his coachman, and received from him the answer which he expected, the young prince said, "Alas! health is but the sport of a dream, and the fear of suffering must take this frightful form. Where is the wise man who, after having seen what he is, could any longer think of joy and pleasure?" The prince turned his chariot and returned to the city.

'A third time he was driving to his pleasure garden through the western gate, when he saw a dead body on the road, lying on a bier, and covered with a cloth. The friends stood about crying, sobbing, tearing their hair, covering their heads with dust, striking their breasts, and uttering wild cries. The prince, again, calling his coachman to witness this painful scene, exclaimed, "Oh! woe to youth, which must be destroyed by old age! Woe to health, which must be destroyed by so many diseases! Woe to this life, where a man remains so short a time! If there were no old age, no disease, no death; if these could be made captive for ever!" Then betraying for the first time his intentions, the young prince said, "Let us turn back, I must think how to accomplish deliverance.'"

'A last meeting put an end to his hesitation. He was driving through the northern gate on the way to his pleasure gardens, when he saw a mendicant who appeared outwardly calm, subdued, looking downwards, wearing with an air of dignity his religious vestment, and carrying an alms-bowl.'

'"Who is this man?" asked the prince.

'"Sir," replied the coachman, "this man is one of those who are called bhikshus, or mendicants. He has renounced all pleasures, all desires, and leads a life of austerity. He tries to conquer himself. He has become a devotee. Without passion, without envy, he walks about asking for alms.'"

'"This is good and well said," replied the prince. "The life of a devotee has always been praised by the wise. It will be my refuge and the refuge of other creatures; it will lead us to a real life, to happiness and immortality."

'With these words the young prince turned his chariot and returned to the city.'

After having declared to his father and his wife his intention of retiring from the world, Buddha left his palace one night when all the guards that were to have watched him were asleep. After travelling the whole night he gave his horse and his ornaments to his groom, and sent him back to Kapilavastu. 'A monument,' remarks the author of the Lalita-Vistara (p. 270), 'is still to be seen on the spot where the coachman turned back.' Hiouen-Thsang (II, 330) saw the same monument at the edge of a large forest, on his road to Kuṣinâgara, a city now in ruins, and situated about fifty miles E. S. E. from Gorakpur.

Buddha first went to Vaisâli and became the pupil of a famous Brahman, who had gathered round him 300 disciples. Having learnt all that the Brahman could teach him, Buddha went away disappointed. He had not found the road to salvation. He then tried another Brahman at Râgagṛiha, the capital of Magadha or Behar, who had 700 disciples, and there too he looked in vain for the means of deliverance. He left him, followed by five of his fellow-students, and for six years retired into solitude, near a village named Uruvilva, subjecting himself to the most severe penances, previous to his appearing in the world as a teacher. At the end of this period, however, he arrived at the conviction that asceticism, far from giving peace of mind and preparing the way to salvation, was a snare and a stumbling-block in the way of truth. He gave up his exercises, and was at once deserted as an apostate by his five disciples. Left to himself he now began to elaborate his own system. He had learnt that neither the doctrines nor the austerities of the Brahmans were of any avail for accomplishing the deliverance of man, and freeing him from the fear of old age, disease and death. After long meditations and ecstatic visions, he at last imagined that he had arrived at that true knowledge which discloses the cause, and thereby destroys the fear of all the changes inherent in life. It was from the moment when he arrived at this knowledge, that he claimed the name of Buddha, the enlightened. At that moment we may truly say that the fate of millions of millions of human beings trembled in the balance. Buddha hesitated for a time whether he should keep his knowledge to himself, or communicate it to the world. Compassion for the sufferings of man prevailed, and the young prince became the founder of a religion which, after more than 2,000 years, is still professed by 455,000,000 of human beings.

The further history of the new teacher is very simple. He proceeded to Benares, which at all times was the principal seat of learning in India, and the first converts he made were the five fellow-students who had left him when he threw off the yoke of the Brahmanical observances. Many others followed; but as the Lalita-Vistara breaks off at Buddha's arrival at Benares, we have no further consecutive account of the rapid progress of his doctrine. From what we can gather from scattered notices in the Buddhist canon, he was invited by the king of Magadha, Bimbisâra, to his capital, Râgagṛiha. Many of his lectures are represented as having been delivered at the monastery of Kalantaka, with which the king or some rich merchant had presented him; others on the Vulture Peak, one of the five hills that surrounded the ancient capital.

Three of his most famous disciples, Sâriputra, Kâtyâyana, and Maudgalyâyana, joined him during his stay in Magadha, where he enjoyed for many years the friendship of the king. That king was afterwards assassinated by his son, Agâtaṣatru, and then we hear of Buddha as settled for a time at Srâvastî, north of the Ganges, where Anâthapiṇḍada, a rich merchant, had offered him and his disciples a magnificent building for their residence. Most of Buddha's lectures or sermons were delivered at Srâvastî, the capital of Koṣala; and the king of Koṣala himself, Prasênagit, became a convert to his doctrine. After an absence of twelve years we are told that Buddha visited his father at Kapilavastu, on which occasion he performed several miracles, and converted all the Sâkyas to his faith. His own wife became one of his followers, and, with his aunt, offers the first instance of female Buddhist devotees in India. We have fuller particulars again of the last days of Buddha's life. He had attained the good age of threescore and ten, and had been on a visit to Râgagṛiha, where the king, Agâtaṣatru, the former enemy of Buddha, and the assassin of his own father, had joined the congregation, after making a public confession of his crimes. On his return he was followed by a large number of disciples, and when on the point of crossing the Ganges, he stood on a square stone, and turning his eyes back towards Râgagṛiha, he said, full of emotion, 'This is the last time that I see that city.' He likewise visited Vaiṣâtlî, and after taking leave of it, he had nearly reached the city of Kuṣinâgara, when his vital strength began to fail. He halted in a forest, and while sitting under a sâl tree, he gave up the ghost, or, as a Buddhist would say, entered into Nirvâṇa.

This is the simple story of Buddha's life. It reads much better in the eloquent pages of M. Barthélemy Saint Hilaire, than in the turgid language of the Buddhists. If a critical historian, with the materials we possess, entered at all on the process of separating truth from falsehood, he would probably cut off much of what our biographer has left. Professor Wilson, in his Essay on Buddha and Buddhism, considers it doubtful whether any such person as Buddha ever actually existed. He dwells on the fact that there are at least twenty different dates assigned to his birth, varying from 2420 to 453 B. C. He points out that the clan of the Sâkyas is never mentioned by early Hindu writers, and he lays much stress on the fact that most of the proper names of the persons connected with Buddha suggest an allegorical signification. The name of his father means, he whose food is pure ; that of his mother signifies illusion ; his own secular appellation, Siddhârtha, he by whom the end is accomplished. Buddha itself means, the Enlightened, or, as Professor Wilson translates it less accurately, he by whom all is known. The same distinguished scholar goes even further, and maintaining that Kapilavastu, the birth-place of Buddha, has no place in the geography of the Hindus, suggests that it may be rendered, the substance of Kapila ; intimating, in fact, the Sânkhya philosophy, the doctrine of Kapila Muni, upon which the fundamental elements of Buddhism, the eternity of matter, the principles of things, and the final extinction, are supposed to be planned. 'It seems not impossible,' he continues, 'that Sâkya Muni is an unreal being, and that all that is related of him is as much a fiction, as is that of his preceding migrations, and the miracles that attended his birth, his life, and his departure.' This is going far beyond Niebuhr, far even beyond Strauss. If an allegorical name had been invented for the father of Buddha, one more appropriate than 'clean-food' might surely have been found. His mother is not the only queen known by the name of Mâyâ, Mâyâdêvî, or Mâyavatî. Why, if these names were invented, should his wife have been allowed to keep the prosaic name of Gopâ (cowherdess), and his father-in-law, that of Dândapâṇi, 'stick-hand?' As to his own name, Siddhârtha, the Tibetans maintain that it was given him by his parent, whose wish (artha) had been fulfilled (siddha), as we hear of Désirés and Dieu-donnés in French. One of the ministers of Daṣaratha had the same name.

It is possible also that Buddha himself assumed it in after-life, as was the case with many of the Roman surnames. As to the name of Buddha, no one ever maintained that it was more than a title, the Enlightened, changed from an appellative into a proper name, just like the name of Christos, the Anointed ; or Mohammed, the Expected. Kapilavastu would be a most extraordinary compound to express 'the substance of the Sânkhya philosophy.' But all doubt on the subject is removed by the fact that both Fabian in the fifth, and Hiouen-Tshang in the seventh centuries, visited the real ruins of that city.

Making every possible allowance for the accumulation of fiction which is sure to gather round the life of the founder of every great religion, we may be satisfied that Buddhism, which changed the aspect not only of India, but of nearly the whole of Asia, had a real founder ; that he was not a Brahman by birth, but belonged to the second or royal caste ; that being of a meditative turn of mind, and deeply impressed with the frailty of all created things, he became a recluse, and sought for light and comfort in the different systems of Brâhman philosophy and theology. Dissatisfied with the artificial systems of their priests and philosophers, convinced of the uselessness, nay of the pernicious influence, of their ceremonial practices and bodily penances, shocked, too, by their worldliness and pharisaical conceit, which made the priesthood the exclusive property of one caste and rendered every sincere approach of man to his Creator impossible without their intervention, Buddha must have produced at once a powerful impression on the people at large, when breaking through all the established rules of caste, he assumed the privileges of a Brahman, and throwing away the splendour of his royal position, travelled about as a beggar, not shrinking from the defiling contact of sinners and publicans. Though when we now speak of Buddhism, we think chiefly of its doctrines, the reform of Buddha had originally much more of a social than of a religious character. Buddha swept away the web with which the Brahmans had encircled the whole of India. Beginning as the destroyer of an old, he became the founder of a new religion."*

* Max Müller, Chips from a German Workshop, Vol. I, p. 210.

According to Buddhist belief when a man dies he is immediately born again, or appears in a new shape, according to his merit or demerit, he may be born in the form of a woman, or a slave, a quadruped, a bird, a fish, an insect, a plant, or even a piece of inorganic matter. He may be born in a state of punishment in one of the many Buddhist hells; or in the condition of a happy spirit or even divinity in heaven; but whatever the position be, and however long he may live in it, the life will have an end, and the individual must be born again, and may again be either happy or miserable—"either a god, or it may be the vilest inanimate object. The Buddha himself, before his last birth as Sakyamuni, had gone through every conceivable form of existence, on the earth, in the air, and in the water, in hell and in heaven, and had filled every condition in human life. When he attained the perfect knowledge of the Buddha, he was able to recall all these existences; and a great part of the Buddhist legendary literature is taken up in narrating his exploits, when he lived as an elephant, as a bird, as a stag, and so forth."—*Goldstücker.*

The Buddhist does not regard these various transmigrations, whether punishments or rewards, as caused by the Creator or Ruler of the Universe. "They do not conceive any god or gods as being pleased or displeased by the actions, and as assigning the actors their future condition by way of punishment or reward." The very idea of a god as creating or in any way ruling the world, is utterly absent in the Buddhist system. God is not so much as denied; he is simply not known." The power that controls the world is expressed by the word *Karma*, literally action, including both merit and demerit. "The future condition of the Buddhist, then, is not assigned him by the Ruler of the Universe; the *Karma* of his actions determines it by a sort of virtue inherent in the nature of things—by the blind and unconscious concatenation of cause and effect."

Buddhism inculcates morality. The most essential virtues are truthfulness, benevolence, kindness, purity, patience, courage, and contemplation. All offensive and gross language is forbidden; nothing is ever to be said to stir up ill-will, or excite enmity, or that would cause quarrels; it is a duty on all occasions to act as a peace-maker. "Humility holds a no less prominent place among Buddhist graces than it does among the Christians."—*Goldstücker, Chamber's Ency.*

Buddhi—Understanding, synonyme of Mahat ; also the name of a daughter of Daksha who became the wife of Dharma.

Budha—(Mercury.) The son of Soma, the moon. *Budha* married *Ilā*, whose sex had been changed by Śiva. Thence the lunar, as distinguished from the solar, line of kings ; and to that point is to be referred many important opinions and results, very widely disseminated. See *Ilā*.

There exists a doubt whether the names of planetary bodies were given to early men, or whether the planets were named after distinguished men of the earliest age. The purắnas give a brief legend, which has been deemed astronomical, but of a doubtful school ; such as reduced Abraham to a constellation. This legend is that *Chandra* (the moon) was placed in the house of *Vrihaspati* (Jupiter) as his pupil, and that Tárá (the lunar path of 27 asterisms) fell in love with *Chandra*, and seduced him while *Vrihaspati* was away at a sacrifice made by Indra (the firmament) ; the result was the birth of *Budha* (Mercury). If there *be* any astronomical meaning, it would imply that the old Chaldeans thought that the moon in some part of its orbit attracted a satellite of Jupiter, detached it from that planet, and was the occasion of its finding an orbit around the sun, as a primary planet. However, this interpretation has great improbabilities.

The poets, and especially Telugu poets, have paraphrased the legend in their own way ; and very freely too. If the parties were men on earth we get at one of the earliest known wars. For, the claim to the parentage and right of *Budha* by Vrihaspati and Chandra, led to a fierce war, dividing gods and men into two parties.

In a variety of works published, writers, though oriental scholars, confound *Budha* and Buddha. This appears so late down as Major Cunningham's book on the Bhilsa Topes ; published in 1855. But the persons are distinct, the sense of the words different, the spelling different, the pronunciation still more so.—*Taylor*.

C

Caste—The term Caste, derived from the Portuguese *Casta*, expressive of the Indian word Játi, has been universally adopted by Europeans to denote the different classes or tribes into which the people of India are divided. "The permanent division of the community into classes, with hereditary professions assigned to each, is one of the most remarkable institutions of Hindustan. There are four great divisions. The most distinguished of all is that of Brahmana or Brahmans, who are said to have come from the mouth of Brahma: the second in rank is that of Kshatriya or Rájas, from the arm of Brahma; the third the Vaisya, or merchants, from the thigh of Brahma; the fourth the Sudras, or workmen, from his foot: all with their females. Each of these four tribes is subdivided into several more; the Sudras especially have an almost endless number of distinctions; such as herdsmen who keep the cows; shepherds who tend the sheep; weavers; five castes of Artizans, viz., carpenters, goldsmiths, blacksmiths, stone-cutters, founders. The several castes of cultivators take precedence of other Sudras, and look with contempt on tradesmen and labourers. There is a Caste of Kaḷḷaru, or robbers, who consider their profession as no way discreditable to themselves or their tribe. Each caste exhibits some particular and local varieties of its own by which it is discriminated from the rest: Some distinguish themselves by the cut and colour of their clothes; some by the manner in which they put them on. But however extravagant their modes and customs are, they never excite from castes of the most opposite habits and fashions the least appearance of contempt or dislike. Upon this point there seems to be the most perfect toleration.

In the South of India there is another division of the different tribes still more general than those which have been yet mentioned. It is that of Right-hand and Left-hand Castes. The greater number of Hindu castes belong either to the Right-hand or the Left. The Brahmans, the Pariahs (or outcastes) and several tribes of the Sudras, are considered neutral, and enjoying all the privileges and honors attached to both hands, they take no part with either. These neutral castes are frequently called upon to arbitrate in the fierce disputes that occur between the Right and Left-hand parties. Both parties lay claim to certain privileges; and when any encroachment is made by either it is followed by tumults that spread through a district, accompanied with every excess; and generally with bloody contests. The Hindu, usually so gentle and timid, seems to change his nature. There is no danger he fears to encounter in maintaining these rights."—*Dubois.*

Dr. Muir in the first volume of his O. S. Texts, has very fully investigated the mythical accounts of the creation of man and of the origin of the four castes. He says "it will be seen from the texts adduced that from a very early period the Indian writers have propounded a great variety of speculations regarding the origin of mankind, and of the classes or castes into which they found their own community divided. The most commonly received of these explanations is the fable which represents the Brahmans, Kshatriyas, Vaisyas and Sudras, to have been separately created from the head, the breast or arms, the thighs, and the feet of the Creator. Of this mythical account no trace is to be found in any of the hymns of the Rig Veda, except one, the Purusha Sūkta."

Dr. Muir is of opinion that this hymn belongs to the most recent portion of the Rig Veda. Mr. Colebrook, Professors Max Müller and Weber concur on this view; which however is controverted by Dr. Haug.

After quoting a great number of texts from the oldest authorities, Dr. Muir remarks. "When we discover in the most ancient Indian writings such different and even discrepant accounts of the origin of man, all put forth with equal positiveness, it is impossible to imagine that any uniform explanation of the diversity of castes could have been received at the period when they were composed, or to regard any of the texts which have been cited as more orthodox and authoritative than the rest. Even, therefore, if we should suppose that the author of the Purusha Sūkta meant to represent the four castes as having literally sprung from separate parts of Purusha's body, it is evident that the same idea was not always or even generally adopted by those who followed him, as a revealed truth in which they were bound to acquiesce. In fact, nothing is clearer than that in all these cosmogonies, the writers, while generally assuming certain prevalent ideas as the basis of their descriptions, gave the freest scope to their individual fancy in the invention of details. In such circumstances, perfect coincidence cannot be expected in the narratives."

The following are the results of Dr. Muir's careful investigation of all the Texts bearing on the subject :—

"The details which I have supplied in the course of this chapter must have rendered it abundantly evident that the sacred books of the Hindus contain no uniform or consistent account of the origin of castes ; but, on the contrary, present the greatest varieties of speculation on this subject. Explanations mystical, mythical, and rationalistic, are all offered in turn ; and the freest scope is given by the individual writers to fanciful and arbitrary conjecture.

First : we have the set of accounts in which the four castes are said to have sprung from progenitors who were separately created ; but in regard to the manner of their creation we find the greatest diversity of statement. The most common story is that the castes issued from the mouth, arms, thighs, and feet of Purusha, or Brahma. The oldest extant passage in which this idea occurs, and from which all the later myths of a similar tenor have no doubt been borrowed, is, as we have seen, to be found in the Purusha Sūkta ; but it is doubtful whether, in the form in which it is there presented, this representation is anything more than an allegory. In some of the texts which I have quoted from the Bhágavata Purána, traces of the same allegorical character may be perceived ; but in Manu and the Purános the mystical import of the Vedic text disappears, and the figurative narrative is hardened into a literal statement of fact. In other passages, where a separate origin is assigned to the castes, they are variously said to have sprung from the words Bhūh, Bhuvah, Svah ; from different Vedas ; from different sets of prayers ; from the gods, and the asuras ; from nonentity, and from the imperishable, the perishable, and other principles. In the chapters of the Vishṇu, Váyu, and Márkaṇḍeya Puránas, where castes are described as coeval with the creation, and as having been naturally distinguished by different gunas, or qualities, involving varieties of moral character, we are nevertheless allowed to infer that those qualities exerted no influence on the classes in whom they were inherent, as the condition of the whole race during the Kṛita age is described as one of uniform perfection and happiness ; while the actual separation into castes did not take place, according to the Váyu Purána, until men had become deteriorated in the Treta age.

Second : in various passages from the Bráhmanas, Epic poems, and Puránas, the creation of mankind is, as we have seen, described without the least allusion to any separate production of the progenitors of the four castes. And whilst in the chapters where they relate the distinct formation of the castes, the Puránas, as has been observed, assign different natural dispositions to each class, they elsewhere represent all mankind as being at the creation uniformly distinguished by the quality of passion. In one of the texts I have quoted, men are said to be the offspring of Vivasvat ; in another his son Manu is said to be their progenitor ; whilst in a third they are said to be descended from a female of the same name. The passage which declares Manu to have been the father of the human race explicitly affirms that men of all the four castes were descended from him. In another remarkable text the Mahábhárata categorically asserts that originally there was no distinction of classes, the existing distribution having arisen out of differences of character and occupation. Similarly, the Bhágavata Purána in one place informs us that in the Kṛita age there was but one çaste ; and this view appears also to be taken in some passages which I have adduced from the Epic poems.

In these circumstances we may fairly conclude that the separate origination of the four castes was far from being an article of belief universally received by Indian antiquity."—Vol. I, p. 160.

Chaidyas—A race of kings, descendants of Chedi, amongst whom were Damagosha and Śiṣupála.

Chaitra—The name of the third lunar month (Feb.-March).

Chaitraratah—A large forest, in the east of Ilávrita.

Chakora—One of the thirty Andhrabhritya kings ; he only reigned six months.

Chakora—The name of a mountain in the eastern ghauts.

Chakra—1, The discus of Vishnu ; a sharp-edged quoit ; Arjuna performed wonderful feats with his chakra. It was with this weapon that Krishṇa slew Śiṣupála. It is always seen in one of the four hands of Vishṇu. The Chakra has also been converted into the prayer wheel of the Buddhists ; 2, The name of one of the chanters of the Sáma Veda.

Chakras—A race of people who about the commencement of our era, extended along the West of India, from the Hindu Kosh to the mouths of the Indus.

Chakravartti—One on whom the Chakra, the discus of Vishnu, abides ; such a figure being delineated by the lines of the hand. The grammatical etymology is 'he who abides in or rules over, an extensive country called a chakra.' Chakravartti is therefore a universal emperor. On the death of such an emperor it was the custom to collect and deposit the ashes of the body, after burning, in a pyramidal monument.—*Wilson.*

Chakravaka—A Brahmani goose : the name of a wise counsellor in the Pancha Tantra ; Hiranyagarbha, the king of the water-fowl, was anxious to make war, when his minister, Chakraváka, made many speeches to prevent it, suggesting that victory was ever doubtful, &c.

Chakshu—One of the four great rivers, made by the division of the Ganges, and which is said in the V. P. to flow into the sea after traversing all the western mountains, and passing through the country of Ketumala.

Chakshu—A prince, the son of Purujánu, one of the descendants of Dwimídha.

Chakshupa—A prince renowned for his valour, the son of Khanitra, one of the descendants of Nedishta.

Chakshusha—The Manu of the sixth Manwantara, son of Ripu by Vrihati. The Márkandeya has a legend of his birth as a son of Kshatriya ; of his being exchanged at his birth for the son of Visranta Rája, and being brought up by the prince as his own ; of his revealing the business when a man, and propitiating Brahma by his devotions, in consequence of which he became a Manu ; In his former birth he was born from the eye of Brahma ; whence his name from Chakshush 'the eye.'

Chakshushas—The first of the five classes of gods in the fourteenth Manwantara.

Chandrayana—Penances, which, according to the Vedánta, cause, not the acquisition of any thing positive, but merely the removal of sin. They are regulated by the moon's age ; and consist in diminishing the daily consumption of food every day, by one mouthful, for the dark half of the month, beginning with fifteen at the full moon, until it is reduced to one at the new moon ; and then increasing in like manner during the fortnight of the moon's increase : there are other forms of this penance.

Champa—The son of Pritulaksha, a descendant of Anu, who founded the city of Champápuri, a city of which traces still remain in the vicinity of Bhaghulpur. Champa is everywhere recognised as the capital of Anga.

Champa—A town on the Ganges in which is a Vihára, or Buddhist convent. It is described in the Dasukumáru as notoriously abounding in rogues.

Chamunda—A name of the consort of Śiva. Her temple is represented as a dreadful place ; whither victims are conveyed to be offered in sacrifice to the cruel goddess. In the drama of Málatí and Mádhava, the heroine Málatí is kidnapped by the priest of Chámunda and carried to the dreaded temple, but is rescued by her lover just as the fatal stroke is about to descend on her.

Chanakko or Chanakya—A brahman of the city of Takkasila who lived about 330 B. C. He is said to have achieved the knowledge of the three Vedas ; could rehearse the *mantra;* was skilful in stratagems, and dexterous in intrigue as well as policy.

After his father's death he became celebrated as the filial protector of his mother. A long legend is told of the way in which he brought up Chandragupta and ultimately placed him on the throne about 315 B. C. When Chandragupta was a wandering adventurer, the ambitious intriguing brahman became his ardent friend, and promised to open for him a pathway to the throne. Nine brothers, called the nine Nandas, then reigned at Magadha. "Chandragupta was looked upon as their half-brother by a Sudra mother. He is called a Takshaka, or descendant of the great snake Seshanága. Feeling unsafe amongst his relatives in Behar he had wandered forth to seek his fortune elsewhere." It was then he met with Chánakya, who in pursuance of his intention to place Chandragupta on the throne "contrived to give dire offence to the nine Nandas." He entered their dining-room unannounced, and with the cool assumption of a powerful brahman, took possession of the place of honour. The kings, having 'their understandings bewildered by fate,' regarded him as a mere wild scholar; and not heeding the remonstrances of their wise minister, they dragged him from his seat with scorn.

"Then Chánakya, blind with indignation, stood up in the centre of the hall, loosened the knot of hair on the top of his head, and thus vowed the destruction of the Nanda race.

'Until I have exterminated these haughty and ignorant Nandas, who have not known my worth, I will not again tie up these hairs.' Having thus declared war he sought out the discontented Chandragupta.

"In the meantime, Rákshasa, who was the prime minister of the Nandas, did all for his princes that could be done either by valour or sagacity. But all in vain, the Nandas 'perished like moths in the flame of Chánakya's revenge.'"

The drama entitled "Mudra Rákshasa," attributed to Visákhadatta, is founded on this story of Chánakya. *Hindu Theatre. Mrs. Manning*; *A. & M. I., Vol. II, p.* 221.

Chandana— A river in Bhagulpúr.

Chandana Dasa —A banker and intimate friend of Rákshasa in the drama of the "Signet of the Minister." He was condemned and dressed for execution, bearing the stake upon his shoulder, followed by his wife and child; when he was rescued, pardoned and made provost of the merchants.

Chandala—An outcaste or pariah; one of the lowest of the mixed tribes descended from a Śudra mother and a Brahman father.

Chando—The name of the bull that protected Chandragupta in infancy.

Chandanodakadundhubi—A Yádava chief called also Bhava, a friend of the Gandharba Tumburu.

Chandragiri—A prince descended from Kusa, the son of Ráma.

Chandrabhaga—The name of a river, that takes its rise in the Himálayás and which Professor Wilson identifies as the Chinab.

Chadragupta—King of Magadha, a most important name, as it has been proved by Professor Wilson and others that he is the Sandracoptus of the Greeks, who visited the camp of Alexander the Great, and we are thus able to determine the chronology satisfactorily. "The relative positions of Chandragupta, Vidmisára, or Bimbisára, and Ajátaśatru, serve to confirm the indentification. Sákya was contemporary with both the latter, dying in the eighth year of Ajátaśatru's reign. The Maháwanśo says he reigned twenty-four years afterwards; but the Váyu makes his whole reign but twenty-five years, which would place the close of it B. C. 526. The rest of the Saiśunága dynasty, according to the Váyu and Matsya, reigned 143 or 140 years; bringing their close to B. C. 383. Another century being deducted for the duration of the Nandas, would place the accession of Chandragupta B. C. 283. Chandragupta was the contemporary of Seleucus Nicator, who began his reign B. C. 310, and concluded a treaty with him B. C. 305. Although therefore his date may not be made out quite correctly from the Pauránic premises, yet the error cannot be more than twenty or thirty years. The result is much nearer the truth than that furnished by the Buddhist authorities. According to the Maháwanśo a hundred years had elapsed from the death of Buddha to the tenth year of the reign of Kálásoko (p. 15). He reigned other ten years, and his sons forty-four, making a total of 154 years between the death of Śákya and the accession of Chandragupta, which is consequently placed B. C. 389, or above seventy years too early. According to the Buddhist authorities, Chan-ta-kutta or Chandragupta, commenced his reign 396 B. C. Burmese Table; Prinsep's Useful Tables. Mr. Turnour, in his Introduction, giving to Kálásoko eighteen years subsequent to the century after Buddha, places Chandragupta's accession B. C. 381, which, he observes, is sixty years too soon; dating, however, the accession of Chandragupta from 323 B. C. or immediately upon Alexander's death, a period too early by eight or ten years at least. The discrepancy of dates, Mr. Turnour is disposed to think, proceeds from some intentional perversion of the Buddhistical chronology." V. P.

Chandrahasa—In the farthest extremity of the Dekhan there lived a Rája who was doomed to the severest adversity. He had a son born at a propitious period, but was himself soon after slain in battle, and his Ráni perished in the funeral pile. The nurse fled away with the infant to Kutuwal, but died herself in three years without having made known the secret of the child's birth. The boy was now quite destitute and suffered much; but one day happening to go to the house of the prime minister, the astrologers present declared that the boy's face had all the signs of royalty. The minister hearing this, determined that the lad should be assassinated. But the men employed for the purpose took compassion on him and resolved not to kill him. He was found in the jungle and adopted by a certain dependant of the Minister, who called the boy Chandrahása because when he laughed it was said his face resembled the moon.

As Chandrahása grew up he was distinguished for his skill and courage, and his achievements came to the ears of the Rája. The Minister became jealous and determined to visit the Zamindar who had adopted Chandrahása, when he discovered that the young man was the very boy he had sent into the jungle to be murdered. Still bent on the youth's destruction he wrote a letter to his son Madan and requested Chandrahása to carry it to the city; the letter was as follows:—

"May my son eat the fruits of youth, and know that this same

Chandrahása is my enemy, and that he is eager to get possession of all my property : Look not you to his youth or comeliness, nor trouble yourself as to whose son he is, or whether he be a man of rank or learning or abilities, but give him *poison*."

As he approached the city he entered a pleasant garden belonging to the Minister, and being very weary, he tied his horse to a tree, laid down in the shade and fell asleep. That very morning the Minister's daughter Bikya, with the Princess and her maids, had come to amuse themselves in the garden. Bikya, wandering away from the others, saw a young man asleep with such a charming face that her heart burnt towards him. Seeing a letter falling from his bosom and perceiving that it was in her father's handwriting, and addressed to her brother, she opened and read it. Having compassion on the youth she determined to alter the letter, and as the word signifying enemy was such that by taking away a single letter she could turn it into a word meaning friend, she did so. The word signifying poison was Bika, which, as the young man was very good-looking, she altered into her own name of Bikya ; and re-sealing the letter placed it again on the youth's bosom, and returned to her companions.

Soon after Chandrahása rose from his sleep, found his way to the house of the Minister, and gave the letter to his son. Madan read the letter with great surprise, but saw that the orders were very positive and that he must obey them without delay.

Chandrahása who was more confounded than any one, was presented with a bridegroom's dress, and directed to prepare himself to be married that evening to the beautiful daughter of the Minister. There was the usual distribution of presents, and great rejoicing throughout the city.

The Minister on his return home was congratulated by every one he met, and "entered his house in a state bordering on madness," when he found what had occurred. His own letter was produced, and as he could not discover the alterations that had been made, he "could only wonder at the greatness of his own blunder." Early next morning he hired some assassins to secrete themselves in the temple of the goddess Durga which was outside the city, and murder the man who should come at evening time to present a golden-pot of incense to the goddess. He then told Chandrahása it was the fixed rule for every man who married into his family to offer a golden-cup of incense at the temple of Durga, and Chandrahása readily promised to comply with the custom that same evening.

But that very day, the Rája, in consequence of a dream, determined to resign his kingly authority, and not knowing of the minister's return sent for Madan, to whom he communicated his intention, and his determination to make Chandrahása his successor. He desired Madan to bring his new brother-in-law to the palace with all speed. Madan gladly set out in search of Chandrahása and found him in the road to the temple of Durga with the golden-cup in his hand ; and having briefly explained to him the urgent necessity for his immediate presence at the palace, he took the cup from his hand and promised to present it himself to the goddess. Madan thus sent back Chandrahása to the palace of the Rája and proceeded alone with the golden-cup to the temple of Durga. On entering it he was cut down by the swords of the assassins and killed on the spot. Chandrahása on arriving at the palace, was crowned by the Rája himself. The minister on hearing how his plot had been again defeated, and his own son killed, destroyed himself in the same temple.—*Wheeler's Mahábhárata.*

Chandraketu—The son of Lakshmana, and king of Chandravaktra, a country near the Himálaya.

Chandrama—A river mentioned in the V. P., but which has not been identified.

Chandrasri—One of the thirty Andhrabhritya kings, who reigned three years. V. P.

Chandrasukta—One of the islands into which the Varsha of Bharata is divided, as enumerated in the Bhágavata and Padma. It has not been identified.

Chandravaloka—A prince descended from Kusa, the son of Ráma.

Chandraswa—One of the three sons of Dhundhumára, who survived the conflict with the demon Dhundu. Dhundu hid himself beneath a sea of sand which king Kuvalayaswa, aided by twenty-one thousand sons, dug up, undeterred by the flames which checked their progress and finally destroyed all but three of them. Kuvalayaswa was hence called Dhundumára. Professor Wilson thinks that the legend originates probably in the occurrence of some physical phenomena, as an earthquake or volcano.

Chanura—A demon who was killed by Krishṇa, after a very severe contest, in which Chanúra was whirled round a hundred times, until his breath was expended in the air, and Krishṇa dashed him on the ground with such violence as to smash his body into a hundred fragments, and strew the earth with a hundred pools of gory mire. V. P.

Charaka—A renowned medical writer of great antiquity. "Charaka appears to have been a person of varied thought and culture, and to have had an earnest desire to teach men so to manage their bodies, as not only to avoid all unnecessary pain on earth; but so as to ensure happiness after death. Charaka states that originally the contents or material of his work was communicated by Atreya to Agnivesa. By Agnivesa it was taught to Charaka, and by him condensed "where it was too prolix and expanded where it seemed too brief." The result of Charaka's labour was a work of considerable extent, no less than one hundred and twenty chapters in eight divisions.—*Mrs. Manning*; *A. and M. I.*, vol. i, *p.* 342, where the reader will find an abstract of Charaka's work; made from the Sanskrit manuscripts of the India Office Library.

Charakas—The students of a Sákhá so denominated from its teacher Charaka.

Charana—A sect pledged to the reading of a certain Sákhá of the Vedas. Charana means an ideal succession of pupils and teachers who learn and teach a certain branch of the Veda. See Gotra.

Charanavyaha—The name of a 'Parisishta' work, which is considered to have been composed later than the Sutras, and representing a distinct period of Hindu literature. See Parisishta.

Chariot—The sun, moon and planets are all represented in the Puránas as having chariots or cars. That of the sun is stated in the V. P. to be nine thousand leagues in length, and the pole of twice that longitude : that of the moon has three wheels and is drawn by ten white horses. The chariot of Mercury is composed of air and fire and is drawn by eight bay horses. The chariots of Mars and Jupiter are of gold.

Charishnu—A son of the sage Kirttimat.

Charudatta—An impoverished brahman who is one of the principal characters in the drama of the Toy Cart. On one occasion Chárudatta says :—

My friend,
The happiness that follows close on sorrow,
Shows like a lamp that breaks upon the night,
But he that falls from affluence to poverty,
May wear the human semblance, but exists
A lifeless form alone.

On being further questioned, Chárudatta declares that he would much prefer death to poverty.

"To die, is transient suffering, to be poor
Interminable anguish."

And he further explains that he does not grieve for the lost wealth :

"But that the guest no longer seeks the dwelling
whence wealth has vanished.

* * * * * * * * * *

And then with poverty comes disrespect ;
From disrespect does self-dependence fail ;
Then scorn and sorrow following, overwhelm
The intellect ; and when the judgment fails
The being perishes. And thus from poverty
Each ill that pains humanity proceeds."

—*A. and M. I., vol. 2, p.* 157.

Charmamandalas—A northern people, living in the district of Mandala or Khanda of Charma. Pliny mentions a king of a people so called, Charmaru rex.

Charmanvati—The name of a river, the Chambal.

Charu, Charudeha, Charudeshna, Charugupta, Charuvinda—Five sons of Krishṇa by Rukmini, one is termed in the V. P. the mighty Cháru.

Charumati—A daughter of Krishṇa by Rukmini.

Charvaka—A philosopher who about the third century, founded a new school of undisguised materialism—maintaining that perception is the one only source of knowledge and means of proof: that while there is body there is thought and sense of pleasure and pain; none when body is not; and hence, as well as from self-conciousness, it is concluded that self and body are identical. In the Vedánta Sára there is a refutation of no less than four followers of Chárváka, who assert his doctrine under various modifications; one maintaining that the gross corporeal frame is identical with soul; another that the corporeal organs constitute the soul; a third affirming that the vital functions do so; and the fourth insisting that the mind and the soul are the same.

Charvaka—A Rákshasa who disguised himself as a mendicant brahman and reviled Yudhishthira at his installation as Rája. The real brahmans, says the Mahábhárata, were so enraged with Chárváka that they looked upon him with such angry eyes that he fell upon the ground like a tree struck with lightning, and was burnt to ashes on the spot.

Chatakas—Pupils of Vaisampáyana. The Váyu states that they were styled Chátakas from Chát 'to divide,' because they shared amongst them their master's guilt. Those pupils of Vaisampáyana were called Chátakas by whom the crime of Brahmanicide was shared.

Chaturunga—A Prince, the son of Romapáda, one of the descendants of Anu.

Chaturmasya—Sacrifices every four months.

Chedi—Son of Kaisika, whose descendants were called the Chaidya kings.

Chedyas—The inhabitants of Chedi, which is usually considered as Chandail, on the west of the Jungle mehals, towards Nagpore. It is known in times subsequent to the Purānas as Ranastambha.

Chhala—A Prince, the son of Dala, one of the descendants of Kusa.

Chhandajas—The vasus and similar divinities. They have the epithet Chhandajá as born in different Manwantaras of their own will.

Chhandas—An Anga of the four Vedas, the one which relates to metre.

Chhaya—The wife of the sun. Sanjna, daughter of Viswakarman, was the wife of the sun and bore him three children, the Manu Vaivaswata, Yama, and the goddess Yami (or the Yamuna river.) Unable to endure the fervours of her lord, Sanjna gave him Chhaya* as his handmaid, and repaired to the forests to practice devotion. The sun supposing Chhaya to be his wife, Sanjna, begot by her three other children, Sanaischara (Saturn); another Manu (Savarni), and a daughter Tapti (the Tapti river.) Chhaya upon one occasion being offended with Yama, the son of Sanjna, denounced an imprecation upon him, and thereby let it be seen that she was not Sanjna, his mother. Chhaya informed the sun that his wife had gone to the wilderness, and he brought her back to his own dwelling. V. P.

Chhandoga-brahmana—In the Brâhmaṇa of the Chhandogas it is evident that, after the principal collection was finished (called the prauḍha or Panchavinśa-brâhmaṇa, *i. e.*, consisting of twenty-five sections,) a twenty-sixth Brâhmaṇa was added which is known by the name of Shadvinśa-brâhmaṇa. This Brâhmaṇa together with the Adbhuta-brâhmaṇa must be of very modern date. It mentions not only temples (Devâyatanâni,) but images of gods (daivata-pratimâ) which are said to laugh, to cry, to sing, to dance, to burst, to sweat and to twinkle. These two have long been supposed to be the only Brâhmaṇas of the Chhandogas,

* That is her shadow or image. It also means shade.

and they constitute, no doubt, the most important part of that class of literature. It is curious, however, that whenever the Brâhmaṇas of the Chhandogas are quoted, their number is invariably fixed at eight. Kumârila Bhaṭṭa says, "in the eight Brâhmaṇas, together with the Upanishads, which the Chhandogas read, no single accent is fixed." —*A. S. L.*

Chhandoga-priests—The second class of priests at sacrifices.

Chikitsa—One of the eight branches of medical science; that which treats of the administration of medicines, or medical treatment in general.

Chintamani—An Epic poem in Tamil, of considerable merit, and regarded as the highest classical authority in that language. It contains the heroic story of a king named Jívagan, and is probably founded on a similar story found in the Mahá Purána, a sacred work of the Jains written in Sanscrit.

Chintámani is a compound of two Sanscrit words *Chintá*, thought or reflection, and *mani* a jewel. It is generally applied to a fabulous gem which is supposed to yield its possessor whatever may be required. The design of the work is to represent the Jaina system in an attractive form.

Chitar—A chief mentioned in the Rig Veda as living with other chiefs near the Sarasvatí.

Chiti—Synonyme of Mahat, "is that by which the consequences of acts and species of knowledge are selected for the use of soul." —*Wilson.* V. P. p. 15.

Chitra—The name of a lunar mansion in Govithi, in the Central Avasthana.

Chitrabaha—A Purána river, not identified.

Chitragupta—The Registrar of Yama; all that die appear before Yama, and are confronted with Chitragupta by whom their actions have been recorded. "Chitragupta is described in the following tasteless and extravagant style in the Vṛihannáradíya Purána. 'The dreadful Chitragupta with a voice like that issuing from the clouds at the mundane dissolution, gleaming like a mountain of collyrium, terrible with lightning-like weapons, having thirty-two arms, as big as three yojanas, red-eyed, long-nosed, his face furnished with grinders and projecting teeth, his eyes resembling oblong ponds, bearing death and disease.' " O. S. T., Vol. V, p. 302.

Chitraka—A prince, the son of Prisni, a descendant of Siní.

Chitraketu—A son of Vasishtha, the great sage, according to the list in the Bhágavata.

Chitrakuta—An isolated hill situated on a river called the Pisani, fifty miles south-east of the town of Banda in Bundelkund. It is a sacred spot crowded with temples, and shrines of Ráma and Lakshmaṇa; celebrated too as the seat of Valmíki, the sage and poet, who became famous in after years as the author of the Rámáyana.

"We have often looked on that green hill: it is the holiest spot of that sect of the Hindu faith who devote themselves to this incarnation of Vishṇu. The whole neighbourhood is Ráma's country. Every head-land has some legend, every cavern is connected with his name; some of the wild fruits are still called *Sítáphal*, being the reputed food of the exiles. Thousands and thousands annually visit the spot, and round the hill is a raised foot-path, on which the devotee, with naked feet, treads full of pious awe."—*Calcutta Review, Vol. XXIII.*

The following extracts from Mr. Griffith's translation of the Rámáyana will serve to show how this sacred character has been acquired:—

"Then, as he saw the morning break,
In answer Bharadvája spake,
'Go forth to Chitrakúṭa's hill,
Where berries grow, and sweets distil:
Full well, I deem, that home will suit
Thee, Ráma, strong and resolute.
Go forth, and Chitrakúṭa seek,
Famed mountain of the Varied Peak.
In the wild woods that gird him round,
All creatures of the chase are found:

Thou in the glades shalt see appear
Vast herds of elephants and deer.
With Sítá there shalt thou delight
To gaze upon the woody height ;
There with expanding heart to look
On river, table-land, and brook,
And see the foaming torrent rave
Impetuous from the mountain cave.
Auspicious hill ! where all day long
The lapwing's cry, the Koïl's song
  Make all who listen gay :
Where all is fresh and fair to see,
Where elephants and deer roam free,
  There, as a hermit, stay."
"Then on from wood to wood they strayed,
O'er many a stream, through constant shade,
As Bharadvája bade them, till
They came to Chitrakúṭa's hill.
And Ráma there, with Lakshmaṇ's aid,
A pleasant little cottage made,
And spent his days with Sítá, dressed
In coat of bark and deerskin vest.
And Chitrakúṭa grew to be
As bright with those illustrious three
As Meru's sacred peaks that shine
With glory, when the gods recline
Beneath them : Śiva's self between
The Lord of Gold and Beauty's Queen."

Chitralekha—The companion and friend of the princess Usha, to whom Usha related her dream, and who by her magic power brought Aniruddha to the palace.

Chitrangada—The son of Sántanu by his wife Satyavati. He was killed when young, in a conflict with a Gandarbhá, who was also named Chitrangada.

Chitrangada—The daughter of the Rája of Manipura who

was married to Arjuna in his travels, but remained in her own city with her son Babhru-váhana, when Arjuna returned to Ḥastinápur.

Chitraratha—The king of the celestial choristers ;

> " On Chitraratha, true and dear
> My tuneful bard and charioteer
> Gems, robes, and plenteous wealth confer
> Mine ancient friend and minister."
>
> —*Griffith's Rámáyana.*

Chitraratha was also the name of the son of Rushadru and father of Saṣavinda who was lord of the fourteen great gems. There was another Chitraratha, son of the Dharmaratha, who drank the Soma juice along with Indra. A fourth Chitraratha is mentioned in the V. P. as the son of Ushṇa, a descendant of Paríkshit.

Chitraratha, Chitrasena, Chitropala—The names of three rivers in the V. P. which have not been yet identified.

Chitravarna—The name of the peacock king in the Panchatantra stories.

Cholas—The inhabitants of the lower part of the Coromandel coast ; so called after them Chólamandala.

Chronology—The Vishṇu Purána says, " Time is a form of Vishṇu : hear how it is applied to measure the duration of Brahma, and of all other sentient beings. Fifteen twinklings of the eye make a Kásh'thá ; thirty Kásh'thás, one Kalá ; and thirty Kalás, one Muhúrtta. Thirty Muhúrttas constitute a day and night of mortals : thirty such days make a month, divided into two half-months : six months form an Ayana (the period of the sun's progress north or south of the ecliptic :) and two Ayanas compose a year. The southern Ayana is a night, and the northern a day, of the gods. Twelve thousand divine years, each composed of (three hundred and sixty) such days, constitute the period of the four Yugas, or ages. They are thus distributed : the Krita age has four thousand divine years ; the Tretá three thousand ; the Dwápara, two thousand ; and the Kali age, one thousand : so those acquainted with antiquity have declared." The period that precedes a Yuga is called a Sandhyá, and it is of as many hundred years as there are thousands in the Yuga : and the period that follows a Yuga, termed the Sandhyánsa, is of similar duration. The interval between the Sandhyá and the Sandhyánsa is the Yuga, denominated Krita, Tretá, &c. The Krita, Tretá, Dwápara and Kali, constitute a great age, or aggregate of four ages : a thousand such aggregates are a day of Brahma, and fourteen Manus reign within that term. Hear the division of time which they measure.

Seven Rishis, certain (secondary) divinities, Indra, Manu, and the kings his sons, are created and perish at one period ; and the interval, called a Manwantara, is equal to seventy-one times the number of years contained in the four Yugas, with some additional years : this is the duration of the Manu, the (attendant) divinities, and the rest, which is equal to 8,52,000 divine years, or to 3,06,720,000 years of mortals, independent of the additional period. Fourteen times this period constitutes a Brahma day, that is, a day of Brahma ; the term (Brahma) being the derivative form. At the end of this day a dissolution of the universe occurs, when all the three worlds, earth, and the regions of space, are consumed with fire. The dwellers of Maharloka (the region inhabited by the saints who survive the world,) distressed by the heat, repair then to Janaloka (the region of holy men after their decease.) When the three worlds are but one mighty ocean, Brahma, who is one with Náráyana, satiate with the demolition of the universe, sleeps upon his serpent-bed—contemplated, the lotus born, by the ascetic inhabitants of the Janaloka—for a night of equal duration with his day ; at the close of which he creates anew. Of such days and nights is a year of Brahma composed ; and a hundred such years constitute his whole life. One Parárddha, or half his existence, has expired, terminating with the Mahá Kalpa called Padma. The Kalpa (or day of Brahma) termed Váráha is the first of the second period of Brahma's existence."

Chunchu—A prince, the son of Harita, a descendant of Harischandra.

Chyavana—A celebrated sage, who in old age was restored to youth by the Aṣvins. The legend is related at length in the Satapatha Brâhmaṇa, and translated by Muir in O. S. T., Vol. V, p. 250. The substance of the story as told in the Mahábhárata is thus given by Muir: "We are there told that the body of Chyavana, when performing austerity in a certain place, became encrusted with an ant-hill; that king Saryāti came then to the spot with his 4,000 wives and his single daughter Sukanyā; that the rishi, seeing her, became enamoured of her and endeavoured to gain her affections, but without eliciting from her any reply. Seeing, however, the sage's eyes gleaming out from the ant-hill, and not knowing what they were, the princess pierced them with a sharp instrument, whereupon Chyavana became incensed, and afflicted the king's army with a stoppage of urine and of the necessary functions. When the king found out the cause of the infliction, and supplicated the rishi for its removal, the latter insisted on receiving the king's daughter to wife, as the sole condition of his forgiveness. Sukanyā accordingly lived with the rishi as his spouse. One day, however, she was seen by the Aṣvins, who endeavoured, but without effect, to persuade her to desert her decrepit husband, and choose one of them in his place. They then told her they were the physicians of the gods, and would restore her husband to youth and beauty, when she could make her choice between him and one of them. Chyavana and his wife consented to this proposal; and, at the suggestion of the Aṣvins, he entered with them into a neighbouring pond, when the three came forth of like celestial beauty, and each asked her to be his bride. She, however, recognized and chose her own husband. Chyavana, in gratitude for his restoration to youth, then offered to compel Indra to admit the Aṣvins to a participation in the Soma ceremonial, and fulfilled his promise in the course of a sacrifice which he performed for king Śaryāti. On that occasion Indra objected to such an honor being extended to the Aṣvins, on the ground that they wandered about among men as physicians, changing their forms at will; but Chyavana refused to listen to the objection, and carried out his intention, staying the arm of Indra when he was about to launch a thunderbolt, and creating a terrific demon, who was on the point of devouring the king of the gods, and was only prevented by the timely submission of the latter."—*Vol. V, p.* 254.

Clepsydra—A water-clock, is thus described in an extract from a commentary, given in a note to the Vishṇu Purána. "A vessel made of twelve Palas and a half of copper, and holding a Prastha, Magadha measure, of water, broad at top, and having at bottom a tube of gold, of four Máshas weight, four fingers long, is placed in water, and the time in which the vessel is filled by the hole in the bottom, is called a Nádika. The common measure of the Nádi is a thin shallow brass-cup, with a small hole in the bottom. It is placed in the surface of water, in a large vessel, where nothing can disturb it, and where the water gradually fills the cup and sinks it." Page 631.

Clouds—Clouds, in the Purának, are of three classes:—1, Ágneya, originating from fire or heat, or in other words evaporation: they are charged with wind and rain and are of various orders; 2, Brahmaja, born from the breath of Brahma; these are the clouds whence thunder and lightning proceed: and 3, Pakshaja, or clouds which were originally the wings of the mountains, and which were cut off by Indra; these are the largest of all, and are those which at the end of the Kalpas and Yugas, pour down the waters of the deluge. The shell of the egg of Brahma, or of the universe, is formed of the primitive clouds. The Vishṇu Purána states that "during eight months of the year the sun attracts the waters and then pours them upon earth as rain." Consequently the Linga Purána observes there is no waste of water in the universe as it is in constant circulation. The Vishṇu Purána adds, "The water that the sun has drawn up from the Ganga of the skies he quickly pours down with his rays, and without a cloud; and men who are touched by this pure rain are cleansed from the soil of sin and never see hell: this is termed celestial ablution." "The water which the clouds shed upon the earth is the Ambrosia of living beings, for it gives fertility to the plants which are the support of their existence. By this, all vegetables grow and are matured, and become the means of maintaining life."

D

Dabhiti—A king mentioned in the Rig Veda who was saved by Indra from being carried off by the Asuras or Dasyus. "Indra burnt all their weapons in a kindled fire, and enriched Dabhiti with their cattle, horses and chariots."

Dadhicha—A celebrated sage who reproved Daksha on the occasion of his great sacrifice, saying, "The man who worships what ought not to be worshipped, or pays not reverence where veneration is due, is guilty of heinous sin."

Dadhikra—The name given in the Rig Veda to a divine horse, described as the straight-going, the graceful-moving, the resplendent, the rapid, the destroyer of enemies like a heroic prince. In a second hymn the Rishi says, "May Aditi, consentient with Mitra and Varuna, render him free from sin who has performed the worship of the steed Dadhikra, when the fire has been kindled at the opening of the dawn."

Dadhividarchas, Dahas—Two tribes of people mentioned in the Vishṇu Purána but not identified.

Dadu—The founder of a Vaishnava sect, who taught that Bhakti, or implicit faith, was more efficacious than subjugation of the passions, charity, or knowledge. Dádú was originally a cotton-cleaner at Ajmír.

Dadu-panthis—The designation of the disciples or followers of the above. One of the Vaishnava sects in Hindustan. It had its origin from Dadu, a cotton-cleaner by profession, who, having been admonished by a voice from heaven to devote himself to a religious life, retired with that view to the Baherana mountain, where, after some time, he disappeared, and no traces of him could be found. His followers believed him to have been absorbed into the Deity. He is supposed to have flourished about A. D. 1600. The followers of Dádú wear no peculiar mark on the forehead, but carry a rosary, and are further distinguished by a round white cap according to some ; but, according to others, one with four corners, and a flap hanging down behind. This cap each man is required to manufacture for himself.—*Wilson.*

Dagoba—A conical erection surmounting relics among the Buddhists. The name is said by Mr. Hardy to be derived from dá, dátu, or dhátu, an osseous relic, and geba or garbha, the womb. These buildings are sometimes of immense height, of circular form, and composed of stone or brick, faced with stone or stucco. They are built upon a platform, which again rests upon a natural or artificial elevation, which is usually reached by a flight of steps. The utmost respect is felt for dágobas among the Buddhists, chiefly because they contain relics of different kinds. Professor Wilson, in his 'Ariana Antiqua,' thus describes the ordinary contents of a dágoba : "The most conspicuous objects are, in general, vessels of stone or metal ; they are of various shapes and sizes ; some of them have been fabricated on a lathe. They commonly contain a silver box or casket, and within that, or sometimes by itself, a casket of gold. This is sometimes curiously wrought. One found by Mr. Masson at Deh Bimaran is chased with a double series of four figures, representing Gautama in the act of preaching ; a mendicant is on his right, a lay-follower on his left, and behind the latter a female disciple ; they stand under arched niches resting on pillars, and between the arches is a bird ; a row of rubies is set round the upper and lower edge of the vessel, and the bottom is also chased with the leaves of the lotus : the vase had no cover. Within these vessels, or sometimes in the cell in which they are placed, are found small pearls, gold buttons, gold ornaments and rings, beads, pieces of white and coloured glass and crystal, pieces of clay or stone with impressions of figures, bits of bone, and teeth of animals of the ass and goat species, pieces of cloth, and folds of Tuz or Bhurj leaf, or rather the bark of a kind of birch on which the Hindus formerly wrote ; and these pieces bear sometimes characters which may be termed Bactrian ; but they are in too fragile and decayed a state to admit of being unfolded or read. Similar characters are also found superficially scratched upon the stone, or dotted upon the metal vessels. In one instance they were found traced upon the stone with ink. Within some of the vessels was also found a liquid, which upon exposure rapidly evaporated, leaving a brown sediment, which was analysed by Mr. Prinsep, and offered some traces of animal and vegetable matters."

The principal dágobas in Ceylon, as we learn from Mr. Hardy, are at Anurádhapura, and it would appear that it was accounted a ceremony of great importance amoug the ancient ascetics to walk round one of these sacred structures. It is regarded by the Hindu Brahmans as a most meritorious walk to circumambulate a temple, raising the person who performs this pious act to a place in the heaven of the god or goddess to whom the temple belongs. The Nepaulese also account it one of the most devout employments in which a Buddhist can be engaged to march round a dágoba, repeating mental prayers, and holding in his right hand a small cylinder fixed upon the upper end of a short staff or handle, which he keeps in perpetual revolution. The reverence in which these structures are held is thus noticed by Mr. Hardy, in his valuable work, entitled 'Eastern Monachism :' "Any mark of disrespect to the dágoba is regarded as being highly criminal, whilst a contrary course is equally deserving of reward. When Elaro, one of the Malabar sovereigns, who reigned in Ceylon B. C. 205, was one day riding in his chariot, the yoke-bar accidentally struck one of these edifices, and displaced some of the stones. The priests in attendance reproached him for the act ; but the monarch immediately descended to the ground, and prostrating himself in the street, said that they might take off his head with the wheel of his carriage. But the priests replied, 'Great king! our divine teacher delights not in torture ; repair the dágoba.' For the purpose of replacing the fifteen stones that had been dislodged, Elaro bestowed 15,000 of the silver coins called kahapana. Two women who had worked for hire at the erection of the great dágoba by Dutugamini were for this meritorious act born in Tawntisa. The legend informs us that on a subsequent occasion they went to worship at the same place, when the radiance emanating from their persons was so great that it filled the whole of Ceylon."

The ground on which a dágoba is held in so high estimation is simply because it contains relics which have from remote times been worshipped by the Buddhists. As far back as the fourth century,

Fa Hian, a Chinese traveller, mentions such a practice as then prevailing. "The bones of Gautama, the garments he used, the utensils he used, and the ladder by which he visited heaven, were worshipped by numbers of devout pilgrims; and happy did the country consider itself that retained one of these precious remains." The most celebrated relic which is still to be found among the worshippers of Gautama Buddha is the DALADÁ (which see). To make a present or offering to a dágoba is viewed as an act of the highest virtue, which will be rewarded both in this world and the next, and will lead to the attainment of *Nirwana* or *annihilation.* Buddha himself declared while on earth, "Though neither flowers nor anything else should be offered, yet if any one will look with a pleasant mind at a dágoba or the court of the bó-tree, he will undoubtedly be born in a DEVA-LOKA (which see); it is unnecessary to say that he who sweeps these sacred places, or makes offerings to them, will have an equal reward; furthermore, should any one die on his way to make an offering to a dágoba, he also will receive the blessedness of the DEVA-LOKAS." Some dágobas are alleged to have the power of working miracles, but this privilege is almost exclusively confined to those which have been built in honor of the *rahats*, or beings who are free from all evil desire, and possess supernatural powers.

"It was not till the year 1837 in which Mr. Jas. Prinsep deciphered the written character of king Asoka's edicts, that anything was known of the Buddhism of ancient India. Then first was it understood when and by whom, and for what purpose, these dágobas were erected."—*A. and M. I.*

Dahana—The name of one of the eleven Rudras, according to the enumeration in the Matsya Purána.

Dahragni—A name of the sage Agastya.

Daityas—Demons. The Daityas are thought to have been, in the epic period, personifications of the Aborigines of India, more particularly of the southern part of the Peninsula; who, to increase the glories of the heroes who conquered them, were represented as giants and demons. They are associated with the Danavas, who bear the same character. In the Puránic period they play a very important part, as the enemies who are constantly at war with the deities for the sake of obtaining the sovereignty of heaven. They are there considered as the descendants of Kaṣyapa and Diti (from whom the name Daitya is called a matronymic). At the churning of the ocean they attempted to seize the cup of Amrita or Ambrosia which was then produced, and was in the hand of Dhanwantari: but Vishṇu, assuming a female form, fascinated and deluded them; and recovering the Amrita from them delivered it to the gods. Sakra and the other deities quaffed the Ambrosia. The incensed demons, grasping their weapons, fell upon them; but the gods, into whom the ambrosial draught had infused new vigour, defeated and put their host to flight; they then fled through the regions of space, and plunged into the subterraneous realms of Pátáḷa. The gods thereat greatly rejoiced, did homage to the holder of the discus and mace, and resumed their reign in heaven. The Daityas then inhabited Pátáḷa. Hiranyakaṣipu was their king, but when deposed by Vishṇu, his illustrious son Prahláda received the sovereignty. The Vishṇu Purána relates other legends of the Daityas obtaining the sovereignty of the earth, and being deluded from the tenets of the Vedas were easily conquered.

Daksha—A celebrated Prajápati, born from the thumb of Brahma; he was the chief of the patriarchs. He had twenty-four daughters by his wife Prasúti, and twenty-seven other daughters who were afterwards stellarised in the lunar mansions. The Váyu Purána contains a full account of the great sacrifice offered by Daksha. One of his daughters, Sati, was married to Śiva; but neither she nor her husband were invited to the sacrifice, as Daksha had been offended with Śiva not long before. Sati, however, attended, and on being affronted threw herself into the flames of the sacrifice and perished.* Śiva exasperated, tore off a lock of his hair and cast it with violence to the ground. It started up in the shape of Víra Bhadra with a thousand hands, whom Śiva sent to destroy the sacrifice. He did so, and according to some accounts cut off Daksha's head. According to the Vishṇu

* Hence in modern times a widow consentary to be bound with the corpse of her husband is called a *Sati*. The common word suttee is not the act of burning, but the female burnt.

Purána, Víra Bhadra, was created from Śiva's mouth, a being like the fire of fate, a divine being with a thousand heads, a thousand feet, &c., &c. It is only the Kási Khanda, however, that makes Sati throw herself into the fire, and Professor Wilson thinks this an improvement indicative of a later age. In other legends she is represented as killing herself on account of a quarrel with her father. The conduct of Víra Bhadra in interfering with and destroying the sacrifice, displeased the gods who were present, and they complained of it to Brahma ; whereupon he with them proceeded to Śiva, interceding on behalf of Daksha. Śiva then went personally to the scene of disorder, and having resuscitated Daksha, whose head could not be found, replaced it by the head of a ram. The exploits of the Rudras on the occasion are particularly specified in the Kurma and Bhágavata Purána. Indra is knocked down and trampled on ; Yama has his staff broken ; Saraswati and the Mátris have their noses cut off. Mitra or Bhaga has his eyes pulled out : Púsha has his teeth knocked down his throat ; Chandra is pummelled ; Vahni's hands are cut off ; Bhrigu loses his beard ; the Brahmans are pelted with stones ; the Prajápatis are beaten ; and the gods and demi-gods are run through with swords or stuck with arrows. Other accounts state that Daksha himself propitiated the mighty god, the holder of the trident, Maheshwara." V. P.

"The sacrifice of Daksha is a legend of some interest, from its historical and archæological relations. It is obviously intended to intimate a struggle between the worshippers of Śiva and of Vishṇu, in which at first the latter, but finally the former, acquired the ascendancy. It is also a favourite subject of Hindú sculpture, at least with the Hindus of the Sáiva division, and makes a conspicuous figure both at Elephanta and Ellora. A representation of the dispersion and mutilation of the gods and sages by Vírabhadra, at the former, is published in the Archæologia, VII, 326, where it is described as the Judgment of Solomon ! a figure of Vírabhadra is given by Niebuhr, Vol. II, tab. 10 : and the entire group in the Bombay Transactions, Vol. I, p. 220. The legend of Daksha therefore was popular when those cavern temples were excavated." V. P.

"Daksha," "says Mrs. Manning," is a shadowy god. He is an Áditya, one of the sons of Aditi.

"Daksha sprang from Aditi, and Aditi from Daksha. In the Rig Veda, Mitra and Varuna are celebrated as the sons of Daksha.

"Mr. Muir relieves us from some of our perplexity concerning this mysterious Daksha, by suggesting that possibly in some of these passages, the word Daksha was used figuratively for strength."—*A. and M. I.*

Daksha-savarni—The name of the Manu of the Ninth Manwantara; described in the Váyu as one of the mind-engendered sons of a daughter of Daksha, by himself and the three gods Brahma, Dharma and Rudra, to whom he presented her on Mount Meru.

Dakshayana—One of the names of the goddess Párvati. It is also the name of a lunar asterism in general. The grammarian Vyádi, author of the Sangraha, is sometimes called Dákshäyana.

Dakshi—The name of the mother of the celebrated Sanscrit grammarian Pánini.

Dakshina—One of the twin daughters of Ruchi and Akúti. These descendants of the first pair are evidently allegorical: thus Yajni (the name of the other twin daughter) is 'sacrifice;' and Dakshiṇá, 'donation' to brahmans. See V. P., Chap. VIII.

Dakshinacharis—A leading division of the sect of Sáktas, the followers of the right-hand ritual; often popularly called the right-hand caste; the followers of the left-hand ritual being termed Vámácharis.

Dala—A prince, the son of Kusa, a descendant of Ráma.

Dalada—The left canine tooth of *Buddha*, the most highly venerated relic among the Buddhists, particularly in Ceylon. To preserve this, the only portion which remains of the body of the holy sage, a temple has been erected, in which it is deposited, being placed in a small chamber, enshrined in six cases, the largest of them being upwards of five feet in height and formed of silver.

All the cases are constructed in the conical shape of a dágoba, and two of them are inlaid with rubies and precious stones. The outer case is ornamented with gold and jewels, which have been offered by devotees. Mr. Hardy describes the relic itself as 'a piece of discoloured ivory or bone, slightly curved, nearly two inches in length, and one in diameter at the base; and from thence to the other extremity, which is rounded and blunt, it considerably decreases in size.' The vihára or temple which contains the sanctuary of this relic, is attached to the palace of the former kings of Kandy. From a work composed on the subject of Buddha's tooth, dating as far back as A. D. 310, it is said that one of the disciples of the sage procured his left canine tooth when his relics were distributed. This much-valued treasure he conveyed to Dantapura, the chief city of Kalinga, where it reminded for 800 years. Its subsequent history we quote from Mr. Hardy's 'Eastern Monarchism:' "The Brahmans informed Pándu, the lord paramount of India, who resided at Pátaliputra, that his vassal, Guhasiwa worshipped a piece of bone. The monarch, enraged at this intelligence, sent an army to arrest the king of Kálinga, and secure the bone he worshipped. This commission was executed, but the general and all his army were converted to the faith of Buddhism. Pándu commanded the relic to be thrown into a furnace of burning charcoal, but a lotus arose from the flame, and the tooth appeared on the surface of the flower. An attempt was then made to crush it upon an anvil, but it remained embedded in the iron, resisting all the means employed to take it therefrom, until Subaddha, a Buddhist, succeeded in its extraction. It was next thrown into the common sewer; but in an instant this receptacle of filth became sweet as a celestial garden, and was mantled with flowers. Other wonders were performed, by which Pándu also became a convert to Buddhism. The relic was returned to Dantapura; but an attempt being made by the princes of Sewet to take it away by force, it was brought to Ceylon, and deposited in the city of Anurádhapura. In the fourteenth century it was again taken to the continent, but was rescued by Prákrama Bahú, IV. The Portuguese say that it was captured by Constantine de Braganza, in 1560, and destroyed; but the native authorities assert that it was concealed at this time at a village in Saffragam. In 1815, it came into the possession of the British Government; and although surreptitiously taken away in the rebellion of 1818, it was subsequently found in the possession of a priest, and restored to its former sanctuary. From this time the keys of the shrine in which it was deposited were kept in the custody of the British agent for the Kandian provinces, and at night a soldier belonging to the Ceylon Rifle Regiment mounted guard in the temple, there being from time to time public exhibtions of the pretended tooth, under the sanction of the British authorities. The relic has since been returned to the native chiefs and priests, by a decree from the Secretary of State for the Colonies."

The Daladá is worshipped with great reverence by all Buddhists, but the inhabitants of Kandy more especially attach the highest importance to the possession of the sacred relic, regarding it as in fact the very glory and security of their country.

Dalaki—One of the four pupils of Sákapúrni, and teacher of the Rig Veda.

Dama—A prince, the son of Narishyanta, whose father Marutta, was a Chakravartti or universal monarch. The Márkaṇḍeya has the following curious story of Dama. His bride Sumaná, daughter of the king Dasárha, was rescued by him from his rivals. One of them Bapushmat, afterwards killed Marutta, who had retired into the woods after relinquishing his crown to his son. Dama in retaliation killed Bapushmat, and made the Pinda or obsequial offering to his father, of his flesh: with the remainder he fed the brahmans of Rakshasa's origin; such were the kings of the solar race. See Vishṇu Purána, Book IV.

Damaghosha—The Raja of Chedi and father of Śiṣupala, q. v.

Damanaka—The name of one of the jackals in the Panchatantra.

Damaliptas, or Tamaliptas—The people at the western mouth of the Ganges, in Medinipur and Tamluk. Tamralipti was a celebrated seaport in the fourth century and retained its character in the ninth and twelfth.

Damayanti—The daughter of Bhíma, Rája of Vidarbha. The name is already familiar to many English readers through Dr. Milman's metrical translation of the story, "Nala and Damayantí"—and a translation in blank verse by Mr. Chas. Bruce, which appeared in *Fraser's Magazine* a few years ago. The story itself is referred to the Vedic period of Hindu history. Damayanti was famous amongst all the Rájas for her radiant charms and exceeding grace. Nala, the Rája of Nishadha, had so often heard of the exquisite loveliness of Damayantí, the pearl of maidens, that he was enamoured without having seen her; and the soul-disturbing Damayantí had in like manner, so often been told of the god-like comeliness and virtues of the hero Nala, that she secretly desired to become his bride. Nala one day wandering in a grove, caught a swan of golden plumage; the bird cried out, 'Slay me not O gentle Rája, and I will so praise thee to Damayantí that she shall think of no other man but thee. So Nala set it free, and the bird flew away with its companions and entered the garden of Rája Bhíma. It took an opportunity of saying to Damayantí, 'O Damayantí, thou art the loveliest of maidens, and Nala is the handsomest of heroes; if the peerless wed the peerless how happy will be the union.' Then the royal maiden whispered, 'Say the same words to Nala.' And the bird flew away to Nishadha and told all to Nala.

Meantime the beautiful maiden grew pale and dejected. She could not sleep, she often wept, she found no joy in banquets or in conversation. The father saw that she must be married, and at the proclamation of her Swayamvara all the Rájas assembled. Nala repairs as a suitor to Vidarbha; but Indra and three other gods become incarnate for the same purpose, and, meeting Nala in the way, they beg him to be the bearer of their message of love. He remonstrates, but at last consents. He delivers it, but Damayantí declares that, even in the presence of the gods, she shall select the noble Nala. The assembly meets, and all the royal suitors are in array; but Damayantí discovers, to her dismay, five Nalas, each of the deities having assumed the form, features, and dress of the king of Nishadha. She utters a supplicatory prayer to the gods to reveal to her the true object of her choice. They are moved with compassion, and stand confessed, their spiritual bodies being distinguished from that of the human hero by their casting no shadow, nor touching the ground, and otherwise. Damayantí throws the wreath of flowers around the neck of the real Nala in token of her choice. The assembly breaks up amid the applause of the gods, and the lamentations of the disappointed suitors. The nuptials are celebrated and Nala and his bride are blessed with two lovely children.

Nala, the model of virtue, and piety, and learning, at length performs the Aśwameda, or sacrifice of a horse, the height of Indian devotion. In the course of time, however, Nala is induced by an evil spirit to play at dice with his brother, ***Pushkara***, and loses his kingdom, his wealth, his very clothes. One stake only remains,—Damayantí herself. This Pushkara proposes, but Nala refuses. The ill-fated pair are driven together into the wilderness all but naked. Nala persuades his wife to leave him, and return to her father's court, but she will not forsake him. The frantic man, however, resolves to abandon her while asleep. He does so. Each passes through a series of strange and stormy adventures, ending in Nala becoming master of the horse to the King of Ayodhya (Oude,) and Damayantí returning to her father's house. After some time, Damayantí, in order to discover the retreat of Nala, proclaims her intention to hold another ***Swayamvara***, and to form a second marriage, though forbidden by the laws of Manu. Rituparṇa, the King of Oude, resolves to become a suitor, and sets forth with his charioteer—the disguised Nala. As they enter the city of Bhíma, Damayantí recognises the sound of her husband's trampling steeds, his driving could not be mistaken by her ear. She employs every artifice to discover her lord ; she suspects the charioteer ; she procures some of his food, and recognises the flavour of her husband's cookery ; she sends her children to him. Nala can conceal himself no longer ; but the jealous thought that his wife was about to take a second husband, rankles in his heart, and he rebukes her with sternness. Damayantí solemnly denies any such design, declaring that she had only employed the artifice to win back her lord. Nala re-assumes his proper form and character—wins back his wife and all that he had lost to his unprincipled brother, and, re-ascending his ancestral throne, recommences a reign of piety, justice and felicity.—*Mrs. Manning, A. & M. I.*

Dambha—Hypocrisy. The son of Adharma (vice,) and Hinsa (violence.)

Damodas—The name of one of the nine divisions of the Atharva Veda.

Danavas—Enemies of the gods, who, "incapable of steadiness and animated by ambition, put forth their strength against the gods. They were the descendants of Kaṣyapa by his wife Danu, hence their name. They were a class of mythological giants; in the Epic period they were probably personifications of the Aborigines of India; in the Puranic period they are regarded as the inhabitant of Pátáḷa and enemies of the gods. See Daityas. —*Thomson.*

Danda—The name of a son of Dharma by Kriya. Also the name of one of the hundred sons of Ikshwáku. Professor Wilson thinks that by these sons of Ikshwáku we are to understand colonies or settlers in various parts of India. In the Padma P., and the Uttara Khanda of the Rámáyana, there is a detailed narrative of Daṇḍa, whose country was laid waste by an imprecation of Bhárgava, whose daughter Daṇḍa had violated. His kingdom became in consequence the Daṇḍaka forest. The Harī Vansa states that Daṇḍa was killed by Sudyumna.

Danda—A measure of time—sixty Vikalás. Sixty Daṇḍas make one siderial day.

Dandaka—An extensive forest near the Godavery, frequently mentioned in the Rámáyana as the scene of Ráma's wanderings. Ráma was living in a hermitage in this forest when Rávaṇa carried off Síta. The river which the unhappy Síta loved was a tributary to the Godavery, running through the dense forests and wild districts not yet entirely explored, which lie to the north of Bombay and stretch away towards Orissa. The plash of the water-fowl bathing in the bright waters of the Godavery is the most cheerful feature of the scene; but, unlike the Gogra, it is skirted by sea-bright hills, with flashing torrents, but hemmed in by the weary woods of "the pathless Daṇḍaka;" where twining creeper plants, hanging and climbing from bough to bough, alone relieve the "forest gloom." The country is said to be still the "pathless Daṇḍaka." A. and M. I., vol II, p. 22.

Dandaka—"A class of metre in Sanskrit which admits an inordinate length of the verse, which may consist of any number of syllables from twenty-seven to nine hundred and ninety-nine; and the specific name varies accordingly. The construction of the metre requires that the first six syllables be short, and the remainder of the verse be composed of cretic feet, or the bacchus. These two kinds of metre are distinguished by different names. A verse consisting of any number of anapæsts within the limitation above mentioned, is also comprehended under this general designation; as are verses of similar length consisting exclusively of iambic or trochaic feet. They have their peculiar denominations."

Dandaniti—Policy; one of the four branches of royal knowledge; originally written by Vishnugupta in six thousand stanzas for the use of the Maurya kings.

Dandis—One of the Vaishnava or Saiva sects among the Hindus, and a legitimate representative of the fourth Asrama or mendicant life, into which the Hindu is believed to enter after passing through the previous stages of student, householder, and hermit. A Brahman, however, does not require to pass through the previous stages, but is allowed to enter at once into the fourth order. The Daṇḍi is distinguished by carrying a small dand or wand, with several projections from it, and a piece of cloth dyed with red ochre, in which the Brahmanical cord is supposed to be enshrined, attached to it; he shaves his hair and beard, wears only a cloth around the loins, and subsists upon food obtained ready-dressed from the houses of the Brahmans once a day only, which he deposits in the small clay-pot that he always carries with him. He should live alone, and near to, but not within a city; but this rule is rarely observed, and, in general, the Daṇḍis are found in cities, collected like other mendicants in *Maths.* The Daṇḍi has no particular time or mode of worship, but employs himself chiefly in meditation and in the study of the Vedânta works. He reverences *Siva* and his incarnations in preference to the other members of the Hindu Triad, and hence the Daṇḍis are reckoned among the Śaivas. They bear the Śiva mark upon the forehead, smearing it with the ***Tripundra,*** that is, a triple transverse line formed with the ashes of fire made with burnt cow-dung. This mark, beginning between the eyebrows and carrying it to their extremity, is made with the thumb reverted between the middle and third fingers. The genuine Daṇḍi, however, is not necessarily of the Śiva or any other sect, and in their establishments they are usually found to adore *Nirguna* or *Niranjana,* the deity devoid of attribute or passion. The Daṇḍis have usually great influence and authority among the Śiva Brahmans of the North of India, and they are the Sanyasis or monastic portion of the Smarta sect of Brahmans in the south.

It is not so much the speculative as the practical Daṇḍis that are worshippers of Śiva, and the form in which they adore him is that of ***Bhairava*** (which see), or Lord of Terror. In the case of those who thus worship Śiva, part of the ceremony of initiation consists in inflicting a small incision on the inner part of the knee, and drawing the blood of the novice as an acceptable offering to the god. The Daṇḍis of every description differ from the great mass of Hindus in their treatment of the dead, as they put them into coffins and bury them, or when practicable cast them into some sacred stream. Hindus of all castes are occasionally found assuming the life and emblems of the order of Daṇḍis. There are even Brahmans who, without connecting themselves with any community, take upon them the character of this class of mendicants. There is, however, a sect of Daṇḍis termed DASNAMIS (which see), which admit none but Brahmans into their order.—*Wilson.*

Danshtrinas—The progeny of Krodavasá, carnivorous animals, birds and fishes—all sharp-toothed monsters.

Dantavaktra—A fierce Asura, the son of prince Vriddhasarman.

Danu—The daughter of Daksha and mother of the Danavas.

Danu—The mother of Vrittra who was slain by Indra, along with her son, and when slaughtered, lay over him like a cow over her calf. O. S. T. Vol. v, p. 95.

Danus—Another name for Danavas, the sons of Dánu.

Danusha—An unerring bow;—one of the fourteen gems obtained at the churning of the milk sea in the second or Kúrma Avatar of Vishnu.

Dapple-skin—The name of the wonderful cow of plenty belonging to the great sage Vasishtha, and which Rája Viswámitra took away by force.

Daradas—The inhabitants of the country along the course of the Indus above the Himálaya, just before it descends to India. This is the locality they occupied in the days of Strabo and Ptolemy, and at the date of the V. P. They reside there still and are now called Durds.

Dabhasayana—A place between Rameshwara and Cape Comorin, where Ráma, reclining on a couch of sacred grass, prayed to the sea for a passage.

Darpa—(Pride). The name of one of the sons of Dharma.

Darsapaurnamasa—One of the five great sacrificial ceremonies: viz., new and full-moon, those at which four priests officiate.

Darsanas—The name given to the six systems of Hindu Philosophy:—

I. The Sánkya system of Kapila, to which is appended
II. The Yoga system of Patanjali.
III. The Nyáya system of Gautama, to which is appended
IV. The Vaiṣeshika system of Kanáda.
V. The Púrva Mimansa system by Jaimini.
VI. The Uttara Mimansa, or Vedánta, by Veda Vyása.

A. & M. I.

Darsapurnamasa—The small festivals held at the new moon and full moon. "In the beginning of the Darsapurnamása sacrifice, the Adhivarya priest having called the cows and calves together, touches the calves with a branch, and says, 'You are like the winds.'"—*Max Müller.*

Daruka—The charioteer of Krishṇa. He was sent to apprise Arjuna of Krishṇa's approaching end, when he was about to quit the body, and "unite himself to his own pure, spiritual, inexhaustible, imperishable and universal spirit—to become Nirguṇa, devoid of all qualities."

Daruna—The name of one of the Narakas, or hells, described in the Purános.

Darvan—The son of Uṣînara, one of the descendants of Anu.

Dasa-bala—Ten powers or modes of wisdom possessed by BUDDHA. Mr. Spence Hardy, to whose excellent works we are indebted for our information on the principles and rites of the BUDDHISTS, thus enumerates the Dasabala, in his 'Manual of Buddhism:'—"1, The wisdom that understands what knowledge is necessary for the right fulfilment of any particular duty, in whatsoever situation; 2, That which knows the result or consequences of karma, or moral action; 3, That which knows the way to the attainment of nirwána or annihilation; 4, That which sees the various sakwalas or systems of worlds; 5, That which knows the thoughts of other beings; 6, That which knows that the organs of sense are not the self; 7, That which knows the purity produced by the exercise of the dhyánas or abstract meditation; 8, That which knows where any one was born in all his former births; 9, That which knows where any one will be born in all future births; 10, That which knows how the results proceeding from karma, or moral action, may be overcome."

Dasa-dandu—Ten prohibitions which are enjoined upon the Buddhist monks to be studied during their noviciate. Mr. Hardy, in his 'Eastern Monarchism,' thus describes them:—"1, The eating of food after mid-day; 2, The seeing of dances or the hearing of music or singing; 3, The use of ornaments or perfumes; 4, The use of a seat or couch more than a cubit high; 5, The receiving of gold, silver, or money; 6, Practising some deception to prevent another priest from receiving that to which he is entitled; 7, Practising some deception to injure another priest, or bring him into danger; 8, Practising some deception in order to cause another priest to be expelled from the community;

9, Speaking evil of another priest ; 10, Uttering slanders, in order to excite dissension among the priests of the same community. The first five of these crimes may be forgiven, if the priest bring sand and sprinkle it in the court-yard of the vihára, and the second five may be forgiven after temporary expulsion."

Dasnami Dandis—The primitive members of the order of Daṇḍis. They are said to refer their origin to SANKARA ACHÁRYA, a remarkable individual who acted a conspicuous part in the religious history of Hindustan. The word Dasnami means ten-named, there being ten classes of mendicants descended from this remarkable man, only three of them, however, having so far retained their purity as to entitle them to be called Sankara's Daṇḍis. These are numerous, especially in and about Benares. The chief Vedántist writers belong to this sect. The most sturdy beggars, as we learn from Professor Wilson, are members of this order, although their contributions are levied particularly upon the Brahmanical class, as whenever a feast is given to the Brahmans, the Daṇḍis of this description present themselves, though unbidden guests, and can only be got rid of by bestowing upon them a share of the viands. Many of them practise the YOGA, and profess to work miracles. The author of the 'Dabistan' speaks of one who could keep his breath suspended for three hours, bring milk from his veins, cut bones with hair, and put eggs into a narrow-mouthed bottle without breaking them.

The remaining members of the Dasnami class, though they have degenerated from the purity of the practice necessary to the original Daṇḍis, are still religious characters, only they have given up the staff or wand, the use of clothes, money, and ornaments ; they prepare their own food, and admit members from any order of Hindus. These Atíts, as they are often called, are frequently collected in *Maths,* as well as the Dandis, but they mix freely in the business of the world ; they carry on trade, and often accumulate property, and some of them even enter into the married state, when they receive the name of Samyogi."—*Wilson.* vol. I, p. 204.

Dasa-sil—*Dasasikha, Dasa-pariji, Dasa-nasanu, Dasa-dandu, Dasa-sil,* the ten obligations binding on the Buddhist priest—to abstain from murder, theft, sexual intercourse, falsehood, intoxicating drink, eating after mid-day, dancing, perfumes, luxury, receiving of gold or silver. The other Dasas relate to the same rules with slight modifications. The Dasa-dandu forbid deceiving or speaking evil of other priests.

Dasaratha—The son of Aja, and father of Ráma. He was the sovereign of Ayodhya or Oude, whose car bore him to the ten quarters of the universe, that is, to the eight points of the compass, and to the zenith and nádir. He was a descendant from Surya, and one of his ancestors, Raghu, had conquered the seven dwípas, or the whole earth.

"There reigned a king of name revered,
To country and to town endeared,
Great Daṣaratha good and sage
Well read in Scripture's holy page ;
Upon his kingdom's weal intent,
Mighty and brave and provident :
The pride of old Ikshváku's seed
For lofty thought and righteous deed.
Peer of the saints for virtues famed,
For foes subdued and passions tamed ;
A rival in his wealth untold
Of Indra and the Lord of Gold.
Like Manu first of kings, he reigned,
And worthily his state maintained.
For firm and just and ever true,
Love, duty, gain he kept in view ;
And ruled his city rich and free,
Like Indra's Amarávatí."—*Griffiths' Ramayan.*

Another Daṣaratha was the son of Múlaka ; a third, the son of Navaratha ; a fourth, the son of Suyaṣas. The name of Daṣaratha, in a similar ancient character to that of Piyadasi's inscriptions, has been found at Gaya amongst Buddhist remains, and like them deciphered by Mr. Prinsep. V. P.

Dasagriva—A name of Rávana, meaning the ten-necked

Dasakumara—The name of a popular collection of stories containing the Adventures of Ten Princes. "They are storiesof common life, relating the adventures of a lively set of people, who kill, cheat, and rob, as it were for diversion;—something indeed after the fashion of pantomimes and farces, which are still popular in Europe."—*Mrs. Manning.* For extracts from these stories, See Works of Professor Wilson, vol. iv.

Dasara—An Annual Festival, called in the north of India the Durga Pújá. It is the most popular, splendid and expensive of any of the Hindu festivals, and takes place in the month *Aswiya,* (the end of September or beginning of October). The preliminary ceremonies occupy several days previous to the three days of worship. "During the whole of this period all business, in many parts of the country, is suspended, and pleasure and festivity prevail...The artisans and labourers offer sacrifices to the tools and implements which they use in their daily work. The labourer brings his plough, hoe, and other instruments, piles them together, and offers to them a sacrifice consisting of incense, flowers, fruits, rice, and similar articles; after which he prostrates himself before them, and then returns them to their places. The mason offers the same adoration and sacrifice to his trowel, his rule, and other instruments. The carpenter is no less pious with regard to his hatchet, his adze, and his plane. The barber, too, collects his razors in a heap, and worships them with similar rites. The writing-master or copyist sacrifices to the iron pencil or style with which he writes; the tailor to his needles; the weaver to his loom; the butcher to his cleaver. The women, at the same time, heap together their baskets, the rice mill, the wooden cylinder with which they bruise the rice, and the other household implements; and fall down before them after having offered the sacrifices above described. In short, every person adores the instrument or tool which he principally uses in gaining his livelihood. The tools are now considered as so many deities; to whom they present their supplications that they would continue propitious, and furnish them still with the means of living. The festival is concluded by erecting a shapeless statue in each village, composed of paste from grain. It is intended to represent the goddess Párvati; and, being placed under a sort of canopy, is carried about and receives the homage of the inhabitants, who flock to render it their adorations."

Many other usages prevail at this festival in different parts of the country. Amongst the Mahrattas, sheep and buffaloes are sacrificed. The chiefs often give money to enable their soldiers to buy sheep to perform sacrifices, which from furnishing them with a good dinner, are by many considered as the most essential ceremonies of the Dasara. The cannon belonging to the army are planted, praised, invoked, and propitiated by several species of offering. Sir John Malcolm states that on the morning of the tenth day, the Péshwa with all his officers and soldiers, used to move out to the camp in the vicinity of the city, each mounted on his best horse, drest in his finest clothes, and with his arms highly polished. Horses, elephants, and camels were all arranged in their gayest trappings, and every corps spread its gaudiest flags and banners. The whole population of the capital, either as actors or spectators, joined in this grand procession, which moved towards the sacred tree, the object of adoration. After the offerings and prayers the Péshwa plucked some leaves of the tree, in which all the cannon and musketry commenced firing. The Péshwa then plucked from a field, purchased for the occasion, a stalk of jowri, on which the whole crowd fired off their arms or shot arrows, and rushing to the field, tore up all the stalks, each person securing some share of the spoil, which he carried home with joy.

Dasarha—A Prince, the son of Nirvriti. In the Linga Purána it is said that Dasárha was the destroyer of the host of copper (faced) foes.

Dasarna—A river mentioned in the Puránas, and identified in the Dhosaun in Bundlekund.

Dasarna—A place mentioned in Kálidása's Cloud Messenger. "Dasárna's fields await the coming shower." Dr. F. E. Hall says it was situated to the east of Chandeyru. Vidisá is described as the capital of the District. Dasárna is said to be derived from Dasa, ten ; and Riṇa, a stronghold or Durga, the Droog of the Peninsula, and means the District of the ten citadels.—*Wilson.*

Dasa-Rupaka—Ten varieties of dramatic performance. See Wilson's Hindu Theatre, vol. i.

Dasra—The name, in later literature, of one of the two Aṣvins.

Dasyus—A name given to the aborigines of India by the first Aryan settlers. The name often occurs in the Rig Veda, where they are described as enemies to be slain.

Dattatreya—An ascetic ; one of the three sinless sons of the patriarch Atri by his wife Anasuya [Atri].

Dattdi—A name of Agastya, in a previous Manwantara.

Dayabhaga—A celebrated Sanscrit treatise on the Hindu Law of Inheritance. Mr. Colebrooke first published a translation of this work, in 1810 ; and a new edition, with valuable notes, was published in 1865 by Mr. Whitley Stokes.

Deva—A divine being, whether resident upon earth or in a deva-loka. Deva is also a divine epithet variously applied but rarely to the superior deities if alone. Maha deva is sometimes met with. The most frequent use of the term is in the plural, and may be translated "Celestials." The Hindu books say there are thirty-three crores of them ; that is, three hundred and thirty millions of celestials ; but this is probably only a figurative expression to denote a great number. They are not demi-gods, as has been stated ; that is not deified human heroes. Rama or Krishṇa is not one of them, but of a higher order. The *devatas* people the paradise of Vishṇu ; but they especially belong to the *Sverga*, the paradise of Indra. They are usually ranged under eight divisions, with a *vasu*, as leader, at the head of each division.

Devabhaga—The son of Sura and one of the nine brothers of Vasudeva.

Devabhuti—The last Sunga prince, the dynasty having consisted of ten, who governed the kingdom for a hundred and twelve years. Devabhúti being addicted to immoral practices, was murdered by his minister, the Kanwa named Vasudeva, who usurped the kingdom.

Devadarsa—A teacher of the Atharva-Veda, a pupil of Kahandha. He had four disciples who taught this veda.

Devagiri—Deogur or Ellora; the mountain of the gods; the Apocopie are said by Ptolemy to be also called mountains of the gods.

Devahuti—A third daughter, according to the Bhágavata of the Manu Swáyambhuva. She was married to the Rishi Kardama, and was mother of the sage Kapila.

Devaka—One of the sons of Ahuka. Also the name of one of the sons of Yudhishthira, the Pándava.

Deva-loka—The six celestial worlds between the earth and the Brahma lokas.

Devaki—The daughter of Devaka, who was married to Vasudeva. No person could bear to gaze upon Devaki, from the light that invested her: the gods, invisible to mortals, celebrated her praises continually from the time that Vishṇu was contained in her person. Before the birth of Krishna "the quarters of the horizon were irradiate with joy as if moonlight was diffused over the whole earth. The virtuous experienced new delight, the strong winds were hushed, and the rivers glided tranquilly, when Janárdana was about to be born. The infant was brought forth and conveyed to a place of safety, to escape from the enraged Kansa who had vowed his destruction. Kansa made unavailing search for the child, and ordered that every boy in whom there were signs of unusual vigour should be slain without remorse." See Krishṇa.

Devakshatra—A prince, the son of Devarata, one of the descendants of Jyamagha.

Devala—A Rishi, the son of Krisaswa. He was a legislator, and has acquired additional celebrity as the grandfather of Panini.

Devamidha—An ancient Rája of the solar race, one of the ancestors of king Janaka.

Devamidhusha—The son of Vrishni; also the name of a son of Hridika.

Devamitra—Also called Sákalya, a teacher of the Rig Veda. He died in consequence of his being defeated by Yajnavalkya in a disputation at a sacrifice celebrated by Janaka.

Devanampriya-Tishya—A king of Ceylon from 307 to 267 B. C. He adopted Buddhism and made it, like Asoka, with whom he was contemporary, the State religion of the island.

Devanika—A prince, the son of Kshemadhanawan, one of the descendants of Kusa.

Devapi—The son of Pratipa, who abdicated the throne and adopted in childhood a forest life ; while an ascetic in the forest he was perverted from the doctrines of the Vedas. The Vishṇu Purána states that he is still in existence.

Devarakshita—The daughter of Devaka, sister of Devaki and aunt of Krishṇa ; also the name of a prince who reigned in a city on the sea-shore over the Kosalas and Tamraliptas.

Devarata—1, A royal sage of the solar race, the name given to Sunaṣepha when he was adopted by Viswámitra. Sunasépha refused to return home with his father Ajigartha, who had offered for 300 cows, to sacrifice him (See Sunaṣepha) and was afterwards enrolled as the adopted son of Viswámitra by the name of Devaráta (Theodotus) ; 2, Also a son of Rája Śuketu ; 3, The name of a son of Karambhi, one of the descendants of Jyámagha ; 4, also a name of Bhíshma.

Devarshis—Divine sages, demi-gods ; their dwelling is the region of the gods.

Devasarman—The name of a brahman who figures in the Panchatantra ; he had no child and his wife was very unhappy in consequence : at length by some mantram the promise of a son was obtained ; the child when born proved to be a snake. It was proposed that the monster should be destroyed, but maternal affection prevailed, and it was reared with tenderness. At the proper age it was married to a brahman girl, and one night was changed into a man, intending to resume its serpent form next morning ; but the girl's father discovering the deserted skin threw it into the fire, and the son-in-law ever after remained in the figure of a man.

Devasavarni—The thirteenth Manu according to the Bhágavata, which differs from the other Purânas in the enumeration.

Devasravas—One of the sons of Sura, and brother of Vasudeva.

Devatithi—A Kuru prince, one of the sons of Akrodhana.

Devavat—A son of Akrura, also a son of Devaka.

Devavriddha—One of the sons of Satwata, said in the Vishṇu Purána to be equal to the gods.

Devayani—The daughter of a Brahman priest named Sukra ; she fell in love with her father's pupil Kanju, and finding her advances rejected, became soured in temper and vindictive in character. One day when out in the jungle with Sarmishta, daughter of the Rája of the Daityas and a number of other young damsels, on reaching a pleasant pool they all threw off their garments and went into the water to bathe, when it so happened that Váyu the god of the wind passed by, and seeing their clothes upon the bank he mingled them up together. Then when the damsels came out of the water, Devayáni and Sarmishta by mistake put on each others' clothes and quarrelled. At last Sarmishta pushed Devayáni into a well and left her there. A Rája named Yayáti, who was hunting in the forest discovered her in the well and extricated her from it. Devayáni, on meeting her maid, said she would never enter the city again. Her father Sukra went to the Rája of the Daityas to obtain an apology from him for his daughter's conduct. Devayáni said to the Rája, "I shall be satisfied upon one condition, that when my father shall give me to a husband, your daughter who pushed me into a well, shall be given to me as a servant." To this the Rája assented, and Devayáni had afterwards the daily attendance of Sarmishta and her maids. One day the whole party were surprised by the Rája Yayáti, who in hot pursuit of a stag burst in upon the damsels. The sight of so much loveliness almost deprived Yayáti of his senses ; but the adventure terminated in Devayáni proposing that he should espouse her, which, on obtaining her father's consent, he did. Two or three years afterwards Sarmishta obtained her revenge by stealing away Yayáti's affections, and Devayáni left him and returned to her father's house.—(*Wheeler's Mahábhárata*). In the V. P. an entirely different account is given.

Devi—The female of a deva. They also may reside either in earth or in a deva loka, and leave the one for the other at will for any important purpose. Also the name of Uma the wife of Śiva.

Devika—The name of a river, the Déva or Goggra.

Devikota—A Puranic city, usually considered to be the modern Devicottah in the Carnatic, which is commonly believed to be the scene of Báṇa's defeat.

Dhamajaya—A Vyása, the arranger of the Vedas in the sixteenth Dwápara.

Dhanaka—A prince, the son of Durdama, a descendant of Yadu.

Dhananjaya—A fierce and venomous many-headed serpent, one of the progeny of Kadru.

Dhanamitra—The name of a wealthy merchant in Kálidása's drama of Sakuntala; the merchant, trading by sea, was lost in a shipwreck; and as he was childless, the whole of his property became by law forfeited to the king. The king ascertained that the merchant's widow was expecting to give birth to a child, and declared that the unborn child had a title to his father's property; a proclamation which was received with acclamations of joy.

Dhana-nando—The youngest son of Kálásoka, king of Pátaliputra. The nine sons succeeded their father in the order of their seniority. The youngest was called Dhana-nando from his being addicted to hoarding treasure. He collected money to the amount of eighty kotís; and to keep it securely he diverted the Ganges from its course, by constructing a dam across it: and in a rock in the bed of the river having caused a deep excavation to be made, he buried the treasure there. Over this cave he laid a layer of stones, and to prevent the admission of water poured molten lead in it. Repeating this process, which made it like a solid rock he restored the river to its former course. This prince was afterwards killed by the brahman Chánakko, who raised Chandragupta to the throne in his stead. As everything in India Chronology depends on the date of Chandragupta, great pains have been taken by Wilson, Max Müller, and others, to determine it accurately.

Dhaneyu—A prince; one of the ten sons of Raudraswa, a descendant of Puru.

Dhanishta—An asterism, or lunar mansion, in Migravithi, in the southern Avashtána.

Dhanur-veda—The science of archery or arms, taught by Bhṛigu.

Dhanwantara—A sage produced from the churning of the ocean, robed in white, and bearing in his hand the cup of Amrita, which was afterwards seized by the Daityas. He is called the physician of the gods. In a second birth he was the son of Dirghatamas, and taught the Ayur Veda, or medical science. He was exempt from human infirmity, and master of universal knowledge. The only work at present existing under the title of Ayar Veda is said to have been revealed by Dhanwantari to his pupil Susruta; Dhanwantari having himself, as he declares, received it from Bramha.

Dhara—A city to the south of the river Godávery, where the celebrated Rája Vikrama resided.

Dharana—Steady thought; retention or holding of the image or idea formed in the mind by contemplation; one of the eight stages by which "Yoga" must be accomplished. See Yoga.

Dharani—A daughter of the Pitris, and wife of Meru. In the Vishṇu Purána she is said to have been well acquainted with theological truth; addicted to religious meditation; accomplished in perfect wisdom, and adorned with all estimable qualities.

Dharbaga—The son of Ajatasatru, king of Maghada, one of the ten Saiṣunágas, the aggregate of whose united reigns amounted to three hundred and sixty-two years.

Dharma—The god of justice ; the Hindu Pluto. See Yama.

Dharma—A Prajápati, one of the mind-engendered sons of Brahma, with form and faculties derived from his corporeal nature. He married thirteen daughters of Daksha. It is evident from the names of these daughters (faith, devotion, &c.) that they are allegorical personages, being personifications of intelligences and virtues and religious rites, and being therefore appropriately wedded to the probable authors of the Hindu Code of religion and morals, or to the equally allegorical representation of that code, Dharma, moral and religious truth. V. P.

Dharma—Virtue, religion, duty, law, moral and religious truth according to the law and the Vedas. Any peculiar or prescribed practice or duty ; thus giving alms, &c., is the *dharma* of a householder : administering justice is the *dharma* of a king ; piety is the *dharma* of a brahman ; courage is the *dharma* of a kshatriya, &c.

Dharma Raja—A name of the eldest of the five Pándavas, Yudhishthira, (q. v.) son of Kunti Devi, by *Yama* ; Pándu, the nominal father, being impotent.

Dhârmadhris—One of the sons of Swaphalka, a descendant of Sini.

Dharmadhwaja—1, A king of Mithila,—who is also called Janaka ; 2, The name of a king of Burdwan, mentioned in the Belata Panchavinsati, as having restored Brahmanism, which had been put aside for the Jaina religion.

Dharmaketu—A prince, the son of Suketana, (according to the Bhágavata list) a descendant of Alarka. In the Vishṇu Purána he is made the son of Sukumára, and in the Agni he appears as the son of Alarka himself.

Dharmanetra—The son of Haihaya, a descendant of Yadu—the tribe in which Krishṇa was born.

Dharmapal—One of the ministers of justice of Mahárája Dasaratha.

Dharmaranya—A Puránic city in the mountainous part of Magadha, the residence of Amurtarajas.

Dharmaranya—Is also the name of the wood to which the god of justice is said to have fled through fear of Sóma the moon-god.

Dharmaratha—A prince, the son of Divaratha. He is said to have drank the Sóma juice along with Indra.

Dharma-sastra—A law book ; the three principal topics of all such are *áchára*, rules of conduct ; *vyavahara*, judicature ; and *práyaschitta*, penance. The Code of Yajjnawalka is termed Dharmasástra ; as is also the Code of Manu.

Dharma-savarni—The Manu of the eleventh Manwantara. One of the mind-engendered sons of a daughter of Daksha, by himself and the three gods Brahma, Dharma, and Rudra, to whom he presented her on Mount Meru.

Dharshtakas—A race of Kshatriyas, some of whom obtained brahmanhood upon earth. V. P.

Dhata—A Rudra, the son of Bhrigu by Khyati.

Dhataki—A prince, the son of Savaṇa, king of Pushkara—an island without mountains or rivers in which men live a thousand years without sickness or sorrow. V. P.

Dhatri—A son of Vishṇu and Lakshmi, married to Ayati, daughter of Meru.

Dhatu—A linguistic root. In European languages if grammar attempts to reduce a word to its last limit, it calls such a limit its 'root,' and a root in grammar thus answers to an element in chemistry, representing the farthest result of analysis attainable by the analyser ; but in Sanskrit grammar,—dhátu, though generally translated root, does not imply that which is expressed by the

European term. The former designates that theoretical form, from which, by conjugational affixes, verbal bases, and by krit affixes nominal bases may be derived. Yet as such derivations may not only be made from those forms which have been collected in lists called Dhátupátha, and may be called primary Dhátus, but also from those derivative forms,—the passives, intensives, causals, desideratives, and denominatives;—even these derivative forms are, to the Hindu grammarian *Dhátus*. To his mind therefore a *dhátu* is not an absolutely last linguistic element; but even a primary dhátu, or that form from which passive and other secondary dhátus could be derived, is to him only that form which, to the *popular* understanding, appeared to be a last limit of derivation."*

Dhatu-Parayana—A celebrated commentary on Dhátus, written by Hemachandra.

Dhaumya—The name of the brahman who was engaged by the Páṇḍavas to be their Purohita or family priest. He also officiated as Hótri and cooked the sacrifice when it was offered. He accompanied the Páṇḍavas on their exile; and on their return performed the inauguratory ceremonies for Rája Yudhishthira; and at the great Aswamedha squeezed milk out of the horse's ear.

Dhava—(Fire). A deity of the class termed Vasu; because they are always present in light or luminous irradiation.

Dhenuka—A demon, fierce and malignant, who in the form of an ass, attacked Bala Ráma when a boy, and began to kick him on the breast with his hinder heels. Bala Ráma however, seized him by both hind legs, and whirling him round till he expired, tossed his carcase to the top of a palm tree from the branches of which it struck down abundance of fruit, like rain drops poured upon earth by the wind. Vishṇu Purána, 517.

Dhi—The wife of the Rudra Manyu.

Dhimat—One of the six sons of Purúravas; the name also of the valiant son of Virat.

Dhishana—A princess of the race of Agni, and wife of Havirdhána.

* Mrs. Manning, A. and M. I.

Dhishnyas—The seven little circles extending in a straight line from the Marjála to the Agnidhra fire.—*Ait. Brah.*

Dhoti or Dhotra—The cloth wrapped round the loins, and universally worn by Hindus. It is spoken of by Nearchus as reaching to the middle of the leg. It is from 2½ to 3½ yards long by 2 to 3 feet broad. "Native sepoys march thirty or forty miles a day in dhótis without fatigue." "In the frescoes on the caves of Ajanta this costume is carefully represented."—*Edin. Rev., Jan.* 1868.

Dhridhaswa—One of the three sons of Kuvalâyaswa, who escaped from the conflict with the demon Dhundu.

Dhrishta—One of the sons of the Manu Vaivaswata. Before their birth the Manu, being desirous of sons offered a sacrifice for that purpose to Mitra and Varuṇa ; but the rite being deranged through an irregularity of the ministering priest, a daughter, Ila, was produced. See Ila and Manu. From Drishta sprang the Kshatriya race of Dharshtakas.

Dhrishtadyumna—A prince, the son of Râja Drupada, in whose reign the possessions of the Pánchálas were divided. Dhrishtadyumna was the brother of Draupadi, who proclaimed the terms of her Swayamvara.

" The gallant Dhrishtadyumna on the plain
Descended, and his father's will proclaimed ;—
Princes, this bow behold ! Yon mark—these shafts—
Who'er with dextrous hand at once directs
Five arrows to their aim ; and be his race,
His person, and his deeds, equivalent
To such exalted union,—He obtains
My sister for his bride. My words are truth.
Thus said, he to the Princess next described
Each royal suitor by his name and lineage,
And martial deeds ; and bade her give the wreath
To him whose prowess best deserved the boon.

Arjuna was the successful suitor, and Draupadi became the wife of the five Pándu brothers. Dhrishtadyumna followed the brothers home, and ascertained that they were not brahmans but Kshatriyas of the royal house of Hastinápura, and soon acquainted his father with the tidings. At the beginning of the great war Dhrishtadyumna was elected commander-in-chief; after several days' fighting, Rája Drupada was slain by Drona, and Dhrishtadyumna vowed that he would be revenged for his father's death by killing Drona. This he did the following day, aided by Bhíma. He was afterwards surprised by Aswatthámа, the son of Drona, while sleeping in the tents of the Páṇḍavas and was barbarously murdered. See Drupada.

Dhrishtaketu—1, The son of Dhrishtadyumna, he commanded the troops of Chedi and Malwa in the great war; 2, The name of a son of Satyadhriti or Sudhriti, king of Mithila, who was celebrated for his piety, and received the designation of "royal saint." 3, A son of Suketu, a descendant of Alarka.

Dhrishtasarman—A prince, one of the sons of Swaphalka, of the family of Anamitru.

Dhrishti—The war minister of Mahárája Dasaratha.

Dhrita—A prince, the son of Dharma.

Dhritamati—A river among those enumerated in the Vishṇu Purána as one of the rivers of Bharata.

Dhritarashtra—The elder son of Krishṇa Dwaipáyana and the widow of Vichitravírya (see Bhíshma), king of Hastinápura, and father of Duryodhana and his ninety-nine brothers. Being blind from birth, he eventually delivered his sceptre to Duryodhana, at whose suggestion he banished the Páṇḍava princes, his own nephews, from his kingdom. It is to him that his charioteer and bard (*súta*), Sanjaya, relates the Bhagavat Gíta, or dialogue between Krishṇa and Arjuna, having received, as he says, from the Vyása, the mystic power of being present while it was carried on. His wife's name was Gándhári, and the chief of her hundred sons were Duryodhana, Duhṣásana, Vikarṇa, and Chitrasena. (Dhritaráshtra is derived from *dhrita*, 'held firm;' and *ráshtra*, a 'kingdom,' 'who tenaciously maintains the sovereignty.' The name, Schlegel observes, may have arisen from his remaining on the throne in spite of his blindness.) (*J. C. Thomson.*) On the death of Duryodhana, who was killed by Bhíma, he meditated revenge, and caused an instrument of strongly constrictive power to be made, which he wore on his person ; and then expressed a strong desire to embrace Bhíma, his nephew, before he died. Krish a being aware of the device (the hug as of a bear) caused a stone image to be substituted ; and as the blind king could not distinguish the difference, he was deceived, and Bhíma escaped.

Dhritaráshtra was also the name of a powerful many-headed serpent, of immeasurable might ; one of the progeny of Kadru.

Dhritarashtri—The daughter of Kaṣyapa, one of the wives of Garuda and mother of geese, ducks, teal and other water-fowl.

Dhritavrata—One of the eleven Rudras. Also the name of a prince, one of the descendants of Anu.

Dhriti—Steadiness. One of the twenty-four daughters of the patriarch Daksha, married to Dharma (righteousness), their son was Niyama (precept). *Dhriti* was also the name of several princes—of a son of Vethavya, king of Mithila ; of a son of Babhru ; and of a son of Vijaya. The wife of Manu, one of the eleven Rudras, was named Dhriti.

Dhritimat—A celebrated sage, the son of Kirthimat, by his wife Dhenuka. Also the name of a son of Yavinara.

Dhruva—The polar star, the pivot of the atmosphere ; on it rests the seven great planets, and on them depend the clouds : the rains are suspended in the clouds and fall for the support of created beings. This source of rain is termed the sacred station of Vishṇu, and the support of the three worlds. Vishṇu Purána, Ch. VIII. From it proceeds the stream that washes away all sin, the river Gunga, embrowned with the unguents of the nymphs of heaven, who have sported in her waters. Having her source in the nail of the great toe of Vishṇu's left foot, Dhruva receives her and sustains her day and night devoutly on his head. V. P.—*Ibid.*

As Dhruva revolves it causes the moon, sun and stars to turn round also ; and the lunar asterisms follow in its circular path, for all the celestial luminaries are bound to the polar star by ærial cords. The rain is evolved by the sun ; the sun is sustained by

Dhruva ; and Dhruva is supported by the celestial porpoise-shaped sphere, which is one with Náráyaṇa. Náráyaṇa, the primeval existent, and eternally enduring, seated in the heart of the stellar sphere, is the supporter of all beings. V. P., Ch. IX.

Dhruva was the son of Uttánapáda and Suníti ; when a child he observed his half-brother Uttama in the lap of his father as he was seated on his throne, and was desirous of ascending to the same place. He was reproved for this by the mother of Uttama, Suṛuchi, the favorite wife of his father. The boy being angry went to the apartment of his own mother, who took him on her lap and asked what had vexed him. Suníti, distressed by the narrative of the boy, said, Suruchi has rightly spoken ; thine, child, is an unhappy fate ; those who are born to fortune are not liable to the insults of their rivals. Yet be not afflicted my child. That the king favors Suruchi is the reward of her merits in a former existence. It is not proper for you to grieve ; a wise man will be contented with that degree which appertains to him ; be amiable, be pious, be friendly, be assiduous in benevolence to all living creatures ; for prosperity descends upon modest worth as water flows towards low ground.

Dhruva answered : "Mother, the words that you have addressed to me for my consolation, find no place in a heart that contumely has broken. I will exert myself to attain such elevated rank that it shall be revered by the whole world." The youth then went forth from his mother's dwelling and applied to seven Munis, whom he found sitting in an adjoining thicket. By their advice he devoted himself entirely to the service of Vishṇu, concentrating his whole mind on this one object. He commenced a course of religious austerities ; resisted all the attempts made to change his purpose ; and was finally elevated by Vishṇu to the skies as the pole-star. V. P.

Dhruva sandhi—One of the sons of Rája Tresandhi, king of Ayódhya, and father of Bharata.

Dhruvasandhi—A prince, the son Pushya, a descendant of Ráma.

Dhruyu—The eldest son of king Yayáti, by his wife Sarmishta ;

called in some of the Puránas, the handmaid of his first wife Devayáni. Dhruyu became king of the western part of his father's dominions.

Dhumaketu—(Comet). An allegorical personage, the son of Krisáswa, by his wife Archish (flame). The deified weapons of the gods were the progeny of Krisáswa. Dhumakétu is also the name of one of the sons of Trinavindu by the celestial nymph Alambushá, who became enamoured of Trinavindu.

Dhumrakesa—One of the five sons of the celebrated Prithu, the universal emperor or Chakra-vertti.

Dhumraksha—One of Rávaṇa's generals, who was killed at the siege of Lanka.

Dhumraswa—The son of Suchandra and king of Vaiṣáli—the city founded by Vaiṣáli, son of Trinavinda. The Buddhists consider Vaiṣáli to be Prayága, or Alláhabad. Among them it is celebrated as a chief seat of the labours of Sakhya and his first disciples.

Dhundu—An Asura, or demon, represented as most formidable. The pious sage Uttanka was much harassed by this demon, and king Kuvalayáswa, inspired with the spirit of Vishṇu, determined to destroy it. In the conflict the king was attended by his sons to the number of twenty-one thousand, and all these with the exception of three perished in the engagement, consumed by the fiery breath of Dhundu. The demon hid himself beneath a sea of sand, which Kuvalayáswa and his sons dug up, undeterred by the flames which checked their progress and finally destroyed most of them. The king was afterwards entitled Dhundumára. The legend is supposed to have originated in some physical phenomena as an earthquake or volcano. V. P.

Dhundumara—The name of Kuvalayáswa, after the conflict above described. In the Rámáyaṇa he is termed the son of Trisanku.

Dhuti—One of the twelve Ádityas who in a former Manwantara were deities called Tushitas ; they entered the womb of Aditi, daughter of Daksha, and were born as the sons of Kaṣyapa, and named the twelve Ádityas.

Dhyana—Profound meditation on Vishṇu. When the image (of Vishṇu) never departs from the mind of the sage, whether he be going or standing, or be engaged in any other voluntary act, then he may believe his retention to be perfect. There are six stages in the attainment of this object: 1, Yama, acts of restraint and obligation; 2, Asana, sitting in particular postures; 3, Praṇáyáma, modes of breathing; 4, Pratyáhára, exclusion of all external ideas; 5, Bhavana, apprehension of internal ideas; 6, Dhárana, fixation or retention of those ideas. Those who thus devote themselves to meditation, must divest their minds of all sensual desire, and have their attention abstracted from every external object, and absorbed with every sense in the prescribed subject of meditation. Patanjali says, 'Restraint of the body, retention of the mind, and meditation, which thence is exclusively confined to one object, is Dhyána.' *See* V. P., p. 657.

Digambara—A naked ascetic, or gymnosophist. The Jains are divided into two principal divisions, Digambaras and Śvetambaras; the former of which appears to have the best pretensions to antiquity, and to have been most widely diffused. The discriminating difference is implied in these terms, the former meaning the sky-clad, that is, naked; and the latter the white-robed, the teachers being so dressed. In the present day, however, the Digambara ascetics do not go naked, but wear coloured garments; they confine the disuse of clothes to the period of their meals, throwing aside their wrapper when they receive the food given them by their disciples.—*Wilson.*

Diksha—Certain ceremonies preliminary to a sacrifice. It also means a new birth—and a rite of initiation.

Diksha—The wife of Ugra, one of the eight Rudras or manifestations of Brahma; or according to the Bhágavata, the wife of Vámadeva, another Rudra.

Dikshaniya Ishti— A curious sacrificial ceremony, apparently suggested by "a feeling nearly akin to belief in original sin. The gods, and especially Vishṇu and Agni, are invoked to come to the offering with the Díksha. 'Grant the Díksha to the sacrifice. Agni as fire, and Vishṇu as the sun, are invoked to cleanse the sacrificer, by the combination of their rays, from all gross and material dross. The worshipper is then covered up in a cloth, on the outside of which is placed the skin of a black antelope ; and, after a certain time has elapsed, and specified prayers have been recited, the coverings are removed, the new birth is considered to have been accomplished, and the regenerated man descends to bathe."*

Dikshavisarjane—A religious ceremony amongst brahmans ; it is customary for a man to allow his hair to grow for six months after his marriage, and then go to his father-in-law's house to have his head shaved ; this act, and the observances which accompany it, is termed Díkshavisarjane.

Dilipa—The son of Ansuman and father of Bhagíratha who brought Ganga down to the earth.

> Ansuman's son, Dilípa famed,
> Begot a son Bhagírath named,
> From him the great Kakutstha rose ;
> From him came Raghu feared by foes.

Dilípa is described in the Raghuvansa as a grand ideal of what a king should be.

> "Tall and broad-shouldered, stout and strong of limb,
> Valour incarnate fixed her throne in him,
> Matchless in beauty and heroic might,
> He towers like Meru in his lofty height.
> Meet for his god-like form, his noble mind
> To worthy studies in his youth inclined.
> Thence great designs inspired his generous soul,
> And mighty deeds with glory crowned the whole."

This monarch was the delight of his subjects, who followed him as their guide, and thereby obeyed the laws of Manu.

> "And well they knew the tax they gladly paid,
> For their advantage on the realm was laid.
> The bounteous sun delights to drink the lakes,
> But gives ten thousand-fold the wealth he takes."

* Mrs. Manning, A. and M. I.

Just as the earth and water, fire and ether, were given by the good Creator for the benefit of all mankind; so was the king, Dilípa, sent to bless his subjects, and find his own happiness in that of others. Theft was unknown in his dominions, and

"He ruled the earth, from rival sceptre free,
Like one vast city girdled by the sea."

But one boon was wanting. He had a lovely queen, but no son.

"Oh! how he longed, that childless king, to see
A royal infant smiling on her knee;
With his dear mother's eyes and face divine,—
A second self to ornament his line!"

In the hope of attaining this boon he resolves to seek his holy guide, the renowned Vasishtha, who now lived far away in a secluded hermitage. His queen goes forth with him, and they travel in a car, which "tells his coming with the music of its bells."

"Fresh on their cheeks the soft wind gently blows,
Wafting the perfume of the woodland rose:
And, heavy with the dust of rifled flowers,
Waves the young branches of the mango bowers.
They hear the peacock's joyous cry; his head
Lifted in wonder at the courser's tread.
They watch the cranes in jubilant armies fly,
Crowning, like flowers, the portals of the sky.
From shady coverts by the way, the deer
Throw startled glances when the car is near.
* * * * * *
Through towns they pass, and many a hamlet fair,
Founded and cherished by their royal care."

Peasants bring them curds and milk; ......the king calls attention to the varied beauties of the woodland scene; and, lost in delight, they reach the end of their journey quite unexpectedly.

"Evening is come, and, weary of the road,
The horses rest before the saints' abode."

The hermitage reminds one of that described in Kálidâsa's play, Sakuntalâ. Hermits from the neighbouring forest have come for grass and fuel; playful fawns are waiting to be fed with rice; young girls are watering the roots of trees, &c.

The king and the queen are most kindly received.

After "food and rest," the sage inquires of the king his wishes, and having heard that

> "Mother earth, whom tears nor prayers have won,
> Is still ungracious, and denies a son,"

and that "the spirits of his fathers pine," seeing no hope of funeral offerings, ...the great Vasishtha falls into profound meditation, and, after a few minutes, announces the cause of the misfortune. The king, Dilípa, had once, thoughtlessly and unconsciously, omitted to pay reverence to "the holy cow," which was lying under a celestial tree near the falls of the Ganges.... Therefore, by way of penance, he and his queen must tend a cow, called Nandinî, in the sacred woods close by; and when they have gained the love of this descendant of the affronted cow, the curse will be removed. The attendance is given faithfully: the queen worships the cow, by walking round her and scattering grain; and the king cannot be persuaded, even by illusive phantoms, to desert his trust. He hastens to the queen;

> "And though she read at once his looks aright,
> He told her all again with new delight.
> Then, at the bidding of the saint, he quaffed
> Of Nandinî's pure milk a precious draught,
> As though, with thirst that rises from the soul,
> He drank eternal glory from the bowl."

At the dawn of day,

> "Swift towards their home the eager horses bound;
> The car makes music o'er the grassy ground.
> They reach the city, where the people wait,
> Longing to meet their monarch, at the gate.
> Dim are his eyes, his cheek is pale, his brow
> Still bears deep traces of his weary vow."

In due time a son was born.

> "There was a glory round the infant's head;

And e'en the unlit torches seemed to shine
As in a picture, with that light divine."

And, when all rites had been duly performed,—

"Still greater glory crowned Dilípa's son."
—*A. and M. I., vol. II, pp.* 99—101.

Kálidása in the Raghuvansa makes Raghu the son of Dilípa and great grandfather of Ráma.

Dina-chariyawa—The daily observances of Buddhist priests. These are very numerous, and are prescribed with minute detail. At the conclusion it is said the priest must maintain a course of good behaviour, he must keep under the five senses, with matured wisdom, and without any haughtiness of either body, speech or mind.

Dipaka—The Illuminator. A figure of poetical rhetoric, throwing "a quickening ray of light upon the colouring of the poet's pictures; for its power it is indebted to arrangement in general, especially to the connection of the single verb, which (to use the expression of the commentator) lights up the whole description."—*Colebrooke.*

Dipavali-habba—A festival instituted in memory of two celebrated giants, Bala-chakravarti and Narak-asura. The latter had become the scourge of the human race and infested the earth with his crimes. Vishṇu at length delivered both gods and men from the terror of this monster, whom he slew after a dreadful combat. The contest ended but with the day. Thus Vishṇu not having it in his power to make his diurnal ablutions before the setting of the sun, had to perform them in the night. The Brahmans in commemoration of this great event, put off their ablutions to the night; and this is the only occasion, in the course of the year, in which they can transgress the ordinance of never bathing after sunset. But this exception of the nocturnal bathing, possesses a high degree of merit, and is conducted with solemnity.

The word *Dipavali-habba* signifies the Feast of Lamps; and the Hindus actually light a great number of lamps round the door of their houses. They make paper lanterns also, which they hang in the streets. The husbandmen celebrate this festival in a different way. Being then the harvest time for grain they assemble in the rágí fields and offer prayers or sacrifices. Some sacrifice to the dunghill which is afterwards to enrich the ground. The offerings consist of burning lamps, fruits, or flowers which are deposited in the mass of ordure.—*Abbé Dubois.*

Diptimat—One of the sons of Krishṇa by Rohiṇí. The Vishṇu Purána says that Krishṇa had one hundred and eighty thousand sons, but the names of only a few are given.

Dirghabahu—A prince, the son of Khatwánga.

Dirghamukha—A crane that figures in the Panchatantra; the name means "long bill."

Dirghatamas—The son of Kásirája and father of Dhanwantari. Another Dírghatamas was the son of Utathaya, and some of the Puránas have an absurd story of the circumstances attending his birth.

Dis—Space, which is said in the Bhágavata to be the deity which presides over the ear. Dis is also the name of a river in the Vishṇu Purána.

Disa—The wife of Bhíma, one of the eight Rudras.

Dishta—One of the sons of Manu Vaivaswata, the son of the celestial luminary.

Diti—A daughter of Daksha, who became one of the wives of Kaṣyapa, and mother of the Daityas, q. v. She is termed the general mother of Titans and malignant beings. Diti having lost her children propitiated Kaṣyapa; and the best of ascetics promised her a boon: on which she prayed for a son of irresistible prowess who should destroy Indra. The Muni granted his wife the gift on one condition, "You shall bear a son," he said, if with thoughts wholly pious, and person entirely pure, you carry the babe in your womb for a hundred years." Diti consented, and during gestation, observed the rules of mental and personal purity. Indra, aware of what was going on, tried to prevent it; and in the last year of the century an opportunity occurred. Diti retired one night to rest without performing the prescribed ablution of her feet, and fell asleep: on which the thunderer divided the embryo in her womb into seven portions. The child thus mutilated, cried bitterly. Indra not being able to console and silence it, divided each of the seven portions into seven, and thus formed the swift-moving deities called Máruts, (winds). "In this myth of Indra destroying the unborn fruit of Diti with his thunder-bolt, from which afterwards came the Máruts or gods of wind and storm, geological phenomena are, it seems, represented under mythical images. In the great mother of the gods is, perhaps, figured the dry earth: Indra the god of thunder rends it open, and there issue from its rent bosom the Máruts or exhalations of the earth, But such ancient myths are difficult to interpret with absolute certainty."—*Gorriseo.*

Divakara—A prince, the son of Prativyoman, of the family of Ikshwáku, q. v.

Divaratha—A prince, the son of Para, a descendant of Anu.

Divaspati—The Indra of the thirteenth Manwantara.

Divijata—One of the sons of Purúravas, according to the list in the Matsya.

Divodasa—1, A king mentioned in the Rig Veda who coveted one of the hundred impregnable cities of the black-skinned Sambara. Indra hurled Sambara from the mountain; he destroyed ninety-nine cities and gave the hundredth to Divodása; 2, A king of Kasi (Benares)—the son of Bhímaratha. There are some curious legends connected with this prince. It is said that Śiva and Párvati, desirous of occupying Kási, which Divodása possessed, sent a teacher named Nikumbha, to lead the prince to the adoption of Buddhist doctrines; in consequence of which he was expelled from the sacred city, and founded another on the banks of the Gomti; or according to other accounts, he took a city on that river from the family of Bhadraṣreṇya; that Durdama the son of Bhadraṣreṇya, recovered the country; that the son of Divodása Pratarddana, subsequently conquered it from his descendants.

Divya—One of the sons of Satwata.

Dosha—The wife of Kalpa, the son of Dhruva.

Dragons—These are represented in the Vishṇu Purána to be the progeny of Surasá; one of the Daityas.

Dravidian—The term applied to designate the five languages of Southern India, viz :—the Tamil, the Telugu, the Canarese, the Malayálim, and the Toulava. South India was formerly called the Drávida country. The Tamil is the most cultivated of the Dravidian tongues ; it contains the largest portion and the richest variety of undoubtedly ancient forms, and the smallest infusion of Sanskrit terms. It is the vernacular of about 12 millions of people. The Telugu ranks next to the Tamil in respect of culture and copiousness ; in point of euphonic sweetness it ranks in the first place. It is the vernacular of about 14 millions. The Canarese occupies the third place. Sanskrit words have been extensively introduced into the modern dialect, and during the reigns of Hyder and Tippu in Mysore, Hindustani words became common ; but the ancient dialect, spoken from about 800 to 1500 A. D. was free from any admixture of foreign terms. It is the vernacular of about 10 millions. The Malayálim ranks next in order and is spoken along the Malabar Coast from Cannanore to Trevandrum by about 3 millions of people. The Toulava is the least important of the five, and is spoken by the smallest number of people.

Drauni—The Vyása of the Dwápara which immediately follows the twenty-eight Dwáparas enumerated in the Vishṇu Purána.

Draupadi—The daughter of Rája Drupada of Pánchála, whose capital was Kámpilya. " She is the heroine of the Mahábhárata." " She is of dark complexion but of exceeding loveliness ; and the only wish we have for her is that we could change her name,—Draupadí ; for it is almost beyond the power of art to invest a heroine with so uncouth an appellation with the poetic charm belonging to her in the Sanskrit."* The reports of the extraordinary beauty of Draupadí attracted many Rájas and chieftains to her Swayamvara. The young Princess was led into the arena, elegantly dressed, adorned with radiant gems, and carrying in her hand the garland which she was to throw over the neck of the hero who might have the fortune to win her to be his wife. Prince Dhṛishṭadyumna stood by the side of his resplendent sister, and proclaimed that whoever shot the arrow through the revolving

* Mrs. Manning. A. and M. I., Vol. ii.

chakra on the first attempt, and struck the eye of the golden fish, should have the princess for his wife. Many Rájas tried to bend the bow but could not. Then the ambitious Karna entered the lists and to the surprise of all bent the bow and fitted the shaft to the string; but the proud Draupadí resolved that no son of a charioteer should be her lord, and cried out, "I wed not with the base-born." Karna was abashed and walked angrily out of the area. Then Śisupála, the Rája of Chedi; and Jarásandha, the Rája of Magadhá, tried one after another to bend the bow, but they both failed. All this time the Páṇḍavas had been standing amongst the crowd disguised as brahmans: suddenly Arjuna advanced and lifted the bow, bent it and drew the cord, then fitting the arrow to the string, he discharged it through the centre of the chakra and struck the eye of the golden fish. A roar of acclamation arose from the vast assembly; the beautiful Draupadí was filled with joy and wonder at the youth and grace of the hero; as commanded by her brother she came forward and threw the garland round the neck of Arjuna, and permitted him to lead her away according to the rule of the Swayamvara.

In the works of H. H. Wilson, Vol. iii, pp. 328—335, the following poetical version of the account of the Swayamvara is given

In Panchála's spacious realm
The powerful monarch Drupada observes
A solemn feast; attending princes wait
With throbbing hearts, his beauteous daughter's choice;
The royal Draupadí, whose charms surpass
All praise, as far as her mild excellence
And mind transcend the beauties of her person.

* * * * * * * * *
* * * * * * * * *

And now the day of festival drew nigh;
When Drupada, whose anxious hopes desired
A son of Páṇḍu for his daughter's lord,
And who had sent his messengers to search
The banished chiefs, still sought by them in vain,
Devised a test—no other force but theirs
He deemed could undergo, to win the bride.

A ponderous bow with magic skill he framed,
Unyielding but to more than mortal strength.
And for a mark he hung a metal plate
Suspended on its axle, swift revolving
Struck by a shaft that from the centre strayed.
This done he bade proclaim—that he whose hand
Should wing the arrow to its destined aim,
Should win the Princess by his archery.
Before the day appointed, trooping came
Princes and chiefs innumerous : 'midst the throng
Duryodhana and all the hundred sons
Of Dhṛitaráshṭra, with the gallant Karṇa,
In haughty cohort at the court appeared.
With hospitable act the king received
His royal guests and fitting welcome gave.
Between the North and East without the gates
There lay a spacious plain ; a fosse profound
And lofty walls enclosed its ample circuit,
And towering gates and trophied arches rose,
And tall pavilions glittered round its borders :
Here ere the day of trial came, the sports
Were held : and loud as ocean's boisterous waves,
And thick as stars that gem the Dolphin's brow,
The mighty city here her myriads poured.
Around the monarch's throne on lofty seats
Of gold with gems emblazoned sat the kings,
Each lowering stern defiance on the rest.
Without the barriers pressed the countless crowd
Or clambering upon scaffolds clustering hung.
Skirting the distance multitudes beheld
The field from golden lattices, or thronged
The high house-tops, whose towering summits touched
The clouds, and like the mountain of the gods
With sparkling peaks streamed radiant through the air.
A thousand trumpets brayed, and slow the breeze
With incense laden wafted perfume round.
Whilst games of strength and skill—the graceful dance,

The strains of music, or dramatic art,
Awoke the gazer's wonder and applause.
Thus sixteen days were passed, and every chief
Of note was present—and the king no more
Could with fair plea his daughter's choice delay.
Then came the Princess forth in royal garb
Arrayed and costly ornaments adorned :
A garland interwove with gems and gold
Her delicate hands sustained—from the pure bath
With heightened loveliness she tardy came,
And blushing in the princely presence stood.
Next in the ring the reverend Priest appeared
And strewed the holy grass and poured the oil,
An offering to the God of Fire, with prayer
Appropriate, and with pious blessings crowned.
Then bade the king the trumpets' clangor cease
And hush the buzzing crowd—while his brave son
The gallant Dhṛishṭadyumna on the plain
Descended and his father's will proclaimed.
"Princes, this bow behold—yon mark—these shafts—
Whoe'er with dexterous hand at once directs
Five arrows to their aim, and be his race,
His person and his deeds equivalent
To such exalted union, He obtains
My sister for his bride—my words are truth."
Thus said, he to the Princess next described
Each royal suitor by his name and lineage
And martial deeds, and bade her give the wreath
To him whose prowess best deserved the boon.
Quick from their gorgeous thrones the kings uprose,
Descending to the conflict, and around
The lovely Draupadí contending pressed ;
Like the bright gods round Śiva's mountain bride.
Love lodged his viewless arrows in their hearts,
And jealous hatred swelled their haughty minds ;
Each on his rivals bent a lowering glance,
And friends till now, they met as deadliest foes.

Alone the kindred bands remained aloof
Who owned Janárdana their glorious chief.
He and the mighty Haláyudha curbed
Their emulous zeal,—and tranquil they beheld
Like furious elephants the monarchs meet ;
Their rage by courteous seeming ill represt
Like fire amidst the smouldering embers glowing
 And now in turn the Princes to the trial
Succeeding past, in turn to be disgraced—
No hand the stubborn bow could bend—they strained
Fruitless each nerve, and many on the field
Recumbent fell, whilst laughter pealed around.
In vain they cast aside their royal robes
And diamond chains and glittering diadems,
And with unfettered arm and ample chest
Put forth their fullest strength—the bow defied
Each chief nor left the hope he might succeed.
Karṇa alone the yielding bowstring drew
And ponderous shafts applied, and all admired.
The timid Draupadí in terror cried,
I wed not with the base-born—Karṇa smiled
In bitterness and upwards turned his eyes
To his great Sire the Sun—then cast to earth
The bow and shafts and sternly stalked away.
 Thus foiled the Princes, through the murmuring crowd
Amazement spread—then Arjuna from where
He and his brethren with the Brahmans placed
Had viewed the scene, advanced to prove his skill—
The priestly bands with wonder struck beheld
Who seemed a student of their tribe aspire
To triumph where the mightiest chiefs had failed—
They deemed the like disgrace would shame the attempt,
And ridicule their race and name assail,
And many a venerable elder strove
To turn the stripling from the hopeless task :
They strove in vain—nor did they all despair—
For many marked his elephantine strength,

His lion port and self-collected soul ;
And fancied that they saw revived in him
The son of Jamadagni : to o'erthrow
Once more the haughty Kshatriya's power and pride.
Unheeding praise or censure, Arjuna
Passed to the field : with reverential steps
He round the weapon circled, next addressed
A silent prayer, to Mahadeo, and last
With faith inflexible on Krishṇa dwelt.
One hand the bow up bore, the other drew
The sturdy cord, and placed the pointed shafts—
They flew—the mark was hit—and sudden shouts
Burst from the crowd long silent : flattering waved
The Brahman scarfs, and drum and trumpet brayed,
And Bard and Herald sung the hero's triumph.

The Páṇḍavas took Draupadí home to their mother, and told her that Arjuna had won the damsel at her Swayamvara, and she became the wife of the five brothers according to the institutions of polyandry, which seemed to have prevailed at a very remote period. The history of Draupadí is henceforth connected with that of the Páṇḍavas. See Arjuna, Bhíma, &c. She at last accompanied her husbands to the Himálaya mountains in the garb of a devotee and died.

Dravina—One of the sons of Prithu, the universal emperor. Also the name of one of the sons of the sage Dhava.

Draviras—The people of the Coromandel Coast, from Madras southwards ; those by whom the Tamil language is spoken.

Dravya—Substance ; thing ; the receptacle or substratum of properties, one of the six *Padárthas,* or categories, into which Kanáda distributes the contents of the universe.

Dridhadhanash—A prince, the son of Senajit, of the family of Hastin.

Dridhanetra—The youngest of the four sons of Viṣwámitra, born when he had retired to the jungles of the south to practice austerities.

And in that solitary spot,
Four virtuous sons the king begot,

Havishyand from the offering named,
And Madhushyand for sweetness famed,
Mahárath, chariot-borne in fight,
And Driḍhanétra, strong of sight."—*Griffiths.*

Dridhasona—A king of Maghada, the son of Susam ; he reigned 48 years.

Dridhayas—One of the sons of Purúravas, according to the Matsya list.

Drishadwati—A river of considerable importance in the history of the Hindus, although no traces of its ancient name exist. V. P., p. 181.

This river is also called Himavat, and is said to be the mother of Prasenajit.

Drishtanta—An illustration, example, or familiar instance ; in the Nyáya system of Gautama, it is a topic on which in controversy both disputants consent ; or "that on regard to which, a man of an ordinary and a man of a superior intellect, entertain the same opinion."

Drona—Son of the Riṣhi Bharadwája, by birth a Brahman, but acquainted with military science, which he received as a gift from Parasuráma (see Ráma.) "Droṇa was no ascetic, and having in childhood shared the lessons and sports of the royal heir of the neighbouring kingdom of Panchála, he felt inclined to live again at that court, now that his old playfellow had become king. Never doubting of a hearty welcome, he presented himself to king Drupada quite unceremoniously, merely saying, 'Behold in me your friend.' His reception however was totally different to what he anticipated.

.... "the monarch sternly viewed
The sage, and bent his brows, and with disdain
His eyeballs reddened ; silent awhile he sat,
Then arrogantly spoke : Brahman, methinks
Thou showest little wisdom, or the sense
Of what is fitting, when thou call'st me friend.
What friendship, weak of judgment, can subsist
Between a luckless pauper and a king?"

"The king of Panchála stares at the idea of friendship between a learned brahman and one to whom the Vedas are a mystery, or between a warrior and one who cannot guide a chariot through the ranks of war; and continues—

> .... he to whose high mandate nations bow,
> Disdains to stoop to friends beneath the throne.
> Hence then with idle dreams; dismiss the memory
> Of other days and thoughts; I know thee not."

Droṇa was too much astonished to speak, but he instantly withdrew from Panchála to Hastinápura, where he was most reverentially welcomed, and was at once entrusted with the instruction of the five young Pándu and the hundred young Kuru princes." Droṇa had in youth been equally instructed in wisdom and in arms; and he taught the young princes to rein the steed, to guide the elephant, to drive the chariot, launch the javelin, hurl the dart, wield the battle-axe, and whirl the mace."* In the Vishṇu Purána, p. 454, Droṇa is called the husband of Kripí, and father of Aswatthámа; afterwards king of the north part of the Panchála country, and a general in the Kuru army. After Bhíshma had been mortally wounded, Droṇa was elected to the command of the army. He promised Duryodhana that he would take Yudhishthira prisoner, but he could not do so as Krishṇa and Arjuna were ever on the alert to prevent it. On the fourth day of his command he killed Viráta and Drupada. Dhrishṭadyumna then vowed to slay Droṇa in revenge for the death of his father Drupada. A combat took place; but it was not till Droṇa was falsely told that his son Aswatthámа was dead, that he laid down his arms, and Dhrishṭadyumna rushed upon him and severed his head from his body.

Dronakas—A term by which, in the Puránas, the inhabitants of valleys, are designated.

Drupada—The son of Prishata, and father of Draupadi, wife of the sons of Pándu. He was king of the Panchálas, and one of the generals of the Pándava army. Being conquered by Droṇa

* Mrs. Manning—Professor Wilson, Oriental Mag., Vol. iii.

he only managed to retain the southern part of his kingdom, from the Ganges to the Charmavati (the modern Chumbal) including the cities Mákandi and Kampilya. "Although Drupada was compelled to acquiesce in the arrangement made by Droṇa, by which his rule was confined to the country south of the Bhágírathí, the partition was the cause of deep mortification, and he long meditated on the means by which he might recover his former power, and be revenged upon his enemy. He especially regretted the want of a son whose youth and valour might compete with Droṇa's disciples, and he visited the chief resorts of the brahmans, in hope to meet with some holy sage, whose more than human faculties might secure him progeny. He found two brahmans of eminent learning and sanctity named Yája and Upayája, and addressed himself to the latter, promising him a million of cows if he enabled him to obtain the son he desired. Upayája, however declined the task and referred him to his elder brother Yája, to whom the king repaired and promised ten millions of kine: with much reluctance he undertook to direct a sacrificial ceremony by which the king should obtain offspring, and called his younger brother to his assistance. When the rite had reached the proper period the queen was invited to partake of it, but she had not completed her toilet and begged the brahmans to delay the ceremony. It was too late, and the sacrifice proceeding without her, the children were born independent of her participation. The son Dhrishṭadyumna appeared with a diadem on his head, in full mail, and armed with a bow and falchion, from the middle of the sacrificial fire. Draupadi, the daughter, from the middle of the vedi or altar, on which the fire had been kindled! she was of very black colour although of exceeding loveliness, and was thence named Krishṇá; the name of the son is derived from the pride and power with which he was endowed from his birth."*

King Drupada was killed by Droṇa on the fourteenth day of the great war.

Duhsala—The daughter of Maharája Dhritaráshtra, who was married to Jayadratha, Rája of Sindhu.

* Wilson's Works, vol. iii, p. 326.

Duhsasana—One of the chief of the hundred sons of Dhritaráshtra. He took part in the great war. It was he who dragged Draupadi into the gambling pavilion by the hair, and insulted her before the assembly. Bhíma vowed to drink his blood; and on the sixteenth day of the great war, after a deadly conflict, Bhíma slew Duhsásana and fulfilled his vow.

Dukha—Pain. The son of Naraka and Vedana.

Dundhubi—A huge giant slain by Báli. When Sugríva wished Ráma to destroy Báli, in order to convince him of the great strength of the latter he showed Ráma the dead body of Dundhubi:—

> "The prostrate corse of mountain size
> Seemed nothing in the hero's eyes;
> He lightly kicked it as it lay
> And cast it twenty leagues away."

Duradarsin—Far-seeing; the name of a Vulture in the Panchatantra, who was the chief minister of the peacock king Chitravarna.

Durdama—The son of Bhadrasrenya, who recovered his father's kingdom from Divodása, q. v.

Durga—The Śakti or wife of the god Śiva, and the goddess of destruction; she is described as terrible in form and irascible in temper. She was the daughter of Himálaya, the sovereign of the snowy mountains. Durgá is often called Káli. In her amiable form she is termed Bhavání. "The adoration of Káli, or Durgá, is however particularly prevalent in Bengal, and is cultivated with practices scarcely known in most other provinces. Her great festival, the Daṣará, is in the West of India, marked by no particular honors, whilst its celebration in Bengal occupies ten days of prodigal expenditure. This festival, the Durgá Pújá, is now well known to Europeans, as is the extensive and popular establishment near Calcutta, the temple of Kálí at Kálí Ghát."

"That human offerings to the dark forms of Śiva and Durgá were sometimes perpetrated in later times, we know from various original sources, particularly from that very effective scene in the drama of Mádhava and Málatí, in which Aghoraghanṭa is represented as about to sacrifice Málatí to Chámuṇḍá, when she is rescued by her lover. No such divinities, however, neither Śiva nor Durgá, much less any of their terrific forms, are even named, so far as we know, in the Vedas, and therefore these works could not be authority for their sanguinary worship. That the practice is enjoined on particular occasions by the Tantras and some of the Puráṇas connected with this branch of the Hindu faith, is, no doubt, true ; but these are works of a much later date."*

"Durgá combines the characteristics of Minerva, Pallas, and Juno. Her original name was Párvatí, but having, by a display of extraordinary valour, defeated a giant named Durgá, she was thenceforth dignified with the name of her conquered foe. This monster is by some supposed to be a personification of vice, and Durgá of virtue, while the struggle typified the action and reaction of good and evil in the world."—*G. Small.* (See Aparṇā, Devī, Kālī, Karālī, Pārvatī, Sati, Yoganidrā.)

Durga—The name of a river flowing from the Vindhya.

Durgadasa—A distinguished commmentator on the Sanskrit Grammar of Vopadeva.

Durgama—Durmada. Two sons of Vasudeva by his wife Rohini.

Durgas—Strongholds. There are four kinds ; three of which are natural from their situation in mountains, amidst water, or in other inaccessible spots ; the fourth is the artificial defences of a village hamlet or city.

Durjayanta—A mountain in the Vishṇu Purána not yet identified.

Durvasas—The great Hindu Cynic ; a celebrated sage, the son of Atri by Anasúyá, and an incarnation of a portion of Śiva. He was wandering over the earth when he beheld in the hands of a nymph of air, a garland of flowers, with whose fragrance he was enraptured. The graceful nymph presented it to the sage, who placed the chaplet upon his brow, and resumed his journey ; soon after he beheld Indra, the ruler of the three worlds, approach, seated on his infuriated elephant Airávata, and attended by the gods. The sage threw the garland of flowers to the king of the gods, who

* H. H. Wilson's Works, vol. ii.

suspended it on the brow of Airávata. The elephant took hold of the garland with his trunk and cast it to the ground. The chief of sages Durvásas, was highly incensed at this treatment of his gift, and thus addressed the sovereign of the immortals. "Thou art an idiot not to respect the garland I gave thee * * * * thy sovereignty over the three worlds shall be subverted, &c." Indra descended from his elephant and endeavoured, but without effect, to appease the sinless Durvásas. Thenceforward the three worlds lost their vigour and fell into decay and ruin. The gods were then oppressed by the Dánavas, had recourse to Vishṇu, and were directed to churn the ocean. Durvásas was a Chiranjívi or immortal man, not limited to one age. In the drama of *Sakuntala*, his curse on that young woman for a slight delay in opening her door to him, brought on her sorrow and disgrace. In like manner, throughout the whole range of Hindu literature, the curse of Durvásas is at hand, to account for every contretemps, mishap or misadventure. A. and M. I.

Duryaman—A prince, the son of Dhrita, a descendant of Druhyu.

Duryodhana—" Difficult to be fought with." The eldest of the Kurus. The eldest of the hundred sons of Dhritaráshtra, and one of the principal actors, among the Kauravas, in the great war... Pándu was the younger brother of Dhritaráshtra, but Yudhishthira his eldest son was born before Duryodhana, and according to the customs of those times had in consequence a prior right to the throne of Hastinápura. This led to constant rivalry between Yudhishthira and Duryodhana for the post of Yuvarája. As the five Pándavas had, on the death of Pándu, come under the guardianship of their uncle Dhritaráshtra, the cousins were brought up together in the old palace of Hastinápura. It is stated in the Mahábhárata that " about this time Duryodhana the eldest of the Kauravas, became very jealous of the strength of Bhíma, and resolved to work evil against him. He attempted to take his life by poison, and throwing him into a lake while stupified from its effect. Bhíma was not however killed but appeared again to play an important part in the struggles of their lives."

"The jealousy and hatred of the Kurus towards the Pándavas increased as they all attained manhood. The father of the Kurus being blind, required a vice king, or Yuvarâjá, *i. e.*, "Little Rája." In this office Yudhishthira was installed, he being entitled to it as eldest son of the late king Pándu. But Duryodhana was highly discontented at this arrangement, and at length persuaded his blind father to send away the Pándavas to the city of Váranávata (the modern Allahabad). Here a splendid house was prepared for them; but hemp, resin, and other combustible substances, were secreted within; for the wicked Duryodhana plotted that the house should be set on fire, and the five Pándavas and their mother burnt to death. Warning, however, was given to these intended victims before they left Hastinápura; and, on taking possession of their splendid new habitation, they had an underground passage made, by which, when the expected fire took place, they all escaped."

Among the poor people whom Kunti had been feasting was a Bhíl woman, with five sons, who, according to the practice of their tribe, drank deeply of intoxicating liquor, and then lay down and slept heavily. The next morning their bodies were found amid the ruins of the conflagration; and it was believed in Hastinápura that the Pándavas had perished, and Duryodhana pretended to mourn their death.

After the Pándavas (q. v.) had conquered their misfortunes "the very splendour of their success revived the dark jealousy of Duryodhana; for he and his brother Duhsásana, and one or two others, plot to deprive the newly-inaugurated king of his territories. They first secure the co-operation of a relative, named Sakuni, who was a noted gambler, and then induce the blind old Mahárája to invite the Pándavas to a gambling festival at Hastinápura. Yudhishthira accepts the invitation, with secret misgiving; for "he was not very skilful in throwing the dice," and he knows that "Sakuni is dwelling in Hastinápura." Of Sakuni, it is said that "he is very skilful in throwing dice, and in playing with dice that were loaded; insomuch, that whenever he played he always won the game." Nevertheless, Yudhishthira feels compelled to go; for "no true Kshatriya can refuse a challenge to war or play." The game they played at seems to have resembled backgammon, "pieces on a board being directed by the throwing of dice." Certain seeds or nuts served as dice ; and dice of this description were used for the guidance of a portion of the religious sacrifice. So that, to throw dice, was not deemed objectionable ; and only when a passion, or the stake immoderate, was it esteemed a vice. It was, of course, contrived that Yudhishthira should be led on to stake and to lose all that he possessed.*

When the Pándavas returned from their second exile it was chiefly owing to Duryodhana that the great war was fought. He rejected all Krishṇa's proposals for peace, though Bhíshma and Drona, as well as his aged father, were anxious that he should accept them... The war commenced.

" The Kuru host entrusted to his care,
The son of Bharadwája marshals ; first
The chiefs of Sindhu, and Kalinga's king,
With the young prince Vikarna on the right
He stations, by Gándhára's martial chivalry ;
With glittering lances armed, and led by Sakuni,
Their sovereign's son, supported. On his left
Duhsásana and other chiefs of fame
Commanded the array : around them rode
Kámboja's horse, Śakas and Yavanas,
On rapid coursers, mighty in the field.
The nations of the north, and east, and south,
Composed his main battalions : in the rear
Secure the monarch marched ; whilst in the van
The gallant Karna led his faithful bands,
Exulting in their sovereign's stately stature,
High raised upon his elephant of war,
And gorgeous shining as the rising sun.
His warriors deemed the gods themselves were weak,
With Indra at their head, to stem his prowess,
And each to each their thoughts revealed, they moved,
Secure of victory, to meet the foe."†

* A. and M. I.

† Wilson's Works, vol. iii, p. 291.

On the last day of the war Bhíma fought Duryodhana in single combat with clubs, and killed him. It is said that he then fulfilled the vow he made to avenge the insult which Duryodhana had offered to Draupadi.

Dushan—A giant slain by Ráma in the forest of Dandaka.

Dushyanta—The eldest son of Anila, and father of the emperor Bharata. The Mahábhárata relates the following legend of this king. "Once upon a time the valiant Rája Dushyanta was hunting in the forest, when he beheld the beautiful Sakuntalá, the adopted daughter of Kanwa the sage; and he prevailed on the damsel to become his wife by a Gandharva marriage, and gave her his ring as the pledge of his troth. Then Dushyanta returned to his own city, whilst Sakuntalá remained in the hermitage of her father. After this Durvásas the sage visited the hermitage of Kanwa, but the thoughts of Sakuntalá were fixed upon her husband, and she heard not the approach of the sage. And Durvásas cursed the damsel, that she should be forgotten by the man she loved; but after a while he relented, and promised that the curse should be removed as soon as Dushyanta saw the ring. When Sakuntalá found that she was with child, she set off for the palace of her husband; but on her way she bathed in a sacred pool, and the ring dropped from her finger and was lost beneath the waters. When she reached the palace of the Rája, his memory had departed from him, and he would not own her to be his wife; and her mother came and carried her away to the jungle, and there she gave birth to a son, who was named Bharata. And it so happened that a large fish was caught by a fisherman, and the ring of Dushyanta was found in the belly of the fish, and carried to the Rája; and Dushyanta saw the ring, and he remembered the beautiful Sakuntalá, who had become his wife by a Gandharva marriage. And the Rája went into the jungle and saw the boy Bharata sporting with young lions and setting at nought the lioness that gave them suck; and his heart burned towards the lad; and presently he beheld the sorrowing Sakuntalá, and he knew that Sakuntalá was his wife, and that Bharata was his son. So Rája Dushyanta took Sakuntalá and Bharata to his own city; and he made Śakuntalá his chief Ráni, and appointed Bharata to succeed him in the Ráj." The story of Sakuntalá is the subject of the beautiful drama of Kálidása, " The Lost Ring."

Dutas—Messengers. The Gananátas or Dútas are divided into three classes; 1, Siva-dutas, who are represented as red, short, and thick like the Bhúta. Their hair-locks twisted together, rest on their heads like a cap, and from their mouths project two great lion's teeth. They have four hands in which they hold, respectively, a snake, a cord, a trident, and a wine-jug; whilst their body is adorned with various ornaments. By means of these messengers Isvara fetches the souls of his devotees at their death to his seat of bliss, called Kailāsa, and that in a Pushpakavimāna, *i. e.*, a self-moving chariot.

2. The Vishṇu-dútas have their hair dressed like the Śiva-dútas, and also like them a lion's teeth, but otherwise they resemble Vishṇu, being of a blue color, and wearing the Tirunāma on their forehead, arms, and breasts; and round their necks a rosary of Tulasimani; whilst they hold in their four hands, respectively, a Sankha, a Chakra, a battle-axe, and a club. Through these messengers Vishṇu fetches the souls of his faithful devotees into his abode of bliss called Vaikuntha.

3. The Yama-dútas, the messengers of Yama, the king of death and hell, are painted quite black, like demons, with horrible faces and great teeth. In their four hands they carry a trident, a club and many ropes; and in their girdles, daggers. Their business consists in carrying the souls of the wicked into Naraka or hell; but they are not allowed to lay hold on any one before his fixed life-time is elapsed, and the souls of the pious they cannot touch at all. When, however, such die as are neither virtuous nor wicked, then it happens that the messengers of Yama and those of Śiva or Vishṇu come into conflict with each other, each party claiming the indifferent souls."

Dwapara—The third Yuga or age, which lasts 2,400 divine years; these are converted into years of mortals by multiplying them by 360, a year of men being a day of the gods—thus $2,400 \times 360 = 864,000$ mortal years, the duration of the Dwápara or third Yuga. The predominant duties of the four Yugas are said to be austere fervour on the Krita age, knowledge in the Tretá, sacrifice in the Dwápara, and liberality alone in the Kali Yuga. O. S. T., vol. i, p. 39.

Dwaraka—The city of Krishṇa; after he had conquered many difficulties in his position, he solicited a space of twelve furlongs from the ocean, and there he built the city of Dwáraka; defended by high ramparts, and beautiful with gardens and reservoirs of water, crowded with houses and buildings, and splendid as the capital of Indra, Amarávati. After Krishṇa abandoned his mortal body, Arjuna conducted his many wives and all the people from Dwáraka, with tenderness and care. The ocean then rose and submerged the whole of Dwáraka except the dwelling of Krishṇa. The Vishṇu Purána says the sea has never been able to wash that temple away, as Krishṇa still abides there. The Mahábhárata declares that the sea did not spare any part whatever. "It is clear, therefore;" says Professor Wilson, "that when the latter was compiled the temple was not standing, and that it was erected between the date of the compilation and the two Puránas. The present shrine, which is held in great repute, stands at the extremity of the peninsula of Guzerat. It is still an object of pilgrimage; it was so in the reign of Akbar; and has been no doubt, from a remote period."

Dwesha—Hatred; one of the five afflictions of the Pátanjali philosophy.

Dwija—Twice-born; a brahman, whose investiture with the sacred thread constitutes, religiously and metaphorically, their second birth. In this sense it may be applied to the Kshatriya and Vaishya.

Dwimidha—One of the sons of Hastin, founder of Hastinápura.

Dwimurddha—One of the Danavas, a son of Kaṣyapa by Danu.

Dwipas—Insular continents, of which there are seven chief, and with the seven seas are supposed to form alternate concentric circles, viz: 1, Jambu Dwípa, surrounded by a salt sea (Lavaṇa); 2, Plaksha, by a sea of sugar-cane juice, (Ikshu); 3, Sálmali, by a sea of wine, (Surá) ; 4, Kusa, by a sea of clarified butter, or ghee, (Sarpi) ; 5, Krauncha, by a sea of curds, (Dugdha) ; 7, Pushkara, by a sea of fresh water. The whole is surrounded by a circular mountain designated Chakravaligiri. An account of the kings, divisions, inhabitants, &c., of these Dwípas will be found in the Vishṇu Purána, Chap. IV, Book I. The geography of the Puránas, says Prof. Wilson, occurs in most of these works ; and in all the main features, the seven Dwípas, seven seas, the divisions of Jambudwípa, the situation and extent of Meru, and the sub-division of Bharata, is the same. It has been stated that the first rudiments and general outline of this fiction, including the circular mountain, are rabbinical, and may be found in the Talmud.

Dwivida—An Asura, the foe of the friends of the gods, which in the form of an ape, committed great devastation. "The whole world, disordered by this iniquitous monkey, was deprived of sacred study and religious rites, and was greatly afflicted." (V. P.) On one occasion, when Bala Ráma was enjoying himself in the groves of Raivata, the monkey Dwivida came there, threw over the wine and groaned at the company. An encounter followed, in which the monkey struck the Yádava on the breast with his paws. Bala Ráma replied with a blow of his fist upon the forehead of Dwivida, which felled him lifeless to the earth. The crest of the mountain on which he fell was splintered into a hundred pieces by the weight of his body, as if the thunderer had shivered it with his thunderbolt. V. P., &c.

Dwivida—One of the sons of the Aṣvins, famed for his beauty.

Dyaus and Prithivi—Heaven and Earth, seemed to have been very ancient Aryan divinities, and are in many passages of the Rig Veda described as the parents of the other gods. There are several hymns specially devoted to their honour. In the hymns, Heaven and Earth are characterized by a profusion of epithets, not only such as are suggested by their various physical characteristics, as vastness, breadth, profundity, productiveness, unchangeableness, but also by such as are of a moral or spiritual nature, as innocuous or beneficent, wise promoters of righteousness.

While Heaven and Earth are described as the universal parents, they are spoken of in other places as themselves created. Thus it is said in the Rig Veda that 'he who produced heaven and earth must have been the most skilful artizan of all the gods.' Indra also is described as their creator ; as having beautifully fashioned them by his power and skill ; as having bestowed them on his worshippers ; as sustaining and upholding them, &c.

"In other passages we encounter various speculations about their origin. In one hymn the perplexed poet inquires which of these two was the first ? and which the last ? How have they been produced ? Sages who knows ? In another hymn the creation of heaven and earth is ascribed to the sole agency of the god Viṣvakarman. Some are of opinion that the functions which in the older Indian Mythology were assigned to Dyaus, were at a later period transferred to Indra. O. S. T., vol. v., pp. 21—34.

Dyumat—One of the sons of the Rishi Vasishtha, according to the list in the Bhágavata, which differs altogether from that in the Vishṇu Purána.

Dyutimat—One of the ten sons of Priyavrata : three of them adopted a religious life : Priyavrata having divided the earth into seven continents, gave them respectively to his other seven sons. Dyutimat was king of Krauncha-dwipa, where the inhabitants resided without apprehension, associating with the bands of divinities.

E

Earth—The Earth, considered as one of the ancient 'elements,' occupies nearly the same place in all the Puránas. The order is, ether, (ákás) air, (váyu) fire, (tejas) water and earth. The order of Empedocles was ether, fire, earth, water, air. The Puránas describe the earth as having been raised from the lowest regions on the ample tusks of the Varáha (boar) avatar. The Bhágavata states that, when the earth, oppressed by the weight of the mountains, sunk down into the waters, Vishṇu was seen in the sub-terrene regions, or Rasátala, by Hiranyáksha, in the act of carrying it off. The demon claimed the Earth, and defied Vishṇu to combat: and a conflict took place in which Hiranyáksha was slain. There are legends which relate the subjugation of the Earth by the mighty Prithu, when he was invested with universal dominion. Prithu levelled or uprooted mountains; defined boundaries on the irregular surface of the Earth; introduced cultivation, pasture, highways, commerce, in a word, civilization. The Vishṇu Purána states, "This Earth, the mother, the nurse, the receptacle, and nourisher of all existent things, was produced from the sole of the foot of Vishṇu. And thus was born the mighty Prithu, the heroic son of Vena, who was the lord of the Earth, and who, from conciliating the affections of the people, was the first ruler to whom the title of Rája was ascribed.

Five chapters in the Vishṇu Purána are devoted to a description of the Earth; its people and countries. Jamba-dwípa is placed in the centre of the seven great insular continents (see DWIPAS) and in the centre of Jamba-dwípa is the golden mountain Meru—the shape of which is variously described in the different Puránas; though all represent it as if enormous size and great beauty. The apples of the Jamba-tree are as large as elephants; from their expressed juice is formed the Jamba river, the waters of which are drunk by the inhabitants; and in consequence of drinking of that stream they pass their days in content and health, neither exposed to decrepitude or decay. Ample details of the Varshas or countries, are given in most of the Purânas, but they are all of an equally fanciful and extravagant character.

The Vishṇu Purána says, "Sesha bears the entire world like a diadem, upon his head * * * * when Ananta, his eyes rolling with intoxication, yawns, then Earth, with all her woods and seas, and mountains, and rivers, trembles." In another place, "At the end of a thousand periods of four ages the Earth is for the most part exhausted. A total dearth then ensues which lasts a hundred years: and in consequence of the failure of food all beings become languid, and at last entirely perish. The eternal Vishṇu then assumes the character of Rudra the destroyer, and descends to re-unite all his creatures with himself. He enters into the seven rays of the sun; drinks up all the waters of the globe, and causes all moisture to evaporate, thus drying up the whole earth. * * * * * The destroyer of all things, Hari, in the form of Rudra, becomes the scorching breadth of the serpent Sésha, and thereby reduces Pátáḷa to ashes. The great fire, when it has burnt all the divisions of Pátála proceeds to the earth, and consumes it also." V. P., 632.

Ear-rings—Among the various articles produced at the churning of the ocean, ear-rings are enumerated; these were taken by Indra and given to Aditi; the daughter of Daksha and wife of Kaṣyapa. The ear-rings were stolen by Naraka, son of the Earth, and conveyed by him to Prágjyotisha, "an impregnable, formidable and unassailable city of the Asuras." Krishṇa attacked the place, overcame all opposition, slew Naraka, recovered the jewelled ear-rings, and returning to the heaven of the gods, restored them to Aditi, who praised Krishṇa in verses which contain some remarkable sentiments. They will be found in the V. P., 584-5.

Egg of the World—In the Rig Veda the Supreme Spirit is represented as producing an egg, and from the egg is evolved a world. At a later period, Brahma is set forth as depositing in the primordial waters an egg shining like gold. The Puránas all contain accounts of the first aggregation of the elements in the form of an egg. The Vishṇu Purána says, "This vast egg, compounded of the elements, and resting on the waters, was the excellent natural abode of Vishṇu in the form of Brahmá ; and there Vishṇu, the lord of the universe, whose essence is inscrutable, assumed a perceptible form, and even he himself abided in it in the character of Brahmá. " Its womb, vast as the mountain Meru, was composed of the mountains ; and the mighty oceans were the waters that filled its cavity. In that egg, O Brahman, were the continents and seas and mountains, the planets and divisions of the universe, the gods, the demons, and mankind. And this egg was externally invested by seven natural envelopes, or by water, air, fire, ether, and Ahankára the origin of the elements, each tenfold the extent of that which it invested ; next came the principle of intelligence ; and, finally, the whole was surrounded by the indiscreet principle : resembling thus the cocoanut, filled interiorly with pulp, and exteriorly covered by husk and rind."

" It seems impossible," says Professor Wilson, " not to refer this notion to the same origin as the widely diffused opinion of antiquity, of the first manifestation of the world in the form of an egg." " It seems" says Bryant, " to have been a favourite symbol, and very ancient, and we find it adopted among many nations." Traces of it occur among the Syrians, Persians and Egyptians ; and besides the Orphic egg amongst the Greeks, and that described by Aristophanes, part of the ceremony in the Dionysiaca and other mysteries, consisted of the consecration of an egg, by which, according to Porphyry, was signified the world."

" The shell of the mundane egg is said to be outside of the seven spheres of which this system is composed : In the V. P. ii, 7, 19 it is said

" These seven spheres have been desçribed by me ; and there are also seven Pátáḷas ; this is the extent of Brahmá's egg. The whole is surrounded by the shell of the egg at the sides, above and below, just as the seed of the wood apple is covered by the rind."

This system, however, it appears is only a very small part of the whole of the universe ; in verse 24 it is added

" There are thousands and ten thousands of thousands of such mundane eggs ; nay hundreds of millions of millions."

"Indian mythology, when striving after sublimity, and seeking to excite astonishment, often displays an extravagant and puerile facility in the fabrication of large numbers. But in the sentence last quoted, its conjectures are substantially in unison with the discoveries of modern astronomy ; or rather they are inadequate representations of the simple truth, as no figures can express the contents of infinite space." Muir, O. S. T., vol. i, p. 504.

Eka—"The one :" a synonym of Mahat, from its singleness. See Mahat.

Ekachakra—One of the renowned Danavas, son of Danu and Kaṣyapa.

Ekachakra—The city in which Bhíma and his mother and brethren were advised by the sage Vyása to reside ; they dwelt there for a long time in the house of a brahman. It was in this city that Bhíma destroyed the cannibal Vaka. "In the neighbourhood there lived a giant,—the same sort of being as the modern earth-goddess of Orissa ; that is a demon who feeds on human beings." One day, it is said, the Páṇdavas heard a great noise in the house in which they were dwelling, and enquiring into its cause, were told that the demon compelled the king of Ekachakra every day to send him a great quantity of provisions ; and that Vaka daily devoured the man as well as the provisions ; and that on that very day the family of the brahman was required to supply the man. While reposing in an inner apartment the Páṇdavas overheard the father, the mother, and the daughter, each urging a separate claim to be allowed to suffer for the rest.

The father commences, saying, that never would he be so base as to give a victim from his house and consent himself to live ; but still he expresses anxiety at not knowing how to provide a place of refuge for his wife, daughter, and little son, after his removal. He cannot, he says, surrender his faithful wife,—the sweet friend given to him by the gods ; nor his daughter,—whom Brahma made to be a bride, and the mother of heroes ; not yet his son : ...but if he offer himself, sorrow will pursue him in the world to come, and his abandoned wife and children will be unable to live without him.

The wife next speaks, and chides her husband for yielding to grief, like one of lowly caste; for, whoever knows the Vedas, must know that—

"Fate, inevitable, orders;—all must yield to death in turn.
Hence the doom, th' irrevocable,—it beseems not thee to mourn.
Man hath wife, and son, and daughter,—for the joy of his own heart;
Wherefore, wisely check thy sorrow,—it is I must hence depart.
'Tis the wife's most holy duty,—law on earth without repeal,—
That her life she offer freely,—when demands her husband's weal."

She goes on to argue, that he can support and guard the children when she is gone, but that she would have no power to guard and support them without him. Deprived of his protection, "rude and reckless men," she says, would come seeking their blameless daughter; and helpless, and beset on every side, she would be unable to check the suit of Sudra lovers... She concludes, by saying, that her honored husband will find another wife, to whom he will be as gentle and kind as he has been to her.

"Hearing thus his wife, the husband fondly clasp'd her to his breast:
And their tears they pour'd together—by their mutual grief oppress'd."

When the daughter overheard the troubled discourse of her parents, she put in her claim to be the offered victim; for, if they died before her, she would sink to bitterest misery: but, if she died to preserve them, she would "then become immortal, and partake of bliss divine."

Whilst they were all thus weeping, the little son opened wide his eyes, and lisped out in broken accents:

"Weep not, father, weep not, mother; oh, my sister, weep not so
First to one, and then to th' other,—smiling went he to and fro.
Then a blade of spear-grass lifting, thus in bolder glee he said:
With this spear-grass will I kill him—this man-eating giant—dead.'
Though o'erpowered with bitterest sorrow, as they heard their prattling boy,
Stole into the parents' bosom—mute and inexpressive joy."

Happily the child's chivalry was not required. After some discussion the brahman reluctantly consented that Bhíma should go himself to the Asura, and he set out with the ordained quantity of provisions, and went on until he came to the banyan tree under which Vaka was accustomed to eat his meals. Bhíma then ate up all the victuals that were in the waggon and refilled it with dirt.

Vaka then came forward ravenous with hunger, and finding nothing but dirt, struck Bhíma in a great rage. They then tore up large trees by the roots and fought together until not a tree was left. They then fought with their fists until the Asura was spent; when Bhíma seized him by the legs and rent him asunder. The date of the story is fixed in the age of Buddhism. Ekachakra has been identified as the modern Arrah. It was occupied by Brahmans who may be regarded as the later representatives of the Aryan population, while the jungle was evidently in the possession of the Asuras or Aborigines.*

Ekadanta—The single-tusked. A name of Gaṇeṣa.

Ekadasi—A ceremony performed on the eleventh day after the death of a relative. During the previous ten days the relatives are supposed to be mourning, and in a state of *asaucha* or impurities, so that no one can communicate with them. When Ekádaṣí is performed the period of uncleanness ceases.

Ekádaṣí is also the eleventh day after the new and full moon, observed by the Vaishnavas as a fast day.

Ekalavya—The king of the Nishádas; he was regarded as invincible by mortals but was attacked and slain by Krishṇa.

Ekapadakas—A nickname or term of derision, found in the geographical accounts of the Puránas; it means one-footed or rather, one-slippered, and is probably an exaggeration of national ugliness, or allusion to some peculiar custom, in the people to whom the term is applied. Professor Wilson thinks that such terms, of which there are many in the Puránas, may have furnished the Mandevilles of ancient and modern times, with some of their monsters.

Ekaparna, Ekapatala—Two of the daughters of Mená, the eminent wife of the great mountain Himavat. They performed great austerities such as could not be accomplished by gods or Dánavas, and distressed both the stationary and moving worlds. Ekaparná (One leaf) fed upon one leaf. Ekapáṭalá took only one páṭalá (Bignonia) for her food. The former was given as a wife

* Mrs. Manning. A. & M. I.

to Asita Devala, the wise teacher of the Yoga. The latter was in like manner bestowed on Jaigishavya. Muir, O. S. T., vol. iv, p. 367.

Ekashtaka—The daughter of Prajápati, who through practising austere-fervour, became the mother of the glorious Indra, and of Soma. According to other authorities, Indra is one of the sons of Kaṣyapa and Dakshâyani. O. S. T., vol. v, p. 80.

Ekavinsa—The name of the collection of hymns created from the northern mouth of Brahma.

Ekoddishta-sradda—Obsequial offerings on account of a kinsman recently deceased. These are performed monthly. The proper period of mourning is ten days, on each of which offerings of cakes and libations of water are to be made to the deceased, augmenting the number of cakes each day, so that in the last day ten cakes are presented.

Elapatra—One of the progeny of Kadru, a powerful serpent, with many heads.

Elephanta—" A small island about 7 miles. in circumference, situated between the island of Bombay and the Mahratta shore, from which it is distant 5 miles, and 7 miles from the castle of Bombay. Its name among the natives is Gorapori ; that by which it is known to Europeans was derived from the figure of an elephant twice the size of life cut out of the solid black rock on the acclivity of a hill about 250 yards from the landing-place. This figure is now completely dilapidated. At a short distance from the elephant stands the figure of a horse, also cut out of the rock. On this island is a remarkable temple-cave. The entrance to this cave, or temple, occurs about half way up the steep ascent of the mountain or rock out of which it is excavated. Its length, measuring from the entrance, which is on the north side, is 130 feet, and its breadth 123 feet ; the floor not being level the height varies from 15 to 17½ feet. The roof was supported by 26 pillars and 8 pilasters, disposed in four rows ; but several of the pillars are broken. Each column stands upon a square pedestal and is fluted, but instead of being cylindrical is gradually enlarged towards the middle. Above the tops of the columns a kind of ridge has been cut to resemble a beam about 12 inches square, and this is richly carved. Along the sides of the temple are carved between 40 and 50 colossal figures varying in height from 12 to 15 feet; none of them are entirely detached from the wall. On the south side, facing, the main entrance, is an enormous bust with three faces, which is supposed to represent the triple deity, Brahma, Vishṇu, and Śiva. The centre face is 5 feet in length. At the west side of the temple is a recess, 20 feet square, having in the centre an altar. The entrance to this recess is guarded by eight naked figures, each 13½ feet high, sculptured in a superior manner. The origin of this cave is quite unknown: it is frequently visited by devotees for the purpose of offering prayers and oblations.—*English Encyclopædia*.

Ellamma—One of the grámadévatas in Southern India—identified with Renuká, wife of Jamadagni, mother of Parasuráma, Ellammá is represented in a sitting posture, with a red skin, a fiery face, and four arms and hands. If any one is bitten by a poisonous serpent he calls on Ellamma for aid. Fishermen when in danger call on Ellamma and make vows to her.

Ellora—A town in the province of Aurangabad, and near to the city of Dowlatabad. In one instance, about a mile to the eastward of the village the side of a great mountain has been excavated, so as to give a level floor 150 feet wide by 270 feet in length. In the centre stands the rock-cut temple called Kailâs, similar in form to the Pagoda at Tanjore It is between 80 and 90 feet high, and is preceded by a large square porch, supported by sixteen columns. In the front of this stands a detached porch, reached by a bridge; and again, in front of the whole, a gateway, connected with the last porch by a rock-cut bridge, and flanked on either side by pillars or deepdans (which word is literally lamp-post.) Two elephants, the size of life, are also mentioned; and all around the court are cloisters, with cells. And the whole,—pillars, cloisters, halls, bridges, and vimâna,—are sculptured out of the rock.—*Mrs. Manning. A. and M. I., Vol. I, p.* 420.

Elu—A dialect of the ancient Singhalese, which differs from the colloquial Singhalese, rather in style than in structure, having been liberally enriched by incorporations from Sanskrit and Pali. Mr. Spence Hardy mentions a number of Buddhist works which are written in Elu.

Emusha—The name of the boar in which Prajápati became incarnate when he raised up the earth and extended it. "Formerly this earth was only so large, of the size of a span. A boar called Emúsha, raised her up. Her lord Prajápati, therefore, prospers him with (the gift of) this pair, the object of his desire, and makes him complete." O. S. T., vol. i, p. 53.

Ettaia—A place in the North-west of India, said to be the scene of a conflict between Krishṇa and Kali; where some fine ruins still exist.

Expiation—The Vishṇu Purána says that "suitable acts of expiation have been enjoined by the great sages for every kind of crime. Arduous penances for great sins, trifling ones for minor offences, have been propounded by Swáyambhuva and others: but reliance upon Krishṇa is far better than any such expiatory acts, as religious austerity or the like. Let any one who repents of the sin of which he may have been culpable, have recourse to this best of all expiations, remembrance of Hari; by addressing his thoughts to Nárayaṇa at dawn, at night, at sunset, and midday, a man shall be quickly cleansed from all guilt: the whole heap of worldly sorrows is dispersed by meditating on Hari; and his worshipper, looking upon heavenly fruition as an impediment to felicity, obtains final emancipation."

"This remembrance of Vishṇu," says Professor Wilson, "is the frequent reiteration of all his names; hence the lower orders of Hindus procure a starling or parrot, that in the act of teaching it to cry Ráma or Krishṇa or Radhá, they may themselves repeat these appellations; the simple recitation of which, even if accidentally, irreverently, or reluctantly performed, is meritorious."

F

Faith—The paramount efficacy of faith is a tenet of the Vedánta school; particularly that branch of it which follows the authority of the Bhagavat Gíta. In that work, and in many of the Puránas, passages relating to faith constantly recur.

Fakir—The word Fakír is derived from an Arabic term signifying "poor people," and belongs strictly to those who profess Mahomedanism, not to Hindus. But the word is sometimes used by Europeans to designate all classes of monks, who subject themselves to austerities and mortifications. Some of them vow to preserve a standing posture during their whole lives, supported only by a stick or rope under their armpits. Some mangle their bodies with scourges or knives. Others wander about in companies, telling fortunes, and in other ways imposing on the people. Some go about as mendicants asking alms in the name of God. *See* Sanyasi.

Feringahi—A name of Párvati or Devi.

Fever—In the Vishṇu Purána, Fever is personified, as an emanation from Maheṣwara, having three feet and three heads, (alluding, says Dr. Wilson, to the three stages of febrile paroxysms, or to the recurrence of tertian ague). Fever fought desperately with Vishṇu in defence of the city of Báṇa. Baladeva, upon whom his ashes were scattered, was seized with burning heat, and his eyelids trembled: but he obtained relief by clinging to the body of Krishṇa. The fever emanating from Śiva was quickly expelled from the person of Krishṇa by fever which he himself engendered. Brahma beholding the impersonated malady, bewildered by the beating inflicted by the arms of the deity, entreated the latter to desist; and the foe of Madhu refrained, and absorbed into himself the fever he had created. The rival fever then departed, saying to Krishṇa, "Those men who call to memory the combat between us shall be for ever exempt from febrile disease."

Fires—According to the Vishṇu Purána there are forty-nine fires. The Agni named Abhimání, who is the eldest born of Brahmá, had, by Swáhá, three sons of surpassing brilliancy, Pávaka Pavámána, and Suchi, who drinks up water : they had forty-five sons, who, with the original son of Brahmá and his three descendants, constitute the forty-nine fires. According to the Vaya Purána, Pávaka is electric, or Vaidyuta fire ; Pavamána is that produced by friction, or Nirmathyaya, and Suchi is solar, or Saura fire. The Bhágavata explains these different fires to be so many appellations of fire employed in the invocations with which different oblations to fire are offered in the ritual of the Vedas.

Fire-Sacrificial—The ceremony of consecrating the fire and hallowing the sacrificial implements is the groundwork of all religious acts amongst the Hindus, and may therefore be particularly described :—" First, the priest smears with cow-dung a level piece of ground four cubits square, free from all impurities, and sheltered by a shed. Having bathed and sipped water, he sits down with his face towards the east, and places a vessel of water with *kuśa* grass on his left ; then, dropping his right knee, and resting on the span of his left hand, he draws with a root of *kuśa* grass a line, one span or twelve fingers long, and directed towards the east. From the nearest extremity of this line he draws another at right angles to it, twenty-one fingers long, and directed towards the north. Upon this line he draws three others, parallel to the first, equal to it in length, and distant seven fingers from each other. The first line is really, or figuratively, made a yellow line, and is sacred to the earth ; the second is red, and sacred to fire ; the third black, and sacred to *Brahma* the creator ; the fourth blue, and sacred to *Indra*, the regent of the firmament ; the fifth white, and sacred to Sóma. He next gathers up the dust from thé edges of these lines, and throws it away towards the north-east, saying, " What was [herein] bad, is cast away :" and he concludes by sprinkling water on the several lines.

Having thus prepared the ground for the reception of the sacrificial fire, he takes a lighted ember out of the covered vessel which contains the fire, and throws it away, saying, "I dismiss far 'away carnivorous fire ; may it go to the realm of *Yama*, bearing "sin [hence]." He then places the fire before him, saying, "Earth! Sky! Heaven!" and adding, "this other [harmless] fire "alone remains here; well knowing [its office], may it convey my "oblation to the gods." He then denominates the fire according to the purpose for which he prepares it, saying, "Fire! thou art named so and so;" and he concludes this part of the ceremony by silently burning a log of wood, one span long and smeared with clarified butter.

He next proceeds to place the *Brahman* or superintending priest. Upon very solemn occasions, a learned *Brahman* does actually discharge the functions of superintending priest; but, in general, a bundle containing fifty blades of *kuśa* grass is placed to represent the *Brahman*. The officiating priest takes up the vessel of water, and walks round the fire keeping his right side turned towards it: he then pours water near it, directing the stream towards the east; he spreads *kuśa* grass thereon; and crossing his right knee over his left without sitting down, he takes up a single blade of grass between the thumb and ring finger of his left hand, and throws it away towards the south-west corner of the shed, saying, "What was herein bad, is cast away." Next, touching the water, resting the sole of his right foot on his left ankle, and sprinkling the grass with water, he places the *Brahman* on it, saying, "Sit on [this] seat until [thy] fee [be paid thee]." The officiating priest then returns by the same road by which he went round the fire; and sitting down again with his face towards the east, names the earth inaudibly.

If any profane word have been spoken during the preceding ceremony, atonement must be now made by pronouncing this text: "Thrice did *Vishṅu* step, and at three strides traversed the "universe: happily was his foot placed on the dusty [earth]." "The meaning is, since the earth has been purified by the contact of *Vishṅu's* foot, may she (the earth so purified) atone for any profane word spoken during this ceremony.

If it be intended to make oblations of rice mixed with milk, curds, and butter, this too is the proper time for mixing them; and the priest afterwards proceeds to name the earth in the following prayer, which he pronounces with downcast look, resting both hands on the ground: "We adore this earth, this auspicious and most excellent earth: do thou, O fire! resist [our] enemies. Thou dost take [on thee] the power [and office] of other [deities]."

With blades of *kuśa* grass held in his right hand, he must next strew leaves of the same grass on three sides of the fire, arranging them regularly, so that the tip of one row shall cover the roots of the other. He begins with the eastern side, and at three times strews grass there, to cover the whole space from north to south; and in like manner distributes grass on the southern and western sides. He then blesses the ten regions of space; and rising a little, puts some wood on the fire with a ladle-full of clarified butter, while he meditates in silence on Brahma, the lord of creatures.

The priest then takes up two leaves of *kuśa* grass, and with another blade of the same grass cuts off the length of a span, saying, "Pure leaves! be sacred to Vishṇu;" and throws them into a vessel of copper or other metal. Again he takes two leaves of grass, and holding the tips between the thumb and ring finger of his right hand, and the roots between the thumb and ring finger of his left, and crossing his right hand over his left, he takes up clarified butter on the curvature of the grass, and thus silently casts some into the fire three several times. He then sprinkles both the leaves with water, and throws them away. He afterwards sprinkles with water the vessel containing clarified butter, and puts it on the fire, and takes it off again, three times, and thus concludes the ceremony of hallowing the butter; during the course of which, while he holds the leaves of grass in both hands, he recites this prayer: "May the divine generator [*Vishnu*] purify thee by means of [this] faultless pure leaf; and may the sun do so, by means of [his] rays of light: be this oblation efficacious."

The priest must next hallow the wooden ladle by thrice turning therein his fore-finger and thumb, describing with their tips the figure of 7 in the inside, and the figure of 9 on the outside of the bowl of the ladle. Then dropping his right knee, he sprinkles water from the palms of his hands on the whole southern side of the fire, from west to east, saying, "*Aditi!* [mother of the gods!] grant me thy approbation." He does the same on the whole western side, from south to north, saying, "*Anumati!* grant me thy approbation;" and on the northern side, saying, "*Saraswati!* grant me thy approbation." And lastly he sprinkles water all round the fire, while he pronounces this text, "Generous sun! approve this rite; approve the performer of it, that he may share its reward. May the celestial luminary, which purifies the intellectual soul, purify our minds. May the lord of speech make our prayers acceptable."

Holding *kuśa* grass in both hands, he then recites an expiatory prayer; and throwing away the grass, he thus finishes the hallowing of the sacrificial implements: a ceremony which necessarily precedes all other religious rites.

He next makes oblations to fire, with such ceremonies, and in such form as are adapted to the religious rite which is intended to to be subsequently performed. The sacrifice, with the three mysterious words, usually precedes and follows the particular sacrifice which is suited to the occasion; being most generally practised, it will be the most proper specimen of the form in which oblations are made.

Having silently burnt a log of wood smeared with clarified butter, the priest makes three oblations, by pouring each time a ladle-full of butter on the fire, saying, "Earth! be this oblation efficacious:" "Sky! be this oblation efficacious:" "Heaven! be this oblation efficacious." On some occasions he makes a fourth offering in a similar mode, saying, "Earth! Sky! Heaven! be this oblation efficacious." If it be requisite to offer a mixture of rice, milk, curds and butter, this is now done; and the oblations, accompanied with the names of the three worlds, are repeated.

There are five fires, which were overcome and demolished by Vishṇu. Their names are the Áhavaniya, Gárhapatya, Dakshina, Sabhya and Ávasathya; of which the three first have a religious, and the other two a secular character. The first is a fire prepared for oblations at an occasional sacrifice: the second is the household fire, to be perpetually maintained: the third is a sacrificial fire, in the centre of the other two, and placed to the south: the Sabhya is a fire lighted to warm a party: and the Ávasathya, the common domestic or culinary fire. Manu, iii, 100, 185, and Kullúka Bhatta's explanation.

Brahmans who devote themselves to the priesthood have to maintain a perpetual fire. They have also to worship fire, making an oblation to it with this prayer : Fire ! seven are thy fuels ; seven thy tongues ; seven thy holy sages ; seven thy beloved abodes ; seven ways do seven sacrifices worship thee. Thy sources are seven. Be content with this clarified butter. May this oblation be efficacious.

The seven tongues of fire are enumerated *Pravaha, Àvaha, Udvaha, Samvaha, Vivaha, Parivaha, Nivaha,* all of which imply the power of conveying oblations, to the deities to whom offerings are made. Fire, like the sun itself, is supposed to emit seven rays ; this perhaps may account for the number seven being so often repeated."—*Colebrooke's Essays, vol. I, p.* 153.

Free-will—The *Mimánsa* philosophy in effect denies the doctrine of free-will ; but endeavours to reconcile the existence of moral evil under the government of an all-wise, all-powerful and benevolent Providence, with the absence of free-will, by assuming the past eternity of the universe, and the infinite renewals of worlds, into which every individual being has brought the pre-dispositions contracted by him in earlier states, and so retrospectively, without beginning or limit.

G

Gabhastimat—One of the nine divisions of Bharata varsha. Also the name of one of the divisions of Patáḷa.

Gachchas—One of the peoples enumerated in the Vishṇu Purána, but not identified.

Gada—1, A son of Vasudeva by Bhadra; 2, The name of Bhíma's formidable weapon.

Gadhi—An incarnation of Indra, born as the son of Rája Kuṣámba. Kuṣámba being desirous of a son, engaged in devout penance to obtain one who should be equal to Indra. Observing the intensity of his devotions, Indra was alarmed, lest a prince of power like his own should be engendered, and determined therefore to take upon himself the character of Kuṣámba's son, Gádhi, the father of Viṣwámitra.

Gahvaras—Dwellers in mountain caves. The mountains from Cabul to Bamian furnish numerous instances of cavern habitations.

Gajavithi—The second division (or Vithi) of the lunar mansions, in the northern Avaṣhtáṇa.

Galava—A Teacher of the white Yajush, a branch of the Yajur Veda, imparted by the sun in the form of a horse.

Games—There are many public games described in the various Puránas; and an account of each will be found under its native name.

Gananathas—Messengers of the gods. See Dútas.

Ganapatyas—The worshippers of Gaṇéṣa, or Gaṇapati; all the Hindus in fact, worship this deity as the obviator of impediments, and never set off on a journey without invoking his protection.

Gandaki—A large river in Oude.

Gandhamadana—A high mountain south of the great mount Meru; an extensive forest of the same name is placed in close proximity to the mountain.

Gandhamadana—One of the generals in Rama's army at the siege of Lanka; he was wounded by the magical weapons of Indrajit and left on the field for dead, but was restored to life by the medicinal herbs brought by Hanuman from the golden hill Rishaba, on the crest of Kailása. Although he is represented as being a large and powerful monkey, he is said to have been the son of Kuvera, the god of wealth

"Of Gandhamádan brave and bold
The father was the Lord of gold."

Gandhamojavaha—A son of Śwaphalka, by his wife Gándiní.

Gandhara—A prince, the son of Aradwat, a descendant of Druhyu. Also, a large country in the west of the Indus, named after Gándhára, famous for its breed of horses; now Kandahar.

Gandharba—One of the nine divisions, or dwípas, of Bharata Varsha.

Gandharbas or Gandharvas—(Southey's Glendoveer's.) A race born from Bramhá, described in the Vishṇu Purána as "born imbibing melody; drinking of the goddess of speech they were born, and thence their appellation." (Gam dhayantah). They are a species of demi-gods or angels, the musicians of heaven, inhabiting Indra loka, the paradise of the deities, and witnesses of the actions of men. They form the orchestra at the banquet of the gods. In the creation of the second Manwantara they are called the illustrious Gandharbas, the children of Arishtá and Kaṣyapa. In the Vishṇu Purána it is said, "in the regions below the earth, the Gandharbas, called Maneyas (or sons of the Muni Kaṣyapa) who were sixty millions in number, had defeated the tribes of the Nágas or snake-gods, and seized upon their most precious jewels, and usurped their dominion." Narmadá, the personified Nerbudda river, was the sister of the Nágas, and on her aid being solicited, she went to Purukutsa, and conducted him to the regions below the earth, where, being filled with the might of the deity, he destroyed the Gandharbas. They originally belong to the latter Epic period, but figure more prominently in the Puránas.

"The Gandharvas or heavenly bards had originally a warlike character, but were afterwards reduced to the office of celestial musicians cheering the banquets of the gods. Dr. Kuhn has shown their identity with the Centaurs in name, origin, and attributes."—*Gorresio.*

Gandharba loka—The region of celestial spirits, the sphere or lóka above the earth to which Súdras are elevated after death.

Gandharba marriage—A form of wedlock requiring no public ceremony, but which is nevertheless, recognised in ancient Hindu law as legal for kings and warriors.

Gandharba veda—The drama, and the arts of music, dancing, etc., of which the Muni Bhárata was the author; and the Artha Sastrum, or Science of Government, as laid down first by Vrihaspati.

Gandharbi—The daughter of Surabhi, and parent of horses.

Gandhari—The daughter of the Rája of Gandhára, who was married to the Mahárája Dhritárástra; she blindfolded herself on hearing that he was blind. She was the mother of the Kauravas, and is represented as a woman of superior character and abilities. She was summoned to the Council to try to overcome the obduracy of her eldest son Duryodhana. The Mahábhárata relates an affecting interview which she had with Krishṇa after the slaughter of her sons in the great war.

Gandini—Daughter of Káṣírájá: the following legend of her birth is told in the V. P., "when the time of delivery arrived the child issued not from the womb, twelve years passed away and still the girl was unborn. Then Káṣírája spoke to the child 'Daughter, why is your birth thus delayed? come forth. I desire to behold you; why do you inflict this protracted suffering upon your mother? Thus addressed, the infant answered, if, father, you will present a cow every day to the brahmans I shall at the end of three years more be born.' The king accordingly presented daily a cow to the brahmans, and at the end of three years the damsel came into the world. Her father called her Gándiní, and he subsequently gave her to Swaphalka when he came to his palace. Gándiní as long as she lived, gave a cow to the brahmans every day."

Gandiva—The name of a miraculous bow which Arjuna received as a present from Agni the god of fire.

Gandusha—One of the ten sons of Súra, and brother of Vásudeva.

Ganesa—The son of *Siva* and *Párvati* the god of good luck, and remover of difficulties and obstacles; addressed at the commencement of all undertakings, and at the opening of all compositions. He is thus the patron of learning. He is called *Ganésa,* as presiding over the troop of deities attendant on Śiva—the *ganas,* or companies of celestials in Śiva's paradise. He is also designated Vináyaka, the god of difficulties. Ganésa is represented by an outrageous figure, half-man and half-elephant, in a sitting posture, with a large belly. His head is that of an elephant, and on it he wears a crown, while his ears are adorned with jewels and his forehead with sacred ashes; of his four arms he elevates two, holding in the left hand a rope and in the right an elephant goad. In his other two hands he holds in the right, a piece of his own elephant's tooth which he once broke himself in a rage, and in the left, a pancake; he is said to be fond of pancakes. His image stands in almost every house, and is worshipped by men and women, with offerings and all the prescribed ceremonies, especially when they are about to begin something important. This eminent position was assigned him as a compensation for the strange head he wears, which was put upon his shoulders when he lost his own, in infancy, by a look of the celestial Sáni—the Hindú Saturn. The goddess, seeing her child headless, was overwhelmed with grief, and would have destroyed Sáni, but Brahma prevented her, telling Sáni to bring the head of the first animal he should find lying with its head northwards. He found an elephant in this position, cut off its head, and fixed it on Ganésa, who then assumed the shape he at present wears. Durgá was but little soothed when she saw her son with an elephant's head; but, to pacify her,

Brahma said that, amongst the worship of all the gods, that of Ganésa should for ever have the preference. Shop-keepers and others paint the name or image of this god over the doors of their shops or houses, expecting from his favour protection and success. He is worshipped especially at the commencement of a wedding, as well as when the bride is presented to the bridegroom. No public festivals, however, in honour of Ganésa are held, nor any temples dedicated to him in Bengal, though stone images of the god are worshipped in the temples on the banks of the Ganges at Benares.

Sir William Jones calls Ganésa the god of wisdom, referring, as a proof, to his having an elephant's head. The Hindús, however, in general, consider the elephant a stupid animal; and to be called "as stupid as an elephant" is a bitter taunt. He corresponds rather to the Roman Janus. In the south Ganésa is usually termed Vigneṣvara as he can prevent literary fame, if his worship be neglected.

When Paraṣuráma, who was a favorite disciple of Śiva, went to Kailasa to visit his master, on arriving at the inner apartments, his entrance was opposed by Gaṇéṣa, as his father was asleep. Paraṣuráma nevertheless urged his way, and the parties came to blows. Gaṇéṣa had at first the advantage, seizing Paraṣuráma in his trunk, and giving him a twirl that left him sick and senseless; on recovering, Ráma threw his axe at Gaṇéṣa, who recognizing it as his father's weapon (Śiva having given it to Paraṣuráma) received it with all humility upon one of his tusks, which it immediately severed, and hence Gaṇéṣa has but one tusk, and is known by the names Ekadanba and Ekadanshtra, (the single-tusked).—*Wilson's Works, Vol. III, p.* 107.

Ganesa—A distinguished Hindu mathematician and astronomer who lived in A. D. 1520.

Ganesa-upa-Purana—The main subject of this work is the greatness of Ganésa; and prayers and formulæ appropriated to him are abundantly detailed. It appears to be a work originating with the Ganapatya sect, or followers of Ganésa. *Preface to Vishnu Purána.*

Ganga—The following is a brief summary of the origin of the Ganges, as detailed in several sections of the first part of the Rámáyana. Ganga was the daughter of Himavat king of mountains, and given by him to the gods.

Ságara king of Ayódhya had by one of his wives sixty thousand sons. Whilst performing the horse sacrifice, the horse was stolen. He commanded his sons to go and search for it. Not finding it on the earth, they dug down to Pátála, where they found the horse feeding, and Kapila Muni near it in profound meditation. On being charged with the theft, he by one glance reduced them all to ashes. On account of their long absence, Ságara sent his grandson, Ansumat, to seek for them. He found their ashes, and the horse feeding near them. Unable to find water to pour on the ashes, he was directed by Kapila (who was a minor incarnation of Vishṇu,) not to pour common water upon them, but now to take the horse and complete his grandfather's sacrifice ; and be assured that his (Ansumat's) grandson should obtain for their ashes the heavenly Ganges. Ságara reigned 30,000 years ; Ansumat 32,000 ; his son Dilípa 30,000 ; his grandson Bhagíratha intent, as his ancestors had been, on bringing down the Ganges, persevered in a long course of austerities. After 1000 years Brahma signified his pleasure by commanding him to ask a boon. He begged that the sons of Ságara might obtain water for their funeral rites ; that, their ashes being wetted by the celestial Ganges, they might ascend to heaven. Brahma granted his request on condition that he prevailed on Śiva to break the fall of the waters ; else the earth would be washed away.

By further austerities he propitiated Śiva, who engaged to receive the goddess, and commanded her to descend. In anger she resolved to bear him down by her stream ; but he, aware of her proud resolve, detained her in his hair. When Bhagíratha applied to him for the waters, Śiva reminded him that his request was only that he should "receive" the Ganges. Bhagíratha engaged in further austerities, and Śiva being pleased with them discharged the waters from his locks in seven streams ; one of which followed the king. As he led the way in a splendid chariot, the Ganges followed ; but, overflowing a sacrifice which Jahnu was performing, the enraged Muni drank up the whole, but was afterwards prevailed upon to discharge it from his ear. Thence the stream followed the king to Pátála, washed the ashes, and liberated his ancestors the sons of Ságara.

Gangadwara—A sacred spot near Himaván, frequented by the Rishis. It is the place where the Ganges descends to the plains, and celebrated as the scene of Daksha's great sacrifice. It is now called Haridwár.

Gara—One of the five sons of Usínara, a descendant of Anu.

Garddhabas, Garddhabhins—A race of kings in the west of India, but not yet satisfactorily identified, though many learned conjectures have been made respecting them.

Garga—An ancient sage, who having propitiated Sesha, acquired from him a knowledge of the principles of astronomical science, of the planets, and of the good and evil denoted by the aspects of the heavens. He is one of the oldest writers on Astronomy amongst the Hindus. According to Mr. Bentley his Sanhita dates 548 B. C. The initiatory rites of Krishṇa and Rama were performed by the sage Garga, who was sent to Gokula by Vasudeva for that purpose. In the Bhágavata Garga describes himself as the Purohita or family priest of the Yádavas. Garga was also the name of one of the sons of Bhavanmanyu.

Gargabhumi, Gargya—Two of the descendants of Alarka, according to the list in the Váyu Purána.

Gargya—A disciple of Bashkali, and teacher of the Rig Veda ; also a Brahman, who, through arduous penance, living upon iron sand for twelve years, became the father of the hero Kálayavana.

Gargya—An etymologist and grammarian of much celebrity in Sanscrit Literature.

Gargyas—The descendants of Gargya, who although Kshatriyas by birth became Brahmans. Professor Wilson says that all the authorities concur in this statement ; thus furnishing an additional instance of one caste proceeding from another.

Garmanas—Hindu or Buddhist priests mentioned by the geographer Strabo. They are represented as feeding on fruits, and wearing only a covering made of the bark of a tree.

Garuda—The king of the feathered tribes and the remorseless enemy of the serpent race. He was the son of Kaṣyapa and Vinatá. Garuda is always represented as the bird on which Vishṇu is carried and described as something between a man and a bird. Garuda is the vehicle of Krishṇa, appearing whenever he is wanted, and conveying his master with incredible speed to the most distant localities. When Krishṇa recovered the jewel mountain, he placed it, with the umbrella of Varuna, upon Garuda, and mounting him himself, he set off to the heaven of the gods to restore the ear-rings of Adití. Garuda is represented as a large white-necked kite or eagle. On the walls of many Vaishnava temples he is represented by the figure of a young man seated, with the palms of the hands closed, and fingers pointed upwards, denoting reverence. "He may be compared with the Símurgh of the Persians, the Anka of the Arabs, the Griffin of chivalry, the Phœnix of Egypt, and the bird that sits upon the ash Yggdrasil of the Edda."—*Griffiths.*

Garuda Purana—Professor Wilson doubts whether a genuine Garuda Puráṇa exists. The one he examined contained no account of the birth of Garuda. Only a brief notice of the creation; and the greater part being occupied with a description of Vratas, or religious observances, of holidays, of sacred places, &c. It contained also treatises on astrology, palmistry, precious stones, and medicine.

Garutwanta—A name of Garuda.

Gathin—The same as Gádhi, q. v.

Gati—(Movement.) An allegorical personage, one of the daughters of Devahúti, and wife of Pulaka.

Gatra—One of the seven pure sages, a son of Vaṣishta.

Gatravat—A son of Krishṇa by Lakshmaṇá.

Gauri—The name of Párvati as a girl before she became the bride of Śiva. Also the name of a wife of Virajas. The wife of

Yuvanáșwas was named Gauri, and having incurred the imprecation of her husband became the Báhudú river.

Gautama Sakya Sinha—See *Buddha*.

Gautama—The founder of the Nyáya school of philosophy. Little is known of his personal history. He was born at Himálaya about the same time as Ráma. He married Ahalyá the daughter of Bramha, and lived as a very austere ascetic, the Rámáyana states, for thousands of years, in a holy hermitage adorned with fruits and flowers, daily performing religious austerities.

One day when the sage was absent from his dwelling, the mighty Indra passed by, and burned with an impure passion for the wife of Gautama; and he entered the hut in the disguise of the sage, and began to entreat Ahalyá: and she, knowing him to be king of heaven, in the wantonness of her heart yielded to his desires. As he was leaving the hermitage Gautama entered, and he was invincible even to the gods through the power of his austerities. Indra was overwhelmed with sadness; and the sage beholding the profligate celestial, addressed him thus; O depraved wretch, assuming my form you have perpetrated this great crime! therefore from this moment you become a eunuch! The sage then pronounced this curse upon his wife Ahalyá; O sinful wretch, for thousands of years shall you remain in this forest, abandoned by all and invisible to all, until Ráma the son of Dașaratha, shall enter here, and you from beholding him shall be cleansed from all sin and again approach me without fear. These words of the illustrious Gautama were all fulfilled. Rámáyana 49. For an account of Gautama's philosophical system, see Nyáya.

Kumárila says: 'In the same manner, if it is said that Indra was the seducer of Ahalyá, this does not imply that the God Indra committed such a crime, but Indra means the sun, and Ahalyá (from ahan and lí) the night; and as the night is seduced and ruined by the sun of the morning, therefore is Indra called the paramour of Ahalyá.'—*Max Müller, A. S. L., p.* 530.

The legend is thus versified by Mr. Griffiths:

"This was the grove—most lovely then—
Of Gautam, O thou best of men,

Like heaven itself, most honoured by
The Gods who dwell above the sky.
Here with Ahalyá at his side
His fervid task the ascetic plied.
Years fled in thousands. On a day
It chanced the saint had gone away,
When Town-destroying Indra came,
And saw the beauty of the dame.
The sage's form the God endued,
And thus the fair Ahalyá wooed :
'Love, sweet! should brook no dull delay,
But snatch the moments when he may.'
She knew him in the saint's disguise,
Lord Indra of the Thousand eyes,
But touched by love's unholy fire,
She yielded to the God's desire

'Now, Lord of Gods!' she whispered, 'flee,
From Gautam save thyself and me.'
Trembling with doubt and wild with dread
Lord Indra from the cottage fled ;
But fleeing in the grove he met
The home-returning anchoret,
Whose wrath the Gods and fiends would shun,
Such power his fervent rites had won.
Fresh from the lustral flood he came,
In splendour like the burning flame,
With fuel for his sacred rites,
And grass, the best of eremites.
The Lord of Gods was sad of cheer
To see the mighty saint so near,
And when the holy hermit spied
In hermit's garb the Thousand-eyed,
He knew the whole, his fury broke
Forth on the sinner as he spoke :
'Because my form thou hast assumed,
And wrought this folly, thou art doomed.

For this my curse to thee shall cling,
Henceforth a sad and sexless thing.'

No empty threat that sentence came,
It chilled his soul and marred his frame,
His might and god-like vigour fled,
And every nerve was cold and dead,

Then on his wife his fury burst,
And thus the guilty dame he cursed :
'For countless years, disloyal spouse,
Devoted to severest vows,
Thy bed the ashes, air thy food,
Here shalt thou live in solitude.
This lonely grove thy home shall be,
And not an eye thy form shall see.
When Ráma, Daśaratha's child,
Shall seek these shades then drear and wild,
His coming shall remove thy stain,
And make the sinner pure again."

Gautama—A Prajápati ; one of the seven Rishis of the seventh Manwantara.

Gavya—All that is derived from the cow ; milk and all preparations of or from milk ; these are proper to be offered as food to deceased ancestors. The sacrifice of a cow or calf formed part of the ancient Śráddha. It then became typical, or a bull was turned loose, instead of being slaughtered.

Gaya—A son of Havirdhána by Dishaṇá a princess of the race of Agni ; also the name of a prince the son of Nahta, descended from Bharata ; also of one of the sons of Sudyumna, after his transformation from Ila to a man.

Gayatri—A metre created from the eastern mouth of Bramha. The Gáyatri is also the holiest verse of the Vedas, not to be uttered to ears profane ; it is a short prayer to the sun, identified as the Supreme, and occurs in the 10th hymn of the 4th section of the third Ashtaka of the Sanhita of the Rig Veda.

"We meditate on that excellent light of the divine sun; may he illuminate our minds." Such is the fear entertained of profaning this text, that copyists of the Vedas not unfrequently refrain from transcribing it, both in the Sanhita and Bháshya. Pious brahmans every morning at sunrise scatter water, purified by the mystical Omkara and consecrated by the Gáyatri; and by this water as by a thunderbolt the foul fiends are scattered.

Gentoos—The name formerly applied by Europeans to the Hindus, especially to the Telugu people.

Ghatasrinjayas—A people from the north-west, amongst the warriors of the Mahábhárata.

Ghatotkacha—The son of Bhíma by a Rákshasí, or female fiend, Hidimbá, whose brother he slew. The scene of these transactions was on the east of the Ganges, and the Rákshasí may therefore mean a princess of some of the bordering tribes east of Hindustan, or between Bhoṭe and Ava; all of whom eating meat, and following other impure practices, might well be considered Rákshasas or cannibals, by the Hindus. Heramba is in fact applied geographically to designate the western portion of Asam. Ghaṭotkacha was slain by Karna with the javelin he had received from Indra. See Karna.—*Wilson's Works, Vol. III, p.* 297.

Ghorata—Terror. One of the properties assigned to perceptible objects by the Sánkya philosophy.

Ghosha—A son of Lambá (an arc of the heavens.)

Ghosha—(Ghoshá.) A female mentioned in the Rig Veda to whom the Aṣvins gave a husband when she was growing old in her father's house. O. S. T., Vol. V., p. 247.

Ghoshavasu—A prince, the son of Palindaka; one of the ten Sungas, who governed the earth for a hundred and twelve years.

Ghritachi—A celestial nymph, one of those frequently engaged in the interruption of the penances of holy sages.

Ghritachi—The wife of Rája Kuṣanábha and queen of Magadha; the mother of a hundred daughters, all of whom Váyu the god of wind, wished to "forsake their mortal lot, and accompany him to the sky," and on their refusal.

> "He heard the answer they returned
> And mighty rage within him burned,
> On each fair maid a blast he sent
> Each stately form he bowed and bent."

They were afterwards married to Bramhadatta, Rája of Kámpilí, and by this means recovered their strength and beauty.

> "Soon as the hand of each young maid
> In Bramhadatta's palm was laid,
> Deformity and cares away
> She shone in beauty bright and gay."—*Griffiths.*

Ghritaprishtha—One of the ten sons of Priyavrata, according to the list in the Bhágavata ; which says that Priyavrata drove his chariot seven times round the earth, and the ruts left by the wheels became the beds of the oceans, separating it into seven Dwípas ; it is uncertain which of them was given to Ghritaprishtha.

Ghriteya—A prince, one of the sons of Randraṣwa, a descendant of Puru,

Ghritasamada—A son of Suhótra, and father of Saunaka who first established the distinctions of the four castes. V. P. 406.

Giri—One of the sons of Swaphalka by his wife Gándiní.

Girigahvaras—A race who lived in caves ; probably between Cabul and Bamian, but their cavern habitations have not been satisfactorily identified.

Girivraja—A city in the mountainous part of Magadha near the wood of Dharmaranya.

Girivraja—The city of Rája Aswapati to which Bharata and Satrughna were sent. The Rájá was the grandfather of the young princes and they were sent to him that they might be out of the way when it was resolved that Ráma should be appointed Yuvarája at Ayódhya.

Gita-Govinda—Songs of Krishṇa. It is also the title of a pastoral mythological dramatic poem in Sanscrit in praise of Krishṇa by Jayadeva. Radha is in it identified with Lakshmi.—*Sir W. Jones.*

Gobhana—A son of Vahni, and grandson of Turvasu, whose line failed and merged into that of Puru, in consequence of the malediction denounced on his son by Yayáti, for refusing to take his father's infirmities on him.

Goghuatas—A people who formerly resided in Gumanta, part of the Konkan about Goa.

Godaveri—The river which still bears that name ; it is so called in all the Puránas.

Gohamukha—A mountain mentioned in the Vishṇu Purána, but not identified.

Gokarna—A famous and venerated region near the Malabar Coast ; celebrated as the scene of Ràja Bhagírath's austerities,

> " The good Bhagírath, royal sage,
> Had no fair son to cheer his age.
> He, great in glory, pure in will,
> Longing for sons was childless still.
> Then on one wish, one thought intent,
> Planning the heavenly stream's descent,
> Leaving his ministers the care
> And burden of his state to bear,
> Dwelling in far Gokarṇa he
> Engaged in long austerity."

Gokula—The village in which the cowherd Nanda resided, when Krishṇa and Balaráma were entrusted to his care, to be brought up as his own children, in order to escape the vengeance of Kansa. It was at Gokula that the female fiend Pútana attempted the life of the child Krishṇa, by giving him her breast to suck ; the infant Krishṇa sucked it with such violence that he drained it of the life and she expired.

Golaka—A disciple of Sákalya, and teacher of the Rig Veda.

Goloka—The highest world of all, and the residence of Krishṇa; represented as indestructible while all else is subject to annihilation. Professor Wilson thinks this is an addition to the original system of seven worlds, in which we have probably some relation to the seven climates of the ancients, the seven stages or degrees of the earth of the Arabs, and the seven heavens of the Mahomedans, if not to the seven Amshaspends of the Parsis. Seven, suggested originally perhaps by the seven planets, seems to have been a favourite number with various nations of antiquity. Amongst the Hindus it was applied to a variety of sacred or mythological objects, which are enumerated in a verse in the Hanumáns Nátaka. Ráma is described there as piercing seven palm-trees with an arrow, in which other groups of seven take fright, as the seven steeds of the sun, the seven spheres, the seven Munis, the seven seas, the seven continents and the seven mothers of the gods.

Gomanta—A mountain in the Western Ghauts; the name is also applied to the country about Goa, the Konkan. The inhabitants are sometimes termed Gomantas."

Gomati—A river in Ayódhya or Oude.

Gomatiputra—One of the Ándhra kings, the son of Sivaswáti, who reigned 21 years.

Gonds, or Khonds—One of the aboriginal or non-aryan tribes of India who now inhabit part of Orissa. They have partially preserved what may be regarded as the primitive religion of Hindustan—a religion that has been designated devil worship, as they sacrifice only to demons or malignant deities.

Gopas—Herdsman; the designation of the inhabitants of Gokula, where Krishṇa spent his early days; they afterwards emigrated to Vrindávana and were the associates of Krishṇa and Balaráma, who joined heartily in whatever sports amused the sons of the herdsmen.

Gopala-kakshas—Tribes of eastern India.

Goparashtra—The district of cowherds, that is of Nomadic tribes. Gova or Kuva is an ancient name of the southern Konkan.

Gopis—The wives of the Gopas or cowherds. Their sports with Krishṇa are narrated in detail in the Vishṇu Purána, as also in the Bhágavata, &c. The Gopis are said to have wept bitterly when he left Gokula for Mathura.

Goswala—One of the five disciples of Sákalya, and teacher of the Rig Veda.

Gotama—One of the twenty-eight Vyásas; the arranger of the Vedas in the twentieth Dwápara.

Gotras—Families or tribes of brahmans. The names of the Gótras were liable to confusion, particularly in later times, when their number had become very considerable. But the respect which the brahmans from the very earliest time paid to their ancestors, and the strictness with which they prohibited marriages between members of the same family, lead us to suppose that the genealogical lists, even at the present day, furnish in their general outlines, a correct account of the priestly families of India. All Brahmanic families who keep the sacred fires are supposed to descend from the seven Rishis. These are :—*Bhrigu, Angiras, Viśvâmitra, Vasistha, Kaśyapa, Atri, Agastya.* The real ancestors, however, are eight in number :—*Jamadagni, Gautama,* and *Bharadvâja, Viśvâmitra, Vasishta, Kaśyapa, Atri, Agastya.* The eight Gótras, which descend from these Rishis, are again subdivided into forty-nine Gótras, and these forty-nine branch off into a still larger number of families. The names gótra, vanṣa, varga, paksha, and gaṇa, are all used in the same sense, to express the larger as well as the smaller families, descended from the eight Rishis.

A Brahman, who keeps the sacrificial fire, is obliged by law to know to which of the forty-nine Gótras his own family belongs, and in consecrating his own fire he must invoke the ancestors who founded the Gótra to which he belongs. Each of the forty-nine Gótras claims one, or two, or three, or five ancestors, and the names of these ancestors constitute the distinctive character of each Gótra. *Max Müller.* A. S. L., p. 80.

Gova—An ancient name of the Southern Konkan; it may imply the district of cowherds, that is of Nomadic tribes.

Govardhana—A mountain near Mathura. The Vishṇu Purána states that Krishṇa thus addressed the Gopas : Cattle and mountains are our gods. Brahmans offer worship with prayer ; cultivators of the earth adore their landmarks, but we, who tend our herds in the forests and mountains, should worship them and our kine. Let prayers and offerings then be addressed to the mountain Govardhana, and kill a victim in due form." * * * * accordingly the inhabitants of Vraja worshipped the mountain, presenting to it curds and milk and flesh : and they fed thousands of brahmans who came to the ceremony. Indra, offended by the loss of his offerings, caused a heavy rain to deluge Gokula. Krishṇa then to calm the troubled cowherds held up the mountain Govardhana as a large umbrella to shelter them and their cattle. For seven days and nights it rained incessantly at Gokula, but the inhabitants were protected by the elevation of the mountain. The threats of Indra having been fruitless, Krishṇa restored the great mountain to its original site. Professor Wilson says that it seems not unlikely that this legend has some reference to the caves or cavern temples in various parts of India. A remarkable representation of it occurs upon the sculptured rocks of Mahabalipur.

Govinda—A name of Krishṇa, given to him by Indra after having preserved the cattle by raising the mountain Govardhana. Govinda is he who knows, finds, or tends cattle. As the Indra of the cows he was called Govinda. Pilgrims invoke Govinda when travelling to Tripati, &c.

Govithi—A division of the lunar mansions : in the Central or Járadgava Avasthána.

Gramadevatas—Tutelar deities which are supposed to protect the fields, villages and towns from evil spirits ; and to ward off all sorts of plagues, famine, pestilence, war, conflagration, and inundation, and are, in short, regarded as beings who can avert much evil, though they may not be able to bestow positive blessings. It is probable they are the gods worshipped by the Aborigines when the Aryans first came to India. In Southern India the Grámadévatas properly so called are Ayenar, with his two wives

Puranic and Pudkalai ; Ellamma, Mariamma, Ankalamma, Bhadrakáli, Pidári, Chámundi, and Durgá.

Gramanis—The seven attendants on the sun's car ; the agents in the distribution of cold, heat, and rain at their respective season. They are also called Yákshas.

Grammar—The Hindus and the Greeks are the only two nations in the whole history of the world which have conceived independently, and without any suggestions from others, the two sciences of Logic and Grammar.* Carefully collecting the facts brought to light by critical and pains-taking observation, they have elaborated a system of Grammar, of gigantic dimensions, far surpassing anything that has ever been effected, in this branch of study, in any country or age of the world. Their greatest and most brilliant champion, in this science, is Páṇini : yet many other grammarians helped to rear the stupendous fabric which now excites the admiration of mankind. And while they emulated the genius of the Greeks in generalising upon the results of their observations, they far outshine them in the correctness and extent of their investigations.† See Páṇini.

Grantha—In the later literature of India, Grantha was used for a volume, and in *granthakuti*, a library, we see clearly that it has that meaning. But in the early literature, *grantha* does not mean *pustaka*, or book ; it means simply a composition as opposed to a traditional work.

Gridhrika—A daughter of Kaṣyapa and his wife Tamra, the parent of vultures.

Grihastha—A householder ; his duties are thus defined in the Vishṇu Purána. " When the scriptural studies appropriate to the student have been completed, and he has received dismissal from his Guru, let the regenerate man enter into the order of the householder ; and taking unto himself, with lawful ceremonies, house, wife, and wealth, discharge to the best of his ability the duties of his station ; satisfying the manes with funeral cakes ; the gods

* Max Muller. † Sherring.

with oblations; guests with hospitality; the sages with holy study; the progenitors of mankind with progeny; the spirits with the residue of oblations; and all the world with words of truth. A householder secures heaven by the faithful discharge of these obligations. There are those who subsist upon alms, and lead an erratic life of self-denial, at the end of the term during which they have kept house. They wander over the world to see the earth, and perform their ablutions, with rites enjoined by the Vedas, at sacred shrines: houseless, and without food, and resting for the night at the dwelling at which they arrive in the evening, The householder is to them a constant refuge and parent: it is his duty to give them a welcome, and to address them with kindness; and to provide them, whenever they come to his house, with a bed, a seat, and food. A guest disappointed by a householder, who turns away from his door, transfers to the latter all his own misdeeds, and bears away his religious merit. In the house of a good man, contumely, arrogance, hypocrisy, repining, contradiction, and violence are annihilated: and the householder who fully performs this his chief duty of hospitality is released from every kind of bondage, and obtains the highest of stations after death."

Gudaras—A class of mendicants, deriving their name from a pan of metal, which they carry about with them, containing fire for burning scented woods at the house of those from whom they receive alms. They do not solicit alms directly, but repeat the word Alakh, "invisible" expressive of the indescribable nature of the deity.

Guha—The Rája of the Bhíls who welcomed Ráma at Sringavera, the border town between the kingdom of Kosala and the country of the Bhíls. After entertaining Ráma with great liberality, the Rája provided a well-furnished boat in which his distinguished guest crossed the Ganges. He also afforded great assistance to Bharata when proceeding to the hermitage of Bharadwája in search of Ráma.

Guhas—The kings of Kalinga and Mahendra; some parts of Orissa and Berar.

Guhyas—The name of a class of demigods who attend on Kuvera the god of wealth, and whose city is Alákapura.

Guna—Quality, virtue, excellence. A property of all created beings ; three are particularized, the

1. Satwa, principles of truth or existence.
2. Rája, passion or foulness.
3. Tamas, darkness or ignorance.

Gupta—A name said in the Vishṇu Purána to be suited to Vaiṣyas and Śudras.

Guptas—A race of kings who reigned in Magadha. They were Rájas of the Vaiṣya caste. Of the existence and power of the Guptas we have recently had ample proofs from inscriptions and coins, as in the Chandragupta and Samudragupta of the Allahabad column, etc., in all which the legends are written in a character prior to the use of the modern Devanágiri and was current probably about the 5th century of our era. See *Vishnu Purána, p.* 480.

Guru—" A spiritual preceptor occupying in some measure the place of the confessor of the middle ages. He is regarded as a representative and vehicle of divine power, and therefore entitled to receive the most implicit obedience from his disciples. The Gurus are a class of priests carefully to be distinguished from the Puróhita, who is a sort of domestic chaplain and *must* be married. The Gurus generally live in celibacy, though some are married. Each caste and sect has its particular Guru, who may be either a Brahman or a Súdra, and who exercises great authority and influence. He superintends those under his jurisdiction and enforces the observance of the rules and customs of the sect. He can expel from caste, and some Gurus can restore those who have been expelled. All Gurus do not possess equal authority. There is a gradation amongst them and the inferior Gurus frequently derive their power from the superior, and are sometimes deposed by them and others appointed.

When the people come into the presence of the Guru, they make the Sāshtānga, *i. e.*, prostration of the eight members, and this, when followed by the Guru's Asirvāda, *i. e.*, benediction, is effectual for the remission of all sins. The look even of a Guru has the same efficacy. The Prasāda, *i. e.*, the present which the Guru confers upon his disciples consists in things otherwise of small value, such as a portion of cow-dung ashes, to beautify the forehead, flowers that were previously offered up to idols, the crumbs from his meals, or the water in which he had washed his feet, which is preserved and sometimes drunk by those who receive it. These and other things of like nature coming from their holy hands, possess the virtue of purifying body and soul from all uncleanness.

But if the benediction of the Guru and the other little tokens of his favour, which he bestows on his disciples, have so wonderful an influence in attracting the respect and reverence of the populace, his *curse* is thought to be not less powerful, and fills them with terror and awe. The Hindus are persuaded that it never fails to take effect, whether justly or unjustly incurred. Their books are full of stories which seem to have been invented for the express purpose of inspiring this belief; and, to add greater force to it, the attendants of the Guru, who are interested in the success of the impostor's game, do not fail to recount many marvellous stories respecting him, of which they pretend to have been eye-witnesses; and to avoid any possibility of detection, they lay the scene of the miracles in some distant country.

The Gurus, in general, rank as the first and most distinguished order of society. Those who are elevated to this great dignity, receive, in most cases, marks of reverence or rather of adoration which are hardly rendered to the gods themselves. But this is not surprising when it is understood that the power of controlling the gods is generally attributed to them, by which it is supposed they have the means of obtaining whatsoever the deities can bestow.

As a rule, the Gurus reside in a kind of monasteries or insulated hermitages, named Matas. The place of residence of the principal Gurus is commonly called Simhāsana, *i. e.*, throne, and that of the inferior ones Pitha, *i. e.*, seat.

The great Gurus never appear in public except with great pomp; but it is when they proceed to a visitation of their district that they are seen surrounded with their whole splendour. They commonly make the procession on the back of an elephant, or seated in a rich palanquin. Some of them have a guard of horse, and are surrounded with troops both cavalry and infantry, armed with pikes and other weapons. Several bands of musicians precede them playing on all the instruments of the country. Flags in all the varieties of colour wave round them, adorned with the pictures of their gods. Some of their officers take the lead, singing odes in their praise, or admonishing the spectators to be prepared to pay the mighty Guru, as he comes up, the honor and reverence which are due to him. Incense and other perfumes are burnt in profusion ; new cloths are spread before him on the road. Boughs of trees, forming triumphal arches, are expanded in many places on the way through which he passes. Bands of young women, the dancing girls of the temples, relieve each other, and keep up with the procession, enlivening it with lewd songs and lascivious dances.

During the visitation, their principal object is to amass money. Besides the fines which are levied from persons guilty of offences or any breaches of the ceremonies of the caste or sect, they often rigorously exact from their adherents a tribute to the utmost extent of their means. This is called Pāda-kānika, *i. e.*, feet offering. There is no affront or indignity which the Gurus are not disposed to inflict on any disciple, who fails, either from inability or unwillingness, to produce the sum at which he is rated, and in the last resort, they threaten to inflict the *curse*. And such is the credulity of the Hindu, and such is the dread of the evils he supposes to spring from the malediction of a Guru, that this extreme denunciation seldom fails to exact the payment.

The dignity of Guru descends, among the married, from father to son ; but upon the death of one who has lived single, a successor is appointed by some one of the grand Gurus, who, in the exercise of this power, generally nominates one of his own dependants."—*Abbe Dubois.*

H

Haihaya, Haya—Two princes of the Yádava race, the sons of Śatajit, the family in which Krishṇa was born.

Haihayas—Descendants of Yadu. They conquered Báhu, and his country was overrun by them, in consequence of which he fled into the forests with his wives. The Haihayas were afterwards almost destroyed by Sagara, the posthumous son of Báhu. There were five great divisions of the Haihaya tribe; but from their common ancestor Yadu they are usually termed Yadavas. These tribes only appear after the Christian era. They are thought to be of Scythian origin. The word háya, a horse, is confirmatory evidence of this.

Haitakas—Causalists; either the followers of the Nyáya or logical philosophy, or Bauddhas, those who take nothing upon authority, and admit nothing that cannot be proved; or it is explained, those who by argument cast a doubt upon the efficacy of acts of devotion.

Hala—A prince, the son of Arishtakarman, one of the thirty Andhrabhritya kings, whose united reigns amounted to four hundred and fifty-six years.

Hansa—A mountain in the north of Meru; projecting from its base like a filament from the root of the lotus. V. P.

Hanuman—1. The son of the wind, or as he is sometimes represented, an incarnation of Váyu the god of the wind. He was the chief general of the monkey king Sugríva, who assisted Ráma in his war with the giant Rávaṇa. When Ráma was in distress at the loss of his wife Síta, Hanumán was employed as a spy; and, after many researches discovered that Síta was kept a close prisoner in Lanka. Four armies of monkeys and bears were dispatched, but only that to the south, under the command of Hanumán, met with any success, and brought back tidings of the lost Síta. The story of Hanumán's adventures in

Lanka is one of the best sustained efforts of pure imagination to be found in the Rámáyana. The exploits of the vast monkey hero, who could swell himself to the size of a mountain, or dwarf himself to the size of a man's thumb; are narrated in a Baron Munchausen style, sometimes ludicrous, sometimes almost sublime. The following incidents may be mentioned:

When Hanumán arrived at the sea-shore, opposite Ceylon, several of his companions offered to leap across, but Hanumán alone was equal to so great a leap.

"Then by Sampati's counsel led
Brave Hanumán who mocked at dread,
Sprang at one wild tremendous leap,
Two hundred leagues across the deep."

Having discovered Síta in a grove of asoka trees attached to Rávaṇa's palace, he gave proofs of his supernatural strength, and was then conducted into the presence of the king, where he announced himself as the ambassador of his master, king Sugríva, who demanded the restoration of Síta on behalf of Ráma. This so irritated Rávaṇa that he ordered Hanumán to be put to death, but Vibhíshana, Rávaṇa's brother, reminded him that the life of an ambassador was always sacred. It was therefore decided that he should be punished by having his tail set on fire. Hanumán then escaped from his guards, jumped on the house-tops with his burning tail, and set the whole city on fire. After having satisfied himself that Síta had not perished in the conflagration, and exhorted her to maintain her spirits and firmness, he bade her adieu, and sprang from a mountain which staggered under the shock and sank into the earth. He then darted through the air, rejoined his companions on the opposite coast, and recounted to them the narrative of his adventures. When the monkeys returned to Sugríva, Ráma learnt the hiding-place of Síta. Hanumán described his interview with her, and to attest the truth of his story, gave Síta's token to Ráma, who praised the monkey general, enquired about the fortifications of Lanka, and soon marched southwards, attended by Hanumán and the monkey army, to fight for Síta's deliverance.

In the course of the battle when Indrajit the bravest of the sons of Rávaṇa, had, by means of magical weapons, inflicted terrible wounds on all the leaders of Ráma's army, Hanumat flew to the Himálaya mountains for four medicinal herbs by which the dead and wounded might be restored ; but the divine plants suspected his object, and rendered themselves invisible. Upon this the irritated monkey chief tore up the mountain peak and carried it with all its contents into the camp of Ráma and Lakshmaṇa ; who with all the dead and wounded generals were instantly restored by the exhalations issuing from the healing plants.

When Lakshmaṇa was dangerously wounded, the physician Susheṇa said that a celebrated medicinal plant (mahaushadi), growing on the northern mountain Gandha-mádana, would cure him, Hanumán undertook to fetch it and accordingly flew there. As he passed over Ayodhya and Nandigramu he was observed by Bharata, who seeing a strange object in the sky prepared to shoot it ; but Hanumán descended, and arresting the arrow, gave Bharata tidings of his brothers. On reaching the mountain Gandha-mádana, he was attacked by a terrible Rákshasa named Kála-nemi, who had been sent by Rávaṇa to kill Hanumán. This demon first took the form of an anchorite, and persuaded Hanumán to drink some water out of a lake where there was a monstrous crocodile. Hanumán, however, killed both the crocodile and Kála-nemi, and afterwards destroyed 30,000 gandharvas who attacked him. He then looked about for the plant, and not finding it, took up the whole mountain bodily in his arms, and deposited it, with its rocks, metals, forests, lions, elephants, and tigers, at the feet of Susheṇa, who knew well where to look for the plant, gathered it, and made Lakshmaṇa breathe its healing exhalations. Hanumán then restored the mountain to its place, killing with his feet and tail more Rákshasas who attacked him on his way while he carried the mountain, and was unable to use his hands.

When Rávana was at last killed Hanumán was sent by Ráma with a message to Síta, and subsequently sent to announce his return to Bharata.*

* Williams ; Indian Epic Poetry. A. and M. I.

"Hanumán, best of monkey kind,
Was son of him who breathes the wind,
Like thunderbolt in frame was he,
And swift as Garuḍ's self could flee."

Hanumán is now regarded as a demi-god, and his whole race as sacred; and because of this monkeys are allowed to multiply indefinitely, and commit mischief of every kind, no one being willing to interfere with them.

Hara—One of the eleven Rudras. Also a name of Śiva, meaning the supremely powerful.

Hari—A name of Vishṇu, as to the origin of which nothing is known.

Hari-hàra-putra—Vishṇu, Śiva's son, because he is said to owe his origin to the union of Śiva and Vishṇu in a female form, called Mohini. A name of Ayenár, the chief male deity among the Gramadévatas. See Ayenár.

Harikesa—The name of one of the seven solar rays.

Haris—A class of deities in successive Manwantaras.

Harischandra—The son of Trisanku, king of Ayodha, a Hindu king of the Solar dynasty, a descendant of Ikshwáku, and a prominent person in the legendary history of ancient India. In the Aitareya Brahmana he is described as a king without a son, though he had a hundred wives. In his house lived, Parvata and Nárada. He asked Nárada 'Tell me what do people gain by a son whom they all wish for?'

Being asked by one verse, Nárada replied in ten verses:

'If a father sees the face of a son, born alive, he pays a debt in him, and goes to immortality.

'The pleasure which a father has in his son is greater than all the pleasures that are from the earth, from the fire, and from the waters.

'Always have the fathers overcome the great darkness by a son; for a self is born from his self; it (the new-born self, the son) is like a ship, full of food, to carry him over.

'What is the flesh? What is the skin? What are the hairs? What the heat? Try to get a son, you Brahmans; he is undoubtedly the world.

'Food is life for men, clothing is protection, gold is beauty, cattle is strength. His wife is a friend, his daughter is a pity; but the son is his light in the highest world.

'As husband he embraces a wife, who becomes his mother, when he becomes her child. Having been renewed in her, he is born in the tenth month.

'A wife is a wife (jâyâ) because man is born (jâyate) again in her. She is a mother (âbhûti) because she brings forth (âbhûti); a germ is hidden in her.

'The gods and the old ages brought great light unto her. The gods said to men: "In her you will be born again."

'There is no life for him who has no son, this the animals also know.

'The path which those follow who have sons and no sorrows, is widely praised and happy. Beasts and birds know it, and they have young ones everywhere.'

Having thus spoken, he said to him: 'Go to Varuṇa the king, and say: May a son be born to me, and I shall sacrifice him to you.' The king assented, he went to Varuṇa the king, and said: 'May a son be born to me and I shall sacrifice him to you.' Varuṇa said, 'Yes.' A son was born to him, called Rohita. Then Varuṇa said to Hariśchandra: 'A son is born to thee, sacrifice him to me.' Hariśchandra said: 'When an animal is more than ten days old, it can be sacrificed. May he be older than ten days and I shall sacrifice him to you.'

Varuṇa assented. The boy was more than ten days old, and Varuṇa said: 'He is older now than ten days, sacrifice him to me.' Hariśchandra said: 'When an animal's teeth come, then it can be sacrificed. May his teeth now come, and I shall sacrifice him to you.'

Varuṇa assented. His teeth came, and Varuṇa said: His teeth have come, sacrifice him to me.' Hariśchandra said: 'When an animal's teeth fall out, then it can be sacrificed. May his teeth fall out, and I shall sacrifice him to you.'

Varuṇa assented; his teeth fell out, and Varuṇa said: 'His teeth have fallen out, sacrifice him to me.' Hariśchandra replied: 'When an animal's teeth come again, then it can be sacrificed. May his teeth come again, and I shall sacrifice him to you.'

Varuṇa assented: His teeth came again, and Varuṇa said: 'His teeth have come again, sacrifice him to me.' Hariśchandra said: 'When a warrior (kshatriya) is girt with his armour, then he can be sacrificed. May he be girt, and I shall sacrifice him to you.'

Varuṇa assented. He was girt, and Varuṇa said: 'He has been girt, let him be sacrificed to me.'

Hariśchandra assented. He addressed his son and said: 'Child, he gave you to me; Death! that I sacrifice you to him.' The son said, 'No!' took his bow, and went to the forest, and lived there for a year.

And Varuṇa seized Hariśchandra, and his belly swelled. This Rohita heard and went from the forest to the village (grama). Indra, in the form of a man, went round him, and said: 'For a man who does not travel about there is no happiness, thus we have heard, O Rohita! A good man who stays at home is a bad man. Indra is the friend of him who travels. Travel.'

Rohita thought, a Brahman has told me to travel, and thus he travelled a second year in the forest. When he went from the forest to the village, Indra, in the form of a man, went round him, and said:

'A traveller's legs are like blossoming branches, he himself grows and gathers the fruit. All his wrongs vanish, destroyed by his exertion on the road. Travel!'

Rohita thought, a Brahman has told me to travel, and thus he travelled a third year in the forest. When he went from the forest to the town, Indra, in the form of a man, went round him, and said:

'The fortune of a man who sits, sits also; it rises, when he rises ; it sleeps, when he sleeps ; it moves well when he moves. Travel !'

Rohita thought, a Brahman has told me to travel, and thus he travelled a fourth year in the forest. When he went from the forest to the town, Indra, in the form of a man, went round him, and said :

' A man who sleeps is like the Kali age ; a man who awakes is like the Dvâpara age ; a man who rises is like the Trêta age ; a man who travels is like the Krita age. Travel !'

Rohita thought, a Brahman has told me to travel, and thus he travelled a fifth year in the forest. When he went from the forest to the town, Indra, in the form of a man, went round him, and said :

' A traveller finds honey, a traveller finds sweet figs. Look at the happiness of the sun, who travelling never tires. Travel !'

Rohita thought, a Brahman has told me to travel, and thus he travelled a sixth year. He met in the forest a starving Rishi, *Ajîgarta*, the son of *Sûyavasa*. He had three sons, *Sunahpuccha*, *Sunahśepha*, and *Sunolângúla*. Rohita said to him : ' Rishi, I give you a hundred cows, I ransom myself with one of these thy sons.' The father embraced the eldest son, and said : ' Not him.' ' Nor him,' said the mother, embracing the youngest. And the parents bargained to give Sunahśepha, the middle son. Rohita gave a hundred, took him, and went from the forest to the village. And he came to his father, and said : ' Father, Death ! I ransom myself by him.' The father went to Varuṇa, and said : ' I shall sacrifice this man to you.' Varuṇa said, ' Yes, for a Brahman is better than a Kshatriya.' And he told him to perform a Râjasûya sacrifice. Hariśchandra took him to be the victim for the day, when the Soma is spent to the gods.

Viśvamitra was his Hotṛi priest, *Jamadagni* his Adhvaryu priest, *Vasishtha*, the Brahman, *Ayâsyu*, the Adyâtri priest. When Sunahśepha had been prepared, they found nobody to bind him to the sacrificial post. And Ajîgarta, the son of Sûyavasa said : ' Give me another hundred, and I shall bind him.' They gave him another hundred, and he bound him. When he had been prepared and bound, when the Aprî hymns had been sung, and he had been led round the fire, they found nobody to kill him. And Ajîgarta, the son of Sûyavasa said : 'Give me another hundred, and I shall kill him.' They gave him another hundred, and he came whetting his sword. Then Sunahśepha thought, 'They will really kill me, as if I was not a man. Death ! I shall pray to the gods.' He went with a hymn to *Prajâpati* (Lord of the world), the first of gods. Prajâpati said to him : 'Agni (fire) is the nearest of gods, go to him. He went with a hymn to Agni, and Agni said to him : '*Savitri* (the progenitor) rules all creatures, go to him.' He went with a hymn to Savitṛi, and Savitṛi said to him : 'Thou art bound for Varuṇa the king,' and Varuṇa said to him : '*Agni* is the mouth of the gods, the kindest god, praise him, and we shall set thee free.' Thus he praised Agni, and Agni said to him : Praise the Viśve Devâh, and we shall set thee free.' Thus he praised the Viśve Devâh, and they said to him : 'Indra is the greatest, mightiest, strongest, and friendliest of the gods, praise him, and we shall set thee free.' Thus he praised Indra, and Indra was pleased, and gave him in his mind a golden car, which Sunahśepha acknowledged by another verse. Indra said to him : 'Praise the *Aśvinau*, and we shall set thee free.' Thus he praised the Aśvinau, and they said to him : 'Praise *Ushas* (dawn), and we shall set thee free.' Thus he praised Ushas with three verses. While each verse was delivered, his fetters were loosed, and Harischandra's belly grew smaller, and when the last verse was said, his fetters were loosed, and Harischandra well again." A. S. L., p. 408-414.

Hariśchandra is represented in all the legends as a king of great uprightness. The following story illustrates this. Once when all the gods and Rishis were assembled in Dévéndra's audience chamber, the latter asked Vasishtha, whether he knew of any one among men on earth who did never lust after another's wife, nor speak a lie ; to which the Rishi replied : "Yes, there is a disciple of mine, king Hariśchandra, he never spoke a lie." On hearing this Visvāmitra called out : "Hariśchandra is a deceiver and liar." Then said Vasishtha : "If Hariśchandra is found to speak the least untruth, I will cease to be a Rishi and to come into this assembly."

"Well," answered Visvámitra, "if I find him altogether truthful, I will give him all the merit of my penance; but I am afraid, you will at once tell him that I am about to try him." Upon this Vasishtha took an oath, that he would not at all go near the king till the matter was settled; and Visvámitra went to Hariśchandra and tempted him in different ways, more especially through women, to speak an untruth; but the king did not swerve from the truth. At last the Rishi asked him far a large sum of money, and having received it, he returned it to him with the request to take care of it till he would require it. After a very long time Visvāmitra came and desired all the money, together with compound interest, which amounted to a sum exceeding the value of his kingdom; but Hariśchandra, in order to pay the sum, sold all he had, and also himself together with his wife and son. Subsequently he was separated from his wife Satyavati, and employed to burn corpses. Then, behold, one day, there comes a woman to have her dead child burnt, and he recognizes her as his wife by her Tāli (the marriage-badge); which he requires of her as his wages for burning the child, and which she will not give away. While they yet talk, there come messengers to seize the woman, because she was suspected of having kidnapped a royal prince who happened to be very similar to her child. Being found guilty, she is condemned to death, and Hariśchandra is ordered to behead her; and he is ready to obey: but, behold, suddenly the sword is turned into flowers, the child becomes alive, and the royal couple are restored to their former glory."

In consequence he was elevated with his subjects to heaven, from whence, having been insidiously led by Nárada to boast of his merits, he was again precipitated. His repentance of his pride, however, arrested his downwards descent, and he and his train paused in mid-air. The city of Hariśchandra is popularly believed to be at times still visible in the skies. The indignation of Vaśishṭha at Viśwámitra's insatiableness produced a quarrel, in which their mutual imprecations changed them to two birds, the Śaráli, a sort of Turdus, and the Baka, or Crane. In these forms they fought for a considerable term, until Brahmá interposed, and reconciled them. The Bhágavata alludes to this story, in its notice of Hariśchandra ; but the Váyu refers the conflict to the reign of a different prince: According to the Śiva Purána, Hariśchandra was an especial worshipper of that deity ; and his wife Satyavatí was a form of Jayá, one of Durga's handmaids.

Harisrava—A river mentioned in the Vishṇu Purána but not identified.

Harita—A prince the son of Yuvanáṣwa from whom the Angirasa Haritas were descended ; also a grandson of Hariśchandra ; one of the five sons of Parávrit, and king of Videha.

Haritas—The descendants of Harita, the son of Yuvanáṣwa. They were brahmans with the properties of Kshatriyas.

Haritas—A class of gods in the twelfth Manwantara ; one of the tribes of Aborigines, who occupy the hills and jungles.

Haritaswa—A son of Sudyumna after his transformation from Ilá into a man.

Hari Vansa—The last portion of the Mahabharata, and believed to be a comparatively recent addition to that work. It is chiefly occupied with the adventures of Krishṇa, but, as introductory to his era it records particulars of the creation of the world, and of the patriarchal and regal dynasties ; done, says Professor Wilson, with much carelessness and inaccuracy of compilation.

Hari-varsha—A country to the north of Hemakuta and south of Nishádha. Also, the name of the nine sons of Agnióthra, king of Nishádha.

Harsha—(Joy). A son of Káma (Love) by his wife Nandi (delight).

Harsha Deva—A king of Kashmír who reigned between A. D. 1113 and 1125, and the reputed author of the play called "Ratnavali, or the necklace," translated by Wilson, in the Hindu Theatre.

Harshavarddhana—A prince, the son of Yajnakrit, one of the descendants of Kshattravriddha.

Haryaksha—One of the five sons of Prithu, according to the Bhágavata enumeration.

Haryanga—A prince, the son of Champa one of the descendants of Anu. Champa was the founder of Champapuri, a city of which traces still remain in the vicinity of Bhágulpúr.

Haryaswa—The son and successor of Dridhaṣwa. Dridhaṣwa was one of the three sons of Kuvalayáṣwa who survived the conflict with the Asura Dhundu, all the others, to the extent of twenty thousand nine hundred and ninety-seven, having perished.

Haryaswa was also the name of a son of Prishadaṣwa; of a son of Drishtakétu; and of a son of Chakshu.

Haryaswas—In the Vishṇu Purána it is stated that Daksha, being commanded by Bramha, created living creatures. The creation and disappearance of the Haryaswas is thus described. "In the first place he willed into existence the deities, the Rishis, the quiristers of heaven, the Titans, and the snake-gods. Finding that his will-born progeny did not multiply themselves, he determined, in order to secure their increase, to establish sexual intercourse as the means of multiplication. For this purpose he espoused Asikní, the daughter of the patriarch Vírana, a damsel addicted to devout practices, the eminent supportress of the world. By her the great father of mankind begot five thousand mighty sons, through whom he expected the world should be peopled, Nárada, the divine Rishi, observing them desirous to multiply posterity, approached them, and addressed them in a friendly tone: 'Illustrious Haryaswas, it is evident that your intention is to beget posterity; but first consider this: why should you, who, like fools, know not the middle, the height, and depth of the world, propagate offspring? When your intellect is no more obstructed by interval, height, or depth, then how, fools, shall ye not all behold the term of the universe?' Having heard the words of Nárada, the sons of Daksha dispersed themselves through the regions, and to the present day have not returned; as rivers that lose themselves in the ocean come back no more."

Haryatma—Called also Uttama, the Vyása of the twenty-first Dwápara."

Hasta—A lunar mansion in Govithi, in the Central Avaṣhthána.

Hastin—The son of Suhótra and founder of the city of Hastinápura.

Hastinapura—Is the name of the ancient capital of the Kurus, frequently mentioned in the Mahábharata. The Vishṇu Purána relates that it was founded by Hastin, washed away by the Ganges—under the reign of Nichakra, who, in consequence of this event, had to remove the seat of his government to Kauśâmbî—and at a later period it was undermined by Balarâma. It was situated on the Ganges, and is placed by Lassen, in his map to the *Indische Alterthuns Kunde*, about 78° long, and 28° 50′ lat.

Hastisima—A river mentioned in the Vishṇu Purána list, but not identified.

Havirbha—(Oblation-born). The wife of the Rishi Pulastya, and mother of Agastya.

Havirdhana—The son of Antarddhána by his wife Sikhandiṇi.

Havishmantas—A class of Pitris, of the corporeal order, living iṇ the solar sphere, sons of Angiras, and Pitris of Kshatriyas. See Pitris.

Havya—According to the Váyu Purána, one of the five sons of Atri after his penance.

Havyavahana—The fire of the gods, the son of Suchi.

Hayasiras—The daughter of Vrishaparvan, the renowned Danava, and wife of Kratu.

Hema—The son of Ushadratha, a descendant of Yayáti. Also the name of a river in the Vishṇu Purána.

Hemachandra—1, The king of Vaisali, a place celebrated amongst the Buddhists as the chief seat of the labours of Sákhya and his first disciples—now Alláhabad; 2, A zealous and able propagator of the Jain doctrines in the twelfth century. He was well versed in the peculiarity of the system which he taught, and may be regarded as a safe guide. He was the author of a useful vocabulary termed the *Abhidana Chintamani*, and of a life of *Maha Víra*. Wilson.

Hemakuta—One of the boundary mountains of the earth, lying to the south of Meru.

Hermit—See Vánaprastha.

Heti—A Rákshas, that always resides in the sun's car during the month of Madha or Chaitra, as one of its seven guardians.

Hidimba—A hideous Asura and cannibal, with yellow eyes and a horrible aspect, but possessed of great strength. He lived in the jungle south of Váranávata, and attacked the Pándavas on their march, but was killed by Bhíma after a severe contest.

Hidimbi—The sister of the above who is described as beautiful, and was afterwards married to Bhíma.

Himavat—The king of mountains. Part of the snowy range. The well-known range of mountains now called the Himálaya, forming the northern barrier of the Indian peninsula, containing the highest elevations in the world. The Imüs or Emodus of classical writers. In Mythology Himavat is husband of the Air-nymph Menaka ; father of the river Gunga and of Durga or Uma, in her descent as Parvati to captivate Śiva, and seduce him from the austerities which he practiced in those mountains. In this personification the name belongs to the Puranic ; as a mountain only, to the Epic.

On account of the majestic height of this mountain range, and the apparent impossibility of reaching its summit, the imagination of the ancient Hindus invested it with the most mysterious properties, and connected it with the history of some of their deities. In the Puránas, Himavat is placed to the south of the fabulous mountain Meru, which stands in the centre of the world, and described as the king of the mountains, who was inaugurated as such when Prithu was installed in the government of the earth. As the abode of Śiva, he is the goal of penitent pilgrims, who repair to his summit in order to win the favours of this terrific god. His wife was Menâ, whom the Pitris or demigods Vairâjas, engendered by the mere power of their thought.

Hindi—One of the tongues of India ; it abounds in Sanskrit words, and has many dialects. Speaking generally the tongues spoken in the whole of upper India, including the Punjab, from the Himálayan to the Vindhyan range, may be said to be Hindi. Also the languages of Kamaon and Garhwal, all along the Sub-Himalayan range as far as the Gogra river; the impure dialect of the Gorkhas; the Brij-Bhasha (or Baka as it is pronounced on the Ganges,) the Panjabi, Multani, Sindi, Jaṭaki, Haruti, Marwari and it is said Konkani. The Bengali is a form of Hindi, but so highly polished as to be classed as a distinct tongue.

Hindus—" The great bulk of the people known by this appellation are the descendants of Scythian and Aryan immigrants, who in bye-gone days, as conquerors, in search of a milder clime, left the cold regions of the north, some off-shoots moving westward and others to the south. Remnants of Scythian languages are found in Beluchistan, and the seat of the great Sanskrit speaking people was long in Kashmir, proving that one great highway to the south, had been along the valley of the Indus, through Kashmir, and the Panjab. But between the valley of the Indus, and that of the Brahmaputra, there are twenty or thirty other passes in the Himálayas, through which the northern races could stream to the genial south. Amongst the first of these immigrants seemingly were the Tamil races, belonging to the Turanian or Tartar family of mankind, a body of whom seem to have followed the course of the Indus and spread themselves over the peninsula. As to the date of their advent, however, history is silent; but there seems no doubt that great branches of the Scythic stock were occupants of India, at the time that it was invaded, and to a considerable extent conquered, by the Sanskrit speaking tribes of the Aryan family. In the north, the subjugation or ousting of the Tamilians from all rank and power was so complete that Sanskrit forms of speech became the language of the country, and the Kashmiri, the Panjabi, the Sindi, the Guzerathi, the Hindustani and the Bengali, all of them with a large admixture of Sanskrit, are sister tongues known as forms of Hindi. South of the Nerbudda, however, it is otherwise. Throughout the peninsula, the languages differ from the Sanskrit in grammar, and only admit Sanskrit words, in the same way that the Anglo-Saxon admitted terms of law and civilization from the Norman French. At the present day, the south of India more largely represents the Tartar, and the north, the Aryan race. But the fair, yellow colored Aryans are to be met with south even to Cape Comorin, and though mixing with the various Tamil nations, races and tribes, for at least two thousand years, in physical form, complexion, intellect and manners, the Brahmanical and other Aryan families are as distinct as when their forefathers first came conquering from the north. The great Aryan migration, however, which seems to have received its first check south of the Aravali, took place between the fourteenth and eighth centuries before our era. Major Cunningham in his learned work on the Bhilsa topes (p. 15) uses the term Aryan in allusion to "the race of Aryya, whose emigrations are recorded in the Zendavesta, who starting from Ericene Vijo, gradually spread to the south-east, over Arya-vartha or Arya-deṣa, the northern plains of India, and to the south-west, over Iran or Persia: he adds that the Medas are called Apìtol by Herodotus. The original meaning of the word is also said to have been equivalent to Upper Noble. It has also, however, been suggested that as the Aryans were originally and essentially an agricultural and therefore a peasant race, they may have derived their name from their plough. The Aryans seem to have brought with them a servile race, or to have had amongst them a social distinction between the noble and the common people which has ever continued. As they conquered southwards, amongst the Tartar races whom they found in the country, they reduced them everywhere to a state of slavery. They named them in fierce contempt Dása or slave, and these formed the true servile race of Manu and other writers. Where the races who had preceded them retained their independence, these proud immigrants styled them M'hlechhas, a term which even to the present day, is intended to comprise every thing that is hateful or vile. In Vedic times, along the western coast of Hindustan dwelt other races, different alike from the Scythic tribes and from the Aryans of the Vedas—earlier colonizers or emigrants, most probably from Assyria and the west,—who had a civilization of their own. Mr. Wheeler divides the history of the Hindus into four great epochs corresponding with the four great changes in their religious belief :—

1—The Vedic age, which was characterised by the worship of the elementary deities, such as Agni and Indra, and appears to have prevailed in the Panjab prior to the disappearance of the Saraswati river in the sand.

2—The Brahmanic age, which was characterised by the worship of Brahma, and appears to have prevailed between the disappearance of the Saraswati in the sand, and the advent of Sakya Muni about B. C. 600.

3—The Buddhist age, which was characterised by the pursuit of Nirváua, and appears to have prevailed from about B. C. 600 to A. D. 800 or 1000.

4—The Brahmanical revival, which was characterised by the worship of incarnations of deities, and appears to have prevailed from about A. D. 800 to the present time."

Professor Wilson writes "The circumstances that are told of the first princes have evident relation to the colonization of India, and the gradual extension of the authority of new races over an uninhabited or uncivilized region. It is commonly admitted, that the Brahmanical religion and civilization were brought into India from without. Certainly, there are tribes on the borders, and in the heart of the country, who are still not Hindus ; and passages in the Rámáyána, and Mahábharata, and Manu, and the uniform traditions of the people themselves, point to a period when Bengal, Orissa, and the whole of the Dakhin were inhabited by degraded or outcaste, that is, by barbarous tribes. The traditions of the Puránas confirm these views : but they lend no assistance to the determination of the question whence the Hindus came ; whether from a central Asiatic nation, as Sir William Jones supposed, or from the Caucasian mountains, the plains of Babylonia, or the borders of the Caspian, as conjectured by Klaproth, Vans Kennedy, and Schlegel. The affinities of the Sanskrit language prove a common origin of the now widely scattered nations amongst whose dialects they are traceable, and render it unquestionable that they must all have spread abroad from some centrical spot in that part of the globe first inhabited by mankind, according to the inspired record. Whether any indication of such an event be discoverable in the Vedas, remains to be determined ; but it would have been obviously incompatible with the Pauráńik system to have referred the origin of Indian princes and principalities to other than native sources. We need not therefore, expect, from them, any information as to the foreign derivation of the Hindus.

We have, then, wholly insufficient means for arriving at any information concerning the ante-Indian period of Hindu history, beyond the general conclusion derivable from the actual presence of barbarous and apparently, aboriginal tribes—from the admitted progressive extension of Hinduism into parts of India where it did not prevail when the code of Manu was compiled—from the general use of dialects in India, more or less copious, which are different from Sanskrit—and from the affinities of that language with forms of speech current in the western world—that a people who spoke Sanskrit, and followed the religion of the Vedas, came into India, in some very distant age, from lands west of the Indus. Whether the date and circumstances of their immigration will ever be ascertained, is extremely doubtful : but it is not difficult to form a plausible outline of their early site and progressive colonization.

The earliest seat of the Hindus, within the confines of Hindusthan, was, undoubtedly, the eastern confines of the Panjab. The holy land of Manu and the Puránas lies between the Drishadwati and Saraswati rivers,—the Caggar and Sursooty of our barbarous maps. Various adventures of the first princes and most famous sages occur in this vicinity ; and the Asramas or religious domiciles of several of the latter are placed on the banks of the Saraswati. According to some authorities it was the abode of Vyása, the compiler of the Vedas and Puránas ; and agreeably to another, when on one occasion, the Vedas had fallen into disuse and been forgotten, the Brahmans were again instructed in them by Saraswata, the son of Saraswati. One of the most distinguished of the tribes of the Brahmans is known as the Saraswata ; and the same word is employed by Mr. Colebrooke, to denote that modification of Sanskrit which is termed generally Prakrit, and which in this case, he supposes to have been the language of the Saraswata nation, 'which occupied the banks of the river Saraswati.' The river itself receives its appellation from Saraswati, the goddess of learning, under whose auspices the sacred literature of the Hindus assumed shape and authority. These indications render it certain, that, whatever seeds were imported from without, it was in the country adjacent to the Saraswati river that they were first planted, and cultivated and reared, in Hindusthan.

The tract of land thus assigned for the first establishment of Hinduism in India, is of very circumscribed extent and could not have been the site of any numerous tribe or nation. The traditions that evidence the early settlement of the Hindus in this quarter, ascribe to the settlers more of a philosophical and religious, than of a secular character, and combine, with the very narrow bounds of the holy land ; to render it possible, that the earliest emigrants were the members, not of a political, so much as of a religious community ; that they were a colony of priests, not in the restricted sense in which we use the term, but in that in which it still applies in India, to an Agrahara, a village or hamlet of Brahmans, who although married, and having families, and engaging in tillage, in domestic duties and in the conduct of secular interests affecting the community, are, still, supposed to devote their principal attention to sacred study and religious offices. A society of this description with its artificers and servants, and, perhaps, with a body of martial followers, might have found a home in the Brahmavarta of Manu, the land which, thence, was entitled 'the holy,' or, more literally, 'the Brahman region,' and may have communicated to the rude, uncivilized, unlettered, aborigines the rudiments of social organization, literature, and religion ; partly in all probability, brought along with them, and partly devised and fashioned, by degrees, for the growing necessities of new conditions of society. Those with whom this civilization commenced would have had ample inducements to prosecute their successful work ; and in the course of time, the improvement which germinated on the banks of the Saraswati was extended beyond the borders of the Jumna and the Ganges.—*Preface to V. P.*

Hiranmaya—A mountainous country lying between the Sevéta and Srinji ranges ; to the north of mount Meru.

Hiranvat—The king of Sweta, installed by his father, the pious king Agnídhra, before he retired to a life of penance at Sálagráma.

Hiranyagarbha—A name of Brahmá, ' he who was born from the golden egg.'

In the Rig Veda Hiranyagarbha is celebrated with all the attributes of supremacy. In the 121st hymn of the tenth book this god is said to have arisen in the beginning, the one lord of all beings, who upholds heaven and earth, who gives life and breath, whose command even the gods obey, who is the god over all gods, and the one animating principle of their being. *O. S. T., Vol. IV, pp.* 13, *ff. V. p.* 355.

Hiranyahasta—The son given by the Asvins to the wise Vadhrimati, in answer to her prayers. O. S. T. v., p. 247.

Hiranyakasipu—A son of Kaṣyapa and Diti, who became king of the Daityas, and usurped the authority of Indra, and exercised of himself the functions of the sun, of the air, of the waters, of fire, and of the moon. Having conquered the three worlds he was inflated with pride, and enjoyed whatever he desired. " He obtained the sovereignty of all the immortals for a hundred million years." (O. S. T., iv, 159.) Prahláda, his son, remained devoted to Vishṇu, and when ordered by his father to be put to death, Vishṇu appeared as his deliverer. Hiraṇyakaṣipu was reconciled to his son, but was notwithstanding put to death by Vishṇu as Narasimha (the man-lion) and Prahláda became the sovereign of the Daityas.

Hiranyaksha—The brother of the above, termed " the invincible." He was destroyed by Vishṇu in his boar incarnation. In the Padma Purána it is said that this occurred in the first, or Matsya avatara : that Vishṇu in the form of a fish entered the ocean and destroyed Hiranyaksha.—*Wilson's Works, Vol. III., p.* 58.

Hiranyanabha—One of the descendants of Ráma, a pupil of Jaimini, and teacher of the Sama Veda. He had a large number of disciples who were termed the northern and eastern chaunters of the Śáman, and founders of schools.

Hiranyaretas—One of the ten sons of Priyavrata, according to the enumeration in the Bhágavata.

Hiranyaroman—A Lókapála, regent of the North, son of Parjanya and Maríchi.

Hlada—One of the four mighty sons of Hiraṇyakasipu.

Hladini—The Gladdener ; the name of one of the seven rivers mentioned in the Rámáyana, in connection with the descent of Ganga. Only two, the Ganges and Indus, are known to geographers.

Homa—A sort of burnt offering which can be made by Brahmans only. It is only made on special occasions, such as the celebration of a festival, the investiture of a young brahman with the sacred thread, marriages, and funerals. The method of making it is as follows : During the utterance of Mantras, five species of consecrated wood, together with the Dharba grass, rice and butter, are kindled and burnt ; and the fire is then kept burning as long as the festival or ceremony lasts. Great efficacy is ascribed to this rite.

Hotri—The priest who recites the hymns at the performance of sacrificial rites.

Hraswarman—One of the kings of Mithila, the son of Suvarṇarman ; sometimes called Hrasvaroma.

Hri—'Modesty,' An allegorical personage represented as one of the daughters of Daksha, and wife of Dharma.

Hridika—A Yádava prince, the son of Swayambhoja, and father of Súra, in whose family Vishṇu took a human form.

Hrishikesa—A name of Vishṇu, meaning 'lord of the senses.'

Humas—The white Huns, or Indo-scythians, who were established in the Punjab and along the Indus, at the commencement of our era, as we know from Arrian, Strabo, and Ptolemy, confirmed by recent discoveries of their coins.

Hutasana—The god of flame.

I

Ida—One of the daughters of Daksha who was married to Kaṣyapa.

Idhmajihwa—One of the ten sons of Priyavrata according to the Bhágavata.

Idvatsara—The name of the third cycle or Yuga, of which five are enumerated, each cycle comprehending sixty-one solar months or 1,830 days.

Ijikas, also Itikas—A people of the South of India.

Ikshula Ikshumati—The name of a river mentioned in the Rámáyana and Vishṇu Purána, but not identified.

Ikshwaku—One of the ten sons of the lawgiver Manu Vaivaswata, considered to be the first prince of the Solar dynasty; he reigned at Ayódha the capital of Kosala, in the second or Treta yuga. He had one hundred sons, and is said to have been born from the nostril of Manu when he happened to sneeze. V. P.

"Ikshwáku was the son of Manu, the first king of Kosala, and founder of the solar dynasty or family of the children of the Sun, the god of that luminary being the father of Manu.'

The following extract from the Rámáyana gives the line of kings from Ikswaku to Bharata.

> "From viewless nature Brahmá rose,
> No change, no end, no waste, he knows.
> A son had he, Maríchi styled,
> And Kasyap was Maríchi's child.
> From him Vivaswat sprang; from him
> Manu whose fame shall ne'er be dim.
> Manu, who life to mortals gave,
> Begot Ikshváku good and brave.
> First of Ayodhyá's kings was he,
> Pride of her famous dynasty.

From him the glorious Kukshi sprang,
Whose fame through all the regions rang.
Rival of Kukshi's ancient fame,
His heir, the great Vikukshi came.
His son was Vāna, lord of might,
His Anaraṇya, strong to fight.
His son was Prithu, glorious name,
From him the good Triṣanku came.
He left a son renowned afar,
Known by the name of Dhundumár.
His son who drove the mighty car
Was Yuvanaṣwa fear'd in war.
He passed away. Him followed then
His son Mándhátá, king of men,
His son was blest on high emprise
Susandhi fortunate and wise.
Two noble sons had he, to wit,
Dhruvasandhi and Prasenajit
Bharat was Dhruvasandhi's son,
And glorious fame that monarch won."—*Griffiths.*

Ila—Before the birth of the sons mentioned above, the Manu, being desirous of sons, offered a sacrifice for that purpose to Mitra and Varuna; but the rite being deranged through an irregularity of the ministering priest, a daughter, Ilá was produced. Through the favour of the two divinities, however her sex was changed, and she became a man named Sudyumna, q. v.

Ilavila—One of the sons of Daṣaratha, who does not appear however to have achieved any distinction.

Ilavila—The daughter of Trinavinda, became the wife of Visravas, and mother of Kuvera the god of wealth.

Ilavrita—One of the nine sons of Agnídhra, king of Jambadwípa. The region in the centre of which Mount Meru is situated was conferred on Ilávrita.

Ilwala—A celebrated demon, the son of Hláda. He is the hero of various legends in the Puránas. He had a cousin of the same name, the son of Viprachitti, who was also distinguished amongst the Danavas.

India, "is bounded on the north and the east by the Himálaya mountains, on the west by the Indus, and on the south by the sea. Its length from Kashmere to Cape Comorin is 1,900 miles; its breadth from Kurrachee to Sudiya, in Assam, 1,500 miles. The superficial contents are 1,287,000 miles, and the population, under British and native rule, is now estimated at 200,000,000. It is crossed from east to west by a chain of mountains called the Vindya, at the base of which flows the Nerbudda. The country to the north of this river is generally designated Hindustan, and that to the south of it the Deccan. Hindustan is composed of the basin of the Indus on one side, and of the Ganges on the other, with the great sandy desert on the west, and an elevated tract now called, from its position, Central India. The Deccan has on its northern boundary a chain of mountains running parallel with the Vindya, to the south of which stretches a table land of triangular form, terminating at Cape Comorin, with the western Ghauts, on the western coast, and the eastern Ghauts, of minor altitude, on the opposite coast. Between the Ghauts and the sea lies a narrow belt of land which runs round the whole peninsula.

Of the ancient history or chronology of the Hindus there are no credible memorials. The history was compiled by poets, who drew on their imagination for their facts, and the chronology was computed by astronomers, who have made the successive ages of the world to correspond with the conjunctions of the heavenly bodies. The age of the world is thus divided into four periods: the *satya yuga* extending to 1,728,000, and the second, or *treta yuga*, to 1,296,000 years; the third, or the *dwápara yuga*, comprises 864,000 years; and the fourth, or *kali yuga* is predicted to last 432,000 years. A *kalpa*, or a day of Brahma, is composed of a thousand such periods, or 4,320,000,000 years. Extravagant as these calculations may appear, they are outdone by the Burmese, who affirm that the lives of the ancient inhabitants extended to a period equal to the sum of every drop of rain which falls on the surface of the globe in three years. The dates given for the first three ages must, therefore, be rejected as altogether imaginary.

while the commencement of the fourth, or present age, which corresponds, to a certain degree, with the authentic eras of other nations, may be received as generally correct.

India is designated by native writers Bharata Varsha, from king Bharat, who is said to have reigned over the whole country. That he did not enjoy universal monarchy in India is certain, though he was doubtless one of the earliest and most renowned of its rulers; but this fact loses all historical value when we are told in the shasters that he reigned ten thousand years, and on his death was transformed into a deer. Thus do we plod our way through darkness and mystery; at every step fact is confounded with fable, and all our researches end only in conjecture. The original settlers are identified with the various tribes of Bhíls, Koles, Gonds, Mínas, and Chúars, still living in a state almost of nature, in the forests of the Soane, the Nerbudda, and the Mahanuddi, and in the hills of Surgúja and Chota Nagpore. Their languages have no affinity with the Sanskrit, and their religion differs from Hinduism. In those fastnesses, amidst all the revolutions which have convulsed India, they have continued to maintain, unchanged, their original simplicity of habits, creed, and speech. They were apparently driven from the plains by fresh colonies of emigrants; and these were in their turn conquered by the Hindus, who brought their religion and language with them from regions beyond the Indus, and, having reduced the inhabitants to a servile condition, branded them with the name of súdras. Of the four Hindu castes, three are designated the twice-born, which seems to indicate that they all belonged to the conquering race, although the term is now applied exclusively to brahmans. In the Institutes of Manu reference is also made to cities governed by súdras, which the twice-born were forbidden to enter, and the allusion evidently applies to súdra chiefs, who continued to maintain their independence after the Hindu invasion.

The Hindus who originally crossed the Indus took possession of a small tract of land, 100 miles north-west of Delhi, about 65 miles by 30, which was considered the residence of gods and holy sages, while the brahmans appear to have subsequently occupied the country north of the Jumna and the Ganges, stretching to the confines of north Behar. The India of the Vedas, of Manu, and the earliest writers was exclusively confined to the region north of the Nerbudda, and comprised but a small portion even of that limited quarter. It was in the north that the four places of greatest sanctity were situated during the early ages, though the Deccan now contains many places of distinguished merit. The north was also the seat of the solar and lunar races, the scene of chivalrous adventures, and the abode of all those who are celebrated in the legends, the mythology, and the philosophy of the Hindus. Even in the polished age in which the Rámáyan and the Mahábhárat were composed, the south was the land of fable, the dwelling of bears and monkeys, and it was not till a very late period that these apes and goblins and monsters were transformed into orthodox Hindus. It must, therefore, be distinctly borne in mind that the revolutions described in the sacred books of the Hindus belong to Hindustan and not to the Deccan."*

Indra—The king of heaven; the king of the Devas; is represented with four arms and hands, with two he holds a lance, in the third one the thunderbolt (Vajrayudha) and the fourth one is empty. Sometimes he is drawn as a white man sitting on an elephant, with the thunderbolt in his right hand and a bow in his left. His reign is to continue one hundred years of the gods, after which another individual from among the gods, the giants, or men, by his own merit, raises himself to this eminence. The sacrifice of a horse one hundred times will, it is said, raise a person to the rank of Indra. The Puránas relate many stories of Indra, who is described as very jealous lest any person should, by sacred austerities or sacrifices, excel him in religious merit, and thus obtain his kingdom. To prevent these devotees from succeeding in their object, he generally sends one of the celestial nymphs to draw away their minds, and thus bring them from their religious observances, induce them to return to a life of sensual gratification. It was Indra who stole the horse consecrated by king Sagara, who was about to perform for the hundreth time the sacrifice of that animal.

* Marshman's History of India, vol. 1.

"Indra plays an important part in each of the three periods of Indian mythology. In the earliest age he seems to have been the unknown mysterious being who inhabited the sky, the firmament between earth and the sun, who rode upon the clouds, who poured forth the rain, hurled the forked lightning upon earth, and spoke in the awful thunder. His character was at once beneficent as giving rain and shade; and awful and powerful in the storm. He is the original of the Jupiter Tonans of the west, and the Thor of the north, and like them rose in the earliest ages to the first place, and the sovereignty among the gods. Fear, a stronger motive among men than gratitude, raised him above the elementary triad. In the Epic period he is the first person of the pure mythological triad, Indra, Agni, and Yama. In the Puránic age, when the powers of a Supreme Being were personified in the superior triad of Brahmá, Vishṇu, and Śiva, Indra's star declines. He is no longer the principal divinity, but only the chief of the inferior deities; and, as such, is at constant war with the giants and demons, by whom he is for a time deposed. A curse from the Rishi Durvása causes his power and that of the deities subject to him gradually to decline; and he is defeated by Krishṇa in a fight for the Párijáta tree, which had been produced at the churning of the ocean, and planted by Indra in his own garden. An amusing account of this battle is given in the Vishṇu-Purána, p. 587. His wife's name is Śachí. He is lord of the eight Vasus. The sage Gautama pronounced upon him the curse of wearing one thousand disgraceful marks which he afterwards turned to eyes. He ravished the daughter of Puloman, whom he slew to avoid his curse. He is borne on a white horse. The rain-bow is supposed to be his bow bent for the destruction of his foes, and thunderbolts are his weapons. The heaven over which he rules, and which the other secondary deities inhabit, is, in the Epic age, called Swarga, and later, Indralóka, or Devalóka. His horse is Uchchhaihshravas; his elephant, Airávata; his city, Amarávati; his palace, Vaijayanta. These details belong to the Puránic age." (Thomson.)

Dr. Muir writes "Indra and Agni are said to be twin brothers. A variety of vague and general epithets are lavished upon Indra. He is distinguished as youthful, ancient, strong, agile, martial, heroic, bright, undecaying, all-conquering, lord of unbounded wisdom and irresistible power and prowess, wielder of the thunderbolt, &c. He has vigour in his body, strength in his arms, a thunderbolt in his hand, and wisdom in his head. * * * * The thunderbolt of Indra is generally described as having been fashioned for him by the Indian Hephaistos, Tvashtri, the artificer of the gods. Another instrument of warfare, a net, is assigned to Indra. 'This world was the great net of the great Sakra. With this net of Indra I envelope them all in darkness.'

"Invoked by his mortal worshippers Indra obeys the summons, and speedily arrives in his chariot to receive their offerings. He finds food provided for his horses, and large libations of soma juice are poured out for himself to quaff. He becomes exhilarated by these libations, which are also frequently described as stimulating his warlike dispositions and energies, and fitting him for his other functions, even for supporting the earth and sky. He is said to have drunk at one draught thirty bowls of soma." * * * * Thus exhilarated by soma juice, "Indra hurries off escorted by troops of Maruts, and sometimes attended by his faithful comrade Vishṇu, to encounter the hostile powers in the atmosphere, who malevolently shut up the watery treasures in the clouds. These demons of drought, called by a variety of names, as Vṛittra, Ahi, Śushna, Namuchi, Pipru, Śambara, Urana, &c., armed on their side also, with every variety of celestial artillery, attempt, but in vain, to resist the onset of the gods. Heaven and earth quake with affright at the crash of Indra's thunder. The enemies of Indra are speedily pierced and shattered by the discharge of his iron shafts. The waters, released from their imprisonment, descend in torrents to the earth, fill all the rivers and roll along to the ocean. The gloom which had overspread the sky is dispersed, and the sun is restored to his position in the heavens.' Constant allusions to these elemental conflicts occur in nearly every part of the Rig Veda; and the descriptions are sometimes embellished with a certain variety of imagery. The clouds are represented as mountains, or as cities or fortresses of the Asuras, or atmospheric demons, which Indra overthrows."

Dr. Muir selects a great variety of passages as specimens of the language in which Indra is most commonly celebrated in the hymns. He adds, "it will be observed that the attributes which are ascribed to him are chiefly those of physical superiority, and of dominion over the external world. In fact he is not generally represented as possessing the spiritual elevation and moral grandeur with which Varuṇa is so often invested." Vol. V., p. 103.

"Thou Indra art a friend, a brother
A kinsman dear, a father, mother.
Though thou hast troops of friends, yet we,
Can boast no other friend but thee.

With faith we claim thine aid divine,
For thou art ours and we are thine.
Thou art not deaf; though far away,
Thou hearest all, whate'er we pray.

Preserve us friend, dispel our fears,
And let us live a hundred years.
And when our earthly course we've run,
And gained the region of the sun,
Then let us live in ceaseless glee,
Sweet nectar quaffing there with thee."

O. S. T., Vol. V., p. 139.

Indrani—The wife of Indra (called also Sáchi) is represented as an ever-blooming virgin, and whilst the dignity of the king of the gods passes from one to another, she remains the wife of each succeeding Devéndra. Indráni, never a mother herself, had a son, Chitraputra, born unto her of a cow, as a reward for the austerities which she practised in honour of Iswara, to the end that he might grant her a son. When Chitraputra was born from the cow, Indráni felt like a woman in travail, and her breasts became full, so that she could nurse the child.

In the Rig Veda one speaker says "I have heard that among all these females Indráni is the most fortunate; for her husband shall never at any future time die of old age." The Aitareya Brahmaṇa alludes to a wife of Indra, called Prásahá. The Śatap. Br. says "Indráni is Indra's beloved wife, and she has a head dress of all forms." O. S. T., Vol. V., p. 82.

Indras of the Manwantara—Each Manwantara has its own Indra. The Indra of the second Manwantara was Vipaschil; of the third, Susanti; of the fourth Śiva (also named Satakrata, as he obtained the honour by his performance of a hundred sacrifices,) of the fifth Vibha; of the sixth, Manojava; of the seventh, Purandara; of the eighth, Báli; of the ninth, Adbhuta; of the tenth, Sánti; of the eleventh, Vrisha; of the twelfth, Rithudáma; of the thirteenth, Divaspati; of the fourteenth, Suchí.

Indra-dwipa—One of the nine portions of the Varsha of Bharata.

Indradyumna—The king of Avanti, who erected the temple of Vishṇu at Purushottama Kshetra, and set up the image of Jagganátha, made for him by Visvakarman.

Indrajit—The bravest and most powerful of the sons of Rávaṇa. His original name was Megha-náda, but was changed by Brahmá to Indrajit, in commemoration of the latter having obtained a victory over Indra. He was skilled in magic, could render himself invisible, possessed enchanted weapons, described as a kind of rope, which when thrown at an enemy became transformed into a serpent, and retained him in its folds. By means of these magical weapons he pierced a great number of warriors and inflicted terrible wounds on all the leaders of Ráma's army; viz., Sugríva, Angada, Níla, Jámbavat, Nala, Tára, Śarabha, Sushena, Panasa, Gandhamadana, Dwivida, Keṣarí, Sampáti, Binata, Rishabha; as well as on Ráma and Lakshmána, leaving them for dead. They were all restored by the exhalations issuing from the healing plants brought by Hanumán from Kailasa. All this occurred after Hanumán had destroyed the great army of Rákshasas sent against him by Rávaṇa, the latter being filled with dismay, ordered his son Aksha to go forth, and he was also slain. Then Rávana filled with grief sent for his famous son Indrajit, and said go you and conquer this evil Monkey. Indrajit then ascended his chariot, drawn by four tigers, and went out at the head of a vast army to fight against the Monkey chief. The combat commenced, but Indrajit could not conquer until he bound Hanumán in the irresistible noose of Brahma. Afterwards Indrajit performed three sacrifices to Agni, and confined Ráma and Lakshmána in his noose, and successfully charged the army of Monkeys. He was ultimately killed by Lakshmána, with an arrow given to him by Indra at the hermitage of Agastya.

Indra-kila—A mountain of the Vishṇu Purána but not identified.

Indra-loka—Amarávati, the heaven of Indra and Kshatriyas, called also Swarga. It was built by Viṣvakarma, the architect of the gods, a son of Brahmá. It is described as eight hundred miles in circumference, and forty miles high. Its pillars are composed of diamonds; all its thrones, beds, etc., of pure gold, as also its palaces. It is surrounded by beauteous gardens and pleasure grounds, interspersed with pools, fountains, etc., while music, dancing, and every sort of festivity entertain the celestial inhabitants. The audience chamber is so large that it accommodates all the three hundred and thirty millions of celestials, together with the forty-eight thousand Rishis, and the multitude of attendants.

Indrapramita—A pupil of Paila and teacher of a Sanhita of the Rig Veda. Indrapramita imparted his Sanhita to his son Mandakeya, and it thence descended through successive generations as well as disciples.

Indra-prastha—The city of the Pándavas situated between Delhi and the Kútub. "The pilgrim who wends his way from the modern city of Delhi to pay a visit to the strange relics of the ancient world which surround the mysterious Kútub, will find on either side of his road a number of desolate heaps, the *debris* of thousands of years, the remains of successive Capitals which date back to the very dawn of history; and local tradition still points to these sepulchres of departed ages as the sole remains of the Ráj of the sons of Pándu, and their once famous city of Indra-prastha."* The Mahábhárata contains a poetical description of the flourishing state of the kingdom under the rule of Rája Yudhishthira. When he resolved on retiring from the world he gave the Ráj of Hastinápur to Paríkshit the son of Abhimanyu, and the Ráj of Indra-prastha to Yuyutsa, the only surviving son of Mahárája Dritaráshtra.

* Wheeler.

Indrasavarni—The Manu of the fourteenth Manwantara, according to the Bhágavata.

Indriyatma—"One with the senses;" a name of Vishṇu, who is described by five appellations.

1. Bhutátma, One with created things.
2. Pradhanátam, One with crude nature.
3. Indriyátma, One with the senses.
4. Paramátma, Supreme spirit.
5. Átma, Soul, living soul animating nature and existing before it.

Indumati Devi—The daughter of the Rája of Vidarbha and wife of Aja. [See Aja.]

Iravat—A son of Arjuna by the serpent nymph Ulupi.

Iravati—The wife of the Rudra Bhava according to the Bhágavata.

Isana—One of the eight Rudras of the Vishṇu Purána whose statue was the air.

Isa—A name of a month occurring in the Vedas, and belonging to a system now obsolete. It is one of the months according to the Vishṇu Purána in which the sun is in his southern declination.

Iswara—Brahma in the neuter form is abstract supreme spirit: and Iṣwara is the Deity in his active nature, he who is able to do, or leave undone, or to do anything in any other manner than that in which it is done. Iṣwara is that which knows all things as if they were present. Mahat is also called Iṣwara from its exercising supremacy over all things. In Southern India Iṣwara is identical with Śiva. All who profess the Śiva mata (the religion of Śiva) regard Iṣwara as the highest god in whose honour they have everywhere built pagodas, and celebrate many festivals. Iṣwara is also the name of one of the Rudras in the Váyu list.

Itihasa—Historical tradition taught by Vyása. It is usually supposed that by the Itihása the Mahábhárata is meant.

Ivilaka—One of the Andhra kings, the son of Lambódara.

J

Jabala—The mother of Satyakáma, who could not tell her son who was his father and to what gotra he belonged; the son had consequently the utmost difficulty in obtaining permission to become a Brahmá chárin. See Satyakáma.

Jabalas—Students of a branch of the Vájasaneyi, or white Yajush.

Jaggannatha*—This is perhaps the most famous form of Krishṇa. The image has no legs, and only stumps of arms. The head and legs are very large. At the festivals, the Brahmans adorn him with silver or golden hands.

Krishṇa having been accidentally killed by Jará, a hunter, he left the body to rot under a tree. Some pious persons, however, collected the bones of Krishṇa and placed them in a box. There they remained till King Indradyumna (a great ascetic) was directed by Vishṇu to form the image of Jaggannátha, and put into its belly these bones of Krishṇa. Viśvakarma (the architect of the gods) undertook to prepare it, on condition that he should be left undisturbed till its completion. The impatient king, however, after fifteen days, went to the spot; on which Viśvakarma desisted from his work, and left the god without hands or feet. The king was much disconcerted, but on praying to Brahmá, he promised to make the image famous in its present shape. Indradyumna then invited all the gods to be present at the setting up of this image. Brahmá himself acted as high priest, and gave eyes and a soul to the god, which completely established the fame of Jaggannátha. This image is said to lie in a pool, near the famous temple at Juggannátha-kshetra (*i. e.* Jagganath's field), near the town of Purí in Orissa, commonly called by the English, Juggernath's Pagoda.

---

* Vulg. "*Juggernath,*" *i. e.* "The Lord of the World."

There are many other temples to Jagannátha in Bengal and other parts of India, besides that in Orissa, built by rich men as works of merit, and endowed with lands, villages, and money, at which the worship of the god is performed every morning and evening.

There are two great annual festivals in honour of the god, viz., the Snán-yátrá in the month Jyaistha (May, June) and the Rath-yáthra in the following month Ásáṛha. These are everywhere most numerously attended; but especially those celebrated at the great temple at Purí. Thither pilgrims from the remotest corners of India flock to pay their adoration at the hallowed shrine. Between two and three thousand persons, it is computed, used to lose their lives on the annual pilgrimages to this temple, and not less than 200,000 worshippers were present at the festivals, from which the Brahmáns draw an immense revenue. Since the withdrawment of the large annual grant, however, which the British Government of India, till very recently, made to the Orissa Temple, the numbers attending these festivals have very greatly diminished. All the land within twenty miles round the "Pagoda" is considered holy; but the most sacred spot is an area of about six hundred and fifty feet square, which contains fifty temples, the most conspicuous of which is a lofty tower, about one hundred and eighty-four feet in height, and about twenty-eight feet square inside, in which the idol, with his brother Bala-Ráma, and his sister Subhadra, is lodged. Adjoining are two pyramidical buildings. In one, about forty square, the idol is worshipped, and in the other, the food prepared for the pilgrims is distributed. These buildings were erected in A. D. 1198. The walls are covered with statues, many of which are in highly indecent postures. The grand entrance is on the eastern side, and close to the outer wall stands an elegant stone column, thirty-five feet in height, the shaft of which is formed of a single block of basalt, presenting sixteen sides. The pedestal is richly ornamented. The column is surrounded by a finely sculptured statue of Hanumán, the monkey chief of the Rámáyana. The establishment of priests and others belonging to the temple has been stated to consist of three thousand nine hundred families, for whom the daily provision is enormous. The holy food is presented to the idol three times a day. His meal lasts about an hour, during which time the dancing girls, the Devadasi, belonging to the temple, exhibit their professional skill in an adjoining building. "At the Suán-yátra (or bathing festival) the god is bathed by pouring water on his head during the reading of incantations. At the Rath-yátrá (or car festival) the carriage, containing the three images (which has sixteen wheels and two wooden horses) is drawn by the devotees, by means of a hawser, for some distance. On this occasion many cast themselves beneath the ponderous wheels and are crushed to death."—*Small, H. S. L., p.* 157.

Jahnu—The son of Suhotra. This prince whilst performing a sacrifice, saw the whole of the place overflowed by the waters of the Ganges; being highly offended at this intrusion, he united the spirit of sacrifice with himself by the power of his devotion, and drank up the river. The gods and sages upon this came to him and appeased his indignation, and re-obtained Gangá from him in the capacity of his daughter.

> "It chanced that Jahnu, great and good
> Engaged with holy offerings stood.
> The river spread her waves around
> Flooding his sacrificial ground.
> The saint in anger marked her pride,
> And at one draught her stream he dried.
> Then god and sage and bard afraid,
> To noble high-souled Jahnu prayed.
> And begged that he would kindly deem
> His own dear child that holy stream.
> Moved by their suit, he soothed their fears,
> And loosed her waters from his ears.
> Hence Gangá through the world is styled
> Both Jahnaví and Jahnu's child."—*Griffiths.*

Jahnu is also the name of a son of Kuru. V. P.

Jahnavi—A name of Gangá as the daughter of Jahnu, as related above.

Jaimini—A pupil of Vyása, and teacher of the Sáma Veda. Also the name of a celebrated author in the South of India, who lived about the thirteenth century. He wrote a free translation from the Sanskrit of the Áswamedhika Parva of the Mahábhárata, detailing the horse sacrifice. This work is acknowledged by all sects to be the finest specimen of Canarese poetry in existence. 'He has read Jaimini' is a proverbial saying, equivalent to 'he is an accomplished man.'

Jainas—The Jainas were a very numerous and important sect in the eighth and ninth centuries of the Christian era. The founder of the system was Rishaba-deva, a Hindu, but the system itself was an off-shoot or after-growth of Buddhism with which it has many leading doctrines in common, but is distinguished from it by its recognition of a divine personal Ruler of all, and by its political leaning towards Brahmanism. The Jainas have left many monuments of their skill and power in the fine temples built in different parts of the Deccan, as well as in the provinces of Mewar and Marwar, which have been designated the cradle of their system. The literature of the Jainas is very extensive, including, besides Puránas of their own, various works in grammar, astronomy, mathematical science, medicine, &c. They were the first who reduced the Canarese language to writing, and cultivated it to a high degree of perfection. The best Epic poem in the Tamil language, the Chintámani, is the work of a Jaina.

"The leading tenets of the Jainas and those which chiefly distinguish them from the rest of the Hindus, are, first, the denial of the divine origin and infallible authority of the Vedas : secondly, the reverence of certain holy mortals, now termed Tirthankara, or saints, who acquired by practices of self-denial and mortification a station superior to that of the gods ; and thirdly, extreme and even ludicrous tenderness for animal life.

"The Jainas are still found in most of the provinces of Upper Hindustan ; in the cities along the Ganges, in Calcutta, but more especially to the westward. They are also numerous in Guzerat, in the upper part of the Malabar Coast, and are scattered throughout the Peninsula. They still form a large and importan division of the population of India. The name of the sect means a follower of Jina, the latter being one of the denominations of their deified saints ; and as another name of these saints is Arhát, the Jainas are also called Arhattas.—*Wilson.*

The following account of Jainism was written in Tamil by Munshi, Sástram Aiyar.* "The Jainas verily believe that their system alone was the primeval system of the world ; that all other systems were derived from it ; that some of the learned professors of their system, by the fault of the time in which they lived, formed various other systems ; that Móksha [bliss] can be obtained in this system and in no other ; that this alone is the true system ; and that all other systems believe falsehood to be truth.

"The Jainas positively affirm that the world exists from all eternity, and that it will exist for ever, without being destroyed, and that it was not created by God, or by any other person. They moreover affirm that this world is divided into three parts, namely, the lower world, the middle world, and the upper world ; and that below this world, there is a world called Adhogati [abyss, the nethermost hell], above which there are seven infernal worlds ; and above those again are ten Pavanalokas, purifying worlds [Purgatories], above which is this world of earth ; above this again is the Jotiloka, world of light [starry world] ; and that in this our world of earth there are two worlds included, namely, the Vyantraloka, world of demons [devils], and the Vidyadharaloka, world of demi-gods ; and again above these are sixteen different kinds of Devalokas, worlds of the gods, over which is the Ahamindraloka, world of Indra ; and above that again is the Mokshaloka, world of bliss ; where dwells the Lord of all these worlds, the Supreme Being, called the Anadi-chitta-para-meshti [Eternal-intellectual-heavenly-dweller.]

"They believe that this earth is sixteen cords high, and seven cords broad ; but this measurement is not within the comprehension of men ; it is known only to the wise. The seas and islands that are situated on the earth cannot be perceived and estimated by man's understanding. They affirm that in the midst of the earth is the great mountain Meru, and that to the South of it is situated the Bharata region, and to the North the Airavata region, and to the East and West is the Videha region. They also affirm that on both sides of Mount Meru are situated the three kinds of Bhogabhumi, fruitful, or felicitous regions ; and that the natives of these regions attain to great age and size ; that they cannot interchange places ; and that while it is day in one of the lands, it is night in the other. The people of Videha also attain to great age and stature.

"The Jainas consider Arugan to be their principal god, and worship him.

* From the Chintámani. By the Rev. H. Bower. Madras, 1868.

The popular name of this god is Jinan; and from this the appellation Jainas is derived. To this god one-thousand and eight sacred names are ascribed. His greatness is such that the three worlds worship and adore him. His knowledge is so great that it extends simultaneously to all things sentient. and unsentient, to things that have been conceived and that will be conceived, to worlds and to worldless spaces. He is powerful to impart the knowledge of his doctrines simultaneously to all kinds of living beings, in their respective language, without the aid of mind, word, or body; and this he does of pure grace, and not from any selfish motives. He does not possess the power [act] of creating anything, or of preserving anything. He is not subject to birth or death. He manifests great grace, and love, and mercy, to all sentient beings. He is of infinite wisdom, of infinite intelligence, of infinite power, and of infinite bliss. It is he that in the beginning, with a view of causing happiness to all living beings, made known the twelve primeval Vedas. He is the possessor of the triple-umbrella. He is without beginning and without end. He is the possessor of the three wheels of justice. He is represented with four holy faces, and as seated in the shade of the ashóka tree. He has forsaken the one hundred and forty-eight actions of life. He has declared that the Veda, the World, Time, Souls, Action, and Virtue are, like himself, imperishable and eternal objects.

"The god Arugan has declared that there is no other god besides himself; that all who worship and adore him will obtain bliss, and that those who do not worship him will not obtain bliss; that all living beings will enjoy the fruits of their good or evil actions; that by preponderance of evil, souls enter hell, and by preponderance of good, they enter the world of the gods; but when good and evil are equally balanced, they are born as human beings; when evil alone exists, they are born as irrational animals; and when both good and evil are destroyed, then they are liberated. Since Arugan has declared these things, the Jains firmly believe them to be true doctrines, and since all other systems have been intermediately introduced by certain persons, they positively affirm them all to be false systems.

"As Time is considered to be eternal, it is indestructable in its nature, and is divided into two sorts, viz., the Utsarpini and the Avasarpini time. The Avasarpini time has six stages, viz., good-good time, good time, good-bad time, bad-good time, bad time, and bad-bad time. In like manner the Utsarpini time has six stages, only that it begins at the bottom of the list with bad-bad time and goes backwards. In the Utsarpini time, beginning from bad-bad time, the age and stature of men increase, as that of the waxing moon. But in the Avasarpini time, beginning from the good-good time, the age and stature of men decrease, as that of the waxing moon. The increase and decrease of stature is up to six thousand Vils [bows], and down to a cubit. The increase and decrease of age will be from three pallams, to fifteen years. This account of pallams is not to be understood by men. In the above specified six divisions of time, the first consists of four krores of krores of oceans of years. The second consists of three krores of krores of oceans of years. The third consists of two krores of krores of oceans of years. The fourth, one krore of krores of oceans of years, save forty-two thousand years. The fifth consists of twenty thousand years. The sixth also consists of twenty thousand years. This account of oceans is not to be understood by men. The stage in which we now live is the fifth, viz., the bad time. When the two sorts of time, viz., the Utsarpini and Avasarpini times run out, it is said to be a Yugam. Utsarpini means the age of increase, and Avasarpani means the age of decrease.

"As the present is the Avasarpini time, we must infer that the three good stages of time have already passed by, and that the Bharata region, and the Airavata region have both been Bhogabhumis, fruitful lands. The people of those times, as before stated, had stature of body, and length of age adequate to the times. The people of those times forty-five days after their birth, became perfect men, and were well up in all sciences, and attained all knowledge by themselves, simply from the plastic power of the time. Moreover in these three stages of time there was no light of the sun or of the moon; but day and night were formed from the reflection and non-reflection of the Kalpaka trees. Those people at death entered the world of the gods, and did not go to hell. And they were not subject to the ordinary physical evils connected with disease, the discharges of the body, &c.

"Thus after the existence of the Bhogabhumi, when yet there was one-eighth of time, in the third stage, fourteen Manus were born. It was in the time of these Manus that the sun and moon, the stars and clouds appeared; division of time into years and months, the equinoctical or solstitial course, the lunar half-month or fortnight, the six seasons, the day of twenty-four hours, and the day as distinguished from night, were instituted; means of warding off the evils arising from wild beasts were discovered; rivers, tanks, reservoirs, mountains, and a variety of means of livelihood were brought into use. Of the above mentioned Manus, the fourteenth is said to have been Nabhi Mahárájah. In the reign of this Manu, as the people were born with the umbilical cord, the name Nabhi was given. In his reign clouds appeared, and it rained. Then appeared trees and various kinds of corn. By this Manu men were taught to eat fruit and grain, and the way of preparing food; and he also pointed out the way of weaving cloths from cotton, and of wearing them; and the use of flowers, garlands, perfumes, and ornaments, to adorn the person, came into vogue.

"This Nabhi Mahárájah is said by some to be Brahma. His consort was Murudeviammal. In his reign was born the first incarnated personage named Vrishabha Tirthankara. After him were born twenty-three Tirthankaras, equal to himself. In their days, the twelve Chakravartis, the nine Baladevas, the nine Vasudevas, and the nine Prativasudevas were all born in the fourth stage. These sixty-three persons were called Salaka purushas, divine personages.

"The twenty-four Tirthankaras, without the instruction of a Guru, were skilled in the circle of the sciences, knew the five Kaliyanas or ceremonies of the gods, were worshipped by the four classes of the gods, and at their very birth were endued with the three kinds of knowledge; they also had the fourth kind of knowledge, by the exercise of which they were cognizant of the thoughts of all living beings, and they also possessed the fifth kind of knowledge called Kevalajnanam [spiritual knowledge,] by which they were instantaneously cognizant of all things done in all the worlds. They sat exalted on the throne in the temple called Sambhavasaranam, constructed by the Devendras. They were the possessors of the triple-umbrella and the Ashoka tree; they were believed in as gods over gods, as omniscient, as lords of the three worlds, as removers of sin and bestowers of heavenly bliss, as persons praised by all living beings, as possessors of divine attributes, as bearing the one thousnd and eight divine appellations, as having the one thousand and eight divine marks on their sacred bodies, and as manifesting abundant grace, love, and mercy to all living beings, and pre-eminent in imparting instruction in their respective languages to the inhabitants of the celestial and the terrestial worlds, to those of the Nagaloka, Vaiyantriloka, and Jotiloka, and also to irrational animals, and inculcating the virtues, such as not killing, &c., prescribed in the twelve Vedas. As these twenty-four Tirthankaras are incarnations of wisdom, and are divine personages who appeared in the world and attained the enjoyment of heavenly bliss, the Jainas consider them to be Swamis equal to the divine-natured Arugan, who exists in this Avasarpini time. And accordingly they build temples in honour of these Tirthankaras, and make images like them of stone, wood, gold, and precious gems, and considering these idols as the god Arugan himself, they perform daily and special pujas [worship], and observe fasts, and celebrate festivals, in their honour.

"They moreover say that in the time of Vrishaba Tirthankara, and in the reign of Baradeswara, the first Chakravarti, the four castes, namely, the Brahman, the Kshatriya, the Vaisya, and the Sudra, were instituted in connection with this system.

"They moreover allege that in the time of Vrishaba Swami, who was the first Tirthankara, the Saiva system was first introduced; and about the same period, by the fault of the time, one hundred and six heterodox sects were established by Marichi, a Prajapati [Patriarch]; and that from the time of Vimalaswami, the 13th Tirthankara, the Vaishnava system was introduced;

and that in the time of Paraswanatha, the 20th Tirthankara, Mahomedanism was established. They also say that there are three hundred and thirty-six false systems of religion.

"They moreover affirm that during the period of the 20th Tirthankara, by the fault of the time, Yagam, animal sacrifice, was first introduced by an Asura named Mahakalesuran; and after the introduction of these Yagams, temples were built for Siva and Vishnu.

"Moreover, as it is declared in the Jaina Vedas that all the gods worshipped by the various Hindu Sects, namely, Siva, Brahma, Vishnu, Ganapati, Subramaniyan, and others, were devoted adherents of the abovementioned Tirthankaras, the Jainas therefore do not consider them as unworthy of their worship; but as they are servants of Arugan, they consider them to be deities of their system, and accordingly perform certain pujas in honour of them, and worship them also.

"As Jaina temples and idols are to be seen in all villages and countries, and in some places even underground, it is evident that the Jaina system, as declared in their Vedas, was the primeval system of the Hindus. As moreover, when the Jaina Vedas are carefully examined, there will be found in them many things calculated to benefit mankind; and since Jaina idols are to be found in all countries; and as the deities worshipped by others are believed to be devotees of Arugan; and as all the precepts of Arugan point only to what is good to all sentient beings; and by the great doctrine that no sentient being whatever, even a tree, should be destroyed; and as there are many things in the system beyond the reach of man's understanding, and which can by no means whatever be comprehended; and as it is evident from their Vedas as well as from experience, that all other systems originated among themselves through the fault of the time, from misunderstanding, and from a variety of other causes; it is evident that this system was the primeval one.

"The Jainas are divided into two parties, the Swetambaras, and Digambaras. Though both parties have the same Veda, they disagree in a few things. The Swetambaras have many internal divisions, and the Digambaras also appear to have a few internal divisions.

"The Jainas are prevalent in the North. Their tenets and observances are the following: They believe that not to kill any sentient being is the greatest virtue; not to tell lies, not to steal other men's goods, not to covet other men's wives, and to desire moderately such things as money, grain, house, garden, land, vehicle, clothing, &c.; these four ordinances they consider of equal importance with the injunction *not to kill.*

"Moreover, not to eat at night, and to drink water strained, are held to be high virtues. And not to drink toddy, or honey, or arrack, are also believed to be important injunctions. They are also forbidden to eat figs, the fruit of the banian, the peepul, the koli and the jujube, as well as the snake-vegetable, the calabash, gunjah (bhàng), opium, onions, assafœtida, garlic, radish, mushroom, &c. Such articles, and others which have much seed in them, they will not so much as think of eating even in an emergency where death is imminent on such abstinence; and any kind of flesh meat they will not even inadvertently touch with the hand.

"These and similar observances are enjoined on those who live in the domestic state; and if we were to write largely upon them many books would be required; we shall, therefore, abridge what we have to say. They have in fact twelve thousand injunctions to observe. But regarding those who live in the ascetic state, as much time will be required both to write and to read, we have not ventured to describe them. However, it is necessary to know that they firmly believe that there is no final liberation [bliss] in the domestic, but only in the ascetic state; nor is liberation to be attained by females, irrational animals, or Sudras, nor by celestial, nor infernal beings; and they moreover hazard the assertion that during the fifth and sixth stages of time there is no liberation for any one; and they show that *Time* alone is the cause of this evil. They also affirm that there are always three less nine krores of Munis [ascetics] on earth.

"The Jainas hold that the function [act, work] of the Divine Being is to exercise love and mercy to all living beings, and reveal to them the Vedas, in order that they may walk according to the precepts enjoined in them; and that the function [act, work] of all living beings is either to do good or evil, and have fruition of their deeds; and that the attainment of heaven or hell is also their own act, and that it is in their own power to renounce sin, and to obtain merit. This they consider to be true doctrine."

According to Mr. Max Müller the Nirwána of the Buddhists is absolute and total annihilation; but the Jainas certainly do not attach any such meaning to the term; it is with them a more defined state of existence than the Moksha of the Hindus. "The Jainas not only affirm that there is such a state, but they define the size of the emancipated souls, the place where they live, their tangible qualities, the duration of their existence, the distance at which they are from one another, their parts, natures and numbers. Those who attain to this nirwána, this extinction of action, this final liberation, do not return to a wordly state, and there is no interruption to their bliss. They have perfect vision and knowledge, and do not depend on works. (Rev. J. Stevenson. The Kalpa Sutra.)

As noticed in the extract given above from Munshi Sastram, the

Jainas are divided into two principal divisions, Digambaras and Swetambaras. The former word means 'sky-clad,' or naked, but in the present day, ascetics of this division wear coloured garments, and confine the disuse of clothes to the period of their meals. Swetambara means 'one who wears white garments;' but the points of difference between these two divisions are far from being restricted to that of dress: it is said to comprehend a list of seven hundred topics, of which eighty-four are considered to be of paramount importance. Amongst the latter are mentioned the practice of the Swetambaras to decorate the images of their saints with earrings, necklaces, armlets, and tiaras of gold and jewels; whereas the Digambaras leave their images without ornaments. Again, the Swetambaras assert that there are twelve heavens and sixty-four Indras; whereas the Digambaras maintain that there are sixteen heavens and one hundred Indras. In the south of India, the Jainas are divided into two castes; in Upper Hindustan, they are all of one caste. It is remarkable, however, that amongst themselves they recognise a number of families between which no intermarriage can take place, and that they resemble, in this respect also, the ancient Brahmanical Hindus, who established similar restrictions in their religious codes.

As regards the pantheon of the Jaina creed, it is still more fantastical than that of the Brahmanical sects, whence it is borrowed to a great extent, but without any of the poetical and philosophical interest which inheres in the gods of the Vedic time. The highest rank amongst their numberless hosts of divine beings—divided by them into four classes, with various sub-divisions—they assign to the deified saints, which they call Jina, or Arhat, or Tirthankara, besides a variety of other generic names. The Jainas enumerate twenty-four Tirthankaras of their past age, twenty-four of the present, and twenty-four of the age to come; and they invest these holy personages with thirty-six superhuman attributes of the most extravagant character. Notwithstanding the sameness of these attributes, they distinguish the twenty-four Jainas of the present age from each other in colour, stature, and longevity. Two of them are red, two white, two blue, two black; the rest are of a golden hue, or a yellowish brown. The other two peculiarities are regulated by them with equal precision, and according to a system of decrement, from Rishabha, the first Jina, who was five hundred poles in stature, and lived 8,400,000 great years, down to Mahâvîra, the 24th, who had degenerated to the size of a man, and was no more than forty years on earth; the age of his predecessor, Pârswanatha, not exceeding one hundred years. The present worship is almost restricted to the two last Tirthankaras; and as the stature and years of these personages have a reasonable possibility, H. T. Colebrooke inferred that they alone are to be considered as historical personages. As, moreover, amongst the disciples of Mahávîra there is one, Indrabhuti, who is called Gautama, and as Gautama is also a name of the founder of the Buddha faith, the same distinguished scholar concluded that, if the identity between these names could be assumed, it would lead to the further surmise that both these sects are branches of the same stock. But against this view, which would assign to the Jaina religion an antiquity even higher than 543 before Christ—the date which is commonly ascribed to the apotheosis of Gautama Buddha—several reasons are alleged by Professor Wilson. As to the real date, however, of the origin of the Jaina faith, as the same scholar justly observes, it is immersed in the same obscurity which invests all remote history amongst the Hindus. We can only infer from the existing Jaina literature, and from the doctrines it inculcates, that it came later into existence than Buddhism.

Jaitra—The name of the chariot of Krishṇa.

Jajali—A pupil of Pathya, and teacher of the Atharva Veda.

Jaleyu—One of the ten sons of Raudraswa, a descendant of Puru.

Jamadagni—One of the seven Rishis, or great sages of the seventh Manwantara, the present period.

Jamadagni—The son of Richíka, was a pious sage, who by the fervour of his devotions, whilst engaged in holy study, obtained entire possession of the Vedas. Having gone to king Prasenajit, he demanded in marriage his daughter Reṇuká, and the king gave her unto him. The descendant of Bhṛigu conducted the princess to his hermitage, and dwelt with her there, and she was contented to partake in his ascetic life. They had four sons, and then a fifth, who was Jámadagnya, (Ráma) the last but not the least of the brethren. Once when her sons were all absent, to gather the fruits on which they fed, Reṇuká, who was exact in the discharge of all her duties, went forth to bathe. On her way to the stream she beheld Chitraratha, the prince of Mrittikávatí, with a garland of lotuses on his neck, sporting with his queen in the water, and she felt envious of their felicity. Defiled by unworthy thoughts, wetted but not purified by the stream, she returned disquieted to the hermitage, and her husband perceived her agitation. Beholding her fallen from perfection, and shorn of the lustre of her sanctity, Jamadagni reproved her, and was exceeding wrath. Upon this there came her sons from the wood, first the eldest, Rumanwat, then Susheṇa, then Vasu, and then Viśwávasu ; and each, as he entered, was successively commanded by his father to put his mother to death ; but amazed, and influenced by natural affection, none of them made any reply : therefore Jamadagni was angry, and cursed them, and they became as idiots, and lost all understanding, and were like unto beasts or birds. Lastly, Ráma returned to the hermitage, when the mighty and holy Jamadagni said unto him, 'Kill thy mother, who has sinned ; and do it, son, without repining.' Ráma accordingly took up his axe, and struck off his mother's head ; whereupon the wrath of the illustrious and mighty Jamadagni was assuaged, and he was pleased with his son, and said, 'Since thou hast obeyed my commands, and done what was hard to be performed, demand from me whatever blessings thou wilt, and thy desires shall be all fulfilled.' Then Ráma begged of his father these boons ; the restoration of his mother to life, with forgetfulness of her having been slain, and purification from all defilement ; the return of his brothers to their natural condition ; and, for himself, invincibility in single combat, and length of days ; and all these did his father bestow.

"It happened on one occasion, that, during the absence of the Rishi's sons, the mighty monarch Kárttavírya, the sovereign of the Haihaya tribe, endowed by the favour of Dattátreya with a thousand arms, and a golden chariot that went wheresoever he willed it to go, came to the hermitage of Jamadagni, where the wife of the sage received him with all proper respect. The king, inflated with the pride of valour, made no return to her hospitality, but carried off with him by violence the calf of the milch cow of the sacred oblation, and cast down the tall trees surrounding the hermitage. When Ráma returned, his father told him what had chanced, and he saw the cow in affliction, and he was filled with wrath. Taking up his splendid bow, Bhárgava, the slayer of hostile heroes, he assailed Kárttavírya, who had now become subject to the power of death, and overthrew him in battle. With sharp arrows Ráma cut off his thousand arms, and the king perished, The sons of Kárttavírya, to revenge his death, attacked the hermitage of Jamadagni, when Ráma was away, and slew the pious and unresisting sage, who called repeatedly, but fruitlessly. upon his valiant son. They then departed ; and when Ráma returned, bearing fuel from the thickets, he found his father lifeless. V. P. See Ráma.

Jambavat—The king of the bears, that killed the lion that slew Prasena, the possessor of the Syamantaka gem. The lion had the jewel in his mouth when he was killed by Jámbavat, who carrying off the gem retired into his cave, and gave it to his son Sukumára to play with. The murder of Prasena having been ascribed to Krishṇa, he determined to recover the gem, and having found the cavern of Jámbavat, he saw the brilliant jewel in the hands of the nurse, who called loudly for help. Hearing her cries Jámbavat came into the cave, and a conflict ensued between him and Krishṇa which lasted twenty-one days. At last Jámbavat was vanquished and acknowledged the divinity of Krishṇa, who then alleviated the bodily pain the bear suffered from the fight. Jámbavat prostrated himself and offered his daughter Jámbavati along with the Syamantaka jewel. Jámbavat was one of the generals in Ráma's army at the siege of Lanka. He was severely wounded by the magical weapons of Indrajit ; but was still conscious, and made known to Hanumán the existence of the four medicinal herbs, that grew at Kailása on the Himálaya mountains, and by virtue of which all the dead and wounded might be restored. Hanumán at once flew to the spot, and brought the mountain peak and all its contents back with him to the camp, and Jámbavat, with the other chiefs were soon made well.

Jamabvati—One of the wives of Krishṇa obtained as related in the preceding article.

Jambu—The name of the rose-apple tree on Mount Gandhamádana, the southern buttress of Mount Meru. From the Jambu-tree the insular continent, Jambu-dwípa derives its appellation. The apples are said to be as large as elephants. V. P.

Jambu-dwipa—The centre of the seven great insular continents, which, with the seven seas, are supposed to form alternate concentric circles. In the centre of Jambu-dwípa is the golden mountain Meru.

Jambumali—The son of the Commander-in-Chief of the Rákshasas, who was sent by Rávaṇa against Hanumán with orders not to return until he had slain the blood-thirsty monkey. But Hanumán took up a large tree and hurled it at the head of his enemy ; afterwards he took up a pillar and threw it at Jambu-máli, dashing him and his chariot to pieces.

Jambunada—The soil in the banks of the river Jambu, absorbing the Jambu juice, and being dried by gentle breezes becomes the gold termed Jambunáda, of which the ornaments of the Siddhas are fabricated.

Jambu river—The apples of the Jambu tree are as large as elephants ; when they are rotten they fall upon the crest of the mountain, and from their expressed juice is formed the Jambu-river, the waters of which are drunk by the inhabitants ; and in consequence of drinking of that stream they pass their days in content and health, being subject neither to perspiration, to foul odours, to decrepitude, nor organic decay. V. P.

Janaka—The Rája of Mithila (the modern Tirhoot) the successor of Nimi, called Janaka from being born without a progenitor. Another Rája of Mithila of the same name, called also Siradharaja, is the more celebrated as the father of Síta.

He received Viswamitra the sage with Ráma and Lakshmána, and exhibited to them the great bow of Śiva, informing them that his daughter Síta was promised to the Rája who could bend the bow. Ráma then bent the bow in their presence and claimed his reward. The Rája invited Dasaratha to the marriage, and proposed to marry his two daughters to Ráma and Lakshmána ; and his two nieces to Bhárata and Satrughna. The sages approved of the marriages of the four damsels to the four sons of Dasaratha. The latter performed a great Sráddha to the ghosts of his deceased ancestors, and gave four lakhs of cows with their calves to the Brahmans, being a lakh for each son, and each cow was adorned with horns of pure gold. The marriage rites were then performed with great pomp and overpowering splendour. (Ramáyana) Janaka was also the name of a king of Magadha, and seems to have been a general title of Mithila kings.

Janakpur—A ruined city in the northern skirts of the Mithila district (Tirhút) and supposed to indicate the site of a city founded by one of the princes of that name.

Jana-loka—The heaven of saints where Sanandana and other pure-minded sons of Brahma reside, situated twenty millions of leagues above Dhruva. During a pralaya or general conflagration of all things at the end of a Kalpa, Jana-loka is beyond the reach of the all-devouring flame ; and the saints who dwell in Maharloka, when the heat of the flames that destroy the world, is felt by them, repair to Jana-loka in thin subtile forms, destined to become re-embodied, in similar capacities as their former, when the world is renewed at the beginning of the succeeding Kalpa. V. P.

Janamejaya—The king of Vaiṣáli, whose father Sómadatta celebrated ten times the sacrifice of a horse. Also a son of Puranjaya, a descendant of Ana. Paríkshit, the son of Kuru, had also a son named Janamejaya ; and another Paríkshit, the son of Abhimanyu, had a son named Janamejaya.

Janarddana—The name of Vishṇu as the one only God, derived from Jana 'men' and Arddana, worship, the object of adoration to mankind.

Janasruti—A king mentioned in the Chhándogya-Upanishad, described as charitably-disposed, the giver of large gifts, and the preparer of much food ; who built houses everywhere that people from all sides might come and feast therein.

Jangalas—One of the aboriginal tribes, dwellers in thickets and jungles. Many of the aborigines were driven into the forests by the Aryan invaders.

Jangams, or Lingayats—One of the forms in which the Linga worship appears, is that of the Lingáyats, Lingawants, or Jangams, the essential characteristic of which is wearing the emblem on some part of the dress or person. The type is of a small size, made of copper or silver, and is commonly worn, suspended in a case, round the neck, or sometimes tied in the turban. In common with the Saivas generally, the Jangamas smear their foreheads with *Vibhúti* (ashes), wear necklaces, and carry rosaries made of the Rudráksha seed. The clerical members of the sect usually stain their garments with red ochre. They are not numerous in upper India, and are rarely encountered except as mendicants, leading about a bull, the living type of Nandi, the bull of Śiva, decorated with housings of various colours and strings of kauṛí shells. The conductor carries a bell in his hand, and, thus accompanied, goes about from place to place, subsisting upon alms. In the South of India the Lingáyats are very numerous, and the officiating priests of the *Śaiva* shrines are commonly of this sect, when they bear the designations of *Àrádhya* and *Pandáram.* The sect is also there known by the name of *Víra Śaiva.* The restorer if not the founder of this faith, was Basava whose history is given in the Basava Purána, q. v.—*H. H. Wilson, Vol. I, p.* 224.

Janma—A birth ; a state of existence ; nativity, one of the branches of the study included in the Brihat-Sanhita.

Jantu—The eldest of the hundred sons of Sómaka. Also the name of a son of Sudanwan.

Jara—An allegorical personage signifying ' old age' ' decay'—mentioned in the Vishṇu Purána as the name of the hunter by whom Krishṇa was slain. He mistook the foot of Krishṇa for part of a deer, and shooting his arrow lodged it in the side. He then said, ' Have pity on me ; I have done this unwittingly, Krishṇa forgave him and sent him to heaven in his own car. Jará was also the name of the female fiend who united the two parts of Jarasandha.

Jaradgava—The southern portion or Avashtháña of the planetary sphere or path of the sun and planets amongst the lunar asterisms.

Jaradgavi—A division of the lunar mansions, occurring in the Central or Vaiswánara Avastháña.

Jarasandha—The son of Vrihadratha, who was born in two parts and put together by the female fiend Jarà. When he grew up he became king of Magadha, and hearing that Krishṇa had killed his son-in-law, he collected a large force and beseiged Mathura; he was defeated, but renewed the attack eighteen times without success. When Yudhiṣhthira was about to perform the Rájasúya, Krishṇa informed him that there was one Rája still to be conquered before he began the great sacrifice, and that was Jarásandha the Rája of Magadha. Krishṇa, Arjuna and Bhíma then disguised themselves as brahmans and journeyed to the city of Magadha, and Bhíma challenged Jarásandha to single combat; the challenge was accepted and after a hard contest the Rája was slain. The story is related at great length in the Mahábharata, but the details are purely mythical.

Jaratkaru—The Vyasa of the twenty-seventh Dwápara.

Jarudhi—One of the mountain ridges which project from the base of Mount Meru, on the western side.

Jataka—A birth; a state of existence; the title of one of the sacred books of the Buddhists, containing an account of Gautama Buddha in 550 different births.

Jatas—One of the five great divisions of the Haiháya tribe.

Jatayu—A son of Syení and Aruṇa. A semi-divine bird, the friend of Ráma, who fought in defence of Síta. He heard her cries in the chariot of Rávana, stopped the chariot and fought desperately with the formidable giant, but was mortally wounded and only lived to make known to Ráma the fate of Síta. The funeral rites of the chief of vultures were carefully performed by Ráma and Lakshmána.

Jathara—A range of mountains running north and south, and connecting the two chains of Nishadha and Níla.

Jatharagni—The name in a previous birth of the Muni Agastya.

Jatharas—A tribe of aborigines inhabiting the mountain range termed Jathara.

Jaughira—An interesting and picturesque place of pilgrimage between Bhagulpúr and Monghír. In the middle of the river there is a romantic rock, with a temple surmounting it sacred to Śiva; while in the mainland, and close to the small town, there is another hill of the same kind, on which temples have been built, some of them of great antiquity. The place has long enjoyed the reputation of being the residence of holy devotees; Mussalman as well as Hindu.

Javali—A renowned logician who at Chitra Kúta endeavoured to persuade Ráma that it was his duty to accept the Ráj when Bharata himself offered it. Ráma regarded his arguments as atheistical and wanting in respect for his deceased father the Mahárája. Javáli ultimately recants. Mr. Wheeler regards the incident as an interpolation to bring forward Buddhism and Atheism for the sake of refuting them.

Jaya—One of the kings of Mithila, the son of Gusruta.

Jayadratha—A descendant of Anu and son of Vrihanmanas. Also the name of a son of Vrihatkarman, a descendant of Hastin.

Jayadhwaja—The king of Avanti; one of chief of the hundred sons of Kárttavírya.

Jayanta—A name applied to one of the Rudras. The Puranic writers apply to the Rudras different appellations of the common prototype, or synonyms of Rudra and Śiva, selected at random from his thousand and eight names.

Jayantpura—A city founded by Nimi, near the Áṣrama of Gautama.

Jayas—In the beginning of the Kalpa twelve gods, named Jayas, were created by Bramha as his deputies and assistants in the creation. They, lost in meditation, neglected his commands; on which he sentenced them to be repeatedly born in each

Manwantara till the seventh. They were accordingly in the several successive Manwantaras, Ajitas, Treshitas, Satyas, Haris, Vaikunthas, Sadyas, and Ádityas.

Jayati—The metre created from the western mouth of Bramha along with the Sáma Véda, the collection of hymns termed Saptadása and the Aitarátra sacrifice.

Jayasena—The son of Adína; one of the descendants of Kuru, Sarvabhauma had a son also named Jayasena.

Jhajhara—A daitya of great prowess, the son of Hiraṇyaksha.

Jillikas—one of the aboriginal or Non-Aryan tribes mentioned in the V. P.

Jimuta—A prince, son of Vyoman, a descendant of Jyámagha.

Jiva—The soul; "Spirit cannot change; intelligence has no knowledge; the soul (*jíva*) knowing things in excess is subject to illusion, and says, 'I act, I see.' If spirit falls into the error of supposing the individual soul, *jíva*, to be itself, as one might suppose a rope to be a snake, it becomes frightened; but so soon as it perceives I am not *jíva*, but the Supreme spirit, (*parátman*) it is released from all fear." *Atma Bodha, quoted in A. and M. I., Vol. I, p.* 212.

Jivata—Man's individual spirit; it is an error to attribute the spirit of life (or man's individual spirit, *jívata,*) to the Supreme Spirit, just as it is an error to take a post for a man. When once the true nature of *jívata* has been recognised *jívata* itself disappears." *Atma Bodha, quoted in A. and M. I. p.* 214.

Jogi—See *Yogi.*

Jumnotree—A sacred spot in the Himálaya mountains, near a junction of three streams. From the bed of the torrent the mountain rises at once to its height, apparently without any very extensive irregularities, and the steepness of the declivity at this point may in some degree be estimated, when it is understood that here, though at the foot of this upper region of the mountain, the very peaks are seen towering above as ready to overwhelm the gazer with the snow from their summit, and, in fact, the avalanches from above fall into the channel of the river. The particular spot which obtains the name of Jumnotree is very little below the place where the various small streams formed on the mountain brow, by the melting of many masses of snow, unite in one, and fall into a basin below. *Balfour's Cyclopædia of India.*

Jnana—"Wisdom," the various epithets applied to it in the Yoga philosophy are that it "requires no exercise," "without the practice of abstract contemplation;" "not to be taught," "not capable of being enjoined" "internally diffused," etc., "of all means knowledge alone is able to effect emancipation; as without fire there can be no cooking, so without *jnana*, science, there can be no final deliverance." *Atma Bodha, A. and M. I., Vol. I, p.* 210.

Jrimbhika—"Yawning," a form or manifestation of Brahmá. V. P. 40.

Jyamagha—A king, celebrated for his devotion to his wife. "Of all the husbands submissive to their wives, who have been or who will be, the most eminent is the king Jyámagha, who was the husband of Saivyá, who was barren: but Jyámagha was so much afraid of her, that he did not take any other wife. On one occasion the king, after a desperate conflict with elephants and horse, defeated a powerful foe, who abandoning wife, children, kin, army, treasure, and dominion, fled. When the enemy was put to flight, Jyámagha beheld a lovely princess left alone, and exclaiming, "Save me, father! Save me, brother!" as her large eyes rolled wildly with affright. The king was struck by her beauty, and penetrated with affection for her, and said to himself, "This is fortunate; I have no children, and am the husband of a sterile bride: this maiden has fallen into my hands to rear up posterity: I will espouse her; but first I will take her in my car, and convey her to my palace, where I must request the concurrence of the queen in these nuptials." Accordingly he took the princess into his chariot, and returned to his own capital.

When Jyámagha's approach was announced, Śaivyá came to the palace gate, attended by the ministers, the courtiers, and the citizens, to welcome the victorious monarch : but when she beheld the maiden standing on the left hand of the king, her lips swelled and slightly quivered with resentment, and she said to Jyámagha, "Who is this light-hearted damsel that is with you in the chariot ?" The king unprepared with a reply, made answer precipitately, through fear of his queen ; This is my daughter-in-law." "I have never had a son," rejoined Saivyá, "and you have no other children. Of what son of yours then is this girl the wife ?" The king disconcerted by the jealousy and anger which the words of Śaivyá displayed, made this reply to her in order to prevent further contention ; "She is the young bride of the future son whom thou shalt bring forth," Hearing this, Śaivyá smiled gently, and said, "So be it ;" and the king entered into his great palace. V. P.

Jyeshta—A lunar month corresponding to May.

Jyeshta—The goddess of misfortune ; produced at the churning of the ocean according to the enumeration in the Uttara Khaṇda of the Padma-Purána.—Also the name of a lunar mansion in Járadgavi in the Central Avashtána.

Jyotiratha—The name of a river mentioned in the Puránas, but not identified.

Jyotisha—"Astronomy ;" an anga of the Vedas, or subsidiary portion of the Vedas. "New moon festivals, and full moon festivals, were integral elements in eariy Hindu worship, and each veda appears to have had a calendar, called jyotisha ; but whether any original copies of these calendars still exist, seems doubtful. They are interesting as being first steps in astronomy, although constructed solely with a view to the regulation of religious ceremonies.

The Súrya Siddhánta, one of the most important of Sanscrit works on Astronomy, has been attacked and defended and explained by competent European scholars."

"M. Biot believed that the Hindus derived their system of nakshatras, or moon stations, from the Chinese ; and Professor Whitney shows that the Hindu nakshatra does not mean the same thing as the Chinese. *siew*. Siew means a single star, whereas nakshatra generally expresses a group of stars, or rather a certain portion of the starry heavens. * * * * The Arab manázil, and the signs of the lunar zodiac, bear a marked resemblance to the Hindu nakshatras, being groups of stars marking out the ecliptic into twelve nearly equal divisions. Such a system, Professor Whitney observes, is as well suited as any that could be devised for a people seeking to define the daily stages of the moon's revolution, without the aid of instruments.

"The path of the moon was in fact marked by twenty-seven stations believed by Hindu observers to be equi-distant. But when a 'new and more exact astronomy had been brought in from the West,' the moon was reduced in significance 'to one of a class of planetary bodies all whose movements were capable of being predicted, and their places at any given time determined, and their conjunctions calculated by an elaborate system of rules. Then first the lesser planets were mentioned by Hindu astronomers, and then first was an observation made by aid of the junction stars, which yielded a trustworthy date. That this must have been not far from A. D. 500 is, Professor Whitney considers, proved.

"The results of this one grand effort, never repeated and never rivalled, are recorded with occasional slight and unexplained modifications, by every succeeding author from century to century. The date coincides with that of the Hindu Astronomer Aryabhata ; and Aryabhata we understand, 'availed himself largely of the progress which the Greeks, (especially Hipparchus) had made in astronomy ; and 'not only improved upon their new theories and inventions, but added also the results of his own independent investigations.'

"The beginning of the sixth century stands out, therefore, as an important era in the history of astronomy in India ; and every fragment of intelligence concerning Aryabhata and his works becomes invested with peculiar importance. (See Appendix, Art. Aryabhata). His idea of the roundness of the earth is thus expressed :—

'The terrestrial globe, a compound of earth, water, fire and air, entirely round, encompassed by a girdle (*the equator*) stands in the air, in the centre of the stellar sphere. Like as a ball formed by the blossoms of the nauclea kadamba is on every side beset with flowerets, so is the earth-globe with all creatures, terrestrial and aquatic.'

"And this globe he believed to have a daily revolution. 'Aryabhata' says Dr. Kern, 'for aught we know was the first, and remained almost the sole astronomer among his countrymen, who affirmed the daily revolution of the earth on its own axis.' He gives the following quotation from one of Aryabhata's works :—

'As a person in a vessel while moving forward, sees an immovable object moving backwards ; in the same manner do the stars, however immovable, seem to move daily.'

Thus showing it is the earth not the stars which move :—

"On another occasion Aryabhata says, 'the sphere of the stars is stationary ; and the earth, making a revolution, produces the daily rising and setting of stars and planets.'

"Mr. Colebrooke states that 'Aryabhata affirmed the diurnal revolution of the earth on its axis ;' that he accounted for it by a wind or current of ærial fluid, the extent of which, according to the orbit assigned to it by him, corresponds to an elevation of little more than a hundred miles from the surface of the earth ; that he possessed the true theory of lunar and solar eclipses, and disregarded the imaginary dark planets of the mythologists and astrologers,—affirming the moon and primary planets (and even the stars) to be essentially dark, and only illumined by the sun.

"But after attaining this excellence, astronomy in India appears to have drifted away from science, for no second correct determination of polar longitude and polar latitude is recorded ; and writers subsequent to Aryabhata confuse astronomy with astrology."* See Bháskaracharya, Varáhamihira, &c.

The popular notion even at the present day is that an eclipse is caused by Ráhu, the demon, attempting to devour a portion of the sun or moon. See Ráhu.

Jyotishtoma—One of the great sacrifices, in which especially the juice of the soma plant is offered for the purpose of obtaining Swarga or heaven.

* Mrs. Manning. A. and M. I., vol. 1, p. 367.

Jyotishmat—The youngest of the ten sons of Priyavrata,—installed by his father king of Kúsa-dwípa. Jyotishmat had seven sons, after whom the seven portions or varshas of the island were named. At the end of all things the seven solar rays dilate to seven suns, one of which is termed Jyotishmat.—*Vishnu Purána.*

Jyotsna—" Dawn"—a form or manifestation of Brahma.

K

Ka—1, A name of Prajápati, the creator of the universe; "Ka is Prajápati; to him let us offer our oblations;" 2, A name given to Daksha; 3, The name of the divinity who presides over the excretory and generative organs.

Kabandha—1, A pupil of the Muni Sumanta who became a teacher of the Sanhitas of the Atharva Veda; 2, A mighty Rákshasa who attacked Ráma and Lakshmána in the forest, and was slain by them. When mortally wounded the Rákshasa informed them that he had originally been a Gandharva, but was changed by the curse of a sage to a Rákshasa until set free by Ráma. He then, assuming his real shape as a Gandharva, counselled Ráma to ally himself to Sugríva, with whose aid he might conquer Rávaṇa. The story is thus translated by Mr. Griffiths.

"A hideous giant then he saw,
Kabandha named, a shape of awe.
The monstrous fiend he smote and slew,
And in the flame the body threw;
When straight from out the funeral flame
In lovely form Kabandha came,
And bade him seek in his distress
A wise and holy hermitess.
By counsel of this saintly dame
To Pampá's pleasant flood he came,
And there the steadfast friendship won
Of Hanumàn the Wind-God's son.
Counselled by him he told his grief
To great Sugríva, Vánar chief,
Who, knowing all the tale, before
The sacred flame alliance swore."

Kabir—The most celebrated of the twelve disciples of the Hindu reformer Rámánand. He produced a great effect in the state of popular belief; assailing the whole system of idolatrous worship, and ridiculing the learning of the Paṇḍits and doctrines of the Śastras, in a style peculiarly suited to the genius of his countrymen. Kabír lived at the beginning of the 15th century. The Bhakta Málá gives an account of his birth and life. The doctrines taught by Kabír are contained in the *Sukh Nidán*, and do not differ much from those of the Vaishnavas. The moral code is short but favorable to morality.—*Wilson's Works, Vol. I, p.* 153.

Kachchas—An aboriginal tribe, the name of which implies that the people dwelt in districts contiguous to water and in marshy spots: such as the province still called Cutch.

Kachhapa—One of the sons of Viṣvámitra.

Kadamba—The name of the tree that grows on Mount Mandara, the flowers of which are said to yield a spirit on distillation, whence Kádambarí is one of the synonyms of wine or spirituous liquor.

Kadru—One of the daughters of Daksha, who was married to Kaṣyapa and had a progeny of a thousand powerful many-headed serpents.

Kaikasi—One of the daughters of Sumáli and Ketumati; Sumáli with his family lived for a long time in Pátaḷa; and once happening to visit the earth he desired his daughter Kaikasi to go and woo Viṣravas, who received her graciously, and she became the mother of the dreadful Rávaṇa, the huge Kumbhakarna, and the two younger brothers, who all grew up in the forest.

Kaikeya—One of the four sons of Śiví, who has given a name to a province and people in the northwest of India.

Kaikeyi—One of the queens of Mahárája Dasaratha, and mother of Bharata. When it was proposed to instal Ráma, the son of Queen Kausalya, as heir apparent, Kaikeyi was pleased, and offered a reward to her slave woman Manthara who brought her the news, saying

> "I joy that Ráma gains the throne,
> Kausalya's son is as mine own."

But the old hag Manthara, who disliked Ráma, excited the jealousy of Kaikeyi by representing the degradation and ruin that would come to Bharata and herself.

> "When Ráma's hand has once begun
> Ayódhya's realm to sway."

This roused her to action and she ran to the chamber of displeasure, sulky and angry. The Mahárája afterwards sought her, and finding her in this state of affliction, protested his love and affection, but she remained silent ; at last in a critical moment she extorted a promise from him and then with "a woman's obstinacy compelled him to keep his word." "He had made the promise and she insisted upon its fulfilment. To all he could urge she had but one answer 'Unless Ráma is exiled and Bharata is installed, you will be stigmatized as a liar and I will take poison.'"

> "The monarch as Kaikeyi pressed
> With cruel words her due request,
> Stood for a time absorbed in thought,
> While anguish in his bosom wrought."

The result was the exile of Ráma ; and when her own son Bharata returned from Girivraja he strongly reproached his mother for what she had done. She lived, however, to rejoice in Ráma's return to his kingdom.

Kaikeyas—The five sons of Dhristakétu, rajah of Kaikeya, are termed the Kaikeyas.

Kailakila Yavanas—A race of kings, who lived when the Greek princes or their Indo-Scythic successors, following the course of the Indus, spread to the upper part of the western coast of the peninsula. From an inscription which has been found dated A. D. 1058, Kilakila, or Kilagila as it is there termed, is called the capital of Márasinha Deva, king of the Konkan.

Kailasa—A mountain situated like Meru, in the lofty regions to the north of the Himálaya, and celebrated in the traditions and myths of India. "Meru and Kailása are the two Indian Olympi. Perhaps they were held in such veneration because the Sanskrit-speaking Indians remembered the ancient home where they dwelt with the other primitive peoples of their family before they descended to occupy the vast plains which extend between the Indus and the Ganges."—*Gorresio.*

In the Puránas Kailása is a fabulous mountain several yójanas in breadth, to the west of Meru. Kailása is described as a mountain of pure silver, brilliantly white, and as the residence of Śiva. In former ages it is said all the mountains had wings; but their flights were productive of so much mischief and danger, that Indra struck off their wings with his thunderbolts, and fixed them in their present position. Kailása is often mentioned in the Rámáyana, as in the region of the sacred lakes, near the northern heights of the Himálayas.

Kaisika—One of the sons of Vidarbha, (q. v.) and grandson of Jyámagha.

Kaitabha—A formidable demon, who with his companion Madhu, sprung from the ear of Vishṇu, when he was sunk in his sleep of contemplation, (Yoganidrá) at the end of the Kalpa; the demons were about to kill Brahmá, when the latter, seeing Vishṇu asleep, with the view of arousing him began to celebrate the praises of Yoganidrá. O. S. T., Vol. IV., p. 371.

Kaivalya—The fourth chapter of the Yóga Sútras, being a treatise on the extatic abstraction or isolation of the soul. The state of emancipation that may be obtained even during life: it is termed jivanmukti; and is the highest state of Yóga before the soul is actually re-absorbed into the Supreme Being. The body still exists, and of course the soul exists within it; but its connection with it is supposed to be entirely broken, and the soul can consequently quit and re-enter the body, and wander about where and as it lists. *J. C. Thomson.*

Kajnghas—An aboriginal tribe mentioned in the Purána lists, but not satisfactorily identified.

Kakamukhas—A nickname or term of derision, meaning crow-faced, applied to designate some of the aboriginal tribes.

Kakas—A tribe of aborigines, dwelling on the banks of the Indus, as it leaves the mountains.

Kakavarna—One of the kings of Magadha, who reigned for thirty-six years ; he was the son of Siṣunaga.

Kakshas—The same as Kachchas.

Kaksheya—One of the ten sons of Raudraswa, a descendant of Puru.

Kakshivat—A young poet and sage, to whom Rája Swanaya on the banks of the river Indus, gave his ten daughters in marriage ; and in return was duly praised in a vedic hymn composed by his enthusiastic son-in-law. Wilson's Rig Veda. He was a worshipper of the Aṣvins, who bestowed on him wisdom, and caused a hundred jars of wine and honied liquor to flow forth from the hoof of their horse as from a sieve. O. S. T., Vol. V, p. 246.

Kakubha—A mountain in Orissa.

Kakud—One of the daughters of Daksha who was married to Dharma.

Kakudmin—A name of Raivata, the prince who went to the heaven of Brahma to consult the god where a bridegroom fit for his lovely daughter should be found.

Kakutstha—In the Treta age a violent war broke out between the gods and the Asúras, in which the former were vanquished. They consequently had recourse to Vishṇu for assistance and propitiated him by their adorations. Náráyana had compassion on them and said, there is an illustrious prince named Puranjaya, the son of a royal sage ; into his person I will infuse a portion of myself, and by him subdue all your enemies. Acknowledging with reverence the kindness of the deity, the immortals quitted his presence, and repaired to Puranjaya to solicit his alliance.

The prince replied, " Let this your Indra, the monarch of the spheres, the god of a hundred sacrifices, consent to carry me upon his shoulders, and I will wage battle with your adversaries as your ally." The gods and Indra readily answered, " So be it ;" and the latter assuming the shape of a bull, the prince mounted upon his shoulder. Being then filled with delight, and invigorated by the power of the eternal ruler of all movable and immovable things, he destroyed in the battle that ensued all the enemies of the gods ; and because he annihilated the demon host whilst seated upon the shoulder (or the hump, Kakud) of the bull, he thence obtained the appellation Kakutstha (seated on the hump). V. P.

Kala—In the Vishṇu Purána the moon's surface is said to be divided into sixteen Kalás or phases ; the moon is also apportioned as a receptable of nectar, into fifteen Kálas or digits, corresponding to the fifteen lunations on the fourteen of which during the wane, the gods drink the amrita, and in the fifteenth of which the Pitris, exhaust the remaining portion. Professor Wilson remarks on the indistinctness of this account, but states that none of the other Puránas make it any clearer. Colonel Warren explains Kála, in one of its acceptations, ' the phases of the moon, of which the Hindus count sixteen.'

Kala—(Kalá.) A gradation or manifestation of the Múla Prakriti ; the principal Kalás are Swáhá, Swadhá, Dakshiná, Swasti, Pushti, Tushti, and others, most of which are allegorical personifications, as Dhriti, fortitude, Pratishta, fame, and Adharma, wickedness, the bride of Mrityu, or death. Aditi the mother of the gods, and Diti, the mother of the demons, are also Kalás of Prakriti. The list includes all the secondary goddesses.—*Wilson's Worhs, Vol. I, p.* 246.

Kala—(Kála.) Time. A form of Vishṇu. " The deity as Time is without beginning and his end is not known : and from him the revolutions of creation, continuance, and dissolution, unintermittingly succeed ; for when, in the latter season, the equilibrium of the qualities (Pradhána) exists, and spirit (Pumán) is detached from matter, then the form of Vishṇu, which is Time, abides." V. P., p. 12.

" This being the case it is asked what should sustain matter and spirit whilst separate, or renew their combination so as to renovate creation ? It is answered, Time, which is when every thing else is not ; and which, at the end of a certain interval, unites Matter, Pradhána, and Purusha, and produces creation. Conceptions of this kind are evidently comprised in the Orphic triad, or the ancient notion of the co-operation of three such principles in creation, as Phanes or Eros, which is the Hindu spirit or Purusha ; Chaos, matter or Pradhána ; and Chronos, or Kála, Time." (Professor Wilson). Kála is also a name of Yama, the Hindu Pluto. " In two remarkable hymns in the Rig Veda we find an altogether new doctrine ; Kála or Time is there described as the source and ruler of all things." O. S. T., Vol. V., p. 407.

Kala—(Kála) Thirty Káshtas make one Kála ; fifteen twinklings of the eye make a Káshta. Kála or Time, is thus computed :

15 Nimishas	=	1 Káshta
30 Káshtas	=	1 Kála
30 Kálas	=	1 Kshana
12 Kshanas	=	1 Muhúrtta
30 Muhúrttas	=	1 day and night.

Kala—(Kála) The name of one of the eleven Rudras according to the Bhágavata ; the son of Vasu Dhruva was named Kála. One of the daughters of Daksha, who was married to Kaṣyapa was named Kála.

Kalajoshakas—One of the aboriginal races mentioned in the Purános.

Kalaka—One of the daughters of Daksha who was married to Kaṣyapa.

Kalakas, Kalakanjas, Kalakeyas—The names applied to a class of Danavas who were powerful, ferocious, and cruel.

Kahlanabha—One of the many sons of Hiraṇyaksha ; also the name of a son of Viprachitti.

Kalanara—A prince, the son of Sabhánara, one of the descendants of Anu.

Kalanjara—A fabulous mountain, is placed in the Purúnas to the north of Meru.

Kala-nemi—The uncle of Rávaṇa ; the latter promised him half his kingdom if he would kill Hanumán. Kála-nemi consequently assumed the form of a devotee and created a magic hermitage on the mountain Gandha-mádana. When Hanumán reached the mountain and perceived Kála-nemi seated like a devotee upon a deer skin, with various rosaries round his neck, and apparently absorbed in meditation, he supposed he saw a devout sage worshipping the linga. Presently Kála-nemi beheld Hanumán, and welcomed him as his guest ; but Hanumán refused food and drink, and would only bathe in the pond which was near. When he dipped his foot in the water it was seized by a crocodile, which however he soon killed ; upon this a beautiful Apsara arose from the dead body, and told Hanumán how she had offended the sage Daksha, and had been cursed to become a crocodile until she should be delivered by Hanumán. She then thanked him for her deliverance and bade him beware of Kála-nemi. Meantime Kála-nemi being assured of the death of Hanumán, was pending over the division of the Ráj of Lanka, when Hanumán suddenly appeared before him and said " O you false hermit I know who you are ;" and seizing him by the feet whirled him round and suddenly let him loose ; he flew through the air to Lanka to the utter surprise of Rávaṇa and his councillors. " Kála-nemi," says Mr. Wheeler, " is a Hindu Alnaschar. He counts upon the pleasure he shall enjoy when taking half the Ráj without considering that Hanumán may be still alive. To this day when a Hindu thinks of future profit without being sure that he will get it, he is often compared with Kála-nemi."

Kalansa—A sub-division of the more important Kalás, or manifestations of Prakriti ; the Kalánsas are all womankind, who are distinguished as good, middling, or bad, according as they derive their being from the parts of their great original in which the Satya, Rajas, and Tamo Guna, or property of goodness, passion and vice predominate.

Kalapa—The name of the fabulous village in which Maru, a descendant of Kusa, has lived for a long period, through the power of devotion, that in a future age he may be the restorer of the Khshatriya race in the solar dynasty. V. P.

Kalasutra—One of the Narakas, or hells, enumerated in the Vishṇu Purána, and described as one of the awful provinces in the kingdom of Yama, terrible with instruments of torture.

Kalavas—One of the aboriginal races mentioned in the Puranas.

Kalayavana—The son of Gargya, as black as a bee, and hence called Kalayavana. He was king of the Yavanas, and having assembled a large army of Mlechchas and barbarians, advanced impatiently against Mathura and the Yádavas. Through the intervention of Krishna Kálayavana was led to enter the cavern in which Muchukunda was sleeping, and was there destroyed. Professor Wilson thinks the story may have originated in some knowledge of the power and position of the Greek Bactrian princes, or their Scythian successors, mixed up with allusions to the first Mahomedan aggressions.

Kalayavi—A disciple of Báshkali and teacher of the Rig Veda.

Kali—A male personification of the Kali age, or the fourth and last age through which the world is now passing. He wished to obtain Damayantí in marriage, and when he found that she had chosen Nala, he was greatly enraged and determined to be revenged. One evening when Nala failed in some ceremonial observance Kali seized the opportunity and straightway entered into him and possessed his inmost soul. Nala had a brother named Pushkara, and Kali said to Pushkara, go you and play at dice with Nala, and I will make you the winner of his Raj. Pushkara challenged Nala to a game at dice, and they sat down to play in the presence of Damayantí. They played for gold and jewels and raiment, for chariots and horses, but Nala was worsted at every throw, for Dwápara embodied the dice, and Kali had mastered him body and soul. Then the faithful friends of Nala prayed him to throw no longer, but he was maddened with the love of play, and shut his ears to all they said. He staked his Raj, and the vestments which he wore, and he lost all to Pushkara. Then followed his exile, see Nala. Kali after this induced Nala to desert Damayantí in the jungle, and this completed his revenge.

Kali—(Káli.) The Moloch of Indian Mythology. A form of Párvati, called Káli, or Mahá-Káli, the consort of Śiva, in his destroying character of Time. As such, she is painted of a black or dark blue complexion. In Calcutta, her images are usually seen of the last-mentioned colour. In plates, she is shown as trampling (as the personification of Eternity) on the body of Śiva (Time). In one hand she holds the exterminating sword, in another a human head; a third points downward, indicating, according to some, the destruction which surrounds her, and the other is raised upwards, in allusion to the figure of regeneration of nature by a new creation. Mr. Ward, however, is of an opinion, which he has expressed respecting others of the deities, but which appears to be much at variance with the character of Káli, who is here annihilating Time itself, *viz.*, that of the two last mentioned hands, one is bestowing a blessing, the other forbidding fear. Whatever her gestures may import, the image of this goddess is truly horrid, as are the devotional rites performed in honor of her. Her wild dishevelled hair reaching to her feet, her necklace of human heads, the wildness of her countenance, the tongue protruded from her distorted mouth, her cincture of blood-stained hands, and her position on the body of Śiva, altogether convey in blended colours so powerful a personification of that dark character she is intended to pourtray, that whatever we may think of their tastes, we cannot deny to the Hindus our full credit for the possession of most extraordinary and fertile powers of imagination. A model of this goddess has the body of a dark blue, the insides of the hands are red, as is also the circlet of hands round the waist. The heads which form the necklace have a ghastly appearance. Her tongue is protruded from her mouth, the sides of which are marked with blood. Her head-dress and other ornaments are splendidly adorned with gems of various kinds. The body of Śiva is white. Káli is also called the goddess of cemeteries, under which form she is described dancing with the infant Śiva in her arms, surrounded by ghosts and goblins (likewise dancing) in a cemetery amongst the dead. A paragraph appeared sometime ago in a Calcutta paper, which stated, that her images, under this form, were now worshipped by the Hindus as a propitiation against the destructive ravages of the cholera. To this ferocious goddess sanguinary sacrifices are made. The *Kalika Purána* which details, in due order and with much precision, the different descriptions of animals that are to be sacrificed, and the length of time by which this insatiate lady will be gratified and kept in good humour by each, ordains that one man (or a lion) will please her for a thousand years, but that by the immolation of *three* men she will graciously condescend to be pleased one hundred thousand years. The sacrificer must repeat the name Kali and pay her the compliment of saying "Hrang, hring, Kali, Kali ! O horrid-toothed goddess ! eat, cut, destroy all the malignant, cut with this axe ; bind, bind, seize, seize, drink blood, spring, secure, secure, salutation to Kali !" Immense sums of money are annually spent in the worship of this terrific deity. There is a celebrated temple dedicated to her at Kali-ghat in the vicinity of Calcutta, or the city of Kali, and impure sacrifices are offered to it ; and on the occasion of the festivals of Kali, her temples are literally swimming with blood. An adequate delineation of the scene, and of the horribly disgusting appearance of the executioners and other attendants of the place is scarcely possible.—*Coleman. Myth. Hind. p.* 94.

Kalidasa—The greatest dramatist, and one of the most celebrated poets of India. He is known to the literary public of Europe especially through his drama *Sakuntala* which, first introduced to the notice of the western world by Sir William Jones (1789,) created so great a sensation throughout Europe, that the early success obtained by Sanskrit studies in England and Germany may be considered due to this master-piece of Sanskrit literature. Another drama of the same poet, and next in renown to *Sakuntala*, is the *Vikramorvaśi*, or the Hero and the Nymph. Besides these works, Hindu tradition ascribes to his authorship a third drama and several poems, which no European critic will believe could ever have sprung from a mind like that of Kálidása. Professor Lassen, in the *Indische Alterthumskunde*, passes the following judgment on this poet : 'Kálidása may be considered as the brightest star in the firmament of Hindu artificial poetry. He deserves this praise on account of the mastery with which he wields the language, and on account of the consummate tact with which he imparts to it a more simple or more artificial form, according to the requirements of the subject treated by him, without falling into the artificial diction of later poets, or over-stepping the limits of good taste ; on account of the variety of his creations, his ingenious conceptions, and his happy choice of subjects ; and not less on account of the complete manner in which he attains his poetical ends, the beauty of his narrative, the delicacy of his sentiment, and the fertility of his imagination.' But although we are enabled by his works to appreciate the merits of this poet, we know little of his personal history. That he lived at Ujjayini or Oujein, and that he was 'one of the nine gems of the court of Vikramáditya,' is all that is related in regard to him. But as there have been several Vikramádityas at Ujjayini, his date is as uncertain as that of any personage of the ancient history of India. Dr. Bháo Dájî, in a learned and ingenious essay 'On the Sanskrit Poet, Kálidása' (*Journal of the Bombay Branch of the Royal As. Soc.*, October 1860), has endeavoured to identify Vikramádityá, the contemporary of Kálidása, with Harsha Vikramádityá, and the great poet would, therefore, have lived in the middle of the sixth century of the Christian era.—*Goldstücker*.

Kalika—One of the daughters of Vaiswánara, the wife of Kaşyapa and mother of the ferocious and cruel Danavas.

Kalikamukha—A distinguished Rákshasa chief, the son of Sumali and Retumatí; he was the uncle of the great giant Rávaṇa, and took part in the mythical battles with the gods.

Kalika Purana—This work contains about nine thousand stanzas in ninety-eight chapters, and is the only work of the series dedicated to recommend the worship of the bride of Śiva, in one or other of her manifold forms as Girija, Devi, Bhadrakáli, Káli, Mahámyá. It belongs therefore to the Sákta modification of Hindu belief, or the worship of the female powers of the deities. The influence of this worship shows itself in the very first pages of the work, which relate the incestuous passion of Brahma for his daughter Sandhya, in a strain that has nothing analogous to it in the Váyu, Linga, or Śiva Puránas.

The marriage of Śiva and Párvati is a subject early described, with the sacrifice of Daksha, and the death of Satí; and this work is authority for Śiva's carrying the dead body about the world, and the origin of the Pithást'hanas, or places where the different members of it were scattered, and where Lingas were consequently erected. A legend follows of the births of Bhairava and Vetála, whose devotion to different forms of Devi furnishes occasion to describe in great detail the rites and formulæ of which her worship consists, including the chapters on sanguinary sacrifices, translated in the Asiatic Researches.—*Wilson.*

Kalinda—The father of Kálindí, the goddess of the Jumna.

Kalindas—One of the tribes of Kshatriyas who from seeing no brahmans became outcasts. O. S. T., Vol. I, p. 482.

Kalindi—1, One of the wives of Krishṇa, the daughter of the Sun, whom Krishṇa met on one of his visits to Indraprastha, and who claimed him as the reward of her penance ; 2, The goddess of the Jumna ; 3, One of the widows of king Asit, and mother of Sagara ;

There came the other widowed queen
With lotus eyes and beauteous mien
Longing a noble son to bear,
And wooed the saint with earnest prayer.
When thus Kálindí fairest dame,
With reverent supplication came,
To her the holy sage replied :
'Born with the poison from thy side,
O happy queen shall spring ere long
An infant fortunate and strong
Then weep no more and check thy sighs
Sweet lady of the lotus eyes.'

Griffiths' Rámáyana.

4. The daughter of the king of the Asuras, who after her father's death offered her kingdom and herself, twin wives, to Mátanga (q. v.) who readily assented, married the damsel, and became king of Pátáḷa.

Kalinga—One of the five sons of Bali. Kalinga is the name of the sea coast west of the mouths of the Ganges, with the upper part of the Coromandel Coast. The inhabitants are called Kalingas.

Kaliya—A serpent king, into whose lake Krishṇa when a boy once leaped, and was severely bitten ; Krishṇa was then exhorted to put forth his celestial vigour, and soon bruised the head of the venomous and powerful snake. Kálíya then prayed for mercy saying, behold I am now without strength, without poison, deprived of both by thee, 'Spare my life.' The snake king was then liberated and sent into the sea.

Kali Yuga—The last age. It consists of 1,200 years of the gods, a year of men being a day of the gods; these divine years may, therefore, be converted into years of mortals by multiplying them by 360, which makes the duration of the Kali Yuga 432,000 years. The date of its commencement is fixed in the thirteenth or fourteenth century B. C., when Vishṇu returned to heaven after his incarnation as Krishṇa. During this age all things will decline, and the deterioration of mankind will be general. The Vedas will be disregarded. The minds of men will be wholly occupied in acquiring wealth; and wealth will be spent solely on selfish gratifications. Women will follow their inclinations and be fond of pleasure. Men of all degrees will consider themselves equal to Brahmans. Cows will be held in esteem only as they supply milk. These are a few of the evils, selected from the long catalogue of them contained in the Vishṇu Purána which are to prevail in the Kali age. A few redeeming properties of the age are, however, mentioned. The efficacy of devotion to Vishṇu is more strikingly manifested. The least moral merit obtains in this age, the greatest reward; and is by all classes most easily displayed. The Kali Yuga is to be followed by the Kṛita Yuga.

Kalki—An Avatára of Vishṇu to be born near the close of the Kali age, when all whose minds are devoted to iniquity shall be destroyed, and righteousness be established on earth; and the minds of those who live at the end of the Kali age shall be awakened and be as pellucid as crystal.

Kalmashapada—A prince, called also Saudasa. Kalmáshapáda, whilst hunting, encountered Śaktri, the son of Vaśísht'ha, in the woods; and on his refusing to make way, struck the sage with his whip. Śaktri cursed the king to become a cannibal; and Viśwámitra, who had a quarrel with Vaśísht'ha, seized the opportunity to direct a Rákshasa to take possession of the king, that he might become the instrument of destroying the family of the rival saint. Whilst thus influenced, Mitrasaha, a Brahman, applied to Kalmáshapáda for food, and the king commanded his cook to dress human flesh, and give it to the Brahman, who, knowing what it was, repeated the curse of Śaktri, that the king should become a cannibal; which taking effect with double force, Kalmáshapáda began to eat men. One of his first victims was Śaktri, whom he slew and ate; and then killed and devoured, under the secret impulse of Viśwâmitra's demon, all the other sons of Vaśiśt'ha. Vaśiśt'ha, however, liberated him from the Rákshasa who possessed him, and restored him to his natural character. V. P. For a somewhat different version of the legend, see O. S. T. Vol. I, p. 414.

Kalpa—A period of time: a great mundane age; a day of Brahmá. The most simple calculation of a Kalpa is its being 1,000 great ages or ages of the gods. Thus 4,320,000 years or a divine age, multiplied by 1,000 is equal to 4,320,000,000 years, or a day or night of Brahmá.

One year of mortals is equal to one day of the gods. 12,000 divine years are equal to a period of four Yugas which is thus made up, viz.:—

Kṛita Yuga,	with its mornings	and evenings,	4,800	divine years.
Tretá Yuga,	,,	,,	3,600	,,
Dvápara Yuga,	,,	,,	2,400	,,
Kali Yuga,	,,	,,	1,200	,,
		making	12,000	divine years.

As a day of the gods is = to one year of mortals, the 12,000 divine years must be multiplied by 360, the assumed number of days in a year, to give the number of the years of mortals in this great period of four Yugas, thus: 12,000 divine years × 360 = 4,320,000 years of mortals. 1,000 of these periods of 12,000 divine, or 4,320,000 human years—*i e.*, 4,320,000,000 human years, are = 1 day of Brahmá, and his night is of the same duration. Within that period of a day of Brahmá, 14 Manus reign, and a Manwantara, or period of Manu, is consequently = the 14th part of a day of Brahmá. In the present Kalpa (= a day of

Brahmá) six Manus, of whom Svayambhuva was the first, have already passed away, the present Manu being Vaivasvata. In each Manwantara seven Rishis, certain deities, an Indra, a Manu, and the kings, his sons, are created and perish. A thousand of the systems of four Yugas, as has been before explained, occur coincidently with these 14 Manwantaras ; and consequently about 71 systems of 4 Yugas elapse during each Manwantara, and measure the lives of the Manu and the deities of the period. At the close of this day of Brahmá a collapse of the universe takes place, which lasts through a night of Brahmá, equal in duration to his day, during which period the three worlds are converted into one great ocean, when the lotus born god, expanded by his deglutition of the universe, and contemplated by the yogis and gods in Janaloka, sleeps on the serpent Śesha. At the end of that night he awakes and creates anew.—*Wilson.*

Kalpa—The name of a son of Dhruva ; also an Anga of the Vedas, containing the Ritual: the ceremonials of the Atharva-Vedas are called the five Kalpas.

Kalpa-sutras—Aphorisms regarding the performance of sacrifices enjoined by the vedas ; written by human authors, and therefore not considered as Śruti or revelation, are yet regarded as of very high authority.

Kama-deva—The Hindu Cupid or Eros, or god of Love, considered to be one of the most pleasing creations of Hindu fiction, is the son of Vishṇu or Krishṇa by Lakshmi, who is then called Máyá or Rukminí. According to another account he was first produced in the heart of Brahmá, and coming out in the form of a beautiful female, was looked upon by Brahmá with amorous emotions. He is usually represented as a handsome youth, sometime conversing with his mother and consort in the midst of his gardens and temples ; sometimes riding by moonlight on a parrot or lory, and attended by nymphs, one of whom bears his banner, which consists of a fish on red ground. Endeavouring to influence Śiva with a passion of love for his wife Párvati, he discharged an arrow at him ; but Śiva, enraged at the attempt reduced him to ashes, or as some say to a mere mental essence, by a beam of fire darted from his central eye. Afterwards the relenting god declared that he should be born again in the form of Pradyumna, son of Krishṇa by Máya or Rukmini. The bow of Kámadeva is made of flowers, with a string formed of bees, and his five arrows are each tipped with the blossom of a flower, which is devoted to and supposed to preside over a sense. He is lord of the Apsarasas. Many names are applied to Káma-deva. He is called the god of desire ; the mind agitator ; the maddener ; the inflamer ; the destroyer of devotional tranquillity.

It is well known that Greek mythology connected Eros, the god of love, with the creation of the universe, somewhat in the same way as Káma is associated with it in the Rig Veda, x. 129. (See Eros in Dr. Smith's Dictionary.) In another hymn of the Atharva beda, Káma, like the Eros of the Greeks and Cupid of the Latins, is described as the god of sexual love. "May Káma, having well-directed the arrow which is winged with pain, barbed with longing, and has desire for its shaft, pierce thee in the heart." &c. O. S. T., Vol. V, p. 407.

Kamagamas—A class of deities of the eleventh Manwantara.

Kamakhya, Kamakshi—The name of a form of Dúrga in the north-east of Bengal. There are some celebrated temples in Assam dedicated to the goddess under this form.

Kamarupa—The name given to the eastern part of Bhárata-varsha. Also the name of a place of pilgrimage in Assam, where the temples referred to in the preceding article are built.

Kambala—One of the many-headed serpent kings, of the progeny of Kádru.

Kambalavarhish—One of the four sons of Andhaka.

Kambojas—A north-western tribe famous for their horses, of which they appear to have possessed a remarkably fine breed. They were conquered by Sagara, who would have destroyed them utterly, but at the request of Vaśiŝht'ha contented himself with imposing on all the vanquished tribes peculiar distinguishing marks, such as shaving their heads, letting their beards grow, &c.

Kameri—The Indian cuckoo, or bird of Káma, whose emblems are peculiarly appropriate, being a bow and arrow composed of roses and jessamine, and other flowers in which no thorns ever lurk. Colonel Tod says "the Kámeri poured forth its monotonous but pleasing notes, from an umbrageous peepul, amidst the stillness of a lovely scene, where the last tints of sunset illuminated the dark hues of the surrounding woods."

Kampilya—One of the five sons of Haryaswa. Their father said these my five (pancha) sons are able (alam) to protect the countries; hence they were called the Pánchálas. Pánchála was at first the country north and west of Delhi, between the foot of the Himálaya and the Chambal. It was afterwards divided iuto northern and southern Pánchála separated by the Ganges. Kampilya was the name also given to part of the country, and was called Kampil by the early Mahommedan invaders. Kampilya was the city of Rája Drupada.

Kamya—Daughter of Kardanea who was married to Priyavrata.

Kamyaka—An extensive forest on the banks of the Saraswati, to which the Pándavas retired, on the occasions of their second exile.

Kanakas—Inhabitants of Múshika, or the country of thieves, a name applied to the pirate coast of Konkan. Professor Wilson thinks it may also designate Malabar where polyandry then as now prevailed.

Kanakhala—The name of the village according to the Linga Purána, where the great sacrifice of Daksha took place. Gangadwára, the place where the Ganges descends to the plains,—or Haridwar, as it is more usually termed, is commonly specified as the scene of action.

Kanchana—The son of Bhíma, a descendant of Pururavas.

Kandarpa—A name of Káma the Indian Cupid.

Kandu—An eminent sage, who practised pious austerities on the lovely borders of the Gomati river. Indra sent the nymph Pramlochá to disturb his penance, and the sweet-smiling damsel diverted the sage from his devotions. They lived together in the valley of Mandura for a hundred and fifty years, wholly given up to enjoyment. Then the nymph requested permission to return to heaven ; but the sage still fondly attached to her, prevailed upon her to remain for some time longer ; and the graceful damsel continued to reside for another hundred years and delight the great sage by her fascinations. Then she again wished to return to the abodes of the gods, and again the Muni desired her to remain. Similar scenes occurred several times.

" On one occasion the sage was going forth from their cottage in a great hurry. The nymph asked him where he was going. ' The day,' he replied, ' is drawing fast to a close : I must perform the Sandhyá worship, or a duty will be neglected.' The nymph smiled mirthfully as she rejoined, ' Why do you talk, grave sir, of this day drawing to a close : your day is a day of many years, a day that must be a marvel to all : explain what this means.' The Muni said, ' Fair damsel, you came to the river-side at dawn ; I beheld you then, and you then entered my hermitage. It is now the revolution of evening, and the day is gone. What is the meaning of this laughter ? Tell me the truth.' Pramlochá answered, ' you say rightly,' venerable Brahman, ' that I came hither at morning dawn, but several hundred years have passed since the time of my arrival. This is the truth.' The Muni, on hearing this, was seized with astonishment, and asked her how long he had enjoyed her society ; to which the nymph replied, that they had lived together nine hundred and seven years, six months, and three days. The Muni asked her if she spoke the truth, or if she was in jest ; for it appeared to him that they had spent but one day together : to which Pramlochá replied, that she should not dare at any time to tell him who lived in the path of piety an untruth, but particularly when she had been enjoined by him to inform him what had passed.

" When the Muni, princes, had heard these words, and knew that it was the truth, he began to reproach himself bitterly, exclaiming, ' Fie, fie upon me ; my penance has been interrupted ; the treasure of the learned and the pious has been stolen from me ; my judgment has been blinded : this woman has been created by some one to beguile me : Brahmá is beyond the reach of those agitated by the waves of infirmity. I had subdued my passions, and was about to attain divine knowledge. This was foreseen by him by whom this girl has been sent hither. Fie on the passion that has obstructed my devotions. All the austerities that would have led to acquisition of the wisdom of the Vedas have been rendered of no avail by passion that is the road to hell.' The pious sage, having thus reviled himself, turned to the nymph, who was sitting nigh, and said to her, 'Go, deceitful girl, whither thou wilt: thou hast performed the office assigned thee by the monarch of the gods, of disturbing my penance by thy fascinations. I will not reduce thee to ashes by the fire of my wrath. Seven paces together is sufficient for the friendship of the virtuous, but thou and I have dwelt together. And in truth what fault hast thou committed? why should I be wrath with thee? The sin is wholly mine, in that I could not subdue my passions: yet fie upon thee, who, to gain favour with Indra, hast disturbed my devotions; vile bundle of delusion.'

"Thus spoken to by the Muni, Pramlochá stood trembling, whilst big drops of perspiration started from every pore; till he angrily cried to her, 'Depart, begone.' She then, reproached by him, went forth from his dwelling, and, passing through the air, wiped the perspiration from her person with the leaves of the trees. The nymph went from tree to tree, and as with the dusky shoots that crowned their summits she dried her limbs, which were covered with moisture, the child she had conceived by the Rishi came forth from the pores of her skin in drops of perspiration. The trees received the living dews, and the winds collected them into one mass. "This," said Soma, "I matured by my rays, and gradually it increased in size, till the exhalation that had rested on the tree tops became the lovely girl named Márishá." V. P.

Kanishtas—A class of deities of the fourteenth Manwantara.

Kanka—One of the sons of Ugraséna.

Kanouj—A city on the banks of the river Sone. The Rámáyana contains an extraordinary legend of its foundation. The Rája Kuṣanábha had a hundred beautiful daughters to whom Váyu the god of wind made some amorous proposals which they rejected, declaring that they would only accept such husband as their father might give them. Váyu then rendered them hunch-backed. Subsequently they were all married to a young Rája, Brahmadatta, who cured them by a touch, and the city in which they dwelt was henceforth called Kanyákubja, the hunch-backed, and still goes by the name of Kanouj.—*See Gritáchí, Kusanábha.*

Kanyakagunas—A race of Aborigines.

Kanyakubja—The city of the Bent Virgins, the modern Kanouj.

Kansa—Rajah of Mathura; he deposed his father Ugraséna; and threatened to slay his cousin Devaki on her wedding day. Vasudeva engaged to deliver up her children to him. He was warned before the birth of Krishṇa, that the latter would take away his life. He accordingly attempted to destroy Krishṇa as soon as he was born; failing in this he ordered that all the worshippers of Vishṇu, young and old, should be slain; and he commanded his warriors to make search for all young children throughout that country, and to slay every male child. He afterwards employed demons to find and kill Krishṇa, and sent Akrúra to bring him to Mathura. Public games were celebrated with great splendour; there was a severe contest in which Krishṇa slew the powerful demon Cháṇúra, and afterwards killed king Kansa himself.

Kansa, Kansavati, Kanki—Daughters of Ugraséna.

Kanwa—1, A teacher of the white Yajush, and founder of several schools for the purpose; 2, The name of a son of Apratiratha from whom the Kaṇwáyana brahmans descended; 3, A son of Ajamídha, a descendant of Hastin.

Kapali, Kaparddi—Two of the eleven Rudras according to the Vishṇu Purána.

Kapalika—The following description of the *Kápalika* is from the *Sankara Vijaya* of *Ànandagiri*:

" His body is smeared with ashes from a funeral pile, around his neck hangs a string of human skulls, his forehead is streaked with a black line, his hair is wove into the matted braid, his loins are clothed with a tiger's skin, a hollow skull is in his left hand (for a cup), and in his right he carries a bell, which he rings incessantly, exclaiming aloud, ho, *Sambhu*, *Bhairava*—ho, lord of Kálí."

Kapi—A prince, the son of Urukshaya, who afterwards became a brahman. V. P., p. 451.

Kapila—A great Rishi, who destroyed the sons of Sagara. When the latter commenced the performance of the solemn sacrifice of a horse, it was guarded by his own sons; nevertheless some one stole the animal, and carried it off into a chasm in the earth. Sagara commanded his sons to search for the steed. They at last found it freely wandering about in Pátáḷa, and at no great distance saw the Rishi Kapila sitting, absorbed in profound meditation, and illuminating the surrounding space with radiance as bright as the splendour of the autumnal sun, shining in an unclouded sky. Exclaiming "This is the villain who has interrupted our sacrifice and stolen the horses, kill him; kill him; they ran towards him with uplifted weapons. The Muni slowly raised his eyes and for an instant looked upon them, and they were reduced to ashes by the sacred flame that darted from his person. Kapila was the founder of the Śánkya school of philosophy. A work said to be written by him, called the Śánkya-Praváchana, or Preface to the Śánkya Philosophy, is still extant, and was printed at Serampore in 1821. The great reverence in which Kapila was held, may be presumed from the fact that he is sometimes considered as an incarnation of the god Agni; and sometimes of Vishṇu himself. He seems to belong only to the Puránic period. See Śánkya. 2, A renowned Danava. 3, One of the serpent kings of the progeny of Kadru. 4, The name of a mountain in the west of Meru. 5, One of the Puránic rivers. 6, A city mentioned in the Puránas.

Kapilasrama—The name of the hermitage of Kapila, on the shore of the island of Sagara, which is still the scene of an annual pilgrimage.

Kapilaswa—One of the three sons of Kuvalayáswa, who survived the great conflict with the demon Dhunda.

Kapotoroman—The son of Vrishta, a descendant of Sini.

Karabhanjikas—An aboriginal mountain tribe of the north.

Karakas, Karatas—Aboriginal tribes enumerated in the Puránas.

Karali—The terrific one ; one of the many names of the consort of Śiva. O. S. T., Vol. IV, p. 364.

Karambhi—A prince, the son of Sakuni of the race of Jyámagha.

Karandhama—The powerful, wealthy, and valiant son of Khaninetra, who when besieged by revolted tributaries is said to have created an army by breathing in his hands ; hence his name.

Karari—Is the worshipper of Devi in her terrific forms, the representative of the *Aghora Ghanta* and *Kápálika*, who as lately as only seven or eight centuries ago, there is reason to suppose, sacrificed human victims to KALI, CHAMUNDA, and other hideous personifications of the Śakti of Śiva.—*Wilson's Works, Vol. I, p.* 264.

Kardama—A Prajápati, who was married to one of the daughters of Daksha named Devahúti. The names given to their daughters show that they are allegorical personifications of intelligences and virtues and religious rites. 2, A son of Pulaha.

Karishakas, Karitis—Aboriginal tribes enumerated in the Puránas.

Karkkotta—One of the serpent kings of the progeny of Kadru.

Karli—Is situated about half way between Poona and Bombay, and is celebrated for the numerous inscriptions in its caves in the Pali language ; of a date estimated at 543 B. C. to 176 A. D. The religion, or divinities or sages mentioned are Buddhist ; the invocation is to the Triad ; no doubt meaning Buddha, Dharma, Sanga. The kings or princes mentioned, Dr. Wilson says, are, Vijara, but Dr. Stevenson, Arodhana, lord of India. Garga, ruler of the Śakas. Of the numerous Buddhist inscriptions in the cave temple at Karli, Drs. Wilson and Stevenson are not quite agreed about the reading. Garga, the "ruler of the Śakas" (Sakya, Buddha's tribe), is mentioned.

The cave temples, in the southern part of India, are classed by Mr. Fergusson into (*a*) the Vihara or monastery caves, which consist of (1) natural caverns or caves slightly improved by art. These are the most ancient, and are found appropriated to religious purposes in Behar and Cuttack; next (2) a verandah, opening behind into cells for the abode of priests, as in Cuttack and in the oldest Vihara at Ajanta; the third (3) has an enlarged hall supported on pillars: the most splendid of these caves are those of Ajanta; though the Dherwarra at Ellora is also fine, and there are same good specimens at Salsette and Junir.

(*b*) Buddhist Chetya caves form the *second* class. These are the temples or churches of the series and one or more of them is attached to every set of caves in western India, though none exist on the eastern side. Unlike the Viharas, all these caves have the same plan and arrangement, and the Karli cave is the most perfect in India. All these consist of an external porch or music gallery, an internal gallery over the entrance; a central aisle, which may be called a nave, roofed by a plain waggon vault, and a semi-dome terminating the nave, under the centre of which always stands a Dagoba or Chaitya. In the oldest temples, the Dagoba consists of a plain central drum surmounted by a hemispherical dome crowned by a Tee, which supported the umbrella of state, of wood or stone.

These two classes comprehend all the Buddhist caves in India.

The *third* class consists of brahmanical caves, properly so called. The finest specimens are at Ellora and Elephanta though some good ones exist also on the island of Salsette and at Mahabalipur.

In form, many of them are copies of, and a good deal resemble the Buddhist Vihara. But they have not been appropriated from the Buddhists, as the arrangement of the pillars and position of the sanctuary are different.

The *Fourth* class consists of rock cut models of structural Brahmanical temples. To this class belong the far famed Kylas at Ellora, the Sivite temple at Doomnar, and the Ruths at Mahabalipur. This last is cut out of isolated blocks of granite, but the rest stand in pits.

The *Fifth* or true Jaina caves occur at Khandagiri in Cuttack and in the southern parts of India, but are few and insignificant. In that in the rock of Gwalior fort, there are cut in the rock a number of rude colossal figures, from 30 to 40 feet high, of one of the Thirtankaras, some sitting and some standing.

The Ajanta, are the most complete series of Buddhist caves in India, without any mixture of Brahmanism, and contain types of all the rest; they are in a ravine or small valley in the ghât south of the Taptee. At Baug in a ravine or small valley in the ghát, on the north side of the valley of the Taptee, are three ancient Buddhistical caves.

The Salsette or Kannari caves in the island of Salsette, are also purely Buddhist, but very inferior to the former. The Kannari caves are excavated in a hill situated in the midst of an immense tract of forest country, and Mr. Fergusson supposes their date about the 9th or 10th century of the christian era.

Dhumnar, about 40 miles S. E. from Neemuch but close to Chundwassa, contains Buddhist caves with a Brahmanical rock temple behind.

The Ellora caves are excavated in a porphyritic green stone or amygdaloid.

The Elephanta caves are cut in a harder rock than those of Ellora.

Those of Dhumnar and Ellora contain a strong admixture of Brahmanism, and those of Elephanta are entirely Brahmanical, though perhaps of the same age as those of Ellora.—*Balfour's Cyclopædia.*

Karma—According to the doctrines of Buddhism the power that controls the universe is Karma, literally Action; consisting of kusala and akusala, or merit and demerit. There is no such monad as an immaterial spirit, but at the death of any being, the aggregate of his merit and demerit is transferred to some other being, which new being is caused by the karma of the previous being, and receives from that karma all the circumstances of its existence. Thus, if the karma be good, the circumstances are favourable, producing happiness, but if it be bad, they are unfavourable, producing misery.

The manner in which being first commenced cannot now be ascertained. The cause of the *continuance* of existence is ignorance, from which merit and demerit are produced, whence comes consciousness, then body and mind, and afterwards the six organs of sense. Again, from the organs of sense comes contact; from contact, desire; from desire, sensation; from sensation, the cleaving to existing objects; from this cleaving, reproduction; and from reproduction, disease, decay, and death. Thus, like the revolutions of a wheel, there is a regular succession of death and birth, the moral cause of which is the cleaving to existing objects, whilst the instrumental cause is karma. It is, therefore, the great object of all beings who would be released from the sorrows of successive birth to seek the destruction of the moral cause of continued existence, that is to say, the cleaving to existing objects, or evil desire. It is possible to accomplish this destruction, by attending to a prescribed course of discipline, which results in an entrance to one of the four paths, with their fruition, that lead, by different modes, to the attainment of nirwána. They in whom evil desire is entirely destroyed are called arhats. The freedom from evil desire ensures the possession of a miraculous energy. At his death the arhat invariably attains nirwána, or ceases to exist.—*Spence Hardy.*

Karmosa—The eldest son of the Patriarch Pulaka. In the Bhágavata he is designated Karmaṣreshta.

Karna—The son of Prithá, or Kunti, by the Phœbus of Hindu mythology. Prithá was the child of a Yádava prince, Śura, who gave her to his childless cousin Kuntibhoja, under whose care she was brought up. One day before her marriage she paid such respect and attention to the great sage Durvásas, a guest in her father's house, that he gave her a charm and taught her an incantation, by virtue of which she was to have a child by any god she liked to invoke. This power she did not suffer to lie idle, but invoked the sun by whom she had a child, born like Minerva ready equipped for the field; armed with a miraculous cuirass and lance. Prithá, afraid of the censure of her relatives, deserted the child, and exposed it in the Jumna. It was found by Dhritaráshtra's charioteer Adhiratha, and nurtured by his wife Rádhá, whence the child was afterwards called Rádheya, though named by his foster parents Vasusheṇa. When he was grown up Indra tricked him out of his armour, by appealing to his generosity in the guise of a brahman. Indra in return conferred upon him enormous strength and changed his name to Karna.—*Monier Williams, I. E. P.*, p. 94.

Karna, though in reality the half-brother of the five Pándava princes, was on more friendly terms with their cousins, the Kurus, and joined Duryodhana and Śakuni in various schemes for destroying the Pāṇḍus. In the great war he became a general in the Kuru army; for five days he had the command of the whole army; he engaged to slay Arjuna, and when the latter went forth to a final battle against him, the armies stopped fighting and the gods descended from heaven. He was finally slain by Arjuna with a crescent-shaped arrow. His widows, children and dependants were treated with great kindness by Arjuna and Yudhisthíra. Karna's relationship to the Páṇḍus was not known by Arjuna at that time, and his death was afterwards lamented by all the brothers.

"The birth of Karna was secret, and he was reputed to be the son of Nandana the charioteer of Dhṛitaráshtra, having been found floating in the river Yamuná, although the son of Prithá by the Sun; he was born in celestial panoply, and with splendid ear-rings, whence his first appellation was Vasusheṇa, or abounding in wealth. Indra disguised as a brahman begged of him his divine coat of mail, in order to obtain it for his own son Arjuna, and from the act of cutting it or detaching it from his body, the prince was named Karna; he is also entitled Vaikarttana from Vikarttana the sun. Indra in return for the armour presented Karna with a javelin freighted with the certain death of one individual whether god, man, or demon. Karna launched it at Ghoṭokacha, the Rákshasa son of Bhíma, and it destroyed him, but left its possessor helpless against the charmed weapons, offensive and defensive, of Arjuna, by whose hand Karna ultimately fell."—*Wilson's Works, Vol. III*, p. 333.

Karnapravaranas—A nickname applied in the Puránas to some of the aboriginal tribes, meaning those who wrap themselves up in their ears.

Karnatakas—The Canarese people; the inhabitants of the centre of the peninsula, the proper Karnata, or Carnatic.

Kartika—The name of one of the lunar months, corresponding to October.

Kartikeya—The Hindu Mars, or god of war, generated from the vivifying principle of Śiva cast into Agni, or Fire, who unable to retain it, cast it into Ganga, or the Ganges. On the banks of this river was born the beautiful boy who was destined to lead the armies of the gods, and to be the destroyer of Táraka, and Súra, a demon who by his austerities, had alarmed both gods and men, and gained the dominion of the universe. When born Kártikeya was nursed by six nymphs called the Krittikás, or Pleiades, who each called him her son, and offering her breast, the child assumed to himself six mouths and received nurture from each. He is considered to be the brother of Gaṇéṣa who was the reputed eldest són of Śiva and Párvatí. He is represented riding on a peacock; sometimes with one face, sometimes with six faces and twelve arms. One account of his birth is as follows: Śiva emitted from his eyes sparks of fire, which being thrown into the lake Saravana, became six infants, who were nursed by the wives of the Rishis who are to be seen in the sky as the Pleiades. When Párvatí saw the children she was so transported with their beauty, and embraced all of them together so forcibly, that their six bodies became one, while their six heads and twelve arms remained. Kártikeya is better known in the south of India as Subramanya, and Tuesday is the weekly day of his devotees. The Skaṇda Purána gives the fullest account of Subramanya, containing his war with Súra, and relates how he was sent by his father to frustrate the sacrifice of Daksha, and, at the instigation of the latter, was delayed in his way by beautiful damsels, who entertained him with song and music. Hence it is the practice still for the dancing girls who serve in the pagodas, to be betrothed and married to him, and then not allowed to marry men though they may prostitute themselves.

Karttavirya—The son of Kritavírya and sovereign of the Kaikaya tribe. He is said to have invaded Lanka and taken

Rávana prisoner. The Vishṇu Purána says that by propitiating the sage Dattatreya he obtained these boons ; a thousand arms ; never acting unjustly ; subjugation of the world by justice, and protecting it equitably ; victory over his enemies ; and death by the hands of a person renowned in the three regions of the universe. With these means he ruled over the earth with might and justice ; and offered ten thousand sacrifices. At the expiration of his long reign (eighty-five thousand years) he was killed by Paraṣurama, as related under *Jamadagni.*

Karundhaka—One of the ten sons of Súra and brother of Vásudeva, in whose family Krishṇa was born.

Karusha—One of the sons of the Manu Vaiwaswata, from whom descended the celebrated warriors termed Kárúshas, who lived in the Paripátra or Vindhya mountains.

Kasa—The son of Suhotra of the family of Áyus, and king of Kásí.

Kaseramat—One of the nine divisions of the Varsha of Bhárata.

Kashtha—One of the daughters of Daksha and wife of Kaṣyapa ; she was the mother of beasts with uncloven hoofs.

Kashtha—Fifteen twinklings of the eye, or Nimishas ; five Kshanas.

Kasi, or Varanasi—Benares, q. v. the sacred city of the Hindus, which they believe to have descended from the gods originally.

Kasina—An ascetic rite among the Buddhists, by which it is supposed that a miraculous energy may be received. There are ten descriptions of this rite,

1. Prathawi........................ earth.
2. Apo............................ water.
3. Tejo .... fire.
4. Váyu .... wind.
5. Níla .... blue.
6. Pita .... golden.
7. Lohita......................... blood red.

8. Odata .... white.
9. Alaka .... light.
10. Akása......................... space.

There are various ceremonies prescribed for the performance of these different kinds of Kasina, and from its practice in any one of its forms, a Buddhist priest expects to derive many advantages. See Hardy's Manual of Buddhism.

Kasiraja—One of the kings of Kási—the son of Kása, an ally of the Pándavas.

Kasis—The people of the Benares district, and that opposite.

Kasmiras—The people of Kashmìr.

Kasya—A prince, the son of Senajit, one of the descendants of Hastin.

Kasyapa—A sage, the son of Maríchi, the son of Brahma, and one of the Prajápatis or progenitors of created things. He married thirteen of the daughters of Daksha; from whom descended the twelve Ádityas; the nymphs of the lunar constellations; the Daityas and Danavas; many classes of animals, etc., etc. His share in creation was thus no unimportant one, as he was the father of the gods and demons, man, beasts, and reptiles. Kaṣyapa was the father of Vivasvat, and he again of Manu. "Righteous was this wise Manu on whom a race was founded. Hence this family of men became known as the race of Manu. Brahmans, Kshatriyas, and other men sprang from this Manu." (O. S. T., Vol. I, p. 125.) "The Chhándogya Upanishad agrees with the above passage from the Mahábhárata, in recognising Manu as the progenitor of the brahmans as well as the other castes." (p. 196.) "Having assumed the form of a tortoise Prajápati created offspring. That which he created, he made; hence the word *kúrma*. Kaṣyapa means tortoise; hence men say all creatures are descendants of Kaṣyapa. This tortoise is the same as Áditya." (Vol. IV, p. 23.)

The Mahábhárata states: "From Kaṣyapa, who was the son of Maríchi, were produced the deities and the Asuras; and he was the source from which all beings sprang. Aditi had twelve sons, beginning with Śakra. The youngest of them was Vishṇu, on whom the worlds are supported." "Ansa, Bhaga, Mitra, Varuna, lord of the waters, Dhátri, Aryaman, Jayanta, Bháskara, Tvashtri, Púshan, Indra, and Vishṇu, who is called the twelfth; these are the twelve Ádityas, the sons of Kaṣyapa, according to tradition (or the veda *sruti*.)" In another passage Vivasvat and Savitṛi occur instead of Jayanta and Bháskara; Tvashtri is placed the eleventh in order, and it adds "the twelfth is called Vishṇu, who though the latest born, surpasses all the Ádityas in his attributes." (Vol. IV, p. 103,104.)

In the Rámáyana the following passage occurs; Visvámitra speaks :—"At this period O Ráma, the divine Kaṣyapa, luminous as fire, glowing, as it were, with splendour, attended by the goddess Aditi, having completed an act of austerity which had lasted for a thousand years of the gods, celebrated thus the praises of the boon-bestowing Madhusúdana. 'Through intense austerity I behold thee the Supreme Spirit, whose essence is austerity, who art a congeries of austerity, the impersonation of austerity, whose wealth is austerity. In thy body, lord, I behold this whole universe; thou art unbeginning, and ineffable; to thee I have resorted as my refuge.' Then Hari, gratified, whose taint of sin had been purged away; 'Ask a boon; may good attend thee; thou art regarded by me as deserving a boon.' Hearing these words of his, Kaṣyapa, the son of Maríchi, replied; 'Sinless lord, become the son of Aditi and myself. Slayer of the Asuras become the younger brother of Śakra. (Indra.) Thou oughtest to succour the gods who are oppressed with grief, Vishṇu, of mighty energy, was accordingly born of Aditi, shaded by an umbrella, in the form of a mendicant, resplendent with a drinking gourd, and a lock of hair on his crown." (*Ibid*, p. 116.)

Kaṣyapa is supposed by some modern writers to be a personification of the remains of the antediluvian race, who took refuge in tho central Asiatic chain, in which traces of his name so plentifully abound, as in the Koh-i-Kas or Caucasus, the Kaspian, and Kashmir. It is asserted that the thirteen Gotras or families of Brahmans owe their origin to as many divine sages called after their names. Kaṣyapa is one of the number. The Asvaláyana Sútra of the Rig Veda contains the enumeration of the Gotras and their sub-divisions, but in a very involved and unintelligible style. The popular enumeration of them, however, is now wholly confined to the South of India, where several of the reputed representatives of these tribes yet exist ; especially about Gooty and Gondavir. Nandavaram, it is said, was a grant to the thirteen Gotras by the sovereign of India, Nanda, in the year of Kali 980 ; but if there be any foundation for the grant, it is of much more recent date, Nanda having lived in the fourth century before the Christian era.—*Hind., Theatre, Vol. II, p.* 11.

Kasyata—A son of Paurnamáṣa, a descendant of one of the daughters of Daksha who was married to one of the Rishis.

Katyayana—A Sanskrit author who lived at the time of and after Pánini and published criticisms on the Sútra of the great grammarian. Max Müller places him in the second half of the fourth century, B. C. Kátyáyana is said to have been a boy of great talent and extraordinary powers of memory. He was able to repeat to his mother an entire play after hearing it once at the theatre ; and before he was even initiated he was able to repeat the Prátiṣákhya which he had heard from byáḷi. He completed and corrected Pánini's Grammar such as we now possess it. Kátyáyana has been identified with Vararuchi (q. v.) the compiler of the doctrines of Saunaka. A. S. L.

Kaukundakas, Kaukattakas, Kaunkanas—Aboriginal tribes inhabiting the mountainous districts of the Konkan and its neighbourhood.

Kaumara Creation—The creation of Rudra or Nílalóhita, a form of Śiva, by Bramhá, and of certain other mind-born sons of Brahmá, termed Sanatkumára, &c., who declining to create progeny, remained, as the name implies, ever boys, kumáras, that is ever pure and innocent ; whence their creation is called the Kaumára. Sanatkumára and his brethren are described in the Śaiva Puránas as Yógis. The Linga Purána has "Being ever as he was born he is called a youth ; and hence his name is well known as Sanatkumára."

Kaumarabhritya—One of the eight branches of medical

science embracing midwifery and the management of children. Vishṇu Purána, p. 407.

Kauravas—The sons of the Maháràja Dhritaráshtra and his wife Gándhári. At an early period they became jealous of their cousins, the Páṇḍavas, who were brought up with them in their father's court. Duryodhana, the eldest of the Kauravas, attempted to take the life of his cousin Bhíma. The chief incidents of their lives are related under their respective names, q. v.

Kausalya—One of the queens of Mahárája Dasaratha and mother of Ráma, of whom she was extremely fond. She was overjoyed when it was decided that Ráma should be installed as heir-apparent, and when Ráma himself informed her that he was to be evicted and Bharata made Yuva-rája, "she fell down to the earth like the bough of a saul tree lopped by the axe of a forester." She urged Ráma to seize the government and slay the Mahárája. She afterwards acknowledged her fault. Bharata declared to her his loyal attachment to Ráma.

Kausambi—An ancient city of Hindustan, which appears as the capital of Vatsa. According to the Rámáyana, it was built by Kusamba, the son of Kusa, a descendant of Ráma. Buchanan, upon the authority of the Bhágavata, ascribes its foundation to Chakra, a descendant of Arjuna ; but neither the Bhágavata nor Vishṇu Purána state that Nimichakra built Kausambi. They only say that when Hastinápura shall be washed away by the Ganges, Nimichakra will reside at Kausambi. From which it is to be inferred, that Kausambi existed at the time that Hastinápura was destroyed. The site of Kausambi, Buchanan supposes to have been that of the ruins ascribed to Hastinápura, but it was most probably lower down in the Doab, bordering upon Magadha on one side, and Koṣala on the other. In the Hindu drama Ratnávali the scene is laid in the palace of King Vatsa at Kauṣámbí. —*Wilson, H. T.*

Kausharavi—A name of Maitreya, a disciple of Paráṣara, who related the V. P. to him.

Kausika—One of the sons of Vásudeva by his wife Vaisali : the half-brother of Krishṇa.

Kausikas—The descendants of Viswámitra. The Gotras, the families or tribes of the Kausika brahmans are given in the V. P., (p. 405) and are said to have been multiplied by intermarriages with other tribes, who were originally of the regal cast, like Viswámitra; but like him, obtained Brahmanhood through devotion. As these Gotras partook more of the character of schools of doctrine, in which teachers and scholars became one family by intermarrying, it shows the interference of the Kshatriya caste, with the Brahmanical monopoly of religious instruction and composition.

Kausiki—A character in the Hindu Drama Agnimitra and Málaviká; the sister of the Rajá's minister Sumati. On one occasion when her brother had to convey the princess Málaviká, she accompanied them, and on their way through the Vindhya mountains they were attacked by foresters, and in the affray Sumati was slain and Málaviká was lost. Kausikí left alone committed her brother's body to the flames, and resumed her journey. Kausikí soon found out Málaviká but forbore to discover herself, confiding in the prophecy of a sage, who had foretold that the princess, after passing through a period of servitude would meet with a suitable match.

Kausiki—The name of the river into which Satyavatí was transformed for following her husband in death. It is now called the Kosi, which rising in Nepal, flows through Puraniya into the Ganges, nearly opposite to Rájamahal.

Kaustabha—The jewel worn by Vishṇu, and which was one of the articles produced at the churning of the ocean.

"And Kaustabha the best
Of gems, that burns with living light,
Upon Lord Vishṇu's breast."

"And Kaustabha the gem
Whose ever beaming lustre glows
In Vishṇu's diadem."

Kautilya—A name of the brahman Chánakya, through whose agency the Nandas were destroyed, and Chandragupta raised to the throne of Palibothra.

Kavasha—The son of Ilúsha by a slave girl. The Rishis, when holding a sacrificial session on the banks of the Saraswati expelled Kavasha from their Sóma sacrifice, saying, how should the son of a slave girl, a gamester, who is no brahman, remain among us? So they drove him into the desert that he might not drink the water of the Saraswati. But a prayer was revealed to him by which he obtained the favour of the waters, and the Saraswati surrounded him on all sides. When the Rishis saw this they said the gods know him let us call him back—*Haug. Ait. Br.*

Kaveri—A river which takes its rise in Coorg, runs through the south of India, and empties itself in the Bay of Bengal. It seems always to have borne the same appellation, being the Chaberis of Ptolemy.

Kavi—1, One of the sons of the Manu Chakshusha; 2, the name of one of the sons of Priyavrata according to the Bhágavata; 3, A son of the Kshatriya Urukshaya, who afterwards became a Brahman.

Kaviraja—The author of the curious poem entitled Raghava-Pándaviya, a remarkable specimen of "studied ambiguity," as it may, at the option of the reader, be interpreted as relating the history of Ráma and the other descendants of Daṣaratha,—or that of Yudhishthira and the other sons of Páṇḍu.—*Colebrooke.*

Kavyas—1, The name given to the descendants of Kavi, as a race of brahmans; 2, One of the classes of Pitris, or progenitors, identified with the cyclic years.

Kekaya—An ancient city supposed to have been in the Panjáb. The king Aṣvapati, (lord of horses) was the father of Rája Daṣaratha's wife Kaikeyi.

Kerala—An ancient name of Malabar proper; the inhabitants are called Keralas.

Kerari—A sect who worshipped Párvatí in her terrific forms, and used to offer up human sacrifices. They used to inflict upon themselves bodily tortures, and pierce their flesh with hooks, &c. Such things are now made a criminal offence.

Kesidhwaja—The celebrated son of Kritadhwaja. He had a cousin named Kháṇḍíkya, who was renowned for religious rites, and the importance he attached to them; while Kesidhwaja regarded spiritual knowledge as the great object of pursuit. The quarrel became so serious that Kháṇḍíkya was expelled from his dominions by Kesidhwaja. The latter, on an occasion of great perplexity, was informed by his counsellors, that none but his enemy Kháṇḍíkya could give him the information he wished to obtain. The desired interview took place, and Kesidhwaja's difficulties were all removed. He, anxious to reward his preceptor, wished him to name the remuneration that would be most pleasing to himself. His friends recommended him to require his whole kingdom to be restored to him. But Kháṇḍíkya, addressing Kesidhwaja said "As it is known that you are learned in the spiritual learning that teaches the doctrine of the soul, if you will communicate that knowledge to me, you will have discharged your debt. Declare to me what acts are efficacious for the alleviation of human affliction." Then Kesidhwaja delivered a discourse on the nature of ignorance and the benefits of the Yóga or contemplative devotion. See V. P., pp. 649—659.

Kesin—A powerful demon, who was ordered by Kansa to destroy Krishṇa. He assumed the form of a horse "spurning the earth with his hoofs, scattering the clouds with his mane, and springing in his paces beyond the orbits of the sun and moon." The formidable demon, however, soon had "his mouth rent open by the arm of Krishṇa, and fell down, torn asunder like a tree struck by lightning; thus he lay separated into two portions, each having two legs, half a back, half a tail, one ear, one eye, and one nostril." Krishṇa was afterwards called Keṣava in honour of this exploit. V. P., p. 540.

Kesini—1, One of the wives of Sagara, who being childless, solicited the aid of the sage Aurva, and the Muni pronounced this boon, that one wife should bear one son, and the other sixty-thousand; and he left it to them to make their election. Kesiní chose to have the single son; 2, The name of the wife of Viṣravas.

Kesini—1, The fair-haired maid servant of Damayanti, who was sent with a message to Nala, and in the interview perceived his divine powers, and reported accordingly to Damayanti.

Ketu—One of the nine planets ; or the sons of Sinhika ; his chariot is drawn by eight horses of the dusky red colour of lac or the smoke of burning straw.

Ketumala—One of the sons of king Agnídhra, and sovereign of Gandhamádana. Also the name of a Varsha or country.

Ketumta—1, A Lókapála, the son of Rajas, regent of the west ; 2, The name of the son of Dhanwantari.

Ketumati—The wife of Sumali, the great Rákshasa chief.

Kevala—1, A prince, the son of Nara ; 2, The name of one of the Puránic countries.

Khandas—1, The name applied to the divisions or portions of the Skanda and Padma Puránas ; 2, The divisions of the Bhárata Varsha.

Khandapani—A prince, the son of Ahínara, of the race of Puru.

Khandava-prastha—A country on the banks of the river Jumna, in which the Páṇḍavas settled and reigned when the Ráj of Bhárata was divided between them and the Kauravas "It was not so much a division of the kingdom as of the family ; one branch remaining at Hastinápur, whilst the other went out to wrest a new country from the Aborigines."

Khandikya—A son of Amitadhwaja, who taught his cousin Kesidhwaja the expiation of a sin, and was by him instructed in the Yóga doctrine.

Khakis—One of the Vaishnava sects of Hindus, of modern origin. Many of them go nearly naked, smearing their bodies with ashes and earth. They add the worship of Hanumán to that of Vishṇu.

Khandas—The elements of sentient existence among the Buddhists, of which there are five constituents.

1. The organized body, or the whole of being apart from mental processes.
2. Sensation.
3. Perception.
4. Discrimination.
5. Consciousness.

The four last *Khandas* are results or properties of the first, which must be understood as including the soul as well as the body. At death the Buddhists believe the Khandas entirely vanish. Gautama says that none of the Khandas, taken separately, are the Ego ; and that taken conjointly they are not the Ego. Yet there is no such thing as an Ego apart from the five Khandas.

Khaninetra, Khanitra—Two princes of the descendants of Nedishṭha ; the priests of the royal family conspired against Khanitra, and were put to death by his ministers.

Khara—The brother of Rávaṇa, who after several unsuccessful contests with Ráma was at length slain by him.

Khasa—One of the daughters of Daksha who was married to Kaṣyapa.

Khasikas, Khasiras—Non-Aryan or Aboriginal tribes in the north-east of Bengal ; or it has been thought that they may be referred to the situation of Kashgar.

Khasrima—A chief of the Danavas, one of the sons of Viprachitti.

Khatwanga—A prince, the son of Visivásaha, called also Dilípa. He rendered important aid to the gods in one occasion, and being asked by them to demand a boon, he enquired 'what is the duration of my life.' 'The length of your life is but an hour,' the gods replied ; on hearing which he descended to the world of mortals, and prayed for final emancipation. Thus he obtained absorption, according to this stanza 'Like unto Khatwánga will be no one upon earth, who having come from heaven, and dwelt amongst men, became united with the three worlds by his liberality and knowledge of truth.

Khonds—A non-aryan or aboriginal tribe in Orissa. Their

condition is in many respects peculiar. They have come less into contact with civilization, and evince greater wildness of deportment, than most of the other non-aryan tribes. "Their religion is very peculiar, and in its whole features entirely distinct from Hinduism. Their supreme god is called BURA-PENNOU the god of light, who created for himself a consort, the earth-goddess called *Tari-Pennou*, the source of evil in the world. The god of light arrested the action of physical evil, while he left man at perfect liberty to reject or receive moral evil. They who rejected it were deified, while the great mass of mankind who received it were condemned to all kinds of physical suffering, with death, besides being deprived of the immediate care of the Creator, and doomed to the lowest state of moral degradation. Bura-Pennou and his consort, meanwhile, contended for superiority, and thus the elements of good and evil came to be in constant collision both in the heart of man and in the world around him. At this point the Khonds diverge into two sects, which are thus described by Major Macpherson in an interesting memoir read before the Asiatic Society, and inserted in their Journal :—" One sect," says he, holds that the god of light completely conquered the earth-goddess, and employs her, still the active principle of evil, as the instrument of his moral rule. That he resolved to provide a partial remedy for the consequences of the introduction of evil, by enabling man to attain to a state of moderate enjoyment upon earth, and to partial restoration to communion with the Creator after death. And that, to effect this purpose, he created those classes of subordinate deities, and assigned to them the office—first, of instructing man in the arts of life, and regulating the powers of nature for his use, upon the condition of his paying to them due worship ; secondly, of administering a system of retributive justice through subjection to which, and through the practice of virtue during successive lives upon earth, the soul of man might attain to beatification. The other sect hold, upon the other hand, that the earth-goddess remains unconquered ; that the god of light could not, in opposition to her will, carry out his purpose with respect to man's temporal lot ; and that man, therefore, owes his elevation from the state of physical suffering into which he fell through the reception of evil, to the direct exercise of her power to confer blessings, or to her permitting him to receive the good which flows from the god of light, through the inferior gods, to all who worship them. With respect to man's destiny after death, they believe that the god of light carried out his purpose. And they believe that the worship of the earth-goddess by human sacrifice, is the indispensable condition on which these blessings have been granted, and their continuance may be hoped for; the virtue of the rite availing not only for those who practice it, but for all mankind.

"In addition to these human sacrifices, which still continue to be offered annually, in order to appease the wrath of Tari, and propitiate her in favour of agriculture, there is a fearful amount of infanticide among the Khond people. It exists in some of the tribes of the sect of Boora to such an extent, that no female infant is spared, except when a woman's first child is female; and that villages containing a hundred houses may be seen without a female child."

The revolting rites of human sacrifice and female infanticide have prevailed from time immemorial among these barbarous people. The British government, however, has happily succeeded in almost completely abolishing these bloody rites. Many children, who had been stolen from their parents, and sold to the Khonds for sacrifice, have been rescued from a cruel death, and put into asylums for Christian education and training. The manner in which the revolting human sacrifices were conducted by the Khonds is thus described by Mr. Fry, a government agent, who has rescued numbers from the sacrificial knife:—"The victim," he inform us, "is surrounded by a crowd of half-intoxicated Khonds, and is dragged around some open space, when the savages, with loud shouts, rush on the victim, cutting the living flesh piece-meal from the bones, till nothing remains but the head and bowels, which are left untouched. Death has by this time released the unhappy victim from his torture; the head and bowels are burnt, and the ashes mixed with grain." These Meriah sacrifices, as they are called, are almost abolished.

Khyati—'Celebrity,' a young and bright-eyed daughter of

Daksha married to the Muni Bhrigu. Khyáti is also the faculty of discriminating objects by appropriate designations ; or the means of individual fruition.—*Wilson's Notes to Vishnu Purána.*

Khumbandas—An order of beings among the Buddhists who are believed to be the attendants of *Virádha* who is one of the four guardian Devas. They are of great size and disgusting form, have blue garments, hold a sword in one hand, and ride on blue horses. They form one of the thirteen orders of intelligence, exclusive of the supreme Buddhas.

Kichaka—The brother of the Rání of Rája Viráta. He insulted Draupadi, and on her complaining to the Rája, followed her to the Council hall, where his influence was so great that the Rája refused to interfere. Draupadi then professed to receive his offers and engaged to meet him at midnight in the dancing room. On his arrival he was seized by Bhíma, who, after a fight, slew him and rolled the body into a ball.

Kikatas—A tribe of aborigines who lived to the east of Saraswati, "they drew no milk to mix with the soma, and by them the sacrificial kettle was never heated."

Kilakila—See Kailakila.

Kimpurusha—One of the nine sons of Agnídhra, king of Jambu-dwípa, to whom his father gave the country of Hémakúta.

Kimpurushas—Demigods, attached to the service of Kuvera, the god of wealth, celestial musicians, represented like centaurs reversed, with human figures and horses' heads.

Kinnaru—A prince, the son of Sunakshatra, of the family of Ikshwáku.

Kinnaras—A race of beings of human shape but with the heads of horses ; different to *Naras*, which are centaurs, or beings with the limbs of horses and human bodies ; created from the limbs of Brahmá. Called also Kimpurushas.

Kiratarjuniya—A poem written by Bháravi on the subject of Arjuna's obtaining celestial arms from Śiva, Indra, and other gods, "by a rigid observance of severe austerities, and afterwards by his prowess in a conflict with Śiva, in which Arjuna prevails: this is the whole subject of the poem, which is ranked among the six excellent compositions in Sanscrit.

Kiratas—Aboriginal tribes dwelling in the East of Bhárata; foresters and mountaineers are intended, the inhabitants to the present day of the mountains east of Hindustan.

Kirtaratha—The son of Rája Pratíndhak, and thirteenth in descent from Mahárája Janaka.

Kirtirat—The great grandson of the above;

> "Mahándhrak's son of boundless might,
> Was Kírtirát who loved the right."

Kirtti—"Fame." A daughter of Daksha, married to Dharma.

Kirttimat—1, A son of the patriarch Angiras. 2, A son of the Manu Uttánapáda. 3, A son of Vasudeva and Devaki, who was killed by Kansa.

Kishkindhya—The monkey city of Báli, the elder brother and enemy of Sugríva. Kishkindhya is supposed to have been situated north of Mysore: "somewhere in that strip of British territory which separates the kingdom of Mysore from the Nizam's territory."—*Cal. Rev.*

Klesa—In the Patanjala philosophy Kleṣa is the term employed to designate the five afflictions of the soul, viz., Ignorance, Selfishness, Love, Hatred, Dread of temporal suffering.

Kodagu—Steep mountains; the name of the country which has been anglicised into Coorg: a country formed by the summits and eastern declivities of the Western Ghauts; about 60 miles in length and 40 in breadth. It comprises 1,585 square miles: covered by forest, save here and there where the clearing of a coffee plantation, or ragi patch, or the park like open glades with their beautiful green sward and varied foliage, afford a charming variety to the landscape. The Koḍagus or Coorgs are supposed to belong to the Dravidian family; and not to have descended from the Pándavas as some have argued, but for which no evidence has been adduced. The Coorgs were probably connected with the

Pándya kingdom which flourished in the South of India perhaps in the fifth century before Christ; but the Mahábhárata Pándavas have nothing to do with this Pándyan kingdom, whose rulers were not Kshatriyas but belonged to the agricultural class.—*Richter's Manual of Coorg*, 1870.

Kokanakas, Kokarakas—The names of aboriginal tribes enumerated in the Vishṇu Purána.

Kolaria—The ancient name for India. In the modern map of India we find indications of the same name in every province from Burmah to Malabar, viz., the Kols of Central India; the Kolas of Katwar; See Dr. Keith Johnston's Index to his Map of India from the Royal Atlas, for a full confirmation of this view, as stated in Mr. W. Hunter's Dissertation in his Dictionary of Non-Aryan Languages.

Kolikod—The ancient and present native name of Calicut.

Kosala—The Rámáyana contains the following description of Koṣala: "In ancient times there was a great country named Koṣala; and that country was happy and joyous, and abounded in cattle, and grain, and riches. And in that country on the banks of the river Sarayú, was a famous city named Ayodhyá; and there all the houses were large and beautifully arranged, and the streets were always watered, and there were very many temples richly decorated, and stately palaces with domes like the tops of mountains, with pleasant gardens full of birds and flowers, and shady groves of trees loaded with delicious fruits, and above all there were the sacred and resplendent chariots of the gods. And the tanks in that city were magnificent beyond all description, and covered with the white lotus; and the bees thirsted for the honey, and the wind drove the white lotuses from the bees as modesty drives away the coy bride from her husband. And the ducks and the geese swam upon the surface of the tanks, or dived under the clear waters; and the brilliant kingfishers, wroth as they beheld their own reflection in the bright wave, and under pretence of catching the fish, they beat the water with their wings. And the plantain trees round the tanks were bending with the weight of the fruit, like reverential pupils bowing at the feet of their preceptors.

The whole city was adorned with gems, so that it resembled a mine of jewels; and it was like unto Amarávati, the city of Indra. It was perfumed with flowers and incense, and decked out with gorgeous banners; and it was ever filled with the sweet sound of music, the sharp twanging of bows, and the holy chaunting of Vedic hymns. The city was encompassed round about with very lofty walls, which were set in with variously-coloured jewels; and all round the walls was a moat filled with water, deep and impassable; and the city gates were strongly barred, and the porticoes of the gates and the towers on the walls were filled with archers, and stored with weapons of every description. Every quarter of the city was guarded by mighty heroes, who were as strong as the eight gods who rule the eight points of the universe, and as vigilant as the many-headed serpents who watch at the entrance of the regions below."

> " On Sarju's bank of ample size,
> The happy realm of Koṣal lies,
> With fertile length of fair champaign
> And flocks and herds and wealth of grain,
> There, famous in her old renown
> Ayódhya* stands, the royal town
> In bygone ages built and planned
> By sainted Manu's princely hand.
> Imperial seat ! her walls extend
> Twelve measured leagues from end to end.
> And three in width from side to side,
> With square and palace beautified.
> Her gates at even distance stand ;
> Her ample roads are wisely planned.
> Right glorious is her royal street,
> Where streams allay the dust and heat.
> On level ground in even row,
> Her houses rise in goodly show :

* " The ruins of the ancient capital of Rama and the children of the Sun, may still be traced in the present Ajudhya near Fyzabad. Ajudhya is the Jerusalem or Mecca of the Hindus." —*Griffiths.*

Terrace and palace, arch and gate,
The queenly city decorate.
High are her ramparts, strong and vast,
By ways at even distance passed,
With circling moat both deep and wide,
And store of weapons fortified."—*Griffiths.*

The name Koṣala is variously applied. Its earliest and most celebrated application is that given above, to the country on the banks of the Sarayú, the kingdom of Ráma, of which Ayodha was the capital. In the Mahábhárata we have one Koṣala in the east, and another in the south; besides the Prak-kosalas and Uttara-koṣalas in the east and north. The Puráṇas place the Koṣalas in the back of Vindhya; and it would appear from the Váyu, that Kusa, the son of Ráma, transferred his kingdom to a more central position; he ruled over Koṣala at his capital of Kusasthali, or Kusávati, built upon the Vindhyan precipices. In later times the country of Koṣala lay south of Oude, for in the Ratnávaḷí the general of Vatsa surrounds the king of Koṣala in the Vindhyan mountains: Ptolemy has a Kouta Koṣala in the south, probably one of the Koṣalas of the Hindus. Wilson's Notes to Vishṇu Purána and Hindu Theatre, Vol. II.

Kotavi—An eighth portion of Rudráṇí, and the tutelary goddess of the Daityas, composed of incantations. The Vishṇu Purána states that as Krishṇa was in the act of casting his discus, to kill Báṇa, the mystical goddess Koṭaví, the magic lore of the demons, stood naked before him, in order to prevent him.

Koutsya—A mythical sage, the disciple of Maharishi Varatanta, who rewarded his tutor with fourteen crores of rupees for the fourteen branches of study completed under him. For the way in which the money was obtained, see RAGHU.

Kratha—The son of Vidarbha; and grandson of Jyámagha, q. v.

Kratu—1, A Prajápati, or one of the mind-born sons of Brahmá and one of the seven glorious spirits who abide in the orb of the sun, scattering light throughout the universe, married to Sannati, daughter of Daksha; 2, A son of Uru, of the race of Dhruva.

Kratusthala—The celestial nymph who resides in the car of the sun during the month Chaitra, as one its seven guardians.

Krauncha—1, The fifth of the seven great insular continents, or dwípas ; the king of this Dwipa was Dyutirnán : it had seven boundary mountains, each in succession twice as lofty as the one preceding it ; the inhabitants resided there without apprehension, associating with the bands of divinities ; the Brahmans were called Pushkaras ; the Kshatriyas, Pushkalas ; the Vaisyas were termed Dhanyas ; and the Sudras, Trishyas.

Kriaswa—1, A sage, who was married to two of the daughters of Daksha ; and the deified weapons of the gods were the progeny of Kriáswa. These are also called the Sastra devatas, gods of the divine weapons ; a hundred are enumerated in the Rámáyaṇa, and they are there termed the sons of Kriáṣwa by Jayá and Vijayá, daughters of the Prajápati, that is of Daksha ; 2, A son of Sahadeva ; 3, A son of Santrataswa.

Krikana, or Krimi—The son of Bhajamána Krimi ; also the name of a son of Uṣínara, a descendant of Anu.

Krimibhojana, Krimisa—The names of the two of the hells or divisions of Naraka below Pátaḷa. The specific punishments of each are described in the Vishṇu Purána, p. 207-9.

Kripa and Kripi—The son and daughter of Satyadhriti, who was a proficient in Military science. Being enamoured of the nymph Urvasi he became the parent of two children, a boy and a girl. The Rája Sántana whilst hunting, found these children exposed in a clump of long Sara grass ; and compassionating their condition took them and brought them up. As they were nurtured through pity (Kṛipá) they were called Kṛipa and Kṛipí. The legend of their birth is thought to be a Puranic invention to explain the origin of their names. The latter became the wife of Drona and mother of Aswatthámau. Kṛipa was one of the Kuru generals. He rebuked Karna for wishing to measure weapons with Arjuna, and advised Duryodhana to conclude a treaty with the Pándavas. When Duryodhana was mortally wounded Kṛipa hastened to him, fetched him water, and inaugurated Aṣwatthâman general. Kṛipa is also called Saradvata.

Krisanu—An archer mentioned in the Rig Veda.

Krishna—The Indian Hercules and Apollo combined. The most renowned demigod of Indian mythology, and most celebrated hero of Indian history, is the eighth Avatára or incarnation of Vishṇu. "Vishṇu was born as Kṛishṇa for the destruction of Kansa, an oppressive monarch, and, in fact, an incarnate Daitya or Titan, the natural enemy of the gods. Kansa being forewarned of his fate seeks to anticipate his destroyer; but Kṛishṇa is conveyed secretly away from Mathurá, the capital of Kansa, and is brought up as the child of a cowherd at Vṛindávan, a pastoral district near Mathurá. It is whilst thus circumstanced that he has been exalted into an object of adoration, and the mischievous follies of the child, the boy, and the lad, are the subject of popular delight and wonder. His male companions are not very prominent in the tale of his youth; but the females, the deified dairy maids, play a more important part in the drama. Amongst the most conspicuous is Rádhá, and she receives scarcely less universal homage than Kṛishṇa himself."*

Kṛishṇa cannot be said to belong really to the Epic age, but almost exclusively to the Puránic. When the story of his life is divested of the marvellous, he will be found to be an historical personage, belonging to that epoch when the Áryan race, leaving the north-western corner of the peninsula, began to make their way by gradual conquests towards the interior and the east. The enemies whom he attacks and subdues are the aborigines of the interior, who, to heighten the glory of the hero, are called giants and demons, Daityas and Dánavas. The Áryans were still a nomad people, pasturing their herds of cattle at the foot of the Himálaya range and in the plains of the Panjáb; and the legend would further lead us to believe that the primitive elementary worship now yielded to the more systematic religion of Bráhmanism and the institutions of caste. His identification with Vishṇu would follow as a natural apotheosis of a monarch and warrior of such fame; but the very legend itself, even as it is given in the Puránas, seems to show that he existed long before the my-

* Wilson's Works, Vol. II, pp. 66,67.

thological triad of Brahmá, Vishṇu, and Śiva had ever been dreamed of. The following is a curtailed account of his birth and actions, borrowed partly from the Puranas, and partly from Monier Williams' Eng.-Sanskrit Dictionary.

The king of the Daityas or aborignes, Áhuka, had two sons, Devaka and Ugrasena. The former had a daughter named Devakí, the latter a son called Kansa. Devaki was married to a nobleman of the Áryan race named Vasudeva (or Anakadundubhi), the son of Śúra, a descendant of Yadu, and by him had eight sons. Vasudeva had also another wife named Rohini. Kansa, the cousin of Devaki, was informed by the saint and prophet Nárada, that his cousin would bear a son, who would kill him and overthrow his kingdom. Kansa was king of Mathurá, and he captured Vasudeva and his wife Devaki, imprisoned them in his own palace, set guards over them, and slew the six children whom Devaki had already borne. She was now about to give birth to the seventh, who was Bala Ráma, the play fellow of Kṛishṇa, and, like him, supposed to be an incarnation of Vishṇu (see Ráma); but by divine agency, the child was transferred before birth to the womb of Vasudeva's other wife, Rohini, who was still at liberty, and was thus saved. Her eighth child was Kṛishṇa, who was born at midnight, with a very black skin (the name Kṛishṇa, as an adjective, means 'black,') and a peculiar curl of hair called the *Shrívatsa*, resembling a Saint Andrew's cross, on his breast. The gods now interposed to preserve the life of this favoured baby from Kansa's vigilance, and accordingly lulled the guards of the palace to sleep with the Yoga-nidra, or mysterious slumber. Taking the infant, its father Vasudeva stole out undiscovered as far as Yamuná, or Jumna river, which seems to have been the boundary between the Áryans and the aborigines. This he crossed, and on the other side found the cart and team of a nomad Áryan cowherd, called Nanda, whose wife, Yaṣodá, had by strange coincidence just been delivered of a female child. Vasudeva, warned of this by divine admonition, stole to her bedside, and placing Kṛishṇa by her, re-crossed the river, and re-entered the palace, with the female baby of Yaṣodá in his arms, and thus substituted it for his own son. When Kansa discovered the cheat, he for a while gave up the affair, and set the prisoners at liberty, but ordered all male children to be put to death. Vasudeva then entrusted Kṛishṇa to the care of Nanda, the cowherd, who took him to the village of Gokula, or Vraja, and there brought him up.

Here Kṛishṇa, and his elder brother Bala Ráma, who joined him, wandered about together as children, and evinced their divine character by many unruly pranks of surprising strength, such as kicking over the cart, which served as conveyance and domicile to Nanda and his family. The female Daitya Pútaná was sent to suckle him, but the refractory baby discovering the trick, showed his gratitude by slaying her. Later in life he vanquished the serpent Káliya in the middle of the Yamuná (Jumna) river. A demon, Arishṭa, assuming the form of a bull; another, Keshin that of a horse; and a third, Kálanemi, all undertook to destroy the boy, but each fell victims to his superhuman strength. Kṛishṇa now incited Nanda and the cowherds to abandon the worship of Indra, and to adopt that of the cows, which supported them, and the mountains, which afforded them pasturage. Indra, incensed at the loss of his offerings, opened the gates of heaven upon the whole race, and would have deluged them, had not our hero plucked up the mountain Govarddhana, and held it as a substantial umbrella above the land. He soon took to repose from his labours, and amused himself with the Gopis, or shepherdesses, of whom he married seven or eight, among whom Rádhá was the favourite, and to whom he taught the round dance called *Rása*, or *Mandala-nrityam.* Meanwhile Kansa had not forgotten the prophecies of Nárada. He invited the two boys, Kṛishṇa and Balaráma, to stay with him at Mathurá; they accepted, and went. At the gates, Kansa's washerman insulted Kṛishṇa, who slew him, and dressed himself in his yellow clothes. He afterwards slew Kansa himself, and placed his father Ugrasena on the throne. A foreign king of the Kála-yavana (Indo-Scythian) race soon invaded the Yadu, or Áryan, territory, whereupon Kṛishṇa built and fortified the town of Dwáraka, in Guzerat, and thither transferred the inhabitants of

Mathurá. He afterwards married Satyabhámá, daughter of Satrájit, and carried off Rukmiṇi, daughter of Bhíshmaka. His harem numbered sixty thousand wives, but his progeny was limited to eighteen thousand sons. When afterwards on a visit to Indra's heaven, he behaved, at the persuasion of his wife, Satyabhámá, in a manner very unbecoming a guest, by stealing the famous parijáṭa tree, which had been produced at the churning of the ocean, and was then thriving in Indra's garden. A contest ensued, in which Kṛishṇa defeated the gods, and carried off the sacred tree. At another time, a female Daitya, Ushá, daughter of Bána, carried off Kṛishṇa's grandson, Aniruddha. His grandfather, accompanied by Ráma, went to the rescue, and though Bána was defended by Śiva and Skanda, proved victorious. Pauṇḍraka, one of Vasudeva's family, afterwards assumed his title and insignia, supported by the king of Benares. Kṛishṇa hurled his flaming discus (*chakra*) at this city, and thus destroyed it. He afterwards exterminated his own tribe, the Yádavas. He himself was killed by a chance shot from a hunter. He is described as having curly black hair, as wearing a club or mace, a sword, a flaming discus, a jewel, a conch, and a garland. His charioteer is Sátyaki ; his city, Dwáraka ; his heaven, Goloka." (Thomson).

Kṛishṇa is the principal speaker in the Bhágavat Gita ; where he expounds the Sánkya system of philosophy to Arjuna. In the great war he took part with the Páṇḍavas, and it was mainly owing to his powerful assistance that the opposite party were vanquished.

Kṛishṇa is known in the Mahábhárata by the following names :—Vásudeva, Keṣava, Govinda, Janárdana, Dámodara, Dáṣára, Näráyana, Hṛishikeṣa, Purushottama, Mádhava, Madhusrúdana and Achyuta.

Krishna—An Asura or Dasyu mentioned in the Rig Veda, who was slain together with his wives that none of his posterity might survive. "Krishṇa means black, and the name may, on this occasion, Professor Wilson thinks, allude to the dark complexioned aborigines. But there is another Krishṇa, even in the Rig Veda, and he and his son Viswaka are members of the

Angirasa family, who may be called Rig Veda aristocrats of good old family descent ; and both father and son appear among the Rishis of the hymns."—*Mrs. Manning, A. & M. I., Vol. I, p.* 65.

Krishna—1, One of the sons of Havirdhána, a descendant of Prithu ; 2, One of the Andhra kings who reigned 10 years.

Krishna—1, The name of one of the Narakas, in which those who live by fraud, &c., are punished ; 2, The name of the Krishṇavéṇa river of the Dakhin, meaning the dark river.

Krishna Misra—The author of Prabodha-Chandrodaya ; or Rising of the Moon of Awakened Intellect. This is a theological and philosophical drama, supposed to have been written about the twelfth century, with the object of establishing the Vedánta doctrine. What others have assailed by reason and argument Krishṇa Misra combats by ridicule. His work is praised by Professor Lassen, who calls it peculiarly Indian, and unlike anything in the literatnre of other countries.—*Mrs. Manning.*

Krishnaveni—The river now called the Krishṇa or Kistna.

Krita—The first Yuga or age ; consisting of four thousand eight hundred divine years, thus :

Kṛita Yuga	4000	
Sandhyá	400	
Sandhyásana	400	
		—4800

If these divine years be converted into years of mortals, by multiplying them by 360, a year of men being a day of the gods, we obtain one million seven hundred and twenty-eight thousand, (1,728,000) ordinary years, the duration of the Kṛita Yuga, accordiug to the Hindu books.

Krita—1, A prince, the son of Kritaratha, king of Mithila ; 2, A son of Sannatimat, to whom Hiraṇyanábha taught the philosophy of the Yoga, and who compiled twenty-four Sanhitas for the use of the Eastern Brahmans who study the Sáma Veda.

Kritadhwaja—The son of Dharmadhwaja ; the Vishṇu Purána says of him that he was a king ever intent upon existent supreme spirit.

Kritagni, Kritavarman, Kritavirya—Three princes, the sons of Dhanaka, of the Yadava race.

Kritaka—1, One of the sons of Vasudeva by his wife Madirá; 2, One of the kings of Magadha.

Kritamala—A river that takes its rise in the Malaya hills.

Kritanjaya—1, The Vyása of the seventeenth Dwápara; 2, A prince, the son of Dharman, of the family of Ikshváku.

Kritanta—The destroyer; a name of Yama, the Hindu Pluto.

Kritanta-dutaru—Yama's officers; frequently represented as hovering, in a frightful shape, over the beds of the dying, to carry off the departing spirit to Pátáḷa.

Kritaratha—One of the kings of Mithila, the son of Pratibhandaka.

Kritavarman—One of the three warriors on the Kaurava side who survived at the end of the great war; the three visited the wounded Duryodhana on the plain of Kurukshetra. He was ultimately slain by Sátyaki at Prabhása.

Kriti—1, The son of Bahuláṣwa, and the last of the kings of Mithila, in whom terminated the family of Janaka.

Kritirata—One of the kings of Mithila, the son of Mahádriti.

Krittika—A lunar mansion in Nágavithi in the Northern Avashtána; when the sun is in the first degree of the lunar mansion, Krittika, and the moon is in the fourth of Viṣákha, it is the great equinox, or holy equinoctial season.

Kritwi—The wife of Anaha, one of the descendants of Hastin.

Kriya—'Devotion', a daughter of Daksha married to Dharma: an allegorical personification of religious rite married to the equally allegorical representation of the Hindu Code, viz., Dharma, moral and religious duty. Wilson's notes to V. P., p. 55; 2, A magical creation, represented in the Vishṇu Puráṇa as a vast and formidable female springing from the southern fire, blazing with ruddy light, and with fiery radiance streaming amidst her hair.

Krodha—1, 'Passion,' represented as a son of Brahmá: one of the allegorical personages occurring in the list of Brahmá's progeny amongst the series of 'virtues and vices;' 2, 'Wrath', a son of Mritha; called in the Vishṇu Purána an inflictor of misery, and one of the progeny of vice; also, as a terrific form of Vishṇu, operating as a cause of the destruction of this world.

Krodhaghara—The chamber of displeasure; an institution still in vogue in Hindu families, wives resorting to it when discontented or angry with their husbands.

Krodhavasa—A daughter of Daksha, married to Kaṣyapa.

Kroshtu—A son of Yadu, the family in which Krishṇa was born.

Kshana—A measure of time, said in the Vishṇu Purána to be equal to thirty kalas; it is often used to express a very minute portion of time, a moment, an instant.

Kshama—'Patience.' One of the daughters of Daksha who was married to the Muni Pulaka.

Kshatradharman—A prince, the son of Sankriti, a descendant of Raji.

Kshatranjas—A king of Magadha, the son of Kshemadarman.

Kshatravriddha—One of the five sons of Áyus, from whose family many names of celebrity proceeded.

Kshatriyas—The second of the four castes, said to have been produced from the breast, some authorities say the arms, of Brahmá; their duty being to protect the earth, the cattle, and brahmans. Kings, governors, and all intrusted with civil and military affairs, in general belong to the Kshatriya caste. Parasuráma vowed that he would extirpate the whole Kshatriya race, and thrice seven times, says the Vishṇu Purána, he cleared the earth of them: a legend, says Professor Wilson, which intimates a violent and protracted struggle between the Brahmans and Kshatriyas for domination in India.

Kshema—'Prosperity.' A son of Dharma by his wife Śantí.

Kshemadhanwan—A prince, the son of Pundaríka, a descendant of Kusa.

Kshemaka—The last prince of the race of Puru: "the race which gave origin to Brahmans and Kshatriyas, and which was purified by regal sages, terminated with Kshemaka in the Káli age."

Kshemya—1, A prince, the son of Ugráyudha, descendant of Dwimídha; 2, A son of Suchi, king of Magadhá.

Kshetrajna—"Embodied spirit," or that which knows the Kshetra, 'body'; a form of Vishṇu, implying the combination of spirit with form or matter, for the purpose of creating.

Kshudraka—A prince, the son of Prasenajit, of the line of Ikshváku.

Kubja—A deformed young female servant of Kansa. Meeting her in the high road carrying a pot of unguent, Krishṇa addressed her sportively, and said 'For whom are you carrying that unguent, tell me lovely maiden, tell me truly.' Kubja, smitten by his appearance, and well disposed towards Hari, replied mirthfully, 'Know you not beloved, that I am the servant of Kansa, and appointed, crooked as I am, to prepare his perfumes.' Krishṇa asked her for some of it, and she gave him and Balaráma as much of the unguent as was sufficient for their persons; and they smeared their bodies with it, till they looked like two clouds, one white and one black, decorated by the many-tinted bow of Indra. Then Krishṇa made her perfectly straight; and when she was thus relieved from her deformity, she was a most beautiful woman; and from gratitude invited Govinda to her house. He promised to go some other time. V. P.

Kuhu—1, A daughter of Angiras. The name means the last day of the moon's wane. The four daughters of Angiras designated phases of the moon; 2, The name of a river in the Himálaya.

Kukkura—A prince, the son of Andhaka. Kukuras, and Kukkuras, are given in the Vishṇu Purána as names of tribes of Bhárata.

Kukshi—The son and successor of Ikshváku, king of Ayodhya; the second of the solar line of kings.

" Manu who life to mortals gave,
Begot Ikshváku good and brave,
First of Ayodhyá's kings was he,
Pride of her famous dynasty.
From him the glorious Kukshi sprang
Whose fame through all the regions rang."—*Griffiths.*

Kukshi—One of the daughters of Priyavrata, the grea progenitor.

Kuladevata—The deity who is the object of hereditary and family worship, and is always one of the leading personages of Hindu mythology, as Śiva, Vishṇu, or Durgá. No house is supposed to be without its tutelary divinity, but the notion attached to this character is now very far from precise.

Kulapavatus—Mountain-ranges in Central India : sometimes termed family mountains or systems ; embracing the various chains described under Mahendra, Malaya, Riksha, Vindhya, &c.

Kulatthas—Aboriginal mountain tribes, described in the Vishṇu Purána as ' ferocious and uncivilized races.'

Kulindas, Kulindapalyakas, Kulutas—Tribes enumerated in the V. P. but not identified.

Kumara—1, A Prajápati, of whom there appear to have been twenty-one ; the Vayu Purána states that they are numerous.

Kumara-sambhava—The Birth of the War God ; a poem by Kálidása, that has been translated into English verse by Mr. Griffiths.

Kumari—A river that rises in the Sáktimat mountains.

Kumbhaka—A suspension of breath by the closing of both nostrils : being part of the brahmanical ritual for obtaining control of the external senses.

Kumbhakarna—A Rákshasa, the son of Viṣravas, and brother of Rávaṇa. He was brought up in the forest with his brothers, and went about eating Rishis. When Brahmá had granted boons to Rávaṇa and Vibhíshaṇa, and was about to confer one on Kumbhakarna, the gods interposed, saying he had eaten seven Apsarases and ten followers of Indra, besides Rishis and men ; and begged that under the guise of a boon stupefaction might be inflicted on him. Brahmá thought on Sarasvatí, who arrived, and by Brahmá's command entered into Kumbhakarna's mouth, to speak for him. Under this influence he asked that he might receive the boon of sleeping for many years, which was granted to him. *O. S. T., Vol. IV, p.* 416.

The description given of Kumbhakarna in the Rámáyana is ridiculously extravagant and exaggerated. At the siege of Lanka when Rávaṇa decided to avail himself of the services of his gigantic brother, the difficulty was to know how to awake him, as he was buried in sleep for six months together, and then only awoke for a short time to gorge himself with enormous quantities of food. The messengers tried to enter his room but were blown away from the door by the wind caused by the deep breathing of the sleeping monster. At last, after violent efforts, they forced an entrance ; and ten thousand Rákshasas made every sort of din in his ears by beating drums, &c. Then they hammered his limbs with mallets, danced upon him, caused a thousand elephants to walk over his body, piled heaps of food under his very nose, all without effect. Nothing availed but the touch of some beautiful women who eventually succeeded in rousing him. Kumbhakarna consented to go out to battle, and displayed extraordinary valour, routing, wounding, and even devouring thousands of the monkey army, but was ultimately conquered and killed by Ráma. The figure of Kumbhakarna is a favourite one in village representations of the siege of Lanka, and he is generally exhibited asleep. I. E. P.

Kumuda—1, One of the six minor Dwípas, situated beyond the sea ; 2, A mountain forming the northern buttress of Mount Meru.

Kumudali—A pupil of Pathya and teacher of the Atharva Veḍa.

Kumadvati—A river that rises in the Vindhya mountains.

Kundaka—A prince, the son of Kshudraka, and grandfather of Sumitra, who was the last of the kings of the family of Ikshváku.

Kundinapur—The capiṭal of Vidarbha, a country of considerable extent and power at various periods. The name remains in Beder, which may have been the ancient capital; but the kingdom seems to have corresponded with the great part of Berar and Kandesh. It is mentioned in the Rámáyana amongst the countries of the south.

Kuntala, Kunthakas—Kuntala is in one place one of the central countries; in another one of the southern; the name is applied in inscriptions to the province in which Kurgode is situated; part of the Adoni district: and consistently with this position it is placed amongst the dependant or allied states of Vidarbha, in the Dasa Kumára.

Kunti or Pritha—The eldest of the five daughters of Súra and Márishá. Súra had a friend named Kuntibhója, to whom as he had no children, he presented in due form, his daughter Kunti. She was married to Páṇḍu, to whom she bore three sons, Yudhishthira, Bhíma, and Arjúna, Páṇḍu, however, had by the curse of a deer, been prevented from having progeny, and she therefore conceived these children by connection with the deities Dharma, Váyu, and Indra respectively. Yudhishthira, as the son of Dharma, is considered justest; Bhíma, Váyu's son, the strongest; and Arjúna, Indra's son, the best bowshot. See KARNA, for an account of Kunti's son before her marriage; 2, Kunti was also the name of a son of Dharmanetra of the *Yádava* race; and of a son of Kratha, of the family of Jyámagha.

Kuntibhoja—A friend of Súra's who adopted his daughter Kunti; he was an ally of the Páṇḍus in the great war.

Kurma Purana—The Purána in which Janárddana, in the form of a tortoise, in the regions under the earth, explained the objects of life—duty, wealth, pleasure and liberation—in communication with Indradyumna, and the Rishis in the proximity of Sakra; which refers to the Lakshmi Kalpa, and contains seventeen thousand stanzas. V. P.

Kurma or Tortoise Avatara—The second of the ten Avatáras of Vishṇu. The legend is that at a very remote period when the gods felt their powers weakened, and were desirous of obtaining Amrita (q. v.) the beverage of immortality, Vishṇu directed them to churn, together with the demons, the milk-sea, by taking the mountain *Mandara* for their staff, and his serpent Vâsuki for their cord, the gods to stand at the tail, and the demons at the head of the serpent; while he himself consented to support the mountain on his back, after having assumed the shape of a gigantic tortoise. The result of this churning of the sea of milk, was, besides the ultimate recovery of the Amrita, the appearance of a variety of miraculous things and beings; but it also led to a violent contest between the gods and demons, in which the latter were defeated. The idea of the lord of creation assuming the shape of a tortoise, and that of sacrificial liquids, especially clarified butter, becoming tortoise-shaped (*Karna*, the word for tortoise, meaning literally, 'badly or slowly going'), occurs also in the Yajurveda; but the legend on which the tortoise-Avatára of Vishṇu is based seems to belong entirely to the post-Vedic period of Hinduism.

Kurmis—Semi-aboriginal cultivators to the south of the Rajputs and Jats.

Kuru—1, One of the sons of Agníd'hra, to whom his father gave the country north of the Sweta mountains, bounded by the Srinagavan range; 2, An ancient king, the son of Samvarṇa, who gave his name to the district Kurukshetra. He was the ancestor of Vichitravírya, the grandfather of the Kurus and Páṇḍavas. Kuru, it is usually supposed, is the prince who gives the designation to Duryodhana and his brothers, thence called Kauravas, in opposition to their cousins the sons of Páṇḍu, termed Páṇḍavas, Kuru being a remote ancestor of both. The Mahábhárata however gives a different account, and derives the term Kaurava from the country, Kuru-jángala, or Kurukshetra (Lassen, Ind. Alt. I, p. 593,) which was subject to the family of Duryodhana, the upper part of the Panjáb beyond Delhi, or Panniput, which is still commonly called by the Hindus Kurukhetr. Kuru, the prince, was descended from Nahusha, the great grandson of Soma, or the moon, by his grandson Puru. The thirteenth descendant of Kuru was Śántanu, who had four sons, Bhíshma, Chitrángada, Vichitravírya, and Vyása. Of these Bhíshma and Vyása lived unmarried, and the other two died without offspring; on which, to prevent the extinction of the family, and conformably to the ancient Hindu law, Vyása had children by his brother's widows. The sons were Dhritaráshtra and Páṇḍu, who became the founders of the two families of the Kauravas and Páṇḍavas. *Wilson's Works, Vol. III, p.* 290.

Kurus—A very ancient people, who seem to have been originally situated in Central and Northern Asia, as the Vishṇu Purána says they inhabited the middle districts of Bhárata. They probably entered India with the Aryans or were a tribe of that great race, and settled in Kurukshetra. With this meaning the name applies to both Kurus and Páṇḍavas—hence Arjuna is called the best of the Kurus. In its particular and exclusive sense the name is given only to that party which adhered to Duryodhana, and opposed the Páṇḍavas, Both names belong to the Epic period.

Kurukshetra—The plain of the Kurus. A tract of land to the east of the Yamuna or Jumna river, in the upper part of the Doab, near the city of Delhi, and the river Saraswati. Hastinápura was its capital.

"The Sarasvati (Sursooty) is an insignificant stream flowing through Sirhind, between the Yamuna and the Shatadru. It eventually loses itself in the sand of the desert, and is, on that account, fabled by the Hindus *to* flow underground into the ocean. It is held, however, as one of the most sacred streams of India. Lassen calls the Doab the Belgium of India. It is the gateway of the peninsula, where the eastern and western races have always met in battle. Here in later days was fought the battle of Pannipat; and here was laid the scene of that war which transferred the sovereignty of middle India from the Kurus to the Páṇḍavas. As it was the gate of India so does it in all probability derive its sacred name from being the first seat of the Áryan race, whence it worked its way from the Indus to the Ganges, and from being retained in their memory with all the respect due to a fatherland." —*J. C Thomson.*

Kurumbas—The aboriginal cultivators of South Kanara.

Kuruvarnakas—The aboriginal people of the forests in the upper part of the Doab.

Kuruvatsa—A prince, the son of Anavaratha, a descendant of Jyámagha.

Kusa—1, Sacrificial grass ; which, on occasion of offerings made to the gods, is placed upon the ground as a seat for them, having its tips towards the east ; 2, the name of the fourth of the great insular continents, or Dwípas ; so named from a clump of Kuṣa grass (Poa) growing there. There reside mankind along with Daityas and Danavas, as well as with spirits of heaven and gods.

Kusa—1, A son of Ráma " Kuṣa and Lava were the twin sons of Ráma and Síta, born after Ráma had repudiated Síta, and brought up in the hermitage of Válmíki. As they were the first rhapsodists the combined name Kusilava signifies a reciter of poems, or an improvisatore, even to the present day." (*Griffiths.*) Kuṣa built Kuṣasthali, on the brow of the Vindhya, the capital of Koṣalá ; the Ragha Vansa describes Kuṣa as returning from Kuṣavati to Ayodhya, after his father's death ; but it seems not unlikely that the extending power of the princes of the Doab, of the lunar family, compelled Ráma's posterity to retire more to the west and south ; 2, A son of Valákáṣwa, a descendant of Purúravas.

Kusadhwaj—The younger brother of Janaka, king of Vidéha.

Kusadhwaja—The king of Kási in the Epic period. According to the Vishṇu Purána he was the brother, and according to the Bhágavata, the son, of Síradhwaja.

Kusagra—The son of Vrihadratha, one of the ancient kings of Kurukshetra.

Kusamba—1, The brother of Vrihadratha, and uncle of Kuságra ; 2, The eldest son of Kuṣa, and founder of Kausambi, afterwards Kanouj.

Kusanabha—The second son of Kuṣá, who also took part in building Kausámbi.

Kusasthali—1, The capital of Ánartta, which was part of Kutch of Guzerat ; it appears to have been the same, or in the same spot, as Dwáraka. The Vishṇu Purána says, " that city Kusasthali which was formerly your capital, and rivalled the city of the immortals, is now known as Dwáraka ; and there reigns a portion of Vișhnu in the person of Baladeva," &c. ; 2, The city built by Kusa on the brow of the Vindhya. (See Kusa.)

Kushidi—A pupil of Paushyinji, and teacher of the Śama veda.

Kushmandas—A class of deities mentioned in the Vișhnu Purána and other Puránas. They are described as taking counsel with Indra how best to interrupt the devout exercises of Dhruva, when, as a child, he commenced the rigorous penance that caused alarm in the celestial regions.

Kusika—According to the Brahmá and Hari Vansa, the father of Gádhi, the incarnation of Indra.

Kusumayudha—A name of Kámadeva, the Hindu Cupid. The word means. "He whose weapons are flowers." O. S. T., Vol. I, p. 112.

Kuthumi—A pupil of Paushyinji and teacher of the Śama Veda.

Kuvalayaswa—The son of Vrihadaswa. This prince, inspired with the spirit of Vishṇu, destroyed the Asura Dhundu, who had harassed the pious sage Uttanka ; and he was thence entitled Dhundumára. In his conflict with the demon he was attended by his sons to the number of twenty-one thousand ; and all these, with the exception of only three, perished in the engagement, consumed by the fiery breath of Dhundu ; a legend originating probably in some earthquake or volcano. V. P.

Kuvera—The Hindu Plutus ; he is the son of Vișravas by Ilavila, and is the god of riches and regent of the north ; the keeper of gold, silver, precious stones, pearls, and all the treasures in the earth, which he gives to those for whom they are destined by Isvara. He is the chief of the Yakshas, and Guhyakas, into whose forms transmigrate the souls of those men who in this life are absorbed in the pursuit of riches. He is represented in external appearance as a mere man, but with a deformed body, of white colour, having three legs and but eight teeth, with a crown on his head, and a club in one of his hands. His whole body is adorned with various ornaments, and his vehicle is a self-moving chariot. The poets have written many stories concerning him, and when they praise a man on account of his riches they compare him to Kuverá. His attendants are Kinneras, who are shaped like men with heads of horses.

Kuvera is said to have performed austerity for thousands of years, in consequence of which he obtained from Brahma as a boon that he should be one of the guardians of the world and the god of riches. He afterwards consulted his father, Viṣravas, about an abode, and at his suggestion took possession of the city of Lanká, which had formerly been built by Visvakarman for the Rákshasas, but had been abandoned by them through fear of Vishṇu, and was at that time unoccupied. O. S. T., Vol. IV, p. 414.

In the Rámáyana Kailása is spoken of as the residence of Kuvera.

"Having quickly passed over that dreadful desert, you shall then see the white mountain, called Kailása, and there the celestial palace of Kuvera, formed by Visvakarman, in colour like a brilliánt cloud, and decorated with gold." O. S. T., Vol. IV, p. 308. And in one passage Śiva is represented as paying a visit to Kuvera on mount Kailása, and as acknowledging the divine character of Ráma. O. S. T., Vol. IV, p. 310. But in general Kuvera is represented as residing in Alaka, (also in the Himálaya) which is termed in the Cloud Messenger the city of the blessed, and is always described as abounding in wealth and magnificence, and being surrounded with a garden of surpassing loveliness, in which was a lake covered with lotuses.

L

Laghu—A measure of time equal to fifteen Káshtas.

Lajja—Modesty—One of the daughters of Daksha, who was married to Dharma.

Lakshmana—One of the sons of Daṣaratha, and brother of Ráma, to whom he was faithfully attached throughout all his vicissitudes.

> Then Lakshman's truth was nobly shown,
> Then were his love and courage known,
> When for his brother's sake he dared
> All perils, and his exile shared.

He followed Ráma to the wilderness and was with him when crowned. The latest incident recorded of him is that he was entrusted with the care of Síta, when she was taken to the hermitage of Válmíki and delivered of twins, Kusa and Lava. In Dr. Muir's O. S. T., Vol. IV, p. 107, the following legend of Lakshmana's death occurs : Time, in the form of an ascetic came to the palace gate of Ráma ; and asked as the messenger of Brahmá, to see Ráma. He was admitted and received with honour, but stated that his message must be delivered in private, and that any one who witnessed the interview would lose his life. Ráma informed Lakshmana of this and desired him to stand outside. * * * * Soon after the irritable Rishi Durvásas came, and insisted on seeing Ráma immediately, under a threat, if refused, of cursing Ráma and all his family. Lakshmana, preferring to save his kinsmen, though knowing that his own death must be the consequence of interrupting the interview of Ráma with Time, entered the palace and reported the Rishi's message to Ráma. Ráma came out, and when Durvásas had got the food he wished and departed, Ráma reflected with great distress on the words of Time, which required that Lakshmana should die. Lakshmana, however, exhorted Ráma not to grieve but to abandon him, and not break his own promise. The counsellors concurring in this advice Ráma abandoned Lakshmana, who went to the river Sarayú, suppressed all his senses, and was conveyed bodily by Indra to heaven.

Lakshmana—One of the wives of Krishṇa.

Lakshmi—"Prosperity." The daughter of Brighu, and bride or Sakti of Vishṇu. The goddess of fortune, wealth and prosperity. She is also represented as the counterpart of Vishṇu. Vishṇu is meaning; she is speech. Vishṇu is understanding; she is intellect. He is righteousness; she is devotion. He is the Creator; she is creation, &c. &c. .... in a word Vishṇu is all that is called male; Lakshmi is all that is termed female; there is nothing else than they. V. P., p. 61. She is represented as having been born from the churning of the ocean, 'rising from the waves, radiant with beauty.' Indra recited a hymn to her praise, calling her the mother of all beings.

Mr. Griffiths thus translates the story of her birth from the Ramáyána and adds a note from Schlegel.

At length when many a year had fled,
Up floated, on her lotus bed,
A maiden fair and tender-eyed,
In the young flush of beauty's pride.
She shone with pearl and golden sheen,
And seals of glory stamped her queen.
On each round arm glowed many a gem,
On her smooth brows, a diadem.
Rolling in waves beneath her crown
The glory of her hair flowed down.
Pearls on her neck of price untold,
The lady shone like burnisht gold.
Queen of the Gods, she leapt to land,
A lotus in her perfect hand,
And fondly, of the lotus sprung,
To lotus-bearing Vishṇu clung.
Her, Gods above and men below
As beauty's Queen and Fortune know.

'That this story of the birth of Lakshmi is of considerable antiquity is evident from one of her names *Kshírábdhi-tanayá*, daughter of the Milky Sea, which is found in *Amarasinha*, the most ancient of Indian lexicographers. The similarity to the Greek myth of Venus being born from the foam of the sea is remarkable.'

'In this description of Lakshmí one thing only offends me, that she is said to have four arms. Each of Vishṇu's arms, single as far as the elbow, there branches into two ; but Lakshmí in all the brass seals that I possess or remember to have seen has two arms only. Nor does this deformity of redundant limbs suit the pattern of perfect beauty.' (Schlegel.)

Mr. Griffith has omitted the offensive epithet four-armed. In a passage quoted by Dr. Muir it is said that when Vishṇu was incarnate as Ráma then Lakshmí became Síta ; and that when he was born as Krishṇa she became Rukminí. O. S. T., Vol. IV, p. 392.

" Lakshmí is not found in the Rig Veda in the sense which the word bears in the later mythology, of a goddess personifying good fortune, though the word itself occurs in a kindred signification." O. S. T., Vol. V, p. 348.

The beautiful goddess is also said to have been produced at the churning of the ocean. In the Brahmá Vaivartta Purána, Lakshmí is said to be a portion of Prakriti ; and in another place is made to issue from the mind of Krishṇa ; in a different part of the work she is described as one of two goddesses into which the first Sarasvati was divided, the two being Sarasvati proper, and Kamala or Lakshmí.—*Wilson's Works, Vol. III, p.* 102.

2, The name of a daughter of Daksha who was married to Dharma.

Lalabaksha—One of the Narakas, that in which those are punished who eat their meals without offering food to the gods, to the manes, or to guests. V. P., p. 208.

Lalita—A distinguished name of the personified female energy. See Sakti.

Lamba—One of the daughters of Daksha and wife of Dharma.

Lambodara—One of the Andhra kings who reigned eighteen years : he was the son of Salakarni the 2nd.

Langalas—One of the aboriginal tribes who dwelt in jungles and forests.

Langali—A pupil of Paushyinji and teacher of the Sáma Veda.

Langalini—A river that has its source in Mahendra.

Lanka—The island of Ceylon, the ancient capital of Rávana, described in the Rámáyana as the capital town of the kings of the race of Pulastya, known as Yakshas. Some pandits in the north of India deny the identity of Lanka and Ceylon.

Laukika—"Worldly," the opposite to Daivika or "Divine" —e. g., The Apsarasas are thus distinguished, thirty-four of them being specified as Laukíka, and ten as Daivika.

Lauhitya—An ancient river mentioned in the Puránas, now part of the Brahmaputra.

Lava—The younger of the twin sons of Ráma by Síta, and king of Sráwastí, in northern Koṣala, by which a part of Oude is commonly understood. He was trained up by his mother in the hermitage of Válmíki, and appears to have become a strong muscular man ; having also acquired great skill in archery. When Ráma sent off a horse, previous to its sacrifice, Kusa and Lava seized it, and maintained their hold till Ráma himself came and recognised his two sons.

Lavana—1, A Rákshasa Chief, the son of Madhu, who reigned at Mathura ; he was killed by Ṡatrughna, who took possession of his capital ; 2, One of the Narakas, (the salt) in which those are punished who associate with women in a prohibited degree.

Lekhas—A class of deities of the sixth Manwantara.

Lesa—A son of Suhotra, of the line of the kings of Kási.

Libations—To be offered to the gods, sages, and progenitors, with the parts of the hand severally sacred to each. The offerer is first to bathe, dress in clean clothes, and scatter water thrice to gratify the gods ; as many times to please the Rishis ; and once to propitiate Prajápati ; he must also make three libations to satisfy the progenitors. For full details see V. P., pp. 302, 303.

Light, or fire—See *Tejas*.

Lila—A pastime ; but mythologically used of certain libidinous amusements of gods among mortals on earth. Krishṇa's adventures with the Gopis and Śiva's pastimes at Madura, are termed Lílas in Sanskrit books.

Linga Purana—The Purána in which Śiva explained the objects of life, viz., virtue, wealth, pleasure, and final liberation at the end of the Agni Kalpa. Professor Wilson says there is nothing in it like the phallic orgies of antiquity : it is all mystical and spiritual. The Linga is twofold, external and internal...... whatever may have been the origin of this form of worship in India, the notions upon which it was founded, according to the impure fancies of European writers, are not to be traced in even Saiva Purános.

Lingam—In grammar means Gender. Mythologically it designates a phallic emblem, and is represented by a cylindrical stone rounded off at the top ; and at the other end inserted in masonry or in the ground, but transfixing another horizontal and flat stone named Yóni. This emblem is placed in the open field, on the way side, and in temples, and worshipped from the Himálayas to Cape Comorin ; and from the mouths of the Ganges to those of the Indus. The worship of the Lingam and Yóni marks the Saivas ; the worship of the Lingam alone denotes the Víra Saivas. The latter attach a further meaning to the word, indicating various heavens or Lokas in the invisible world. The uppermost is the Brahmá, or sometimes Śiva lingam ; concerning which metaphor is exhausted.

Lingadhari—One who wears a small lingam on his person, usually in a little silver box, hanging on his breast from a string round the neck ; or sometimes fastened to his right arm.

Lobha—" Covetousness," a son of Brahmá—being one of his progeny of virtues and vices as enumerated in the Vishṇu Purána. In another part of the same Purána, Lobha is described as the son of Dharma by one of the daughters of Daksha ; also as the son of Adharma (vice) and it states that he was married to Nikriti, and their progeny was Krodha, Hinsa, &c.

Lohitas—A class of deities in the twelfth Manwantara.

Lokakshi—One of the pupils of Paushyinji, and a teacher of the Sáma Véda.

Lokaloka—The mountain belt beyond the sea of fresh water; the circular boundary between the world and void space. The mountain range encircling the world is termed Lokáloka, because the world is separated by it from that which is not world. The Mahommedan legends of Koh Kaf, 'the stony girdle that surrounds the world,' are evidently connected with the Lokáloka of the Hindus. According to the Śiva Tantra, the El dorado, at the foot of the Lokáloka mountains, is the play-ground of the gods. V. P., p. 202.

Loka Palaka—World-protector, an epithet constantly given by Hindu writers to a rajah.

Loka-palas—The rulers stationed by Brahmá for the protection of the different quarters of the world: they are termed the regents of the east, south, west and north. In another part of the Vishṇu Purána eight are mentioned as regents of the spheres; or eight deities in that character; Indra, Yama, Varuna, Kuvera, Vivaswat, Soma, Agni, and Váyu.

Lokas—The seven spheres above the earth.

1. Prájapatya or Pitri loka.
2. Indra loka, or Swerga.
3. Marutloka, or Diva loka, heaven.
4. Gandarbha loka, the region of celestial spirits, called also Maharloka.
5. Janaloka, or the sphere of saints.
6. Tapaloka, or the world of the seven sages.
7. Brahmá loka, or Satya loka, the world of infinite wisdom and truth.

For a full account of these lokas, see the Vishṇu Purána, pp. 212—215. In the Brahmá Vaivartta Purána another Loka is mentioned as the residence of Krishṇa denominated Goloka; it is far above the three worlds, and has, at five hundred millions of yojanas below it, the separate Lokas of Vishṇu and Śiva, Vaikunta and Kailas. This region is indestructible, while all else is subject to annihilation, and in the centre of it abides Krishṇa, of the colour of a dark cloud, in the bloom of youth, clad in yellow raiment, splendidly adorned with celestial gems, and holding a flute. He is exempt from Máya and all qualities, eternal, alone, and the Paramátma, or supreme soul of the world.

Lomaharshana—A name of Súta.

M

Mabali—A name of Bali, q. v.

Mabalipuram—A sacred place 34 miles north of Madras called the Seven Pagodas.

Mada—Insanity. One of the progeny of Brahmá, Vishṇu Purána, p. 50.

Madayanti—The wife of the Rája Saudása, q. v.

Madhava-Madhu—The names of two of the months as they occur in the Vedas, and belonging to a system now obsolete; corresponding to the lunar months Mágha and Pálguṇa, or December and January.

Madhava—A name of Krishṇa, which may be either derived as a patronymic from Matha, who is mentioned among his ancestors, or be considered equivalent to Madhusúdana. 'Slayer of Madhu.'

Madhavacharya—The founder of a school of philosophy, opposed to the system of Vyása in the Brahmá Sútras; and that contained in the last portion of the Bhágavat Gíta; maintaining that the Divine being and the soul of man (Paramátma and Jívátma) are two, separate and distinct. Hence his system is spoken of as the Dvaita. It closely resembles that termed the Sátwata which was revived by Rámánuja chárya and is now found to prevail to some extent in all large communities. See Sátwata.

Madhavas—The name of a tribe, descendants of Madhu the son of Vrisha.

Madhu—1, One of the sons of Kárttavírya; 2, A son of Vrisha; 3, A son of Devakshatra. All the above are of the race of Yádu to whose family, the Yádavas, Krishṇa belonged; 4, The name of a formidable Rákshasa chief, termed a great demon, probably one of the aborigines, who was killed by Krishṇa.

Madhuvana—The grove of Madhu, the demon referred to above. After his death Satrughna founded a city on the spot, which was called Mathura : this became celebrated as a holy shrine, and it was here that Dhruva performed penance.

Madhwacharya—A celebrated Vaishnava teacher, who is placed by Professor Wilson in the thirteenth century.

Madhyandina—A teacher of the white Yájush.

Madira—One of the wives of Vasudeva.

Madra—1, One of the four sons of Sivi ; who has given a name to a province and tribe in the north of India ; 2, The name of a river that rises in the Vindhya mountains.

Madrabhujingas, Madras, Madreyas—Tribes of people mentioned in the Puránas but not yet satisfactorily identified.

Madri—One of the wives of Páṇḍu, and mother of Nakula and Sahadeva, by the celestial twin-sons, the Aswini.

Magadha—The modern Behar. A celebrated country in the Puránas, which furnish lists of the kings who reigned over it.

Magadha—The bard and herald of the Hindus, being attached to the state of all men of rank to chaunt their praises, celebrate their actions, and commemorate their ancestry. *Wilson.* The name of a herald, a bard who was produced at the sacrifice performed by Brahmá at the birth of Prithu.

Magha—A lunar mansion in Ásharbhí, in the Central Avasthána.

Magha—The name of one of the lunar months corresponding to December.

Mahabali—A name of Bali, q. v.

Mahabhadra—One of the four great lakes, the waters of which are partaken of by the gods. The Bhágavata calls it a lake of honey.

Mahabharata—This huge epic, which is in all probability later in date than the Rámáyana, and consists of about 220,000 long lines, is rather a cyclopædia of Hindú mythology, legendary history, and philosophy, than a poem with a single subject. It is divided into eighteen books, nearly every one of which would form a large volume ; and the whole is a vast thesaurus of national legends, said to have been collected and arranged by *Vyása* (the supposed compiler of the Vedas and Puránas), a name derived from a Sanskrit verb, meaning "to fit together," or "arrange."

The following is an outline of the leading story, though this occupies little more than a fifth of the whole work, numerous episodes and digressions on all varieties of subjects being interspersed throughout the poem :—

According to the legendary history of India, two dynasties were originally dominant in the north—called *Solar* and *Lunar*, under whom numerous petty princes held authority, and to whom they acknowledged fealty. The most celebrated of the Solar line, which commenced in *Ikshváku*, and reigned in Oude, was the Ráma of the Rámáyaṇa. Under this dynasty the Bráhmaṇical system gained ascendancy more rapidly and completely than under the Lunar kings in the more northern districts, where fresh arrivals of martial tribes preserved an independent spirit among the population already settled in those parts.

The most famous of the Lunar race, who reigned in Hastinápura, or ancient Delhi, was *Bharata,* whose authority is said to have extended over a great part of India, and from whom India is to this day called by the natives Bhárat-varsha (the country or domain of Bharata.) This Bharata was an ancestor of *Kuru*, the twenty-third in descent from whom was the Bráhman *Kríshna Dwaipáyana Vyása* (the supposed author of the Mahábhárata), who had two sons, *Dhritaráshtra* and *Pándu.* The former, though blind, consented to assume the government when resigned by his younger brother Páṇḍu, and undertook to educate, with his own hundred sons, the five reputed sons of his brother. These five sons were,—1st, Yudhishthira (*i. e.*, "firm in battle"); 2nd, Bhíma (*i. e.*, "terrible"); 3rd, Arjuna (*i. e.*, "upright"); 4th, Nakula (*i. e.*, "a mungoose"); 5th, Sahadeva (*i. e.*, "a twining plant.")

The three first were born from Páṇḍu's wife, Prithá, or Kunti, but were really her children by three gods, viz., Dharma, Váyu and Indra respectively. The two last were children of his wife Mádrí, by the Aṣviní-Kumáras, or "twin-sons," *i. e.*, of the Sun. As, however, Páṇḍu had acknowledged these princes as his sons, the objection to their birth was overruled by his example. Páṇḍu (*i. e.*, "the pale") was probably a leper, and so incapable of succession.

To make the genealogy more clear it may be shown in a tabular form as drawn up by Professor M. Williams.

Atri, the *muni*, generally reckoned among the seven Rishis or sages.
Soma, (or Chandra) the moon.
Budha (or Mercury) married Ilá, daughter of Ikshwaku.
Pururuvas (or Aila) married the nymph Urvaṣi.
Âyus.
Nahusha.
Yayáti (husband of Śarmishtha and Devayáni.)

Line of Puru.

Puru (king in Prakshthána.)
Dushyanta (h. of Śakuntala).
Bharata.
Hastin (built Hastinápur).
Kuru.
Śántanu.

Line of Yadu.

Yadu.
Vṛishni.
Devarata.
Andhaka.
Sura.
Vasudeva, brother of Kunti or Pritha.
Krishna and Balarama, with whom the line becomes extinct. They were contemporary with the sons of Pándu and Dhritarashtra.

Line of Puru and Kuru—continued.

Santanu—Satyavati.

- Chitrangada.
- Vichitra-vírya son of both died childless.
- Vyása son of Satyavati married the two widows of Vichitra-vírya.
- Bhíshma called Santanava and Gangeya as son of Santanu by Ganga.

Children of Vyása:

- Dhritarashtra—Gandhari.
  - Duryodhana and 99 other sons.
- Kunti or Pritha—Pandu—Madri.
  - Karna, Yudhishthira. Bhima Arjuna Nakula Sahadeva.
- Vidura called Kshattri.

The characters of the five Páṇḍavas are drawn with much artistic delicacy, and maintained consistently throughout the poem. The eldest, Yudhishthira, is a pattern of justice, integrity, and chivalrous honour and firmness. Bhíma is a type of brute courage and strength, of gigantic stature, impetuous and irascible; he is capable, however, of warm, unselfish love, and shows devoted affection for his mother and brothers. Arjuna, who is the chief hero of the poem, is represented as a man of undaunted courage, and, at the same time, generous, modest, and tender-hearted; of super-human strength, withal, and matchless in arms and athletic exercises. Nakula and Sahadeva are amiable, noble-minded, and spirited. All five are as unlike as possible to the hundred sons of Dhritaráshtra, commonly called the Kuru princes, or Kauravas, who are represented as mean, spiteful, dishonourable, and vicious. The cousins, though so uncongenial in character, were educated together at Hastinápur by a Brahman named Droṇa, who found in the Páṇḍu princes apt scholars. Their education finished, a grand tournament is held, at which the cousins display their skill in archery, the management of chariots, horses, &c. Arjuna especially distinguishes himself by prodigies of strength and skill; but suddenly a stranger enters the lists, named Karṇa, who, after performing the same feats, challenges Arjuna to single combat. But each champion is obliged to tell his name and pedigree, and Karṇa's parentage being doubtful (he was really the illegitimate son of Prithá, by Surya (the sun), and, therefore, half-brother of Arjuna), he is obliged to retire ignominiously from the arena. Thus publicly humiliated, Karṇa joins the party of their enemies, the Kurus, to whom he renders important service. Enraged at the result of this contest, the Kurus endeavour to destroy the Páṇḍavas by setting fire to their house; but they, warned of their intention, escape by an under-ground passage to the woods. Soon after, in the disguise of mendicant Brahmans, they repair to the *Swayamvara* of Draupadí, daughter of Drupada, king of Panchála. Arjuna, by the exhibition of his gymnastic skill, wins the favour of the lovely princess, who becomes his bride. Strengthened by Drupada's alliance, the Páṇḍu princes throw off their disguise, and the king, Dhritaráshtra, is induced to settle all differences by dividing his kingdom between them and his own sons, the Kurus. Yudhishthira, however, afterwards stakes and loses his whole territory at dice. His brothers then pass twelve years in the woods, in disguise, after which the war is again renewed. Krishṇa, king of Dwáraka, in Guzerat (an incarnation of Vishṇu), joins the Páṇḍavas, as charioteer to Arjuna. The rival armies meet near Delhi. The battle, which lasts for eighteen days, terminates in favour of the Páṇḍavas, who recover their possessions, and the elder brother is elevated to the throne; Duryodhana and all the Kurus being slain in the conflict.

Thus the undivided kingdom of Hastinápur became the possession of the sons of Páṇḍu; but they were so grieved by the dreadful slaughter which their ambition had occasioned, that they resigned their power. Their famous ally, Krishṇa—who previous to his founding the city of Dwáraka, had been expelled from Mathura (Muttra), the seat of his family—was accidentally killed in a thicket, and his sons, driven from their paternal possessions, sought refuge beyond the Indus.* See Bhágavat Gíta, Paudavas, Arjuna, &c.

Mahabhoja—A pious prince, the son of Sátwatu. The name is sometimes read Mahabhága.

Mahadeva—A Rudra—the name of the eighth manifestation of the Rudra—an account which Wilson says is grounded apparently on Saiva or Yogi mysticism; 2, A name of Śiva.

Mahajwala—The name of one of the Narakas, in which the crime of incest is punished.

Mahamaya—The king of Atala, the first of the seven regions of Pátáḷa.

Mahamoha—"Extreme illusion," causing addiction to the enjoyments of sense; one of the five kinds of obstruction to the soul's liberation; or as they are called in the Patanjala philosophy, one of the five afflictions—the 'five-fold Ignorance' of the Vishṇu Purána.

Mahan—One of the eleven Rudras.

* Williams. Indian Epic Poetry.

Mahanabha—A daitya of great prowess, one of the sons of Hiranyáksha.

Mahanada—A river in Orissa.

Mahanandi—One of the ten Saiṣunága kings of Magadha, the son of Nandivarddhana.

Mahanila—A powerful many-headed serpent. One of the progeny of Kadru.

Mahantu—A prince, the son of Dhímat ; he lived during the Swáyambhuva Manwantara.

Mahapadma—1, A prince, the son of Mahananda ; his name was Nanda, but he was remarkably avaricious. He was born of a Súdra woman, and after him the kings of the earth were to be all Súdras. Like Parasurama he endeavoured to annihilate the Kshatriya race, and brought the whole earth under one umbrella. He and his descendants, termed the nine Nandas, reigned a hundred years ; when the dynasty was overturned by the Brahman Kautilya (also called Chánakya and Chanaki) who placed Chandragupta on the throne. (See the Mudra Rakshasa, Hindu Theatre, Vol. 2.)

2. The name of one of the progeny of Kadru, a powerful many-headed serpent.

Mahapurusha—Great or supreme spirit ; purusha meaning that which abides or is quiescent in body ; incorporated spirit. It is a name applied to Vishṇu ; who is any form of spiritual being acknowledged by different philosophical systems : he is the Brahmá of the Vedanta, the Iswara of the Patanjala, and the Purusha of the Sánkhya school.

Maharashtra—The name in the Puránas of the Mahratta country.

Mahar-loka—The heaven of celestial spirits, the sphere of saints, situated at the distance of ten million leagues above Dhruva : the inhabitants dwell in it throughout a Kalpa or day of Brahmá. Those who are distinguished for piety, abide, at the time of dissolution, in Mahar-loka, with the Pitris, the Manus, the seven Rishis, the various orders of celestial spirits, and the gods. Then at the end of a Kalpa, when the heat of the flames that destroy the world reaches to Mahar-loka, the inhabitants repair to Janaloka, within subtile forms, destined to become re-embodied, in similar capacities as their former, when the world is renewed at the beginning of the succeeding Kalpa. This continues throughout the life of Brahmá ; at the expiration of his life all are destroyed ; but those who have thus attained a residence in the Brahma-loka by having identified themselves in spirit with the Supreme, are finally resolved into the sole existing Brahmá. See Wilson's Notes to V. P., p. 633.

Mahamagha—The occurrence of the full moon in or about the asterism Magha, with other astronomical incidents, which occur once in twelve years, and which time is auspicious for bathing. At Khumbakhonam there is a large tank, the water of which is supposed to rise once in twelve years, on the above occasion, and when people in great numbers assemble from distant places to bathe and obtain remission of sins.

Maharoman—One of the kings of Mithila, the son of Kritaráta.

Mahaswat—A prince, the son of Amarsha, a descendant of Ráma.

Mahat—Intellect ; the first product of Pradhána, sensible to divine, though not to merely human organs, is, both according to the Sánkhya and Purána doctrines, the principle called Mahat, literally the Great, explained as 'the production of the manifestation of the qualities :' Mahat, the Great principle, is so termed from being the first of the created principles, and from its extension being greater than that of the rest. Mahat is also called Iswara, from its exercising supremacy over all things. The Puránas generally attribute to Mahat, or Intelligence, the act of creating. Mahat is therefore the divine mind in creative operation, the *νους ὁ διακοσμων τε παντων αἰτιος* of Anaxagoras ; an ordering and disposing mind, which was the cause of all things. See Wilson's Notes to V. P., p. 15.

Mahatala—The fifth of the seven divisions of Pátáḷa, with a sandy soil, embellished with magnificent palaces, in which dwell numerous Dánavas, Daityas Yakshas, and the great snake-gods.

Mahavichi—The name of one of the Narakas beneath the earth.

Mahavira—1, One of the sons of Priyavrata, according to the Bhágavata; the one who had Krauncha-dwípa assigned to him; 2, A son of Savana, king of the seventh dwípa; 3, The name of a division of Pushkara dwípa.

Mahavira—The twenty-fourth Tírthankara of the Jains. His first birth, which occurred at a period indefinitely remote, was as Nayasára, headman of a village in the country of Vijáya. His piety and humanity elevated him next to the heaven called Saudharma, where he enjoyed happiness for some oceans of years. He was next born as Marichi, the grandson of the first Tírthankara Rishaba, thence transferred to the Brahmaloka, whence he returned to earth as a worldly-minded and sensual brahman, the consequence of which was his repeated births in the same caste, each birth being separated by an interval passed in one of the Jain heavens, and each period of life extending to many lakhs of years. He then became Viṣvabhuta, prince of Rajagṛiha, and next a Vásudeva named Triprishta (q. v.) then a chakravartti Priyamitra (q. v.) then a Nandana leading a life of devotion.

On the return of the spirit of Nandana to earth it first animated the womb of the wife of a brahman, but Mahendra, disapproving of the receptacle as of low caste, transferred it to the womb of Triṣalá the wife of Siddhárta, of the family of Iksváku, and prince of Ravana, in Bharatakshetra. Mahavira was born on the thirteenth of the light fortnight of Chaitra: the fifty-six nymphs of the universe assisted at his birth, and his consecration was performed by Śakra and the other sixty-three Indras. The name given by his father was Varddhamána, as causing increase of riches and prosperity, but Śakra gave him also the appellation of Mahávíra as significant of his power and supremacy over men and gods.

Mahávíra married Yaṣodá, daughter of the prince Samaravíra. By her he had a daughter Priyadarṣana, who was married to Jamali, a prince, one of the saint's pupils, and founder of a schism. Siddhartha and his wife died when their son was twenty-eight years old, on which Mahavíra adopted an ascetic life, the government devolving on his elder brother Nandivarddhana. After ten years of abstinence and self-denial at home he commenced an erratic life, and the attainment of the degree of a Jina.

During the first six years of his peregrinations, Mahávíra observed frequent fasts of several month's duration, during each of which he kept his eyes fixed upon the tip of his nose, and maintained perpetual silence. He was invisibly attended by a Yaksha named Siddhārtha, who, at the command of Indra watched over his personal security, and where speech was necessary acted as spokesman. In his travels he acquired a singular follower named Goṣála, a man of low caste who acted as a sort of buffoon.

It is not the duty of a Jain ascetic to inflict tortures on himself: his course of penance is one of self-denial, fasting, and silence; and pain, however meritorious its endurance, must be inflicted by others, not himself. Mahávíra voluntarily exposed himself to maltreatment at the hands of various savage tribes, offering no resistance, but rather rejoicing in his sufferings. At the end of the ninth year he relinquished his silence in answer to a question put by Goṣála, but continued engaged in the practice of mortification and in an erratic life.

In the course of twelve years and six months he attained the *Kevala*, or *only knowledge*. This occurred under a Sál tree, on the north bank of the Rijupalika. Indra instantly hastened to the spot accompanied by thousands of deities, who all did homage to the saint. He commenced his instructions on a stage erected for the purpose by the deities, a model of which is not uncommonly represented in Jain temples. The following is the introductory lecture ascribed to Mahávíra by his biographer.

"The world is without bounds like a formidable ocean; its cause is action (*Karma*) which is as the seed of the tree. The being, (*Jíva*) invested with body, but devoid of judgment, goes like a well-sinker ever downwards, by the acts it performs, whilst the embodied being which has attained purity goes ever upwards by its own acts, like the builder of a palace. Let not any one injure life, whilst bound in the bonds of action; but be as assiduous in cherishing the life of another as his own. Never let any one speak falsehood, but always speak the truth. Let every one who has a bodily form avoid giving pain to others as much as to himself. Let no one take property not given to him, for wealth is like the external life of men, and he who takes away such wealth commits as it were murder. Associate not with women, for it is the destruction of life; let the wise observe continence, which binds them to the Supreme. Be not encumbered with a family, for by the anxiety it involves the person separated from it falls like an ox too heavily laden. If it be not in their power to shun these more subtle destroyers of life, let those who desire so to do avoid at least the commission of all gross offences."

When Mahávíra's fame began to be widely diffused, it attracted the notice of the brahmans of Magadha, and several of their most eminent teachers undertook to refute his doctrines. Instead of effecting their purpose, however, they became converts, and constituted his Gaṇadharas, heads of schools, the disciples of Mahávíra, and teachers of his doctrines, both orally and scripturally.

The period of his liberation having arrived, Mahávíra resigned his breath, and his body was burned by Śakra and other deities, who divided amongst them such parts as were not consumed by the flames, as the teeth and bones, which they preserved as relics; the ashes of the pile were distributed amongst the assistants; the gods erected a splendid monument on the spot, and then returned to their respective heavens.—*Wilson's Works, Vol. I, p.* 304.

Mahavirya—1, A prince, the son of Vrihaduktha, one of the kings of Mithila; 2, A son of Bhavanmanyu, a descendant of Bharata.

Mahavishuba—The great equinox when the sun is in the third degree of Viṣakhá and the moon is in the head of Krittiká. At this time offerings are to be presented to the gods and to the manes, and gifts are to be made to the Brahmans by serious persons. Liberality at the equinoxes is always advantageous to the donor. V. P., p. 225.

Mahayajnas—The great Sacrifices, the great obligations, or as Sir W. Jones terms them sacraments, are but five: viz:—

1. Bramhayajna, sacred study;
2. Pitriyajna, libations to the manes;

3. Devayajna, burnt offerings to the gods ;
4. Baliyajna, offerings to all creatures ;
5. Uriyajna, hospitality.

The Prajápatiyajna, or propagation of offspring, and Satyajna, observance of truth, are apparently later additions.—*Wilson's Notes to V. P.*

Mahayuga—The aggregate of four Yugas or ages : viz :—

Kṛiti Yuga........4000
Sandhya..... 400
Sandhyánsa. 400
——4800

Tretá Yuga.......3000
Sandhya...... 300
Sandhyánsa. 300
——3600

Dwápara Yuga........2000
Sandhya..... 200
Sandhyánsa. 200
——2400

Kali Yuga.......1000
Sandhya..... 100
Sandhyánsa. 100
——1200

If these divine years are converted into years of mortals, by multiplying them by 360, a year of men being a day of the gods we obtain the years of which the Yugas of mortals are respectively said to consist :

4800×360=1,728,000
3600×360=1,296,000
2400×360= 864,000
1200×360= 432,000

A Maháyuga-4,320,000

So that these periods resolve themselves into very simple elements ; the notion of four ages in a deteriorating series expressed by descending arithmetical progression, as 4, 3, 2, 1 : the conversion of units into thousands ; and the mythological fiction that these were divine years, each composed of 360 years of men.

It does not seem necessary to refer the invention to any astronomical computations, or to any attempt to represent actual chronology.—*Wilson's Notes to V. P.*

Mahendra—1, One of the seven main chains of mountains in Bhárata. Mahendra is the chain of hills that extends from Orissa and the northern Circars to Gondwána, part of which, near Ganjam, is still called Mahendra Malei, or hills of Mahendra ; 2, The name of a star in the tail of the celestial porpoise ; 3, The name of a river mentioned in the Puránas.

Maheswara—A name of Śiva, 'the great Lord.'

Maheyas—People living near the Mahi river.

Mahi—A river, the Mahy of Western Malwa.

Mahikas, or Mahishas—Supposed to be the ancient name for the inhabitants of Mysore.

Mahinasa—One of the eleven *Rudras.*

Mahishakas—An ancient name of the people of Mysore.

Mahishmat—A prince of the Yada race, the son of Sahanji.

Mahishmati—A city on the road to the south (Mahábhárata, Udyoga Parva) which is commonly identified with Chulí Maheṣwar, on the Narmada.

Mayodaya—The ancient name of the city of Kanouj, q. v.

Mahyuttaras—A people to the north of the river Mahí.

Mainaka—A son of Himávat and Mená ; the brother of Ganga and Párvatí.

Maitreya—1, A disciple of Paráṣara, to whom the Vishṇu Purána is related in reply to his inquiries ; he is also one of the chief interlocutors in the Bhágavata, and is introduced in the Mahábhárata, (Vana Parva, S. 10) as a great Rishi, or sage, who denounces Duryodhana's death. In the Bhágavata he is also termed Kausharavi ; 2, A son of Mítráyu, from whom the Maítreya Brahmans were descended.

Maitreyas—A tribe of Brahmans descended from Mitráyu.

Maitri—Friendship, daughter of Daksha, wife of Dharma.

Makara—A huge amphibious monster, usually taken to be the shark or crocodile, but depicted in the signs of the zodiac with the head and forelegs of an antelope, and the body and tail of a fish. It is the ensign of the god of love. Varuna, the god of the sea, rides upon it through the waves, showing it to have been a *fish* of some sort. It is now the name of a shark in many parts of India.

Makandi—The capital of Southern Pánchála, the country north of the Ganges as far as to the Chambal.

Maladas, Malajas, Malas—Tribes of people enumerated in the Puránas, but not satisfactorily identified.

Malavas—An aboriginal tribe dwelling along the Páripátra mountains.

Malaya—One of the seven chief chains of mountains in Bhárata; the southern portion of the Western Ghauts.

Malyavan—One of Śiva's principal attendants, who for interceding for one of his fellow-servants Pushpadanta (q. v.) was sentenced to a similar punishment—namely, to leave the paradise of Kailása and be born as a human being. After a due interval Mályaván was born at Pratishta, under the name of Gunádhya.—*Wilson's Works, Vol. III, p.* 152.

Malyavan—A mountain at the base of Meru, to the east.

Malayas—The aboriginal tribes of the Southern Ghauts.

Malina—The son of Tansu, a descendant of Puru.

Mallarashtra—A name given in the Puránas to the Mahratta country.

Mallas—In Bhíma's Dig-Vijaya we have two people of this name, both in the east, one along the foot of the Himálaya, and the other more to the south.

Manas—Mind; that which considers the consequences of acts to all creatures, and provides for their happiness. It is sometimes used as a synonym of Mahat.

Manasa—1, A form of Vishṇu, when he was born of Sambhúti, along with the gods Abhútarajasas, in the Rawala Manwantara; 2, One of the four great lakes, the waters of which are partaken of by the gods.

Manasottara—A prodigious range of mountains, running in a circular direction (forming an outer and an inner circle,) situated in Pushkara, the seventh Dwípa. The mountains are represented as 50,000 leagues high, and on the eastern face of the summit, the city of Indra is situated; that of Yama in the southern face; that of Varuna in the west, and that of Soma in the north.

Manaswini—The wife of Mikránda, the great Muni.

Manasya—A prince, the son of Mahánta, who reigned over India in the first, or Swayambhuva Manwantara.

Mancha—A raised platform, with a floor and a roof, ascended by a ladder. V. P., p. 553.

Mandahara—A minor Dwípa; the Bhágavata and Pádma name eight such islands, peopled for the most part by Mlechchhas, but who worship Hindu divinities.

Mandara—The mountain which was used by the gods as a churning stick, at the churning of the sea of milk.

Mandehas—Terrific fiends who attempt every night to devour the sun. The night is called Usha, and the day is denominated Vyushta, and the interval, between them is called Sandhyá. On the occurrence of the awful Sandhyá, the Mándehas do their utmost to devour the sun; for Brahmá denounced this curse upon these terrific fiends, that without the power to perish they should die every day (and revive by night,) and therefore a fierce contest occurs daily between them and the sun. V. P. The Váyu says the Mandehas are three crores in number. Professor Wilson says the story seems to be an ancient legend imperfectly preserved in some of the Puránas.

Mandhatri—A prince, the son of Yuvanáṣwa, of whose birth the Vishṇu Purána relates the following extraordinary legend. Yuvanáṣwa had no son, at which he was deeply grieved. The Munis instituted a religious rite to procure him progeny, one night during its performance, the sages, having placed a vessel of consecrated water upon the altar, had retired to repose. It was past midnight when the king awoke, exceedingly thirsty ; and unwilling to disturb any of the holy inmates of the dwelling, he looked about for something to drink. In his search he came to the water in the jar, which had been endowed with prolific efficacy by sacred texts, and he drank it. When the Rishis arose and found that the water had been drunk, they inquired who had taken it, and said, 'The queen that has drunk this water shall give birth to a mighty and valiant son.' 'It was I,' exclaimed the Rája 'that unwittingly drank the water ;' and accordingly, in due course, the Rája gave birth to a child from his right side. Indra became its nurse ; and hence the boy was named Mándhátṛi. The boy grew up and became a mighty monarch. He married Bindumatí, and had by her three sons and fifty daughters. The latter were all married to the sage Saubhari, q. v.

Mandukeya—A teacher of the Rig Veda, the son of Indrapramati who imparted his Sanhita to his son, and it thence descended through successive generations as well as disciples.

Mangala—The fiery-bodied Mars, son of the Rudra Sárva and his wife Vikesi.

Mani—A powerful serpent, one of the progeny of Kadru.

Manidhanga—The king of a tract of country near the Vindhya mountains.

Manojava—1, The son of the Rudra Isána ; 2, (Hanumán.) The son of the Vasu Anila (Wind) Manojava means 'swift as thought ;' 3, The Indra of the sixth Manwantara was called Manojava.

Manmatha—A name of the Indian Cupid, the son of Vishṇu, called also Káma, q. v. He is represented as the cause of sensual love both in mortals and celestials, but more especially in the female sex : whilst his wife, Rati, inflames the fire in the male sex—like Venus of old.

Mantra—A hymn of invocation or form of prayer in the Sanskrit language. Mantras are used in the performance of every religious rite. They are of various sorts, invocatory, evocatory, deprecatory, conservatory. They are beneficent or hurtful, salutary or pernicious. By means of them it is believed that great and various effects may be produced. Some are for casting out evil spirits; some for inspiring love or hatred, for curing diseases or bringing them on, for causing death or averting it. Some are of a contrary nature to others, and counteract their effect: the stronger overcoming the influence of the weaker. Some are potent enough, it is said, to occasion the destruction of a whole army: while there are others which the gods themselves are constrained to obey.

The Puróhitas, or domestic chaplains, of all Hindus, understand them best. They are indispensably necessary to them for accompanying the ceremonies which it is their office to conduct. But Brahmáns generally are conversant with these formulæ; and when rallied upon the present state of their Mantras, wholly divested as they are of their boasted efficacy and power, they answer that this loss of their influence is to be attributed to the Kali yuga; the age of the world in which we now live, the iron age, the time of evil and misfortune in which everything has degenerated. See Dubois.

Manu—The head or ruler of an extensive period of time, termed a Manwantara. Each Kalpa, or creation of the world, is divided into fourteen Manwantaras or intervals, over which a Manu presides. Six of these periods have passed; the first Manu was Swáyambhuva; the second Swarochisa, the third Auttami; the fourth Tamasa; the fifth Raivata; the sixth Chakshusha; these six Manus have passed away; the Manu who presides over the seventh, which is the present period, is Vaivaswata, the son of the sun, the wise lord of obsequies. The Vishṇu Purána contains an account of the Manwantaras yet to come; and the names of the Manus who will preside over each. The Jainas have also fourteen Manus to whom they give names different to those in the Hindu Puránas.

Manu—The Noah of the Hindus. The Śatapatha Brahmana contains an important legend of the deluge, but speaks of Manu simply, without assigning to him any patronymic, such as Vaivaswata, so that it is uncertain which Manu is referred to. O. S. T., Vol. I, p. 217. Monier Williams writes of him as the seventh Manu, or Manu of the present period, called Vaivaswata, and regarded as one of the progenitors of the human race. He is represented as conciliating the favour of the Supreme in an age of universal depravity. Dr. Muir gives a translation of the legend in his Orig. Sans. Texts, Vol. I, p. 182 ; Prof. Max Müller has also translated it on his An. Sans. Lit., p. 425. The following translation is from Prof. M. Williams' Indian Epic Poetry.

"It happened one morning that they brought water to Manu, as usual, for washing his hands. As he was washing a fish came into his hands. It spake to him thus : 'Take care of me and I will preserve thee.' Manu asked, 'From what wilt thou preserve me.' The fish answered, 'A flood will carry away all living beings ; I will save thee from that.' He said, 'How is thy preservation to be accomplished' ? The fish replied, 'while we are small, we are liable to constant destruction, and even one fish devours another ; thou must first preserve me in an earthen vessel ; when I grow too large for that dig a trench, and keep me in that. When I grow too large for that, thou must convey me to the ocean ; I shall then be beyond the risk of destruction.' So saying, it rapidly became a great fish, and still grew larger and larger. Then it said, 'After so many years the deluge will take place ; then construct a ship, and pay me homage, and when the waters rise, go into the ship, and I will rescue thee.' Manu therefore, after preserving the fish as he was directed, bore it to the ocean ; and at the very time the fish had declared he built a ship and did homage to the fish. When the flood rose he embarked in the ship and the fish swam towards him, and he fastened the ship's cable to its horn. By its means he passed beyond this northern mountain. The fish then said 'I have preserved thee ; now do thou fasten the ship to a tree. But let not the water sink from under thee while thou art on the mountain. As fast as it sinks do thou go down with it'. He therefore so descended ; and this was the manner of Manu's descent from the northern mountain. The flood had carried away all living creatures. Manu alone was left. Wishing for offspring he diligently performed a sacrifice. In a year's time a female was produced. She came to Manu. He said to her, 'Who art thou ?' She answered, 'Thy daughter.' He asked, 'How lady art thou my daughter?' She replied, 'The oblations which thou didst offer in the waters, viz., clarified butter, thick milk, whey and curds; from these hast thou begotten me. I can confer blessings.' With her he laboriously performed another sacrifice, desirous of children. By her he had offspring, called the offspring of Manu; and whatever blessings he prayed for were all granted to him."

"From this interesting legend we learn that, according to its author's belief, Manu was not the creator of mankind, as some later accounts considered him to have been, but himself belonged to an earlier race of living beings, which was entirely destroyed by the deluge which is described. The legend regards him as a representative of his generation, who for some reason, perhaps his superior wisdom, or sanctity, or position, was selected out of the crowd of ordinary mortals to be rescued from the impending destruction. That he was regarded as a mere man, and not as a being of a superior order, is shown by the fact of his requiring the aid of a higher power to preserve him. A supernatural fish, apparently some divine person, conceived as taking the form of a creature which would be perfectly secure and at home in the midst of the raging waters, undertook to deliver him, and guided the ship on which he was directed to embark, through all dangers to its destined haven. No one but Manu took refuge in the ship, for he alone, the story expressly records, was preserved, while all the other living beings were overwhelmed. Finding himself the sole survivor when the waters subsided, he became desirous of progeny; and with intense devotion performed certain religious rites in the hope of realizing his wish through their efficacy. As a result of his oblations, a woman arose from the waters into which they had been cast. A male and a female now existed, the destined parents of a new race of men who sprang from their union,—a union the fruitfulness of which was assured by their assiduous practice of sacred ceromonies. From Manu and Iḍā, we are expressly told, the race known as that of Manu, *i. e.*, the race of men, was produced. The legend says nothing whatever of this race being originally characterized by any distinction of castes, or about four sons, the ancestors of Brahmans, Kshatriyas, Vaisyas, and Sudras being born to Manu and Iḍá. We must therefore suppose that the author of the legend intends to represent the early race of mankind, or at least the first inhabitants of Bharatavarsha, as descended from one common progenitor without any original varieties of caste, however different the professions and social position of their descendants afterwards became. We are consequently entitled to regard this legend of the Śatapatha Brahmana as at variance with the common fable regarding the separate origin of the Brahmans, Kshatriyas, Vaisyas and Sudras."—*Muir. O. S. T., Vol. I, p.* 185.

Manu—The great Hindu law-giver who lived about 800 B. C. The institues of Manu, or code of laws still extant, is sometimes attributed to Swayambhuva the first Manu. The Manu of the present period is sometimes considered the author of the Dharmashastra, the code which bears his name. "The name belongs to the Epic and Puranic periods. In the former we may trace in it the remains of the tradition of a first man, alike progenitor, or even creator, like Prometheus, of his descendants, and law-giver. We should conceive its historical value to be the allusion to some legendary personage, such as every nation can boast of, who first wakes his country-men from barbarism and a wild life, to the light of civilization and systematic government." *Thomson.* Manu was " a legislator and saint, a son of Brahmá, or a personification of Brahmá himself, the creator of the world and progenitor of mankind. Derived from the root *man* to think, the word means originally *man*, the thinker, and is found in this sense in the Rig Veda.

" Manu as a legislator is identified with the Cretan Minos ; as progenitor of mankind with the German Mannus : ' Celebrant carminibus antiquis, quod unum apud illos memoriæ et annalium genus est, Tuisconem deum terra editum, et filium Mannum, originem gentis conditoresque. TACITUS, Germania, Cap. II."—*Griffiths.*

Manu—1, The name, according to the Bhágavata of one of the eleven Rudras ; 2, A sage, the son of Krisáswa and Dhishana.

Manwantara—A period equal to seventy-one times the number of years contained in the four Yugas, with some additional years : this is the duration of the Manu, the (attendant) divinities, and the rest, which is equal to 852,000 divine years, or to 306,720,000 years of mortals, independent of the additional period. Fourteen times this period constitutes a Brahmá day, that is a day of Brahmá, or a Kalpa.

Margashirsha—The month which comprises the latter half of November and the former half of December. "It is otherwise called *Agraháyana* "the commencement of the year;" and although the Hindus now begin their year in the month *Vaisháka* (April, May) we find in Prinsep's Useful Tables, part II, p. 18, that in Bentley's opinion, this month would have begun the year, before the use of a fixed calendar in India, between B. C. 693 and 451.

Maricha—A Daitya, the son of Sunda.

Marichi—1, A Prajápati, one of the nine Brahmá rishis, or mind-born sons of Brahmá ; he was married to Sambhúti (fitness) one of the daughters of Daksha. Their son, Kaṣyapa, had an extensive posterity ; 2, The chief of the Maruts, or personified winds.

Marichigarbhas—A class of deities belonging to the ninth Manwạntara.

Marisha—The daughter of the sage Kaṇdu, and the nymph Pramlocha. An account of her birth has been given under Kaṇdu : in a previous existence she was the widow of a prince, and left childless at her husband's death : she prayed to Vishṇu that in succeeding births she might have honorable husbands and a son equal to a patriarch amongst men. The prayer was granted and she was married to the Prachétasas.

Markandeya—The son of the Rishi Mrikanda.

Markandeya Purana—This Purána contains an account of the nature of Vásudeva, and an explanation of some of the incidents described in the Mahábhárata. It was narrated in the first instance by the Muni Márkandeya, and in the second place by certain fabulous birds, of heavenly descent, profoundly versed in the Vedas. It contains a long episodical narrative of the actions of the goddess Dúrga, and furnished the pomp aud circumstance of the great festival of Bengal, the Dúrga Pújá, or public worship of that goddess. Professor Wilson says this Purána has a character different from that of all the others; it contains few precepts, moral or ceremonial. Its leading feature is narrative, and it presents a succession of legends, most of which, when ancient, are embellished with new circumstances; and when new, partake so far of the spirit of the old, that they are disinterested creations of the imagination, having no particular motives.

Marriage—The forms of marriage are eight, the Brahmá, Daiva, the Ársha, Prájápatya, Asura, Gandharba, Rakshasa and Paiṣacha. These different modes of marriage are described by Manu III, 27, &c. The Vishṇu Purána describes the kind of maiden that should be selected by the man who has finished his studies, and proposes to enter into the married state. She should be a third of his own age; one who has not too much hair, but is not without any; one who is not very black nor yellow complexioned, and who is not from birth a cripple or deformed: he must not marry a girl who is vicious or unhealthy, of low origin or labouring under disease; one who has been ill brought up; one who talks improperly; one who inherits some malady from father or mother; one who has a beard, or is of a masculine appearance; one who speaks thick or thin, or croaks like a raven; one who keeps her eyes shut, or has the eyes very prominent; one who has hairy legs, or thick ankles; or one who has dimples in her cheeks when she laughs;* let not a wise and prudent man marry a girl of such a description; nor let a considerate man wed a girl of a harsh skin; or one with white nails; or one with red eyes; or with very fat hands and feet; or one who is a dwarf, or who is very tall; or one whose eyebrows meet, or whose teeth are far apart and resemble tusks.

Marshti, Marshtimat—Two of the sons of Śarana of the family of Vasudeva.

* For the credit of Hindu taste it is to be noticed that the commentator observes the hemistich in which this clause occurs is not found in all copies of the text.—*Prof. Wilson.*

Marttikavatas—Princes of Mrittikavatí.

Maru—1, The son of Síghra, a descendant of Ráma. In the Vishṇu Purána it is stated that Maru is, through the power of devotion, (Yóga) still living in the village called Kalápa, and in a future age will be the restorer of the Kshatriya race in the solar dynasty ; 2, The name of the son of Hariyaṣwa, king of Mithila.

Marubhaumas—The inhabitants of Marubhúmi, the desert ; an aboriginal tribe occupying the sandy deserts of Sindh.

Marudeva—A prince, the son of Supratítha, a descendant of Ikshváku.

Marut-loka—The heaven of the winds and Vaisyas.

Maruts—The winds. The sons of Diti, who having lost her children prayed for a son of irresistible prowess who should destroy Indra. The Muni Kaṣyapa granted his wife the great boon she solicited, but with one condition ; that she should be pregnant a hundred years, and maintain a rigid observance of all religious rites during the whole period. Indra watched for an opportunity of frustrating her intentions, and in the last year of the century, an opportunity occurred. Diti retired one night to rest without performing the prescribed ablution of her feet, and fell asleep : on which Indra divided the embryo in her womb into seven portions. The child, thus mutilated, cried bitterly. Indra failing to silence it again divided each of the seven portions into seven, and thus formed the swift-moving deities called Marutas (winds.) They derived this appellation from the words with which Indra had addressed them (Marodih, weep not,) and they became forty-nine subordinate divinities, the associates of the weilder of the thunderbolt. V. P. This legend, says Professor Wilson, occurs in all the Puránas in which the account of Kasyapa's family is related. The Vishṇu Purána in another place, says the winds were the children of Marutwatí. The Maruts are said to have given Bharata a son named Bharadwája. q. v. Among the lesser gods, an important share of adoration is enjoyed by a group avowedly subordinate to Indra,—involving an obvious allegory,—the Maruts, or Winds, who are naturally associated with the firmament. We have, indeed, a god of the wind, in Váyu ; but little is said of him, and that chiefly in association with Indra, with whom he is identified by scholiasts on the Veda. The Maruts, on the contrary, are frequently addressed as the attendants and allies of Indra, confederated with him in the battle with Vṛitra, and aiding and encouraging his exertions. They are called the sons of Pṛiṣni, or the earth, and also Rudras, or sons of Rudra : the meaning of which affiliations is not very clear, although, no doubt, it is allegorical. They are also associated, on some occasions, with Agni ; an obvious metaphor, expressing the action of wind upon fire. It is also intimated that they were, originally, mortal, and became immortal in consequence of worshipping Agni, which is also easy of explanation. Their share in the production of rain, and their fierce and impetuous nature, are figurative representations of physical phenomena.—*Wilson.*

Marutta—1, A celebrated Chakravartti, or universal monarch, the son of Avikshit. A Sanskrit verse thus sets forth the splendour of his proceedings :—"There never was beheld on earth a sacrifice, equal to the sacrifice of Marutta : all the implements and utensils were made of gold. Indra was intoxicated with the libations of Soma juice, and the Brahmans were enraptured with the magnificent donations they received. The winds of heaven encompassed the rite as guards, and the assembled gods attended to behold it." Marutta reigned 85,000 years, according to the Markendaya Purána ; 2, A son of Karandhama, a descendant of Turvasa.

Marutwati—One of the daughters of Daksha, who was married to Dharma.

Matali—The charioteer of Indra. It was he who was sent to convey Yayáti to heaven, when Indra invited him thither. The Padma Purána relates a philosophical conversation that took place between the king and Mátali, in which the imperfection of all corporeal existence, and the incomplete felicity of every condition of life are discussed. These attributes belong, it is said, even to the gods themselves, for they are affected with disease, subject to death, disgraced by the passions of lust and anger, and are consequently instances of imperfection and of misery. Various degrees of vice are then described, and their prevention or expiation are declared to be the worship of Śiva or Vishṇu, between whom there is no difference; they are but one, as is the case indeed with Brahmá also; for 'Brahmá, Vishṇu, and Maheṣwara are one form, though three gods; there is no difference between the three: the difference is that of attributes alone.' See Yayáti.

Matanga—A brahman mentioned in the Daṣakumára who was killed while trying to preserve the life of another brahman. On reaching the city of souls, Yama said to Chandragupta 'This man's hour is not yet come. He died in defence of a brahman. That one virtuous act effaces all his former sins. Let him behold the penalty paid to the wicked, and then restore him to his former body.' Returning to life his adventures were still more remarkable. Aided by a prince whom he met in the forest he penetrated the path to Pátáḷa. On arriving near the city, he cast himself into the flames of a fire he had prepared and rose again in an angelic form. A damsel richly arrayed and numerously attended, who said her name was Kálindí, daughter of the king of Asuras, and that she had come with the concurrence of her council to offer the kingdom and herself, twin wives, to his espousal. Mátanga married her and became king of Pátáḷa.—*Wilson's Works, Vol. IV, p.* 174.

Mathura—A holy city, founded by Satrughna, (the younger brother of Ráma.) It is situated in the banks of the Yamuná, where a demon at one time resided, named Madhu. His son the Rakshas Lavaṇa, was slain by Satrungha, who afterwards built the shrine which obtained celebrity as a purifier from all sin. It was in this place that Dhruva's penance was performed.

Mati—Understanding—that which discriminates and distinguishes objects preparatory to their fruition by the soul. It is often used to signify mind, intelligence, knowledge, wisdom.

Matinara—The son of Rikska, the fifteenth in descent from Puru. V. P.

Matsya—1, The name of one of the Minor Dwípas; 2, A teacher of the Rig Veda, a disciple of Vedamitra.

Matsya, or fish Avatara—The first of the ten Avataras of Vishṇu. When, at the end of the last mundane age, the Bhágavata Purána relates, Brahmá, the first god of the Trimúrti, had fallen asleep, a powerful demon, *Hayagríva*, stole the Vedas which had issued from the mouth of Brahmá, and lay by his side. About that time, a royal saint, *Satyavrata*, had by his penance attained the rank of a Manu, and Vishṇu, who had witnessed the deed of Hayagrîva, and intended to slay him, assumed for this purpose the form of a very small fish, and glided into the hands of the saint when the latter made his daily ablutions in the river. Manu, about to release the little fish, was addressed and asked by it not to expose it to the danger that might arise to it from the larger fish in the river, but to place it in his water-jar. The saint complied with its wish ; but in one night the fish grew so large, that at its request he had to transfer it to a pond. Yet soon the pond also becoming insufficient to contain the fish, Manu had to choose a larger pond for its abode ; and, after successive other changes, he took it to the ocean. Satyavrata now understood that the fish was no other than *Náráyana* or Vishṇu, and, after he had paid his adoration to the god, the latter revealed to him the imminence of a deluge which would destroy the world, and told him that a large vessel would appear to him, in which he was to embark together with the seven Rishis, taking with him all the plants and all the seeds of created things. Manu obeyed the behest of the god : and when the water covered the surface of the earth, Vishṇu again appeared to him in the shape of a golden fish with a single horn, 10,000 miles long ; and to this horn Manu attached the vessel, by means of Vishṇu's serpent serving as a cord. While thus floating in the vessel, Manu was instructed by the fish-god in the philosophical doctrines and the science of the supreme spirit ; and after the deluge had subsided, the fish-god killed Hayagrîva, restored the Vedas to Brahmá, and taught them to the Manu Satyavrata, who in the present mundane age was born under the name of *Srâddhadeva*, as the son of Vivasvat. A fuller account of this Avatâra is given in the *Matsya-Purâna*, where the instruction imparted to Manu by the fish-god includes all the usual detail contained in a Purána (q. v.,) that relating to creation, the patriarchs, progenitors, regal dynasties, the duties of the different orders, and so forth. In the Mahábhárata, where the same legend occurs, but without either that portion concerning Hayagrîva, or the instruction imparted by the fish, there is, besides minor variations, that important difference between its story and that of the Puránas, that the fish is not a personification of Vishṇu, but of Brahmá, and that the deluge occurs in the present mundane age, under the reign itself of the Manu, who is the son of Vivasvat. The origin of this Avatára is probably a kindred legend, which occurs in the *Sathapatha brâhmana,* of the White Yajurveda; but there the fish does not represent any special deity, and the purpose of the legend itself is merely to account for the performance of certain sacrificial ceremonies.—[MANU.]

Matsya Purana—This Purána, after the usual prologue of Súta and the Rishis, opens with the account of the Matsya or 'fish' Avatára of Vishṇu, in which he preserves a king named Manu, with the seeds of all things, in an ark, from the waters of that inundation which in the season of a Pralaya overspreads the world. Whilst the ark floats fastened to the fish (Vishṇu) Manu enters into conversation with him, and his questions, and the replies of Vishṇu, forms the main substance of the compilation. The first subject is the creation, which is that of Brahmá and the patriarchs; the regal dynasties are next described; and then follow chapters on the duties of the different orders, &c. The account of the universe is given in the usual strain. Saiva legends ensue; as the destruction of Triparásura; the war of the gods with Taraka and the Daityas, and the consequent birth of Kartikeya, with the various circumstances of Uma's birth and marriage, the burning of Kamadeva; the destruction of the Asuras Maya and Andhaka; interspersed with the Vaishnava legends of the Avatáras. There are also chapters on law and morals, and one which furnishes directions for building houses and making images. See Vishṇu Purána, Preface.

Matsyas—The people of Dinajpur, Rangpur, and Cooch Behar. There are, however, two Matsyas, one of which according to the Yantra Samrát, is identifiable with Jaypur. In the Dig Vijaya of Nakula the Matsyas are placed farther to the west or in Guzerat.

Maudga—A teacher of the Sáma Veda, and disciple of Devadersa.

Maudgalyas—A class of Brahmans descended from Mudgala : they, as well as the Kanwas, were all followers or partisans of Angiras.

Maunas—A dynasty of kings, consisting of eleven sovereigns ; and forming part of the seventy-nine princes mentioned in the Vishṇu Purána as to reign over the earth for one thousand three hundred and ninety years.

Mauneyas—A name of the Gandharbas, dwelling in the regions below the earth, sixty millions in number, who defeated the tribes of the Nágas, or snake-gods, seizing upon their most precious jewels and usurping their dominion.

Mauryas—A race of kings of Magadha commencing with Chandragupta, whose dynasty lasted for a hundred and thirty-seven years.

Maya—A powerful Dánava, of some note as the father of Vajrakámá and Mahodárí.

Maya—Illusion. "Know that matter is illusion, and the great deity the possessor of illusion. The vedantists say that Brahmá, the self-resplendent, the supremely happy, and the one sole essence, assumes, unreally, the form of the world through the influence of his own illusion." O. S. T., Vol. III, p. 195. "In the spirit of the Berkeleyan theory they affirm that matter exists not independent of perception ; and that substances are indebted for their seeming reality to the ideas of the mind. All that we see is Máya, deception, illusion. There are no two things in existence ; there is but one in all. There is no second ; no matter ; there is spirit alone. The world is not God, but there is nothing but God in the world."—*Wilson's Works, Vol. II, p.* 98.

Maya—'Deceit' ; 1, A daughter of Adharma (vice) ; 2, A daughter of Anrita (falsehood).

Mayadevi—The supposed wife of the Asura Sambara, who rescued Pradyumna when he was thrown into the sea as an infant, and swallowed by a fish (See Pradyumna.) She had deluded

Sambara for the purpose of protecting and rearing Pradyumna to whom she was afterwards married, and returned with him to Dwáraka to the great joy of Rukmini and Krishṇa.

Medha—'Intelligence'; 1, One of the three sons of Priyavrata who adopted a religious life; remembering the occurrences of a prior existence they did not covet dominion, but diligently practised the rites of devotion, in due season, wholly disinterested, and looking for no reward. V. P. 2, A daughter of Daksha who was married to Dharma.

Medatithi—One of the sons of Priyavrata who became king of Plaksha dwípa. He had seven sons, and the Dwipa was divided amongst them, each division being named after the prince to whom it was subject, the people enjoyed uninterrupted felicity, being sinless, V. P., p. 197.

Medhavin—A prince, the son of Sunaya, of the race of Puru.

Mekala—A Rishi, the father of the river Narmadá; thence called Mekala and Mekalakanya: the mountain where it rises is also called Mekaládri.

Mekalas—A tribe which according to the Puránas live in the Vindhya mountains: this locality is confirmed by mythological personations. The Rámáyana places the Mekalas amongst the Southern tribes.

Mena—A daughter of the Pitris, acquainted with theological truth and addicted to religious meditation; accomplished in perfect wisdom and adorned with all estimable qualities. She was married to Himávat, and was the mother of Mainάka and of Ganga, and of Párvati or Umá; 2, A river.

Menaka—A divine nymph; one of the ten Apsarasas who are specified as of the Daivika or divine class, and whose principal occupation is the interruption of the penances of holy sages.

Mendicant—See Vánaprastha.

Meru—In the earlier Epic period this is probably the name given to the high table-land of Tartary, to the north of the Himálaya range, from the neighbourhood of which the Aryan race may originally have pushed their way southwards into the peninsula, and thus have preserved the name in their traditions as a relic of the old mountain worship.* In the Puránas it is described as the golden mountain in the centre of Jambu-dwípa. Its height is eighty-four thousand Yójanas ; and its depth below the surface of the earth sixteen thousand. Its diameter at the summit is thirty-two thousand Yójanas ; (the yojana is nine miles) and at its base sixteen thousand ; so that this mountain is like the seed cup of the lotus of the earth. V. P. Prof. Wilson in a note states "the shape of Meru according to this description, is that of an inverted cone ; and by the comparison to the seed cup its form should be circular : but there seems to be some uncertainty upon this subject amongst the Pauránics. The Pádma compares its form to the bell-shaped flower of the Dhatura. The Váyu represents it has having four sides of different colours ; or white on the east, yellow on the south, black on the west, and red on the north : but notices also various opinions of the outline of the mountain, which, according to Atri, had a hundred angles : to Bhrigu a thousand ; Savarni calls it octangular ; Bhaguri quadrangular ; and Varsháyani says it has a thousand angles : Gálana makes it saucer-shaped ; Garga, twisted, like braided hair : and others maintain that it is circular. The Linga makes its eastern face of the colour of ruby ; its southern, that of the lotus ; its western, golden ; and its southern coral. The Matsya has the same colours as the Váyu and both contain this line 'Four-coloured, golden, four cornered, lofty : but the Váyu compares its summit in one place to a saucer ; and observes that its circumference must be thrice its diameter. The Matsya also says the measurement is that of a circular form but it is considered quadrangular. According to the Buddhists of Ceylon, Meru is said to be of the same diameter throughout. Those of Nepal consider it to be shaped like a drum."

On the summit of Meru is the vast city of Brahmá, extending fourteen thousand leagues and renowned in heaven ; and around it in the cardinal points and the intermediate quarters ; are situated

*Thomson.

the stately cities of Indra and the other regents of the spheres. Mount Meru is in short the Olympus of India.

Merubhutas—See Marubhaumas.

Merumandara—A mountain to the south of Meru with a large Pípal tree on its summit.

Meru-savarnis—The Manus from the ninth to the twelfth Manwantaras ; described in the Váyu as the mind-engendered sons of a daughter of Daksha, by himself and the three gods Brahmá, Dharma, and Rudra, to whom he presented her on Mount Meru ; whence they are called Meru-sávarṇis. They are termed Sávarṇis from their being of one family.

Mimansa Darsana—"The founder of the Mímánsá School was *Jaimini*, of whose history very little is known. He is described as a short young man, of light complexion, wearing the dress of a mendicant, and living at Nílavata-Múla. He was born at Dwaita-vana. His father, Śákatayana, was author of a Sanskrit dictionary, and his son, Krití, wrote certain verses in the Deví-Bhágavata.

There are about twenty-six works extant, illustrating the Mímánsá system, the chief of which are the Sútras of Jaimini ; the Bháshya, by Shávara (and comments thereon by Bhatta, Váchaspati Mishra and Ránaka) ; the Satíka-Śástra-Dípiká, by Sóma-Nátha ; the Dharma-Dípiká ; the Mímánsá-Súra ; and the Mímánsá Sangraha.

From the three last-named works chiefly we gather the following abridgment of the system of Jaimini. He taught that God is to be worshipped only through the incantations of the Vedas : that the Vedas were uncreated, and contained in themselves the proofs of their own divinity, the very words of which were unchangeable. His reasonings on the nature of material things were similar to those of Gautama, insisting that truth is capable of the clearest demonstration, without the possibility of mistake. Creation, preservation, and destruction, he represented as regulated by the merit and demerit of works ; while he rejected the doctrine of the total destruction of the universe. He maintained that the images of the gods were not real representations of these beings, but only given to assist the mind of the worshipper ; that the mere forms of worship had neither merit nor demerit in them ; and that the promises of the Sástra to persons who presented so many offerings, so many prayers, &c., were only given as allurements to duty.

He directed the person, who sought final emancipation, to cherish a firm belief in the Vedas, as well as persuasion of the benefits of religion, and the desire of being engaged in the service of the gods ; and then, by entering upon the duties of religion, and by degrees ascending through the states of a student, a secular, and a hermit, he would be sure to obtain final absorption in Brahmá.

Of the three divisions of the Veda, the first, called the *Karma Kánda*, or " practical part," relates to religious *ceremonies* (including moral and religious obligations.) This portion Jaimini has attempted to explain in his *Sútras*, and in the *Púrva* Mímánsá (*i. e.*, *former* " Mímánsá," which is commonly referred to when the term " *Mímánsá*" simply is used,) so called in distinction from the *Uttara* (or latter) Mímánsá ascribed to Vyása, which is the the same as the Vedánta, and is founded on the *Juána Kánda* (or theological part) of the Vedas, treating of the *spiritual* worship of the Supreme Being or soul of the Universe.

Sound, says Jaimini, in opposition to the Nyaiyikas, who deny this, is *uncreated* and *eternal*, and is of two kinds, viz., *simple* sound, or that which is produced by an impression on the air without requiring an agent, as the name of God ; and *compound* (smybolized or audible) sound. Thus, the state of the sea, in a perfect calm, represents simple, uncreated sound ; but the sea, in a state of agitation, illustrates sound as made known by an agent.

Symbols, of sounds, or letters, are eternal and uncreated ; as is also the meaning of sounds. For instance, when a person has pronounced *ka*, however long he may continue to utter *ka*, *ka*, it is the same sound, sometimes present and sometimes absent ; but sound is never new. Its manifestation alone is new by an impression made upon the air. Therefore *sound is God* (Brahmá), and the *world* is nothing but *name*.

The Veda has no human origin, but contains in itself the evidence of divine authorship, and comes forth as the command of a monarch. It is incumbent on men to receive also, as divine, those works (of the sages) which are found to agree with the Veda, to contain clear definitions of duty, and to be free from contradictions.

What is religion? That which secures happiness. And it is the duty of man to attend to the duties of religion, not only on this account, but in obedience to the commands of God. The divine law is called *Vidhi*.

Should any one say, then I have nothing to do with other kinds of instruction, since this alone is divine. To that it is replied, that forms of praise, motives to duty, and religious observances, are auxiliaries to the divine law, and have, therefore, a relative sanctity and obligation.

There are five modes of ascertaining the commands of God, viz: (1), the subject to be discussed is brought forward; (2), questions respecting it are stated; (3), objections are started; (4), replies to these objections are given; and (5), the question is decided. He who acts in religion according to the decision thus come to, does well; and so does he who rejects what will not bear this examination; but he who follows rules which have been hereby condemned, labours in vain.

Those actions from which future happiness will arise are called religious, or good, because productive of happiness; and those which tend to future misery are called evil, on account of their evil fruits. Hence, according to Jaimini, actions of themselves have in them neither good nor evil. Their nature can only be inferred from the declarations of the Veda respecting them, or from future consequences. The Hindús appear to have no just idea of *moral evil.*

Of all the works on the Civil and Canon Law, that of *Manu* is to be held in the greatest reverence, for Manu composed his work after a personal study of the Veda. Other sages have composed theirs from mere comments.

From the evidence of things which God has afforded, especially the evidence of the senses, mistakes cannot arise either respecting secular or religious affairs. When there may exist error in this evidence, it will diminish, but cannot destroy the nature of things.

If there be an imperfection in seed, the production may be imperfect, but its nature will not be changed. The seat of error and inattention is to be found in this reasoning faculty, and not in the senses ; error arising from the confused union of present ideas *(anubhava)* with recollection.

Some affirm that ideas are received into the understanding separately, and never two at the same instant. This is incorrect ; for it must be admitted, that while one idea is retained, there is an opening left in the understanding for the admission of another. Thus, in arithmetical calculations, "one added to one makes two."

The Veda has, in some parts, forbidden all injury to sentient beings, and in others has prescribed the offering of bloody sacrifices. Jaimini explains this apparent contradiction by observing that some commands are general, and others particular : that the former must give way to the latter, as a second knot always loosens, in a degree, the first. So, when it is said that Saraswatí is altogether white, it is to be understood, not literally, but generally, for the hair and eyebrows of the goddess are not white. Therefore, in cases where general commands are given, they must be observed with those limitations which are found in the *S'ástra.*

The promises of reward contained in the *S'ástra* upon a minute attention to the different parts of duty, have been given rather as an incitement to its performance than with the intention of entire fulfilment. He who has begun a ceremony, but has, by circumstances, been unable to finish it, shall yet not be unrewarded.

The benefits resulting from the due performance of civil and social duties are confined to this life. Those connected with the performance of religious duties are to be enjoyed in a future state, while some meritorious actions, or virtues, reap their reward both in the present and the future life.

Works give birth to invisible consequences—either propitious or otherwise—according to their nature ; and, besides works, there is no other sovereign or judge. These consequences, ever accompanying the individual, as the shadow the body, appear in the next birth, in accordance with the time and manner in which those actions were performed in the preceding birth. "Works rule, and men by them are led or driven, as the ox with a hook in its nose."

The progress of all actions, whether they originate in the commands of the Śástras, or in the customs of a country, are as follows :—First, the act is considered and resolved on in the mind ; then it is pursued by means of words ; and, lastly, it is accomplished by executing the different constituent parts of the action. Hence it follows that religion and irreligion refer to thoughts, words, and actions. Some actions, however, are purely those of the mind, or of the voice, or of the body. The virtue or vice of all actions depend on the state of the heart.

The doctrine that, at a certain period, the whole universe will be destroyed at once, is incorrect. The world had no beginning, and will have no end. As long as there are works, there must be birth, as well as a world like the present, to form a theatre on which they may be performed, and their consequences either enjoyed or endured.

One of the sages of the Mímánsá school thus expresses himself :—' God is simple sound. To assist the pious in their forms of meditation (or incantations). He is represented as light ; but the power of liberation lies in the sound ' God—God.' When the repeater is perfect, the incantation, or name repeated, appears to him in the form of simple light or glory.

The objects of worship, which are within the cognisance of the senses, are to be received ; for without *faith* religious actions are destitute of fruit. Therefore, let no one treat an incantation as a mere form of alphabetic signs, nor an image as composed of the inanimate material, lest he should be guilty of a serious crime.' —*Small, H. S. L.*

Minaratha—A prince, the son of Anenas, a king of Mithila, of the family of Janaka.

Misrakesi—One of the Apsarasas, a Laukíka nymph.

Mithi—A prince, the son of Nimi, the legend of whose birth is thus related in the Vishṇu Purána. As Nimi left no successor, the Munis, apprehensive of the consequences of the earth being without a ruler, agitated the embalmed body of Nimi, and produced from it a prince who was called Janaka, from being born without a progenitor. In consequence of being produced by agitation.

(Mathana) he was further termed Mithi. The Rámáyana places a prince named Mithi between Nimi and Janaka, whence comes the name Mithila.

Mithila—The modern Tirhoot. Mithila is celebrated in the Puránas as the country over which the descendants of Ikshváku reigned for a long period. Mithi, from whom the country derived its name, was the grandson of Ikshváku.

Mitra—1, One of the twelve Ádityas, the one who presides over the organs of excretion ; 2, A sage, one of the seven sons of Vasishtha. V. P.

Mitra is the god of the day. Mitra is said to represent the sun by day, and Varuna the setting luminary. " Mitra re-appears in the Zendavesta as the well-known Mithra, who is the angel presiding over and directing the course of the sun."—*Quarterly Review, July* 1870.

Mitrasaha—A prince, the son of Sudása. Having gone into the woods to hunt, he fell in with two tigers by whom the forest had been cleared of the deer. The prince slew one of these tigers with an arrow. At the moment of expiring the form of the animal was changed, and it became that of a fiend of a fearful figure and hideous aspect. Its companion, threatening the prince with its vengeance, disappeared. After some interval Saudása celebrated a sacrifice which was conducted by Vasishtha. At the close of the rite Vasishtha went out ; when the Rákshasa, the fellow of the one that had been killed in the figure of a tiger, assumed the semblance of Vasishtha, and came and said to the king " now that the sacrifice is ended, you must give me flesh to eat ; let it be cooked and I will presently return. Having said this he withdrew, and transforming himself into the shape of the cook, dressed some human flesh which he brought to the king, who, receiving it on a plate of gold, awaited the re-appearance of Vasishtha ; as soon as the Muni returned the king offered to him the dish. Vasishtha knowing it to be human flesh was surprised at such an insult, and in his anger denounced a curse upon the Rája, transforming him into a cannibal. " It was yourself replied the Rája to the indignant sage, who commanded this food to be prepared." Vasishtha, having recourse to meditation then detected the whole truth : but though the curse was partially withdrawn, the Rája became a cannibal every sixth watch of the day for twelve years, and in that state wandered through the forests and devoured multitudes of men. On one occasion he met with a brahman and his wife : seizing the husband, and regardless of the wife's reiterated supplications, he ate the brahman as a tiger devours a deer. He returned to his wife Madayanti at the expiration of the period of his curse, but suffered from the imprecation of the brahman's wife. V. P.

Mitravrinda—One of the seven beautiful wives of Krishṇa.

Mitraya—1, A scholar of Súta's and teacher of the Puránas and legendary lore : he was also a composer of one of the Sanhitas afterwards collected into the Vishṇu Purána ; 2, The son of Divodáṣa, from whom the Maítreya brahmans were descended.

Mlechchas—Outcastes. The Vishṇu Purána states that various Kshatriya races were degraded by Sagara, by being deprived of established usages and the study of the Vedas ; and thus separated from religious rites, and abandoned by the brahmans, these different tribes became Mlechchas.

Moha—1, 'Dulness' or 'Stupefaction,' a property of sensible objects ; a kind of ignorance ; or illusion produced by the notion of property or possession, and consequent attachment to objects, as children and the like, as being one's own. Moha also occurs in the Bhágavata and Matsya Purána amongst a series of Brahma's progeny, or virtues and vices ; Moha is there translated by Wilson to mean Infatuation.

Mohini—Vishṇu in a female form. The product of Śiva's union with Móhini was Ayeṉar, the only male among the Gráma-dévatas.

Moksha—Absorption into the Deity. The Hindu idea of supreme blessedness. It is only those who attain to a full knowledge of the nature of the deity, the soul, the intellect, &c., derived from meditation, the teaching of the guru, experience, penance, &c., or the exalted ascetic, who, by austerities is said to have annihilated his passions, and freed his soul from earthly desire, that is considered ripe for this final emancipation or Móksha.

Monotheism—In the Vishṇu Purána it is said, ' the only one God, Janárddana takes the designation of Brahmá, Vishṇu, and Śiva, accordingly as he creates, preserves or destroys. This, says Professor Wilson, is the invariable doctrine of the Puránas, diversified only according to the individual divinity to whom they ascribe identity with Paramátmá or Parameswara. In the Vishṇu Purána this is Vishṇu ; in the Saiva Puránas, as in the Linga, it is Śiva ; in the Brahmá-vaivartta it is Krishṇa. The identification of one of the hypostases with the common source, the triad, was an incongruity not unknown to the other theogonies ; for Cneph amongst the Egyptians, appears on the one hand to have been identified with the Supreme Being, the indivisible unity, whilst on the other he is confounded with both Eureph and Ptha, the second and third persons of the triad of hypostases. Cudworth, Vol. I, p. 4–18.

Moon—The Vishṇu, Váyu, and Pádma Puránas all relate in detail the legend of the churning of the ocean, and state that the cool-rayed moon was one of the products of the operation ; it was seized by Mahádeva. The Vishṇu Purána says that the chariot of the moon has three wheels, and is drawn by ten horses, of the whiteness of the jasmine, five in the right half of the yoke and five in the left. The horses drag the car for a whole Kalpa. During the dark half of the month nectar and ambrosia are accumulated in the moon, and these are drunk by thirty-six thousand divinities during the light fortnight ; the Pitris are nourished by it in the dark fortnight ; vegetables with the cool nectary aqueous atoms it sheds on them ; and through their development it sustains men, animals, and insects ; at the same time gratifying them with its radiance. V. P., p. 239. The orb of the Moon, according to the Linga Purána is only congealed water.

Mrigavithi—A division of the lunar mansions, in the southern Avashtána.

Mrida—A prince, the son of Nripanjaya, of the race of Puru.

Mrigasiras—A lunar mansion, in Gajavithi of the northern Avashtána.

Mrigavyadha—One of the eleven Rudras, according to the enumeration in the Matsya Purána.

Mrikanda—The son of Vidhátri and Niryati, descendants of the daughters of Daksha who were married to the Rishis.

Mrittikavati—A city in Malwa, near the Parnáṣá river, whose sovereigns were the Bhojas, descendants of Satwata.

Mritya—1, 'Death,' one of the progeny of Brahmá; he is also represented in the same work, the Vishṇu Purána, as the son of Bhaya and Maya; and his children are thus given Vyadhi (disease), Jará (decay), Soka (sorrow), Trishna (greediness), and Krodha (wrath); 2, The name of one of the eleven Rudras, in the Váyu list; 3, A Vyasa in the sixth Dwápara age.

Muchukunda—One of the sons of Mándhátṛi, called the 'king of men,' who in a battle between the gods and demons, had contributed to the defeat of the latter; and being overcome with sleep he solicited of the gods as a boon, that he should enjoy a long repose. 'Sleep long and soundly, said the gods, and whoever disturbs you shall be instantly burnt to ashes by fire emanating from your body.' The black king, Kályavana, met with this fate, by a stratagem of Krishṇa; and Muchukunda having fallen down and worshipped Krishṇa as the undecaying, illimitable and imperishable being, departed to Gandhamádana to perform penance, and obtain emancipation from all existence. Another account states that "Muchukunda carried on war against the Buddhists till he was too weary to fight any longer; whereupon he sought the grateful seclusion of the Guttikonda cave. In this peaceful and salubrious spot he fell asleep; it was a sleep of the greatest profundity, and lasted for some centuries. In an evil moment for the Buddhists they entered the cave in pursnit of Krishṇa, and disturbed the placid slumbers of Muchukunda. After a nap of some hundreds of years, he was not a man to be trifled with; so he rose up in the exuberance of his renovated energies and extirpated the obnoxious Buddhists." *A. & M. I.*

Muda—'Pleasure,' a son of Dharma by one of the daughters of Daksha, Santósha (Joy).

Mudgala—1, A sage mentioned in the Mahábhárata, who had lived a life of poverty, piety, and self-restraint, offering hospitality to thousands of brahmans, according to his humble means, with the grain which he gleaned like a pigeon, and which (like the widow of Zarephath's oil) never underwent diminution. At length another sage called Durvásas, famous in Hindu tradition for his irascible temper, came to prove Mudgala's powers of endurance ; and six times devoured all the food which the hospitable saint possessed. Finding that the temper of his host was altogether unaffected by these trials, Durvásas expressed the highest admiration of his virtue, and declared that he would go bodily to heaven. As he spoke these words a messenger of the gods arrived in a celestial car, and called upon Mudgala to ascend to a state of complete perfection. The sage, however desired first to learn the advantages and drawbacks of the heavenly state, and the messenger proceeded to tell him first what kind of people go there, viz ; those who have performed austerities or celebrated great sacrifices, the truthful, the orthodox, the righteous, the self-restrained, the meek, the liberal, the brave, &c. These celestial abodes were, he said, shining, glorious, and filled with all delights. There is seen the vast-golden mountain Meru, and the holy garden Nandana, &c., where the righteous disport. There hunger, thirst, weariness, cold, heat, fear, are unknown ; there is nothing disgusting or disagreeable ; the scents are delightful ; the sounds are pleasant to the ear and mind ; there is no sorrow, nor lamentation, nor decay, nor labour, nor envy, nor jealousy, nor delusion. There the blessed are clothed with glorious bodies, which are produced by their works, and not generated by any father or mother. Their garlands are fragrant and unfading ; they ride in aerial cars. Beyond these regions there are, however, others of a higher character—those to which the Rishis, who have been purified by their works, proceed. Still further on are those where the Ribhus, who are gods even to the gods, dwell, and where there is no annoyance occasioned by women, or by envy arising from the sight of worldly grandeur. The blessed there do not subsist on oblations, nor do they feed upon ambrosia ; they have celestial and not coarse material bodies. These eternal gods of gods do not desire pleasure ; they do not change with the revolutions of Kalpas (great mundane ages). How can they then be subject either to decay or death ? They experience neither joy, nor pleasure, nor delight, neither happiness nor suffering, neither love nor hatred. That highest state, so difficult to attain, and which is beyond the reach of those who seek after pleasure, is desired even by the gods. This celestial felicity, the messenger says, is now within Mudgala's reach,—the fruit of his good deeds. The speaker next, according to his promise, explains the drawbacks of the heavenly state. As the fruit of works done on earth is enjoyed in heaven, whilst no other new works are performed there from which new rewards could spring, this enjoyment is cut off from its root, and must therefore come to an end. For this world is the place for works, while the other is the place for reward. This loss of gratifications to which the heart has become devoted, and the dissatisfaction and pain which arise in the minds of those who have sunk to a lower estate, from beholding the more brilliant prosperity of others, is intolerable. To this must be added the consciousness and the bewilderment of those who so descend, and the fear of falling which they experience when their garlands begin to fade. Such are the defects which attach to all existence till it is absorbed in Brahmá. But the state of those who have fallen from heaven is not altogether without compensation. As a result of their previous good deeds they are born in a condition of happiness ; though, if they are not vigilant, they sink still lower. Having given this explanation, the messenger of the gods invites Mudgala to accompany him to paradise. The saint, however, after consideration, replies that he can have nothing to do with a state of happiness which is vitiated by so great defects, and the termination of which is followed by so great misery. He has therefore no desire for heaven ; and will seek only that eternal abode where there is no sorrow, nor distress, nor change. He then asks the celestial messenger what other sphere there is which is free from all defects. The messenger replies, that above the abode of Brahmá is the pure eternal light, the highest sphere of Vishṇu who is regarded as the supreme Brahmá. Thither none can proceed who are devoted to objects of sense, or who are the slaves of dishonesty, avarice, anger, delusion or malice; but only the unselfish, the humble, those who are indifferent to pain and pleasure, those whose senses are under restraint, and those who practice contemplation and fix their minds on the deity. The sage then dismissed the messenger of the gods, began to practise ascetic virtues, becoming indifferent to praise and blame, regarding clouds, stones and gold as alike. Pure knowledge led to fixed contemplation; and that again imparted strength and complete comprehension, whereby he attained supreme eternal perfection. O. S. T., Vol. V, pp. 324—6.

Mudgala—2, A teacher of the Rig Veda; 3, One of the five sons of Hariyaswa, king of Panchála.

Mudita—One of the five kinds of BHAVANA or meditation, in which the Buddhist priests are required to engage. The *mudita* is the meditation of joy, but it is not the joy arising from earthly possessions. It feels indifferent to individuals, and refers to all sentient beings. In the exercise of this mode of meditation, the priest must express the wish, "May the good fortune of the prosperous never pass away; may each one receive his own appointed reward."

Muhurtta—1, A measure of time, thirty Kalás, according to the Vishṇu Purána. Other Puránas say that a Muhurtta is twelve kshanas, and that one kshana contains thirty kalás. The Bhágavata states that two Narikas make one Muhurtta; 2, The name of a daughter of Daksha.

Muka—A Daitya, the son of Upasanada, famous in Puránic legend.

Mukhyas—A class of deities to come in the ensuing or eighth Manwantara.

Mula—The nineteenth lunar mansion, in Ajavíthi, of the Southern Avashthána.

Mulaka—The son of Aṣmaka. The Vishṇu Purána states that when the warrior tribe was extirpated upon earth, he was surrounded and concealed by a number of females; whence he was denominated Nárí-kavacha (having women for armour.) Múlaka, or 'the root' refers also to his being the stem whence the Kshatriya races again proceeded. V. P. and note, p. 383.

Mummies—The Vishṇu Purána states that the corpse of Nimi was preserved from decay by being embalmed with fragrant oils and resins, and it remained entire as if it were immortal. This, says Professor Wilson, shows that the Hindus were not unacquainted with the Egyptian art of embalming dead bodies, though such a practice would be thought impure in the present day.

Mundas—A dynasty of kings, consisting of thirteen, who are said in the Vishṇu Purána to be sovereigns of the earth for upwards of two hundred years; Wilford regards them as Huns, the Morunda of Ptolemy. Notes to Vishṇu Purána.

Muni—1, Any great sage or Rishi. In Southern India they are said to be forty-eight thousand: they are supposed to be holy persons who by different kinds of austerities have acquired great gifts, and power to bless and curse most effectually. The accounts given of them are rather contradictory; they are said to need neither sleep nor rest, neither food nor drink; and yet that they perform severe penance before God continually; 2, The name of a daughter of Daksha who was married to Kaṣyapa.

Munjakesa—A teacher of the Atharva Veda, and founder of a school. Sometimes Munjakeṣa is regarded as another name for Babhra.

Mura—A demon of great power who had seven thousand sons. He defended Pragjyotisha by surrounding the environs with nooses as sharp as razors, but Krishṇa cut them to pieces by throwing his discus, Sudarsana, amongst them. He afterwards slew the demon and burnt all his sons, like moths, with the flame of the edge of his discus.

Murdhabhishikta—An anointed Rájah. Hindu rájahs were formerly consecrated by having water from a sacred stream mixed with honey, ghee, and spirituous liquor, as well as two sorts of grass and the spirits of corn, poured on their heads while seated on a throne prepared for the purpose. The term applies to the *Kshatriya* as the caste from which kings are taken.

Murtti—' Form' a daughter of Daksha, married to Dharma.

Murundas—See Mundas.

Musala—A club, born of Sambu for the destruction of the Yadavas. Ugrasena had the club, which was of iron, ground to dust, and thrown into the sea; but the particles of dust there became rushes (eraká). There was one part of the iron club which was like the blade of a lance, and which the Andhakas could not break; this, when thrown into the sea, was swallowed by a fish; the fish was caught, the iron spike was extracted from its belly, and was taken by a hunter named Jará, by whom Krishṇa was subsequently killed.

Mushtika—A demon celebrated as a great wrestler. At the games of Mathura, when Kansa hoped to destroy Krishṇa, Balabhadra wrestled with Mushtika and at last killed him.

N

Nabha—A powerful Danava, the son of Viprachitti by Sinhika, the sister of Hiraṇyakasipu.

Nabhaga-nedishta—One of the sons of the Manu Vaivaswata; his name means 'no share,' and in the Aitareya Brahmana he is said to have been excluded from all share of his inheritance on the plea of his being wholly devoted to a religious life. The Bhágavata says that having protracted his period of study beyond the usual age, his brothers appropriated his share of the patrimony. On his applying for his portion they consigned their father to him, by whose advice he assisted the descendants of Angiras in a sacrifice, and they presented him with all the wealth that was left at its termination. Rudra claimed it as his; and Nabhaga acquiescing, the god confirmed the gift, by which he became possessed of an equivalent for the loss of territory.

Nabhaga—1, The son of the preceding; he became a Vaisya through carrying off and marrying the daughter of a Vaisya; it appears from this that a race of Vaisya princes was recognised by early traditions; 2, A son of Sruta, a descendant of Sagara; 3, A son of Yayáti.

Nabhas, Nabhasya—1, A name of the months, Srávana and Bhádra, corresponding to July and August, the names occur in the Vedas and belong to a system now obsolete; 2, The son of Nala, a descendant of Kusa.

Nabaswati—The wife of Antarddhána, a descendant of Pritha.

Nabhi—One of the nine sons of Agnídhra, to whom the country of Hímahwa was assigned.

Nachiketas—A philosopher, the son of Gautama, mentioned in the Katha Upanishad, of whom Dr. Roer says, "the enthusiasm and intimate conviction which Nachiketas shows about the infinite superiority of what is good to the pleasures of the world, and the firmness which he maintains amidst all the allurements which are placed before him, bears some resemblance to the energy of mind with which Plato, in the first and second books of his 'Republic,' shows that justice has an incomparable worth, and ought to be preserved under any circumstances."* In an interview with Yama, who promised Nachiketas any boon, the latter requested to be instructed in the nature of the soul, Yama objected saying, even gods have doubted and disputed on this subject, for it is not easy to understand it. But Nachiketas could not be persuaded to think any other boon worth asking for.†

Naga—1, A mountainous ridge in the north of Meru ; 2, A serpent, one of the progeny of Kadru ; 3, Originally the Cobra-capella, or Colubernaga.

Nagadwipa—A division of Bhárata Varsha.

Nagas—The 'Snake gods,' children of Kadru. In mythology these beings have human heads and the bodies of serpents : they are one thousand in number and bear jewels in their heads. They are the sons of Kaṣyapa and Kadru, subject to Vishṇu's bird, Garuda, and inhabiting part of Pátáḷa, called Naga-loka, the capital of which is Bhógavati. When they were deprived of their power by the Gandharbas, they despatched their sister, Narmadá, to solicit the aid of Purukutsa, and she conducted him to the regions below the earth where being filled with the might of the deity he destroyed the Gandharbas. The snake gods, in acknowledgment of Narmadá's services, conferred upon her as a blessing, that whoever should think of her and invoke her name, should never have any dread of the venom of snakes.

Nagas—"The *Saiva Sannyâsís* who go naked are distinguished by this term. They smear their bodies with ashes, allow their hair, beards, and whiskers to grow, and wear the projecting braid of hair, called the *Jâtá* ; like the *Vairáji Nágas*, they carry arms, and wander about in troops, soliciting alms, or levying contributions. The *Saiva Nágas* are chiefly the refuse of the *Dandi* and

* Bibliotheca Indica, Vol. XV, p. 91.

† A. and M. I., Vol. I, p. 136.

Atit orders, or men who have no inclination for a life of study or business: when weary of the vagrant and violent habits of the *Nága*, they re-enter the better disposed classes, which they had first quitted. The *Saiva Nágas* are very numerous in many parts of India."—*Wilson.*

Nagas—The designation of nine kings who reigned in Padmávati.

Nagavithi—1, A division of the lunar mansions in the Northern Avashthána; 2, The milky way, daughter of Yámí (night).

Nagna—A Jain mendicant; a naked ascetic.

Nagnas—Apostates. The Rig, Yajur, and Sáma Vedas, constitute the triple covering of the several castes, and the sinner who throws this off is said to be naked or apostate. The three Vedas are the raiment of all orders of men, and when that is discarded they are left bare. (V. P.) Wilson in his notes, adds, ascetics whether of the Buddha or Digambara order of Jains, are literally Nagnas, "going naked." The qualified application of it, however, was rendered necessary by the same practice being familiar to ascetics of the orthodox faith. To go naked was not necessarily the sign of a heretic, and therefore his nudity was understood to be rejecting the raiment of holy writ. Thus the Váyu Purána extends the word to all ascetics, including naked brahmans, who practice austerities fruitlessly, that is heretically or hypocritically.

Nagnajiti—One of the wives of Krishṇa, termed in the Vishṇu Purána the virtuous Nagnajití.

Nahusha—1, The son of Ambarísha; 2, The eldest of the five sons of Áyus, who having attained the rank of Indra, compelled the Rishis to bear his litter, and was cursed by them to fall from his state and re-appear upon earth as a serpent. From this form he was set free by philosophical discussions with Yudhishtira, and received final liberation; 3, The name of one of the progeny of Kadru, a powerful many-headed serpent.

Naigama—A teacher of the Rig Veda, a pupil of Sákapúrṇi.

Naigameya—One of the sons of Kumára.

Naikaprishtas—An aboriginal tribe mentioned in the Puránas, so termed probably in derision ; it means having more than one back.

Naishadha—A tract of country near the Vindhya mountains.

Nakhis—Religious mendicants who practice various austerities, never cut their finger nails, and wear the *Saiva* marks.

Nakshatra-Yoginis—The chief stars of the lunar mansions, or asterisms in the moon's path : these are fabled to have been the twenty-seven daughters of Daksha, who became the virtuous wives of the moon.

There are twenty-seven divisions of the lunar orbit ; each marking the motion of the moon in one lunar day. Such is their simple reference, astronomically ; but the Hindu astrologers make them of great practical consequence, from their assumed good or evil influence. They reckon from the first degree of Aries, in the old Astronomy.

1. Asvini, the ram's head.......................good.
2. Bharini...bad.
3. Critica, Pleiades..............................very bad.
4. Rohini, hyades................................good.
5. Mrigasiras, a triple star....................good.
6. Ardra, one star...............................bad.
7. Punar vasu, four stars......................good.
8. Pushya, nebula in Cancer..................good.
9. Aslesha, five stars...........................bad.
10. Magha, cor leonis...........................good.
11. Purvap'halguni, two stars.................medium.
12. Uttara P'halguni, two stars...............medium.
13. Hasta, five stars.............................good.
14. Chitra, one star..............................bad.
15. Swati, one star...............................good.
16. Visáka, four stars...........................bad.
17. Anuradha, four stars........................good.
18. Jyeshṭa, three stars.........................bad.
19. Mula, eleven stars, cor scorpionis.........very bad.
20. Purvashadha, four stars....................medium.
21. Uttara shadha, three stars.................good.

22. Sravana, three stars........................good.
23. Dhanishta, four stars........................bad.
24. Satabhisha, a hundred stars................bad.
25. Purva bhadrapada, two stars...............medium.
26. Uttara bhadrapada, two stars..............medium.
27. Revati, thirty-two stars.......................good.

These influences refer principally to marriages. The Nakshatras are classified as *deva*, divine; *manushya*, human; *rakshasa*, savage; if the two parties to be married are born in the same class, it is well: if one asterism be divine, the other human, it may pass; but divine and savage is a cross that may not be permitted.

An intercalary *abhijit*, one-fourth of a Nakshatra, is sometimes introduced between 21 and 22 for astrological purposes, or to make up a complete cycle of the moon's motion.—*Taylor*.

Nakta—A prince, the son of Prithu, who reigned over one of the divisions of Bharatavarsha in the first or Swáyambhuva Manwantara.

Nakula—One of the sons of Páṇḍu by his wife Mádrí, though really begotten by the elder of the two Asvinan (see Páṇḍu). He is half-brother to Sahadeva, the son of Dasra, by the same mother, and nominally brother to the three other Páṇḍavas. He is always referred to as one of the wisest of mortals.

Nala—The king of Nishada, whose history forms part of the third book of the Mahábhárata and is called the *Nalopakhyanam*. Nala possessed all the noble qualities and acquirements that could distinguish an Indian monarch. The king of Berar had an only daughter, the most beautiful and accomplished of her sex—the gentle Damayanti. Nala and Damayantí became mutually enamoured of each other from the mere fame of each other's virtues. Damayanti preferred Nala to Indra, Sani, and two other demi-gods who became incarnate for the purpose of attending the *Swayamvara* of the princess. Incensed at Damayanti's refusal to marry him, Sani, a malevolent being, persecuted the royal couple with great hatred, and caused Nala to lose his kingdom by gambling, and to be banished to the wilderness; and as his faithful consort could not be persuaded to return to her father, he took her with him into the forest; but not being willing to cause her so much suffering as a life in the woods involves, he resolved to leave her alone when she was sleeping under a tree, thinking she would then return to her father's house. But this she did not do; lamenting, she sought her husband, and when she could not find him she went to a certain king and became maid of honour to the queen; whilst Nala wandered about and became so black he could no longer be recognised as king Nala. Finally he became cook to the king at whose court Damayanti lived; and was such a skilful cook that his skill in cooking has become a proverb; and after all he was recognised by his faithful spouse as king Nala; and having soon recovered his former pleasing appearance he also regained his throne. See Damayanti; 2, The name of a prince, the son of Yadu; 3, The name of a river that falls into the Ganges.

Nalakanakas—A people mentioned in the Puránic lists but not identified.

Nalini—The name of one of the five streams formed by the Ganges after it escaped from Śiva.

Nama—Literally name: the term applied to the tridental mark which the Vaishnavas wear on their forehead, the mark, or figure, is called Tirunáma, 'holy name' it is an imitation of Vishṇu's trident almost like the Hebrew character shin. It consists of two white lines, extending from the hair to the eyebrows, and then leading to the nose where they meet, and a red perpendicular line between them from the nose to the hair.

Namasivaya—The principal Mantra of the Saivas, called Panchákshara five characters, and means 'O Śiva, be praised:' or 'Adoration to Śiva.'

Namuchi—A powerful Danava, one of the sons of Viprachitti. This Asura was a friend of Indra; and taking advantage of his friend's confidence, he drank up Indra's strength along with a draught of wine and soma. Indra then told the Aṣvins and Sarasvatí that Namuchi had drunk up his strength. The Aṣvins and Sarasvatí, in consequence gave Indra a thunderbolt in the form of a foam, with which he smote off the head of Namuchi. The Aṣvins then drank the soma mixed with blood and wine, from the belly of Namuchi and transferred it pure to Indra ; and by transferring it they delivered Indra. O. S. T., Vol. V, p. 94.

Nanda—1, The chief of the cowherds, and brother of Radha. He was the foster father of Krishṇa, as it was to his care the infant Krishṇa was committed when Kansa sought to destroy the child ; 2, One of the sons of Vasudeva ; 3, The son of Mahananda, and sometimes called Mahapadma, because he was avaricious. He brought the whole earth under one umbrella, and had eight sons, or descendants rather, according to Professor Wilson, who governed for a hundred years ; when the brahman Kautilya overthrew the dynasty and placed Chandragupta on the throne. The Mudra Rakshasa illustrates this affair.

Nandana—The grove of Indra, situated to the north of Mount Meru.

Nandayania—A pupil of Báshkali and teacher of the Rig Veda.

Nandi—The snow white bull, the attendant and favourite vehicle of Śiva. It is represented on a pedestal crouching in front of Saiva fanes ; the head turned towards the small door of the shrine. On one occasion Nandi, by assuming the likeness of Śiva, caused a blush on the cheeks of Párvati, and for this offence, Śiva sent his vehicle down to earth to do penance ; hence the mountain Nandi-durga—(Nandidroog.) Another mission to earth was in the person of the elder Basava.

Nandi—'Delight,' the wife of Dharma and mother of Hersha (joy.)

Nandimukhas—A class of Pitris : there seems to be some uncertainty about the character of the Nándímukhas ; and they are addressed both as Pitris and gods ; being in the former case either the ancestors prior to the great grand-father, ancestors collectively, or a certain class of them ; and in the latter being identified with the Viṣwadevas. The term Nándímukha is also applied to the rite itself, or to the Vriddhi Śráḍḍa, and to one addressed to maternal ancestors. See Wilson's Notes to Vishṇu Purána, p. 315.

Nandivardhana—1, The son of Urdávasu, king of Mithila; 2, The son of Janaka, king of Magadha; The son of Udayaṣwa, king of Magadha.

Nara—Paramátma: the waters it is said were the progeny of Nara; that is they were the first productions of God in creation.

Nara—1, A pious sage, the son of Dharma by Múrtti; 2, A prince, the son of Gaya; 3, A prince, the son of Sudhriti; 4, One of the sons of Bhavanmanyas of the royal family of Bharata.

Nara—'Bodily forms' in which spirit is enshrined; and of which the waters, with Vishṇu resting upon them, are a type. Waters, the first product of Nara. Vishṇu Purána, p. 28.

Narada—A Prajápati or divine Rishi, born from the hip of Brahmá; the invention of the véna, or Indian lyre, is attributed to Nárada; also a code of laws, and one of the eighteen Puránas entitled Náradiya Purána. In the Brahmá Purána he is called the smooth-speaking Nárada, and his likeness to Orpheus is carried still further by a descent which he made from heaven to visit Pátáḷa, the nether regions. In Manu and in the Vishṇu Purána he is called a Prajápati, in the Mahábhárata he is one of the Gandharbhas. It was he who dissuaded the sons of Daksha from multiplying their race; they accordingly scattered themselves through the regions of the universe to ascertain its extent, &c., and the patriarch Daksha finding that all his sons had vanished was incensed and denounced an imprecation on Nárada. It was Nárada who informed Ḳansa that the supporter of the earth Vishṇu, was going to become incarnate as the eighth child of Devaki. When Nárada visited Krishṇa he presented him with the flower Párijáta from the world of the gods. Krishṇa gave it to Rúkmini, which so excited the jealousy of one of his favourite mistresses Satyabháma, that in order to appease her, Krishṇa went to the heaven of the gods and brought away the tree itself that bore the flower. In mythology Nárada is often described as bearing a resemblance to Hermes or Mercury, being engaged in conveying messages and causing discord among the gods and men. He is usually represented as sitting in a fire, having his hands folded over his head, and stretching his legs also towards his head, his arms and legs being tied together with a girdle.

Narada Purana—This Purána is related by Nárada and gives an account of the Vrihas Kalpa. It is communicated to the Rishis at Naimisháraṇya, on the Gamati river. Professor Wilson regards it as a sectarial and modern compilation intended to support the doctrine of Bhakti, or faith in Vishṇu. It contains a number of prayers addressed to one or other form of that divinity ; a variety of observances and holidays connected with his adoration ; and different legends, some perhaps of an early, others of a more recent date, illustrative of the efficacy of devotion to Hari. There are the stories of Dhruva and Prahláda, the latter told in the words of the Vishṇu Purána ; whilst the second portion of it is occupied with a legend of Mohiní, the will-born daughter of a king called Rukmángada ; beguiled by whom the king offers to perform for her whatever she may desire. She calls upon him either to violate the rule of fasting on the eleventh day of the fortnight, a day sacred to Vishṇu, or to put his son to death ; and he kills his son, as the lesser sin of the two. This shews the spirit of the work. Its date may also be inferred from its tenor, as such monstrous extravagancies in praise of Bhakti are certainly of modern origin. One limit it furnishes itself, for it refers to Śuka and Paríkshit, the interlocutors of the Bhágavata, and it is consequently subsequent to the date of that Purána : it is probably considerably later, for it affords evidence that it was written after India was in the hands of the Mohammedans. In the concluding passage it is said, "Let not this Purána be repeated in the presence of the 'killers of cows' and contemners of the gods." It is possibly a compilation of the sixteenth or seventeenth century. Vishṇu Purána. Preface.

Naraka—Hell ; of which twenty-eight different divisions are enumerated, said to be situated beneath the earth, below Pátáḷa and to be terrific regions of darkness, of deep gloom, of fear, and of great terror. In the Vishṇu Purána, Vol. II, c. 6, they are particularly described, with the crimes punished in them respectively. The gods in heaven are beheld by the inhabitants of hell as they move with their heads inverted ; whilst the gods, as they cast their eyes downwards, behold the sufferings of those in hell ; the commentator observes that the sight of heavenly bliss is given to the lost to exacerbate their sufferings ; whilst the inflictions of hell are exhibited to the gods, to teach them disregard of even heavenly enjoyments, as they are but of temporary duration. Heaven is that which delights the mind ; hell is that which gives it pain ; hence vice is called hell ; virtue is called heaven. V. P.

Naraka—1, A son of Anrita (falsehood) and Nikriti (immorality) ; 2, A Danava, one of the sons of Viprachitti ; 3, A son of the Earth who ruled over the city of Prágjyotisha. Indra went to Dwáraka and reported to Krishṇa the tyranny of Naraka. Having heard this account, the divine Hari, mounting Garuda, flew to Prágjyotisha ; there a fierce conflict took place with the troops of Naraka, in which Govinda destroyed thousands of demons ; and when Naraka came into the field, showering upon the deity all sorts of weapons, the wielder of the discus cut him in two with his celestial missile. Naraka being slain, Earth bearing the two earrings of Aditi, approached the lord of the world and said, " When I was upheld by thee in the form of a boar, thy contact then engendered this my son. He whom thou gavest me has now been killed by thee ; take therefore these two earrings and cherish his progeny. Forgive the sins which Naraka has committed." Krishṇa then proceeded to redeem the various gems from the dwelling of Naraka. In the apartments of the women he found sixteen thousand and one hundred damsels, who became Krishṇa's wives ; in the palace were six thousand large elephants each having four tusks ; twenty-one lakhs of horses of Kámbója and other excellent breeds ; these Govinda dispatched to Dwáraka, in charge of the servants of Naraka. The umbrella of Varuna, the jewel mountain which he also recovered, he placed upon Garuda ; and mounting himself, and taking Satyabháma with him, he set off to the heaven of the gods to restore the earrings of Aditi. V. P.

Narantaka—One of the sons of the giant Rávaṇa who was killed at the seige of Lanka.

Naras—'Centaurs,' or beings with the limbs of horses and human bodies, created by Brahmá along with Kinnaras, Rakshasas, &c. V. P., p. 42.

Narasinha Avatara—The fourth incarnation of Vishṇu, in the form of a man-lion (*nara* a man, and *Sinha* a lion.) One of the two doorkeepers of Vishṇu's paradise, (see *Varaha*) came down to earth as a monarch, named Hiranyakasipu. He was cruel, tyrannical, unjust; particularly so towards his son named Prahláda. But he had obtained from Bramhá, by severe penance, the boon that he should not be slain by any created being; in consequence of which he became very proud, and required all persons to honor him by saying. "Om Hiranya" (Adoration to Hiranya); and those who would not say so he ordered to be punished. His son Prahláda, who was a devout worshipper of Vishṇu, would not obey his father's order, but continued to say "Om namah" (meaning by Om Vishṇu). Hiranya remonstrated with him because of this, but in vain. Then he attempted to punish and kill him, but in vain: Prahláda was struck heavily but did not feel the strokes; he was cast into the fire, but was not burnt; he was trampled on by elephants, but continuing to think of Vishṇu he was not hurt: he was thrown fettered into the sea, but a fish carried him safely to shore. At last, when Prahláda did not cease praising Vishṇu, and asserted that he was everywhere and in everything, Hiranya retorted. "If so why dost thou not show him unto me?" Upon this Prahláda rose and struck a column of the hall in which they were assembled; and behold, there issued from it Vishṇu, in a form which was half-man and half-lion, and tore Hiranya to pieces. V. P.

Narayana—1, A name of Vishṇu, meaning 'he whose place of abiding was the deep.' The waters are called Nárá, because they were the offspring of Nárá (the supreme spirit); and as in them his first (Ayana) progress (in the character of Brahmá) took place, he is thence named Nárâyaṇa; 2, A sage, the son of Dharma by Murtti; 3, A prince, the son of Bhumimitra, of the Káṇwa dynasty.

Narishyanta—1, One of the sons of the Manu Vaivaswata; 2, The son of Marutta, the fourteenth of the posterity of Dishṭa.

Narika—A measure of time, fifteen Laghus.

Narikavacha—A name of Múlaka, q. v.

Narmada—The river Narbadda, the Namadus of Ptolemy. It rises in the Vindhya, or in the Riksha mountains, taking its origin in Gondwana. Mythologically the personified Narmada was the sister of the Nágas, and had a son named Trasadasya.

Narttaka—A dancer, who also performs extraordinary feats of strength and agility.

Nata—An actor; in popular acceptation it comprehends jugglers, buffoons, and persons practising sleight of hand, and exhibiting feats of agility.—*Wilson.*

Navala—The daughter of the patriarch Vairája, and wife of the Manu Chakshusha.

Navaratha—A prince, the son of Bhímaratha.

Naya—(Polity) a son of Dharma by Kriya.

Nedishta—One of the sons of the Manu Vaivaswata.

Nichakra—A prince, the son of Asíma Krishṇa, who when Hastinápura was washed away by the Ganges, removed the capital to Kauṣámbí.

Nidagha—A son of Pulastya and disciple of Ribhu; to him Ribhu willingly communicated perfect knowledge. The residence of Pulastya was at Víranagara, on the banks of the Devíká river. "In a beautiful grove adjoining to the stream, the pupil of Ribhu, Nidágha, conversant with devotional practices, abode. When a thousand divine years had elapsed, Ribhu went to the city of Pulastya, to visit his disciple. Standing at the doorway, at the end of a sacrifice to the Viśwadevas, he was seen by his scholar, who hastened to present him the usual offering, or Arghya, and conducted him into the house; and when his hands and feet were washed, and he was seated, Nídágha invited him respectfully to eat, (when the following dialogue ensued):—

" *Ribhu.* 'Tell me, illustrious Brahman, what food there is in in your house; for I am not fond of indifferent viands.'

" *Nidágha.* ' There are cakes of meal, rice, barley, and pulse in the house ; partake, venerable sir, of whichever best pleases you.'

" *Ribhu.* ' None of these do I like ; give me rice boiled with sugar, wheaten cakes, and milk with curds and molasses.'

" *Nidágha.* ' Ho dame, be quick, and prepare whatever is most delicate and sweet in the house, to feed our guest.'

" Having thus spoken, the wife of Nidágha, in obedience to her husband's commands, prepared sweet and savoury food, and set it before the Brahman ; and Nidágha, having stood before him until he had eaten of the meal which he had desired, thus reverentially addressed him :—

" *Nidágha.* Have you eaten sufficiently, and with pleasure, great Brahman ? and has your mind received contentment from your food ? Where is your present residence ? Whither do you purpose going ? and whence, holy sir, have you now come ?

" *Ribhu.* ' A hungry man, Brahman, must needs be satisfied when he has finished his meal. Why should you inquire if my hunger has been appeased ? When the earthly element is parched by fire, then hunger is engendered ; and thirst is produced when the moisture of the body has been absorbed (by internal or digestive heat.) Hunger and thirst are the functions of the body, and satisfaction must always be afforded me by that by which they are removed ; for when hunger is no longer sensible, pleasure and contentment of mind are faculties of the intellect : ask their condition of the mind then, for man is not affected by them. For your three other questions, Where I dwell ? Whither I go ? and whence I come ? hear this reply. Man, (the soul of man) goes everywhere, and penetrates everywhere, like the ether ; and is it rational to inquire where it is ? or whence or whither thou goest ? I neither am going nor coming, nor is my dwelling in any one place ; nor art thou, thou ; nor are others, others ; nor am I, I. If you wonder what reply I should make to your inquiry why I made any distinction between sweetened and unsweetened food, you shall hear my explanation. What is there that is really sweet or not sweet to one eating a meal ? That which is sweet, is no longer so when it occasions the sense of repletion ; and that which is not sweet, becomes sweet when a man (being very hungry) fancies that it is so. What food is there that first, middle, and last is equally grateful. As a house built of clay is strengthened by fresh plaster, so is this earthly body supported by earthly particles ; and barley, wheat, pulse, butter, oil, milk, curds, treacle, fruits, and the like, are composed of atoms of earth. This therefore is to be understood by you, that the mind which properly judges of what is or is not sweet is impressed with the notion of identity, and that this effect of identity tends to liberation,'

" Having heard these words, conveying the substance of ultimate truth, Nidágha fell at the feet of his visitor, and said, ' Shew favour unto me, illustrious Brahman, and tell me who it is that for my good has come hither, and by whose words the infatuation of my mind is dissipated.' To this, Ribhu answered, ' I am Ribhu, your preceptor, come hither to communicate to you true wisdom ; and having declared to you what that is, I shall depart. Know this whole universe to be the one undivided nature of the supreme spirit, entitled Vásudeva.' Thus having spoken, and receiving the prostrate homage of Nidágha, rendered with fervent faith, Ribhu went his way." V. P., p. 53-55.

Nidra—Sleep ; a form of Brahmá. In the Uttara Khanda of the Pádma Purána, Nidrá is entered as one of the products of the churning of the ocean.

Nighna—The son of Anamitra, and father of Satrájit, to whom the divine Áditya, the sun, presented the Syamantaka gem.

Nikriti—(Immorality.) A daughter of Adharma (vice.)

Nikumbha—A prince, the son of Haryyasva.

Nila—Blue. 1, A range of mountains in Orissa ; 2, A central range to the north of Meru, running east and west ; 3, A son of Yadu ; 4, A son of Ajamídha.

Nilalohita—A name of Rudra, from the Vaishnava Puránas, which give only one original form, instead of eight as in the Vishṇu Purána, and to which the name of Nílalohita, the blue and red or purple complexioned, is assigned.

Nilini—The wife of Ajamídha.

Nimisha—A measure of time—a twinkle of the eye—a second; according to the Bhágavata, three Lavas.

Nimi—One of the three distinguished sons of Ikshváku. He instituted a sacrifice that was to endure a thousand years, and applied to Vasishtha to offer the oblations. Vasishtha in answer said, that he had been pre-engaged by Indra for five hundred years, but that if the Rája would wait for some time, he would come and officiate as superintending priest. The king made no answer, and Vasishtha went away, supposing that he had assented. When the sage had completed the performance of the ceremonies he had conducted for Indra, he returned with all speed to Nimi, purposing to render him the like office. When he arrived, however, and found that Nimi had retained Gautama and other priests to minister at his sacrifice, he was much displeased and pronounced upon the king, who was then asleep, a curse to this effect, that since he had not intimated his intention, but transferred to Gautama the duty he had first entrusted to himself, Vasishtha, Nimi should thenceforth cease to exist in a corporeal form. When Nimi woke, and knew what had happened, he in return denounced as an imprecation upon his unjust preceptor, that he also should lose his bodily existence, as the punishment of uttering a curse upon him without previously communicating with him. Nimi then abandoned his bodily condition. The spirit of Vasishtha also leaving his body, was united with the spirits of Mitra and Varuna for a season, until, through their passion for the nymph Urvaśí, the sage was born again in a different shape. The corpse of Nimi was preserved from decay by being embalmed with fragrant oils and resins, and it remained as entire as if it were immortal. When the sacrifice was concluded, the priests applied to the gods, who had come to receive their portions, that they would confer a blessing upon the author of the sacrifice. The gods were willing to restore him to bodily life, but Nimi declined its acceptance, saying, "O deities, who are the alleviators of all worldly suffering, there is not in the world a deeper cause of distress than the separation of soul and body: it is therefore my wish to dwell in the eyes of all beings, but never more to resume a corporeal shape!" To this desire the gods assented, and Nimi was placed by them in the eyes of all living creatures; in consequence of which their eyelids are ever opening and shutting. V. P.

Nipa—A prince, the son of Para, a descendant of Hastin.

Niramitra—1, One of the Páṇḍavas, the son of Nakulá; 2, The son of Khaṇḍapáni; 3, The son of Ayutáyus.

Nirmalas—One of the divisions of the SIKHS who profess to dedicate themselves exclusively to a religious life. They lead a life of celibacy, and disregard their personal appearance, often going nearly naked. They do not assemble together in colleges, nor do they observe any particular form of Divine service, but confine their devotion to speculative meditation on the perusal of the writings of Nának, Kábír, and other unitarian teachers. They are always solitary, supported by their disciples, or wealthy persons who may happen to favour the sect. The *Nirmalas* are known as able expounders of the *Vedanta philosophy*, in which Brahmans do not disdain to accept of their instructions. They are not a very numerous body on the whole; but a few are almost always to be found at the principal seats of Hindu wealth, and particularly at Benares.—*Wilson's Works, Vol. I.*

Nirmanaratis—A class of deities who belong to the eleventh Manwantara.

Nirrita—One of the eleven Rudras, according to the Váyu list.

Nirukta—An Anga of the Vedas, containing a glossarial comment.

Niruktakrit—The name of the pupil to whom Sákapúrṇi gave his glossary (Nirukta) of the Rig Veda.

Niruta—A giant; a regent or guardian of the south-west point of the world. He is represented as of a green colour, and is said to have been raised to the dignity he enjoys in consequence of his severe penance. On his head he wears a crown, and on his forehead Śiva's sign of sacred ashes. Of his four hands one is empty, and in the other three he holds respectively a banner with the sign of a fish, a ring, and a wine jug: his vehicle is a crocodile

Nirvritti—A prince, the son of Vrishni, a descendant of Jyámagha.

Nirwana—The blowing out. Extinction. The summum-bonum of Buddhism. It was long thought that Nirwána simply meant final beatitude, the emancipation of the soul from the body: its exemption from further transmigration, and re-union with the deity. Some still maintain this view, and regard Nirwána as synonymous with Móksha; the absorption of the individual soul into the divine essence; which the Hindus represent as the highest goal of their religion and philosophy. But it has been shown by Mr. Spence Hardy, Mr. Max Müller, and other high authorities, that Nirwána means utter annihilation, or the destruction of all elements which constitute existence. There are four paths, an entrance into any of which secures either immediately, or more remotely, the attainment of *Nirwána.* They are; (1,) *Sowán,* which is divided into twenty-four sections, and after it has been entered there can be only seven more births between that period and the attainment of *Nirwána,* which may be in any world but the four hells; (2,) *Sakradágámi,* into which he who enters will receive one more birth. He may enter this path in the world of men, and afterwards be born in *déva-lóka;* or he may enter it in a *déva-lóka,* and afterwards be born in the world of men. It is divided into twelve sections; (3,) *Anágámi,* into which he who enters will not again be born in a *káma-lóka*; he may, by the apparitional birth, enter into a *brahma-lóka,* and from that world attain *Nirwána.* This path is divided into forty-eight sections; (4,) *Arya* or *Aryahat,* into which he who enters has overcome or destroyed all evil desire. It is divided into twelve sections.

Those who have entered into any of the paths can discern the thoughts of all in the same, or preceding paths. Each path is divided into two grades; 1, The perception of the path; 2, Its fruition or enjoyment. The mode in which Nirwána, or the destruction of al. the elements of existence, may be reached, is thus pointed out by Mr. Spence Hardy, in his 'Eastern Monachism:' "The unwise being who has not yet arrived at a state of purity, or who is subject to future birth, overcome by the excess of evil desire, rejoices in the organs of sense, Áyatana, and their relative objects, and commends them. The Áyatanas therefore become to him like a rapid stream to carry him onward toward the sea of repeated existence; they are not released from old age, decay, death, sorrow, &c. But the being who is purified, perceiving the evils arising from the sensual organs and their relative objects, does not rejoice therein, nor does he commend them, or allow himself to be swallowed up by them. By the destruction of the 108 modes of evil desire he has released himself from birth, as from the jaws of an alligator; he has overcome all attachment to outward objects; he does not regard the unauthorized precepts, nor is he a sceptic; and he knows that there is no ego, no self. By overcoming these four errors, he has released himself from the cleaving to existing objects. By the destruction of the cleaving to existing objects he is released from birth, whether as a brahmá, man, or any other being. By the destruction of birth he is released from old age, decay, death, sorrow, &c. All the afflictions connected with the repetition of existence are overcome. Thus all the principles of existence are annihilated, and that annihilation is Nirwána."

Nisatha—A son of Balaráma by his wife Revatí.

Nischara—One of the seven Rishis in the second Manwantara.

Nishadas—Inhabitants of the Vindhya mountains—barbarians. Nishadha was the country of Nala, and has consequently attained celebrity, but its situation has not been certainly determined; it was not far from Vidarbha (Berar) as that was the country of Damayanti.

Nishadha—1, A range of mountains to the south of Meru; one of the central ranges, next to Meru, running east and west, and extending one hundred thousand Yojanas; 2, A prince, the son of Atithi, and grandson of Kusa.

Nisitha—A son of Kalpa; the name means 'the middle of night.'

Nisunda—A Daitya, the son of Hláda.

Nitala—One of the seven regions of Pátála.

Nivata-kavachas—Danavas, to the number of thirty millions, residing in the depths of the sea. The Mahábhárata describes their destruction as one of the exploits of Arjuna. The Vishṇu Purána says they were born in the family of the Daitya Prahláda.

Niyama—The second stage of Yoga, being self-restraint, of which five kinds are specified :—

1. Purity of mind and body
2. Cheerfulness under all circumstances
3. Religious austerity
4. The repetition of incantations
5. The association of all religious ceremonies with the Supreme Being.

These are also designated five duties or obligations, namely purity, contentment, devotion, study of the Vedas, and adoration of the Supreme.

Niyama—Precept. A son of Dharma by one of the daughters of Daksha.

Niyati—The daughter of Meru who was married to Vidhátri.

Niyat—The wife of Mahán one of the eleven Rudras.

Niyodhaka—A prize-fighter, either as a wrestler or boxer or a swordsman—in some parts of India he also fights with gauntlets armed with steel spikes.—*Wilson*.

Nrichaksha—A prince, the son of Richa, of the race of Puru.

Nriga—A son of the Manu Vaivaswata ; the Linga Purána relates his transformation to a lizard by the curse of a brahman.

Nripanjaya—1, A prince, the son of Suvíra ; 2, The son of Medhavin of the race of Puru.

Nriyajna—One of the five great obligations or sacrifices, viz., that of hospitality ; a duty on which great stress is laid.

Nyagrodha—One of the sons of Ugrasena.

Nyaya—Logic. One of the six schools or systems of Philosophy of the Hindus.

The Nyáya system was originally taught by Gautama, of whose personal history, however, but little is known. From the Rámáyana and the Puránas, we learn that he was born at Himálaya, about the same time as Ráma, *i. e.*, at the commencement of the *Treta* Yuga (or second age of the world); that he married Ahalya, the daughter of Brahmá (q. v.) He is said to have lived as a very austere ascetic, first at Pryága (now Allahabad), then in a forest at Mithilá (Muttra), and latterly (after the repudiation of of his wife) in the Himálayan mountains. His son, Satánanda, was priest to Janaka, king of Mithilá the father of Sítá, the wife of Ráma. From the above statements we may see how little reliance can be placed on the historical veracity of the Puránas. These works assure us that Gautama, though he lived in the second or silver age, married a daughter of Brahmá ; but they meet the anachronism by affirming that all the sages live through the four Yugas (the Satya, Tretà, Dwápas, and Kalí,) into which the Hindus divide the whole course of the world's existence.

"The *Nyáya* offers the sensational aspect of Hindu Philosophy. In saying this, it is not meant that the Nyáya confines itself to sensation, excluding emotion and intellection ; nor that the other systems ignore the fact of sensation ; but that the arrangement of this system has a more pointed regard to the fact of the five senses than the others have, and treats the external more frankly as a solid reality.

"The word Nyáya means 'propriety or fitness,' and the system undertakes to declare the *proper method* of arriving at that knowledge of the truth, the fruit of which, it promises, is the chief end of man. The name is also used, in a more limited application, to denominate the proper method of setting forth *argument.* This has led to the practice of calling the Nyáya the '*Hindu Logic,*' a name which suggests a very inadequate conception of the scope of the system. The Nyáya system was delivered by Gautama in a set of aphorisms, so very concise, that they must, from the first, have been accompanied by a commentary, oral or written. The aphorisms of the several Hindu systems, in fact, appear designed, not so much to *communicate* the doctrine of the particular schools, as to *aid*, by the briefest possible suggestions, the memory of him to whom the doctrine shall have been *already* communicated. To this end they are in general admirably adapted. The sixty aphorisms, for example, which constitute the first of Gautama's Five Lectures, present a methodical summary of the whole system, while the first aphorism, again, of the sixty, presents a summary of these sixty. The first aphorism is as follows :—From knowledge of the truth in regard to evidence, the ascertainable, doubt, motive, example, dogma, confutation, ascertainment, disquisition, controversy, cavil, fallacy, perversion, futility, and occasion for rebuke,—there is the attainment of the *Summum Bonum.*

" In the next aphorism, it is declared how knowledge operates mediately in producing this result. 'Pain, birth, activity, fault, false notions,—since, on the successive departure of these in turn, there is the departure of the antecedent one, there is Beatitude.' That is to say, when *knowledge of the truth* is attained to, '*false notions*' depart ; on their departure, the '*fault*' of concerning one's-self about any external object ceases ; thereupon the enlightened sage ceases to 'act ;' then, there being no *actions* that call for either reward or punishment, there is no occasion, after his death, for his being *born again* to receive reward or punishment ; then, not being born again, so as to be liable to pain, there is no room for '*pain*,' and the absence of pain is the Nyáya conception of the *Summum Bonum.*"

As to the instruments adapted to the acquisition of a knowledge of the truth, Gautama teaches that " proofs" *i. e.*, (instruments of right knowledge,) " are the senses, the recognition of signs, the recognition of likenesses, and speech (or testimony.")

The *objects* in regard to which we have to obtain right knowledge, by means of the appropriate instruments, he enumerates as follows :—" Soul, body, sense, sense-object, knowledge, the mind, activity, fault, transmigration, fruit, pain, and beatitude,—these are the objects regarding which we are to seek for right knowledge." Here it is to be carefully observed that the *soul* is spoken of as an entirely different entity from the *mind.* Dugald Stewart tells us that the mind can attend to only one thought at a time. Gautama, recognising the same fact, but speaking of the *known* invariably as the *soul*, accounts for the fact in question by assuming that there is an *instrument*, or internal organ, termed the *mind*, through which alone knowledge can reach the soul, and which, admitting only *one thought at a time*, the Naiyáyika inferred must be no larger than an *atom*.

"Pleasure, pain, desire, aversion, volition, and knowledge," says Gautama, "are that whereby we recognise the (*átman*);" and, again, "the sign" (whereby we infer the existence) "of the mind" (manas) "is the not arising of cognitions" (in the soul) "simultaneously." Thus the *soul* may be practically regarded as corresponding to the thinking principle, and the *mind* (manas) to the faculty of attending to one, and only one, thing at a time; it being further kept in remembrance that the Naiyáyika reckons the mind to be a *substance* and not a *faculty*.

"In the list of the objects regarding which right knowledge is to be obtained, the next after *mind*, is *activity*. This is defined as 'that which originates the [utterance of the] voice, the [cognitions of the] understanding, and the [gestures of the] body.' This activity, we have seen under Aph. II., Gautama regards with an evil eye, as the cause of birth, which is the cause of pain, which it is the *summum bonum* to get permanently rid of.

He further holds that it is through our own '*fault*' that we are active; and he tells us that faults (or failings) have this characteristic, that they cause 'activity.' These faults are classed under the heads of affection, aversion, and stolidity or delusion, each of which he regards as a fault or defect, inasmuch as it leads to actions, the recompense of which, whether good or evil, must be received in some birth, or state of mundane existence, to the postponement of the great end of entire emancipation."

The immediate obstacle to "emancipation" *mokshá*, or *apavarga*, namely, "transmigration" pretyabháva, he next defines as "the arising again" *punarutpatti*. • "Pain," *duhka*, he defines as "that which is characterised by uneasiness," and absolute deliverance therefrom is "emancipation." This *summum bonam* is to be obtained by an abnegation of all action, good or bad."—*Small, H. S. L.*

O

Oblations—The householder after pouring libations to the gods, sages, and progenitors, is to offer oblations with fire, not preceded by any other rite, to Brahmá. Oblations are made with such ceremonies, and in such form, as are adapted to the religious rite which is intended to be subsequently performed. The residue of oblations to be offered to Indra, Yama, Varuna, and Soma, at the four cardinal parts of his dwelling; and in the north-east quarter it is to be presented to Dhanwantari. See V. P., p. 304.

Obsequies—See Sráddha.

Ocean—*Churning of.* See Amrita.

Odra—The ancient name of Orissa.

Oghavati—The name of a river in the Puránas, that has not been identified.

Om or Omkara—A combination of letters invested by Hindu mysticism with peculiar sanctity. In the Vedas it is said to comprehend all the gods; and in the Puránas it is directed to be prefixed to many sacred formulas. The syllable Om, says the Pádma Purána is the leader of all prayers; and to be employed in the beginning of all prayers. According to the same authority one of the mystical imports of the term is the collective enunciation of Vishṇu expressed by A, of Srí, his bride, intimated by U, and of their joint worshipper designated by M. A whole chapter of the Váyu Purána is devoted to this term. It is said to typify the three spheres of the world, the three holy fires, the three steps of Vishṇu, &c. It is identified with the supreme undefinable deity, or Brahmá. In the Bhágavat Gíta it is said "Repeating Om, the monosyllable, which is Brahmá, and calling me to mind;" The form or sensible type of Vasudeva, is considered to be the monosyllable Om. Mr. J. C. Thomson says, a more probable origin of the word is that it is composed of the initials of the three personifications of the triad of elements, which is a much more ancient trinity than that of Brahmá, Vishṇu and Śiva. The A would then represent Agni, or fire ; the U Varuna, water ; and the M Marut, wind or air. The reverence attached to this monosyllable may be inferred from the fact that some transcribers of MSS. have been afraid to write the awful word itself, and have substituted some other.

Oshta-karnakas—A nickname or term of derision, or derived from some exaggeration of national ugliness, applied to some of the aborigines of India. It means having lips extending to their ears.

Oxydracæ—The Sudra people of in the west, or north-west, towards the Indus. Pliny has Sudraci for the people who formed the limit of Alexander's eastern conquests, or those hitherto inaccurately called Oxydracæ.

P

Padmakalpa—A Maha Kalpa—a day of Brahmá already expired.

Padmanabha—Lotus-navel ; with the addition of Svámi, a name of Náráyana in the Malayalam country. One of the titles of the Travancore rajah was ' the slave of Padmanábha.'

Padmapurana—A very voluminous work containing fifty-five thousand slokas. These are divided amongst five books or Khandas ; 1, The Srishti Khanda, or section on Creation ; the Bhumi Khanda, a description of the Earth ; the Swarga Khanda, a chapter on Heaven ; Pátáḷa Khanda, a chapter on the regions below the earth ; and 5, Uttara Khanda, the last or supplementary chapter. There is also current a sixth division, the Kriyá Yoga Sára, a treatise on the practice of devotion.

The denominations of these divisions of the Pádma Purána convey but an imperfect and partial notion of their contents. In the first, or section which treats of creation, the narrator is Ugraśravas the Súta, the son of Lomaharshaṇa, who is sent by his father to the Rishis at Naimisháráṇya to communicate to them the Purána, which, from its containing an account of the lotus (padma), in which Brahmá appeared at creation, is termed the Padma or Pádma Purána. The Súta repeats what was originally communicated by Brahmá to Pulastya, and by him to Bhíshma. The early chapters narrate the cosmogony, and the genealogy of the patriarchal families, much in the same style, and often in the same words, as the Vishṇu ; and short accounts of the Manwantaras and regal dynasties : but these, which are legitimate Pauráṇik matters, soon make way for new and unauthentic inventions, illustrative of the virtues of the lake of Pushkara, or Pokher in Ajmir, as a place of pilgrimage.

The Bhúmi Khánda, or section of the earth, defers any description of the earth until near its close, filling up one hundred and twenty-seven chapters with legends of a very mixed description, some ancient and common to other Purános, but the greater part peculiar to itself, illustrative of Tírthas, either figuratively so termed—as a wife, a parent, or a guru, considered as a sacred object—or places to which actual pilgrimage should be performed.

The Swarga Khánda describes in the first chapters the relative positions of the Lokas or spheres above the earth, placing above all Vaikuntha, the sphere of Vishṇu; an addition which is not warranted by what appears to be the oldest cosmology. Miscellaneous notices of some of the most celebrated princes then succeed, conformably to the usual narratives; and these are followed by rules of conduct for the several castes, and at different stages of life. The rest of the book is occupied by legends of a diversified description, introduced without much method or contrivance; a few of which, as Daksha's sacrifice, are of ancient date, but of which the most are original and modern.

The Pátáḷa Khánda devotes a brief introduction to the description of Pátáḷa, the regions of the snake-gods; but the name of Ráma having been mentioned, Śesha, who has succeeded Pulastya as spokesman, proceeds to narrate the history of Ráma, his descent and his posterity; in which the compiler seems to have taken the poem of Kálidása, the Raghu Vanśa, for his chief authority. An originality of addition may be suspected, however, in the adventures of the horse destined by Ráma for an Aśwamedha, which form the subject of a great many chapters. When about to be sacrificed, the horse turns out to be a Brahman, condemned by an imprecation of Durvásas, a sage, to assume the equine nature, and who, by having been sanctified by connexion with Ráma, is released from his metamorphosis, and despatched as a spirit of light to heaven. This piece of Vaishnava fiction is followed by praises of the Śrí Bhágavata, an account of Krishṇa's juvenilities, and the merits of worshipping Vishṇu. These accounts are communicated through a machinery borrowed from the Tantras: they are told by Sadáśiva to Párvati, the ordinary interlocutors of Tantrika compositions.

The Uttara Khánda is a most voluminous aggregation of very heterogeneous matters, but it is consistent in adopting a decidedly

Vaishnava tone, and admitting no compromise with any other form of faith. The chief subjects are first discussed in a dialogue between king Dilípa and the Muni Vasishtha; such as the merits of bathing in the month of Mágha, and the potency of the Mantra or prayer addressed to Lakshmi Náráyana. But the nature of Bhakti, faith in Vishṇu—the use of Vaishnava marks on the body—the legends of Vishṇu's Avatáras, and especially of Ráma—and the construction of images of Vishṇu—are too important to be left to mortal discretion: they are explained by Śiva to Párvati, and wound up by the adoration of Vishṇu by those divinities. The dialogue then reverts to the king and the sage; and the latter states why Vishṇu is the only one of the triad entitled to respect; Śiva being licentious, Brahmá arrogant, and Vishṇu alone pure. Vasishtha then repeats, after Śiva, the Mahátmya of the Bhagavat Gíta; the merit of each book of which is illustrated by legends of the good consequences to individuals from perusing or hearing it. Other Vaishnava Mahátmyas occupy considerable portions of this Khánda, especially the Kártíka Mahátmya, or holiness of the month Kártíka, illustrated as usual by stories, a few of which are of an early origin, but the greater part modern, and peculiar to this Purána.

The Kriyá Yoga Sára is repeated by Súta to the Rishis, after Vyása's communication of it to Jaimini, in answer to an inquiry how religious merit might be secured in the Kalí age, in which men have become incapable of the penances and abstraction by which final liberation was formerly to be attained. The answer is, of course, that which is intimated in the last book of the Vishṇu Purána—personal devotion to Vishṇu: thinking of him, repeating his names, wearing his marks, worshipping in his temples, are a full substitute for all other acts of moral or devotional or contemplative merit.

The different portions of the Pádma Purána are in all probability as many different works, neither of which approaches to the original definition of a Purána. There may be some connexion between the three first portions, at least as to time; but there is no reason to consider them as of high antiquity. They specify the Jains both by name and practices; they talk of Mlechchhas, 'barbarians,' flourishing in India; they commend the use of the frontal and other Vaishnava marks; and they notice other subjects which, like these, are of no remote origin. The Pátáḷa Khánda dwells copiously upon the Bhágavata, and is consequently posterior to it. The Uttara Khánda is intolerantly Vaishnava, and is therefore unquestionably modern. It enjoins the veneration of the Sálágram stone and Tulasí plant, the use of the Tapta-mudra, or stamping with a hot iron the name of Vishṇu on the skin, and a variety of practices and observances undoubtedly no part of the original system. It speaks of the shrines of Srí-rangam and Venkatádri in the Dekhin, temples that have no pretension to remote antiquity; and it names Haripur on the Tungabhadra, which is in all likelihood the city of Vijayanagar, founded in the middle of the fourteenth century. The Kriyá Yoga Sára is equally a modern, and apparently a Bengali composition. No portion of the Pádma Purána is probably older than the twelfth century, and the last parts may be as recent as the fifteenth or sixteenth.—*Wilson.*

Padmavati—A titular name which may be understood of *Lakshmi*, as seated on a lotus-flower (padma) it is commonly used to designate a goddess of the Jainas; especially at some shrines of the eastern and western Chalukyas; corresponding with the northern part of Telingána and the southern Mahratta provinces.

Padmavati—A city amongst the Vindhya hills.

Pahlavas—A northern or north-western nation, often mentioned in Hindu writings, in Manu, the Rámáyana, the Puránas, &c. They were not a Hindu people, and may have been some of the tribes between India and Persia.

Pahnavas—Probably the same as the Pahlavas. Border tribes on the confines of Persia. They were conquered by Sagara, but spared on the intercession of Vasishtha, the family priest of Sagara.

Paila—The compiler of the Rig Veda; a disciple or co-adjutor of Vyása in arranging the Vedas. Professor Wilson thinks the tradition records the first establishment of a school, of which the Vyása was the head, and Paila and the other persons named were the teachers.

Pakayajna—A sacrifice, in which food is offered; one that may be made by a Súdra. It implies either the worship of the Viśwadevas, the rites of hospitality, or occasional oblations, as building a house, the birth of a child, or any occasion of rejoicing.

Paksha—A lunar fortnight; fifteen days of thirty Muhúrttas each.

Pakshaja—One of the three classes of clouds; those which were originally the wings of the mountains, and which were cut off by Indra.

Palaka—A protector or ruler; *loka palaka* is an epithet applied to a king. *Dik-palaka* is a regent of one of the eight points of the heavens: each point being supported by one of the *ashta dik gajas*, or elephant caryatides. The names of the dik-palakas are Indra, E., Varuna, W., Kuvera, N., Yama, S., Isáni, N.E., Niruta, S.W., Váyu, N.W., Agni, S.E.

Palaka—The son of Pradyóta, king of Magadhá. There were five kings of the house of Pradyóta, who reigned for a hundred and thirty-eight years.

Palasini—A river from the eastern portion of the Himálaya, a feeder of the Mahánada.

Palin—One of the sons of Prithu.

Palita—A prince, the son of Parávrit: he was the brother of Jyámagha, and ruled over Videha.

Pampa—A river, that rises in Rishyamuka in the Dekkin.

Panchadasa hymns—A collection of hymns, created along with the Yajur Veda from the southern mouth of Brahmá.

Panchajana—A demon in the form of a couch shell, who lived in the sea of Prabhása, and was killed by Krishṇa, in order that the son of Sandípani might be rescued.

Panchajanya—The name of Krishṇa's conch. It was made of the bones of the giant Panchajana. When Krishṇa was getting up his military acquirements, the son of his áchárya, or tutor, Sandípani, was drowned in the sea of Prabhása, and carried down to the bottom by the said giant. Krishṇa plunged in, dived down, slew the giant, brought up his bones to make a conch of, and restored his son to the grieving tutor.

Panchanga—The Hindu Calendar, Panchánga means five members. It contains five principal heads, namely, the days of the month, the sign in which the moon is each day to be found, the day of the week, the eclipses, and the place of the planets. It likewise marks the good days and the evil ; those on which one may journey towards any of the four cardinal points ; for each point of the compass has its lucky and unlucky days ; and a person who might to-day travel very successfully towards the north, would expose himself to some grievous danger if he took a southward course. It farther contains a vast number of predictions of all sorts which would be too tedious for this place.

Panchala—The country north and west of Delhi, between the foot of the Himálaya and the Chambal. It was afterwards divided into northern and southern Pánchála separated by the Ganges. The name is derived from the five (páncha) sons of Hariyaswa, who were able (alam) to protect the countries ; and hence they were termed the Pánchálas.

Pancha-lakshana—An epithet applied to the Puránas, meaning 'that which has five characteristic topics ;' these are primary creation, or cosmogony ; secondary creation, or the destruction and renovation of worlds ; including chronology ; 3, Genealogy of gods and patriarchs ; 4, Reigns of the Manus, or periods called Manwantaras ; and, 5, History, or such particulars as have been preserved of the princes of the solar and lunar races, and of their descendants to modern times.

Pancha Tantra—The collection of Fables and stories termed Pancha Tantra or Panchopákhyána, is one of the oldest in the world. It was translated from Sanskrit into Persian in the sixth century ; and from Persian into Arabic in the ninth century ; it was afterwards rendered into Hebrew, Greek, Latin and Syriac ; from these versions successive translations were made into all the languages of modern Europe, until it became universally known as Pilpay's Fables.

The narrator of the stories is in the Arabic version called Bidpai; in the Sanscrit original no name similar to this occurs; but it is certain that the name Pilpay, by which the work is known in Europe, is a corruption of Bidpai.

The Arabic translation of the Pancha Tantra is called Kalila wa Damna; it is thus designated in allusion to two jackals which act a conspicuous part in the first story of the Arabic version, and which we recognise in the Sanskrit and Canarese under the forms Karataka and Damanaka.

The most admired Persian translation is not that which was first made, but the one written at the beginning of the sixteenth century, and known under the title of Anwár-i-soheili; which was afterwards rendered into Turkish with the designation of Humáyun Námeh.

With the exception of the Bible and the Pilgrim's Progress, there is probably no work that has been translated into so many languages as the Pancha Tantra. In India it has retained its popularity to the present time, and is found in some form in all the spoken dialects of the country.

The Sanskrit epitome of the Pancha Tantra is termed the "Hitópadésa," or "Salutary Instruction." This has been translated into English by Sir William Jones and by Sir Charles Wilkins.

"Its popularity" says Professor Johnson, "through so many ages, amidst such various nations, is evidence of intrinsic merit; and the pictures of domestic manners and human nature which it presents, however tinctured by national peculiarities, must have been recognised as universally true, as well as diverting; or they would not have been naturalized in the west as well as in the east. In the maxims also which the tales serve to illustrate, there must have been much which secured the acquiescence of all mankind, or the remarks would have been left to enlighten the moralists of India alone. These merits, however, were such as admitted of transfusion into other languages; the merits of its composition are those which have chiefly recommended its preservation by the Press, and its circulation amongst the cultivators of Sanskrit literature."

There is a great diversity in the manuscript copies of the Pancha Tantra. Many differences occur in the various stories. In some versions the residence of the king is in Mahilaropya, a city in the south of India, which Professor Wilson identifies with St. Thomé. The Canarese version of the Pancha Tantra follows the Hitópadésa in making the residence of the king in Pátaliputra on the Ganges.

The king had three sons who were deficient in ability and application. He made this known to his counsellors and sought their advice ; asking them "of what use is a son who has neither knowledge nor virtue ? of what use is a cow who has no milk with her calf, &c. ? A learned brahman who was present offered to relieve the king of his anxiety by taking the princes to his house and instructing them perfectly. He then composed in their benefit these five chapters ; Mitra Bhéda, Dissension of friends ; Mitra Prápti, acquisition of friends ; Kakolukíya, inveterate enmity ; Labda Nashta, loss of advantage ; Asamprekshya karitwa, inconsiderateness. Through reading these the princes became in six months highly accomplished, and the five tantras were famous throughout the world.

An analytical account of the Pancha Tantra is contained in the Works of H. H. Wilson, Vol. IV.

Pandava—Patronymic from Páṇḍu, applied first to his five sons, and then generally to their party or army. Also to Arjuna in particular.

Pandavas—The five sons of the *Rája* Páṇḍu. After their father's death they returned to Hastinápur, and were kindly received by their uncle Dritaráshtra ; they were brought up with their cousins the Kauravas, in the old palace of Hastinápur ; but from the days of their early youth the sons of Dritaráshtra were ever jealous of the sons of Páṇḍu. Duryodhana, the eldest of the Kauravas, attempted to take the life of Bhíma. Soon after, a famous Brahman preceptor, named Drona, arrived at the city of Hastinápur. Their Uncle Bhíshma engaged him to instruct the Kauravas and Páṇḍavas in arms and sciences. Drona took great pains in teaching all the young men, but especially in teaching the Páṇḍavas. To Yudhishthira he imparted the use of the spear, but that young prince became more renowned for wisdom and goodness than for deeds of arms. To Arjuna he taught the use of the bow, and Arjuna became the most famous archer of his time. To Bhíma he taught the use of the club, for Bhíma was a young man of great appetite and enormous strength, and could wield the club right lustily. To Nakula he taught the whole art of taming and managing horses, and to Sahadeva Astronomy and the use of the sword. Drona instructed the Kauravas in like manner, as well as his own son Aswatthâma. But of all his pupils the most beloved was Arjuna, for he was the most perfect of all; and thus, while Duryodhana, the eldest of the Kauravas was jealous of all the Páṇḍavas, he was the most jealous of Arjuna.

This feeling increased and led to many quarrels; ultimately to the exile of the Páṇḍavas, who were sent by Dritaráshtra to the city of Varanávata. Here Duryodhana plotted their destruction by having them invited to a house built of combustible materials, with the intention of setting it on fire at night when they were all asleep. A retainer of his, Purochana, was the agent sent to effect this. The plot was discovered; an underground passage was dug through which they might escape; and Bhíma set on fire the house of Purochana; the flames reached the house of the Páṇḍavas, who were conducted by Bhíma through the passage underground, and went into the jungle with their mother Kuntí. They afterwards lived as mendicant brahmans in the city of Ekachakra (q. v.) Their subsequent history embraces the events which led to the Great War in the plain of Kurukshetra; the details of which will be found under the names of the various actors in it. The brothers at last assumed the garb of devotees, and after passing through many lands, they reached the Himálaya mountains, and there died one after the other, and were transported to the heaven of Indra. The fine description of the renunciation of their kingdom by the five brothers, and their journey towards Indra's heaven, has been well translated by Monier Williams :—

> When the four brothers knew the high resolve of king Yudhishthira,
> Forthwith with Draupadí they issued forth, and after them a dog
> Followed; the king himself went out the seventh from the royal city,
> And all the citizens and women of the palace walked behind;

But none could find it in their heart to say unto the king, 'Return.'
And so at length the train of citizens went back, bidding adieu.
Then the high-minded sons of Pándu and the noble Draupadí
Roamed onwards, fasting with their faces towards the east; their hearts
Yearning for union with the Infinite; bent on abandonment
Of worldly things. They wandered on to many countries, many a sea
And river. Yudhishthira walked in front, and next to him came Bhima,
And Arjuna came after him, and then, in order, the twin brothers.
And last of all came Draupadí, with her dark skin and lotus-eyes –
The faithful Draupadí, loveliest of woman, best of wives—
Behind them walked the only living thing that shared their pilgrimage,
The dog—And by degrees they reached the briny sea. There Arjuna
Cast in the waves his bow and quivers. Then with souls well-disciplined
They reached the northern region, and beheld with heaven-aspiring hearts
The mighty mountain Himavat. Beyond its lofty peak they passed
Towards the sea of sand, and saw at last the rocky Meru, king
Of mountains. As with eager steps they hastened on, their souls intent
On union with the Eternal, Draupadí lost hold of her high hope,
And faltering fell upon the earth.

"One by one the others also drop, till only Bhíma, Yudhishthira, and the dog are left. Still Yudhishthira walks steadily in front, calm and unmoved, looking neither to the right hand nor to the left, and gathering up his soul in inflexible resolution. Bhíma, shocked at the fall of his companions, and unable to understand how beings so apparently guileless should be struck down by fate, appeals to his brother, who without looking back explains that death is the consequence of sinful thoughts and too great attachment to worldly objects; and that Draupadí's fall was owing to her excessive affection for Arjuna; Sahadeva's (who is supposed to be the most humble-minded of the five brothers) to his pride in his own knowledge; Nakula's (who is very handsome) to feelings of personal vanity; and Arjuna's to a boastful confidence in his power to destroy his foes. Bhíma then feels himself falling, and is told that he suffers death for his selfishness, pride, and too great love of enjoyment. The sole survivor is now Yudhishthira, who still walks steadily forward, followed only by the dog.

When with a sudden sound that rang through earth and heaven, came the god
Towards him in a chariot, and he cried, "Ascend, O resolute prince."
Then did the king look back upon his fallen brothers, and address'd
These words unto the Thousand-eyed, in anguish—"Let my brothers here
Come with me. Without them, O God of Gods, I would not wish to enter
E'en heaven; and yonder tender princess Draupadí, the faithful wife,
Worthy of happiness, let her too come. In mercy hear my prayer."

Upon this, Indra informs him that the spirits of Draupadí and his brothers are already in heaven, and that he alone is permitted to ascend there in bodily form. Yudhishthira now stipulates that his dog shall be admitted with him. Indra says sternly, "Heaven has no place for those who are accompanied by dogs (Śwavatám) ;" but Yudhishthira is unshaken in his resolution, and declines abandoning the faithful animal. Indra remonstrates—"You have abandoned your brothers and Draupadí ; why not forsake the dog ?" To this Yudhishthira haughtily replies, "I had no power to bring them back to life ; how can there be abandonment of those who no longer live ?"

The dog, it appears, was his own father Dharma in disguise (Mahaprasthánika-parva.) Reassuming now his proper form he praises Yudhishthira for his constancy, and they enter heaven together. There, to his surprise, he finds Duryodhana and his cousins, but not his brothers or Draupadí. Hereupon he declines remaining in heaven without them. An angel is then sent to conduct him across the Indian Styx (Vaitaraṇí) to the hell where they are supposed to be. The scene which now follows may be compared to the Necyomanteia in the eleventh book of the Odyssey, or to parts of Dante.

"The particular hell to which Yudhishthira is taken is a dense wood, whose leaves are sharp swords, and its ground paved with razors. The way to it is strewed with foul and mutilated corpses. Hideous shapes flit across the air and hover over him. Here there is a horror of palpable darkness. There the wicked are burning in flames of blazing fire. Suddenly he hears the voices of his brothers and companions imploring him to assuage their torments, and not desert them. His resolution is taken. Deeply affected, he bids the angel leave him to share their miseries. This is his last trial. The whole scene now vanishes. It was a mere illusion, to test his constancy to the utmost. He is now directed to bathe in the heavenly Ganges ; and having plunged into the sacred stream, he enters the real heaven, where at length, in company with Draupadí and his brothers, he finds that rest and happiness which were unattainable on earth."*

* Indian Epic Poetry, p. 29 to 31.

Pandu—The second son of the Vyása, Krishṇa Dwaipáyana and Ambáliká one of the widows of Rája Vichitravirya,—the Pale, was the half-brother of Dhritáráshṭra who was blind. "The reason given for these defects is curious. Ambiká, (the mother of Dhritáráshṭra) was so terrified by the swarthy complexion and shaggy aspect of the sage Vyása, that when he visited her she closed her eyes, and did not venture to open them while he was with her. In consequence of this assumed blindness her child was born blind. Ambáliká, on the other hand, though she kept her eyes open, became so colourless with fright, that her son was born with a pale complexion. Páṇḍu seems in other respects to have been good looking."* He was the father of the five Páṇḍava princes Yudhishṭhira, Bhíma, Arjuna, Nakula, and Sahadeva. He married Kunti, or Pritha, and sometime afterwards his uncle Bhíshma, wishing him to take a second wife, "made an expedition to Śalya, king of Madra, and prevailed upon him to bestow his sister Mádri upon Páṇḍu, in exchange for vast sums of money and jewels."† But as Páṇḍu had incurred a curse from a deer which he shot, he was prevented from having progeny himself, and the Páṇḍava princes were therefore begotten respectively by the gods Dharma, Vayu, Indra, and the twin Aswinau.

Páṇḍu was carefully educated by his uncle Bhíshma, who afterwards installed him as Rája of Bhárata. The Rája Páṇḍu was a great warrior, and is said to have undertaken a campaign which would have extended his empire over all Hindustan, from the Punjab to Bengal, and from the slopes of the Himálayas to the Vindhya mountains. But he was addicted to hunting, and he went with his two wives to the Himálaya mountains; but his life there is filled with mythical details which may be passed over. While the five princes were still children, Páṇḍu, forgetting the curse of the sage whom he had killed in the form of a deer, ventured one day to embrace his wife Mádri, and died in her arms. She and Kunti then had a dispute for the honour of becoming a sati (suttee) which ended with Mâdri burning herself with her husband's corpse.‡

Pandu or Prana—A son of Dhatrí and Áyatí, who was

* Indian Epic Poetry, p. 92. † Ibid. ‡ Ibid.

married to Pundaríka, and was the ancestor of Uṣanas the preceptor of the Daityas.

Panini—" The greatest known grammarian of ancient India, whose work on the Sanskrit language has up to the present day remained the standard of Sanskrit grammar. Its merits are so great, that Páṇini was ranked among the Rishis, or inspired seers, and at a later period of Sanskrit literature, was supposed to have received the fundamental rules of his work from the god Śiva himself. Of the personal history of Páṇini nothing positive is known, except that he was a native of the village Salâtura, situated north-west of Attock, on the Indus—whence he is also surnamed Sálaturíya—and that his mother was called Dâkshî, wherefore, on his mother's side, he must have been a descendant of the celebrated family of Daksha. A tale-book, the *Kathâsaritságara* (*i. e.*, the ocean for the rivers of tales,) gives, indeed, some circumstantial account of the life and death of Páṇini ; but its narrative is so absurd, and the work itself of so modern a date —it was written in Cashmere, at the beginning of the twelfth century—that no credit whatever can be attached to the facts related by it, or to the inferences which modern scholars have drawn from them. According to the views expressed by Goldstücker (*Pánini, his place in Sanskrit Literature:* London, 1861,) it is probable that Páṇini lived before Sâkyamuni, the founder of the Buddhist religion, whose death took place about 543 B. C., but that a more definite date of the great grammarian has but little chance of ascertainment in the actual condition of Sanskrit philosophy. The grammar of Páṇini consists of eight Adhyâyas, or books, each book comprising four Pádas, or chapters, and each chapter a number of Sûtras (q. v.,) or aphoristical rules. The latter amount in the whole to 3996 ; but three, perhaps four, of them did not originally belong to the work of Páṇini. The arrangement of these rules differs completely from what a European would expect in a grammatical work, for it is based on the principle of tracing linguistic *phenomena*, and not concerned in the classification of the linguistic *material*, according to the so-called parts of speech. A chapter, for instance, treating of a prolongation of vowels, will deal with such a fact whenever it occurs, be it in the formation of bases, or in conjugation, declension, composition, &c. The rules of conjugation, declension, &c., are, for the same reason, not to be met with in the same chapter or in the same order in which European grammars would teach them ; nor would any single book or chapter, however apparently more systematically arranged—from a European point of view—such as the chapters on affixes or composition, suffice by itself to convey the full linguistic material concerned in it, apart from the rest of the work. In a general manner, Páṇini's work may therefore be called a natural history of the Sanskrit language, in the sense that it has the strict tendency of giving an accurate description of facts, instead of making such a description subservient to the theories according to which the linguistic material is usually distributed by European grammarians. Whatever objections may be raised against such an arrangement, the very fact of its differing from that in our grammars makes it peculiarly instructive to the European student, as it accustoms his mind to survey language from another point of view than that usually presented to him, and as it must induce him, too, to question the soundness of many linguistic theories now looked upon as axiomatic truths. As the method of Páṇini requires in a student the power of combining many rules scattered all over the work, and of combining, also, many inferences to be drawn from these rules, it exercises, moreover, on the mind of the student an effect analogous to that which is supposed to be the peculiar advantage of the study of mathematics. The rules of Páṇini were criticised and completed by Kátyáyana, who, according to all probability, was the teacher, and therefore the contemporary of Patanjali ; and he, in his turn, was criticised by Patanjali, (q. v.,) who sides frequently with Páṇini. These three authors are the canonical triad of the grammarians of India ; and their works are, in truth, so remarkable in their own department, that they exceed in literary merit nearly all, if not all, grammatical productions of other nations, so far as the two classes are comparable. The rules of Páṇini were commented on by many authors. The best existing commentary on them is that called the *Kasikavritti*, by Vámana Jayáditya, which follows these rules in their original order. At a later period, attempts were made to arrange the rules of Páṇini in a manner which approaches more to the European method ; the chief work of this category is the *Siddhánta Kaumutí*, by Bhaṭṭóji-díkshita. Páṇini mentions, in his Sútras, several grammarians who preceded him, amongst others, Sákatayana. Manuscripts of a grammar ascribed to a grammarian of this name exist in the Library of the India Office in London, and in the Library of the Board of Examiners at Madras. On the ground of a few pages only of the latter an attempt has been very recently made to prove that this grammar is the one referred to by Páṇini, and therefore older than the work of the latter. But the facts adduced in proof of this hypothesis are so ludicrously weak, and the reasoning upon them so feeble and inconclusive, whereas the evidence in favour of the comparatively recent date of this work is so strong, that no value whatever can be attached to this hasty hypothesis. For the present, therefore, Páṇini's work still remains the oldest existing grammatical work of India, and probably of the human race. The Sútras of Páṇini with a modern commentary by two native pandits, and with extracts from the *Vârttikas* of Kâtyâyana and the *Mahâbhâshya* of Patanjali, were edited at Calcutta in 1809. This edition, together with the modern commentary, but with garbled extracts from the extracts mentioned, was re-printed at Bonn in 1839–1840 by Dr. O. Bochtlingk, who added to it remarks of his own and some indices. For the literature connected with Páṇini, see Colebrooke's preface to his *Grammar of the Sanskrit Language* (Calc. 1805,) and Goldstücker's *Páṇiṇi*, &c., as mentioned above."—*Chambers' Encyclopædia, VII*, 231.

Pannagari—A teacher of the Rig Veda, who was previously a pupil of Bashkáli.

Papa—The name of one of the Narakas.

Para—The son of Anga, a descendant of Anu ; also a son of Prithusena, a descendant of Hastin ; and of Samara, in the same line.

Para or Para—A river in Malwa, the Párvatí.

Para—Supreme, infinite ; and Pára, the farther bank or limit, the point that is to be attained by crossing a river or sea, or figuratively the world or existence. Vishṇu, then, is Pára, that which nothing surpasses ; and Pára, the end or object of existence ; he is Apára pára, the farthest bound of that which is illimitable, or space and time : he is Param parabhyah, above or beyond the highest being, beyond or superior to all the elements : he is Paramartha rúpí, or identical with final truth, or knowledge of soul : he is Brahmá pára, the object or essence of spiritual wisdom. Parapárabhuta is said to imply the farther limit (Pára) of rudimental matter. See Wilson's Notes to Vishṇu Purána, 113.

Paradas—See Pahlavas.

Paramanu—A measure of time, equal to one Anu.

Param—The duration of Brahmá's life, consisting of a hundred of his years.

Paramatma—A name of Vishṇu, meaning 'supreme spirit.'

Parameshthin—The son of Indrayumna, a descendant of Bharata.

Paramiksha—A son of Anu.

Paran—The heavenly one, in Tamil. It corresponds with Brahm, or Para Brahm of the Upanishads. In the South there has been a controversy whether Vishṇu or Śiva is Paran, or the supreme Being.

Pararddham—1, Half of the duration of Brahmá's life ; 2, That number which occurs in the eighteenth place of figures, enumerated according to the rule of decimal notation.

Paras—A class of deities, consisting of twelve, to appear in the ninth Manwantara.

Parasara—A great sage, the son of Śakti, and grandson of Vaṣishtha. In order to avenge the death of his father, who had been devoured by a Rákshas, he commenced a sacrifice to effect the destruction of all the Rákshasas, but was dissuaded from it by his grandsire ; who showed him that his father's death was the work of destiny. Pulastya taught him the Vishṇu Purána, which he related to Maitareya, to convey the truths that the world was produced from Vishṇu ; that it exists in him ; that he is the cause of its continuance and cessation ; that he is the world. Paráṣara was also the Vyása of the twenty-sixth Dwápara, and a teacher of a branch of the Rig Veda, and of the Sáma Veda.

Buchanan has noticed the incompatibility of Paráṣara's genealogy with his being, as it is stated, cotemporary with Śántanu, king of Hastinápur, that prince being the 44th in descent from Atri, who is cotemporary with Vaṣishtha, who again is but three generations anterior to Paráṣara ; he supposes therefore that many generations in the line of Vaṣishtha must have been omitted. It is not necessary, however, to attempt to reconcile these incongruities, for the coetaneous existence of Atri and Vaṣishtha is less chronological than mythological, or perhaps, as they are both enumerated amongst the stars of the great bear, astronomical ; it extends throughout the Manwantara ; their immediate successors, who hold a sacred character, enjoy a like longevity, and are similarly cotemporary, at any period, with their ancestry and posterity ; if we consider them as mere mortals we must suppose that Paráṣara preceded the great war by three generations, Krishṇa Dwaipáyana Vyása, his son, being the father of Dhritaráshtra, Páṇḍu, and Vidura, by the widows of Vichitravírya. Vyása was, however, cotemporary with his grandson and their descendants, agreeably to the above system of saintly immortality. Mr. Bentley places Paráṣara, about 575, B. C., (Hindu Astronomy) ; Buchanan, about 1300, B.C., (Genealogies of the Hindus) ; and Wilford, 1391, B.C., (As. Res. IX, 87) ; Wilson's Works, III, 123.

2, A second Paráṣara is the author of a celebrated code of laws ; he is mentioned by Yajnavalka in his standard work, and often quoted by the commentaries ; 3, There is a third of the same name the reputed author of a Tantra ; and, 4, A fourth, the author of an astronomical work.

Parasikas—The people of Pars, or Persians.

Parasarama or Rama—of the axe (Paruṣa). See Ráma.

Paravatas—A class of deities of the Second Manwantara.

Paravrij—An outcast mentioned in the Rig Veda who was blind and lame, but restored to sight and the power of walking by the Aṣvins. O. S. T., V, 246.

Paravrit—A prince, the son of Rukmakavacha, and father of Jyámagha.

Parijata tree—A celestial tree, produced at the churning of the ocean, from the whirlpool of the deep, the delight of the nymphs of heaven, perfuming the world with its blossoms. Krishṇa, at the desire of his wife Satyabháma carried off this tree from the gardens of Indra. Śachí excited Indra to prevent its removal. A conflict ensued between the gods and Krishṇa, which is narrated at great length in the Hari V., and with some variations in the Vishṇu Purána. Krishṇa was victorious, and took the tree to Dwáraka where it was planted in Satyabháma's garden. When Krishṇa abandoned his mortal body the tree proceeded to heaven again along with the Sudharman palace.

Parikshit—The son of Abhimanyu and grandson of Arjuna. After the destruction of the Kurus the child (Paríkshit) was killed in the womb of his mother Uttará, by the magic Brahmá weapon hurled by Aswatthámau, but restored to life again by Krishṇa. When the Pándava princes determined to renounce the world and retire into the forest, the Rájah Yudhishthira gave the Ráj of Hastinápur to Paríkshit. The commencement of the Kali age is placed at the beginning of the reign of Paríkshit, though according to the usual notions it commenced from the death of Krishṇa. The Vyása who arranged or compiled the Puránas flourished during the reign of Paríkshit. The prince himself died of the bite of a snake, according to the Maha Bhárata, and it is said the Bhágavata Purána was related to him between the bite and its fatal effect. The king had incurred the imprecation of a hermit by which he was sentenced to die of the bite of a venomous snake, at the expiration of seven days ; and in preparation for this event, he repaired to the banks of the Ganges ; thither also went the gods and sages to witness his death. Amongst the latter was Suka the son of Vyása ; and it was in reply to Paríkshit's question " what should a man do who is about to die" that he narrated the

Bhágavata, as he had heard it from Vyása ; believing that nothing secures final happiness so certainly as to die while the thoughts are wholly engrossed by Vishṇu. V. P.

Parinamin—That which may be modified, one of the definitions of Pradhána, q. v.

Paripatra—1, A range of mountains the northern portion of the Vindhya chain ; 2, A prince, the son of Ahínagu, a descendant of Kusa.

Pariplava—A prince, the son of Sukhibala, or Sukhinala, of the race of Puru.

Pariyatra—A mountain range, to the west of Meru, called in the Vishṇu Puráṇa the limitative mountains in the west. It is said in Wilson's notes to be the same as Paripátra, the northern and western portion of the Vindhya.

Parivatsara—One of the five Cyclic years, or Yugas, q. v.

Parjanya—The thundering rain god. There are several hymns in the Rig Veda which celebrate Parjanya, as the procreative and stimulating fructifier. "The winds blow, the lightnings fall, the plants shoot up ; the heaven fructifies ; food is produced for all created things, when Parjanya, thundering, replenishes the earth with moisture." Parjanya forms the subject of two papers by Dr. G. Bühler, containing a comparison of Parjanya with the Lithuanian god Perkunas, the god of thunder. Dr. Bühler holds Parjanya to have been decidedly distinct from Indra. "Taking a review of the whole, we find that Parjanya is a god who presides over the lightning, the thunder, the rain, and the procreation of plants and living creatures. But it is by no means clear whether he is originally a god of the rain or a god of the thunder." He inclines, however, to think that from the etymology of his name, and the analogy between him and Perkunas, he was originally the thunder god. In his German essay, his conclusion is that Parjanya is "the god of thunderstorms and rain, the generator and nourisher of plants and living creatures."—*Muir, O. S. T., V*, 142.

Parjanya is also represented as the brother of Aditi, and husband of Prithiví, the Earth. He is also described as the father of Soma, and the protector of the Soma plant.

2, A Lókapála, the regent of the north and king of clouds ; 4, The wife of Maríchi, whose son became a Lókapála.

Parna—One of the fifteen teachers of the White Yajush.

Parswanatha—The twenty-third of the Tírthankaras, or deified saints of the Jainas in the present era. He and Mahávíra, the twenty-fourth, are regarded with the greatest veneration throughout Hindustan. At Belupura, near Benares, there is a temple honoured as the birth-place of Páraswanátha.

Parvana Sraddhas—Ancestral oblations, or the worship of progenitors, at certain lunar periods.

Parvas—Days of periodical impurity when a wise man must desist from the study of the Vedas.

Parvasa—Called also Sarvagas the son of Paurnamása, and brother of Kaṣyapa.

Parvasi—The wife of Parvasa, and mother of Yajnaváma and Kaṣyata, who were both founders of Gotras or families.

Parvati—The daughter of Himálaya and spouse of Mahádeva. Her name was changed to Durgá (q. v.) ; she is also called Deví, Uma, &c. Dr. Muir quotes various passages to show the dignity to which this goddess has eventually been elevated in the estimation of her worshippers ; and that she has now attained a far higher rank in the Indian pantheon than was originally enjoyed by the daughter of Daksha and Himavat. O. S. T., IV, 372.

Parvatiyas—A designation of many of the aboriginal tribes of India, meaning "dwellers in mountains," from Parvati, a mountain.

Pasupati—A name of Śiva. There is a treatise on the Páṣupata worship, or worship of Śiva by Páṣupati.

Pasupati—One of the eight Rudras, the one who has the place of fire.

Pasuyajna—One of the five great sacrificial ceremonies ; the sacrifice of a horse or animal. See Aṣwamedha.

Patala—The lowest of the seven regions in the interior of the earth, extending downwards ten thousand yojanas. These seven are Atala, Vitala, Nitala, Gabhastimat, Mahátala, Sútala, and Pátála. Their soil is severally white, black, purple, yellow, sandy, stony, and of gold. They are embellished with magnificent palaces, in which dwell numerous Dánavas, Daityas, Yakshas, and great snake gods. The Muni Nárada, after his return from those regions to the skies, declared amongst the celestials that Pátála was much more delightful than Indra's heaven. 'What' exclaimed the sage, 'can be compared to Pátála, where the Nágas are decorated with brilliant and beautiful and pleasure-shedding jewels;' and who will not delight in Pátála where the lovely daughters of the Daityas and Danavas wander about, fascinating even the most austere; where the rays of the sun diffuse light, and not heat, by day; and where the moon shines by night for illumination, not for cold; where the sons of Danu, happy in the enjoyment of delicious viands and strong wines, know not how the time passes? There are beautiful groves and streams and lakes where the lotus blows; and the skies are resonant with Köil's song. Splendid ornaments, fragrant perfumes, rich unguents, the blended music of the lute and pipe and tabor; these and many other enjoyments are the common portion of the Danavas, Daityas, and snake-gods, who inhabit the regions of Pátála.

Below the seven Pátálas is the form of Vishnu, from the quality of darkness, which is called Sesha. Vishnu Purána, p. 205.

Patala, Patanga—The names of two of the seven suns into which the solar rays dilate at the great Pralaya, when Vishnu assumes the character of Rudra the destroyer, and descends to reunite all his creatures with himself.

Pataliputra or Palibothra—The metropolis of Magadha.

Pathya—A teacher of the Sáma Veda.

Patumat—One of the Andhra kings of Magadha, the son of Meghaswáti.

Patumitra—One of the kings of Mekalá, a country in the Narbada. Vishnu Purána, p. 479.

Paulomi—The wife of Brighu, a descendant of the daughters of Daksha.

Paulomas—Distinguished Danavas ; powerful, ferocious and cruel. The Vishṇu Purána states that Puloma, who was married to Kaṣyapa, bore him thirty thousand of them.

Paundraka—A Vasudeva, who assumed the insignia and style of Krishṇa, and was supported by his friend and ally the king of Kásí. Krishṇa marched against them and destroyed them both. The son of the king of Kásí then sent a magical being against Krishṇa ; but the discus, Sudarsana, speedily destroyed it, with the army of Kásí, and the demi-gods attendant upon Śiva : the discus afterwards set on fire the city of Benares consuming it and its inhabitants. In this legend, says Professor Wilson, we have a contest between the followers of Vishṇu and Śiva intimated, as, besides the assistance given by the latter to Paundraka, Benares has been from all time, as it is at present, the high place of the Saiva worship.

Paundras—The inhabitants of Pundra, a western province of Bengal.

Pauras—A race of kings whose dynasty continued three hundred years. Vishṇu Purána, p. 477.

Puravas—Descendants of Puru.

Pauravi—A title, attached to the second Rohini, wife of Vasudeva, to distinguish her from the first, the mother of Balaráma.

Paurnamasa—The son of Maríchi and Sambhúti.

Paurnamasi—The day of full moon one of the seasons when gifts are meritorious.

Pausha—The name of one of the lunar months, corresponding to December.

Paushinji—A teacher of the Sáma Veda.

Pavaka, Pavamana—Two of the brilliant sons of Agni. According to the Váyu Purána Pauvamána is the fire produced by friction, or Nirmathaya ; and Pávaka is electric or Vaidyata fire. The Bhágavata makes these two fires the sons of Antarddhána. When dominion over different provinces of creation was assigned to different beings, Pávaka was made chief of the Vásus.

Pavitras—One of the five classes of deities of the fourteenth Manwantara.

Payoshni—A river which the Vishṇu Purána says rises from the Riksha mountains; but the Váyu and Kúrma bring it from the Vindhya range. There are several indications of its position in the Mahábhárata, but none very precise. Its source appears to be near that of the Krishúa; it flows near the beginning of the Dandaka forest, which should place it rather near to the sources of the Godáverí; it passes through Vidarbha or Berar, and Yudhishthira having bathed in it, comes to the Vaidúrya mountain and the Narbadá river. These circumstances make it likely that the Payín Gangá is the river in question.

Phalguna—A lunar month corresponding nearly to January.

Pindaraka—A Tírtha. A village in Guzerat, still held in reverence from the following legend connected with it. The three sages Viswamitra, Kanwa, and Nárada were here observed by some boys who determined to play a trick upon them. They accordingly took a boy named Sámba, and having dressed him as a damsel, conducted him to the sages, and with deep respect enquired, what child will this female, the wife of Babhra, who is anxious to have a son give birth to. The sages, knowing what was done, replied, "She will bring forth a club that shall crush the whole of the Yádava race." The boys related all that had occurred to Ugrasena; and as foretold a club was produced from the belly of Sámba. Ugrasena had the club which was of iron, ground to dust, and thrown into the sea; but the particles of dust there became rushes; one part, which could not be broken, was swallowed by a fish; the fish was caught, the iron spike was extracted from its belly, and was taken by a hunter named Jará. This hunter afterwards shot Krishṇa with an arrow tipped with the iron spike. So was it determined by fate. V. P.

Pindas—Balls of food, offered at Sráddas. They are made of boiled rice, sesamum seeds, honey and butter; various kinds of fruit of pulse, and of grain, water, frankincense, sugar and milk, are also mixed up in them at times; the size differs from that of a fowl's egg to that of a cocoanut; but the Piṇḍa is usually of such a magnitude as to be conveniently held in the hand.

Pingala—One of the eleven Rudras, according to the enumeration in the Matsya Purána.

Pipal Tree—Ficus religiosa: the one in Vipula mountain, on the west of Meru, is said in the Vishṇu Purána to spread over eleven hundred yójanás.

Pippala—The name of one portion of Jambu-dwípa, according to the Mahábhárata; the other portion is called Sása; the two are reflected in the lunar orb as in a mirror.

Pippalada—A disciple of Devadarsa and teacher of the Atharva Veda.

Pipru—One of the demons of drought, represented in the Rig Veda as one of the malevolent powers in the atmosphere, to encounter whom Indra marches forth accompanied by the Maruts, and sometimes attended by Vishṇu. The dreadful battles which are described are evidently personifications of the storms which occur at the bursting of the monsoons in India.

Pisacha—A daughter of Daksha, and wife of Kaṣyapa.

Pisacha Marriage—A marriage in which a damsel is neither purchased, nor seduced, nor carried away captive, but simply taken at a disadvantage; an outrage, says Mr. Wheeler, "far more likely to be committed amongst a peaceful community than amongst a race of chivalrous warriors, like the Kshatriyas." "If a damsel found herself likely to become a mother, without being able to furnish a satisfactory reason for her maternity, she would naturally plead that she had been victimised by a Pisácha; and probably from this circumstance the term came to be applied to all cases in which a damsel had been taken at a disadvantage by a mortal lover." In modern times the belief is still common in the rural districts of India that such events occur.

Pisachas—Evil spirits or demons, supposed to haunt the earth and inhabit trees and forests. The term is constantly applied to the wild mountain tribes, the aborigines. One of the hymns of the Rig Veda calls upon Indra to destroy the tawny coloured fearfully roaring Pisáchas, and to annihilate the Rákshasas.

Pisachika—A river that has its rise on the Riksha mountains.

Pithastanas—Fifty-one places where, according to the Tantras, the limbs of Satí fell, when scattered by her husband Śiva, as he bore her dead body about, and tore it to pieces, after she had put an end to her existence at Daksha's sacrifice. This part of the legend seems to be an addition to the original fable, and bears some analogy to the Egyptian fable of Isis and Osiris. At the Pitha stánas of Jiválákmukhí, Vindhyavásini, Kálighát, and others, temples are erected to the different forms of Devi or Satí, not to the phallic emblem of Śiva, which if present, is there as an accessory and embellishment, not as a principal, and the chief object of worship is a figure of the goddess; a circumstance in which there is an essential difference between the temples of Dúrga and shrines of Osiris.—*Wilson's Notes to Vishnu Purána.*

Pitri-loka—One of the seven spheres above the earth, the heaven of Pitris and Brahmans.

Pitris—Progenitors; born from the side of Brahmá; they are also called the sons of Angiras. In the divisions of the celestial sphere the path of the Pitris is said in the Vishṇu Purána to be in the north of Agastya, and south of the line of the Goat; exterior to the Vaiswánara path. The Pitris derive satisfaction from ancestral offerings in the day of the new moon. A Srádda at certain seasons will content them for a thousand years. The songs of the Pitris are said to confer purity of heart, integrity of wealth, prosperous seasons, perfect rites, and devout faith; all that men can desire. The various descriptions of food, &c., that should be offered to deceased ancestors, are mentioned in the Vishṇu Purána.

Pitrayajna—Obsequial rites; or libations to the manes; one of the great obligations or sacrifices.

Pivari—The wife of Vedaṣiras; they had many children, who constituted the family, or Brahmanical tribe of Bhárgavas, sons of Bhrigu.

Piyadasi, or Piyadasano—An Indian king identified both by name and circumstances, with Aṣóka. There are many inscriptions on columns and rocks, by a Buddhist prince, in an ancient form of letter and the Pálí language, found in India ; and many of these are attributed to Aṣóka. Their purport agrees with his character, and their wide diffusion with the traditionary report of the number of his monuments. His date is near that of Antiochus the Great. See Wilson's Notes to Vishṇu Purána, p. 470.

Plaksha—One of the seven Dwípas, or great insular continents ; surrounded with a sea of sugar cane juice or Ikshu ; the king was named Midhatithe ; the Dwípa was divided amongst his seven sons, and each division was named after the prince to whom it was subject. The several kingdoms were bounded by as many ranges of mountains, in which the sinless inhabitants ever dwell, along with celestial spirits and gods ; in them are many holy places ; and the people there live for a long period, exempt from care and pain, and enjoying uninterrupted felicity. There are also in the seven divisions of Plaksha seven rivers flowing to the sea, whose names alone are sufficient to take away sin ; the people who drink of their waters are always contented and happy ; and there is neither decrease nor increase amongst them. Vishṇu Purána, p. 197.

Pongal, or Sankranti—The Pongāl is the greatest of the unsectarian festivals of the Hindus. It is celebrated at their astronomical new year when the sun enters Capricorn about the 11th of January ; and lasts three days ; during which the Hindus employ themselves in mutual visits and compliments, something in the same manner as the Europeans do on the first day of the year. The feast of the Pongāl is a season of rejoicing for two special reasons. The first is, that the month of Magha, *i. e.*, December—January, every day in which is unlucky, is now over ; and the other, that it is succeeded by a month, each day of which is lucky.

For the purpose of averting the evil effect of the baleful month of Magha, about four o'clock in the morning, a sort of Sannyásis, *i. e.*, penitents, go from door to door of every house, beating on a plate of iron or copper, which produces a piercing sound. All who sleep, being thus roused, are counselled to take wise precautions, and to guard against the evil presages of the month, by expiatory offerings, and sacrifices to Śiva, who presides over it. With this view, every morning, the women scour a space of about two feet square before the door of the house, upon which they draw several white lines with flowers ; and upon these they place several little balls of cow-dung, sticking in each a citron blossom. These little balls are probably designed to represent Vighnéṣvara, the remover of obstacles, whom they desire to propitiate with the flower. Each day these little lumps of cow-dung, with their flowers, are picked up and preserved in a private place, till the last day of the month Magha ; and when that comes, the women, who are alone charged with this ceremony, put the whole in a basket, and march from the house, with musical instruments before them, clapping their hands, till they reach some waste place where they dispose of the relics.

Then, with the first day of the new month begins the festival, the first day of which is called Bhōgi Pongāl, *i. e.*, Indra's Pongāl, and it is kept by inviting the near relations to an entertainment, which passes off with hilarity and mirth.

The second day is called Sūrya Pongāl, *i. e.* Pongāl of the sun, because it is set apart in honour of the sun. Married women, after purifying themselves by bathing, which they perform by plunging into the water without taking off their clothes, and coming out all wet, set about boiling rice with milk, in the open air, and not under any cover ; and when it begins to simmer, they make a loud cry, all at once, repeating the words : Pongāl, Pongāl ! The vessel is then lifted off the fire, and set before the idol of Vighnéṣvara, which is placed close by, and after having been offered to the image, part of the rice is given to the cow ; and the remainder distributed among the people.

This is the great day of visits among the Hindus. The salutation begins with the question, "has the milk boiled ?" to which the answer is, "it has boiled ;" and from this the festival takes its name "Pongāl" *i. e.* "boiling."

The third day is called the Pongāl of cows. On it they mix in a great vessel filled with water, some saffron, cotton seeds, and leaves of the Margosa tree ; and then going several times round all the cows and oxen belonging to the house, they springle them with the water, as they turn to the four cardinal points ; and make the Sáshtānga, or prostration of the eight members, before them four times. This ceremony is performed by the men only. Next the cows are all dressed out, their horns being painted with various colours, and garlands of flowers and foliage put round their necks and over their backs. They likewise add strings of cocoanuts and other fruits, which are soon shaken off by the brisk motion of the animals, which these trappings occasion, and are picked up by children and others, who follow the cattle on purpose, and greedily eat what they gather, as something sacred. The cattle then, being driven in herds through the villages, and made to scamper about from side to side by the jarring noise of many sounding instruments, are, during the remainder of the day, allowed to feed at large without a keeper ; and whatever trespasses they commit are suffered to pass without notice or restraint.

At the conclusion of the festival they take the idols from the temples, and carry them in pomp to the place where the cattle have been again collected. The girls of pleasure, named Devadasis, who are found at all ceremonies, are also not wanting here. *Abbé Dubois.*

Prabha—The daughter of Swarbhána, and wife of Namuchi ; according to the Matsya Purána she was the wife of the sun, by whom he had Prabhata ; according to the Bhágavata she was the wife of Kalpa, who had by her Pratáh, (dawn) Madhyadina, (noon) and Sáya, (evening.)

Prabhakara—A Rishi of the house of Atri, who married the ten daughters of Raudráswa, a descendant of Puru.

Prabhasa—(Light.) 1, One of the deities called Vásus, because they are always present in light, or luminous irradiation ; 2, A place of pilgrimage in the west of India on the coast of Guzerat, near the temple of Sómanath, and town of Pattan Sómanath. In the Mahábhárata it is placed near Dwáraka. It was visited by Arjuna, and afterwards by Balaráma during the great war. Before the destruction of Dwáraka Krishṇa issued a proclamation that all the people of the city should go to the sea-shore at Prabhása and pay their devotions to the deity of Dwáraka.

Prabhata—A son of Vivaswat, the Sun, by his wife Prabhá.

Prachetas—1, A deity who presides over the tongue ; 2, A son of Duryáman, a descendant of Druhya ; 3,

Prachetasas—The ten sons of Práchínaverhis, who, instructed by their father, plunged into the depths of the ocean, and with minds wholly devoted to Náráyana, the sovereign of the universe, were engrossed by religious austerity for ten thousand years : on which, Vishṇu, being pleased with them, appeared to them amidst the waters, of the complexion of the full-blown lotus leaf. Beholding him mounted on the king of birds, Garuda, the Prachetásas bowed down their heads in devout homage ; when Vishṇu said to them, "Receive the boon you have desired ; for I, the giver of good, am content with you, and am present." The Prachetásas replied to him with reverence, and told him that the cause of their devotions was the command of their father to effect the multiplication of mankind. The god, having accordingly granted to them the object of their prayers, disappeared, and they came up from the water.

The Prachetásas took to wife Márishá (q. v.) and from her was born the eminent patriarch Daksha, who had in a former life been born as a son of Brahmá. Vishṇu Purána.

Prachinaverhis—The eldest of the six sons of Havirdhána ; he was a great prince and patriarch by whom mankind was multiplied after the death of Havirdhana ; he was called Prachínaverhis from his placing upon the earth the sacred grass, pointing to the east. He married Savarṇá, the daughter of the ocean, who was the mother of ten sons, styled Prachetásas, who were in the sea for ten thousand years. Vishṇu Purána.

Prachinvat—A prince, the son of Janamejaya, and grandson of Puru.

Pradarsanas—A class of deities of the third Manwantara.

Pradhana—Primary or crude matter ; a form of Vishṇu ; it is also designated Prakriti, Nature ; it comprehends both causes and effects ; it is durable, self-sustained, undecaying ; the mother of the world ; without beginning ; and that into which all that is produced is resolved. Pradhána, when unmodified, is according to the Sankhyas and Pauránics, nothing more than the three qualities in equilibrio, or goodness, foulness, and darkness neutralising each other. Sankhya Karika, p. 52.

Pradhanatma—A name of Vishṇu, meaning, one with crude nature, or Viswabhávana.

Pradosha—A son of Kalpa, and Doshá. Pradosha had two brothers Niṣítha and Vyushta ; the three names mean the beginning, middle and end of night.

Pradyota—A king of Magadha, son of the minister Simika, who having killed his sovereign placed his son Pradyóta on the throne ; the dynasty lasted one hundred and thirty-eight years.

Pradyumna—The son of Krishṇa and Rukminí—the incarnate Indian Cupid. He is called in the South Manmatha (the confounder of the mind) and in the North of India, Káma (Desire.) He is said to be the mental son of Vishṇu, and to have become incarnate in Pradyumna, the first born of the 108,000 sons of Krishṇa. His history is thus related in the Vishṇu Purána.

"When Pradyumna was but six days old, he was stolen from the lying-in chamber by Sambara, terrible as death ; for the demon foreknew that Pradyumna, if he lived, would be his destroyer. Taking away the boy, Sambara cast him into the ocean, swarming with monsters, into a whirlpool of roaring waves, the haunt of the huge creatures of the deep. A large fish swallowed the child, but he died not, and was born anew from its belly : for that fish, with others, was caught by the fishermen, and delivered by them to the great Ásura Sambara. His wife Máyádeví, the mistress of his household, superintended the operations of the cooks, and saw, when the fish was cut open, a beautiful child, looking like a new shoot of the blighted tree of love. Whilst wondering who this should be, and how he could have got into the belly of the fish, Nárada came to satisfy her curiosity, and said to the graceful dame, "This is the son of him by whom the whole world is created and destroyed, the son of Vishṇu, who was stolen by

Sambara from the lying-in chamber, and tossed by him into the sea, where he was swallowed by the fish. He is now in thy power; do thou, beautiful woman, tenderly rear this jewel of mankind." Thus counselled by Nárada, Máyádeví took charge of the boy, and carefully reared him from childhood, being fascinated by the beauty of his person. Her affection became still more impassioned when he was decorated with the bloom of adolescence. The gracefully moving Máyávatí then, fixing her heart and eyes upon the light-minded Pradyumna, gave him, whom she regarded as herself, all her magic (and illusive) powers.

Observing these marks of passionate affection, the son of Krishṇa said to the lotus-eyed Máyádeví, "Why do you indulge in feelings so unbecoming the character of a mother?" To which she replied, "Thou art not a son of mine; thou art the son of Vishṇu, whom Kála Sambara carried away, and threw into the sea: thou wast swallowed by a fish, but wast rescued by me from its belly. Thy fond mother, O beloved, is still weeping for thee." When the valiant Pradyumna heard this he was filled with wrath, and defied Sambara to battle. In the conflict that ensued, the son of Mádhava slew the whole host of Sambara. Seven times he foiled the delusions of the enchanter, and making himself master of the eighth, turned it against Sambara, and killed him. By the same faculty he ascended into the air, and proceeded to his father's house, where he alighted, along with Máyávatí, in the inner apartments. When the women beheld Pradyumna, they thought it was Krishṇa himself. Rukminí, her eyes dimmed with tears, spoke tenderly to him, and said, "Happy is she who has a son like this, in the bloom of youth. Such would be the age of my son Pradyumna, if he was alive. Who is the fortunate mother adorned by thee? and yet from thy appearance, and from the affection I feel for thee, thou art assuredly the son of Hari."

At this moment Krishṇa accompanied by Nárada, arrived; and the latter said to the delighted Rukminí, "This is thine own son, who has come hither after killing Sambara, by whom, when an infant, he was stolen from the lying-in chamber. This is the virtuous Máyávatí, his wife, and not the wife of Sambara. Hear the reason. When Manmatha, the deity of love, had perished,* the goddess of beauty, desirous to secure his revival, assumed a delusive form, and by her charms fascinated the demon Sambara, and exhibited herself to him in various illusory enjoyments. This thy son is the descended Káma ; and this is the goddess Ratí, his wife. There is no occasion for any uncertainty : this is thy daughter-in-law." Then Rukminí was glad, and Keśava also ; the whole city resounded with exclamations of joy, and all the people of Dwáraká were surprised at Rukminí's recovering a son who had so long been lost.

Pradyumna is represented as a man, with a crown on his head ; and his ears, neck, breast, arms, hands, feet, and the remaining part of his body, are adorned with various ornaments of pearls, precious stones, gold and silver. On his shoulders he wears a Bāhupattai, *i. e.*, a shoulder-girdle. In one of his hands he holds a bow of sugar-cane, with a string of insects ; and in the other an arrow, ready for discharge. On his back he carries a quiver, with five sorts of arrows, consisting of five kinds of flowers. His standard is a fish ; his vehicle, a parrot ; and the color of his body, yellow. Ratí his wife, is represented as a female with long black hair, braided into a pigtail that reaches to the ground. Like her husband, she wears also a crown, and is on the whole adorned and equipped similar to him.

Prahlada—The son of Hiraṇyakaṣipu, a daitya, but from the influence of a prior existence, a worshipper of Vishṇu. In the war between the gods and demons, however, he takes part with his family, and is killed by the discus of Vishṇu. He is again born of the same parents, and with the same name, and is then the Prahláda who is the hero of the usual story, the pious son of an impious father, the latter of whom was destroyed by Vishṇu in the Naṛisiṇha or man-lion avatára, and the former was raised to the rank of Indra for life, and finally united with Vishṇu. The V. P., contains a full account of the cruelties to which Prahláda was subjected by his father in order to compel him to renounce the

*When he was reduced to ashes by a fiery glance from Siva, in resentment of his inflaming him with passion for Uma.

worship of Vishṇu ; but all in vain ; he remains firm throughout. It is said in the Bhágavata that Hiraṇyakaṣipu at last asks his son, why, if Vishṇu is everywhere, he is not visible in a pillar in the hall where they are assembled. He then rises and strikes the column with his fist, on which Vishṇu, in a form which is neither wholly a lion nor a man, issues from it, and a conflict ensues, which ends in Hiraṇyakaṣipu's being torn to pieces. V. P., Book I, Chap. XX.—*Wilson's Notes.*

Prajani—A prince, the son of Pransa, descendant of Nedishta.

Prajapatis—Progenitors of mankind. The seven mind-born sons of Brahmá, viz ; Brighu, Pulastya, Angíras, Maríchi, Daksha, Atri, and Vaṣishta. Considerable variety prevails in this list ; " but the variations are of the nature of additions made to an apparently original enumeration of but seven." The names of Pulaka and Kratu, occur in some. The Vishṇu Purána gives nine names. The Pádma Purána substitutes Kardama for Vaṣishtha. The Matsya agrees with Manu in adding Nárada to the list. Others include Adharma, and Ṛuchi, and Gautama. " Altogether therefore we have seventeen instead of seven. The simple statement that the first prajápatis sprang from the mind or will of Brahmá, has not contented the depraved taste of the mystics ; and in some of the Puránas they are derived from various parts of Brahmá's body.—*See Wilson's Notes, p.* 50.

Prajapati-yajna—Propagation of offspring ; a recent addition to the five great obligations of Manu.

Prajapatya—1, A particular sacrifice performed before appointing a daughter to raise issue in default of male heirs ; 2, A sort of penance, eating once a day for three days in the mornings, once in the night for three nights, subsisting three days on food given as alms, and fasting three days more.

Prajna—A synonymn of Mahat. That by which the properties of things are known.

Prakrita—Primary Creation : Elemental Dissolution : Nature. The general resolution of the elements into their primitive source. Prakṛita is generally translated Nature. See Pradhána.

Prakriti—The goddess nature ; the female principle ; the passive agent in creation. Vishṇu as Purusha, combines with Prakrití, and engenders creation.

Pralaya—" Dissolution." The dissolution of all things is of four kinds : Naimittaka, occasional ; Prakrittika, elemental ; Atyantika, absolute ; Nitya, perpetual. 1, The first occurs when the sovereign of the world reclines in sleep ; 2, In the second the mundane egg resolves into the primary element from whence it was derived ; 3, Absolute non-existence of the world is the absorption of the sage through knowledge, into the supreme spirit ; 4, Perpetual destruction is the constant disappearance, day and night, of all that are born. Vishṇu Purána.

Professor Wilson states, " the first is called Naimittaka, ' occasional' or ' incidental,' or Bráhmya, as occasioned by the intervals of Brahmá's days ; the destruction of creatures, though not of the substance of the world, occurring during his night. The general resolution of the elements into their primitive source, or Prakriti, is the Prákritika destruction, and occurs at the end of Brahmá's life. The third, the Absolute or final, is individual annihilation ; Móksha ; exemption for ever from future existence. The Bhágavata here notices the fourth kind, Nitya, or constant dissolution ; explaining it to be the imperceptible change that all things suffer, in the various stages of growth and decay, life and death. The various conditions of beings subject to change are occasioned by that constant dissolution of life which is rapidly produced by the resistless stream of time, taking everything perpetually away."

Pramlocha—A celestial nymph. One of the Apsarasas, of the Daivika, or divine class, of whom there are ten enumerated. It was Pramlocha, who interrupted the penance of Káṇḍu, and remained on earth with him for so many years. See Káṇḍu.

Pramoda—Pleasure. A son of Brahmá. The virtues and vices are enumerated as the progeny of Brahmá.

Prana—1, A measure of time equal to a respiration, six respirations make one vikála ; 2, A son of Dhátri and Ayati ; 3, One of the seven Rishis of the third Manwantara.

Pranayama—Suppression of breathing. It is performed by three modifications of breathing : the first act is expiration, which is performed through the right nostril, whilst the left is closed with the fingers of the right hand : this is called Rechakas, the thumb is then placed upon the right nostril, and the fingers raised from the left, through which breath is inhaled ; this is called Púraka : in the third act both nostrils are closed, and breathing suspended ; this is Kumbhaka : and a succession of these operations is the practice of Práṇáyáma.

Pransu—1, One of the ten sons of the Manu Vaivaswata ; 2, The son of Vatsapri.

Prapti—One of the wives of Kansa.

Prasada—(Favour) one of the sons of Dharma.

Prasena–The son of Nighana and brother of Satrájit. It was to Satrájit the Sun presented the Syamantaka gem which he wore on his neck. Satrájit, fearing that Krishṇa would ask him for the jewel transferred it to his brother Prasena. But though the jewel was an inexhaustible source of good to a virtuous person, if it were worn by a man of bad character it would cause his death. Prasena having taken the gem, and hung it about his neck, mounted his horse and went to the woods to hunt. In the chase he was killed by a lion. The precious gem afterwards came into the possession of Akrúra.

Prasenajit—1, A prince, the son of Kuṣáṣwa ; 2, The son of Susandhi, of the family of Ikshváku.

> " Susandhi fortunate and wise.
> Two noble sons had he, to wit
> Dhruvasandhi and Prasenajit."

Professor Wilson places this prince, the twenty-fourth of the line of Ikshváku, in the sixth century before Christ.

Prasraya—(Affection.) One of the allegorical sons of Dharma (moral and religious duty.)

Prastara—A prince, the son of Udgítha, a descendant of Bharata.

Prastutas—A class of deities of the sixth Manwantara.

Prasusraka—A prince, the son of Maru, a descendant of Kuṣa. In the Vishṇu Purána it is said that Maru is still living in the village called Kalápa.

Prasuti—One of the daughters of the Manu Swáyambhuva, who was married to Daksha ; they had twenty-four daughters, all plainly allegorical, being personifications of intelligence and virtues and religious rites.

Pratah—(Dawn.) The son of Kalpa and Prabhah.

Pratarddana—The son of Divodása, (king of Benares) so named from destroying the race of Bhadraṣrenya. He had various other appellations, as Satrájit, 'the victor over his foes,' from having vanquished all his enemies : Vatsa, or 'child,' from his father's frequently calling him by that name ; Ritadhwaja, 'he whose emblem is truth,' being a great observer of veracity ; and Kuvalayáṣwa, because he had a horse called Kuvalaya. Vishṇu Purána, p. 408. In the notes it is said that from the scanty and ill-digested notices in other Puránas it appears that Divodása, on being expelled from Benares, took some city and district on the Gomati, from the family of Bhadraṣrenya ; that Durdama recovered the country ; and that Pratarddana again conquered it from his descendants.

Pratibandhaka—A king of Mithila, the son of Maru, of the family of Janaka.

Pratibimba—'Reflection' a form of Brahmá. V. P., p. 40, note 15.

Pratihara—A prince, the son of Parameshtín, of the race of Bharata.

Pratihartta—The son of Pratihára, and father of Bhava, of the race of Bharata.

Pratikshatra—1, A king of Kási, the son of Kshatravriddha ; 2, A son of Saíma, of the Yadava race.

Pratipa—The son of Dilípa, a descendant of Kuru.

Pratisarga—Secondary creation—that which took place at the commencement of the present Kalpa ; water, and even the earth, being in existence, and consequently having been preceded by the creation of Mahat and the elements.

Pratisukya—A short section of the Vedas ; or more strictly, a collection of phonetic rules, peculiar to one of the different branches of the four Vedas.—*Müller, A. S. L., p.* 119.

Pratishthana—The capital city of Sudyumna ; situated on the eastern side of the confluence of the Ganges and Jumna ; the country between which rivers was the territory of the direct male descendants of Vaivaswata. In consequence of his having been a female formerly, Sudyumna was excluded from any share in his paternal dominions ; but his father, at the suggestion of Vasishtha, bestowed upon him the city Pratishthána, and he gave it to Purúravas.

Prativahu—The youngest son of Swaphalka.

Prativindya—One of the sons of Yudhishthira by Draupadi.

Prativyoman—A prince, the son of Vatsavyuha, of the family of Ikshváku.

Pratyahara—Restraining the organs of sense from susceptibility to outward impressions, and directing them entirely to mental perceptions. This is one of the means for effecting the entire subjugation of the senses ; and if they are not completely controlled the sage cannot accomplish his devotions.

Pratyaya Sarga—Intellectual creation of the Sánkhya philosophy ; the creation of which we have a notion, or to which we give assent ; in contradistinction to organic creation, or that existence of which we have no sensible perception. In its specific sub-divisions it is the notion of certain inseparable properties in the four different orders of beings : obstruction, or solidity in inanimate things ; inability or imperfection in animals ; perfectibility in man ; and acquiescence or tranquil enjoyment in gods. V. P., Notes. 37.

Pratyusha—(Daybreak.) One of the deities called Vásus.

Prava—One of the daughters of Daksha who was married to Kaşyapa.

Pravaha—The name of one of the winds ; so termed because it bears along the planets, which turn round, like a disc of fire, driven by the aerial wheel.

Pravilasena—One of the kings of Andhra, the son of Tálaka.

Pravira—1, The son of Prachinvat, or according to the Mahábhárata the son of Puru ; 2, One of the sons of Hariyaṣwa, a descendant of Hastin.

Prayag—The Hindu name of Allahabad.

Prayaschitta—'Expiation' or 'sacred philosophy,' created from the eastern mouth of Brahmá.

Prekshagara—House of seeing ; a sort of theatre ; a place made for seeing the sacrifice ; a sort of stockade used as a place where spectacles could be witnessed.

Preta-rat—The Lord of the dead ; a name of Yama, the Hindu Pluto.

Prishadaswa—A prince, the son of Anaraṇya.

Prishadhra—One of the sons of the Manu Vaivaswata, who, in consequence of the crime of killing a cow was degraded to the condition of a Súdra. This story, says Professor Wilson, has been modified apparently at different periods, according to a progressive horror of the crime. The Vishṇu Purána simply states the fact. The Váyu says he was hungry, and not only killed, but ate the cow of his spiritual preceptor Chyavana. In the Markaṇḍeya he is described as being out a hunting, and killing the cow of the father of Babhravya, mistaking it for a Gavaya or Gayal. The Bhágavata, as usual, improves upon the story, and says that Prishadhra was appointed by his Guru Vasishtha to protect his cattle. In the night a tiger made his way into the fold, and the prince in his haste, and in the dark, killed the cow upon which he had fastened, instead of the tiger. In all the authorities the effect is the same, and the imprecation of the offended sage degraded Prishadhra to the caste of a Súdra. According to the Bhágavata, the prince led a life of devotion, and perishing in the flame of a forest, obtained final liberation. The obvious purport of this legend, and of some that follow, is to account for the origin of the different castes from one common ancestor.

Prishata—The youngest of the hundred sons of Somaka.

Prishtaja—One of the sons of Kumára.

Prisni—A prince, the son of Anamitra.

Pritha, or Kunti—The daughter of Súra, and wife of Páṇḍu. For her history see KUNTI; also KARNA.

Prithivi—Earth, as one of the elements in Hindu philosophy, where it is said to be produced from the rudiment of smell. The waters becoming productive, engendered the rudiment of smell; whence an aggregate (earth) originates, of which smell is the property. V. P., p. 16.

Prithivi—Earth personified as a goddess. The Vishṇu Purána contains a hymn of adoration addressed by the goddess to Náráyana when he was incarnate as a boar, and descended to the subterrene regions. When Prithu took up his divine bow Ajagava, and marched forth to assail the Earth, the latter, assuming the figure of a cow, fled hastily from him, and traversed, through fear of the king, the regions of Brahmá and the heavenly spheres; but wherever went the supporter of living things, there she beheld Vaiṇya with uplifted weapons; overcome with apprehension the goddess Earth addressed Prithu, who made Swáyambhuva Manu, a calf to milk the Earth for the benefit of mankind. By granting life to the Earth, Prithu was as her father, and she thence derived the patronymic Prithivi (the daughter of Prithu). There are many mystifications in the Puránas of the original simple allegory, which typified the Earth as a cow who yielded to every class of beings the milk they desired, or the object of their wishes. V. P., Notes. See DYAUS.

Prithu—1, The most distinguished individual of this name was the son of Veṇa (q. v.) engendered by friction from the right arm of his dead father (V.P., 101.) He was resplendent in person as if the blazing deity of Fire had been manifested. At the birth of Prithu all living creatures rejoiced: and Veṇa, delivered by his birth from the hell named Put, ascended to the realms above. The mighty Prithu was invested by the gods with universal dominion, and soon removed the grievances of the people whom his father had oppressed. They complained of the want of edible fruits and plants, and said they were suffering from famine. On hearing this Prithu took up his divine bow, Ajagava, and soon extorted a promise from the Earth to supply mankind with all that was necessary for their sustenance. The legend of Prithu occurs in most of the Purânas, and all the versions are essentially the same. See Vishṇu Purâna, p. 104.

2. A prince, the son of Prastára.

3. A prince, the son of Anenas, and grandson of Kakutsha.

4. A prince, the son of Para, a descendant of Hastin.

5. A prince, the son of Anaraṇya, and father of Triṣanku of the line of Ikshvâku.

> " Anaraṇya, strong to fight,
> His son was Prithu, glorious name,
> From him the wise Triṣanku came."

Prithudana, Prithujaya, Prithukarman, Prithukirtti, Prithusravas, Prithyasas—Six princes, the most renowned of the million sons of Saṣavindu.

Prithugas—A class of deities of the sixth Manwantara.

Prithuloksha—A prince, the son of Chaturanga, a descendant of Anu.

Prithurukman—The brother of Jayámagha, and son of Parávrit, a descendant of Sasavindu.

Priti—'Affection'—One of the daughters of Daksha who was married to the sage Pulastya.

Priya—A princess in the city of Kapila, who was seized with white leprosy and taken to a distant jungle, and placed in a large cave where she was supplied with fire, fuel, and all kinds of food. At the same time, Ráma, Rája of Benares, was seized with the same disorder, and abandoned his Ráj, retiring to the same jungle. Subsequently he found a remedy in the root, leaves, fruit, and bark of a certain tree, and his body became pure as gold. Ultimately he fell in with Priya, cured her leprosy, and married her ; and they resided in the city of Koli. Wheeler's Notes to the Mahábhárata.

Priyamitra—After Tripṛishta, (q. v.), had been born as a lion, and had migrated through various forms, he became the Chakravartti Priyamitra in the division of the world Mahavideha. After a victorious reign of eighty-four lakhs of years he became an ascetic for a further period of a hundred lakhs, and was then translated to one of the higher heavens.—*Wilson, I, 292.*

Priyavrata—The eldest son of the divine Manu Swáyambhuva. He married Kámya the daughter of the patriarch Kardama, and had by her two daughters, Samrat and Kukshí, and ten sons, wise, valiant, modest and dutiful, named Agnídhra, Agnibáhu, Vapushmat, Dyutimat, Medha, Medhatithi, Bhavya, Savala, Putra, and the tenth was Jyotishmat, illustrious by nature as by name. These were the sons of Priyavrata, famous for strength and prowess. Of these, three, or Medha, Putra, and Agnibáhu, adopted a religious life: remembering the occurrences of a prior existence, they did not covet dominion, but diligently practised the rites of devotion in due season, wholly disinterested, and looking for no reward. V. P.

Priyavrata having divided the earth into seven continents, gave them respectively to his other seven sons. According to the Bhágavata, he drove his chariot seven times round the earth, and the ruts left by the wheels became the beds of the oceans, separating it into seven Dwípas. To Agnídhra he gave Jambudwípa; to Medhatithi he gave Plaksha-dwípa: he installed Vapushmat in the sovereignty over the Dwípa of Sálmali; and made Jyotishmat king of Kuśa-dwípa: he appointed Dyutimat to rule over Krauncha-dwípa; Bhavya to reign over Sáka-dwípa: and Savala he nominated the monarch of the Dwípa of Pushkara.

Proshakas, Proshtas—Inhabiters of valleys, a designation of some aboriginal tribes.

Pudkalai—One of the wives of Ayanas.

Pujari—An inferior priest who officiates in the pagodas, offering sacrifices, and receiving those offerings which are brought by the people in fulfilment of vows.

Puje—Adoration of the deity; worship of the gods with various ceremonies and offerings: the term is also applied to the respect or homage paid to superiors.

Pulaka—A Prajápati. One of the mind-born sons of Brahmá; he was married to Kshamá (Patience) one of the daughters of Daksha, by whom he had three sons, Karmasa, Arvarivat, and Sahishna.

Pulastya—Another Prajápati who was also one of the mind-born sons of Brahmá. It was he who appeared to Paráșara, and communicated to him the Vishṇu Puráņa, as a summary or compendium of Puranic traditions. Pulastya was married to Príti, (Affection) one of the daughters of Daksha. In the Vishṇu Puráņa it is said their son, now known as the sage Agastya, was called in a former birth, or in the Swáyambhuva Manwantara, Dattoli. The Váyu specifies three sons of Pulastya Dattoli, Vedabāhu, and Viníta; also a daughter, Sadwati, married to Agni. Pulastya is considered as the ancestor of the Rákshasas, as he is the father of Visravas, the father of Rávana and his brethren.

Pulimat—One of the Andhra kings, the son of Gomatiputra: he reigned twenty-eight years.

Pulindaka—One of the ten Sungas, who reigned at Magadha for a hundred and ten years after the Mauryan dynasty. Pulindaka was the son of Ardraka, and only reigned three years.

Pulindas—A name applied to any wild or barbarous tribe; in the Vishṇu Purāna it refers to the people of the deserts along the Indus: but Pulindas are met with in many other positions, especially in the mountains and forests across Central India, the haunts of the Bhíls and Gonds. Ptolemy places the Pulindai along the banks of the Narmada. Notes to Vishṇu Puráņa, 186.

Puloma—One of the daughters of Vaiswánara; the other was named Kálika; both were married to Kașyapa, and became the mothers of sixty-thousand distinguished Dánavas, who were powerful, ferocious, and cruel.

Puloman—1, A Dánava; one of the distinguished sons of Kașyapa and Danu; 2, A son of Viprachitti, and father of Sáchí the wife of Indra.

Pulomarchish—The last of the Andhrabhritya kings; the

Vishṇu Purána states that there were thirty of them whose united reigns amounted to four hundred and fifty-six years.

Pulomavit—One of the Andhra kings, the son of Swátikarna: he reigned thirty-six years.

Puman—Incorporated spirit; the same as Purusha. In the Notes to the Vishṇu Purána it is said the meaning is that Vishṇu is any form of spiritual being that is acknowledged by different philosophical systems; or that he is the Brahmá of the Vedánta, the Iswara of the Pátanjala, and the Purusha of the Sánkhya school.

Punarvasu—1, A lunar mansion in Airávati, in the Northern Avashthána; 2, A Yádava chief, the son of Abhijit.

Pundarika—1, One of the serpent-kings, of the progeny of Kádru; 2, A prince, the son of Nabhas, a descendant of Kúṣa.

Pundarika—(Pundaríká.) 1, A daughter of Vaṣishtha, and wife of Práṇa; 2, One of the Apsarases.

Pundarikaksha—A name of Viṣhnu, occurring in the first line of the Vishṇu Purána; it means having eyes like a lotus, or heart-pervading; or Pundaríka is explained, 'supreme glory,' and Aksha imperishable.

Pundra—1, A prince, one of the sons of Bali a descendant of Anu; 2, The name of a fabulous city between the Himavat and Hemakúta mountains.

Pundras—The inhabitants of the western provinces of Bengal; sometimes the term designates the provinces themselves, and includes the districts of Dinájpur, Rangpur, Bírbhúm, Burdwan, Midnapur, the jungle Mehats, &c.

Punul—The Tamil name of the sacred thread worn by the Brahmáns, Kshatriyas and Vaisyas.

Punya—1, (Merit.) A daughter of the sage Kratu, according to the Váyu list; 2, A river in Behar, now termed Pun-pun.

Punyajanas—A class of Rákshasas, who destroyed Kuṣasthali, the capital of Kakudmin, surnamed Raivata, whilst he was on a visit to the region of Brahmá.

Pur—One of the synonyms of Mahat, defined in the Vishṇu Purána to be "that by which the concurrence of nature occupies and fills all bodies."

Puraka—A modification of breathing so termed ; the act is performed as follows : the thumb is placed in the right nostril, and the fingers raised from the left, through which breath is inhaled.

Puranas—There are eighteen large treatises so designated. The following is a list of them :—

1. Brahmá Purána.
2. Pádma Purána.
3. Vishṇu Purána.
4. Vayavíya Purána.
5. Sri Bhágavata.
6. Nárada, or Náradíya Purána.
7. Markaṇḍa, or Markaṇḍeya Purána.
8. Agni Purána.
9. Bhavishya Purána.
10. Brahmá Vaivartta Purána.
11. Linga Purána.
12. Varáha Purána.
13. Skanda Purána.
14. Vámana Purána,
15. Kúrma Purána
16. Matsya Purána.
17. Gáruda Purána.
18. Brahmáṇḍa Purána.

A brief account of the contents of each of the above will be found under their separate titles. The Preface to the Vishṇu Purána by Dr. Wilson contains the following excellent remarks on their general character.

"The different works known by the name of Puránas are evidently derived from the same religious system as the Rámáyana and Mahábhárata, or from the mytho-heroic stage of Hindu belief. They present, however, peculiarities which designate their belonging to a later period, and to an important modification in the progress of opinion. They repeat the theoretical cosmogony of the two great poems; they expand and systematize the chronological computations; and they give a more definite and connected representation of the mythological fictions, and the historical traditions. But besides these and other particulars, which may be derivable from an old, if not from a primitive era, they offer characteristic peculiarities of a more modern description, in the paramount importance which they assign to individual divinities, in the variety and purport of the rites and observances addressed to them, and in the invention of new legends illustrative of the power and graciousness of those deities, and of the efficacy of implicit devotion to them. Śiva and Vishṇu, under one or other form, are almost the sole objects that claim the homage of the Hindus in the Puránas; departing from the domestic and elemental ritual of the Vedas, and exhibiting a sectarial fervour and exclusiveness not traceable in the Rámáyana, and only to a qualified extent in the Mahábhárata. They are no longer authorities for Hindu belief as a whole; they are special guides for separate and sometimes conflicting branches of it, compiled for the evident purpose of promoting the preferential, or in some cases the sole worship of Vishṇu or of Śiva.

"That the Puránas always bore the character here given of them, may admit of reasonable doubt; that it correctly applies to them as they now are met with, the following pages will irrefragably substantiate. It is possible, however, that there may have been an earlier class of Puránas, of which those we now have are but the partial and adulterated representatives. The identity of the legends in many of them, and still more the identity of the words—for in several of them long passages are literally the same—is a sufficient proof that in all such cases they must be copied either from some other similar work, or from a common and prior original. It is not unusual also for a fact to be stated upon the authority of an 'old stanza,' which is cited accordingly; shewing the existence of an earlier source of information: and in very many instances legends are alluded to, not told; evincing acquaintance with their prior narration somewhere else. The name itself, Purána, which implies 'old,' indicates the object of the compilation to be the preservation of ancient traditions, a purpose in the present condition of the Purânas very imperfectly fulfilled. Whatever weight may be attached to these considerations, there is no disputing evidence to the like effect afforded by other and unquestionable authority. The description given by Mr. Colebrooke of the contents of a Purána is taken from Sanskrit writers. The Lexicon of Amara Sinha gives as a synonym of Purána, Pauchalakshanam, 'that which has five characteristic topics :' and there is no difference of opinion amongst the scholiasts as to what these are. They are, as Mr. Colebrooke mentions ; 1, Primary creation, or cosmogony ; 2, Secondary creation, or the destruction and renovation of worlds, including chronology ; 3, Genealogy of gods and patriarchs ; 4, Reigns of the Manus, or periods called Manwantaras ; and 5, History, or such particulars as have been preserved of the princes of the solar and lunar races, and of their descendants to modern times. Such, at any rate, were the constituent and characteristic portions of a Purána in the days of Amara Sinha, fifty-six years before the Christian era ; and if the Purânas had undergone no change since his time, such we should expect to find them still. Do they conform to this description ? Not exactly in any one instance ; to some of them it is utterly inapplicable ; to others it only partially applies. There is not one to which it belongs so entirely as to the Vishṇu Purána, and it is one of the circumstances which gives to this work a more authentic character than most of its fellows can pretend to. Yet even in this instance we have a book upon the institutes of society and obsequial rites interposed between the Manwantaras and the genealogies of princes, and a life of Krishṇa separating the latter from an account of the end of the world, besides the insertion of various legends of a manifestly popular and sectarial character. No doubt many of the Purânas, as they now are, correspond with the view which Col. Vans Kennedy takes of their purport. "I cannot discover in them," he remarks, "any other object than that of religious instruction." The description of the earth and of the planetary system, and the lists of royal races which occur in them, he asserts to be "evidently extraneous, and not essential circumstances, as they are entirely omitted in some Purânas, and very concisely illustrated in others; while, on the contrary, in all the Puránas some or other of the leading principles, rites, and observances of the Hindu religion are fully dwelt upon, and illustrated either by suitable legends or by prescribing the ceremonies to be practised, and the prayers and invocations to be employed, in the worship of different deities." Now, however accurate this description may be of the Puránas as they are, it is clear that it does not apply to what they were when they were synonymously designated as Pancha-lakshanas, or 'treatises on five topics;' not one of which five is ever specified by text or comment to be "religious instruction." In the knowledge of Amara Sinha the lists of princes were not extraneous and unessential, and their being now so considered by a writer so well acquainted with the contents of the Puránas as Col. Vans Kennedy, is a decisive proof that since the days of the lexicographer they have undergone some material alteration, and that we have not at present the same works in all respects that were current under the denomination of Puránas in the century prior to Christianity.

"The inference deduced from the discrepancy between the actual form and the older definition of a Purána, unfavourable to the antiquity of the extant works generally, is converted into certainty when we come to examine them in detail; for although they have no dates attached to them, yet circumstances are sometimes mentioned or alluded to, or references to authorities are made, or legends are narrated, or places are particularized, of which the comparatively recent date is indisputable, and which enforce a corresponding reduction of the antiquity of the work in which they are discovered. At the same time they may be acquitted of subservience to any but sectarial imposture. They were pious frauds for temporary purposes: they never emanated from any impossible combination of the Brahmans to fabricate for the antiquity of the entire Hindu system any claims which it cannot fully support. A very great portion of the contents of many, some portion of the contents of all, is genuine and old. The sectarial interpolation or embellishment is always sufficiently palpable to be set aside, without injury to the more authentic and primitive material; and the Puránas, although they belong especially to that stage of the Hindu religion in which faith in some one divinity was the prevailing principle, are also a valuable record of the form of Hindu belief which came next in order to that of the Vedas ; which grafted hero-worship upon the simpler ritual of the latter ; and which had been adopted, and was extensively, perhaps universally, established in India at the time of the Greek invasion. The Hercules of the Greek writers was indubitably the Balaráma of the Hindus ; and their notices of Mathurá on the Jumna, and of the kingdom of the Suraseni and the Pandæan country, evidence the prior currency of the traditions which constitute the argument of the Mahábhárata, and which are constantly repeated in the Puránas, relating to the Paṇḍava and Yádava races, to Krishṇa and his contemporary heroes, and to the dynasties of the solar and lunar kings.

"The theogony and cosmogony of the Puránas may probably be traced to the Vedas. They are not, as far as is yet known, described in detail in those works, but they are frequently alluded to in a strain more or less mystical and obscure, which indicates acquaintance with their existence, and which seems to have supplied the Puránas with the groundwork of their systems. The scheme of primary or elementary creation they borrow from the Sánkhya philosophy, which is probably one of the oldest forms of speculation on man and nature amongst the Hindus. Agreeably, however, to that part of the Pauráṇik character which there is reason to suspect of later origin, their inculcation of the worship of a favourite deity, they combine the interposition of a creator with the independent evolution of matter, in a somewhat contradictory and unintelligible style. It is evident too that their accounts of secondary creation, or the developement of the existing forms of things, and the disposition of the universe, are derived from several and different sources ; and it appears very likely that they are to be accused of some of the incongruities and absurdities by which the narrative is disfigured, in consequence of having attempted to assign reality and significancy to what was merely metaphor or mysticism. There is, however, amidst the unnecessary complexity of the description, a general agreement amongst them as to the origin of things, and their final distribution ; and in many of the circumstances there is a striking concurrence with the ideas which seem to have pervaded the whole of the ancient world, and which we may therefore believe to be faithfully represented in the Purânas.

"The Pantheism of the Purânas in one of their invariable characteristics, although the particular divinity, who is all things, from whom all things proceed, and to whom all things return, be diversified according to their individual sectarial bias. They seem to have derived the notion from the Vedas: but in them the one universal Being is of a higher order than a personification of attributes or elements, and, however imperfectly conceived, or unworthily described, is God. In the Purânas the one only Supreme Being is supposed to be manifest in the person of Śiva or Vishṇu, either in the way of illusion or in sport; and one or other of these divinities is therefore also the cause of all that is, is himself all that exists. The identity of God and nature is not a new notion; it was very general in the speculations of antiquity, but it assumed a new vigour in the early ages of Christianity, and was carried to an equal pitch of extravagance by the Platonic Christians as by the Saiva or Vaishṇava Hindus. It seems not impossible that there was some communication between them. We know that there was an active communication between India and the Red Sea in the early ages of the Christian era, and that doctrines, as well as articles of merchandise, were brought to Alexandria from the former. Epiphanius and Eusebius accuse Scythianus of having imported from India, in the second century, books on magic, and heretical notions leading to Manichæism, and it was at the same period that Ammonius instituted the sect of the new Platonists at Alexandria. The basis of his heresy was, that true philosophy derived its origin from the eastern nations: his doctrine of the identity of God and the universe is that of the Vedas and Purânas; and the practices he enjoined, as well as their object, were precisely those described in several of the Purânas under the name of Yóga. His disciples were taught "to extenuate by mortification and contemplation the bodily restraints upon the immortal spirit, so that in his life they might enjoy communion with the Supreme Being, and ascend after death to the universal parent." That these are Hindu tenets the following pages will testify; and by the admission of their Alexandrian teacher, they originated in India. The importation was perhaps not wholly unrequited; the loan may not have been left unpaid. It is not impossible that the Hindu doctrines received fresh animation from their adoption by the successors of Ammonius, and especially by the mystics, who may have prompted, as well as employed, the expressions of the Purāṇas. Anquetil du Perron has given, in the introduction to his translation of the 'Oupnekhat,' several hymns by Synesius, a bishop of the beginning of the fifth century, which may serve as parallels to many of the hymns and prayers addressed to Vishṇu in the Vishṇu Purána.

"But the ascription to individual and personal deities of the attributes of the one universal and spiritual Supreme Being, is an indication of a later date than the Vedas certainly, and apparently also than the Rámáyana, where Ráma, although an incarnation of Vishṇu, commonly appears in his human character alone. There is something of the kind in the Mahábhárata in respect to Krishṇa, especially in the philosophical episode known as the Bhagavat Gítá. In other places the divine nature of Krishṇa is less decidedly affirmed; in some it is disputed or denied; and in most of the situations in which he is exhibited in action, it is as a prince and warrior, not as a divinity. He exercises no superhuman faculties in the defence of himself or his friends, or in the defeat and destruction of his foes. The Mahábhárata, however, is evidently a work of various periods, and requires to be read throughout carefully and critically before its weight as an authority can be accurately appreciated. As it is now in type—thanks to the public spirit of the Asiatic Society of Bengal, and their Secretary, Mr. J. Prinsep—it will not be long before the Sanskrit scholars of the continent will accurately appreciate its value.

"The Purānas are also works of evidently different ages, and have been compiled under different circumstances, the precise nature of which we can imperfectly conjecture from internal evidence, and from what we know of the history of religious opinion in India. It is highly probable, that of the present popular forms of the Hindu religion, none assumed their actual state earlier than the time of Śankara Ácharya, the great Śaiva reformer, who flourished, in all likelihood, in the eighth or ninth century. Of the Vaishnava teachers, Rámánuja dates in the twelfth century, Madhwácharya in the thirteenth, and Vallabha in the sixteenth; and the Puránas seem to have accompanied or followed their innovations, being obviously intended to advocate the doctrines they taught. This is to assign to some of them a very modern date, it is true; but I cannot think that a higher can with justice be ascribed to them. This, however, applies to some only out of the number, as I shall presently proceed to specify.

"Another evidence of a comparatively modern date must be admitted in those chapters of the Puráṇas which, assuming a prophetic tone, foretell what dynasties of kings will reign in the Kalí age. These chapters, it is true, are found but in four of the Puráṇas, but they are conclusive in bringing down the date of those four to a period considerably subsequent to Christianity. It is also to be remarked, that the Váyu, Vishṇu, Bhágavata, and Matsya Puráṇas, in which these particulars are foretold, have in all other respects the character of as great antiquity as any works of their class.

"The invariable form of the Puráṇas is that of a dialogue, in which some person relates its contents in reply to the inquiries of another. This dialogue is interwoven with others, which are repeated as having been held on other occasions between different individuals, in consequence of similar questions having been asked. The immediate narrator is commonly, though not constantly, Lomaharshaṇa or Romaharshaṇa, the disciple of Vyása, who is supposed to communicate what was imparted to him by his preceptor, as he had heard it from some other sage. Vyása, as will be seen in the body of the work, is a generic title, meaning an 'arranger' or 'compiler.' It is in this age applied to Krishṇa Dwaipáyana, the son of Paráṣara, who is said to have taught the Vedas and Puránas to various disciples, but who appears to have been the head of a college or school, under whom various learned men gave to the sacred literature of the Hindus the form in which it now presents itself. In this task the disciples, as they are termed, of Vyása were rather his colleagues and coadjutors, for they were already conversant with what he is fabled to have taught them ; and amongst them, Lomaharshaṇa represents the class of persons who were especially charged with the record of political and temporal events. He is called Súta, as if it was a proper name ; but it is more correctly a title ; and Lomaharshaṇa was 'a Súta,' that is, a bard or panegyrist, who was created, according to the text, to celebrate the exploits of princes ; and who, according to the Váyu and Pádma Puráṇas, has a right by birth and profession to narrate the Puráṇas, in preference even to the Brahmans. It is not unlikely therefore that we are to understand, by his being represented as the disciple of Vyása, the institution of some attempt, made under the direction of the latter, to collect from the heralds and annalists of his day the scattered traditions which they had imperfectly preserved ; and hence the consequent appropriation of the Puráṇas, in a great measure, to the genealogies of regal dynasties, and descriptions of the universe. However this may be, the machinery has been but loosely adhered to, and many of the Puráṇas, like the Vishṇu, are referred to a different narrator." *Preface to V. P.*

"The Puráṇas are uniformly stated to be eighteen in number. It is said that there are also eighteen Upa-Puráṇas, or minor Puráṇas, but many of them are not now procurable. The following eighteen are specified in the Deví Bhágavata :—

1.	Sanatkumára.	10.	Kálika.
2.	Nárasinha.	11.	Sámba.
3.	Naradiya.	12.	Nandi.
4.	Śiva.	13.	Saura.
5.	Durvasasa.	14.	Páráṣara.
6.	Kapila.	15.	Áditya.
7.	Manava.	16.	Máheṣwara.
8.	Ausanaṣa.	17.	Bhargava.
9.	Varuṇa.	18.	Vasishtha.

Of the contents of these books very little is known. There are many local legends of particular temples which are sometimes designated Upa-Puráṇas. Many ancient notions and traditions are preserved in the Puráṇas, but they have been so much mixed up with sectarian views, intended to favour the popularity of particular forms of worship, or articles of faith, that they cannot be received as authorities for the mythological religion of the Hindus at any remote period."

Purandara—The Indra of the seventh (the present) Manwantara.

Puranjaya—1, A king of Ayodhya ; son of Vikukshi, whose reign preceded that of Ikshváku. Puranjaya assisted the gods in their contest with the Asuras. As he destroyed the demon host whilst seated on the hump of a bull, he obtained the appellation Kakutstha, q. v ; 2, A prince, the son of Srinjaya ; 3, A Yavana chief, the son of Vindhyaṣakti.

Puravati—A river not identified.

Purohita—A family priest, or chaplain. "The most ancient name for a priest by profession," says Prof. Max Müller "is Puróhita, which means *prepositus* or *prœses*. The Puróhita, however, was more than a priest. He was the friend and counsellor of the chief, the minister of the king, and his companion in peace and war. The original occupation of the Puróhita may have consisted in the performance of the usual sacrifices ; but, with the ambitious policy of the Brahmans, it soon became a stepping stone to political power."

The office of a Puróhita now-a-days is, in the words of the Abbé Dubois, to prognosticate what are good and what are evil days for beginning any affair, or for putting it off ; to avert, by Mantras or prayers, the pernicious effects of maledictions or the influence of malign constellations ; to assign names to new born children and calculate their nativity ; to bless new houses, wells, or tanks ; to purify temples and consecrate them ; to imbue idols with the divine essence : all these ceremonies, and many others of smaller importance, are the province of the Brahmans called Puróhitas.

The most important of the ceremonies over which they preside are those of marriages and burials. They are so complex that an ordinary Brahman would be found incapable of performing them. A regular study is necessary for the exactness and precision which they require ; and Mantras are requisite of which the greater part are ignorant. The Puróhitas alone are accomplished in the management of these rites, the detail of which they have in writing, in certain formularies, which they permit nobody to see, not even the other Brahmans. Indeed the principal Mantras that are used are not reduced into writing, from the fear that some other Brahmans might acquire them, and so become their rivals, to the diminution of their exclusive profits. The father teaches them to his son, and thus they pass from generation to generation in one family. This shows that it is self-interest rather than superstition which occasions this reserve. By hindering the other Brahmans from learning these ceremonies and the corresponding Mantras, the Puróhitas render themselves more necessary to the people, and to the Brahmans themselves, who cannot dispense with their services on many occasions.

One of the highest privileges attached to the profession of the Puróhita is the exclusive right of publishing the Hindu Almanac. There are but few who are found capable of making the calculations ; perhaps one or two only in a district. It is not upon a knowledge of the motions of the heavenly bodies that the Hindu Almanac is compiled, but upon the approximation and agreement of numerous tables and formulæ of great antiquity, and therefore the calculation is very complicated, and much time, attention, and labour is required to arrive at exact conclusions.

On the first day of the year, the Puróhita assembles the principal inhabitants of the place where he lives. In their presence he announces, by sound of trumpet, who is to be supreme over the stars. He determines also the quantity of rain and of drought, and foretells, in short, whether it is to be a year of health or of disease ; whether the deaths or the births shall predominate, and many other contingencies of equal importance.

The Puróhita is essentially a family priest and a religious preceptor. Amongst the poorer classes he may officiate for very many families, in which case he employs assistants, and gives them a stipulated share of the gifts and other perquisites which he may receive. But amongst the richer classes, the duties of a Puróhita are confined to a single family, and under such circumstances his influence becomes paramount in the household. He performs all the necessary religious rites and ceremonies for the members of the family, and imparts religious instruction from the sacred books. At the same time, he is the repository of all the family secrets, and the confidential and authoritative counsellor in all times of doubt and difficulty. He is also frequently engaged in more secular matters, such as the settlement of disputes ; and in modern times a Hindu Zemindar or Rája has occasionally employed his Puróhita as an ambassador or envoy.

Purnasa—(Parnasa). A river that rises in the Páripátra mountain.

Purnotsanga—One of the thirty Andhrabhritya kings, the son of Sri Sátakarni ; his reign lasted eighteen years.

Puru—1, One of the sons of the Manu Chakshusha ; 2, the youngest son of king Yayáti, who consented to give his youth and vigour to his father, and receive in exchange Yayáti's infirmities. After Yayáti had had a thousand years experience of the vanity of sensual pleasures, he restored his youth to Puru, and installed him in the sovereignty of Pratishthána. The descendants of Puru were numerous and celebrated ; and included the Páṇḍavas and Kauravas. See page 367.

Puruhotia—A prince, the son of Anuratha, one of the descendants of Jyámagha.

Purujanu—One of the kings of Kámpilya, the son of Suṣánti.

Purukutsa—A king, who reigned in the banks of the Narmada, to whom the Vishṇu Puráṇa was repeated. He was the son of Mándhátri, and assisted the snake-gods by destroying the Gandharbas in the regions below the earth.

Purumidha—One of the sons of Hastin, the founder of Hastinápur.

Pururavas—The son of Budha and Sudyumna (Ila.) He was a prince renowned for liberality, devotion, magnificence, love of truth, and for personal beauty. Urvaṣí having incurred the imprecation of Mitra and Varuṇa, determined to take up her abode in the world of mortals; and descending accordingly, beheld Purúravas. As soon as she saw him she forgot all reserve, and disregarding the delights of Swarga, became deeply enamoured of the prince. Beholding her infinitely superior to all other females in grace, elegance, symmetry, delicacy, and beauty, Purúravas was equally fascinated by Urvaṣí : both were inspired by similar sentiments, and mutually feeling that each was every thing to the other, thought no more of any other object. Confiding in his merits, Purúravas addressed the nymph, and said, "Fair creature, I love you; have compassion on me, and return my affection." Urvaṣí, half averting her face through modesty, replied, "I will do so, if you will observe the conditions I have to propose." "What are they?" inquired the prince; "declare them." "I have two rams," said the nymph, "which I love as children; they must be kept near my bedside, and never suffered to be carried away: you must also take care never to be seen by me undressed; and clarified butter alone must be my food." To these terms the king readily gave assent.

After this, Purúravas and Urvaṣí dwelt together in Alaká, sporting amidst the groves and lotus-crowned lakes of Chaitraratha, and the other forests there situated, for sixty-one thousand years. The love of Purúravas for his bride increased every day of its duration; and the affection of Urvaṣí augmenting equally in fervour, she never called to recollection residence amongst the immortals. Not so with the attendant spirits at the court of Indra; and nymphs, genii, and quiristers, found heaven itself but dull whilst Urvaṣí was away. Knowing the agreement that Urvaṣí had made with the king, Viswavasu was appointed by the Gandharbas to effect its violation; and he, coming by night to the chamber where they slept, carried off one of the rams. Urvaṣí was awakened by its cries, and exclaimed, "Ah me! who has stolen one of my children? Had I a husband, this would not have happened! To whom shall I apply for aid?" The Rája overheard her lamentation, but recollecting that he was undressed, and that Urvaṣí might see him in that state, did not move from the couch. Then the Gandharbas came and stole the other ram; and Urvaṣí, hearing it bleat, cried out that a woman had no protector who was the bride of a prince so dastardly as to submit to this outrage. This incensed Purúravas highly, and trusting that the nymph would not see his person, as it was dark, he rose, and took his sword, and pursued the robbers, calling upon them to stop, and receive their punishment. At that moment the Gandharbas caused a flash of brilliant lightning to play upon the chamber, and Urvaṣí beheld the king undressed: the compact was violated, and the nymph immediately disappeared. The Gandharbas, abandoning the rams, departed to the region of the gods.

Having recovered the animals, the king returned delighted to his couch, but there he beheld no Urvaṣí; and not finding her anywhere, he wandered naked over the world, like one insane. At length coming to Kurukshetra, he saw Urvaṣí sporting with four other nymphs of heaven in a lake beautified with lotuses, and he ran to her, and called her his wife, and wildly implored her to return. "Mighty monarch," said the nymph, "refrain from this extravagance. I am now pregnant: depart at present, and come hither again at the end of a year, when I will deliver to you a son, and remain with you for one night." Purúravas, thus comforted, returned to his capital. Urvaṣí said to her companions, "This prince is a most excellent mortal: I lived with him long and affectionately united." "It was well done of you," they replied; "he is indeed of comely appearance, and one with whom we could live happily for ever."

When the year had expired, Urvaṣí and the monarch met at Kurukshetra, and she consigned to him his first-born Áyus; and these annual interviews were repeated, until she had borne to him five sons. She then said to Purúravas, "Through regard for me, all the Gandharbas have expressed their joint purpose to bestow upon my lord their benediction: let him therefore demand a boon." The Rája replied, "My enemies are all destroyed, my faculties are all entire; I have friends and kindred, armies and treasures: there is nothing which I may not attain except living in the same region with my Urvaṣí. My only desire therefore is, to pass my life with her." When he had thus spoken, the Gandharbas brought to Purúravas a vessel with fire, and said to him, "Take this fire, and, according to the precepts of the Vedas, divide it into three fires ; then fixing your mind upon the idea of living with Urvaṣí, offer oblations, and you shall assuredly obtain your wishes." The Rája took the brasier, and departed, and came to a forest. Then he began to reflect that he had committed a great folly in bringing away the vessel of fire instead of his bride ; and leaving the vessel in the wood, he went disconsolate to his palace. In the middle of the night he awoke, and considered that the Gandharbas had given him the brasier to enable him to obtain the felicity of living with Urvaṣí, and that it was absurd in him to have left it by the way. Resolving therefore to recover it, he rose, and went to the place where he had deposited the vessel ; but it was gone. In its stead he saw a young Áṣwattha tree growing out of a Śami plant, and he reasoned with himself, and said, " I left in this spot a vessel of fire, and now behold a young Áṣwattha tree growing out of a Śami plant. Verily I will take these types of fire to my capital, and there, having engendered fire by their attrition, I will worship it." V. P.

Having thus determined, he took the plants to his city, and prepared their wood for attrition, with pieces of as many inches long as there are syllables in the Gáyatrí ; he recited that holy verse, and rubbed together sticks of as many inches as he recited syllables in the Gáyatrí. Having thence elicited fire, he made it threefold, according to the injunctions of the Vedas, and offered oblations with it, proposing as the end of the ceremony reunion with Urvaṣí. In this way, celebrating many sacrifices agreeably to the form in which offerings are presented with fire, Purúravas obtained a seat in the sphere of the Gandharbas, and was no more separated from his beloved. Thus fire, that was at first but one, was made threefold in the present Manwantara by the son of Ilá."

Purúravas is also called Vikrama ; and the legend forms the subject of Kálidása's drama. " Vikrama and Urvaṣí ; or the Hero and Nymph." The legend as related in the Satapatha Brahmana differs from the above in several particulars. An explanation of the myth is given by Max Müller in his Comparative Mythology,* " One of the myths of the Veda which expresses this

Chips from a German Workshop, Vol. II, p. 101.

correlation of the Dawn and the Sun, this love between the mortal and the immortal, and the identity of the morning dawn and the evening twilight, is the story of Urvaṣí and Purúravas......Urvaṣí was originally an appellation and meant dawn." Another explanation is that Purúravas personifies the sun ; while Urvaṣí is the morning mist. Urvaṣí is an Apsarasas ; and the Apsarasas are "personifications of the vapours which are attracted by the sun, and form into mists or clouds." Dr. Goldstücker holds therefore that the legend represents the absorption by the sun of the vapour floating in the air. When Purúravas becomes distinctly visible, Urvaṣí vanishes ; because when the sun shines forth, the mist is absorbed.

Purusha—Spirit. The first form of Vishṇu. Mahat is also called Purusha from its abiding within the body.

Purushottama—A common title of Vishṇu, implying supreme best spirit.

Purva-bhadrapada—A lunar mansion in Vaiswánarí, in the Southern Avashthána.

Purvachitti—One of the Apsarasas ; of the Daivika or divine class.

Purvaja—An appellation of Vishṇu, meaning produced or appearing before creation ; the Orphic πρωτογονος : animating nature and existing before it.

Purvashada—A lunar mansion in Ajávithi, in the Southern Avashthána.

Purvaphalguni—A lunar mansion in Arshabhi, in the Central Avashthána,

Pushan—A solar deity. "Púshan is a protector and multiplier of cattle and of human possessions in general. As a cow-herd he carries an ox-goad, and he is drawn by goats. In character he is a solar deity, beholds the entire universe, and is a guide on roads and journeys, and to the other world. He is called the lover of his sister Súrya. He aids in the revolutions of day and night ; and shares with Soma the guardianship of living creatures. He is invoked along with the most various deities, but most frequently with Indra." He is the lord of all things moving and stationary, the inspirer of the soul, an unconquerable protector and defender, and is besought to give increase of wealth. He is said to regard and to see clearly and at once all creatures. He is not only the tutelary god of travellers, but also, like Savitṛi and Agni, and the Greek Hermes, αψυχοπομπος, who conducts departed spirits on their way to the other world. Many hymns are addressed to Púshan, some of which are translated by Dr. Muir, (O. S. T., V, p. 174) "from which it will appear that the character of this god is not very distinctly defined; and that it is difficult to declare positively what province of nature or of physical action he is designed to represent, as is at once manifest in the case of Dyaus, Pṛithivi, Agni, Indra, Parjanya, and Súrya."

Some of the hymns in the Rig Veda are exclusively devoted to the celebration of Púshan. The single or detached verses of other hymns in which he is mentioned are numerous. He is mentioned as 'abounding in wealth,' as 'bringing blessings' as 'most bountiful,' 'beneficient,' 'distinguished by all divine attributes.' He is associated with Savitṛi, and is described as moving onward under his impulse, and as knowing and perceiving all creatures. In some hymns Púshan is connected with the marriage ceremonial, being besought to take the bride's hand and lead her away, and to bless her in her conjugal relation.

Pushkalas—The designation of Kshatriyas in Krauncha Dwípa.

Pushkara—The last of the seven great insular continents, or Dwípas, encompassing the sea of milk, and being itself surrounded by a sea of fresh water. Pushkara is represented as a terrestial paradise; where all the inhabitants are happy, and rejoice in total exemption from sickness and decay. They live a thousand years undisturbed by anger or affection. There is neither virtue nor vice, killer nor slain: there is no jealousy, envy, fear, hatred, covetousness, nor any moral defect; neither is there truth or falsehood. V. P. 201.

Pushkara—1, One of the sons of Bharata; he was king of Gandhára, residing at Pushkaravati; 2, The brother of Nala, who engaged him in the gambling match which cost him his kingdom. (See NALA.)

Pushkaras—The designation of brahmans in Krauncha Dwípa.

Pushkaravarttakas—A designation of the class of clouds Pakshaja ; so termed from their including water in their vortices ; they are the largest and most formidable of all, and are those which, at the end of the Yugas and Kalpas, pour down the waters of the deluge.

Pushkarin—A prince the son of Urukshaya, a descendant of Bharata.

Pushkarini—The daughter of the patriarch Anaranya, and mother of the Maṇu Chákshusha.

Pushpadanta—One of Śiva's principal attendants. "On the summit of Kailása, a lofty peak of the Himálaya range, resided the mighty deity Maheṣwara, attended by innumerable spirits and genii, and worshipped even by the superior divinities. The daughter of the mountain monarch, and the spouse of Mahadeva, propitiated her lord by her celestial strains ; and, being pleased by her adulations, he proffered her whatever boon she might request. Her only demand was to receive instruction from his lips, and to hear from him such narrations as were yet unknown to the immortals or herself.. Śiva, giving orders that no person should be admitted, proceeded to reveal to the goddess those narratives which illustrate the felicity of the gods, the troubles of mankind, and the intermediate and varying conditions of the spirits of earth and heaven.

It happened that Pushpadanta came to the palace gate and was refused admission by the warder. As he was a great favourite with his master and had always ready access to his person, the refusal excited his astonishment and curiosity ; and, rendering himself invisible, he passed in, determined to ascertain why entrance was so rigorously barred. In this manner having come to where Śiva and Bhaváni were seated, he over-heard all the marvellous stories repeated by the deity. When these were concluded, he retired as he had entered, unobserved, and going home communicated the narrative to his wife Jayá, it being impossible to keep wealth or secrets from a woman. Jayá, equally unable to preserve silence, communicated what she had heard to her fellow attendants on Párvatí ; and the affair soon became known to the goddess and her lord. As the punishment of impertinence, Pushpadanta was condemned to a human birth, and his friend Málÿavan, who presumed to intercede for him, was sentenced to a like fate. Being, however, subdued by the distress of Jayá, the offended goddess fixed a term to their degradation, and thus spake. 'When Pushpadanta, encountering a Yaksha, who has been doomed by Kuvera to haunt the Vindhya mountains as a goblin, shall recollect his original condition, and shall repeat the tales he has rashly over-heard, the curse shall no more prevail.' So saying, she ceased, and the two culprits, instantly, like a flash of lightning, blazed and disappeared.

After a due interval Pushpadanta was born at Kauṣámbí as Vararuchi, and when arrived at years of discretion found the goblin, and recollecting his origin, repeated to him the seven great narratives of Śiva, each comprehending a hundred thousand verses.—*Wilson's Works, III*, 160-163.

Pushpadantha—One of the serpent kings ; of the progeny of Kadru.

Pushpaka—The name of Ráma's car.

Pushpatmitra—The first king of the Sunga Dynasty ; he reigned at Mekala, a country on the Narbada ; he was the general of the last Maurya prince, whom he put to death, and ascended the throne himself ; the dynasty lasted a hundred and twelve years.

Pushpavat—A prince, the son of Rishabha.

Pushpottara—One of the heavens of the Jainas. When Priyamitra returned to the earth in the Bhárata division as Nandana, after an existence of twenty-five lakhs of years, he was raised to the dignity of king of the gods in the Pushpottara heaven, in which capacity he preserved his ancient faith, offering flowers to, and bathing daily, the hundred and eighty images of the Arhats. Such exalted piety was now to meet with its reward, and the pains of existence were to be terminated in the person of the Tírthankara Mahávíra or Varddhamána.—*Wilson, I*, 293.

Pushti—'Thriving' ; 1, A daughter of Daksha and wife of Dharma ; 2, A daughter of Paurṇamása.

Pushya—1, A prince, the son of the saintly king Yajnawalkya; 2, The eighth lunar mansion; in Airávata, in the Northern Avashthana.

> "The morning dawned with cloudless ray
> On Pushya's high auspicious day,
> And Cancer with benignant power
> Looked down on Ráma's natal hour."

Puskola—The palm leaf upon which the native books are written in Ceylon.

Putana—A female fiend or Asura, the daughter of Bali; she was known as a child killer, and attempted the life of Krishṇa when he was an infant, but was killed herself in the act.

Putra—One of the three sons of Priyavrata who adopted a religious life; remembering the occurrences of a prior existence, he did not covet dominion, but diligently practiced the rites of devotion.

Puyavaha—One of the Narakas, that in which crimes of violence, &c., are punished.

R

Radha—One of Krishṇa's favourite mistresses. The Gíta Govinda is a poem on their attachment to each other. The poet opens the first interview of Krishṇa and Rádha with an animated description of a night in the rainy season, in which Krishṇa is represented as a wanderer, and Rádha, daughter of the shepherd Naṇda, is sent to offer him shelter in their cottage. Naṇda thus speaks to Rádha "The firmament is obscured by clouds ; the woodlands are black with Tamála trees ; that youth who roves in the forest will be fearful in the gloom of night ; go, my daughter, bring the wanderer to my rustic mansion." Such was the command of Naṇda the herdsman, and hence arose the love of Rádha and Madhava.*

Raga—Love. One of "the five afflictions" in the Patanjala philosophy ; the other four are Avidya, Asmitá, Dwesha, and Abhinivesa.

Raghu—A distinguished mythical Mahárája of the solar race, the son of Dilípa, and sovereign of Ayodhya, celebrated for his learning, his riches, his bravery, and his uniform success. The Raghuvansa narrates his wonderful achievements and varied conquests, and concludes with the following legend. A brahman named Koutsya, a disciple of the great Rishi Varatanta, having completed his course of studies, asked his guru what acknowledgment he should make to show his gratitude. The tutor professed himself satisfied with the services the disciple had rendered ; the latter, however, insisting on bestowing a gift, the guru asked for fourteen crores of rupees. For this enormous sum Koutsya applied to Mahárája Raghu, who having just emptied his treasury by the performance of the sacrifice termed Visvajit-yajna, determined to conquer Kubera (the god of riches), who was so alarmed at the prospect that he at once sent innumerable crores to the Mahárája.

---

* Tod's Rajast'han, Vol. I, p. 540, which contains a beautiful engraving of Krishṇa and Rádha.

The money was then given to the brahman, who in return blessed the king with the promise of a good son, and in due course the illustrious *Aja* was born.

Raghu—1, A prince of the lunar race, the son of Dírghabáhu ; 2, One of the sons of Yadu, the founder of the Yádava race.

Raghuvansa—An epic poem by Kálidása. The poem describes the exploits of a line of princes descended from the Sun, of whom Ráma was the boast and ornament. It has been translated into Latin by Stenzler, and into French by M. Hippolyte Fauche. The Idylls from the Sanskrit by Mr. T. H. Griffiths are chiefly taken from the Raghuvansa. See DILIPA.

Rahat—One who is entirely free from evil desire, and in consequence possessed of supernatural powers.

Rahu—One of the nine planets of the Hindus ; an imaginary being supposed to cause the eclipses of the sun and moon. Ráhu according to the Pádma Purána and Bhágavata, was the son of the Dánava Viprachitti ; at the churning of the sea of milk he insinuated himself amongst the gods, and obtained a portion of the Amrita or nectar ; the sun and the moon observed the theft, and informed Vishṇu of it, who, as a punishment beheaded the Daitya ; the head became immortal in consequence of the Amrita having reached the throat, and was transferred as a constellation to the skies ; and as the sun and moon detected his presence amongst the gods and made known his theft, Ráhu pursues them with implacable hatred, and his efforts to seize them are the causes of eclipses ; Ráhu typifying the ascending and descending nodes. Ráhu is also called the king of meteors. The Vishṇu Purána states that eight black horses draw the dusky chariot of Ráhu, and once harnessed are attached to it for ever. On the Parvas (the nodes, or lunar and solar eclipses) Ráhu directs his course from the sun to the moon and back again from the moon to the sun, taking up the circular shadow of the earth.

Rahula—A prince, the son of Sákya. A name, says Dr. Wilson, of considerable chronological interest ; for Sákya is the name of the author or reviver of Buddhism, whose birth appears to have occurred in the seventh, and death in the sixth century before Christ (B. C. 621—543.) Sákya, as the twenty-second of the line of Ikshváku is contemporary with Ripunjaya, the last of the kings of Magadha. The chronology is not easily adjusted, but it is not altogether incompatible. The Buddhists always consider their teacher Sákya to be descended from Ikshváku. In Tibet, where several sects of Buddhists are found, some of them profess themselves to be followers of Ráhula.

Raivata—1, One of the sons of Priyavrata according to the Bhágavata list, and the Manu of the fifth Manwantara. Four Manus were descended from Priyavrata, who in consequence of propitiating Vishṇu by his devotions, obtained these rulerships of the Manwantara, for his posterity. The Markaṇḍeya contains a legend of the birth of Raivata, as the son of king Durgama, by the nymph Revatí, sprung from the constellation Revatí.

2. An appellation of one of the eleven Rudras.

3. A name of Kakudmin (q. v.) the eldest of the sons of Revatí ; he visited Brahmá, and gave his daughter in marriage to Balaráma.

4. The name of a mountain.

Raja—A prince, the son of Virája a descendant of Bharata. Rája is derived from Ráj, to shine or be splendid.

Rajadhidevi—A daughter of Súra, who was married to Jayasena, king of Avantí.

Rajagaha—A city near Benares, celebrated as the residence of Gautama Buddha, and the place where he died.

Rajagriha—The ancient capital of Magadha or Behár, containing many remarkable ruins.

Rajarshis—Royal Rishis, or princes who have adopted a life of devotion, as Viswámitra, Ikshváku, and others ; they dwell in the heaven of Indra.

Rajas—The quality of foulness, passion, activity.

Rajas—One of the seven sages, according to the enumeration in the Vishṇu Purána ; they were all the sons of Vaṣishta.

Rajyavarddhana—A prince, the son of Dama, a descendant of Marutta.

Rajavat—The son of Dyutimat, of the race of Bhrigu.

Raji—One of the five sons of Áyus. He is celebrated for having assisted the gods in their contest with the demons, and " by his numerous and formidable weapons" securing to them the victory. In consequence of this Indra resigned his throne to Raji.

Rajni—The daughter of Raivata and wife of Vivaswat.

Raka—1, One of the phases of the moon, represented as one of the four daughters of Angiras ; 2, The day when the moon is quite round.

Rakhi—A bracelet used as an armlet, or preservative against evil (Ráksha) consisting of a piece of thread or silk or some more costly material, bound round the wrist or arm, with an appropriate prayer. Besides its application to children to avert the effects of evil eyes, or to protect them against Dains or witches, there is one day in the year, the Rákhí Purnimá, or full moon in the month of Sravan (July—August) when it is bound upon the wrists of adults, by friendly or kindred brahmans, with a short prayer or benediction. The Rákhí is also sent sometimes by persons of distinction, and especially by females, to members of a different family or race to intimate a sort of brotherly or sisterly adoption. Colonel Tod received the bracelet from three queens in Rajasthan, and after he returned to his own country set a high value on these testimonies of friendly regard.—*(Wilson.)*

In his Annals he says, " The festival of the Rákhí is in spring, and whatever its origin it is one of the few when an intercourse of gallantry of the most delicate nature is established between the fair sex and the cavaliers of Rajasthan. Though the bracelet may be sent by maidens, it is only on occasion of urgent necessity or danger. The Rájput dame bestows with the Rákhí the title of adopted brother ; and while its acceptance secures to her all the protection of a '*cavaliere serventé*,' scandal itself never suggests any other tie to his devotion. He may hazard his life in her cause, and yet never receive a smile in reward, for he cannot even see the fair object who, as the brother of her adoption, has constituted him her defender. But there is a charm in the mystery of such connexions, never endangered by close observation, and the loyal to the fair may well attach a value to the public recognition of being the Rákhí-bund Bháe, the 'bracelet-bound-brother' of a princess. The intrinsic value of such pledge is never looked to, nor is it requisite it should be costly, though it varies with the means and rank of the donor, and may be of flock silk and spangles, or gilt chains and gems. The acceptance of the pledge and its return is by the *kalchli* or corset of simple silk, or satin, or gold brocade and pearls. In shape or application there is nothing similar in Europe, and as defending the most delicate part of the structure of the fair, it is peculiarly appropriate as an emblem of devotion.

The emperor Humáyún was so pleased with this courteous delicacy in the customs of Rajasthan, on receiving the bracelet of the princess Kurnavati, which invested him with the title of her brother, and uncle and protector to her infant, that he pledged himself to her service. He proved himself a true knight, and abandoned his conquests in Bengal when called on to redeem his pledge. Many romantic tales are founded on the gift of the Rákhí. See Tod's Rajasthan, I, 312.

Rakshas—The son of Khasá, and father of the Rákshasas.

Rakshasa-ritual—By violence. Manu says, the seizure of a maiden by force, whilst she weeps and calls for assistance, after her kinsmen and friends have been slain in battle or wounded, and their houses broken open, is the marriage called Rákshasa.

Rakshasas—Giants. They are said in the Vishṇu Purána to be the descendants of Pulastya, through Rákshas. They are also represented in the same work as having proceeded from Brahmá; beings of hideous aspect, and with long beards. They hastened to the deity; such of them as exclaimed "Oh! preserve us," were thence called Rákshasas (from Raksha to preserve); others who cried out, "let us eat," were denominated Yakshas from (yaksha to eat.)

"In their earliest conception," says Mr. J. C. Thomson, "they seem to be those unknown creatures of darkness, to which the superstition of all ages and races has attributed the evils that attend this life, and a malignant desire to injure mankind. In the Epic period they seem to be personifications of the aborigines of India, presented under the terrible aspect of vampires flying through the air, sucking blood, &c., in order to heighten the triumphs of the Aryan heroes who subdued them. In this character they play a very prominent part on the Rámáyaṇa, the beautiful epic of Válmíki. Here they are led by Rávaṇa, the king of Lanka, which is supposed to be the island of Ceylon and its capital, and they are subdued by Dasaratha Ráma the hero of the poem. In the Puránic period they are infernal giants, the children of the Rishi Pulastya, and enemies of the gods. They are then divided into three classes :—

1. The slaves of Kuvera the god of wealth, and guardians of of his treasures.
2. Malevolent imps whose chief delight is to disturb the pious in their devotions.
3. Giants of enormous proportions, inhabiting Naraka, or hell, and hostile to the gods. In the second Manwantara they are the sons of Kaṣyapa and Khasá."

The most celebrated Rákshakas are Rávaṇa, and his brothers Kumbhakarna and Vibhíshana, an account of whom will be found under their respective names.

Rama—This name belongs altogether to the epic period, and is given to three persons of considerable historical importance, whose mighty deeds won for them the privilege of being considered incarnations of Vishṇu. The first is *Parasuráma,* or Rama of the Axe. He is considered as the sixth Avatára of Vishṇu, and belongs to the period of the first struggle between the Brahmans and the Kshatriyas, the hierarchy and the government.

He is said to have been the son of a certain Muni called Jamadagni ; (q. v.) but as his mother Kenuka was a lady of the Kshatriya caste, and as the children follow the caste of their mother, he is not, like his father, a Brahman by birth, although he espoused the Brahman cause, and afterward himself became a Muni. The legend relates that the princess, his mother, having committed a sin, his father commanded his sons to put her to death.

All refused except Ráma, the youngest, who seized his axe and felled her to the ground. In reward for this triumph of duty over feeling he received the gift of invincibility. Afterwards when Kártavírya, king of the Haiheyas, coveted the divine cow Kámadhénu which belonged to the Muni, and took it from him by force, when he was on a visit to Jamadagni, Ráma went forth to recover the cow, and soon killed the robber king. The sons of Kártavírya, to revenge his death, attacked the hermitage of Jamadagni, when Ráma was away, and slew the pious and unresisting sage, who called repeatedly but fruitlessly, upon his valiant son. Ráma returned to bewail his father's unmerited fate, and having lighted his funeral pile, vowed that he would extirpate the whole Kshatriya race. "Thrice seven times did he clear the earth of the Kshatriya caste," says the Mahábhárata ; Paraṣuráma was born at the beginning of the Treta Yuga (Second age.)

2. The second Ráma is the most celebrated of all. He is sometimes designated *Dasaratha Ráma* or Ramachandra, the son of Dasaratha, king of Ayodhya (Oude), born at the close of the Tréta Yuga. He belongs historically to the age when the Áryan race, already settled in the north, pushed their conquests towards the southern part of the peninsula, and introduced into those wild districts civilization and agriculture, which are typified as Sítá, to whom Ráma was married, and who is represented in the Vishṇu Purána as having been found in the earth. She was the daughter of Janaka, king of Mithila (q. v.) and Ráma received her for his strength in breaking the bow of Mahéshwara, in that king's palace. She was carried off by Rávaṇa, and the war which ensued for her recovery is the subject of Válmiki's epic, the Rámáyaṇa. Having built a bridge across the ocean, and destroyed the whole Rákshasa nation, he recovered his bride Sítá, whom their ten-headed king Rávaṇa had carried off, and returned to Ayodhyá with her, after she had been purified by the fiery ordeal from the soil contracted by her captivity, and had been honoured by the assembled gods who bore witness to her virtue. Ramachandra (the moon-like-Ráma) is the seventh incarnation of Vishṇu, born into the world at the end of the second or Treta age, for the purpose of destroying the demons who infested the earth.

3. *Balaráma*, the strong Ráma, born at the end of the Dwápara, or third age, as the seventh son of Vasudeva and Devakí, but mystically transferred from the womb of the latter to that of Vasudeva's other wife Rohini, and thus saved from the hands of Kansa. He was the brother and playfellow of Krishṇa; the sharer in his toils and his glory. He is sometimes regarded as an incarnation of the serpent Ánanta or Sesha; sometimes called the eighth incarnation of Vishṇu. He is also termed the Hercules of Indian Mythology.

Ramagiri—A mountain near Nagpur, now called Ram-tek.

Ramanaka—One of the eight islands enumerated in the Bhágavata, as peopled by Mlechchhas, who worship Hindu divinities.

Ramanuja—A celebrated Vaishnava teacher, who lived some time in the twelfth century.

Ramayana—One of the great Epic poems of the Hindus, the other being the Mahábhárata. It is perhaps impossible to fix the exact period at which either of them was composed; though it is evident from internal evidence that both are productions of a *post-vedic* age. The Rámáyaṇa was the more ancient of the two Indian Epics. Probably neither it nor the Mahábhárata, nor any of the productions of antecedent ages, were committed to writing till long after their original composition. In the fourth chapter of the first book of the Rámáyaṇa, we meet with special reference to the ministrels and reciters, by whom, like the Greek *ῥαψῳδοί*, the ancient Hindu poems, previous to the invention of writing in India, were preserved and transmitted from age to age.

The word Rámáyaṇa means the adventures of Ráma, who was one of the incarnations of Vishṇu, the Preserver, and is still a favourite deity in most parts of India, more especially in the districts of Oude and Bahár, where Krishṇa has not supplanted him. There were three Rámas in Hindu mythology, viz., Parasu-Ráma, Ráma-Chandra, and Bala-Rama, all avatars (or incarnations) of Vishṇu. The last is the Indian Hercules, and as the elder brother of Krishṇa, appears frequently in the Mahábhárata. Parasu-Ráma, as the son of the sage Jamadagni, is the type of Brahmanism, arrayed in opposition to the Kshatriyas, or military caste. He is introduced once into the Rámáyaṇa, but only to exhibit his inferiority to the real hero of the work, viz., Ráma-Chandra, who, as the son of Dasaratha, a prince of the solar dynasty, typifies the conquering Kshatriyas, advancing towards the south, and subjugating the barbarous aborigines, who are represented by Rávaṇa and his followers.

There are many poems bearing the name of Rámáyaṇa—all relating to the same hero—but by far the most complete and famous is the lengthy epic, the authorship of which is attributed to *Vâlmíki.*

It narrates the banishment of Ráma, under the surname of Chandra (the moon,) a prince belonging to the dynasty of the kings of Ayodhya ; his wanderings through the southern peninsula ; the seizure of his wife, Sítá, by the giant ruler of Ceylon (Rávaṇa) ; the miraculous conquest of this island by Ráma, aided by Sugríva, king of the monkeys (or foresters—the word *bandar* meaning both,) or *Rákshasas* as they are also called, and by Vibhíshaṇa, the brother of Rávaṇa ; the slaying of the ravishing demon by Ráma, and recovering of Sítá ; and the restoration of Ráma-Chandra to the empire of his ancestors at Ayodhya.

No mention is made of Ráma in the Vedas, but he may be regarded as the first real Kshatriya hero of the *post-vedic* age ; and looking to the great simplicity of the style of the Rámáyaṇa, the absence of any reliable allusion to Buddhism as an established fact, and to the practices known to have prevailed in India as early as the fourth century before Christ, as well as from other considerations, " we cannot," says Monier Williams (Essay on Indian Epic Poetry,) " be far wrong is asserting that a great portion, if not the whole, of the Rámáyaṇa, as we have now it, must have been current in India as early as the fifth century before Christ."

Válmíki's work consists of 24,000 ṣlokas (or distichs,) divided into seven books, which are again sub-divided into chapters. It may be divided into three principal parts, or periods, corresponding to the three chief epochs in the life of Ráma. (I.) The account of his youthful days ; his education and residence at the court of his father Dasaratha, king of Ayodhya ; his happy marriage to Sítá; and his inauguration as heir-apparent or Crown Prince. (II.) The circumstances that led to his banishment; the description of his exile and residence in the forests of Central India. (III.) His war with the giants or demons of the south for the recovery of his wife Sítá, who had been carried off by their chief Rávaṇa; his conquest and destruction of Rávaṇa, and his restoration to the throne of his father.

In the first two sections of the poem, there is little of extravagant fiction; but in the third, the poet mars the beauty of the descriptions by the wildest exaggeration and hyperbole.

The poem seems to be founded on historical fact; and the traditions of the south of India uniformly ascribe its civilization, the subjugation, or dispersion of its forest tribes of barbarians, and the settlement of civilised Hindus, to the conquest of Lanká (Ceylon) by Ráma.

[A good analysis of the Rámáyaṇa will be found in Monier Williams' Indian Epic Poetry, 1863. An abridged English translation has been published by Mr. Talboys Wheeler, forming the second volume of his History of India, 1869. The first English translation was made by Carey and Marshman, at Serampore, when they printed the first volume containing the first book of the poem, in 1806.

An excellent translation, into English verse, of the First and Second Books has just been published (1870–71) by Mr. R. T. Griffiths, M. A., Principal of the Benares College, already favorably known by his Idylls from the Sanskrit.]

Rambha—1, One of the five sons of Áyus; 2, One of the Apsarasas, of the Laukika class, of whom thirty-four are specified.

Ramya—One of the nine sons of king Agnídhra, and who became king of the countries situated between mount Meru and the Níla mountain.

Ramyaka—A district to the north of Meru, extending from the Níla or blue mountains to the Sweta or white mountains.

Ranaṇjaya—A prince, the son of Kritanjaya, of the family of Ikshváku.

Ranastambha—A country to the west of the jungle Mehals towards Nagpur ; known in the Puránas as Chedí.

Rantideva—The son of Sankrití, who is described in the Bhágavata as a prince of great liberality. According to a legend preserved in the Megha Dúta his sacrifices of kine were so numerous that their blood formed the river Charmanvati, the modern Chambal.

Rantinara—A prince, the son of Riteya, descendant of Puru.

Rasa dance—A fabled dance of Krishṇa with the Gopis, in which it is said the circle of the dance could not be constructed, as each of the Gopis attempted to keep in one place, close to the side of Krishṇa ; he therefore took each by the hand, and when their eyelids were shut, by the effects of such touch, the circle was formed. Professor Wilson says, Krishṇa, in order to form the circle takes each damsel by the hand and leads her to her place ; there he quits her ; but the effect of the contact is such that it deprives her of the power of perception, and she contentedly takes the hand of her female neighbour, thinking it to be Krishṇa's. The Bhágavata is bolder and asserts that Krishṇa multiplied himself, and actually stood between each pair of damsels.

Rasaloma—The wife of one of the eleven Rudras, Mahinasa.

Rasatala.—One of the divisions of Pátáḷa, as enumerated in the Bhágavata, Pádma Puráṇa and Váyu.

Rasayana—One of the eight branches of medical science, that which treats of alchemical therapeutics.

Rasa Yatra—An annual festival celebrated in various parts of India, in the month of Kártika, upon the sun's entrance into Libra, by nocturnal dances, and representations of the sports of Krishṇa. Some of the earliest labourers in the field of Hindu mythology have thought this circular dance to typify the dance of the planets round the sun, (Maurice) but there seems to be no foundation for such a notion. See Wilson's Notes to Vishṇu Purána, 534.

Rasollasa—The spontaneous or prompt evolution of the juices of the body, independently of nutriment from without; this is termed one of the eight perfections or Siddhis.

Rashtrapala—One of the sons of Ugrasena.

Rashtrapali—A daughter of Ugrasena.

Rathachitra—A river mentioned in the Puránas but not yet identified.

Rathakrit—One of the Yakshas, or guardians of the sun for the month of Sukra.

Rathantara—1, A teacher of the Rig Veda and pupil of Satyasri; 2, The portion of the Sáma Veda which proceeded from the eastern mouth of Brahmá.

Rathinara—One of the Angirasas, or warrior priests, a Kshatriya by both parents, who became a brahman by profession.

Rati—The wife of Káma, the Hindu Cupid who was killed by Śiva for daring to discharge an arrow at him. Rati's Lament is one of the Idylls from the Sanskrit, translated by Mr. Griffiths from the fourth canto of Kálidása's Kumára Sambhava, or Birth of the War-god.

Ratnagarbha—A commentator on the Visnṇu Purána. His book is entitled Vaishnavakúta Chandriká, 'the moon-light of devotion to Vishṇu;' but his date has not been ascertained.

Ratri—Night. One of the forms of Brahmá. Prof. Wilson says "the notions of night, day, twilight, and moon-light, being derived from Brahmá, seem to have originated with the Vedas. All the authorities place night before day, and the Asuras or Titans before the gods, in the order of appearance, as did Hesiod, and other ancient theogonists."

Ratula—A prince, the son of Suddhodana of the family of Ikshváku.

Rauchya—The Manu of the thirteenth Manwantara, and son of the Prajápati Ruchi by the nymph Máninί. According to the Matsya and Pádma, the ninth Manu was named Rauchya.

Raudraswa—A prince, the son of Ahamyáti, descendant of Puru.

Raurava—One of the Narakas, that in which falsehood and perjury are punished.

Ravana—A celebrated Rákshaka, the son of Visravas. He was the king of Ceylon, and his great power and influence have been represented in Hindu poetry by the ascription to him of ten heads and twenty arms. His character is described as libidinous and cruel. His great exploit was the abduction of Síta, the wife of Ráma, in whose absence she was carried through the air by Rávaṇa to Ceylon. He was ultimately, after a hard struggle, killed by Ráma, who invaded the island in order to rescue Síta.

But as this terrible Rákshasa occupies a large space in the mythology of India it is necessary to relate his story in more detail. Rávaṇa was the Rája of the Rákshasas. He devoted many years to the performance of religious austerities ; and by the power of those austerities he secured the favour of Brahmá, who at his request rendered him invulnerable to gods and demons. Rávaṇa then considered himself to be immortal ; the gods and demons were unable to harm him ; men and beasts were so much beneath his notice that he had not stooped to pray for immunity from their attacks. Accordingly he oppressed the gods ; not indeed the Brahmanical gods Brahmá, Vishṇu, and Śiva, but the ancient gods of the Rig Veda, whom he compelled to do as he pleased. Death was not allowed to afflict his subjects the Rákshasas ; the burning sun was required to shine mildly over his city ; the Moon was obliged to be always at the full throughout his Ráj ; the seasons came and went at his command ; Fire ceased to burn in his presence ; and the Wind was forced to blow gently. Accordingly the gods, with Indra at their head, complained to Brahmá of Rávana's insolence. Brahmá, who acknowledged the superiority of Vishṇu, by conducting them to the ocean of milk, where he abode, and the gods propitiated Vishṇu whom they could not see, with loud praises. Then Vishṇu the Lord of the world, appeared with his shell, chakra, mace, and lotus, in his four hands ; and his wife Lakshmí sitting upon his knees. The gods fell prostrate before him and sought relief from Rávaṇa ; as Brahmá was unable to recall the gift of invulnerability, Vishṇu promised to overthrow him by mortals and monkeys, as Rávaṇa in his pride, had not requested Brahmá to secure his life from them. Vishṇu further said, "I will take advantage of this omission, and cause the destruction of Rávaṇa without casting aside the blessing which has been bestowed on him by Brahmá ; I will go to Ayodhya, and divide myself into four parts, and take my birth as the four sons of Mahárája Dasaratha. Thus by becoming man I shall conquer in battle Rávaṇa, the teror of the universe, who is invulnerable to the gods ; go you meantime upon the earth, and assume the shape of monkeys and bears, that you may render me service in my battle with Rávaṇa."

Accordingly Vishṇu became incarnate as Ráma, and early in life began to destroy the Rákshasas. When Rávaṇa heard that Ráma had slain the two celebrated Rákshasa chiefs, Kara and Dúshana, he entered the arena of conflict, proceeded to Panchavati, and visited the hermitage of Ráma as a mendicant brahman, and made proposals to Síta, declaring that he was Rávaṇa and that she should be his chief Ráni. When the proposal was rejected with indignation and disdain, he assumed his proper shape, and carried off Síta by force through the air to Lanka ; his chariot was stopped by Jatáyus, whom he slew, and conducted Síta to his palace. All his efforts to seduce Síta were ineffectual, and after long fighting, in which the army of monkeys and bears were engaged against the Rákshasas, Rávaṇa was slain by Ráma. See Ráma, Síta, &c.

Raya—The name of one of the six sons of Purúravas, according to the list in the Bhágavata.

Rayananiya—The son of Lokákshi, a distinguished teacher of the Sáma-veda, and author of a Sanhita still extant.

Rebha—A Rishi who had been hidden by maglignant demons, bound, overwhelmed in the waters, (a well, according to the commentator,) for ten nights and nine days, and abandoned until he was nearly if not entirely dead ; the Aṣvins drew him up as soma juice is raised with a ladle.—*O. S. T., V*, 245.

Rechaka—One of the three modifications of breathing in the practice of Pránáyáma : the first act is expiration, which is performed through the right nostril whilst the left is closed with the fingers of the right hand; this is called Rechaka.

Renuka—The daughter of Reṇu, and wife of Jamadagni, q. v. She was the mother of Paraṣuráma, and an account of her death and restoration to life will be found under Jamadagni.

Revanta—In the Vishṇu Purána Revanta is said to be a son of the sun by his wife Sanjna; according to other accounts he was the son of Vivaswat and Rajni.

Revata—The son of Ánartta, king of the country called after his father Anartta, who dwelt at the capital denominated *Kusasthali*—in Guzerat.

Revali—The daughter of Raivata, whose loveliness was such that no one could be found on earth worthy of her hand. Her father therefore repaired with her to Brahmá, to consult the god where a fit bridegroom was to be met with. When they arrived the quiristers Háhá, Húhú, and others, were singing before Brahmá; and Raivata, waiting till they had finished, imagined the ages that elapsed during their performance, to be but as a moment. At the end of their singing Raivata prostrated himself before Brahmá and explained his errand. He was informed that many successions of ages had passed away while he had been listening to the heavenly songsters; that a portion of Vishṇu was then reigning on earth in the person of Balaráma at Dwáraka which had formerly been his own capital of Kusasthali. Raivata returned with his daughter to earth, where he found the race of men dwindled in stature, reduced in vigour, and enfeebled in intellect. He bestowed his unequalled daughter on Balaráma, who beholding the damsel of excessively lofty height, shortened her with the end of his ploughshare and she became his wife. The object of this legend, says Professor Wilson, is obviously to account for the anachronism of making Balaráma cotemporary with Raivata; the one early in the Treta age, and the other at the close of the Dwápara. V. P.

Revati—A lunar mansion in Vaiswánarí, in the southern Avasthána.

Ribhu—An ancient vedic deity, not now worshipped. "The practical portion of the Vedas consists of little else than detached prayers addressed with a few exceptions to divinities no longer worshipped, some of whom are even unknown. There is one for instance named Ribhu, of whose history, office, or even name, a person might ask in vain from one end of India to the other."—*Wilson's Works, Vol. II, p*. 48.

Ribhu—One of the mind-born sons of Brahmá; of the ninth or Kaumára creation; these, declining to create progeny, remained, as the name of the first implies, ever boys, Kumáras; that is, ever pure and innocent; whence their creation is called the Kaumára. Ribhu, being a son of the supreme Brahmá was of a holy character and acquainted with true wisdom. Nidágha, the son of Pulastya, was his disciple, and to him Ribhu communicated perfect knowledge. The residence of Pulastya was at Víranagara, a large handsome city on the banks of the Devíka river. Nidágha lived in a grove adjoining to the stream. When a thousand years had elapsed, Ribhu went to the city of Pulastya to visit his disciple; and after having fully explained to him the principles of unity departed. After the expiration of another thousand years Ribhu returned to his disciple and perfected him in divine knowledge.

Ribhus—The sons of Sudhanvan, who on account of their artistic skill attained to immortality and divine honours. They are said to have made Indra's chariot and horses, restored their own parents to youth, &c. They are represented as *fabricating* hymns also. "These Ribhus are said to have made into four a single new sacrificial cup which Tvashṭri had formed. This exhibition of skill was performed by command of the gods, and in consequence of a promise that its accomplishment should be rewarded by exaltation to divine honours. Tvashṭri is represented as becoming ashamed, and hiding himself among the goddesses, when he saw this alteration of his work, and as resenting this change in his own manufacture as a slight to himself, and as having in consequence sought to slay his rivals. In another place, on the contrary, he is said to have applauded their design, and admired the brilliant results of their skill."—*Muir, O. S. T., Vol. V, p*. 227.

"It was part of the Vedic creed that holy men, as in the case of *Ribhus*, might attain the condition of gods. These intimations, however, are incidental and vague, and all that we can positively conclude from them is that the Vedas recognised after the dissolution of the body, the life of the soul which animated it, and its continued existence in some heavenly sphere."—*Wilson, V*, 345.

Ribhus—A class of deities of the sixth Manwantara.

Richa—A prince, the son of Sunı́ta, of the race of Puru.

Richas—The hymns of the Rig Veda, which were recited by the priests termed Hotri.

Richeya—One of the sons of Raudraṣwa, of the race of Puru.

Richika—A sage, of the descendants of Bhrigu, who demanded in marriage Śatyavatí, the daughter of king Gádhi. The king was very unwilling to give his daughter to a peevish old brahman, and demanded of him as the nuptial present, a thousand fleet horses, whose colour should be white, with one black ear. Richíka, having propitiated Varuṇa, the god of ocean, obtained from him, at the holy place called Áswatírtha, a thousand such steeds; and giving them to the king espoused his daughter. See JAMADAGNI, also SATYAVATI.

Rig Veda—The oldest and most important of the four Vedas. "As long as man continues to take an interest in the history of his race, and as long as we collect in libraries and museums the relics of former ages, the first place in that long row of books which contains the records of the Áryan branch of mankind, will belong for ever to the Rig Veda."* The hymns of the Rig Veda are amongst the oldest writings known to mankind, they are generally short, and are addressed to the great powers of nature, to Indra, the god of the firmament; to Fire, to the Sun, to the Moon; and as regards the latter, they are more especially devoted to the praise of the Sóma, or Moon plant, the juice of which plays a prominent part in many of the Vedic hymns. This juice was probably fermented, and formed into an exhilarating or intoxicating beverage, which was held in very high esteem.

* Max Muller.

" The total number of hymns in the Rig Veda is about 1,020. Their composition was doubtleess the work of many men and of long periods of time. They bear evident marks of having been handed down by tradition, and although they were collected and arranged in their present forms about ten centuries before the Christian era, a long time must have passed before they were brought together by the sage, who from his performance of this work is called Vyása, the arranger.

" The language of the hymns, besides being archaic, is very involved and elliptical, abounding with epithets of which it is difficult to see the force, and with metaphors and comparisons which are by no means obvious. It ' teems with words which require a justification.' The hymns consequently demand, as Mr. Müller observes, a similar treatment to that bestowed upon the interpretation of ancient inscriptions ; a careful collection of all grammatical forms, and a thorough comparison of all passages in which the same word occurs. The metre of the hymns is a very important guide to the correct reading of the text, but this presents so many apparent anomalies that its rules are variously explained. The hymns of the Rig Veda contain very little poetry of an agreeable or elevated order. The chief desires expressed are for riches, victory, and various temporal blessings. Moral sentiments rarely occur ; the hymns addressed to Varuna contain the most.

Often passages among the Mantras of the Veda are in the form of a dialógue, and in such cases, the discoursers were alternately considered as Rishi and Devata.

Mr. Müller after working for more than twenty years at his translation of the Rig Veda, thus writes :—" My work is a mere contribution towards a better understanding of the Vedic hymns, and though I hope it may give in the main, a right rendering of the sense of the Vedic poets, I feel that in many points my translation is liable to correction, and will sooner or later be replaced by a more satisfactory one."

" With regard to the character and style of these hymns on which so much labour has been expended, it may be remarked that they contain very little poetry of an agreeable or elevated order: nothing whatever that could be compared for a moment with the Psalms of David. "As mere literary productions, apart from their archaic value, we doubt if any man could be found to read them. Snatches of poetry may here and there be found; a grand and elevated tone mixed with the most familiar and, to modern taste, most ignoble and unsuitable allusions. The mere reading of some of them conveys the impression that they are not fully understood, and sets the mind inquiring as to the meaning which may lie concealed in them. The following hymn, addressed to Agni the god of fire, and the Maruts, or the Storm-gods, is one of the most readable in the present volume:—

1. Thou art called forth to this fair sacrifice for a draugh tof milk; with the Maruts come hither O Agni!

2. No god indeed, no mortal, is beyond the might of thee, the mighty one; with the Maruts, &c., &c.

3. They who know of the great sky, the Visve Devas without guile; with the Maruts, &c.

4. The wild ones who sing their song, unconquerable by force; with the Maruts, &c.

5. They who are brilliant, of awful shape, powerful, and devourers of foes; with the Maruts, &c.

6. They who in heaven are enthroned as gods, in the light of the firmament; with the Maruts, &c.

7. They who toss the clouds across the surging sea; with the Maruts come hither, &c.

8. They who shoot with their darts across the sea with might; with the Maruts, &c.

9. I pour out to thee for the early draught the sweet juice of Soma; with the Maruts, &c."—*Sat. Review*, 1869.

Rijiswan—A king mentioned in the Rig Veda, the friend of Indra, and who conquered the Dasyu Krishṇa on the banks of the Ansumatí.

Rijrasva—A person mentioned in the Rig Veda, who had been made blind by his cruel father, for slaughtering one hundred and one sheep, and giving them to a she-wolf to eat: the wolf having supplicated the Aṣvins on behalf of her blind benefactor, they restored sight to Rijráṣva.—*O. S. T., V*, 245.

Rijudesa—A son of Vasudeva by his wife Devakí.

Riksha—1, A descendant of Bhrigu, the Vyása of the twenty-fourth Dwápara, sometimes called also Valmíka.

2. A prince, the son of Ajamídha.
3. A prince, the son of Akrodhána, a descendant of Kuru.
4. A chain of mountains in Gondwána.

Rina—A Vyása in the eighteenth Dwápara.

Ripu, Ripunjaya—Two of the sons of Slishti and Suchcháya, grandsons of Dhruva.

Rishabha—The son of king Nabhi by his queen Meru. Rishabha had a hundred sons, the eldest of whom was Bharata; having ruled with equity and wisdom and celebrated many sacrificial rites, he resigned the sovereignty of the earth to the heroic Bharata, and, retiring to the hermitage of Pulastya, adopted the life of an anchoret, practising religious penance, and performing all prescribed ceremonies, until, emaciated by his austerities so as to be but a collection of skin and fibres, he put a pebble in his mouth and naked went the way of all flesh. V. P. In a note Wilson adds 'the great road' 'the road of heroes.' The pebble was intended either to compel perpetual silence, or to prevent his eating. The Bhágavata adverts to the same circumstances, and gives more details of Rishabha's devotion, and connects him with the spread of Jain doctrines in the western parts of the peninsula. Rishabha is the name of the first Tírthankara, or Jain saint of the present era.

Rishabha—2, One of the seven Rishis of the second Manwantara; 3, A prince, the son of Kuṣágra; 4, A mountain on the north of Meru.

Rishabha—5, One of the generals in Ráma's army at the siege of Lanka; he was severely wounded by the magical weapons of Indrajit, and left apparently dead on the battle field; but was restored to life by the healing plants brought by Hanuman from the golden hill called Rishabha.

Rishabha—6, The name of a golden hill on the very crest of Kailása; on which grew four medicinal herbs, by virtue of which the dead and wounded might be restored to life.

Rishis—Great Sages. Seven are enumerated; they are the same as the Prajápatis, q. v. One of the Rishis is an attendant on the sun in each month of the year, along with one of the Ádityas, Gandharbhas, Apsarasas, Yakshas, etc. The Vishnu Purána says there are three kinds of Rishis, or inspired sages; royal Rishis, or princes who have adopted a life of devotion, as Viswámitra; divine Rishis, or sages who are demi-gods also, as Nárada; and Brahman Rishis, or sages who are the sons of Brahmá, or Brahmans, as Vasishtha and others. Mr. J. C. Thomson writes "in the Epic period Rishi is merely a name for historical personages, distinguished for their piety and wisdom, either by their acts or their writings. In the Puránic period the Rishis, *par excellence*, are seven primeval personages, born of Brahmá's mind, and presiding, under different forms, over each Manwantara." The word Rishi is derived from rish, an old vedic root meaning 'to see.'

Rishis—The constellation of the Great Bear. For an account of its revolutions see the Vishṇu Purána, p. 485, and Wilson's learned notes on the subject.

Rishika, Rishikulya—A river that rises in the Mahendra mountain and flows into the sea near Ganjam.

Rishikas—A people placed by the Rámáyana both in the north and in the south; Arjuna visits the former and exacts from them eight horses.

Rishyamukha—A mountain in the Dekhin where the Pampa rises, the abode of the monkeys, and the temporary abode of Ráma.

Rishya-sringa—A horned sage, celebrated in the first book of the Rámáyana.

He was the son of Vibháṇḍak, a Rishi descended from Kaṣyapa.

> "Bred with the deer that round him roam,
> The wood shall be that hermit's home.
> To him no mortal shall be known
> Except his holy sire alone."

He was thus brought up in the forest with his father and saw no other human being until he attained early manhood. At a season of great drought, Somapád, king of Anga, enquired what should be done to cause rain, when the brahmans said,

> " By every art O monarch try
> Hither to bring Vibháṇḍak's child,
> Persuaded, captured or beguiled,
> And when the boy is hither led
> To him thy daughter duly wed."

After much deliberation as to the way in which the " wondrous boy" should be induced to leave his father's home, the poem proceeds,

> " Then this shall be the plan agreed,
> That damsels shall be sent,
> Attired in holy hermit's weed
> And skilled in blandishment,
> That they the hermit may beguile
> With every art and amorous wile,
> Whose use they know so well,
> And by their witcheries seduce
> The unsuspecting young recluse
> To leave his father's cell.
>
> Then when the boy with willing feet
> Shall wander from his calm retreat,
> And in that city stand,
> The troubles of the king shall end
> And streams of blessed rain descend
> Upon the thirsty land.
>
> Thus shall the holy Rishyaṣring
> To Somapád the mighty king
> By wedlock be allied;
> For Śántá, fairest of the fair,
> In mind and grace beyond compare,
> Shall be his royal bride."

All this took place accordingly.

"In ships with wondrous art prepared
Away the lovely women fared,
And soon beneath the shade they stood
Of the wild lonely dreary wood.
And there the leafy cot they found
Where dwelt the devotee
And looked with eager eyes around
The hermit's son to see.

* * * * * * * *

Forth came the hermit's son to view
The wondrous sight to him so new,
And gazed in rapt surprise,
For from his natal hour till then
On woman or the sons of men
He ne'er had cast his eyes.

The scheme was successful. On the following day when his father went as usual to the forest, Rishyaṣring eagerly sought his charming visitants and accompanied them to their "lovely home."

Vibháṇḍak returned to his cottage in the evening to learn the will of fate—

"A stately ship, at early morn,
The hermit's son away had borne.
Loud roared the clouds as on he sped,
The sky grew blacker overhead ;
Till as he reached the royal town,
A mighty flood of rain came down,
By the great rain the monarch's mind
The coming of his guest divined.
To meet the honoured youth he went,
And low to earth his head he bent.
And sought, with all who dwelt within
The city walls, his grace to win.
He fed him with the daintiest fare,
He served him with unceasing care,

And gave to be the Brahman's bride
His own fair daughter, lotus-eyed.
Thus loved and honoured by the king,
The glorious Brahman Rishyaṣring
Passed in that royal town his life
With Śántá his beloved wife."—*Griffiths' Rámáyana.*

Rita—1, Truth. The son of Dharma, by one of the daughters of Daksha ; 2, A king of Mithila, the son of Vijaya.

Ritadhaman—The Manu of the thirteenth Manwaṇtara, according to the list in the Pádma and Matsya Puránas.

Ritadhwaja—1, One of the eleven Rudras, according to the enumeration in the Bhágavata ; 2, One of the designations of Pratarddana, meaning he whose emblem was truth, being a great observer of veracity.

Riteya—A prince, the eldest of the ten sons of Raudraṣwa, a descendant of Puru.

Ritu—The Manu of the twelfth Manwantara.

Ritudhaman—The Indra of the twelfth Manwantara.

Ritujit—One of the kings of Mithila, the son of Anjana.

Rituparna—A prince, the son of Ayutáṣwa.

Rochana—A wife of Vasudeva.

Rodha—One of the Narakas ; that for the punishment of the crimes of causing abortion, killing a cow, plundering, &c.

Rohini—1, The wife of Vasudeva. Kansa, king of Mathura, captured Vasudeva and his wife Devakí, imprisoned them in his own palace, set guards over them, and slew the six children whom Devakí had already borne. She was now about to give birth to the seventh, who was Balaráma, the playfellow of Krishṇa, and like him, supposed to be an incarnation of Vishṇu ; but by divine agency the child was transferred before birth to the womb of Vasudeva's other wife, Rohiṇi, who was living in Gokula.

2. One of the wives of Krishṇa.
3. The name of the wife of one of the Rudras.
4. The daughter of Surabhi, and parent of horned cattle.
5. A lunar mansion in Gajavithi, in the northern Avashtháṇa.

Rohita—1, The Manu, according to some of the Puránas, of the ninth Manwantara ; 2, The son of Harischandra, q. v.

Rohitaswa—Called also Rohita. The son of Harischandra, q. v. Traces of his name appear in the strongholds of Rotas, in Behar, and in the Panjab. The Bhágavata has a legend of his having been devoted to Varuṇa before his birth, by his father, who having on various pleas deferred offering his son as promised, was afflicted by a dropsy. Rohita at last purchased Sunahṣephas who was offered as a victim in his stead.

Romaharshana—A disciple of Vyása, and the narrator of the Puránas. See Súta.

Romanas, Ropanas—A people mentioned in the Puránas ; it has been conjectured that the Romans may be meant.

Romapada—1, A son of Vidarbha and the princess rescued by Jyámagha, (q. v.) ; 2, A prince, the son of Chitraratha.

Ruchi—One of the Prajápatis or mind-born sons of Brahmá. He was married to Akúti, who bore him twins, Yajna and Dakshina, who afterwards became husband and wife, and had twelve sons, the deities called Yámas, in the Manwantara of Swá yambhuva.

Ruchiradhi—A prince, the son of Sankrite, of the race of Bharata.

Ruchiraswa—A prince, the son of Senajit, descendant of Hastin.

Rudhirandha—One of the Narakas, designed for incendiaries, treacherous friends, soothsayers, &c.

Rudra—An agent in creation ; who sprang from the forehead of Brahmá, radiant as the noontide sun, fierce, and of vast bulk, and of a figure which was half-male, half-female. At the command of Brahmá, Rudra became two-folds disjoining his male and female natures. His male being he again divided into eleven persons, of whom some were agreeable, some hideous, some fierce, some mild : and he multiplied his female nature manifold, of complexions black or white. This is considered by Professor Wilson to be the primitive form of the legend.

The Vishṇu Purána gives another account, as follows :

In the beginning of the Kalpa, as Brahmá purposed to create a son, who should be like himself, a youth of a purple complexion appeared, crying with a low cry, and running about. Brahmá, when he beheld him thus afflicted, said to him, "Why dost thou weep?" "Give me a name," replied the boy. "Rudra be thy name," rejoined the great father of all creatures : "be composed ; desist from tears." But, thus addressed, the boy still wept seven times, and Brahmá therefore gave to him seven other denominations ; and to these eight persons regions and wives and posterity belong. The eight manifestations, then, are named Rudra, Bhava, Sarva, Iṣána, Paṣupati, Bhíma, Ugra, and Mahádeva, which were given to them by their great progenitor. He also assigned to them their respective stations, the sun, water, earth, air, fire, ether, the ministrant Brahman, and the moon ; for these are their several forms.

The Váyu details the application of each name severally. These eight Rudras are therefore but one, under as many appellations, and in as many types. The Pádma, Márkaṇḍeya, Kúrma, Linga, and Váyu agree with the V. P., in the nomenclature of the Rudras, and their types, their wives, and progeny.

Rudra—A name of Śiva ; one of the five great lords or faces of Śiva, the name Rudra occurs in the Rig Veda as one of the inferior gods.

Rudrakali—A form of Uma, in which she accompanied Vírabhadra when he was sent by Śiva to spoil the sacrifice of Daksha.

Rudraksha—A rosary, or string of beads, the fruit of the eleocarpus, resembling in form, size, and colour, the nutmeg, but with a rough surface. The meaning of the word is Rudra's (*i. e.*, Śiva's) eye, and then also tear. It is said that Śiva once, in a war with the Asúras, having burned three cities, wept at the loss of lives involved, and the tears falling to the ground, sprung up as shrubs, producing berries, which were thence called Rudráksha.

Rudra-loka—The heaven above Brahmá-loka.

Rudrani—The wife of the Rudra Dhritavrata.

Rukmakavacha—A Yádava prince, the son of Siteyas.

Rukmisha—The grandson of the preceding Yádava king.

Rukmin—The son of Bhishmaka, king of Vidarbha. He had a beautiful sister named Rukminí, with whom Krishṇa fell in love and selected in marriage ; but her brother, who hated Krishṇa, would not assent to the espousals. The father then affianced Rukminí to Siṣupála. In other to celebrate the nuptials, Jarásandha and other princes, the friends of Siṣupála, assembled in Kundina, the capital of Vidarbha ; and Krishṇa, attended by Balaráma and many other Yádavas, also went to witness the wedding. When there Krishṇa contrived to carry off the princess, leaving Ráma and his kinsmen to sustain the weight of his enemies. The sovereigns who had assembled to be present at the marriage, indignant at the insult, exerted themselves to kill Krishṇa ; and Rukmin, vowing that he would never enter Kundina until he had slain him in fight, pursued and overtook him. In the combat that ensued Krishṇa destroyed with his discus the whole host of Rukmin, and would have put him to death, but was withheld by the entreaties of Rukminí. Rukmin, thus spared, built the city Bhojakata, and in pursuance of his vow, ever after dwelt therein. He was ultimately killed by Balaráma in a quarrel which occurred at a game of dice.

Rukmini—The sister of the above. After the defeat of Rukmin, Krishṇa married Rukminí in due form, having first made her his own by the Rákshasa ritual, V. P. According to the Bhágavata, Rukminí sent to invite Krishṇa to carry her off, and instructed him how to proceed. She was the mother of Pradyumna. On the death of Krishṇa she and four other of his wives burnt themselves with his body.

Rupa—A river, from the Saktimat mountain.

Rupavahikas, Rupavasikas—People mentioned in the Puránas as Southern tribes, probably in the vicinity of the Rupa river.

Ruruka—A prince, the son of Vijaya, and ancestor of Sagara.

Rushadra—The son of Swáhi, and grandfather of Sasavinda.

S

Sabhanara—One of the sons of Anu.

Sadacharas—Fixed observances; the institutions or observances of the pious; the perpetual obligations of a householder, consisting of daily purifications, ablutions, libations, and oblations; hospitality, obsequial rites, ceremonies to be observed at meals, at morning and evening worship, and on going to rest.

Sadakanta, Sadanira—Puránic rivers, the latter is said to flow from Páripátra.

Sadaswa—A prince, the son of Samara.

Sadhus—Saints; just or pious men; those who are free from all defects.

Sadhya—A daughter of Daksha and one of the wives of Dharma.

Sadhyas—A class of demi-gods, the sons of Sádhya; according to the Váyu the Sádhyas are the personified rites and prayers of the Vedas, born of the metres and partakers of the sacrifices. It also enumerates them amongst the gods of the present Manwantara.

Sadnova—The youngest son of the Rája of Chitapur, who was thrown into a cauldron of boiling oil for delaying to join his father in an expedition against Arjuna. Sadnova prayed to God, and the oil became quite cold. Sadnova came out unhurt and went with the army to fight against Arjuna, but he and all his brethren were slain.

Sadwati—The daughter of Pulastya and wife of Agni.

Sagara—The son of Báhu or Báhuka. His birth is thus narrated in the Vishṇu Purána. Báhu was vanquished by the tribes of Haihayas and Tálajanghas, and his country overrun by them; in consequence of which he fled into the forests with his wives. One of these was pregnant, and being an object of jealousy to a rival queen, the latter gave her poison to prevent her delivery. The poison had the effect of confining the child in the womb for seven years. Báhu, having waxed old, died in the neighbourhood of the residence of the Muni Aurva. His queen having constructed his pile, ascended it with the determination of accompanying him in death ; but the sage Aurva, who knew all things, past, present, and to come, issued forth from his hermitage, and forbade her, saying, "Hold! hold! this is unrighteous ; a valiant prince, the monarch of many realms, the offerer of many sacrifices, the destroyer of his foes, a universal emperor, is in thy womb ; think not of committing so desperate an act!" Accordingly, in obedience to his injunctions, she relinquished her intention, The sage then conducted her to his abode, and after some time a very splendid boy was there born. Along with him the poison that had been given to his mother was expelled ; and Aurva, after performing the ceremonies required at birth, gave him on that account the name of Sagara (from Sa, 'with,' and Gara, 'poison.') The same holy sage celebrated his investure with the cord of his class, instructed him fully in the Vedas, and taught him the use of arms, especially those of fire, called after Bhárgava.

When the boy had grown up, and was capable of reflection, he said to his mother one day, "Why are we dwelling in this hermitage? where is my father? and who is he?" His mother, in reply, related to him all that had happened. Upon hearing which he was highly incensed, and vowed to recover his patrimonial kingdom, and exterminate the Haihayas and Tálajanghas, by whom it had been overrun. Accordingly when he became a man he put nearly the whole of the Haihayas to death, and would have also destroyed the Śakas, the Yavanas, Kámbojas, Páradas, and Pahnavas, but that they applied to Vaṣiṣhtha, the family priest of Sagara, for protection. Vasiṣhṭha regarding them as annihilated (or deprived of power), though living, thus spake to Sagara: "Enough, enough, my son, pursue no farther these objects of your wrath, whom you may look upon as no more. In order to fulfil your vow I have separated them from affinity to the regenerate tribes, and from the duties of their castes." Sagara, in compliance with the injunctions of his spiritual guide, contented himself therefore with imposing upon the vanquished nations peculiar distinguishing marks. He made the Yavanas shave their heads entirely: the Śakas he compelled to shave (the upper) half of their heads; the Páradas wore their hair long; and the Pahnavas let their beards grow, in obedience to his commands. Them also, and other Kshatriya races, he deprived of the established usages of oblations to fire and the study of the Vedas; and thus separated from religious rites, and abandoned by the Brahmans, these different tribes became Mlechchhas. Sagara, after the recovery of his kingdom, reigned over the seven-zoned earth with undisputed dominion.

Sumati the daughter of Kaṣyapa, and Keṣiní the daughter of Rája Viderbha, were the two wives of Sagara. Being without progeny, the king solicited the aid of the sage Aurva with great earnestness, and the Muni pronounced this boon, that one wife should bear one son, the upholder of his race, and the other should give birth to sixty thousand sons; and he left it to them to make their election. Keṣiní chose to have the single son; Sumati the multitude: and it came to pass in a short time that the former bore Asamanjas, a prince through whom the dynasty continued; and the daughter of Vinatá (Sumati) had sixty thousand sons.

"The elder consort bare
A son called Asamanj, the heir.
Then Sumati, the younger, gave
Birth to a gourd,* O, hero brave,
Whose rind, when burst and cleft in two,
Gave sixty thousand babes to view."

The son of Asamanjas was Anṣumat.

Asamanjas was from his boyhood of very irregular conduct. His father hoped that as he grew up to manhood he would reform; but finding that he continued guilty of the same immorality, Sagara abandoned him. The sixty thousand sons of Sagara followed the example of their brother Asamanjas. The path of virtue and piety being obstructed in the world by the sons of

* Ikshváku, the name of a king of Ayodhyá, who is regarded as the founder of the solar race, means also a *gourd*. Hence perhaps the myth.—GRIFFITHS.

Sagara, the gods repaired to the Muni Kapila, who was a portion of Vishṇu, free from fault, and endowed with all true wisdom. Having approached him with respect, they said, "O lord, what will become of the world, if these sons of Sagara are permitted to go on in the evil ways which they have learned from Asamanjas! Do thou, then, assume a visible form, for the protection of the afflicted universe." "Be satisfied," replied the sage, "in a brief time the sons of Sagara shall be all destroyed."

At that period Sagara commenced the performance of the solemn sacrifice of a horse, which was guarded by his own sons: nevertheless some one stole the animal, and carried it off into a chasm in the earth. Sagara commanded his sons to search for the steed; and they, tracing him by the impressions of his hoofs, followed his course with perseverance, until coming to the chasm where he had entered, they proceeded to enlarge it, and dug downwards each for a league. Coming to Pátáḷa, they beheld the horse wandering freely about, and at no great distance from him they saw the Rishi Kapila sitting, with his head declined in meditation, and illuminating the surrounding space with radiance as bright as the splendours of the autumnal sun, shining in an unclouded sky. Exclaiming, "This is the villain who has maliciously interrupted our sacrifice, and stolen the horse! kill him! kill him!" they ran towards him with uplifted weapons. The Muni slowly raised his eyes, and for an instant looked upon them, and they were reduced to ashes by the sacred flame that darted from his person.

"Then all the princes lofty souled,
Of wondrous vigour, strong and bold,
Saw Vásudeva standing there
In Kapil's form he loved to wear,
And near the everlasting God,
The victim charger cropped the sod.
They saw with joy and eager eyes
The fancied robber and the prize,
And on him rushed the furious band
Crying aloud, stand, villain! stand!

'Avaunt ! avaunt ! great Kapil cried,
His bosom flushed with passion's tide ;
Then by his might that proud array
All scorched to heaps of ashes lay." '*

When Sagara learned that his sons, whom he had sent in pursuit of the sacrificial steed, had been destroyed by the might of the great Rishi Kapila, he despatched Anṣumat, the son of Asamanjas, to effect the animal's recovery. The youth, proceeding by the deep path which the princes had dug, arrived where Kapila was, and bowing respectfully, prayed to him, and so propitiated him, that the saint said, "Go, my son, deliver the horse to your grandfather ; and demand a boon ; thy grandson shall bring down the river of heaven on the earth." Anṣumat requested as a boon that his uncles, who had perished through the sage's displeasure, might, although unworthy of it, be raised to heaven through his favour. "I have told you," replied Kapila, "that your grandson shall bring down upon earth the Ganges of the gods ; and when her waters shall wash the bones and ashes of thy grandfather's sons, they shall be raised to Swarga. Such is the efficacy of the stream that flows from the toe of Vishṇu, that it confers heaven upon all who bathe in it designedly, or who even become accidentally immersed in it : those even shall obtain Swarga, whose bones, skin, fibres, hair or any other part, shall be left after death upon the earth which is contiguous to the Ganges." Having acknowledged reverentially the kindness of the sage, Anṣumat returned to his grandfather, and delivered to him the horse. Sagara, on recovering the steed, completed his sacrifice ; and in affectionate memory of his sons, denominated Sagara the chasm which they had dug.

Sagara is still the name of the ocean, and especially of the Bay of Bengal, at the mouth of the Ganges. V. P.

* It appears to me that this my third story has reference to the volcanic phenomena of nature. Kapil may very possibly be that hidden fiery force which suddenly unprisons itself and bursts forth in volcanic effects. Kapil is, moreover, one of the names of Agni, the god of Fire.—GORRESIO.

Sahadeva—1, The fifth and youngest son of Páṇḍu by his wife Madri, but mystically begotten by Dasra, the younger of the two Aswinau. He is considered as the *beau ideal* of masculine beauty. He was taught Astronomy and the use of the sword by Droṇa. When the Paṇḍavas applied for service to the Rája Virata, Sahadeva was made master of the cattle, and caster of nativities and teller of fortunes ; 2, A prince, the son of Srinjaya ; 3, The son of Harshavarddhana ; 4, A son of Sudása ; 5, A son of Jarásandha ; 6, The son of Divákara, of the family of Ikshváku.

Sahajanya—A divine nymph ; one of the ten in the class termed Daivika.

Sahanji—A prince, the son of Kuntí.

Saharaksha—The fire of the Asuras ; the Bhágavata explains the different fires to be so many appellations of fire employed in the invocations with which different oblations to fire are offered in the ritual of the Vedas.

Sahas, Sahasya—The names of two of the months, occurring in the Vedas and belonging to a system now obsolete.

Sahasrabala—A prince, a descendant of Kusa, according to the lists in the Matysa, Linga, &c.

Sahasrajit—1, The eldest son of Yadu ; 2, One of the sons of Bhajamána.

Sahishna—1, One of the sons of the patriarch Pulaka ; 2, A son of Vanakapívat, and father of Kámadeva.

Sahya—One of the seven principal chains of mountains in Bharata ; the northern portions of the Western Ghauts, the mountains of the Konkan.

Saindhava, or Saindhavayana—A teacher of the Atharva Veda, and founder of a school of brahmans.

Saindhavas—1, The inhabitants of Sindh, and Western Rajpootána ; 2, A school of brahmans.

Saineyas—The descendants of Siní, a branch of the Yádavas.

Sainhikeyas—A class of Dánavas, the sons of Viprachitti and Sinhiká.

Saisikatas—Inhabitants of mountainous regions and sandy deserts.

Saisiri—A teacher of the White Yajush. V. P., 281.

Saisiriya—A teacher of the Rig Veda, a disciple of Vedamitra, called also Sákalya.

Saisunaga—A king of Magadha, and founder of the dynasty of that name, consisting of ten kings. He relinquished Benares to his son and established himself at Girivraja in Behar, where he is said to have reigned forty years.

Saiva Purana—The fourth Purána in the enumeration given in the Vishṇu Purána. In some lists it is omitted, and when that is the case it is replaced by the Váyu, or Vayuvíya. When the Saiva is specified, as in the Bhágavata, then the Váyu is omitted ; intimating the possible identity of these two works. This Purána contains the genealogies of the patriarchs, a description of the universe, and the incidents of the first six Manwantaras ; intermixed with legends and praises of Śiva. A long account of the Pitris or progenitors is also peculiar to this Purána ; as are stories of some of the most celebrated Rishis, who were engaged in the distribution of the Vedas. See VÁYU PURÁNA.

Saivya—The wife of king Satadhanu, and a woman of great virtue. The legend of her life is peculiar to the Vishṇu Purána and is thus narrated. She was devoted to her husband, benevolent, sincere, pure, adorned with every female excellence, with humility, and discretion. The Rája and his wife daily worshipped the god of gods, Janárddana, with pious meditations, oblations to fire, prayers, gifts, fasting, and every other mark of entire faith, and exclusive devotion. On one occasion when they had fasted on the full moon of Kártika, and had bathed in the Bhagirathí, they beheld, as they came up from the water, a heretic approach them, who was the friend of the Rája's military preceptor. The Rája, out of respect to the latter, entered into conversation with the heretic ; but not so did the princess ; reflecting that she was observing a fast, she turned from him, and cast her eyes up to the sun. On their arrival at home, the husband and wife, as usual, performed the worship of Vishṇu, agreeably to the ritual. After a time the Rája, triumphant over his enemies, died ; and the princess ascended the funeral pile of her husband.

In consequence of the fault committed by Satadhanu, by speaking to an infidel when he was engaged in a solemn fast, he was born again as a dog. His wife was born as the daughter of the Rája of Káśí, with the knowledge of the events of her pre-existence, accomplished in every science, and endowed with every virtue. Her father was anxious to give her in marriage to some suitable husband, but she constantly opposed his design, and the king was prevented by her from accomplishing her nuptials. With the eye of divine intelligence she knew that her own husband had been regenerate as a dog, and going once to the city of Vaidiṣá, she saw the dog, and recognised her former lord in him. Knowing that the animal was her husband, she placed upon his neck the bridal garland, accompanying it with the marriage rites and prayers : but he, eating the delicate food presented to him, expressed his delight after the fashion of his species ; at which she was much ashamed, and, bowing reverently to him, thus spake to her degraded spouse : " Recall to memory, illustrious prince, the ill-timed politeness on account of which you have been born as a dog, and are now fawning upon me. In consequence of speaking to a heretic, after bathing in a sacred river, you have been condemned to this abject birth. Do you not remember it ?" Thus reminded, the Rája recollected his former condition, and was lost in thought, and felt deep humiliation. With a broken spirit he went forth from the city, and falling dead in the desert, was born anew as a jackal. In the course of the following year the princess knew what had happened, and went to the mountain Koláhala to seek for her husband. Finding him there, the lovely daughter of the king of the earth said to her lord, thus disguised as a jackal, " Dost thou not remember, oh king, the circumstance of conversing with a heretic, which I called to thy recollection when thou wast a dog ?" The Rája, thus addressed, knew that what the princess had spoken was true, and thereupon desisted from food, and died. He then became a wolf ; but his blameless wife knew it, and came to him in the lonely forest, and awakened his remembrance of his original state. " No wolf art thou," she said, " but the illustrious sovereign Satadhanu. Thou wast then a dog, then a jackal, and art now a wolf." Upon this, recollecting himself, the prince abandoned his life, and became a vulture; in which form his lovely queen still found him, and aroused him to a knowledge of the past. "Prince," she exclaimed, "recollect yourself: away with this uncouth form, to which the sin of conversing with a heretic has condemned you!" The Rája was next born as a crow; when the princess, who through her mystical powers was aware of it, said to him, "Thou art now thyself the eater of tributary grain, to whom, in a prior existence, all the kings of the earth paid tribute." Having abandoned his body, in consequence of the recollections excited by these words, the king next became a peacock, which the princess took to herself, and petted, and fed constantly with such food as is agreeable to birds of its class. The king of Káṣí instituted at that time the solemn sacrifice of a horse. In the ablutions with which it terminated the princess caused her peacock to be bathed, bathing also herself; and she then reminded Satadhanu how he had been successively born as various animals. On recollecting this, he resigned his life. He was then born as the son of a person of distinction; and the princess now assenting to the wishes of her father to see her wedded, the king of Káṣí caused it to be made known that she would elect a bridegroom from those who should present themselves as suitors for her hand. When the election took place, the princess made choice of her former lord, who appeared amongst the candidates, and again invested him with the character of her husband. They lived happily together, and upon her father's decease, Satadhanu ruled over the country of Videha. He offered many sacrifices, and gave away many gifts, and begot sons, and subdued his enemies in war; and having duly exercised the sovereign power, and cherished benignantly the earth, he died, as became his warrior birth, in battle. His queen again followed him in death, and, conformably to sacred precepts, once more mounted cheerfully his funeral pile. The king then, along with his princess, ascended beyond the sphere of Indra to the regions where all desires are for ever gratified, obtaining ever-during and unequalled happiness in heaven, the perfect felicity that is the rarely realised reward of conjugal fidelity."

Saivya—A celebrated legendary king of ancient India, of whom an affecting story is related of a hawk and a dove.

" Saivya, a king whom earth obeyed,
Once to a hawk a promise made,
Gave to the bird his flesh and bone
And by his truth made heaven his own."

" Learn from that tale, the Hawk and Dove,
How strong for truth was Saivya's love
Pledged by his word the monarch gave
His flesh the suppliant bird to save."

" The following is a free version of this very ancient story, which occurs more than once in the Mahábhárata.

THE SUPPLIANT DOVE.

Chased by a hawk there came a dove
With worn and weary wing,
And took her stand upon the hand
Of Káśí's mighty king.

The monarch smoothed her ruffled plumes
And laid her on his breast,
And cried, ' No fear shall vex thee here,
Rest, pretty egg-born, rest !

Fair Káśí's realm is rich and wide,
With golden harvests gay,
But all that's mine will I resign
Ere I my guest betray.'

But panting for his half-won spoil
The hawk was close behind,
And with wild cry and eager eye
Came swooping down the wind :

' This bird,' he cried, my destined prize,
'Tis not for thee to shield :
'Tis mine by right and toilsome flight
O'er hill and dale and field.

Hunger and thirst oppress me sore,
 And I am faint with toil :
Thou shouldst not stay a bird of prey
 Who claims his rightful spoil.

' They say thou art a glorious king,
 And justice is thy care :
Then justly reign in thy domain,
 Nor rob the birds of air.'

Then cried the king : ' A cow or deer
 For thee shall straightway bleed,
Or let a ram or tender lamb
 Be slain, for thee to feed.

Mine oath forbids me to betray
 My little twice-born guest :
See how she clings with trembling wings
 To her protector's breast.'

' No flesh of lambs,' the hawk replied,
 ' No blood of deer for me ;
The falcon loves to feed on doves,
 And such is Heaven's decree.

But if affection for the dove
 Thy pitying heart has stirred,
Let thine own flesh my maw refresh,
 Weighed down against the bird.'

He carved the flesh from off his side,
 And threw it in the scale,
While women's cries smote on the skies
 With loud lament and wail.

He hacked the flesh from side and arm,
 From chest and back and thigh,
But still above the little dove
 The monarch's scale stood high.

He heaped the scale with piles of flesh,
 With sinews, blood, and skin,

And when alone was left him bone
He threw himself therein.

Then thundered voices through the air ;
The sky grew black as night ;
And fever took the earth that shook
To see that wondrous sight.

The blessed Gods, from every sphere,
By Indra led, came nigh ;
While drum and flute and shell and lute
Made music in the sky.

They rained immortal chaplets down,
Which hands celestial twine,
And softly shed upon his head
Pure Amrit, drink divine.

Then God and Seraph, Bard and Nymph
Their heavenly voices raised,
And a glad throng with dance and song
The glorious monarch praised.

They set him on a golden car
That blazed with many a gem ;
Then swiftly through the air they flew,
And bore him home with them.

Thus Káśí's lord, by noble deed,
Won heaven and deathless fame ;
And when the weak protection seek
From thee, do thou the same.

—GRIFFITHS. *Scenes from the Rámáyan, &c.*

2. Saivya was also the name of a king of the Sivis, who was an ally of the Paṇḍavas ; the Silex of the Greeks.

Saivya—1, The wife of Hariṣchandra, (q. v.) whose heroic fortitude was shown in her patient endurance of the long series of severe trials to which she and her husband were subjected by Viṣvámitra.

"According to the Markaṇḍeya Purána, Hariṣchandra gave up his whole country, and sold his wife and son, and finally himself, in satisfaction of Viṣvámitra's demands for money. The sufferings of Hariṣchandra, his wife, and son, are very pathetically depicted, and the effect of the various incidents is heightened with great artistic skill. The story, in fact, appears to me one of the most touching to be found in Indian literature. Hariṣchandra, the Purána tells us, was a royal Rishi who lived in the Tretá age, and was renowned for his virtues, and the universal prosperity, moral and physical, which prevailed during his reign. On one occasion, when hunting, the king heard a sound of female lamentation which proceeded, it appears, from the sciences who were becoming mastered by the austerely-fervid sage Viṣvámitra, in a way they had never been before by any one else; and were consequently crying out in alarm at his superiority. In fulfilment of his duty as a Kshattriya to defend the weak, and inspired by the god Ganeṣa, who had entered into him, Hariṣchandra exclaimed "'What sinner is this who is binding fire in the hem of his garment, while I, his lord, am present, resplendent with force and fiery vigour?' He shall to-day enter on his long sleep, pierced in all his limbs by arrows, which, by their discharge from my bow, illuminate all the quarters of the firmament." Viṣvámitra was provoked by this address. In consequence of his wrath the sciences instantly perished, and Hariṣchandra, trembling like the leaf of an aṣvattha tree, submissively represented that he had merely done his duty as a king, which he defined as consisting in the bestowal of gifts on eminent Brahmans and other persons of slender means, the protection of the timid, and war against enemies. Viṣvámitra hereupon demands a gift as a Brahman intent upon receiving one. The king offers him whatever he may ask: Gold, his own son, wife, body, life, kingdom, good fortune. The saint first requires the present for the Rájasúya sacrifice. On this being promised, and still more offered, he asks for the empire of the whole earth, including everything but Hariṣchandra himself, his wife and son, and his virtue which follows its possessor wherever he goes.* Harișchandra joyfully agrees. Vișvámitra then requires him to strip off all his ornaments, to clothe himself in the bark of trees, and to quit the kingdom with his wife Saivyá and his son. When he is departing the sage stops him and demands payment of his yet unpaid sacrificial fee. The king replies that he has only the persons of his wife, his son, and himself left. Vișvámitra insists that he must nevertheless pay; and that "unfulfilled promises of gifts to Brahmans bring destruction." The unfortunate prince, after being threatened with a curse, engages to make the payment in a month; and commences his journey with a wife unused to such fatigues, amid the universal lamentations of his subjects. While he lingers, listening to their affectionate remonstrances against his desertion of his kingdom, Vișvámitra comes up, and being incensed at the delay and the king's apparent hesitation, strikes the queen with his staff, as she is dragged on by her husband. All this Harișchandra endures with patience, uttering no complaint. Then the five Vișvedevas, merciful gods, exclaimed, "'To what worlds shall this sinner Vișvámitra go, who has thrust down this most excellent of sacrifices from the royal dignity? Whose faith shall now sanctify the soma-juice poured out with recitation of texts at the great sacrifice, that we may drink it, and become exhilarated'?" Vișvámitra heard what they said, and by a curse doomed them to become men; he relented, however, so far as to exempt them from having offspring, and from other family ties and human weaknesses, and promised that they should eventually be restored to their pristine position as gods.

---

* Compare Manu's very striking verses, which may be freely rendered as follows :—

"Our virtue is the only friend that follows us in death;
All other ties and friendships end with our departing breath.
Nor father, mother, wife, nor son beside us then can stay,
Nor kinsfolk :—virtue is the one companion of our way.
Alone each creature sees the light, alone the world he leaves;
Alone of actions, wrong or right, the recompense receives.
Like log or clod, beneath the sod their lifeless kinsman laid,
His friends turn round and quit the ground; but virtue tends the dead.
Be then a hoard of virtue stored, to help in day of doom;
By virtue led, we cross the dread, immeasurable gloom."

They in consequence became partailly incarnate as the five Páṇḍus, the sons of Draupadí. Resuming the story of Hariṣchandra, the writer tells us that he then proceeded with his wife and little son to Benares, imagining that this divine city, as the special property of Śiva, could not be possessed by any mortal. Here he found the relentless Viṣvámitra waiting for him, and ready to press his demand for the payment of his sacrificial gift, even before the expiration of the full period of grace. In this extremity Saivyá the queen suggests with a sobbing voice that her husband should sell her. On hearing this proposal Hariṣchandra swoons, then recovers, utters lamentations, and swoons again, and his wife, seeing his sad condition, swoons also. While they are in a state of unconsciousness, their famished child exclaims in distress, "O father, father, give me bread ; O mother, mother, give me food : hunger everpowers me ; and my tongue is parched." At this moment Viṣvámitra returns, and after recalling Hariṣchandra to consciousness by sprinkling water over him, again urges payment of the present. The king again swoons, and is again restored. The sage threatens to curse him if his engagement is not fulfilled by sunset. Being now pressed by his wife, the king agrees to sell her, adding, however, "If my voice can utter such a wicked word, I do what the most inhuman wretches cannot perpetrate." He then goes into the city, and in self-accusing language offers his queen for sale as a slave. A rich old Brahman offers to buy her at a price corresponding to her value, to do his household work. Hariṣchandra's heart was torn, and he could make no reply. The Brahman paid down the money, and was dragging away the queen by the hair of her head, when her little son Rohitáṣva, seeing his mother about to be taken away from him, began to cry, and laid hold of her skirts. The mother then exclaims : " 'Let me go, let me go, venerable sir, till I look upon my son. I shall hardly ever behold him again. Come, my darling, see thy mother now become a slave. Touch me not, young prince ; I may no longer be handled by thee.' Seeing his mother dragged away, the child ran after her, his eyes dimmed with tears, and crying 'mother.' The Brahman purchaser kicked him when he came up ; but he would not let his mother go, and continued crying "mother, mother.' The queen then said to the Brahman, 'Be so kind, my master, as to buy also this child, as without him I shall prove to thee but a useless purchase. Be thus merciful to me in my wretchedness; unite me with my son, like a cow to her calf.'* The Brahman agrees: 'Take this money and give me the boy.'" When his wife and son were being carried away, Hariṣchandra broke out into lamentations: "'She, my spouse, whom neither air, nor sun, nor moon, nor stranger had beheld, is now gone into slavery. This my son, a scion of the solar race, with his delicate hands and fingers, has been sold. Woe to me, wicked wretch that I am.'"—*O. S. T., Vol. I, pp.* 379-383.

2. Saivyá was the name of the wife of king Jyámagha. Her history will be found in the account of her husband. [JYÁMAGHA.]

Saka—One of the seven Dwípas, or great insular continents; it is surrounded with a sea of milk. In this Dwípa there are seven mountains and seven sacred rivers. There grows a large Saka (teak) tree, frequented by the Siddhas and Gandharbas, the wind from which, as produced by its fluttering leaves, diffuses delight. The inhabitants are described as sinless and happy.

Sakalya—A teacher of the Rig Veda. He is said in the Vishṇu Purána to have divided the Sanhita, or collection of hymns, given to him, into five Sanhitas, which he distributed amongst as many disciples, who became founders of schools for teaching the truths of the Veda.

Sakapurni—(Called also Rathantara.) A teacher of the Rig Veda, who divided the original Sanhita into three portions, and added a glossary (Nirukta) constituting a fourth. See Vishṇu Purána, 277.

Sakas—The Sakai and Sacæ of classical writers; the Indo-Scythians of Ptolemy; Turks or Tartar tribes, who established themselves about a century and a half before our era, along the western districts of India, from the Hindu Koh to the mouths of the Indus. Professor Wilson thinks they were not improbably

* The whole of this reads like a scene from "Uncle Tom's Cabin."

connected with our Saxon forefathers. Sixteen kings of this race are mentioned in the Vishṇu Purána which also mentions their conquest by Sagara, along with the Yavanas and Kambojas.

Sakha—One of the sons of Kumára, and grandson of Agni.

Sakha—A branch (*i. e.*, of the Veda considered as a tree); it means sometimes a division or part; sometimes an edition or recension. A Sákhá generally comprised a Sanhita and a Bráhmaṇa.

Sakra—1, A name of Indra, (q. v.); 2, One of the twelve Ádityas.

Sakra—The powerful god, an epithet of Indra.

Saktas—The worshippers of the Śakti, the power or energy of the divine nature in action, are exceedingly numerous amongst all classes of Hindus. This active energy is, agreeably to the spirit of the mythological system, personified, and the form with which it is invested, considered as the especial object of veneration, depends upon the bias entertained by the individuals towards the adoration of Vishnu or Śiva. In the former case the personified Śakti is termed Lakshmí, or Mahá Lakshmí, and in the latter, Parvatí, Bhavání, or Durgá. Even Sarasvatí enjoys some portion of homage, much more than her lord, Brahmá, whilst a vast variety of inferior beings of malevolent character and formidable aspect receive the worship of the multitude. The bride of Śiva, however, in one or other of her many and varied forms, is by far the most popular emblem in Bengal and along the Ganges.

The worship of the female principle, as distinct from the divinity, appears to have originated in the literal interpretation of the metaphorical language of the *Vedas*, in which the *will or purpose to create* the universe is represented as originating from the creator, and co-existent with him as his bride, and part of himself. Thus in the *Rig Veda* it is said, "That divine spirit breathed without afflation, single with (*Svadhá*) her who is sustained within him; other than him nothing existed. First desire was formed in his mind, and that became the original productive seed," and the *Sáma Veda*, speaking of the divine cause of creation, says, "He felt not delight, being alone. He wished another, and instantly became such. He caused his own self to fall in twain, and thus became husband and wife. He approached her, and thus were human beings produced." In these passages it is not unlikely that reference is made to the primitive tradition of the origin of mankind, but there is also a figurative representation of the first indication of *wish* or *will* in the Supreme Being. Being devoid of all qualities whatever, he was alone, until he permitted the wish to be multiplied, to be generated within himself. This wish being put into action, it is said, became united with its parent, and then created beings were produced. Thus this first manifestation of divine power is termed *Ichchhárúpa*, personified desire, and the creator is designated as *Svechchhámaya*, united with his own will, whilst in the *Vedánta* philosophy, and the popular sects, such as that of KABÍR, and others, in which all created things are held to be illusory, the Śakti, or active will of the deity, is always designated and spoken of as *Máyá* or *Mahámáyá*, original deceit or illusion.

Another set of notions of some antiquity which contributed to form the character of the Śakti, whether general or particular, were derived from the *Sánkhya* philosophy. In this system nature, Prakṛiti, or *Múla Prakriti*, is defined to be of eternal existence and independent origin, distinct from the supreme spirit, productive though no production, and the plastic origin of all things, including even the gods. Hence *Prakriti* has come to be regarded as the mother of gods and men, whilst as one with matter, the source of error, it is again identified with *Máya*, or delusion, and as co-existent with the supreme as his Śakti, his personified energy, or his bride.

These mythological fancies have been principally disseminated by the *Puránas*, in all which *Prakriti*, or *Máya* bears a prominent part. The aggregate of the whole is given in the *Brahmá Vaivartta Purána*, one section of which, the Prakṛiti *Khanda*, is devoted to the subject, and in which the legends relating to the principal modifications of the female principle are narrated.—*Wilson*.

Sakti—Energy. Potency. Mythologically the word means consort of a deity. Parvati is the Śakti of Śiva. Sarasvati the

Sakti of Brahmá. The Sakṭi is said to have originated in God, the Supreme Being. From the first Śakti nine others are derived who are called Navasakti. They for their arrogance, were banished from heaven to earth; and when here obtained the office of protecting mankind from demons; hence temples are erected and festivals celebrated in their honour. They are in fact the Grámadevatas so often mentioned. The Śakti is worshipped in the pagodas under the form of the Śivalinga. There are many special forms of Sakti-worship, some of them accompanied with the grossest obscenities. The Abbé Dubois terms one of them an "occult sacrifice, secret and abominable." The Śakti worship is to a certain extent sanctioned by the Puránas, but it is especially prescribed in certain works called Tantras. The female forms of Rudra, white and black, are termed in the Vishṇu Purána, Śaktis.

Sakti, Saktri—A celebrated sage, the son of Vaṣiṣhtha. King Kalmáshapáda, one day met Śakti, in a narrow path in a thicket and desired him to stand out of his way. The sage refused; on which the rája beat him with his whip, and Śakti cursed him to become a Rakshas, or cannibal. The Rája in this transformation killed and ate its author, Sakti, and all the other sons of Vaṣiṣhtha. Paráṣara was a posthumous son of Śakti. In the twenty-fifth Dwápara Sakti was the Vyása.

Sakuni—1, The son of the Rája of Gandhára, who conducted his sister Gandhárí to the city of Hastinápur to be married to Rája Dritaráshtra. He was very skilful in throwing dice, and in playing with dice that were loaded; so that he always won the game. At the celebrated gambling match when Yudhishthira lost all his property, himself, his brothers and his wife, it was Sakuni who threw the dice and won every game, and obliged the Páṇḍavas to go into exile. Sakuni plotted with Duryodhana to seize Krishṇa, when the latter revealed his divinity and disconcerted the whole.

Sakuni—2, A Daitya of great prowess, one of the sons of Hiraṇyáksha.

Sakuni—A female fiend or Asura, the daughter of Bali, and sister of Pútaná.

Sakuntala—The daughter of the celebrated Rishi Visvámitra, by one of the Apsarasas named Menaká, who was sent from heaven by Indra to allure the sage from his solitary penance. "Visvámitra yielded and lived with Menaká in connubial bliss for some years. When Visvámitra returned to his ambitious austerities, Menaká went back to heaven, and their child, Sakuntala, was adopted by the Rishi Kanwa, and brought up at his hermitage, in a forest to the south of Hastinápura, the city in which were reigning the princes of the Lunar line. To Dushyanta, the reigning monarch, it was decreed by the celestials, the daughter of Menaká should be married;"*. the plot of Kálidása's drama of "Sakuntala or the Lost Ring," is arranged to bring about the marriage.

Sakwala—A mundane system; being the space to which the light of a sun extends, each sakwala, of which there is a great number, including a heaven, earth, hells, &c.

Sakya, or Sakyamuni—The author or reviver of Buddhism, whose birth appears to have occurred in the seventh, and death in the sixth century before Christ (B. C. 621-543). He was the son of Suddhodana, king of Kapila-vastu, or of Magadha (Behar.) See Buddha and Gautama.

Sala—One of the sons of Báhlíka, of the family of Kuru.

Salagrama—A holy place of pilgrimage, often mentioned, but the locality is unknown. The kings Agnídhra, Bharata, and others, are said to have retired thither to a life of penance. The term Sálagráma is usually applied to a stone, an ammonite, which is supposed to be a type of Vishṇu, and of which the worship is enjoined in some books. Ammonites are found chiefly in the Gandak river, and Professor Wilson thinks that the Sálagráma Tírtha was probably at the source of that stream, or at its confluence with the Ganges. He adds that its sanctity, and that of the stone, are probably of comparatively modern origin.

Salaka—One of the eight branches of medical science; that which treats of external organic affections; this and Salya constitute surgery.

* Mrs. Manning, A. and M. I.

Saligotra—A teacher of the Sáma-veda; he was the son of Lángali and established six schools.

Salin—One of the fifteen teachers of the white Yájush.

Salisuka—A king of Magadha, of the Maurya dynasty, the son of Sangata.

Saliya—A disciple of Vedamítra and teacher of the Rig Veda.

Salmali—One of the Dwípas or seven great insular continents into which the Purános divide the world. In this Dwípa there are seven mountain ranges abounding in precious gems and medicinal herbs. There are seven rivers whose waters wash away sins. A large Sálmalí (silk cotton) tree grows in this Dwípa and gives it its name. The Dwípa is sourrounded by the Súra sea (sea of wine) of the same extent as itself.

Salwas, or Salyas—Are placed by the Váyu and Matsya amongst the central nations, and seem to have occupied part of Rájasthan, a Sálwa Rája being described in the Vishṇu Purána as engaging in hostilities with the people of Dwáraka in Guzerat.

Salya—The first of the eight branches of medical science, that which treats of the extraction of extraneous bodies. Śalya and Saláka constitute surgery.

Salya—1, A Danava, the son of Viprachittí renowned for great strength; 2, The Rája of Madra. He sold his sister Mádrí to be wife to Páṇḍu. He was Rája of one of the mountain tribes occupying the southern slopes of the Himálayas. At the beginning of the great war he was on the side of the Páṇḍavas, but afterwards deserted them, and drove the chariot of Karna in his combat with Arjuna. He obtained the command of the army for one day, the last of the war, and was slain by Yudhishthira.

Samadhi—The result of meditation; or that state of mind when there is an absence of all idea of individuality, when the meditator, the meditation, and the thing or object meditated upon, are all considered to be but one. According to the text of Patanjali: 'Restraint of the body, retention of the mind, and meditation, which thence is exclusively confined to one object is Dhyána; the idea of identification with the object of such meditation, so as if devoid of individual nature, is Samádhi. The word is sometimes used to express the power that enables its possessor to exercise an entire control over all his faculties, and keep them in perfect restraint.

Saman—The name of the third Veda. See Sama-veda.

Samanera—The novice of Buddhism, from sranana, an ascetic. He must be at least eight years of age, and must have received the consent of his parents to his abandonment of the world. The vows of the Sámanéra are not in any case irrevocable, and there are many circumstances that make his yoke less onerous than that of the stricter communities among the western celibates.

Samanodakas—People who are related or connected only by presentations of water. V. P., p. 316.

Samara—The eldest of the hundred sons of Nípa, and king of Kampilya in the Doab. The Matsya makes Samara the son of Káṣya.

Samaravira—A king in Bharatakshetra, whose daughter Yaṣodá was married to prince Varddhamána, who afterwards became the distinguished Jaina saint Mahávíra.

Sama-veda—Sáman is the name of third Veda, which in the Bhágavat Gíta is called the best of the three. It appears to be little more than a recast of the Rich, (see Rig Veda) consisting chiefly of the same hymns, broken up and arranged so as to be chanted during the various expiatory ceremonies. Thus, while the Rich is said to be in regular metre to be recited aloud ; and the Yájush consists chiefly of prose to be inaudibly muttered, the Sáman contains a certain rhythm, or mode, which was sung to music, and the name is also generally employed to designate a hymn.

The principal part of the Sáma-veda is that entitled Árchika. It comprises prayers arranged in six chapters ; sub-divided into half chapters and into sections, ten in each chapter, and usually containing exactly ten verses each. The same collection of prayers, in the same order, but prepared for chanting, is distributed in seventeen chapters, under the title of *Grámageya gána*. Another portion of the Sáma-veda, arranged for chanting, bears the title of Aranya-gana, and is sub-divided in the same manner as the Árchika.

There are four Bráhmanas of this Veda, received by four different schools. One is denominated *Shadvinsa*, probably from its containing twenty-six chapters. Another is called the *Adbhuta Bráhmana*. But the best known is that entitled the Tandya, and an exposition of it by Sáyanácharya. Its principal Upanishad is the Chhandogya, divided into eight chapters. Another is called the *Kena Upanishad*. These works are disquisitions on abtruse and mystical theology. The *Kena* has been translated by Rammohan Roy. SMALL. H. S. L.

Samba—A son of Krishṇa by his wife Jambavati, celebrated for his great strength. At the Swayamvara of the daughterof Duryodhana, the princess was carried off by Sámba. Duryodhana, Karna, Bhíshma, Drona, and other celebrated chiefs, incensed at his audacity, pursued him and took him prisoner. When the Yádavas heard of the occurrence, they prepared for war; but Balaráma undertook alone to procure the liberation of Sámba; he succeeded by threatening to throw the city of Hastinápura into the River. Sámba for deceiving and ridiculing the Rishis was cursed to bring forth an iron pestle, which was broken and thrown into the sea; a spike of it, that could not be broken, was swallowed by a fish; the fish was caught, and the spike extracted by a hunter named Jará, who tipped his arrow with the spike. Krishṇa was ultimately killed with this arrow. V. P.

Sambara—1, An ancient aboriginal king mentioned in the Rig Veda as a black-skinned enemy, who dwelt forty years on the mountains and possessed a hundred impregnable cities. These cities were coveted by one of Indra's white-complexioned friends, the 'hospitable Divodása.' Divodása was repulsed, and obliged to hide himself in the water; but Indra to give him pleasure, struck off the head of Sambara. Sambara lived in Udavraja, "a country into which the waters flow." He believed himself invulnerable: but Indra discovered him when issuing from the mountain, and scattered the hundreds and thousands of his hosts. For the mighty Divodása, Indra, who dances with delight in battle, destroyed ninety cities. Indra hurled Sambara from the mountain; ninety-nine cities he destroyed; the hundredth he gave to Divodása.—*Wilson's Rig Veda*.

Sambara—2, A great Asura or demon, 'terrible as death,' who knowing that Pradyumna, if he lived, would be his destroyer, carried off the infant and threw him into the ocean. Pradyumna was preserved by a fish and rescued. When he reached manhood and heard, what Sambara had done ; he challenged the demon, and after a terrible conflict, killed him. V. P.

Sambara—3, One of the demons who personify drought ; they are described in the Rig Veda as shutting up the watery treasures in the clouds, until Indra attacks them and after severe contests overcomes them, and the clouds discharge their imprisoned waters on the thirsty earth.

" And now the clouds disperse, the blue
Of heaven once more comes forth to view.
The sun shines out, all nature smiles,
Redeemed from Vrittra's powers and wiles;
The gods, with gratulations meet,
And loud acclaim, the victor greet ;
While Indra's mortal votaries sing
The praises of their friend and king."

—*O. S. T., Vol. V, p.* 135.

Sambhala—A village celebrated as the birth-place of the sage Kalki, who was endowed with eight superhuman faculties.

Sambhu—1, One of the eleven Rudras ; 2, The wife of Dhruva.

Sambhuta—A prince, the son of Trasadasyu.

Sambhuti—' Fitness.' A daughter of Daksha and wife of Marichi.

Samika—One of the sons of Súra and brother of Vasudeva.

Sampadvasa—One of the seven principal solar rays—the one which supplies heat to the planet Mars.

Sampara—A prince, the son of Samara.

Samparayana—One of the fifteen teachers of the White Yojush, who founded various new schools.

Sampati—The son of Syení and brother of Jatáyu. It was he who informed Hanumán that Rávaṇa had carried Síta to Lanka.

Samrat—1, The Manu of any particular period; 2, One of the daughters of Priyavrata, by his wife Kámya.

Samudra—The king of rivers.

Samudra—The daughter of Samudrá by his wife Velá. Samudrá was married to Prachínàvarshish, and became the mother of the ten Prachetasas.

Samvara—A son of Kaṣyapa and Danu, and one of the most celebrated Daityas. He is called in the Vishṇu Puráṇa the mightiest of enchanters, to whom Hiranyakaṣipu had recourse, when he was himself unable to influence or destroy his son Prahláda. Samvara undertook to effect his destruction, but all his schemes were frustrated.

Samvarana—A prince, the son of Riksha, and father of Kuru.

Samvatsara—1, The name of the first of the five Cycles or Yugas, consisting of twelve years; 2, The lord of times and seasons.

Samvit—That in which all things are found or known, and which is found or known in all things. A synonym of Mahat.

Samya—An original property of man. One of the eight perfections or Siddhis, defined in the notes to the Vishṇu Purána as sameness of degree.

Samyati—A son of Prachinvat or Bahugava, of the race of Puru.

Samyoga—The union of contiguity, in opposition to that of identification or perfect unity—*Tadaikyam*.

Sanaischara, Saturn—The son of Rudra and Suvarchalá. Saturn is also represented in the Vishṇu Purána as the son of the sun and his handmaid Chháya, and is said to move slowly along in a car drawn by piebald steeds.

Sanaka, Sanandana, Sanatana, Sanatkumara—Sons of Rudra, who declining to create progeny, remained, as the name of the last implies, ever-boys, kumárás, that is, ever pure and innocent; whence their creation is called the Káumara.

Sanakadi, Sampradayis—One of the *Vaishnava* sects among the Hindus. They worship ***Krishna*** and ***Radha*** conjointly, and are distinguished from other sects by a circular black mark in the centre of the ordinary double streak of white earth ; and also by the use of the necklace and rosary of the stem of ***Tulasi***. The members of this sect are scattered throughout the whole of Upper India. They are very numerous about Mathura, and they are also among the most numerous of the Vaishnava sects in Bengal.

Sandansa—One of the Narakas, the hell of pincers ; into which falls the violator of a vow, and one who breaks the rules of his order.

Sandhya—Twilight ; a form of Brahmá ; also the name of the period preceding a Yuga. In the Vishṇu Purána it is said, " The night is called Ushá, and the day is denominated Vyush'ta, and the interval between them is called Sandhyá. On the occurrence of the awful Sandhyá, the terrific fiends termed Mandehas, attempt to devour the sun ; for Brahmá denounced this curse upon them, that, without the power to perish, they should die every day (and revive by night), and therefore a fierce contest occurs daily between them and the sun. At this season pious Brahmans scatter water, purified by the mystical Omkára, and consecrated by the Gáyatri, and by this water, as by a thunderbolt, the foul fiends are consumed. When the first oblation is offered with solemn invocations in the morning rite, the thousand-rayed deity shines forth with unclouded splendour. Omkára is Vishṇu the mighty, the substance of the three Vedas, the lord of speech ; and by its enunciation those Rákshasas are destroyed. The sun is a principal part of Vishṇu, and light is his immutable essence, the active manifestation of which is excited by the mystic syllable Om. Light effused by the utterance of Omkára becomes radiant, and burns up entirely the Rákshasas called Mandehas. The performance of the Sandhyá (the morning) sacrifice must never therefore be delayed, for he who neglects it is guilty of the murder of the sun. Protected thus by the Brahmans and the pigmy sages called Bálakhilyas, the sun goes on his course to give light to the world.

Sandipani—The tutor of Krishṇa and Balaráma ; who was so astonished at their rapid progress that he thought the sun and moon had become his scholars. When they had acquired all that he could teach and enquired what fee he demanded, he requested them to give him his dead son drowned in the sea of Prabhása. The sea said, 'I have not killed the son of Sándípani ; a demon named Panchajana, who lives in the form of a conch shell, seized the boy ; he is still under my waters.' Krishṇa then plunged into the sea ; and having slain the demon, took the conch shell as his horn ; the boy was also restored to life and given to his father.

Sandhyansa—The name of the period succeeding a Yuga.

Sandilya—A celebrated teacher of whom Mr. Max Müller says, "It was an epoch in the history of the human mind when the identity of the masculine self and the neutral Brahmá was for the first time perceived, and the name of the discoverer has not been forgotten. It was Sándilya who declared that the self within our heart is Brahmá, and this tenet, somewhat amplified, is quoted as Sándilya's wisdom." The age in which he lived is not given. —*A. S. L., p.* 323.

Sandracottus—See Chandragupta.

Sangata—One of the ten Mauryas, descendants of Chandragupta, whose dynasty at Mithila lasted a hundred and thirty-seven years.

Sangha—An assembly or chapter of Buddhist priests.

Sangha-bheda—The causing of a division among the priesthood.

Sangha disesa—A class of priestly misdemeanours.

Sanghamitta—A princess, the daughter of the grandson of Chandragupta, who on being left by her husband became a priestess, and was the first who visited Ceylon.

Sangramajit—One of the sons of Krishṇa, by his wife Saivya or Mitravinda.

Sanhataswa—A prince, the son of Nikumbha.

Sanhitas—Collections of Hymns. By a Sanhita is generally understood a collection or compilation. The Sanhitas of the Vedas are collections of hymns and prayers belonging to them, arranged according to the judgment of some individual sage who is therefore regarded as the originator and teacher of each. The Vishṇu Purána mentions the names of the principal teachers of the Sanhitas of the Vedas and of their disciples and the schools founded by them.

Sanhlada—The youngest of the four sons of Hiraṇyakasipu, distinguished for his heroism, and termed the augmentor of the Daitya race.

Sani—Saturn. See Sanaischara above.

Sanjaya—The minister and charioteer of Mahárája Dhritaráshtra. He was sent on an embassy to the Páṇḍavas, and is, says Mr. Wheeler, evidently the type of an ancient diplomatist. His object was to induce the Páṇḍavas to return to Hastinápur, without giving them any distinct pledge that their Ráj would be restored to them. He was surprised at the greatness of their preparations for war. The Páṇḍavas received him in Council, and he delivered the message of the Mahárája ; to which Yudhishthira replied that whoever is wise would never give his consent to a war on trivial grounds ; but that when war seemed to be inevitable it would be useless in them to humiliate themselves to the dust for the sake of concord. "He, however, who is intent upon a war of malice is always in a fever, and the fever burns stronger and stronger in his heart day by day, until he can feel no pleasure in the ordinary gratifications of the world." As for Dhritaráshtra we acknowledge him to be our Mahárája, and we know that he is kind and benevolent, and averse to doing evil ; but for the sake of humouring his son Duryodhana, and keeping on good terms with him, the Mahárája stoops to act deceitfully towards us, and would entrap us into his presence by mere offers of protection." Krishṇa spoke to the same effect, Yudhishthira then gave costly presents to the envoy Sanjaya, both for himself and some of his old friends, to whom he sent kind messages. The mission however was a fruitless one, and when the war broke out, Sanjaya was employed to inform the blind Mahárája of every event that transpired during its progress. It was Sanjaya who recited the Bhagavat Gíta ; 2, A prince, the son of Supárṣwa ; 3, the son of Pratikshatra ; 4, A prince of the family of Ikshváku, son of Ranaṇjaya.

Sanjna—The daughter of Viṣvakarman, was the wife of the sun and bore him three children, the Manu (Vaivaswata), Yama, and the goddess Yamí (or the Yamuná river). Unable to endure the fervours of her lord, Sanjná gave him Chháyá his handmaid, and repaired to the forests to practise devout exercises. The sun, supposing Chháyá to be his wife Sanjná, begot by her three other children, Sanaiṣchara (Saturn), another Manu (Sávarṇi), and a daughter Tapatí (the Tapti river). Chháyá, upon one occasion, being offended with Yama, the son of Sanjna, denounced an imprecation upon him, and thereby revealed to Yama and to the sun that she was not in truth Sanjná, the mother of the former. Being further informed by Chháyá that his wife had gone to the wilderness, the sun beheld her by the eye of meditation engaged in austerities, in the figure of a mare (in the region of Uttara Kuru.) Metamorphosing himself into a horse, he rejoined his wife, and begot three other children, the two Áṣvins and Revanta, and then brought Sanjná back to his own dwelling. To diminish his intensity, Viṣvakarman placed the luminary on his lathe, to grind off some of his effulgence; and in this manner reduced it an eighth, for more than that was inseparable. The parts of the divine Vaishṇava splendour, residing in the sun, that were filed off by Viṣwakarman, fell blazing down upon the earth, and the artist constructed of them the discus of Vishṇu, the trident of Śiva, the weapon of the god of wealth, the lance of Kártikeya, and the weapons of the other gods: all these Viṣvakarman fabricated from the superfluous rays of the sun. V. P.

Sankalpa—1, One of the prajápatis, according to the Kúrma list; 2, A daughter of Daksha and wife of Dharma.

Sankana—A prince, the son of Kalmáshapáda according to the Rámáyana.

Sankara—1, A name of Śiva; 2, A renowned Dánava, son of Kaṣyapa and Danu.

Sankara Acharya—The great Saiva Reformer, who flourished, it is supposed, in the eighth or ninth century; Professor Wilson is of opinion that of the present popular forms of the Hindu religion, some assumed their actual state earlier than the above date. Sankara Áchárya was a distinguished professor of the Vedanta and Advaita system. He was a native of Kérala or Malabar, of the tribe of Nambúri brahmans, and in the mythological language of the sect an incarnation of Śiva.

"In Malabar, he is said to have divided the four original tribes into seventy-two, or eighteen sub-divisions each, and to have assigned them their respective rites and duties. Notwithstanding this, he seems to have met with particular disrespect, either on account of his opinions, or his origin, or his wandering life. On his return home, on one occasion, his mother died, and he had to perform the funeral rites, for which his relations refused to supply him with fire, and at which all the Brahmans declined to assist. Sankara then produced fire from his arm and burnt the corpse in the court-yard of the house, denouncing imprecations to the effect, that the Brahmans there should not study the Vedas, that religious mendicants should never obtain alms, and that the dead should always be burnt close to the houses in which they had resided—a custom which is said to have survived him.

"All accounts concur in representing Sankara as leading an erratic life, and engaging in successful controversy with various sects, whether Saiva, or Vaishṇava, or of less orthodox opinions as the Buddhists and Jainas. In the course of his peregrinations, he established several Maths, or convents, under the presidencies of his disciples, particularly one, still flourishing at Sringeri, or Sríngiri, on the western ghats, near the sources of the Tungabadra. Towards the close of his life, he repaired as far as Kashmir, and seated himself, after triumphing over various opponents, on the throne of Sarasvati. He next went to Badarikásrama, and finally to Kedarnáth, in the Himálaya, where he died at the early age of thirty-two. The events of his last days are confirmed by local traditions, and the Pítha, or throne of Sarasvati, on which Sankara sat, is still shown in Kashmir; whilst at the temple of Śiva at Badari, a Malabar Brahman, of the Nambúri tribe, has always been the officiating priest.

"The influence exercised by Sankara in person, has been perpetuated by his writings, the most eminent of which are his Bhashyas, or commentaries on the Sútras or Aphorisms of Vyása. A commentary on the Bhagavat Gíta, is also ascribed to him, as is one on the Nrisinha Tapaníya Upanishad, and a cento of verses in praise of Durga. The Saundarya Lahari is likewise said to be his composition." See VÉDÁNTA.

Sankarshana—A name of Balaráma, given to him in consequence of his being extracted from his mother's womb to be transferred to that of Rohiṇí.

Sankasya—A country in the Doab, near Mainpuri.

Sankha—1, A powerful many-headed serpent, one of the progeny of Kadru ; 2, one of the minor Dwípas, peopled by Mlechhas who worship Hindu deities ; 3, A conch shell, one of the principal weapons of Vishṇu.

Sankhakuta—One of the mountain ridges on the north of Meru.

Sankhanata—A prince, the son of Vajranábha, a descendant of Ráma.

Sankhapada—One of the eight Lókapálas, and son of the patriarch Kardama by Sruti. He is the regent of the south.

Sankhya—One of the six Śastras properly so called. It is ascribed to the Muni Kapila. It is the principal of the six philosophical schools of India. This system say some, is an attempt to account for the existence of the universe without the deity, by asserting the principle of duality, or in other words, the co-existence of spirit and matter. Dr. Ballantyne gives the following outline of the system. " The Sánkhya makes a step in advance of the Nyáya by reducing the external from the category of *substance* to that of *quality*. *Souls alone* are, in the Sánkhya, regarded as *substances ;* whatever *affects* the soul being arranged under the head of a quality—1, pleasing ; 2, displeasing ; or 3, indifferent. This mode of viewing the universe may be designated the emotional view of things.

The word Sánkhya means " *numeral*, *rational* or *discriminative*." The system promises beatitude as the reward of that discrimination which rightly distinguishes between soul and nature. The meaning to be attached to these two words will be explained presently.

The *Sánkhya* system was delivered by *Kapila* in a set of aphorisms no less concise than those of the *Nyáya*. He begins by defining the *chief end of Man*. His first aphorism is as follows :—" Now the complete (or highest) end of man." By the three kinds of pain are meant—1, diseases, griefs, &c., which are intrinsic or inherent in the sufferer ; 2, injuries from ordinary external things ; and 3, injuries from things supernatural or meteorological. In his nineteenth aphorism, he declares that the bondage (*bandha*) under which the soul, or individual man (purusha), groans, is due to its conjunction with nature (prakṛiti) ; and this bondage is merely *seeming*, because soul is " ever essentially a pure and free intelligence."

In his fifty-ninth aphorism, he says again of the soul's bondage —" It is merely verbal, and not a reality, since it resides in [the soul's organ] the *mind* [and not in the soul or self] ;" on which the Hindu commentator remarks,—" That is to say, since bondage, &c., resides only in the mind (*chitta*), all this, as far as concerns the soul [*purusha*], is merely *verbal*, because it is merely a *reflexion*, like the redness of a [pellucid] crystal [when a China rose is near it], but not a *reality*, with no false imputation like the redness of the China rose itself."

Of *nature*, which thus, by conjunction, makes the soul *seem* to be in bondage when it is really *not*, he gives, in his sixty-second aphorism, the following account :—" Nature (prakṛiti) is the state of equipoise of goodness (*sattwa*), passion (*rajas*), and darkness (*tamas*) ; from nature [proceeds] intellect (*mahat*), from intellect self-consciousness (*ahankára*), from self-consciousness the five subtile elements (*taumátra*), and both sets [external and internal] of organs (*indriya*), and from the subtile elements the gross elements (*sthúla-bhâta*), [then, besides, there is] soul (*purusha*) ; such is the class of twenty-five."

We may add further, that, in aphorism 105, we are told that " experience (*bhoga*) [whether of pleasure or pain, liberation from both of which is desiderated], *ends with* [the discrimination of] *thought* [*i. e.*, soul as contra-distinguished from nature] ;" that *a plurality of souls* is asserted (in opposition to the *Vedánta*) in another aphorism (150), viz. : " From the diverse allotment of birth, &c., the plurality of souls [is to be inferred];" and, finally, that the *Sánkhya* system explicitly repudiates the charge of *annihilation*, aphorism 47 declaring that, "In neither way [whether as a means or as an end] is this [viz., annihilation], the soul's aim."

Mr. J. C. Thomson writes, "The Sánkhya is divided into three classes:—1, The pure Sánkhya, which, if it admits, does not mention, a deity or Supreme Being, but considers the material essence as the plastic principle of all things, and is therefore called *nirishwara* or atheistical. Its text books are the 'Sánkhya-pravachana,' and the 'Tattwa Samása,' both attributed to Kapila himself, and the 'Sánkhya-káríka,' to his disciple Ishwara Krishṇa. Asuri and Panchashika are also mentioned as the earliest followers of this system; 2, The Yoga system, called *seshwara*, or theistical, founded by Patanjali, whose Yoga-sútras are its text book, and followed by the author of the Bhágavat Gítá; 3, The Puránic school, a corrupt mixture of the other two. (Lit., 'rational,' from *Sânkhya*, 'reasoning, computation.')

Sankhyayana—A teacher of the Rig Veda.

Sankranta—The beginning of the year or a month, and the name of the festival which is commonly called Pongal, (q. v.)

Sankriti—1, A prince, the son of Sankriti; 2, The son of Nara, descendant of Bharata.

Sanku—One of the sons of Ugrasena.

Sankusiras—A powerful Dánava—one of the sons of Kaṣyapa and Danu.

Sannati—Humility; one of the daughters of the patriarch Daksha, who was married to the Muni Kratu.

Sannatimat—A prince, the son of Sumati.

Sannyasi—An ascetic; the last of the four conditions of life prescribed for brahmans. These four conditions are: 1, That of the Brahmachári or bachelor, who, from the time of his investment with the sacred cord, is required to tend the sacred fires and to follow his studies under, or in the presence of, his preceptor; 2, That of the Grihasta or householder, who, from his marriage, must strictly observe his religious duties, maintain the sacred fires, and liberally practise hospitality for the support of the other three orders ; 3, That of the Vánaprastha or recluse, who, with or without his wife, relinquishes domestic life, retires to the desert, feeding on leaves, roots and fruits, or on the hospitality of the second order, and continues to perform his daily rites ; 4, That of the Sannyási or ascetic, who performs no rite whatever, and appears sometimes in a state of nudity ; who has renounced social life, with all its enjoyments and attachments, and subjected his passions ; who lives on what is given him unasked, and remains in a village only one day, in a town not more than three days, and in a city only five ; lest his mind become secularized.

Sansapayana—A teacher of the Puránas, and composer of a " fundamental Sanhita," the substance of which is included in the Vishṇu Purána.

Sanskaras—The ten essential ceremonies of Hindus of the first three castes ; viz., three before birth ; then, " At the birth of a child the father should feed two brahmans, seated with their faces to the east ; and according to his means offer sacrifices to the gods and progenitors. Let him present to the manes balls of meat mixed with curds, barley, and jujubes, with the part of his hand sacred to the gods, or with that sacred to Prajápati. Let a brahman perform such a Śraddha, with all its offerings and circumambulations, on every occasion of good fortune."

" Next, upon the tenth day (after birth), let the father give a name to his child,—the first term of which shall be the appellation of a god ; the second, of a man ; as Śarman or Varman ; the former being the appropriate designation of a brahman ; the latter, of a warrior ; whilst Gupta and Dása are best fitted for the names of Vaiṣyas and Śúdras. A name should not be void of meaning ; it should not be indecent, nor absurd, nor ill-omened, nor fearful ; it should consist of an even number of syllables ; it should not be too long, nor too short, nor too full of long vowels, but contain a proportion of short vowels, and be easily articulated. After this and the succeeding initiatory rites, the purified youth is to acquire religious knowledge, in the mode that has been described, in the dwelling of his spiritual guide."

Santana—Mercury. The son of the Rudra Ugra.

Santanu—A king of the lunar race, the thirteenth in descent from Kuru, the prince who gives the designation to Duryodhana and his brothers, thence called Kauravas, their cousins, the sons of Páṇḍu being termed Páṇḍavas. Śántanu had four sons, Bhíshma, Chitrángada, Vichitravírya and Vyása. Of these the eldest and youngest both lived unmarried, the other two Chitrángada and Vichitravírya both died without issue ; on which, to prevent the extinction of the family, and in accordance with the ancient Hindu law, Vyása begot offspring on his brother's widows. The sons were Dhritaráshtra and Páṇḍu. Dhritaráshtra had a hundred sons by Gandhárí, the princess of Gandhára, of whom Duryodhana was the eldest. Páṇḍu had five sons, the celebrated princes Yudhishthira, Bhíma, Arjuna, and the twin brothers Nakula and Sahadeva. Of these the first was remarkable for his piety and integrity ; the second for his gigantic bulk and strength. Arjuna was eminent for his valour, and was the particular friend of Krishṇa—*Wilson, Vol. III, p.* 291. See VIDURA.

Santarddana—A prince, the son of Dhrishtaketu, rája of Kaikeya, or according to the Pádma, king of Kashmír.

Santateyu—A prince, the son of Randraswa, of the house of Puru.

Santati—The son of Alarka, who became king and succeeded his father as sovereign of Benares, but whose reign was only that of an ordinary mortal, though his father is said to have reigned as a youthful monarch for sixty thousand and sixty hundred years.

Santi—1, Placidity, a property of sensible objects, according to the Sánkhya philosophy ; 2, The Indra of the tenth Manwantara ; 3, A brahman, pupil of Angiras, who having suffered the holy fire to go out in his master's absence, prayed to Agni, and so propitiated him, that he not only relighted the flame but desired Sánti to demand a further boon ; 4, A prince, the son of Níla ; 5, A daughter of Daksha, 'Expiation,' and wife of Dharma.

Santideva—A daughter of Devaka, who was married to Vasudeva.

Santosha—Content. The son of Dharma by his wife Tushti, (Resignation) one of the daughters of Dharma.

Sapeijon—A teacher of the white Yajush and founder of several schools.

Sapindana—An ancestral Śráddha, performed at the expiration of twelve months after the death of a person. The practices of this rite are the same as those of the monthly obsequies, but a lustration is made with four vessels of water, perfumes, and sesamum ; one of these vessels is considered as dedicated to the deceased, the other three to the progenitors in general ; and the contents of the former are to be transferred to the other three, by which the deceased becomes included in the class of ancestors to whom worship is to be addressed with all the ceremonies of the Śráddha.

Sapindas—Relations connected by offerings of cakes to common ancestors ; they extend to seven degrees, ascending or descending.

Saptadasa—A collection of hymns created from the western mouth of Brahmá, along with the Sáma Veda, &c.

Sarabhanga—A celebrated devotee described in the Rámáyana. He was visited by Indra and invited to return with him to heaven ; and when asked afterwards by Ráma the reason of Indra's coming to his hermitage, Sarabhanga replied, " O Ráma, the sovereign of the gods or demons came to take me to the heaven of Brahmá, which I have gained by my severe austerities ; but knowing that you were not far off I would not depart to heaven until I had seen you." Sarabhanga then said, " Behold, now while I put off this body, as a serpent casts its slough !" Then the sage prepared a fire, offered ghee, and entered the flame ; the fire consumed his body ; and a youth, bright as the fire, was instantly produced ; and in this shape, Sarabhanga sought the heaven of the sages who had devoted their lives to religious austerities, and passing by the heaven of the gods, he ascended to the heaven of Brahmá.

Saradwat—The husband of Ahalya and father of Satyadhriti.

Sarama—A daughter of Daksha and wife of Kaṣyapa ; she is said to be the mother of canine animals. Vishṇu Purána, 122.

Saranu—One of the ministers of Rávaṇa, who was sent with Súka to spy out the army of Ráma, and obtain information of the chief heroes and counsellors. See SÚKA.

Saranu—One of the sons of Vaṣudeva, by his wife Rohiní.

Saranyu—The daughter of Tvashṭṛi, who was given in marriage to Viṿaswat, the son of Aditi. Saraṇyú became the mother of the two Aṣvins. Dr. Muir quotes the following text: " Saraṇyú, the daughter of Tvashṭṛi, bore twins to Vivaswat. She then substituted for herself another female of similar appearance, and fled in the form of a mare. Vivaswat in like manner, assumed the shape of a horse and followed her. From their intercourse sprang two Aṣvins, while Manu was the offspring of Savarṇá (or 'the female of like appearance.')" Another text is : "Tvashṭṛi had twin children, Saraṇyú and Trisiras. He gave Saraṇyú in marriage to Vivaswat, to whom she bore Yama and Yamí, who were also twins. Creating a female like herself without her husband's knowledge, and making the twins over in charge to her, Saraṇyú took the form of a mare and departed. Vivaswat, in ignorance, begot, on the female who was left, Manu, a royal Rishi, who resembled his father in glory." But discovering that the real Saraṇyú had gone away, he followed her in the shape of a horse, and from their intercourse sprang the two Kumáras (youths) Násatya and Dasra, who are lauded as Aṣvins (sprung from a horse.)—*Muir, O. S. T., Vol. V, p.* 228.

Sarasvat—A river god, the consort of Sarasvati, who rolls along his fertilizing waters, and is invoked by the worshippers who are seeking for wives and offspring, as well as for plenty and protection.—*O. S. T., V,* 340.

Sarasvata—1, A sage who related the Vishṇu Purána to Paráṣara ; 2, A Vyása in the ninth Dwápara age. In the notes to the Vishṇu Purána, a legend is given from the Mahábhárata in which it is said " that during a great drought the Brahmans, engrossed by the care of subsistence, neglected the study of the sacred books, and the Vedas were lost. The Rishi Sárasvata alone, being fed with fish by his mother Sarasvatí, the personified river so named, kept up his studies, and preserved the Hindu scriptures. At the end of the famine the Brahmans repaired to him to be taught, and sixty thousand disciples again acquired a knowledge of the Vedas from Sárasvata. This legend appears to indicate the revival, or more probably the introduction, of the Hindu ritual by the race of Brahmans, or the *people* called Sárasvata; for according to the Hindu geographers, it was the name of a nation, as it still is the appellation of a class of Brahmans who chiefly inhabit the Panjab. The Sárasvata Brahmans are met with in many parts of India, and are usually fair-complexioned, tall, and handsome men. They are classed in the Játi málás, or popular lists of castes, amongst the five Gaura Brahmans, and are divided into ten tribes: they are said also to be especially the Purohits or family priests of the Kshatriya or military castes: circumstances in harmony with the purport of the legend, and confirmatory of the Sárasvatas of the Panjab having been prominent agents in the establishment of the Hindu religion in India. The holy land of the Hindus, or the primary seat, perhaps, of Brahmanism, has for one of its boundaries the Sarasvatí river." V. P., 285.

Sarasvata—A dialect of Sanscrit; the term is employed by Mr. Colebrooke to designate that modification of Sanscrit, which is generally termed Prakṛit.

Sarasvatas—A tribe of brahmans, which occupied the banks of the river Sarasvati. See above, under Sarasvata.

Sarasvati—The consort of Brahmá and the goddess of wisdom, knowledge, science, art, learning and eloquence, the patroness of music and inventor of the Sanscrit language and Devanagari letters. 'She is represented as a young female, of fair complexion, with four arms and hands. In one of the two right hands she holds a flower, which she offers to her husband, by whose side she is continually standing, and in the other a book of palm leaves, indicating that she is fond of learning, and imparts knowledge to those who study. In one of her two left hands she holds a string of pearls, called Sivamâla, which serve her as a rosary, and in the other a damaru, or small drum. An annual festival is celebrated in her honour. She dwells among men, but her special abode is Brahmá lóka, with Brahmá her husband.'

The name Sarasvati means flowing, and is applied to a celebrated river as well as to the goddess of speech. The river rises in the mountains north-east of Delhi. Sarasvati was also the name of one of the daughters of Daksha who was married to Dhárma.

" Sarasvati, by the standard mythological authorities, is the wife of Brahmá, and the goddess presiding over letters and arts. The Vaishṇavas of Bengal have a popular legend that she was the wife of Vishṇu, as were also Lakshmí and Gangá. The ladies disagreed ; Sarasvati, like the other prototype of learned ladies, Minerva, being something of a termagant, and Vishṇu, finding that one wife was as much as even a god could manage, transferred Sarasvati to Brahmá, and Gangá to Śiva, and contented himself with Lakshmí alone. It is worthy of remark that Sarasvati is represented as of a white colour, without any superfluity of limbs, and not unfrequently of a graceful figure, wearing a slender crescent on her brow, and sitting on a lotus."—*Wilson's Works, Vol. II, pp.* 187-8.

" Sarasvati is a goddess of some, though not of very great importance, in the Rig Veda. As observed by Yáska, she is celebrated both as a river and a deity. She was no doubt primarily a river deity, as her name, " the watery," clearly denotes, and in this capacity she is celebrated in a few separate passages. Allusion is made in the hymns and in the Brahmanas to sacrifices performed on the banks of this river, and the adjoining Dhrishdavati : and the Sarasvati in particular seems to have been associated with the reputation for sanctity which was ascribed to the whole region, called Brahmavartta, lying between those two small streams, and situated immediately to the westward of the Jumna. The Sarasvati thus appears to have been to the early Indians what the Ganges (which is only twice named in the Rig Veda) became to their descendants. When once the river had acquired a divine character, it was quite natural that she should be regarded as the patroness of the ceremonies which were celebrated on the margin of her holy waters, and that her direction and blessing should be invoked as essential to their proper performance and success. The connection into which she was thus brought with sacred rites may have led to the further step of imagining her to have an influence on the composition of the hymns which formed so important a part of the proceedings, and of identifying her with Vách, the goddess of speech. At least, I have no other explanation to offer of this double character and identification.

Sarasvati is frequently invited to the sacrifices along with other goddesses Ilá, Mahí, Varutrí, who however were not, like her, river nymphs, but personifications of some department of religious worship or sacred science.

In many of the passages where Sarasvati is celebrated, her original character is distinctly preserved. Thus in two places she is mentioned along with rivers, or fertilizing waters. She is spoken of as having seven sisters, as one of seven rivers, and as the mother of streams. In another place she is said to pour on her fertilizing waters, to surpass all other rivers, and to flow pure from the mountains to the sea. She is called the best of mothers, of rivers, and of goddesses.

In the later mythology, as is well known, Sarasvati was identified with Vách, and became, under different names, the spouse of Brahmá, and the goddess of wisdom and eloquence, and is invoked as a Muse. In the Mahábhárata she is called the mother of the Vedas, and the same is said of Vách in the Taitt. Br. In the Sántiparva it is related that when the Brahmarshis were performing austerities, prior to the creation of the universe, " a voice derived from Brahmá entered into the ears of them all ; the celestial Sarasvati was then produced from the heavens."—*O. S. T., V*, 337-343.

Saragu or Sarju—A river, commonly identified with the Devá ; but though identical through great part of their course, they rise as different streams, and again divide and enter the Ganges by distinct branches.

Sardhawa—Confidence. One of the Charitas, or states of mind, which the Buddhist priest is taught to cultivate. The priest who has attained this condition is known by his being always cheerful ; by the pleasure he has in hearing the sacred writings, and by the general excellence of his conduct.

Sarmajaya—A prince, the son of Swaphalka.

Sarman—An appropriate name for a brahman, affixed to the appellation of a god ; both to be given by the father the tenth day after the birth of the child. Vishṇu Purána, 297.

Sarmishta—The daughter of Vrishaparvan, and one of the wives of king Yayáti. She was the mother of Puru, who gave his youth to his father, receiving in exchange Yayáti's infirmities.

Sarpa—The name of one of the eleven Rúdras according to the Váyu list.

Sarpi—The wife of the Rudra Śiva, whose place is the air.

Saru—One of the sons of Vaṣudeva by his wífe Rohini.

Sarva—One of the eight modifications or manifestations of Rudra ; the one whose station is the earth. Vishṇu Purána, 58.

Sarvabhauma—A prince, the son of Vidúratha, a descendant of Kuru.

Sarvaga—(1, A son of the sage Paurnamása, of the race of Maríchi ; 2, one of the Páṇḍava princes, the son of Bhíma.

Sarve'svara—One of the names of the Supreme Being, meaning "The Lord of all." Ziegenbalg writes, "When the Hindus speak of the highest Divine Being as altogether spiritual and immaterial, they talk quite reasonably. They take for unquestionable truth all that Christians believe of God's nature and attributes, saying that there is but one God, who is purely spiritual, incomprehensible, eternal, almighty, omniscient, all-wise, holy, true, just, gracious, and merciful ; who creates, upholds, and governs all ; who has pleasure in dwelling with mankind and making them happy, both in this world and the world to come ; wherefore to serve him is happiness. The names they give to this Divine Being are altogether expressive of divine attributes."

Saryatas—Sons of Sáryátas, descendant of Raivata, who through fear of the Rákshasas took refuge in forests and mountains, and afterwards, according to the legends, became renowned in all regions.

Saryati—1, One of the sons of the great Manu Vaivaswata ; 2, A son of Nahusha, according to the list in the Linga Puráṇa.

Sasa—A portion of Jambu-dwípa, reflected in the lunar orb as in a mirror.

Sasada—The son of Ikshváku, who on the death of his father succeeded to the sovereignty of Ayodhya, or as the Vishṇu Purána has it, to the dominion of the earth.

Sasadharman—One of the Mauryan kings, or descendants of Chandragupta, king of Magadhá.

Sasavinda—A prince, the son of Chitrarathra ; celebrated as the lord of the fourteen great gems ; or articles the best of their kind, seven animate and seven inanimate ; a wife, a priest, a general, a charioteer, a horse, an elephant, and a body of foot soldiers ; or instead of the last three, an excutioner, an encomiast, a reader of the vedas : and a chariot, an umbrella, a jewel, a sword, a shield, a banner, and a treasure. The Vishṇu Purána states that he had a hundred thousand wives and a million of sons !

Sastra-devatas—Gods of the divine weapons ; a hundred are enumerated in the Rámáyana, and they are there termed the sons of Kriaswa by Jaya and Vijaya, daughters of the Prajápati, that is, of Daksha.

Saswata—One of the kings of Mithila, the son of Sruta.

Satabali—A distinguished general in the army of the monkey king Sugríva.

Satabhisha—A lunar mansion in Mrigavithi in the southern Avashthána.

Satadhanu—1, A king in the olden time celebrated on account of the great virtue of his wife Saivyá, under whose name the history of Satadhanu will be found' ; 2, One of the sons of Hridika, of the Yádava race.

Satadru—"The hundred channelled," the river Sutledj. It is the Zardras of Ptolemy, the Hesidrus of Pliny. Notes to Vishṇu Purána.

Satadyumna—1, One of the ten sons of the Manu Chákshusha ; 2, One of the kings of Mithila, the son of Bhánumat.

Satajit—1, One of the kings of Bhárata, the son of Rája ; 2, A son of Sahasrajit of the Yádava race ; 3, One of the sons of Bhajamána.

Satakarni—The name or title of several Andhra princes.

Satananda—The son of Gautama by Ahalya. According to the Rámáyaṇa, Satánanda was the family priest of Janaka, the father of Síta.

Satanika—1, One of the Páṇḍava princes, the son of Nakula ; 2, The son of Janamejaya, king of Bhárata ; 3, The son of Vasudána, of the race of Puru.

Satapatha-Brahmana—An appendix to the White Yajur Veda, which describes a variety of solemn sacrifices in which the juice of the Soma plant is the chief ingredient. It also contains various theories of creation and wild legends which show that "the old Sanskrit philosophers found it extremely difficult to determine the difference between gods and men."

"Considered religiously the Satapatha-Brahmana appears to offer a thorough type of scepticism. Man makes gods, god makes a chief god, the chief god (Prajápati) makes the world and gods. But the gods were mortal. Rites and austerities were invented which insure immortality. Death becomes alarmed. Death is promised that only without the body shall gods or men become immortal. But after the gods have become immortal, they are unable to determine which among them shall be greatest."*

The contents of the Satapatha-Brahmana are somewhat heterogeneous, and amongst other curious stories there is one relating to the Deluge, which has been already given under the article MANU.

Satarupa—The female portion of Brahmá, who, after detaching from himself the property of anger, in the form of Rúdra, converted himself into two persons, the first male, or the Manu Swáyambhuva, and the first woman, or Satarúpa : Professor Wilson says, "The division of Brahmá into two halves, designates, as is very evident from the passage in the Vedas given by Mr.

* Mrs. Manning. A. and M. I.

Colebrooke, the distinction of corporeal substance into two sexes; Viráj being all male animals, Satarúpa, all female animals. Satarúpa, the bride of Brahmá, of Viráj, or of Manu, is nothing more than beings of varied or manifold forms, from Sata, 'a hundred,' and rúpa, 'form'; explained by the annotator in the Hari Vansa by Anantarúpa, of infinite shape, and Vividharúpa, of diversified shape, being as he states, the same as Máyá 'illusion,' or the power of multiform metamarphosis." Vishṇu Purána, 53.

Sata Sankhyas—A class of deities in the tenth Manwantara.

Satavalaka—A pupil of Sakapurni and teacher of the Rig Veda.

Satayus—One of the six sons of Purúravas.

Sati—Truth; one of the daughters of Daksha, and wife of Bhava. The Vishṇu Purána says she abandoned her corporeal existence in consequence of the displeasure of Daksha: and was afterwards the daughter of Himavan by Mená; and in that character, as the only Umá, the mighty Bhava again married her. Urged by her Mahéswara went to the sacrifice of Daksha; the different Puránas furnish contradictory accounts of her share in the transaction and of the way in which she met her death.

Satrughna—The youngest of the four divine sons of Dasaratha, king of Ayodhya. Satrughna killed the Rákshasa chief Lavaṇa, and took possession of his capital Mathura. After the destruction of the Rákshasas had been completed, Satrughna re-ascended to heaven with his three brothers.

Satrajit—The son of Nighna and friend of the divine Áditya, the Sun. The Vishṇu Purána relates the following legend respecting him:—"On one occasion, Satrájit, whilst walking along the sea-shore, addressed his mind to Súrya, and hymned his praises; on which, the divinity appeared and stood before him. Beholding him in an indistinct shape, Satrájit said to the Sun: "I have beheld thee, lord, in the heavens, as a globe of fire. Now do thou show favour unto me, that I may see thee in thy proper form." On this, the Sun, taking the jewel called Syamantaka from off his neck, placed it apart; and Satrájit beheld him of a dwarfish stature, with a body like burnished copper, and with slightly reddish eyes. Having offered his adorations, the Sun desired him to demand a boon ; and he requested that the jewel might become his. The Sun presented it to him, and then resumed his place in the sky. Having obtained the spotless gem of gems, Satrájit wore it on his neck ; and, becoming as brilliant, thereby, as the Sun himself, irradiating all the regions with his splendour, he returned to Dwáraka. The inhabitants of that city, beholding him approach, repaired to the eternal male, Purushottama,—who, to sustain the burthen of the earth, had assumed a mortal form (as Krishṇa),—and said to him : "Lord, assuredly the (divine) Sun is coming to visit you." But Krishṇa smiled, and said : "It is not the divine Sun, but Satrájit, to whom Áditya has presented the Syamantaka gem ; and he now wears it. Go and behold him without apprehension." Accordingly, they departed. Satrájit, having gone to his house, there deposited the jewel, which yielded, daily, eight loads of gold, and, through its marvellous virtue, dispelled all fear of portents, wild beasts, fire, robbers, and famine.

Satrájit was ultimately killed by Satadhanwan in order to obtain possession of the jewel.

Satwata—A prince of the Yádava race, whose descendants were termed Satwatas.

Satya—The quality of goodness, or purity, knowledge, quiescence. An incarnation of Vishṇu in the third Manwantara.

Satyabhama—The daughter of Satrájit and one of the wives of Krishṇa. In consequence of some aspersions cast on the character of Krishṇa relating to the disappearance of the Syamantaka gem, Satrájit reflected that he had been their cause, and to conciliate Krishṇa gave him to wife his daughter Satyabháma. When the jewel was recovered, Balabhadra claimed it as his property jointly with Krishṇa, while Satyabháma demanded it as her right, as it had originally belonged to her father. She afterwards desired to possess the Parijáta tree, which Krishṇa accordingly removed from heaven to Dwáraka, though strongly opposed by Indra and the other gods.

Satyadhrita—A prince, the son of Pushpavat.

Sataydhriti—1, One of the kings of Mithila, the son of

Mahávírya ; 2, The son of Sarana ; 3, The son of Dhritimat ; 4, The son of Satánanda : and a proficient in military science. Being enamoured of the nymph Urvaṣí, Satyadhriti was the parent of two children, a boy and a girl ; who were found exposed in a clump of long Sara grass, by the Rája Santana whilst out hunting.

Satyadhwaja—A prince, the son of Urjjavaha, king of Mithila.

Satyahita—A teacher of the Rig Veda.

Satyajit—One of the kings of Mágadha, the son of Sanhita.

Satyaka—A prince, the son of Sini.

Satyakarman—One of the kings of Anga, the son of Dhritavrata.

Satyaketu—A king of Káṣí, the son of Sukamara, a descendant of Alarka.

Satyaloka—The world of infinite wisdom and truth, the inhabitants of which never again know death. It is said in the Vishṇu Purána to be situated one hundred and twenty millions of leagues above Dhruva.

Stayanetra—A sage, one of the sons of Atri, according to the series in the Váyu.

Satyaratha—One of the kings of Mithila, the son of Mínaratha.

Satyarathi—The son and successor of the above.

Satyas—A class of deities in the third Manwantara. (See Jayas.)

Satyasravas—A teacher of the Rig Veda.

Satyavak—One of the noble sons of the Manu Chákshusha.

Satyavan—The son of a blind old king who had been driven from his throne and was living in the forest as a hermit, when Savitrí, the lovely daughter of king Aswapati saw Satyaván and loved him. She was warned by a seer to overcome her attachment as Satyaván was a doomed man having only one year to live. But Savitrí replies :—

> Whether his years be few or many, be he gifted with all grace
> Or graceless, him my heart hath chosen, and it chooseth not again.

They are therefore married and the bride strives to forget the ominous prophecy ; out as the last day of the year approaches, her anxiety becomes irrepressible. She accompanied her husband to the forest on the fatal morning with a heavy heart ; while he was cutting wood a thrill of agony suddenly shot through his temples, and he called out to his wife to support him—

> Then she received her fainting husband in her arms, and sate herself
> On the cold ground, and gently laid his drooping head upon her lap ;
> Sorrowing she called to mind the sage's prophecy, and reckoned up
> The days and hours. All in an instant she beheld an awful shape
> Standing before her, dressed in blood-red garments, with a glittering crown
> Upon his head : his form, though glowing like the sun, was yet obscure,
> And eyes he had like flames, a noose depended from his hand, and he
> Was terrible to look upon, as by her husband's side he stood
> And gazed upon him with a fiery glance. Shuddering she started up
> And laid her dying Satyavan upon the ground, and with her hands
> Joined reverently, she thus with beating heart addressed the shape ;
> Surely thou art a god, such form as thine must more than mortal be,
> Tell me, thou god-like being, who thou art, and wherefore thou art here?

The figure replies that he is Yama, king of death ; that her husband's time has come, and that he must bind and take his spirit.

> Then from her husband's body forced he out and firmly with his cord
> Bound and detained the spirit, like in size and length to a man's thumb.
> Forthwith the body, reft of vital being, and deprived of breath,
> Lost all its grace and beauty, and became ghastly and motionless.

After binding the spirit, Yama proceeds with it towards his own quarter, the South. The faithful wife follows him closely. Yama bids her go home and prepare her husband's funeral rites ; but she persists in following, till Yama, pleased with her devotion, grants her any boon she pleases *except* the life of her husband. She chooses that her husband's father, who is blind, may recover his sight. Yama consents, and bids her now return home. Still she persists in following. At last, overcome by her constancy, Yama grants a boon without exception. The delighted Savitrí exclaims—

> 'Nought, mighty king, this time hast thou excepted ; let my husband live ;
> Without him I desire not happiness, nor even heaven itself :
> Without him I must die.' 'So be it, faithful wife,' replied the king of death,
> 'Thus I release him ; and with that he loosed the cord that bound his soul.'*

—See Savitrí.

Satyavati—The daughter of king Gádhí, who was demanded

* William's Indian Epic Poetry, pp. 37—39.

in marriage by an elderly brahmin name Richíka. The king would only consent to give his daughter on the condition that the sage should give him as the nuptial present, a thousand fleet horses whoso colour should be white with one black ear. Richíka, having propitiated Varuṇa, the god of the ocean, obtained from him, at (the holy place called) Aṣwatírtha, a thousand such steeds, and, giving them to the king, espoused his daughter.

In order to effect the birth of a son, Richíka prepared a dish of rice, barley, and pulse, with butter and milk, for his wife to eat; and, at her request, he consecrated a similar mixture for her mother, by partaking of which, she should give birth to a prince of martial prowess. Leaving both dishes with his wife,—after describing, particularly, which was intended for her, and which for her mother,—the sage went forth to the forests. When the time arrived for the food to be eaten, the queen said to Satyavatí: "Daughter, all persons wish their children to be possessed of excellent qualities, and would be mortified to see them surpassed by the merits of their mother's brother. It will be desirable for you, therefore, to give me the mess your husband has set apart for you, and to eat of that intended for me; for the son which it is to procure me is destined to be the monarch of the whole world, whilst that which your dish would give you must be a brahman, alike devoid of affluence, valour, and power." Satyavatí agreed to her mother's proposal; and they exchanged messes.

When Richíka returned home, and beheld Satyavatí, he said to her: "Sinful woman, what hast thou done? I view thy body of a fearful appearance. Of a surety, thou hast eaten the consecrated food which was prepared for thy mother: thou hast done wrong. In that food I had infused the properties of power, and strength, and heroism; in thine, the qualities suited to a brahman,—gentleness, knowledge, and resignation. In consequence of having reversed my plans, thy son shall follow a warrior's propensities, and use weapons, and fight, and slay. Thy mother's son shall be born with the inclinations of a brahman, and be addicted to peace and piety." Satyavatí, hearing this, fell at her husband's feet, and said: "My lord, I have done this thing through ignorance. Have compassion on me: let me not have a son such as thou hast foretold. If such there must be, let it be my grandson, not my son." The Muni, relenting at her distress, replied: "So let it be." Accordingly, in due season, she gave birth to Jamadagni; and her mother brought forth Viṣvámitra. Satyavatí afterwards became the Kauṣikí river. V. P.

Satyavrata—A king of Ayodhyá, the seventh in descent from Ikshváku, who obtained the appellation of Triṣanku, and was degraded to the condition of a Cháṇḍála or outcaste. The Vishṇu Purána states that: "During a twelve years' famine, Triṣanku provided the flesh of deer, for the nourishment of the wife and children of Viṣvámitra; suspending it upon a (spreading) fig-tree on the borders of the Ganges, that he might not subject them to the indignity of receiving presents from an outcaste. On this account, Viṣvámitra, being highly pleased with him, elevated him, in his living body, to heaven.

In a Note, Professor Wilson remarks, "The occurrence of the famine, and Satyavrata's care of the wife and family of Viṣvámitrá, are told, with some variations, in the Váyu, which has been followed by the Brahmá and Hari Vamṣa. During the famine, when game fails, he kills the cow of Vaṣiṣhtha; and, for the three crimes of displeasing his father, killing a cow, and eating flesh not previously consecrated, he acquires the name of Triṣanku (tri, 'three," ṣanku, 'sin.') Vaṣiṣhtha refusing to perform his regal inauguration, Viṣvámitra celebrates the rites, and, on his death, elevates the king, in his mortal body, to heaven. The Rámáyaṇa relates the same circumstance, but assigns to it a different motive,—Viṣvámitra's resentment of the refusal of the gods to attend Triṣanku's sacrifice. That work also describes the attempt of the gods to cast the king down upon earth, and the compromise between them and Viṣvámitra, by which Triṣanku was left suspended, head downwards, in mid-air, forming a constellation in the southern hemisphere, along with other new planets and stars formed by Viṣvámitra. The Bhágavata has no allusion to this legend, saying that Triṣanku is still visible in heaven. The Váyu furnishes some further information from an older source: Both my copies have a blank, where it is marked; and a similar passage does not elsewhere occur: but the word should probably be *nisha*, and the whole may be thus rendered : " Men acquainted with the Puránas recite these two stanzas : 'By the favour of Visvámitra, the illustrious Trisanku shines in heaven, along with the gods, through the kindness of that sage. Slowly passes the lovely night in winter, embellished by the moon, decorated with three watches, and ornamented with the constellation Trisanku.' " This legend is, therefore, clearly astronomical, and alludes, possibly, to some reformation of the sphere by Visvámitra, under the patronage of Trisanku, and in opposition to a more ancient system advocated by the school of Vasishtha. It might be no very rash conjecture, perhaps, to identify Trisanku with Orion, the three bright stars of whose belt may have suggested the three Sankus (stakes or pins) which form his name.

" The seven ancient rishis or saints, as has been said before, were the seven stars of Ursa Vajor. The seven other new saints which are here said to have been created by Visvámitra, should be seven new southern stars, a sort of new Ursa. Von Schlegel thinks that this mythical fiction of new stars created by Visvámitra may signify that these southern stars, unknown to the Indians as long as they remained in the neighbourhood of the Ganges, became known to them at a later date when they colonised the southern regions of India."—GORRESIO.

Satyayajna—The observance of truth ; one of the great obligations of brahmans.

Saubhari—A devout sage, learned in the Vedas, of whom the following extraordinary legend is narrated. He spent twelve years immersed in a lake, the sovereign of the fish in which, named Sammada, had a very numerous progeny. His children and his grandchildren were wont to frolic around him, in all directions ; and he lived amongst them happily, playing with them night and day. Saubhari, the sage, being disturbed, in his devotions, by their sports, contemplated the patriarchal felicity of the monarch of the lake, and reflected : " How enviable is this creature, who, although born in a degraded state of being, is ever thus sporting cheerfully amongst his offspring and their young ! Of a truth, he awakens, in my mind, the wish to taste such pleasure ; and I, also, will make merry amidst my children." Having thus resolved, the Muni came up, hastily, from the water, and, desirous of entering upon the condition of a householder, went to Mándhátṛi, to demand one of his daughters as his wife. As soon as he was informed of the arrival of the sage, the king rose up from his throne, offered him the customary libation, and treated him with the most profound respect. Having taken a seat, Saubhari said to the Rája: "I have determined to marry. Do you, king, give me one of your daughters, as a wife? Disappoint not my affection. It is not the practice of the princes of the race of Kakutstha to turn away from compliance with the wishes of those who come to them for succour. There are, O monarch, other kings of the earth to whom daughters have been born; but your family is, above all, renowned for observance of liberality in your donations to those who ask your bounty. You have, O prince, fifty daughters. Give one of them to me; that so I may be relieved from the anxiety I suffer through fear that my suit may be denied."

When Mándhátṛi heard this request, and looked upon the person of the sage, emaciated by (austerity and) old age, he felt disposed to refuse his consent: but, dreading to incur the anger and imprecation of the holy man, he was much perplexed, and, declining his head, was lost awhile in thought. The Rishi, observing his hesitation, said: "On what, O Rája, do you meditate? I have asked for nothing which may not be readily accorded. And what is there that shall be unattainable to you, if my desires be gratified by the damsel whom you must needs give unto me?" To this, the king, apprehensive of his displeasure, answered and said: "Grave sir, it is the established usage of our house to wed our daughters to such persons only as they shall, themselves, select from suitors of fitting rank; and, since this your request is not yet made known to my maidens, it is impossible to say whether it may be equally agreeably to them as it is to me. This is the occasion of my perplexity; and I am at a loss what to do." This answer of the king was fully understood by the Rishi, who said to himself: "This is merely a device of the Rája, to evade compliance with my suit. He has reflected that I am an old man, having no attractions for women, and not likely to be accepted by any of his daughters. Even be it so : I will be a match for him." And he then spake aloud, and said : " Since such is the custom, mighty prince, give orders that I be admitted into the interior of the palace. Should any of the maidens, your daughters, be willing to take me for a bridegroom, I will have her for my bride. If no one be willing, then let the blame attach alone to the years that I have numbered." Having thus spoken, he was silent.

Mándhátṛi, unwilling to provoke the indignation of the Muni, was accordingly, obliged to command the eunuch to lead the sage into the inner chambers ; who, as he entered the apartments, put on a form and features of beauty far exceeding the personal charms of mortals, or even of heavenly spirits. His conductor, addressing the princesses, said to them : " Your father, young ladies, sends you this pious sage, who has demanded of him a bride ; and the Rája has promised him, that he will not refuse him any one of you who shall choose him for her husband." When the damsels heard this, and looked upon the person of the Rishi, they were equally inspired with passion and desire, and, like a troop of female elephants disputing the favours of the master of the herd, they all contended for the choice. " Away, away, sister !" said each to the other : " this is my election ; he is my choice ; he is not a meet bridgeroom for you ; he has been created, by Brahmá, on purpose for me, as I have been created in order to become his wife ; he has been chosen, by me, before you ; you have no right to prevent his becoming my husband." In this way arose a violent quarrel amongst the daughters of the king, each insisting upon the exclusive election of the Rishi ; and, as the blameless sage was thus contended for by the rival princesses, the superintendent of the inner apartments, with a downcast look, reported to the king what had occurred. Perplexed, more than ever, by this information, the Rája exclaimed : " What is all this ? And what am I to do now ? What is it that I have said ? And, at last, although with extreme reluctance, he was obliged to agree that the Rishi should marry all his daughters.

Having then wedded, agreeably to law, all the princesses, the sage took them home to his habitation, where he employed the chief of architects, Viṣvakarman,—equal, in taste and skill, to

Brahmá himself,—to construct separate palaces for each of his wives: he ordered him to provide each building with elegant couches, and seats, and furniture, and to attach to them gardens and groves, with reservoirs of water, where the wild-duck and the swan should sport amidst beds of lotus flowers. The divine artist obeyed his injunctions, and constructed splendid apartments for the wives of the Rishi; in which, by command of Saubhari, the inexhaustible and divine treasure called Nanda took up his permanent abode; and the princesses entertained all their guests and dependants with abundant viands of every description and the choicest quality.

After some period had elapsed, the heart of king Mándhátṛi yearned for his daughters; and he felt solicitous to know whether they were happily circumstanced. Setting off, therefore, on a visit to the hermitage of Saubhari, he beheld, upon his arrival, a row of beautiful crystal palaces, shining as brilliantly as the rays of the sun, and situated amidst lovely gardens and reservoirs of pellucid water. Entering into one of these magnificent palaces, he found and embraced a daughter, and said to her, as the tears of affection and delight trembled in his eyes: "Dear child, tell me how it is with you. Are you happy here, or not? Does the great sage treat you with tenderness? Or do you revert, with regret, to your early home?" The princess replied: "You behold, my father, how delightful a mansion I inhabit,—surrounded by lovely gardens and lakes, where the lotus blooms, and the wild swans murmur. Here I have delicious viands, fragrant unguents, costly ornaments, splendid raiment, soft beds, and every enjoyment that affluence can procure. Why, then, should I call to memory the place of my birth? To your favour am I indebted for all that I possess. I have only one cause of anxiety, which is this: my husband is never absent from my dwelling; solely attached to me, he is always at my side; he never goes near my sisters; and I am concerned to think that they must feel mortified by his neglect: this is the only circumstance that gives me uneasiness."

Proceeding to visit another of his daughters, the king, after embracing her, and sitting down, made the same enquiry, and received the same account of the enjoyments with which the princess was provided. There was, also the same complaint, that the Rishi was wholly devoted to her, and paid no attention to her sisters. In every palace, Mándhátṛi heard the same story, from each of his daughters, in reply to his questions; and, with a heart overflowing with wonder and delight, he repaired to the wise Saubhari, whom he found alone, and after paying homage to him, thus addressed him: "Holy sage, I have witnessed this thy marvellous power. The like miraculous faculties I have never known any other to possess. How great is the reward of thy devout austerities!" Having thus saluted the sage, and been received by him, with respect, the Rája resided with him for some time, partaking of the pleasures of the place, and then returned to his capital.

In the course of time, the daughters of Mándhátṛi bore to Saubhari a hundred and fifty sons; and, day by day, his affection for his children became more intense, and his heart was wholly occupied with the sentiment of self. "These my sons," he loved to think, "will charm me with their infant prattle; then they will learn to walk; they will, then, grow up to youth, and to manhood; I shall see them married, and they will have children; and I may behold the children of those children." By these and similar reflections, however, he perceived that his anticipations every day outstripped the course of time; and, at last, he exclaimed: "What exceeding folly is mine! There is no end to my desires. Though all I hope should come to pass for ten thousand or a hundred thousand years, still new wishes would spring up. When I have seen my infants walk; when I have beheld their youth, their manhood, their marriage, their progeny; still my expectations are unsatisfied, and my soul yearns to behold the descendants of their descendants. Shall I even see them, some other wish will be engendered; and, when that is accomplished, how is the birth of fresh desires to be prevented? I have at last, discovered, that there is no end to hope, until it terminates in death; and that the mind which is perpetually engrossed by expectation can never be attached to the supreme spirit. My mental devotions, whilst immersed in water, were interrupted by attachment to my friend the fish. The result of that connexion was my marriage; and insatiable desires are the consequences of my married life. The pain attendant upon the birth of my single body is now augmented by the cares attached to fifty others, and is further multiplied by the numerous children whom the princesses have borne to me. The sources of affliction will be repeatedly renewed by their children, and by their espousals, and by their progeny, and will be infinitely increased : a married life is a mine of individual anxiety. My devotions, first disturbed by the fish of the pool, have since been obstructed by temporal indulgence ; and I have been beguiled by that desire for progeny which was communicated to me by association with Sammada. Separation from the world is the only path of the sage to final liberation : from commerce with mankind innumerable errors proceed. The ascetic who has accomplished a course of self-denial falls from perfection, by contracting worldly attachments. How much more likely should one so fall, whose observances are incomplete ! My intellect has been a prey to the desire of married happiness : but I will, now, so exert myself, for the salvation of my soul, that exempt from human imperfections, I may be exonerated from human sufferings. To that end, I will propitiate, by arduous penance, Vishṇu, the creator of the universe, whose form is inscrutable, who is smaller than the smallest, larger than the largest, the source of darkness and of light, the sovereign god of gods. On his everlasting body, which is both discrete and indiscrete substance, illimitably mighty, and identical with the universe, may my mind, wholly free from sin, be ever steadily intent, so that I may be born no more ! To him I fly for refuge ; to that Vishṇu who is the teacher of teachers, who is one with all beings, the pure eternal lord of all, without beginning, middle, or end, and besides whom is nothing." V. P.

Saudasa—A prince, the son of Sudása ; named also Mitrasaha, to which the reader is referred for the legend of his life.

Saumitri—A teacher of the Sáma Veda.

Saumya—A division of the Varsha of Bhárata.

Saunahotra—A Rishi, the son of Sunahotra. On one occasion Indra himself went to a sacrifice of the Rishi in order to please him. The great Asuras, thinking that Indra was above, and wishing to take him, surrounded the sacrificial enclosure. Indra, however, perceived it, and taking the guise of the Rishi, he went away. The Asuras, seeing the sacrificer again, seized Saunahotra, taking him for Indra. He pointed out Indra to them and was released by the Asuras.—*A. S. L.*, 231.

Saunaka—1, A teacher of the Atharva Veda ; 2, The son of Ghritsamada according to the Vishṇu Purána, but Professor Wilson remarks that this is probably an error, as several other Puránas agree in making him the son of Sunaka. It was Saunaka who established the distinctions of the four castes. See A. S. L., 232–36.

Saurashtras—The people of Surat ; the Surastrene of Ptolemy.

Sauvirai—The nations of Sindh, and Western Rájputána.

Savala—One of the sons of Priyavrata, who was nominated by his father to be the monarch of the Dwípa of Pushkara.

Savalaswas—Daksha, at the command of Brahmá, is said to have created various living creatures. His first four thousand sons, termed Haryaswas, were dissuaded by Nárada from propagating offspring, and dispersed themselves throughout the universe. Daksha then created a thousand other sons, named Savaláswas, who were desirous of engendering posterity, but were dissuaded by Nárada, in a similar manner. They said to one another "what the sage has observed is perfectly just." We must follow the path that our brothers have travelled, and when we have ascertained the extent of the universe, we will multiply our race. Accordingly they scattered themselves through the regions, and, like rivers flowing into the sea, they returned not again.

Savana—One of the seven sons of the Muni Vaṣiṣhtha.

Savarna—1, The daughter of the ocean who was married to king Práchínaverhis, to whom she had been previously betrothed. She was the mother of the Prachetasas, q. v. ; 2, The "female of like appearance" who was substituted by Saraṇyú, when she fled from Vivaswat. Savarṇá became the mother of Manu.—*O. S. T., Vol. V*, p. 228.

Savarni—A Manu, the son of the sun by his maid Chháya. He is to be the Manu of the eighth Manwantara.

Savibhasa—One of the seven suns into which the solar rays dilate at the end of the day of Brahmá when the world is destroyed.

Savitri—"A king, named Aswapati, sighed for offspring, and after praying in vain for eighteen years, the gods of heaven sent him a daughter, who grew up so "bright in her beauty," that she appeared like a child of the Immortals; and the princes around were so dazzled, that none dared to ask for her as a bride.

"So passing fair the young Sávitri grew
That all adored her but none thought to woo.
No lovelier nymph e'er left her native skies
To dazzle mortals with her heavenly eyes;
And how might e'en the proudest chieftain dare,
To woo a Princess so divinely fair."

This distressed her father, and he said that she must go now and make choice herself.

"Meekly bowed the modest maiden, with her eyes upon the ground,
And departed, as he bade her, with attendants troop'd around.
Many a hermitage she travers'd, riding in a gold-bright car;
Many a wilderness and forest, holy places near and far."

"When she came back she told of a blind old king, driven from his throne by a ruthless kinsman, living with his beloved wife in a grove; and his brave son, Satyaván, her heart has chosen. "Satyaván," she says, "has all my love."

At this announcement a Rishi, who happened to be present, exclaims, in distress, that she would choose care and grief, in choosing Satyavan. He is

"Learned as the gods' own teacher,—glorious as the sun is he:
With the earth's untiring patience, and great Indra's bravery."

He is noble,

"True, and great of soul,
Bountiful is he, and modest,—every sense does he controul.
Gentle, brave, all creatures love him,—keeping in the righteous way,
Number'd with the holy hermits,—pure and virtuous as they."

But alas! in a year, counting from this day, "Satyaván will die." On hearing this, the king considers a marriage out of the question, and says: "Go, then, my dearest child, and choose again." But his daughter replies:

"Be he virtuous or worthless,—many be his days, or few,—
Once for all I choose my husband: to that choice will I be true."

The sage and her father give way to her decided wishes: and in due time the young couple are married, and live in great happiness with the hermits in the grove. Sâvitrî, the bride, put aside her jewels, and wore the coarse raiment usually adopted by hermits; and, by her meekness and affection, won the hearts of all with whom she dwelt.

> "Sadly, sadly as she counted, day by day flew swiftly by,
> And the fated time came nearer when her Satyavan must die.
> Yet three days and he must perish, sadly thought the loving wife,
> And she vowed to fast, unresting, for his last three days of life."

Her husband's father feared that the trial would be too great for her, but she answered: "Firm resolve has made me vow it; firm resolve will give me strength." She kept her vow, and maintained her fast; and when the third day dawned, and the fire of worship was kindled, and the morning rites performed, she reverently saluted the aged Brâhmans and her husband's honoured parents, but still refused food. Presently, her husband takes his axe upon his shoulder to perform his daily task of felling trees. She begs him to let her go also; he replies:

> "All unknown to thee the forest; rough the part and weary thou:
> How, then, will thy feet support thee, fainting from thy fasting vow?"
> "Nay, I sink not from my fasting, and no weakness feel to-day;
> I have set my heart on going: oh! forbid me not, I pray!"

Sâvitrî has always kept her sad secret from her husband; and he has, therefore, no idea of her real reason for wishing to accompany him. He, however, consents, and calls her attention to the lovely woods, stately peacocks, and flowers of brilliant hue; but she can look only upon him, and mourn for him as one about to die. She gathers cooling fruits, and he makes the woods resound with the strokes of his hatchet. But, soon a thrilling agony shoots through his temple......She sits down upon the ground, and he rests his head upon her breast, and sleeps. But,—

> "Sudden, lo! before Sâvitrî stood a great and awful One;
> Red as blood was his apparel, bright and glowing as the sun.
> In his hand a noose was hanging; he to Satyavan stood nigh,
> And upon the weary sleeper fix'd his fearful, glittering eye."

This awful apparition was Yama, god of Death, come to bind and take the spirit of Satyavan. Having done this, he moved towards the south, Sâvitrî closely following. Yama tries to persuade her to go back ; but she says, no : wherever her husband goes, there she will go also. Yama praises her sweet speech, and offers her any boon except the life of Satyavan ; and she begs that the blind king, her father-in-law, may be restored to sight, but without relinquishing her first request. Yama tries again and again to get rid of her, and says she wlll faint.

> " Can I faint when near my husband ? where he goes my path shall be.
> I will follow where thou leadest ;—listen once again to me."

Nothing can induce her to return without Satyavan ; and at length "love conquers death." Yama relents ; the happy wife hastens to where her husband's dead body lay, and, leaning upon her faithful bosom he awakes again to sense and life. A very touching conversation follows, during which he gradually recovers his recollection ; but his wife, avoiding any full explanation of what had been occurring, says :

> " Night's dark shadows round us fall ;
> When the morrow's light returneth, dearest ! I will tell thee all.
> Up, then, and away, I pray thee,—come unto thy parents, love !
> See ! the sun long time has vanish'd, and the night grows black above."

And accordingly they return to the hermitage, when Satyavan finds his father no longer blind ; and every kind of happiness awaits them."*—See SATYAVAN.

Savitri—1, One of the twelve Ádityas, the sun. " Savitri has established the earth by supports ; Savitri has fixed the sky in unsupported space : Savitri has milked the atmosphere, restless (or noisy) as a horse [or, Savitri has extracted from the atmosphere the ocean, &c., restless as a horse ;]—the ocean fastened on the unpassable expanse. Savitri, son of the waters, knows the place where the ocean supported, issued forth. From him the earth, from him the atmosphere, arose ; from him the heaven and earth extended." The sun also whose place is on the sky is called Savitri. 2, The Vyása of the fifth Dwápara age.

Senajit—One of the kings of Hastinápura, the son of Viswajit.

Senani—One of the eleven Rudras according to the enumeration in the Matsya Purána.

* A. & M. I. Indian Epic Poetry.

Serpents—These are represented in the Vishṇu Purána as the progeny of Kadru, they are described as powerful and many-headed; and some as fierce and venomous. The chief are mentioned by name.

Sesha—Eternal matter in which Vishṇu reposes during the night of Bramhá when the destructive power only is in operation. It is represented as an immense snake, forming by its many coils, a bed on which Vishṇu sleeps, and with its thousand heads erect, to form a canopy over Vishṇu's head, and to present the idea of defence against any invasion of the sleeper's repose. *Sésha* is also said to support the eight elephants which support the world. The name Sésha is considered by Sir William Jones and others to designate abstract eternity, but the emblem does not altogether correspond with the Egyptian hieroglyphic used for this purpose. The literal meaning is primal serpent, and many of the Hindu legends introduce this snake. In the Puránas there is an account of a dispute between it and *Váyu*, regent of the wind. The latter blew with all his strength against the thousand peaks of Mount Meru, and Sésha covered every one of the peaks, each by one of his thousand heads. The sanctity of Tripiti, a hill in the north of Mysore is derived from a traditionary version of this legend. Váyu is said to have ceased blowing for a time when Sésha lifted up one head to ascertain the cause, and Váyu suddenly blew off the exposed peak, which was carried through the air and fell at Tripiti, conferring on the place the sanctity of Mount Meru. At the Seven Pagodas, near Madras, there is a good sculpture of Sésha in one of the hill caves. The subject is a favorite one with the Vaishnavas. Sir C. Wilkins thus describes one in the north of India, the rock of Ichangiri in the province of Behar. Among the images carved in relief in the surface of the rock, is one of *Hari*, (a title of Vishṇu) of gigantic dimensions, recumbent upon a coiled serpent, whose heads, which are numerous, the artist has contrived to spread into a kind of canopy over the sleeping god; and from each of its mouths issues a forked tongue, seeming to threaten instant death to any whom rashness might prompt to disturb him. The whole lies almost clear of the block on which it is hewn. It is finely imagined and is executed with great skill. The Hindus believe that at the end of every kalpa (creation) all things are absorbed in the deity, and that in the interval of another creation he reposeth himself upon the serpent Sésha (duration), who is also called *Ananta*, (endless), q. v.

" Sésha, worshipped by all the gods, supports the whole region of the earth like a diadem, and is the foundation of Pátáḷa. The Siddhantas, or scientific astronomical works of India, however, maintain that the earth is unsupported."—*O. S. T., Vol. IV, p.* 96.

Sesha—One of the Prajápatis.

Siddhartha—A prince of the family of Ikshváku. He was king of Pavana in Bharatakshetra when by supernatural agency he was made the father of the great Tírthankara Mahávíra, q. v.

Siddhas—Pure and holy beings, exempt from covetousness and concupiscence, love and hatred, taking no part in the procreation of living beings, and detecting the unreality of the properties of elementary matter. The Vishṇu Purána states that eighty-eight thousand of these chaste beings tenant the regions of the sky, north of the sun, until the destruction of the universe.

Siddhi—Perfection ; One of the daughters of Daksha, married to Dharma.

Siddhis—The eight perfections ; 1, *Rasollása*, the spontaneous or prompt evolution of the juices of the body, independently of nutriment from without ; 2, Tṛipti, mental satisfaction, or freedom from sensual desire ; 3, Sámya, sameness of degree ; 4, Tulyatá, similarity of life, form, and feature ; 5, Viṣoká, exemption alike from infirmity or grief ; 6, Consummation of penance and meditation, by attainment of true knowledge ; 7, The power of going everywhere at will ; 8, The faculty of reposing at any time or in any place. These attributes are alluded to, though obscurely, in the Váyu, and are partly specified in the Márkaṇḍeya Purána.

Sighra—1, A prince, the son of Agnivara, descendant of Kuṣa ; 2, A river.

Sikhandini—The wife of Antarddhána, descendant of Prithu.

Siksha—An Anga, or subsidiary portion of the Vedas, containing the rules of reciting the prayers, the accents and tones to be observed, &c.

Sindhu—A river of Bhárata Varsha; there are several rivers of this name, as well as the Indus; there is one of some note, the Kálí Sindh in Malwa.

Sindhu—A country near the forest of Káma. It was the Rája of Sindhu, Jayadrathu, who visited Draupadi, in the absence of her husbands, and attempted to carry her away.

Sindhudwipa—One of the kings of Ayodhya, the son of Ambarísha.

Sinhika—One of the daughters of Kaṣyapa, and wife of Viprachitti. She was the sister of the celebrated Danava Hiraṇyakaṣipu.

Sini—One of the Bhoja princes of Mrittikávaṭi, the son of Sumitra.

Sinivali—1, The name of the day when the new moon is first visible; 2, One of the daughters of Angiras.

Sipraka—The first Andhra king; and founder of the Andhrabhritya dynasty. He had previously been minister to Suṣarman, the last of the Kaṇwa kings of Magadha, against whom Siprak conspired, and assumed the sovereignty himself.

Siradhwaja—A name of Janaka, king of Mithila, celebrated as the father of Síta.

Sisira—A teacher of the Rig Veda.

Sisumara—Porpoise. The symbol for the celestial sphere. The porpoise-like figure of the celestial sphere is upheld by Naráyaṇa, who himself, in planetory radiance, is seated in its heart; whilst the son of Uttanápada, Dhruva, in consequence of his adoration of the lord of the world, shines in the tail of the stellar porpoise. Vishṇu Purána, 230.

Sisunaga—One of the kings of Magadha, who relinquished Benares to his son, and established himself at Girivraja, in Behar.

Sisupala—The son of Damaghosha, king of Chedí. This prince was in a former existence the unrighteous but valiant monarch of the Daityas, Hiraṇyakaṣipu, who was killed by the divine guardian of the creation (in the man-lion Avatara.) He was next the ten-headed sovereign Rávaṇa, whose unequalled prowess, strength, and power, were overcome by the lord of the three worlds Ráma ; when born again as Siṣupála, he renewed with greater inveteracy than ever, his hostile hatred towards the god surnamed Puṇḍaríkáksha, a portion of the Supreme Being who had descended to lighten the burden of the earth, and was in consequence slain by him : but because his thoughts were constantly engrossed by the Supreme Being, Siṣupála was united with him after death ; V. P. The death of Siṣupála is thus related in the Mahábhárata : "now the custom was at the beginning of a Rájasúya to declare who was the greatest and strongest of all the Rájas there assembled, in order that the Argha might be given to him ; and Bhíshma, as ruler of the feast, declared that the honour was due to Krishṇa, who was the greatest and strongest of them all. But Siṣupála, the Rája of Chedí, was exceedingly wroth with Krishṇa, for when he was betrothed to the beautiful Rukminí, Krishṇa had carried her away and made her his own wife. So Siṣupála arose and threw the whole assembly into an uproar, and he said with a loud voice :—" If the honour be due to age, it should have been given to Vaṣudeva ; if it be due to him who has the greatest Raj, it should have be given to Rája Drupada ; if it be due to the youth of loftiest mind, it should have been given to Rája Duryodhana ; if it be due to the greatest preceptor, it should have been given to Drona ; and if it be due to the greatest saint, it should have been given to Vyása : but shame be upon this assembly, who hath given that honour to a cowherd, who was the murderer of his own Rája." Having thus spoken, Siṣupála and his friends who were with him made a great tumult. Yudhishthira and Bhíshma then reasoṇed with Siṣupála, but he would not heed their words, and drew his sword, and threatened to slay all the guests and spoil the sacrifice. Yudhishthira and his brethren then rose to fight against Siṣupála, but Bhíshma withheld them ; and Siṣupála in his rage abused Bhíshma and Krishṇa in such opprobrious terms that the whole assembly were alarmed. At last Krishṇa said :—" I have hitherto restrained my hand, because this man is my own kinsman, but I can bear with his words no longer." And thus speaking he whirled his chakra furiously at Siṣupála, and severed his head from his body ;

and Sisupála fell dead upon the ground, and his sons carried away his body and burnt it upon the funeral pile. Thus Krishṇa saved the Rájasúya of Yudhishthira by the slaughter of Sisupála; for had Rája Yudhishthira been set at defiance by a Rája who had not been conquered, the Rájasúya would have been imperfect and of no avail."

Sita—The daughter of Janaka, king of Mithila, (Síradhwaja.) She is called earth-born, as having been turned up from the soil by a plough, as Janaka was ploughing a spot to prepare for a sacrifice. She was promised in marriage to the Rája who could bend the great bow of Śiva; many distinguished Rájas attempted the feat, but could not succeed; "now when Ráma saw the bow he lifted it with one hand from the ground playfully, while a great multitude looked on in amazement. Then Ráma bent the bow till it broke in the midst, and the noise was like the crash of a falling mountain, so that the bystanders were stunned and fell down. After this Sítá was married to Ráma. The story of their honeymoon in the Rámáyana, is supposed to be an interpolation of recent date. When Ráma had to go into exile Sítá avowed her determination to accompany him to the jungle. Ráma objected to this, but at length yielded to her earnest entreaties. They met with many adventures in their jungle life which are described in great detail in the Rámáyana. They rested in the cave of the sage Atri, whose wife Anásúya gave Sítá an ointment to render her young and "beautiful for ever." On one occasion she besought Ráma to pursue a beautiful deer, his brother Lakshmana remaining behind for her protection. Sounds of distress were heard as if proceeding from Ráma, and Sítá taunted Lakshmana with unconcern for his brother until he left her. Then Rávaṇa, by whose contrivance all this had come about, entered the hut as a brahman mendicant, assumed his true form, and addressed Sítá, who replied to him with anger, and Rávaṇa carried her off by force to Lanka, where she was discovered by Hanumán in the Asóka garden. While being carried by Rávaṇa through the air, which she filled with cries and lamentations, she saw five monkeys sitting in the mountain named Risha-mukhá, and threw down her ornaments amongst them in the hope that they might find their way to Ráma. They were found by Sugríva and by him shown to Ráma. Sítá wrathfully refused to receive the addresses of Rávaṇa, who threatened to slay her. She had an interview with Hanumán, and was finally rescued by Ráma ; but had to pass through a severe ordeal before she was received as pure after being imprisoned in the palace of Rávaṇa. She entered the fire and the god Agní attested her purity. She was then installed as Rání with great splendour. She had two children Lava, and Kuṣa.

Siteyus—A prince, the son of Uṣanas, (q. v.)

Siva—The third deity in the Hindu triad. Wilson says that Śiva is the same as Vishṇu in the character of destroyer of creation. He also personifies reproduction, as Hindu philosophy excludes the idea of total annihilation without subsequent regeneration. Hence he is sometimes identified with Brahmá the first person in the triad.

Śiva is the particular god of the Tantrikas, or followers of the books called Tantras. His worshippers are termed Saivas, and although not so numerous as the Vaishnavas, exalt their god to the highest place in the heavens, and combine in him many of the attributes which properly belong to the other deities. According to them, Śiva is Time, Justice, Fire, Water, the Sun, the Destroyer and Creator. As presiding over generation, his type is the Linga, or Phallus, the origin probably of the Phallic emblem of Egypt and Greece. As the god of generation and of justice, which latter character he shares with the god Yama, he is represented riding a white bull. His own colour, as well as that of the bull, is generally white, referring probably to the unsullied purity of justice. His throat is dark-blue ; his hair of a light reddish colour, and thickly matted together, and gathered above his head like the hair of an ascetic. He is sometimes seen with two hands, sometimes with four, eight, or ten, and with five faces. He has three eyes, one being in the centre of his forehead, pointing up and down. These are said to denote his view of the three divisions of time, past, present, and future. He holds a trident in his hand to denote, as some say, his relationship to water, or according to others, to show that the three great attributes of Creator, Destroyer, and Regenerator are combined in him. His loins are enveloped in a tiger's skin. In his character of Time, he not only presides over its extinction, but also its astronomical regulation. A crescent or half-moon on his forehead indicates the measure of time by the phases of the moon ; a serpent forms one of his necklaces to denote the measure of time by years, and a second necklace of human skulls marks the lapse and revolution of ages, and the extinction and succession of the generations of mankind. He is often represented as entirely covered with serpents, which are the emblems of immortality. They are bound in his hair, round his neck, wrists, waist, arms, and legs ; they serve as rings for his fingers, and earrings for his ears, and are his constant companions. Śiva has more than a thousand names, which are detailed at length in the sixty-ninth chapter of the Śiva Puráṇa. The following list of the principal of these will give the best idea of his character and attributes. The auspicious one. The Lord of the Universe. The Destroyer, a personification of time that destroys all things. The Reproducer, the Conqueror of life and death, and Cause of life and being. The Disperser of the Tears of mortals."—*Williams.*

Siva—1, The wife of the Rudra Iṣána ; 2, The wife of Anila, (Wind.)

Sivas—A class of deities in the third Manwantara.

Sivaskandha—One of the Andhra kings, the son of Sivasri Satakarni.

Sivasti—Another of the Andhra kings.

Siva-Upa-Purana—The Śiva Upa-puráṇa contains about six thousand stanzas, distributed into two parts. It is related by Sanatkumára to Vyása and the Rishis at Naimisháraṇya ; and its character may be judged of from the questions to which it is a reply. "Teach us," said the Rishis, "the rules of worshipping the Linga, and of the god of gods adored under that type : describe to us his various forms, the places sanctified by him, and the prayers with which he is to be addressed." In answer, Sanatkumára repeats the Śiva Purána, containing the birth of Vishṇu and Brahmá ; the creation and divisions of the universe ; the origin of all things from the Linga ; the rules of worshipping it and Śiva ; the sanctity of times, places, and things, dedicated to him ; the delusion of Brahmá and Vishṇu by the Linga ; the rewards of offering flowers and the like to a Linga ; rules for various observances in honour of Mahádeva ; the mode of practising the Yoga ; the glory of Benares and other Saiva Tírthas ; and the perfection of the objects of life by union with Maheṣwara. These objects are illustrated, in the first part, with very few legends ; but the second is made up, almost wholly, of Saiva stories, as the defeat of Tripurásura ; the sacrifice of Daksha ; the births of Kárttikeya and Gaṇeṣa, (the sons of Śiva), and Nandi and Bhṛingaríti (his attendants), and others ; together with descriptions of Benares and other places of pilgrimage, and rules for observing such festivals as the Śivarátri. This work is a Saiva manual, not a Purána.—*Wilson.*

Sivi—1, A Daitya, the son of Sanhráda ; 2, The Indra of the fourth Manwantara ; 3, A prince, the son of Usínara.

Skambha—The Supporter or Upholder ; an appellation of the Supreme Being. In a hymn of the Atharva Veda, Skambha is considered like Purusha, as a vast embodied being co-extensive with the universe, and comprehending, in his several members, not only the different parts of the material world, but a variety of abstract conceptions, such as austere fervour *(tapas,)* faith, truth, and the divisions of time. He is distinct from, and superior to, Prajápati, who founds the worlds upon him. The thirty-three gods are comprehended in him, and arose out of nonentity, which forms his highest member, and, as well as entity, is embraced within him. The gods who form part of him, as branches of a tree, do him homage, and bring him tribute. He is identified with Indra ; and perhaps also with the highest Brahmá, who is mentioned in verses 32–34, 36, and in the first verse of the next hymn, x. 8, 1. In verse 36, however, this Brahmá is represented as being born (or, perhaps, developed) from toil and *tapas*, whilst in x. 8, 1, the attributes of the Supreme Deity are assigned to him. In compositions of this age, however, we are not to expect very accurate or rigorous thinking, or perfect consistency :—

In Skambha are contained the worlds, austere fervour, and the ceremonial. Skambha, I clearly know thee to be contained entire in Indra. In Indra are contained the worlds, austere fervour, and the ceremonial. Indra, I clearly know thee to be contained entire in Skambha. When the Unborn first sprang into being, he attained to that independent dominion, than that which nothing higher has ever been. Reverence be to that greatest Brahmá, of whom the earth is the basis, the atmosphere the belly, who made the sky his head, of whom the sun and the ever-renewed moon are the eye; who made Agni his mouth, of whom the wind formed two of the vital airs, and the Angirasas the eye, who made the regions his organs of sense. Skambha established both these [worlds], earth and sky, the wide atmosphere, and the six vast regions; Skambha pervaded this entire universe. Reverence to that greatest Brahmá who, born from toil and austere fervour (*tapas*,) penetrated all the worlds, who made soma for himself alone. How is it that the wind does not rest? How is not the soul quiescent? Why do not the waters, seeking after truth, ever repose? The great being [is] absorbed in austere fervour in the midst of the world, on the surface of the waters. To him all the gods are joined, as the branches around the trunk of a tree. Say who is that Skambha to whom the gods, with hands, feet, voice, ear, eye, present continually an unlimited tribute? By him darkness is dispelled; he is free from evil; in him are all the three luminaries which reside in Prajápati. He who knows the golden reed standing in the waters is the mysterious Prajápati.

Professor Goldstücker adds that Skambha "seems to mean the fulcrum of the whole world, in all its physical, religious, and other aspects. The object of the hymn being to inquire what this fulcrum is, from the answer given to the various questions it seems to follow that it is there imagined to be the primitive deity, or the *primitive* Veda, the word *brahman* in the neuter implying both. From this *primitive* Veda, not visibly but really (*sat*) existing, not only all the gods, worlds, religious rites, &c. were derived, but also the existing three Vedas and the Atharvan were 'fashioned.'" —*O. S. T.*, *V*, 384.

Skanda—1, A name of Kartikeya, the son of Śiva and Párvati, and the Mars of Hindu mythology. For the legend of his birth, see Kartikeya. In a note to the Megha Dúta, Professor Wilson writes, " Several instances of the solitary production of offspring occur in the Hindu as well as in the Grecian mythology. Thus as Pallas sprang from the brow of Jupiter, we have Skanda generated solely by the deity Śiva : Gangá springs from the head of the same deity, and Ganeṣa is the self-born son of the goddess Párvati. The miraculous birth of the warrior deity, Skanda, was for the purpose of destroying Táraka, an Asura or demon, who, by the performance of continued and severe austerities, had acquired powers formidable to the gods. The excentric genius of Southey has rendered it unnecessary, by his poem 'The curse of Kehâma,' for me to explain the nature or results of these acts of devotion. The germ of Skanda was cast by Śiva into the flame of Agni, the god of fire ; who, being unable to sustain the increasing burden, transferred it to the goddess Gangá : she accordingly was delivered of the deity, Skanda ; who was afterwards received and reared, among thickets of the Sara reed (Saccharum Sara), by the six daughters of a king, named Krittiká ; or according to other legends, by the wives of seven great Rishis or Saints. In either case, they form in astronomy the asterism of the Pleiades. Upon his coming to maturity, Skanda encountered and killed the demon, who had filled the reign of Indra with dismay :—

Emissumque imâ de sede Typhoëa terrâ,
Cœlitibus fecisse metum.—*Works IV*, 353.

Skanda—2, The son of the Rudra Paṣupati, by his wife Swáha.

Skanda Purana—" The Skánda Purána is that in which the six-faced deity (Skánda) has related the events of the Tatpurusha Kalpa, enlarged with many tales, and subservient to the duties taught by Maheṣwara. It is said to contain eighty-one thousand one hundred stanzas : so it is asserted amongst mankind."

It is uniformly agreed that the Skánda Purána, in a collective form, has no existence ; and the fragments, in the shape of Sanhitás, Khándas, and Máhátmyas, which are affirmed, in various parts of India, to be portions of the Purána, present a much more formidable mass of stanzas than even the immense number of which it is said to consist. The most celebrated of these portions, in Hindusthan, is the Háśí Khánda, a very minute description of the temples of Śiva in or adjacent to Benares, mixed with directions for worshipping Maheṣwara, and a great variety of legends explanatory of its merits and of the holiness of Káśí. Many of them are puerile and uninteresting; but some are of a higher character. The story of Agastya records, probably in a legendary style, the propagation of Hinduism in the south of India; and, in the history of Divodása, king of Káśí, we have an embellished tradition of the temporary depression of the worship of Śiva, even in its metropolis, before the ascendancy of the followers of Buddha. There is every reason to believe the greater part of the contents of the Káśí Khánḍa anterior to the first attack upon Benares by Mahmud of Ghizni. The Káśí Khánḍa alone contains fifteen thousand stanzas.—*Wilson*.

Slishti—One of the sons of the great sage Dhruva, by his wife Śambhu.

Smaya—Wonder. A son of Dharma.

Smriti—Tradition, as distinguished from Sruti, revelation. The Veda is regarded as revelation; and what is called the whole body of the law is regarded as tradition. "This distinction may be of some importance as an illustration of the national belief in inspiration; and it may throw some light on that era in the history of Sanskrit literature when inspiration was supposed to end and tradition to begin."* Mr. Max Müller makes a similar remark, and discusses the subject in his History of Sanskrit Literature.

Smriti—1, Memory. One of the daughters of Daksha, married to the Muni Angiras; 2, The faculty of recognising all things, past, present, or to come.—*Wilson's Notes to Vishnu Purána*.

Soka—Sorrow: one of the children of Mritya (Death.)

Soma—Reference has been already made to the important share which the exhilarating juice of the soma-plant assumes in bracing Indra for his conflict with the hostile powers in the atmosphere, and to the eagerness of all the gods to partake in this beverage.

* Talboys Wheeler.

Soma is the god who represents and animates this juice, an intoxicating draught which plays a conspicuous part in the sacrifices of the Vedic age. He is, or rather was in former times, the Indian Dionysus or Bacchus. Not only are the whole of the hymns in the ninth book of the Rig Veda, one hundred and fourteen in number, besides a few in other places, dedicated to his honour, but constant references to the juice of the Soma occur in a large proportion of the other hymns. It is clear therefore, as remarked by Prof. Whitney, that his worship must at one time, have attained a remarkable popularity. 'The simple-minded Arian people, whose whole religion was a worship of the wonderful powers and phenomena of nature, had no sooner perceived that this liquid had power to elevate the spirits, and produce a temporary frenzy, under the influence of which the individual was prompted to, and capable of, deeds beyond his natural powers, than they found in it something divine ; it was to their apprehension a god endowing those into whom it entered with god-like powers ; the plant which afforded it became to them the king of plants ; the process of preparing it was a holy sacrifice ; the instruments used therefore were sacred. The high antiquity of this cultus is attested by the references to it found occurring in the Persian Avesta ; it seems however to have received a new impulse on Indian territory.'

With the decline of the Vedic worship however, and the introduction of new deities and new ceremonies, the popularity of Soma gradually decreased, and has long since passed away ; and his name is now familiar to those few Brahmans only, who still maintain in a few places the early Vedic observances.

A great variety of divine attributes and operations are ascribed to Soma. 'He is addressed as a god in the highest strains of adulation and veneration ; all powers belong to him ; all blessings are besought of him as his to bestow.* In a passage where the joys of paradise are more distinctly anticipated and more fervently implored than in most other parts of the Rig Veda, Soma is addressed as the god from whom the gift of future felicity is expected.

* Whitney, J. A. O. S., III, 299.

Soma exhilarates Varuṇa, Mitra, Indra, Vishṇu, the Maruts, the other gods, Váyu, Heaven and Earth. Both gods and men resort to him saying that his juice is sweet, by him the Ádityas are strong and the earth vast. He is the friend, helper, and soul of Indra, whom he succours in his conflicts with Vrittra. He rides in the same chariot with Indra, but has winged mares of his own and a team-like Váyu.—*O. S. T.*, *V*, 258-67.

In the post-vedic age the name Soma came to be commonly applied to the moon and its regent, who is represented as the son of Atri ; the monarch of the stars and planets, of brahmans and of plants, of sacrifices and of penance. The Vishṇu Purána has the following legend : Soma celebrated the Rájasúya (sacrifice) ; and, from the glory thence acquired, and the extensive dominion with which he had been invested, he became arrogant (and licentious,) and carried off Tárá, the wife of Bṛihaspati, the preceptor of the gods. In vain Bṛihaspati sought to recover his bride ; in vain Brahmá commanded, and the holy sages remonstrated : Soma refused to relinquish her. Uṣanas, out of enmity to Bṛihaspati, took part with Soma. Rudra, who had studied under Angiras, (the father of Bṛihaspati,) befriended his fellow-student. In consequence of Uṣanas, their preceptor, joining Soma, Jambha, Kujambha, and all the Daityas, Dánavas, and other foes of the gods, came also to his assistance ; whilst Indra and all the gods were the allies of Bṛihaspati.

Then there ensued a fierce contest, which, being on account of Táraká (or Tárá,) was termed the Tárakámaya or Táraká war. In this, the gods, led by Rudra, hurled their missiles on the enemy ; and the Daityas with equal determination assailed the gods. Earth, shaken to her centre by the struggle between such foes, had recourse to Brahmá, for protection ; on which he interposed, and, commanding Uṣanas, with the demons, and Rudra, with the deities, to desist from strife, compelled Soma to restore Tárá to her husband. Finding that she was pregnant, Bṛihaspati desired her no longer to retain her burthen ; and, in obedience to his orders, she was delivered of a son, whom she deposited in a clump of long Munja-grass. The child, from the moment of its birth, was endued with a splendour that dimmed the radiance of every other divinity ; and both Bṛihaspati and Soma, fascinated by his beauty, claimed him as their child. The gods, in order to settle the dispute, appealed to Tárá ; but she was ashamed, and would make no answer. As she still continued mute to their repeated applications, the child (became incensed, and) was about to curse her, saying : " Unless, vile woman, you immediately declare who is my father, I will sentence you to such a fate as shall deter every female, in future, from hesitating to speak the truth." On this, Brahmá again interfered, and pacified the child, and then, addressing Tárá, said : " Tell me, daughter, is this the child of Bṛihaspati or of Soma ?" " Of Soma," said Tárá, blushing. As soon as she had spoken, the lord of the constellations—his countenance bright, and expanding with rapture,—embraced his son, and said : " Well done, my boy ! Verily, thou art wise." And, hence, his name was Budha.

' He who knows.' Much erroneous speculation has originated in confounding this Budha, the son of Soma, and regent of the planet Mercury,—' he who knows,' ' the intelligent,'—with Buddha, any defied mortal, or ' he by whom truth is known ;' or as individually applicable, Gautama or Śákya, son of Rája Śuddhodana, by whom, the Buddhists themselves aver, their doctrines were first promulgated. The two characters have nothing in common ; and the names are identical, only when one or other is mis-spelt. This Budha was the founder of the lunar race. The Brahmá Purána and Hari Vansa have a legend of the birth of Soma, the moon, from the Rishi Prabhákara of the race of Atri.—*Wilson.*

Soma—One of the deities called Vasus, because they are always present in luminous irradiation.

Somadatta—A king of Vaiṣálí, the son of Kriṣaswa. He is famed for his having celebrated ten times the sacrifice of a horse.

Ṣomaka—One of the kings of Magadha, the son of Sahadeva.

Somapas—A class of Pitris, " drinkers of the acid juice."

Soma-plant—A plant constantly mentioned in the vedic ritual, and corresponding to the Homa of the Zendavesta, but it is uncertain what plant was originally intended by the name. "It is described as 'a creeper, of a dark colour, sour, without leaves, milky, and pulpy externally; it causes phlegm and vomiting, and is a favourite food of goats,' see Müller, Zeitscher, d. D. M. G. ix. It is said to come from the north, and to be bought of barbarian tribes; but the soma of the 'Veda' is no longer known in India. Dr. Haug says that 'the plant at present used by the sacrificial priests of the Dekkhan is not the soma of the Vedas, but appears to belong to the same order. It grows on hills in the neighbourhood of Poona, to the height of about four or five feet, and forms a kind of bush, consisting of a certain number of shoots, all coming from the same root; their stem is solid like wood, the bark greyish, they are without leaves, the sap appears whitish, has a very stringent taste, is bitter but not sour; it is a very nasty drink, but has some intoxicating effect.' (Ait. Br., Vol. II., p. 489). "The ceremonial writers allow the plant *pútíka*, Guilandina Bonduc, to be used as a substitute for the soma. The Parsees of Bombay use the branches of a particular tree, obtained from Persia in a dried state."*

In the Rig Veda the soma plant is said to have been brought to the earth by a falcon. In another passage it is declared to have been brought by the daughter of the Sun from the place where it had been nourished by Parjanya, the rain-god, when the Gandharvas took it and infused into it sap.

Somasarmman—One of the Mauryan kings of Magadha.

Somasushmapana—The Vyâsa of the twenty-third Dwápara age.

Soma-tirtha—A place of pilgrimage in the west of India, on the coast of Guzerat, near the celebrated temple of Somanath, and town of Pattan Somanath. Its name is derived from the legend that Soma the moon, was there cured of the consumption brought upon him by the imprecation of Daksha, his father-in-law. The place is also called **Prabhása**.

Somayajna—Offerings and libations of the juice of the acid asclepias.

* Quarterly Review, July 1870.

Sona—The Sone river rising in Maináka or Amarakantak, and flowing east to the Ganges.

Sonitapura—The city of Báṇa, considered to be the modern Devicotta in the Carnatic.

Sraddha—Faith : One of the daughters of Daksha, married to Dharma, or according to some authorities to Angiras.

Sraddha—An obsequial or funeral sacrifice ; but it also implies offerings to the progenitors of an individual and of mankind, and always forms part of a religious ceremony on an occasion of rejoicing or an occasion of prosperity, this being termed the Abhyudaya or Vriddhi Sráddha.

"The offerings of the Hindus to the Pitris partake of the character of those of the Romans to the lares and manes, but bear a more conspicuous part in their ritual. They are said indeed by Manu to be of more moment than the worship of the gods. These ceremonies are not to be regarded as merely obsequial ; for independently of the rites addressed to a recently deceased relative,—and, in connexion with him, to remote ancestors, and to the progenitors of all beings,—which are of a strictly obsequial or funeral description, offerings to deceased ancestors, and the Pitris in general, form an essential ceremony, on a great variety of festive and domestic occasions. The Nirṇaya Sindhu, in a passage referred to by Mr. Colebrooks* specifies the following Sráddhas ; 1, The Nitya, or perpetual ; daily offerings to ancestors in general ; 2, The Naimittika, or occasional ; as the Ekoddishṭa, or obsequial offerings on account of a kinsman recently deceased ; 3, The Kámya, voluntary : performed for the accomplishment of a special design ; 4, The Vṛiddhi ; performed on occasions of rejoicing or prosperity ; 5, The Sapiṇḍana ; offerings to all individual and to general ancestors ; 6, The Párvaṇa Sráddha ; offerings to the manes, on certain lunar days called Párvans, or day of full-moon and new-moon, and the eighth and fourteenth days of the lunar fortnight ; 7, The Goshṭhí ; for the advantage of a number of learned persons, or of an assembly of Brahmans,

* Asiatic Researches, Vol. VII.

invited for the purpose ; 8, The Śuddhi ; one performed to purify a person from some defilement,—an expiatory Sráddha ; 9, The Karmánga ; one forming part of the initiatory ceremonies, or Samskáras, observed at conception, birth, tonsure, &c. ; 10, The Daivika ; to which the gods are invited ; 11, The Yátrá Sráddha ; held by a person going a journey ; and, 12, The Pushṭi Sráddha ; one performed to promote health and wealth. Of these, the four which are considered the most solemn are the rite performed for a parent, or near relative, lately deceased ; that which is performed for kindred, collectively ; that observed on certain lunar days ; and that celebrated on occasions of rejoicing.

The following extract from Mr. Talboys Wheeler's History of India, Vol. II, gives a very complete view of this subject.

" The Sráddha, or feast of the dead, is perhaps one of the most primitive, as it certainly is one of the most simple, of all the Vedic rites that have been handed down from a period of remote antiquity to the present day. It originated in the crude idea already indicated, that the spirit or ghost had a separate existence after death, and that it might be gratified or propitiated with offerings of food. This idea certainly involved a belief in the prolonged existence of the spirit in a future state of being ; but in its origin it had no connection with the doctrine of future rewards and punishments. It is rather to be traced to the old world belief, which has existed in all ages, and which still lingers in the imagination of even a philosophic and material generation, that the spirits of the departed hover at times near those persons and places which were associated with their earthly careers, and are gratified by any tribute of respect which may be paid to their memory.

The Sráddha, or feast of the dead, was thus in its earliest form a pleasing expression of natural religion, which long preceded the advent of a priestly caste, or the introduction of a systematic ritual. But, like every other popular ceremonial which has been handed down amongst the Hindus from the Vedic period, it has been recast in a Brahmanical mould ; and it is in this latter form that the institution appears in the Epics as well as in the laws of Manu. It consists of three distinct rites :—

1st—The daily Sráddha, to be performed in propitiation of the Pitris, or ghosts of remote ancestors.

2nd—The monthly Sráddha, to be performed in propitiation of the more immediate paternal ancestors.

3rd—The funeral Sráddha, to be performed within a certain period after death, or the hearing of the death, of a near kinsman.

It should also be remarked that Sráddhas are likewise performed on other occasions, and notably at the celebration of any marriage ceremony.

The daily Sráddha was an offering either of boiled rice, or of milk, roots, and fruit, or of water only, to the Pitris, or remote ancestors. This ceremonial has been already described, and it will be only necessary to add that in modern practice it is considered sufficient to pour water out of a particular vessel every day as a drink-offering to the Pitris.

The monthly Sráddha may be considered under four separate heads :—

1st—Ceremonies to be performed at a monthly Sráddha.

2nd—Persons to be entertained at the monthly Sráddha.

3rd—Persons to be excluded from the monthly Sráddha.

4th—Relative merits of the different kinds of victuals which may be offered at a monthly Sráddha.

The ceremonies at the monthly Sráddha, as described in the Institutes of Manu, are of a very intelligible character ; and seem to have been laid down for the purpose of converting the old Vedic offering of food and water into a great feast to the Brahmans. The monthly Sráddha was performed on the dark day of the moon, that is, when the sun and moon are in conjunction. A sequestered spot was selected, such as was supposed to be pleasing to the ghosts ; and then the invited Brahmans were conducted to their allotted seats, which had been purified with kusa grass, and were presented with garlands of flowers and sweet perfumes. The officiating Brahman then satisfied the three Vedic deities,—Agni, Soma, and Yama,—by pouring an oblation of ghee upon the sacred fire. He then proceeded to satisfy the ancestors of the giver of the Sráddha. He first sprinkled water on the ground with his right hand, and then formed three balls or cakes of boiled rice, which are called piṇḍas. One of these cakes is presented to each of the three immediate paternal ancestors, namely, the father, the grandfather, and the great-grandfather. The offering of piṇḍas, however, is said to be extended to the fourth, fifth, and sixth degrees of paternal ancestors in the ascending line, by the simple process of wiping the hand with kusa grass after offering the piṇḍas to the ancestors of the first, second, and third degree. This ceremony was followed by a great feast to the Brahmans, consisting of vessels filled with rice, together with broths, potherbs, milk and curds, ghee, spiced puddings, milky messes of various sorts, roots of herbs, ripe fruits, and savoury meats ; and during the feast, passages were read from the Sástras. The remains of the cakes were to be eaten by a cow, a Brahman, or a kid ; or to be cast into water or fire ; but the wife of the householder was to eat the middle of the three cakes, in order that she might become the mother of a son, who should be long-lived, famous, strong-minded, wealthy, and the father of many sons. When the Brahmans had duly feasted, the householder gave a feast to the kinsmen of his father, and afterwards to the kinsmen of his mother. In cases of poverty, however, the offering of water seems to be considered a sufficient satisfaction of the spirits of the six paternal ancestors.

As regards the persons to be invited to the monthly Sráddha, great stress is laid by the code upon the entertainment of learned Brahmans, and the exclusion of ignorant ones from the Sráddha ; but it is added that if such learned Brahmans cannot be found, certain relatives may be entertained. This last expression is somewhat obscure, and may possibly imply that the Sráddha was originally eaten by the kinsmen, and that the introduction of learned Brahmans was a later idea.

Manu's catalogue of the persons who were to be excluded from a monthly Sráddha is of a very miscellaneous character ; and is chiefly valuable from the illustrations which it furnishes of the Brahmánical notion of impure or immoral characters. The catalogue may be re-distributed under four general heads, according to the four different grounds upon which the individuals specified have been respectively excluded, namely, moral, religious, physical and professional.

The persons to be excluded from a Sráddha on moral grounds, are:—

"A Brahmachári who has not read the Veda; a Brahmán who has committed theft; one who opposes his preceptor; a younger brother married before the elder; an elder brother not married before the younger; one who subsists by the wealth of many relatives; the husband of a Súdra; the son of a twice-married woman; a husband in whose house an adulterer dwells; one who teaches the Veda for wages; one who gives wages to such a teacher; the pupil of a Súdra; the Súdra preceptor; a rude speaker; the son of an adulteress born either before or after the death of her husband; a forsaker of his mother, father, or preceptor without just cause; a man who forms a connection with great sinners; a house-burner; a giver of poison; an eater of food offered by the son of an adulterer; a suborner of perjury; a wrangler with his father; a drinker of intoxicating spirits; one of evil repute; a cheat; the husband of a younger sister married before the elder; an injurer of his friend; a father instructed in the Veda by his own son; one who diverts watercourses; a seducer of damsels; a man who delights in mischief; a Brahman living as a Súdra; one who observes neither approved customs nor prescribed duties; a constant and importunate asker of favours; one who is despised by the virtuous; the husband of a twice-married woman; a Brahman of bad manners; and an ignorant Brahman."

The persons to be excluded from a Sráddha on religious grounds, are:—

"Those who profess to disbelieve in a future state; a Brahman who has performed many sacrifices for other men; those who worship images for gain; one who deserts the sacred fire; one who omits the five great sacraments; a contemner of Brahmans; a despiser of scripture; and one who sacrifices only to the inferior gods."

The persons to be excluded from a Sráddha on physical grounds, are :—

"Those with whitlows on their nails ; those with black-yellow teeth ; a consumptive man ; a man who has lost an eye ; a man with elephantiasis ; an impotent man ; an epileptic man ; one with erysipelas ; a leper ; a lunatic ; a blind man ; a club-footed man."

The persons to be excluded from a Sráddha because of their trade or profession, are :—

"Physicians ; gamesters ; usurers ; dancers ; sellers of meat ; those who live by low traffic ; a public servant of the whole town ; a public servant of the Rája ; a feeder of cattle ; a seller of the moon-plant ; a navigator of the ocean ; a political economist ; an oil man ; one who employs gamesters for his own benefit ; a seller of liquors ; a maker of bows and arrows ; the keeper of a gambling-house ; a common informer ; a tamer of elephants, bulls, horses, or camels ; one who subsists by astrology ; a keeper of birds ; one who teaches the use of arms ; one who builds houses for gain ; a messenger ; a planter of trees for pay ; a breeder of sporting dogs ; a falconer ; one who supports himself by tillage ; a shepherd ; a keeper of buffaloes ; and one who removes dead bodies for pay."

The food that is given to such men at a Sráddha becomes base and impure ; and the giver of the Sráddha will be punished in the next life.

The foregoing catalogues of persons who are to be excluded from a Sráddha are very suggestive. In the first place it will be noticed that Manu classifies immorality, heresy, and deviation from caste rule, with physical evils, such as leprosy, blindness, and elephantiasis ; and this intermingling is more perceptible in the original text, where no attempt has been made to separate the precepts under different heads. This strange confusion of sin and disease appears to have originated in the old idea, connected with the dogma of the transmigration of the soul, that disease was the punishment of sins committed either in this life or in a previous state of existence.

The peculiar usages which seem to have originated some of the precepts are also well worthy of notice. Thus it has been seen that it was considered wrong for a younger brother or a younger sister to be married before an elder brother or an elder sister ; a notion which could only find a place amongst a people who believed that the marriage of a daughter was a duty which every parent was bound to fulfil. It has also been seen that a woman who married a second husband was held in great abhorrence ; and to the present day the marriage of a Hindu widow, even when her first husband has died before the marriage has been consummated, is regarded with a national antipathy which education and legislation have done but little to remove. It is also somewhat curious that Manu should exclude a constant and importunate asker of favours from a Sráddha ; from which it would appear that askers of favours were as constant and importunate in the age of Manu as they are in our own time.

Amongst the persons whom Manu directed should be excluded on religious grounds are to be found those who sacrifice only to the " inferior gods." This expression of " inferior gods" seems to suggest a religious opposition. Indeed it is not impossible that Manu is alluding to the old Vedic deities, who were treated by the Brahmans as subordinate to their god Brahmá. The injunction against the Brahmans who performed many sacrifices for other men, may have been aimed at the mercenary priests who sacrificed for hire. The injunction against those who worshipped images for the sake of gain is involved in more obscurity, inasmuch as there does not appear to be any satisfactory reference to images in the hymns of the Rig Veda ; although it is easy to conceive that such a form of worship must sooner or later find expression.

The exclusion of men who followed certain trades or professions from the entertainment given at a Sráddha, furnishes in like manner some striking illustrations of the old opposition between the priest and the soldier, the Brahman and the Kshatriya, which seems to be more or less identical with the opposition between the Brahmans and the Vedic Aryans. Thus amongst the ancient Kshatriyas, gambling was a favourite pastime, and certainly was not regarded as a vice, excepting when carried to a vicious excess and terminating in the ruin of a family. Even Yudhishthira, who is represented in the Mahábhárata as an incarnation of Dharma, or goodness, and who was apparently regarded as a model Rája, is actually said to have disguised himself as a Brahman, and in that guise to have taught the art of dice to the Rája of Viráta. But Manu excludes from the Sráddha every gambler, and every man who keeps a gambling-house or employs gamblers. Then again the Kshatriyas revelled in wine and flesh-meat ; but Manu excludes the sellers of wine and meat from the Sráddha. The most significant precepts however are those which exclude the makers of bows and arrows, the tamers of horses, and those who taught the use of arms ; for the bow was the favourite weapon of the Kshatriyas, and the taming of horses was regarded as a royal accomplishment ; whilst two of the most patriarchal characters in the Mahábhárata, Bhíshma and Drona, are said to have trained Páṇḍu and Dritarashtra, and their sons, the Páṇḍavas and Kauravas, in the use of different kinds of weapons. The exclusion of navigators is equally curious. Navigation was certainly known to the Vedic Aryans, and is even recognised by Manu ; but it has always been regarded with peculiar horror by the Brahmans ; and consequently it is referred to the three first Yugas or ages, but discountenanced in the age of Kali. The exclusion of physicians seems to have originated in the idea that they must be impure from having to deal with impure things.

As regards the food to be offered to the ghosts at the monthly Sráddha, the precepts in Manu are also significant. The old primitive custom of offering fish and flesh is sufficiently recognized, but at the same time it is urged that the ghosts prefer a more simple and Brahmanical diet, such as milk and honey. At a later period it was declared that the feasting on flesh-meat at a Sráddha was forbidden in the Kali age.

The funeral Sráddha, which is performed after the death of a kinsman, is in every respect similar to the monthly Sráddha, and consequently calls for no detailed description. The code lays down certain laws as regards the purification of the survivors, but they are devoid of historical significance. The ceremonies which accompanied and followed the death of Mahárája Dasaratha sufficiently illustrate the popular ideas and customs which still prevail.

It will be seen from the foregoing data that the old Vedic belief in the worship of ancestors has been strangely Brahmanized by the compilers of the code. The monthly Sráddha, whilst ostensibly celebrated in honour of deceased ancestors, is in reality nothing more than an entertainment given to the Brahmans. Again, the original idea appears to have originated in a child-like belief that the food and water sustain and refresh the spirit of the departed; whilst, according to the more modern Brahmanical doctrine, the performance of a Sráddha delivers the soul of the dead person from the custody of Yama, the judge of the dead, and translates it to the heaven of the Pitris, or ancestors; there to remain until the merits of its previous life on earth are all exhausted, and then to return again to earth and re-animate another body. Thus it is the current belief that without the Sráddha the soul of the deceased cannot ascend to the heaven of the Pitris and take up its abode there." Chapter IX.

Sraddha—Religious Faith. Personifications of abstract ideas are not uncommon in the Rig Veda, one hymn of which, x. 151, is addressed to Śraddhá, or religious faith. By her it is said the sacrificial fire is kindled, and by her the oblation is offered up. She is asked to prosper the liberal worshippers of the gods, and to impart faith; and is said to be an object of adoration in the morning, at noon, and at sunset. In the Váj Sanhita it is said that faith is obtained by gifts, and truth by faith. In the same work it is declared that 'Prajápati beholding, made a distinction between the forms of truth and falsehood, connecting disbelief with the latter, and faith or belief with the former.' This declaration that truth is the only proper object of faith, has a far deeper signification than this ancient writer could possibly have assigned to it, viz., that it is the ultimate truth, and not the so-called orthodoxy of any proposition, which can alone entitle it to reception.

Śraddhá is also celebrated in the Taitt. Br., where we are told that through Śraddhá, a god obtains his divine character; that the divine Śraddhá is the support of the world, that she has Káma (or the fulfilment of desire) for her calf, and yields immortality as her milk ; that she is the first-born of the religious ceremonial, and the sustainer of the whole world ; and she, who is the supreme mistress of the world, is besought to bestow immortality on her worshippers.—*O. S. T., V*, 347.

Sravaka—(From the Sanskrit *śru*, to hear) is the name of the disciples of Buddha, who, through the 'hearing' of his doctrine, and by practising the four great Buddhistic truths, attain to the qualification of an Arhat, or Buddhist saint. From among the number of the disciples of Buddha, 80 are called the *Mahâśrâvakas*, or the great Śrâvakas. The Śrâvakas are entitled to the predicate *Ayushmat*, or 'one possessed of (long) life.'

Sravana—1, The lunar month which nearly corresponds with July ; 2, A lunar mansion in Mrigavíthi in the southern Avashthána.

Sravasta—A prince, the son of Yuvanáswa, who built the city of Śravasti, in Koṣala or Oude ; a city of some sanctity in the estimation of the Buddhists.

Sri—A name of Lakshmi, q. v.

"In the Vishṇu, Garuda, Linga, and Padma Purános, Śri is said to have been born the daughter of the divine sage Bhrigu, the son of Maríchi, who sprang from the mind of Brahmá, and to have obtained Vishṇu for her husband. But she is more generally considered to be the female energy of that god, and therefore to be exempt from birth. 'Śri is inseparable from Vishṇu, for wherever Vishṇu is there also is Śri ; he is the sun and she its splendour ; he is the moon and she its radiance ; Govinda is the ocean and Kamala the tide ; he is the day and she the night : all that is masculine is Vishṇu, and all that is feminine is Śri.'"*

Srideva—One of the daughters of Devaka, married to Vásudeva.

Sridhara Swami—A commentator in the Bhágavata and in the Vishṇu Purána.

Srijavana—One of the sons of Dyutimat.

* Col. Vans Kennedy. A. and H. M.

Sringa—A Rishi, the story of whose life is related in the Rámáyana. He passed the earlier years of his life in the hermitage of his father, in the jungle, and had consequently never seen the face of a woman. He was enticed from his father's hermitage by damsels sent from the Rája of Anga : on his arrival there he caused rain to fall in abundance ; and was married to Sántá the daughter of the Rája ; and was subsequently engaged to perform the Aswamedha of Mahárája Dasaratha.—[RISHYASRINGA.]

Sringavera—The modern Sungroor, the frontier town between Koṣala and the Bhíl country. When Ráma was going into exile, he and Síta halted there, and were hospitably received by Guha, the Rája of the Bhíls.

Sringi—A range of mountains to the north of Meru.

Srinjaya—1, The fourth king of Vaisáli, son of Dhúmaráṣwa ; 2, A son of Súra, and brother of Vasudeva ; 3, The son of Kálánara ; 4, A king of Mágadha, son of Haryaṣwa.

Srinjayas—A people from the north-west, among the warriors of the Mahábhárata.

Srisaila—A mountain near the Krishna.

Sritala—One of the seven regions of Pátála, according to the enumeration in the Váyu.

Sruta—1, (Sacred tradition) A son of Dharma by Medhá ; 2, The son of Bhagíratha ; 3, A son of Krishṇa by Kálindí.

Srutadeva—A daughter of Súra, and wife of Vriddháṣarman, king of Kárusha—the parents of the fierce Asura Dantavaktra.

Srutakarman—One of the Páṇḍavas, the son of Sahadeva, the youngest of the Páṇḍava princes.

Srutakirtti—A daughter of Súra, married to Dhrishtaketu, Rája of Kaikeya.

Srutakirtti—One of the Páṇḍavas the son of Arjuna.

Srutanjaya—One of the kings of Mágadha, the son of Senajit.

Srutasena—One of the sons of Paríkshit.

Srutasoma—The son of the Páṇḍava prince Bhíma.

Srutasuras—The daughter of Súra, who was married to Damaghosha, king of Chedí.

Srutavat—One of the kings of Mágadha, the son of Somápi. In some lists called Srutasuras, and said to have reigned 67 years.

Srutayus—1, One of the kings of Ayodhya, the son of Bhánumítra, a descendant of Kúsa ; 2, A king of Mithila, son of Arishtanemí ; 3, The youngest son of Purúravas.

Sruti—(From the Sanscrit *śru*, hear, hence, literally, the hearing, or that which is heard) is, in Sanscrit Literature, the technical term for all those works which are considered to have been revealed by a deity. It applies, therefore, properly speaking, only to the Mantra and Brâhmana portion of the Vedas ; but at a later period, it is applied likewise, if not especially, to the Upanishads. It means Revelation, as distinguished from Smriti, Tradition. "The distinction" says Max Müller, "between Sruti, (revelation), and Smriti, (tradition) is a point of vital importance for the whole Brahmanic system, and will be found significant in a historical point of view." "The distinction between Sruti and Smriti, revelation and tradition, had been established by the Brahmans previous to the rise of Buddhism, or, at all events, previous to the time when the Sútra style began to be adopted in Indian literature. There existed, previous to the Sútra period, a body of literary works propagated by oral tradition, which formed the basis of all later writings on sacred subjects, and which by the Brahmans was believed to be of divine origin. The idea expressed by the word *śru*, to hear, *i. e.*, to receive by inspiration, is known in the Brahmanas."—*A. S. L.*, 107.

Sruti—The daughter of Atri, married to the Prajápati Kardama.

Stambha—1, A phonetic variety of the same dhátu or root as Skambha, (q. v.) ; 2, One of the seven Rishis of the second Manwantara.

Sthaleyu Sthandileyu—Two of the ten sons of Raudraṣwa, king of Mithila.

Stoma and Stuti—Hymns and prayers, created from the eastern and other mouths of Brahmá.

Subahu—A king of Mathura, the son of Śatrughna.

Subala—A mountain in the island of Lanká, on which Hanumán alighted when he "took a gigantic spring, and by his prodigious strength leaped over the wide ocean," as described in the Rámáyaṇa.

Subhadra—The sister of Krishṇa. Arjuna fell in love with her, and with the consent of Krishṇa eloped with her, but afterwards returned to Dwáraká where they were formally married with great splendour. She was easily reconciled to Draupadí and became the mother of Arjuna's son Abhimanyu, (q. v.)

Subhasa—One of the kings of Mithila, the son of Sudhanwan.

Subhumi—One of the sons of Ugrasena.

Suchandra—A king of Vaiṣáli, son of Hemchandra.

Sucharu—One of the sons of Krishṇa by his wife Rukminí.

Suchchaya—The wife of Slishti, a son of Dhruva.

Suchi—1, One of the sons of the Agni named Abhimáni, the eldest born of Brahmá : Suchi was one of the three fires ; the genealogy is different in the Bhágavata ; 2, The son of Satadyumna, king of Mithila ; 3, One of the sons of Andhaka ; 4, The son of Vipra, king of Mágadha ; 5 The Indra of the fourteenth Manwantara.

Suchi—The parent of water-fowl ; daughter of Kaṣyapa by his wife Támra.

Suchiravas—One of the twelve Prajápatis.

Sudarsana—A prince of the family of Ikshváku, and sovereign of Ayodhya.

Sudasa—The son of Sarvakáma, a descendant of Sagara ; 2, A king of Mágadha, the son of Chyavana.

Suddhodana—A prince of the family of Ikshváku who, from his connection with Sákya, the author or reviver of Buddhism, is ascertained to have lived in the seventh century before Christ.

Sudeshna—One of the sons of Krishṇa by Rukmíní.

Sudeva—1, A son of Chunchu ; 2, A son of Devaka, of the Yadava race.

Sudhaman—A Lokapála, regent of the east quarter, the son of Virajas and Gauri.

Sudhamas—A class of deities of the third and tenth Manwantaras.

Sudhamans—A class of thirty-three gods in the thirteenth Manwantara.

Sudhanush—A son of the patriarch Kuru who gave his name to the holy district Kurukshetra.

Sudhanwan—1, A king of Mithila, the son of Sáswata ; 2, A king of Mágadha, the son of Satyadhrita.

Sudharman—The hall of Indra, which was given by Krishṇa to Ugrasena, for the assemblage of the race of Yadu : it was conveyed by Váyu to the Yadavas, the chiefs of whom thenceforth possessed this celestial court, emblazoned with jewels, and defended by the arms of Govinda. After the death of Krishṇa the Sudharman palace returned to heaven along with the Párijáta tree.

Sudharmas—A class of divinities of the ninth Manwantara ; the class consisted of twelve.

Sudhis—A class of twenty-seven deities belonging to the fourth Manwantara.

Sudhriti—A prince of the solar dynasty, the son of Rájgavarddhana.

Sudra dynasty—This was founded by Chandragupta in the first half of the fourth century B. C. The dynasty lasted one hundred and thirty-seven years. Chandragupta is the same person as Sandracottus, who, according to Justin, had seized the throne of India after the prefects of Alexander had been murdered. Seleucus found him as sovereign of India when, after the taking of Babylon, and the conquest of the Bactrians, he passed on into India. Seleucus however did not conquer Sandracottus, but after concluding a league with him, marched on to make war against Antigonus.

Sudraka—The first Andhra prince, who reigned seventy-three years at Mágadha.

Sudras—The lowest of the four castes, said in the Vishṇu Purána to have been produced from the feet of Brahmá; but in another part of the same work the distinctions are ascribed to voluntary election, to accident, or to positive institutions; their duties are said to be to wait on the three upper castes; and by that means to earn their subsistence; they may also engage in trade and mechanical labour.

Sudyumna—See Ilá; who was transformed into a man named Sudyumna; at a subsequent period he was again transformed to a woman, in the vicinity of the hermitage of Budha, who saw and espoused her, and had by her a son named Purúravas. After his birth the Rishis prayed to Vishṇu, and through his favour Ilá once more became Sudyumna. In consequence of his having been formerly a female, Sudyumna was excluded from any share in his paternal dominions; but his father, at the suggestion of Vasishtha, bestowed upon him the city of Pratishthána, and he gave it to Purúravas. V. P.

Sugandhi—One of the bond maids of Vasudeva.

Sugriva—The monkey chieftain in the Rishya-mukha mountain, who received Ráma and Lakshmana when they were trying to discover Síta, and showed her ornaments, which she had purposely dropped in her flight, to Ráma. He then related the story of his grievances against his brother Báli, and solicited Ráma's aid, Ráma had afforded evidence of his superhuman strength and skill.

"Then high Sugríva's spirit rose,
Assured of conquest o'er his foes.
With his new champion by his side,
To vast Kishkindhyá's cave he hied.
Then summoned by his awful shout,
King Báli came in fury out,
First comforted his trembling wife,
Then sought Sugríva in the strife.
One shaft from Ráma's deadly bow,
The monarch in the dust laid low.
Then Ráma bade Sugríva reign
In place of royal Báli slain."—*Griffiths.*

When Báli was dying he acknowledged his fault, and asked his brother's forgiveness, commending his son Anga and his wife Tára to Sugríva's care. The latter, when reinstated on the throne at Kishkindhya invited Ráma and Lakshmana to live with him there. This invitation Ráma was unable to accept on account of his vow ; but after the rainy season, Sugríva summoned his armies to assist Ráma in conquering the Rákshasas and recovering Síta. He marshalled his troops in four great divisions. The first he sent north under Vinata. The second, south, under various generals, especially Hanuman, and Jámbavat. The third, west, under Sushena. The fourth, east, under Sátabali.

When Hanuman returned with tidings that Síta was a prisoner in Lanka, Sugríva set forth at the head of his army to aid in effecting her deliverance. Sugríva was wounded by Rávana, and afterwards suffered greatly from the wounds inflicted by the magical weapons of Indrajit, the brave son of Rávana. Sugríva was restored by the medicinal herbs brought by Hanuman from Kailása. After the death of Rávana, Sugríva accompanied Ráma and Lakshmana on their return to Ayodhya on the self-moving car Pushpaka.

Sugrivi—One of the " six illustrious daughters" of Kasyapa, who became the parent of horses, camels, and asses.

Suhma—A son of Báli, who gave his name to his descendants and the country they inhabited. Of Suhma it may be remarked that it is specified in the Siddhánta Kaumudí as an example of Paniní's rule, by which Nagara, compounded with names of countries in the east becomes Nágara, as Sauhmanágara produced, &c., in a city of Suhma. *Wilson's Notes to V. P.*

Suhmas—The Suhmas and Prasahmas were found in the east by Bhíma ; and Suhma is elsewhere said to be situated east of Bengal, towards the sea, the king and the people being Mlechchhas, that is, not Hindus ; it would correspond therefore with Tiperah and Arracan.

Suhotra—Three of this name are mentioned in the Vishnu Purána, and in all the best authorities ; 1, Suhotra, great grandson of Amávasa, father of Jahnu, (q. v.) and ancestor of Visvámitra and the Kauṣikas ; 2, Suhotra, son of Kshattravriddha, grandson of Ayus and progenitor of the Kási kings ; 3, Suhotra, the son of Vrihatkshatra, grandson of Vitatha, and parent of Hastin. The Brahmá Purána in some degree, and the Hari Vansa in a still greater, have made most extraordinary confusion in the instance of this name.—*Wilson's Notes to V. P.* Another Suhotra is mentioned as the son of Sudhanush, and another as the son of Sahadeva, both in the same line of Hastin.

Sujati—A Yádava prince, the son of Vítihotra. The Sujatas form a tribe in Central India at the present day.

Sujyeshta—A king of Magadha, the son of Agnimitra.

Suka—One of the ministers of Rávaṇa, who, having assumed the form of a monkey, was sent by his master, with another minister, Sárana, to go and spy out the army of Ráma, and bring him word as to the names and characters of his chief heroes and counsellors. They were seized and carried into the presence of Ráma, who ordered them to return and tell all they had seen to Rávaṇa ; he also threatened to follow himself and reduce Lanka to a heap of ashes. When Rávaṇa heard the message, he exclaimed, 'Not though all the world came out to fight against me, will I ever restore Sítá to Ráma ?' When Súka counselled a different course, he was dismissed from the service, and went to the jungle where he passed the remainder of his life as a devotee.

Sukala—The wife of a Vaiṣya, who, having gone on a pilgrimage, left her in great affliction, and her female friends came to console her ; Sukalá continuing to mourn for her absent lord, Kámadeva and Indra attempted to seduce her but were foiled, and she remained faithful to her husband, who returned from pilgrimage and received blessings from heaven in recompense of the virtues of his wife. This story is said in the Pádma Puránas to have been recited by Vishṇu to king Veṇa, in illustration of the truth that a wife may be considered as a Tírtha.—*Wilson's Works, III*, 35.

Sukalins—Sons of Vasishtha, and Pitris of Súdras. The Matsya specifies them as amongst the incorporeal Pitris.

Sukanya—The daughter of the Rája Saryáti, who was married to the sage Chyavana ; (q. v.)

Sukara—One of the Narakas ; the swine hell, for the murderer of a brahman, the stealer of gold, and drinker of wine.

Sukarman—A teacher of the Sáma-veda : he and his father Sumantri, studied the same Sanhita under Jaiminí.

Sukarmans, Sukarmas—Two classes of deities of the thirteenth and twelfth Manwantaras respectively.

Suketu—1, One of the kings of Mithila, the son of Nandwarddhana ; 2, One of the Kási princes, the son of Sunítha.

Sukha—Enjoyment ; the son of Dharma, by one of the daughters of Daksha, Siddhi, Perfection.

Suki—The daughter of Tamra and wife of Kaṣyapa, who gave birth to parrots, owls, and crows.

Sukra—1, The son of Bhava ; 2, One of the seven sages of the third Manwantara, sons of Vasishtha ; 3, One of the sons of Havirdhána ; 4, The planet Venus, (or her regent) whose vast car is drawn by earth-born horses, is equipped with a protecting fender and a floor, armed with arrows, and decorated by a banner ; 5, The name of a month occurring in the Vedas, belonging to a system now obsolete.

Sukra—The priest and preceptor of the Daityas. In days of old when the Daityas and Devatás were at war, Sukra was the priest and preceptor of the Daityas, and Vrihaspati, the priest of the Devatás, and Kanju, the son of Vrihaspati, became a pupil in the house of Sukra. He passed his time very pleasantly with Devayáni, the daughter of Sukra ; they were constantly together singing, conversing, &c., until Devayáni began to feel a deep love for her father's pupil. The Daityas were angry that their priest Sukra should teach the son of the priest of their enemy : and one day when Kanju was taking his tutor's cows to pasture, the Daityas carried him off. Sukra compelled them, at the request of Devayáni, to restore him. When Kanju had finished his studies and was about to return to his father's house, Devayáni suggested that he should demand her of her father in marriage : but Kanju refused saying he regarded her as his sister. (See DEVAYÁNI.) The daughter of the Rája of the Daityas pushed Devayána into a well, at which Sukra's anger was excited, and he threatened to forsake the Daityas. The Rája was alarmed; he and his council humbled themselves to Sukra, and made his daughter servant to Devayáni. The aid of Sukra was implored by Rávaṇa before he took the field against Ráma. Súkra taught him certain mantras, and directed him to offer sacrifice in a secret place, and repeat the mantras, whereupon certain weapons would come out of the fire, and render him invincible; but Súkra warned him that he must observe a strict silence throughout, or the sacrifice would be devoid of all power. Rávaṇa arranged accordingly; but Ráma, hearing what his enemy was about to do, sent Angada and Hanumán with an army of monkeys to obstruct the sacrifice, which they succeeded in doing.

Sukriti—The son of Prithu, a descendant of Hastin.

Sukshatra—A king of Magadha, the son of Niramitra.

Suktimat—One of the seven chains of mountains in Bhárata; the east and north portions of the Vindhya range.

Suktimati—A river in Cuttack.

Sukumara—A prince, the son of Dharmaketu, a descendant of Alarka.

Sulapani—The sovereign of the Bhútas, or evil spirits; appointed when the various provinces of creation were assigned to different beings.

Sulomadhi—The name, according to the Bhágavata, of the last Andhra prince.

Sumalya—One of the nine Nandas, kings of Magadha.

Sumanas—1, The son of Ura and grandson of the Manu Chákshusha; 2, The son of Haryaswa.

Sumanasas—A class of deities of the twelfth Manwantara.

Sumantra—The chief counsellor of Mahárája Dasaratha, who made known the ancient prophecy that the Aswamédha was to be performed by the Rishi Sringa. He pacified the infant Ráma with a mirror. He was sent by Vasishtha to summon the Mahárája to the installation of Ráma ; but Kaikeyi desired him to bring Ráma into their presence, and on his arrival she informed him of a previous promise of the Mahárája's, and stated that he was to go into exile. Sumantra reproached her but to no purpose ; he then drove Ráma and Sítá out of Ayodhya in the royal chariot, and on his return to the palace delivered Ráma's parting message to Dasaratha.

Sumantu—1, A teacher of the Atharva-veda, who had studied under the learned Vyása. He was the son of Jaimini ; 2, A prince, the son of Jahnu.

Sumati—1, The fifth Tírthankara, or Jain saint of the present era ; 2, A son of Bharata, a most virtuous prince ; he resigned the kingdom for the life of an ascetic, and died at the holy place Sálagráma ; he is said in the Vishṇu Purána to have been afterwards born again as a Brahman in a distinguished family of ascetics ; 3, A son of Janamejaya, king of Vaiṣáli ; 4, The son of Suparswa, king of Hastin ; 5, The son of Dridhasena, king of Magadha ; 6, A teacher of the Puránas.

Sumati—1, A daughter of the sage Kratu, married to Yajnaváma, the founder of a Gotra ; 2, A daughter of Vinata, and wife of Sagara, who gave birth to sixty thousand sons, who were all destroyed by the sage Kapila.—[SAGARA.]

Sumedhasas—A class of deities of the fifth Manwantara.

Sumitra—1, One of the sons of Vrishni ; 2, The last of the descendants of Ikshváku.

Sumitra—One of the wives of Mahárája Dasaratha, and mother of Lakshmaṇa and Satrughna.

Sun—The Vishṇu Purána contains a long description of the sun's chariot, and horses, his diurnal course, his northern and southern declinations, the way in which his destruction is daily attempted by the Mandehas, (q. v.) It also shows that the sun is the cause of rain by evaporation. A mystical account is furnished of the functions of the sun : his wives and children are enumerated. Then it is stated that to diminish his intensity, Viṣvakarman placed the luminary on his lathe, and ground off some of his effulgence, in this way reducing it an eighth. The sun is represented as the son of Aditi, a daughter of Daksha; and as the father of Vaivaswata, the founder of the Solar dynasty. He is said to have revealed the white Yajush to Yajnawalkya, and to have given the Syamantaka gem to Satrájit. At the end of the world he is to dilate into seven suns, and set the universe on fire.

Sunahotra—A great Muni, the son of Bharadvaja. See a passage quoted in A. S. L. for "a strange and startling mixture of legendary and historical matter," connected with the family of this Muni.

Sunahsephas—The story of Sunahṣepha is told by different authorities, with several variations. As the author of various Súktas in the Rich, he is called the son of Ajígarta. The Rámáyana makes him the middle son of the sage Richíka, sold to Ambarisha, king of Ayodhyá by his parents, to be a victim in a human sacrifice offered by that prince. He is set at liberty by Viṣvámitra; but it is not added that he was adopted. The Bhágavata concurs in the adoption, but makes Sunahṣepha the son of Viṣvámitra's sister, by Ajígarta, of the line of Bhṛigu, and states his being purchased, as a victim, for the sacrifice of Hariṣchandra. The Váyu makes him a son of Richíka, but alludes to his being the victim at Hariṣchandra's sacrifice. According to the Rámáyana, Viṣvámitra called upon his sons to take the place of Sunahṣepha, and, on their refusing, degraded them to the condition of Cháṇḍálas. The Bhágavata says, that fifty only of the hundred sons of Viṣvámitra were expelled their tribe, for refusing to acknowledge Sunahṣepha or Devarata, as their elder brother. The others consented; and the Bhágavata expresses this:—

"They said to the elder, profoundly versed in the Mantras, "We are your followers:" The Rámáyana also observes, that Sunahṣepha, when bound, praised Indra with Richas, or hymns of the Rig Veda. The origin of the story, therefore,—whatever may be its correct version,—must be referred to the Vedas; and it, evidently, alludes to some innovation in the ritual, adopted by a part only of the Kausika families of Brahmans."

Sunaka—A king of Kási, the son of Ghritsamada.

Sunakshatra—The son of Marudeva, of the family of Ikshváku.

Sunanda—A servant of Vishṇu, who was sent by that deity to convey king Bharata, after resigning his crown to his son, to Vaikuṇṭha. On the way Bharata asked him to describe the regions which they traversed, and Sunanda accordingly told him the situation and extent of the different Lokas or spheres above the earth.

Sunanda—The sister of the Rája of Chedi, who received Damayanti as a companion.

Sunaman—One of the sons of Ugrasena.

Sunaya—1, A king of Mithila, the son of Rita ; 2, The son of Pariplava, of the race of Puru.

Sunda—One of the Daityas, the son of Nisunda, and father of Marícha and Táraká.

Sundara—One of the thirty Andhrabhritya kings, the son of Pravilasena.

Sungas—A dynasty of ten kings who ruled in Magadha for a hundred and twelve years.

Sunika—The prime minister of Ripunjaya, king of Magadha, who having killed his sovereign placed his son Pradyota upon the throne.

Sunita—One of the kings of Magadha, the son of Suvala.

Sunitha—1, A king of Kási, the son of Santali and grandson of the celebrated Alarka : 2, The son of Susheṇa, of the race of Puru.

Sunitha—The daughter of Mrityu, who was married to Anga, and became the mother of Veṇa, who was inaugurated by the Rishis as monarch of the earth.

Sunrita—The wife of Uttánapáda, son of Dhruva.

Sunyabandhu—A son of Trinavinda, by the celestial nymph Alambushá.

Suparna—A name of Garuda, the king of the feathered tribes.

Suparswa—A mountain in Jambudwípa, forming the northern buttress of Mount Meru.

Suparswa—1, A king of Mithila, the son of Srutáyus ; 2, A king of Hastinápura, the son of Dridhanemi.

Suprattha—A king of the country south of Meru, the son of Bhanuratha, descendant of Ikshváku.

Sura—1, The eldest son of Karttavírya, the Yádava prince ; 2, The son of Devamidhusha who was married to Márishú, and became the father of Vasudeva ; 3, A son of Vidúráthu, also a Yádava.

Surabhi—The name of the cow produced from the churning of the ocean, the fountain of milk and curds, worshipped by the divinities, and beheld by them with minds disturbed and eyes glistening with delight. V. P. It is termed the cow of plenty, able to grant every wish ; 2, A daughter of Daksha and wife of Kaṣyapa.

Surasa—1, One of the daughters of Daksha, who was married to Kaṣyapa ; 2, The name of a river not identified.

Surasena—1, The son of Satrughna, who, with his brother Subáhu, reigned at Mathura, after the ascent of their father to heaven ; 2, One of the sons of Kárttavírya.

Surasenas—The inhabitants of Mathura, the Suraseni of Arrian.

Suratha—1, The son of Jahnu, descendant of Kuru ; 2, The son of Kundaka, of the line of Ikshváku.

Sureswara—One of the eleven Rudras according to some of the lists. There is a great variety in the appellations of the Rudras, arising from the writers applying to them indifferent names of the common prototype, or synonyms of Rudra or Śiva, selected at will from his thousand and eight names according to the Linga Purána.

Surochish—One of the seven sons of the sage Vasishtha, according to the enumeration in the Bhágavata.

Surpa-nakha—The sister of Rávaṇa, who admired the beauty of Ráma, and used various efforts to induce him to marry her. Ráma jestingly advised her to marry his younger brother Lakshmana. She threatened to devour Sítá, and rushing on her in a phrensy of passion, Lakshmana had to interfere, and with his scemitar cut off the ears and nose of Surpa-nakha. She then fled to her brother Khara, who vowed vengeance for the treatment she had received: but he and his army of Rákshasas all perished in the attempt, being slain by Ráma. Surpa-nakha then went to Rávaṇa, and urged him to carry off Sítá.

Surupas—A class of divinities of the fourth Manwantara.

Surya—The Sun. The mythical ancestor of the Rájas of Koṣala. This deity seems, "under different names to have always held a high place amongst the primitive gods of every nation, by virtue of its prominence in the heavens and the extent to which its influence is felt upon earth. Its daily course and its annual course, its welcome rising in the morning, and its glorious setting in the evening, must all have excited the keenest curiosity amongst a child-like and inquisitive people; and at the same time, the imagination was left to account for the existence of phenomena which in a non-scientific age, are altogether beyond human ken. Thus it seems extremely probable that one of the earliest efforts of poetical genius was to personify the sun as the deity of light, travelling through the blue ether in a golden chariot which all men might see, drawn however by steeds which were invisible to the outward eye, but which were easily assumed to be white, resplendent, and beautiful beyond expression. In the Vedas the attributes of this deity are frequently the same as those of Agni, especially that of originating and diffusing light; but still the sun stands forward as a deity altogether distinct from Fire, when described as journeying through the firmament in an upward and downward course, and especially in his character of measuring days and nights. This god is apparently addressed under a variety of names—but in the Epics he is chiefly known by the name of Súrya, and was regarded as the great ancestor of the solar race who appear in the Rámáyana."—*Wheeler.*

1. By lustrous heralds led on high,
   The omniscient Sun ascends the sky,
   His glory drawing every eye.

2. All-seeing Sun, the stars so bright,
   Which gleamed throughout the sombre night,

Now scared, like thieves, slink fast away,
Quenched by the splendour of thy ray.

3. Thy beams to men thy presence shew ;
Like blazing fires they seem to glow.

4. Conspicuous, rapid, source of light,
Thou makest all the welkin bright.

5. In sight of gods, and mortal eyes,
In sight of heaven thou scal'st the skies.

6. Bright god, thou scann'st with searching ken
The doings all of busy men.

7. Thou stridest o'er the sky ; thy rays
Create, and measure out, our days ;
Thine eye all living things surveys.

8. 9. Seven lucid mares thy chariot bear,
Self-yoked athwart the fields of air,
Bright Sūrya, god with flaming hair.

10. That glow above the darkness we
Beholding, upward soar to thee,
For there among the gods thy light
Supreme is seen, divinely bright.

—*O. S. T., V.* 160.

Susandhi—A prince, the son of Prasuṣruta, a descendant of Kusa.

Susanti—1, The son of Sánti, king of Hastinápura ; 2, The Indra of the third Manwantara.

Susarman—One of the four kings of Magadha of the Kanwa dynasty.

Susarman—The Rája of Trigarta. He proposed to the Kauravas to invade the kingdom of Viráta. After the plan of the campaign had been decided on, he challenged the Rája Viráta to single combat, defeated and captured him. Susarmas was afterwards taken prisoner himself by Bhíma. In the great war he and his four brothers challenged Arjuna to battle in the first day of Drona's command. The five brothers were vanquished by Arjuna ;

on the following day Susarman sent a second challenge to Arjuna to fight in the southern quarter of the plain ; Arjuna accepted the challenge, and it was during his absence on this occasion that his son, the young and heroic Abhimaṇyu was slain.

Sushena—1, One of the sons of Vasudeva, who was killed by Kansa ; 2, The son of Vrishṇimat, of the race of Puru ; 3, One of the sons of Krishṇa by his wife Rukminí ; 4, A distinguished physician in the Rámáyana, who restored the dead monkeys to life by herbs brought from the Himálaya mountains.

Sushna—A name of Vrittra, the demon who personifies drought, and is also called Ahi.

" The lightnings then began to flash,
The direful thunderbolts to crash,
By Indra proudly hurled.
The gods themselves with awe were stilled
And stood aghast ; and terror filled
The universal world.
* * * * * * * *
Now bound by Śushṇa's spell no more,
The clouds discharge their liquid store ;
And long by torrid sunbeams baked,
The plains by copious showers are slaked ;
The rivers swell and sea-wards sweep
Their turbid torrents broad and deep.
The peasant views with deep delight,
And thankful heart, the auspicious sight,
His leafless fields so sere and sad,
Will soon with waving crops be clad,
And mother earth now brown and bare,
A robe of brilliant green will wear."

—*O. S. T., Vol. V, p.* 135.

Sushumna—One of the seven principal rays of the sun ; that which supplies heat to the moon.

Susravas—One of the Prajápatis, according to the enumeration in the Váyu Purána.

Susruta—1, A king of Mithila, the son of Subhása; 2, A teacher of medical science, the reputed author of a celebrated work in Sanskrit still extant.

Susti—A goddess, who is propitiated with offerings when children are troublesome. When the infant Ráma cried for the moon and could not be quieted, it was said the goddess Sustí was unpropitious.

Susuma—A king of Magadha, the son of king Dharma.

Suta—A generic term for chroniclers and bards. The bard and herald of the Hindus, being attached to the state of all men of rank to chaunt their praises, celebrate their actions, and commemorate their ancestry. Also the name of a celebrated pupil of Vyása, from whom he learned many historical and legendary traditions. It was to Súta that the great Muni communicated the Puránas. Súta had himself six scholars who acquired distinction.

Sutala—One of the seven divisions of Pátáḷa, that with a stony soil, but embellished with magnificent palaces.

Sutanu.—One of the five daughters of Ugrasena.

Sutapas—One of the seven pure sages according to the enumeration in the Vishṇu Purána, sons of the great sage Vaìshtha.

Sutapas—A class of deities of the eighth Manwantara.

Sutara—The daughter of Swaphalka.

Sutikshana—An ascetic who figures in the Rámáyana, as of extraordinary merit on account of his austerities. When Ráma and Síta visited him in his hermitage in the forest they found him covered with mud, and his head covered with matted hair; his body reduced to bones and skin. He was absorbed in profound forgetfulness of all things earthly; but when Ráma paid his respects the sage at once embraced him, and bestowed his blessings on him.

Sutra—" (From the Sanscrit *siv*, to sew, literally, therefore, a thread or string) is, in Sanscrit Literature, the technical name of aphoristic rules, and of works consisting of such rules. The importance of the term will be understood from the fact, that the *groundworks* of the whole ritual, grammatical, metrical, and philosophical literature of India are written in such aphorisms, which therefore constitute one of the peculiarities of Hindu authorship. The object of the Sútras is extreme brevity; and, especially in the oldest works of this class, this brevity is carried to such an excess, that even the most experienced would find it extremely difficult, and sometimes impossible, to understand these aphorisms without the aid of commentaries, which, however, are fortunately never wanting, wherever a work is written in this style. Though there is no positive evidence as to the cause or causes which gave rise to this peculiarity of Hindu composition, the method of teaching in ancient India—an account of which is afforded in some of the oldest works—renders it highly probable that these Sútras were intended as memorial sentences which the pupil had to learn by heart, in order better to retain the fuller oral explanation which his teacher appended to them. But it is likewise probable that this method of instruction itself originated in the scarcity or awkwardness of the writing material used, and in the necessity, therefore, of economising this material as much as possible; for that writing was known and practised at the remotest period of Hindu antiquity, is now placed beyond a doubt, though a startling theory was propounded, some years ago, to the effect that writing was unknown in India, even at the time of the great grammarian Pâṇini. The manner, however, in which up to this day, the Hindus are in the habit of keeping the leaves of their books together, seems to throw some light on the name given to this aphoristic literature. The leaves—generally narrow, and even at the present time often being dried palm leaves, on which the words are either written with ink or scratched with a style—are piled up, and, according to the length of the leaves, pierced in one or two places, when, through the hole or holes, one or two long *strings* are passed to keep them together. The name of Sútra was probably, therefore, applied to works, not because they represent a thread or string of rules, but on account of the manner in which these works were rendered fit for practical use; just as in German a volume is called *Band*, from its being 'bound.' That a habit deeply rooted outlives necessity, is probably also shewn by these Sútra works; for while the oldest works of this class may be called

Sútras by necessity, there are others which convey the suspicion that they merely imitated the Sútra style after the necessity had passed away, more especially as they do not adhere to the original brevity of the oldest Sútras ; and the Sútras of the Buddhists, conspicuous for their prolixity, could scarcely lay claim to the term, if compared with the Sútra of the Brahmanical literature."—GOLDSTUCKER.

The Sútra period of Sanscrit literature is fixed by Max Müller at from 600 to 200, B. C., the characteristic of the period is that the Brahmanical writers used very curt and dry sentences, or Sútras, for expressing their thoughts. Numerous Sútra works by different authors are still extant, among which the Vyákarna Sútras of Pâṇini, and the Vedánta Sútras of Vyása, occupy a prominent place.

Suttee—" (An English corruption from the Sanscrit *sati*, a virtuous wife) means the practice which prevailed in India, of a wife burning herself on the funeral pile, either with the body of her husband, or separately, if he died at a distance.

The practice of Suttee is based by the orthodox Hindus on the injunctions of their Sástras, or sacred books, and there can be no doubt that various passages in their Puránas (q. v.,) and codes of law *countenance* the belief which they entertain of its meritoriousness and efficacy. Thus, the *Brahmá-Purána* says : 'No other way is known for a virtuous woman after the death of her husband ; the separate cremation of her husband would be lost (to all religious intents). If her lord die in another country, let the faithful wife place his sandals on her breast, and, pure, enter the fire. The faithful widow is pronounced no suicide by the recited text of the Rig Veda.' Or the code of *Vyâsa :* 'Learn the power of that widow who, learning that her husband has deceased, and been burned in another region, speedily casts herself into the fire,' &c. Or the code of *Angiras :* 'That woman, who, on the death of her husband, ascends the same burning pile with him, is exalted to heaven, as equal in virtue to Arundhati (the wife of Vaṣishtha). She who follows her husband (to another world) shall dwell in a region of joy for so many years as there are hairs on the human body, or 35 millions. As a serpent-catcher forcibly draws a snake from his hole, thus drawing her lord (from a region of torment), she enjoys delight together with him. The woman who follows her husband to the pile expiates the sins of three generations on the paternal and maternal side of that family to which she was given as a virgin...No other effectual duty is known for virtuous women, at any time after the death of their lords, except casting themselves into the same fire. As long as a woman (in her successive transmigrations) shall decline burning herself, like a faithful wife on the same fire with her deceased lord, so long shall she be not exempted from springing again to life in the body of some female animal. When their lords have departed at the fated time of attaining heaven, no other way but entering the same fire is known for women whose virtuous conduct and whose thoughts have been devoted to their husbands, and who fear the dangers of separation.' But however emphatically these and similar passages recommend a wife to burn herself together with her deceased husband, it should, in the first place, be observed, that *Manu*, who, among legislators of ancient India, occupies the foremost rank, contains no words which enjoin, or even would seem to countenance, this cruel practice; and, secondly, that no injunction of any religious work is admitted by the orthodox Hindus as authoritative, unless it can shew that it is taken from, or based on, the revealed books, the Vedas. An attempt has of late years been made by Rája Râdhâkant Deb, to shew that, in a text belonging to a particular school of the Black Yajurveda, there is really a passage which would justify the practice of suttee; but in the controversy which ensued on this subject between him and the late Professor H. H. Wilson, it clearly transpired that the text cited by the learned Rája is of any thing but indubitable canonicity; moreover, that there is a verse in the Rig Veda which, if properly read, would enjoin a widow not to burn herself, but, after having attended the funeral ceremonies of her husband, to return to her home, and to fulfil her domestic duties; and it seems, at the same time, that merely from a misreading of a single word of this verse from the Rig Veda, that interpretation arose which ultimately led to a belief and an injunction so disastrous in their results. That

79

an immense number of widows have fallen victims to this erroneous interpretation of the oldest Vedic text, is but too true. Some thirty years ago, however, the East India Company took energetic measures to suppress a practice which it was perfectly justified in looking upon as revolting to all human feelings, and which it would have likewise been entitled to consider as contrary to the spirit of the Vedic religion. This practice may now be said to have been successfully stopped ; for though, from habit and superstition, even now-a-days cases of suttee occur, they are extremely rare ; and all reports agree that the enlightened natives everywhere, except, perhaps, in certain native states, support the action of government to repress this evil of bygone times.—*Chambers' Encyclopædia.*

Suvala—A king of Magadha, the son of Sumati.

Suvama—The beautiful river ; identified by Wilford with the Ram-gangá.

Suvarchala—The wife of Rudra, the Rudra who was the first of the eight manifestations.

Suvarna—A prince, the son of Antaríksha, of the family of Ikshváku.

Suvarnaroman—One of the kings of Mithila, the son of Maharoman.

Suvibhu—One of the Kaṣya princes, the sixth in descent from Alarka, rája of Benares.

Suvira—1, One of the sons of Sivi ; 2, One of the Kaurava princes, the son of Kshemya.

Suvrata—A king of Magadha, whose reign is said to have lasted 60 years : he was the son of Rája Kshemya.

Suyasas—One of the kings of Magadha, son of the Buddhist king Asokavarddhana, (q. v.)

Suyodhana—A name sometimes given (euphemistically) to Duryodhana, the eldest of the hundred sons of Dhritaráshtra, and who as the representative of the others is painted in the darkest colours, and embodies all their bad qualities. Many Hindus regard him as the visible type of Vice, or the evil principle in human nature, for ever doing battle with Virtue, or the good and divine principle, symbolised by the five sons of Páṇḍu. At Duryodhana's birth various evil omens of the usual hackneyed description occurred ; jackalls yelled, donkeys brayed, whirlwinds blew, and the sky seemed on fire. Dhritaráshtra alarmed, called his ministers together, who recommended him to abandon the child, but could not persuade him to do so.*

Swabhavas—The characteristics, or inherent properties, of the Gunas (or qualities) by which they act, as soothing, terrifying, stupifying, &c.

Swabhojana—One of the Narakas ; that for the punishment of the religious student who sleeps in the day ; and for those who though mature, have to be instructed in sacred literature by their children.

Swadha—1, Oblation : one of the daughters of Daksha, and wife of the Pitris ; 2, One of the wives of Angiras ; 3, The wife of one of the eleven Rudras.

Swaha—1, Offering : one of the daughters of Daksha, who was married to Agni ; 2, The wife of the Rudra Paṣupati.

Swahi—One of the Kroshtri princes, son of Vrijinívat, and grandson of Yadu.

Swamabhak—One of the seven suns, into which the seven solar rays dilate at the end of the day of Brahmá.

Swaphalka—A sage of great sanctity ; wherever he dwelt, there famine, plague, dearth, and other visitations were unknown ; wherever rain was wanted his presence secured the blessing. He was married to the daughter of Kásirája, named Gándiní, (q. v.), whose remarkable birth has already been related. Gándiní, as long as she lived, gave a cow to the brahmans every day. Akrúra was their son ; and his birth therefore proceeded from a combination of uncommon excellence. V. P., 432.

* Williams' Indian Epic Poetry.

Swaraj—One of the seven principal solar rays, that which supplies heat to the planet Saturn.

Swarat—Brahmá, the Creator.

Swarbhanu—1, A renowned Dánava, son of Kaşyapa ; 2, One of equal celebrity, the son of Viprachitti.

Swarga—1, The son of Rudra Bhíma ; 2, Paradise, on Mount Meru, the seat of the righteous, and where the wicked do not arrive even after a hundred births.

Swar-loka—The planetary sphere, extending from the sun to Dhruva, explained in the Puránas to be heaven.

Swarnaprastha—One of the eight minor Dwípas, situated beyond the sea, and inhabited by Mlecchas, but who worship Hindu divinities.

Swarochisha—The Manu of the second Manwantara ; so named from the splendour of his appearance when born. He was the son of the nymph Varuthiní by the Gandharba Káli. The seven Rishis of the period were the Manu's sons.

Swarupas—Forms of things : the distinctions of biped, quadruped, brute, bird, fish, and the like.

Swastyatreyas—A race of brahmans, celebrated for their sanctity ; a branch of the lunar race.

Swati—A lunar mansion in Govithi, in the Central Avashthána.

Swayambhoja—A Yádava chief, the son of Pratikshatra.

Swayambhu—1, Brahmá ; a synonym of Mahat, so termed from its being ungenerated ; 2, the Vyása of the first Dwápara.

Swayambhuva—The Manu, born of and one with Brahmá ; Brahmá converted himself into two persons, the first male, or the Manu Swayambhuva, and the first woman or Satarúpa.

Swayamvara—Self-choice. The public choice of a husband. The most popular of all the forms of marriage which prevailed amongst the Vedic Aryans. The Swayamvara, says Mr. Wheeler, was evidently an institution of the Kshatriyas, resembling in a remarkable degree the tournaments of the age of chivalry.

The man who gained the day became the husband of the damsel. The Mahábhárata contains a long narrative of the Swayamvara of Draupadi. The Swayamvara emphatically belongs to the old Vedic period, and is distinctly recognised in the hymns of the Rig Veda. The institution is an exaggerated expression of the age of chivalry.—*Wheeler*.

"The Swayamvara, the free, or self-election of a husband, was a not uncommon practice amongst the Hindus, and forms the subject of frequent description both in ancient and modern poetry: the Princes being assembled in a public place with appropriate ceremonies, the Princess performed the tour of the circle, and signified her preference by throwing a garland of flowers upon the neck of the successful competitor; the marriage rite was subsequently performed as usual. It may be easily supposed that the preference was not always the suggestion of the moment, and grew out of previous acquaintance: thus Damayanti adopted this mode of choosing Nala in concert with her lover; Tarávati chose Chandraṣekara by the guidance of her nurse; and the Princess of Kanoj invited Prítha Rai to her Swayamvara. The consequences may also be easily conjectured, and mortified vanity, or disappointed expectation must often have engendered personal hostility: the result may not unfrequently have been long and widely felt; and though neither the Swayamvaras of Draupadi or Damayanti may have been attended with any remarkable events, the choice of the Princess of Kanoj was less innoxious: for the animosity which it excited between her father and her lord, laid India bare to Mohammedan aggression, and paved the way for European ascendancy."—*Wilson's Works, III*, 324.

Sweta—1, A serpent king, one of the progeny of Kadru; 2, A range of mountains north of Meru.

Sweta-dwipa—The white or silver island, the abode of Vishṇu. Colonel Wilford bestowed great pains on the verification of these fictitious Dwípas, which he imagined to represent actual divisions of the globe. The white or silver island, or island of the moon, was the island of great Britain, according to him. Still, says Wilson, his essays on these subjects, contain much curious and interesting matter.

Syadvadis—" Assertors of probabilities, or of what may be ;" a designation of the Jainas.

Syala—A Yádava chief, who publicly offended Gargya, the Brahman, and led the latter to adopt a course of austerities to obtain a son who should be a terror to the tribe of Yadu. See Kálayavana.

Syama—One of the sons of Súra.

Syama (Syaṃa)—The black goddess ; one of the names of Párvati.

Syamantaka Gem—A jewel of great celebrity which insured its possessor, if a good man, safety, prosperity and happiness. It was presented by the Sun to Satrájit who wore it on his neck, and became thereby as brilliant as the sun himself. Satrájit, fearing that Krishṇa would ask him for the jewel, transferred it to his brother Prasena ; and as Prasena's character was bad it caused his death ; he being killed by a lion when hunting. The lion taking the jewel in his mouth was about to depart, when he was killed by Jámbavat, the king of the bears, who carried off the gem to his cave and gave it to his son Sukumára to play with. Krishṇa was suspected of having murdered Prasena to get possession of the jewel. To clear himself Krishṇa tracked the jewel to the bear's cave, and after a conflict with Jámbavat which lasted twenty-one days, recovered the jewel. Jámbavat then recognised Krishṇa's divinity, and gave him his daughter Jambavatí in marriage. The jewel was again restored to Satrájit, who was killed by Satadhanwan for the sake of it. Krishṇa resolved that Satadhanwan should relinquish the prize, pursued him, put him to death, but found not the jewel, as it had been given to Akrúra to keep. Balabhadra thought Krishṇa was deceiving him and quarrelled with his brother on account of it.

Akrúra retained the precious jewel fifty-two years, and in consequence enjoyed immunity from all kinds of evil, the whole country partaking of the benefit. This led Krishṇa to conjecture that Akrúra had the gem in his possession ; and in a full assembly Akrúra owned to it and offered it to Krishṇa ; but it was decided that it should remain with Akrúra, who wore it publicly ever after as a garland of light. V. P.

Syamayani—A teacher of the Yajur Veda, and chief of the northern class.

Syeni—A daughter of Kaṣyapa, and the parent of hawks.

T

Tadaikyam—Union ; perfect union ; or identification of one with another. "The mind of man is the cause both of his bondage and his liberation : its addiction to the objects of sense is the means of his bondage ; its separation from objects of sense is the means of his freedom. The sage who is capable of discriminative knowledge must therefore restrain his mind from all the objects of sense, and therewith meditate upon the Supreme Being, who is one with spirit, in order to attain liberation ; for that supreme spirit attracts to itself him who meditates upon it, and who is of the same nature, as the loadstone attracts the iron by the virtue which is common to itself and its products. Yet the union that takes place is only that of contiguity, (Samyoga) not that of identification or unity, Tadaikyam. Vishṇu Purána and note.

Taksha—The son of Bhárata ; he was Rája of Gandhára, residing at Takshaṣíla.

Tala—One of the Narakas—that for the punishment of adultery, murder, &c.

Talajangha—A prince of the Yádava race ; the father of a hundred sons, who were called Tálajanghas : they conquered Bahu, but were afterwards subdued by Sagara. They were a branch of the Haihayas.

Talaka—One of the Andhra kings, the son of Hála.

Talatala—The fourth of the seven regions of Pátáḷa : Máya reigns over Talátala, having been raised to that dignity after the destruction of his three cities by Śiva.

Tamas—1, The quality of darkness, ignorance, inertia.

Ignorance is said to be five-fold ; in this definition Tamas, or obscurity, is the first thing of which it consists ; 2, One of the Narakas ; 3, A Yádava prince, the son of Prithuṣravas.

Tamasa—1, A Manu, the son of Priyavrata ; the Manu of the fourth Manwantara ; 2, A river, the Touse. It was on the banks of this river that Ráma halted the first night of his exile ; when the Máháraja had been carried back to Ayodhya, and the people would keep with the chariot of Ráma. They all spent the night on the banks of the river Tamasa, and at early morning Ráma rose from his bed of leaves, and with Síta and Lakshmana left before the people awoke.

Tamisra—Gloom : the fourth quality of Ignorance in the definition which makes it five-fold.

Tamra—1, One of the daughters of Daksha, married to Kasyapa ; 2, A river.

Tamrapakshi—A son of Krishṇa by his wife Rohiní.

Tamraparni—A river in Tinnevelly, which rises at the southern extremity of the Western Ghauts.

Tamravarna—One of the nine portions of the Varsha of Bhárata.

Tamrayani—A teacher of the white Yájush, and founder of a school.

Tandri—Sloth ; a form of Brahmá.

Tanmatra—The rudiment or type of an element ; the characteristic property of an element.

Tansu—A prince, the son of Rantináru, a descendant of Puru ; called also Tansurodha.

Tantra—A religious text book : the principal rites and formulæ connected with the adoration of *Prakriti* or *Sakti* are derived from the works known by the collective term of Tantras. The followers of the Tantras profess to consider them as a fifth *Veda*, and attribute to them equal antiquity and superior authority. "The Tantras are a class of books of which little is known in Europe, but which, until English education began in India, were the creed of a large proportion of Hindus. Old Pandits in Bengal will still maintain that the Tantric was the grandest religion of all, only it was beyond human nature to carry it out ; for it is based on the idea that we should practice every kind of excess to the utmost, and yet carry a mind fixed on the Supreme Being in the midst of it all. He who worshipped God with purity of life was but a *pásu*, a mere beast ; while he who worshipped him in orgies of drunkenness and licentiousness was a víra, a hero. The Tantric rites were not long ago very prevalent in Bengal, and though, as western culture and the study of English spread, such ideas and rites retreat into obscurity, the Tantras were but the lowest step of that progressive degradation which we traced from the simple and elevated nature-worship of the Rig Veda."* The observances they prescribe have indeed, in Bengal, almost superseded the original ritual. The question of their date is involved in considerable obscurity. From the practices described in some of the Puránas, particularly that of the *Diksha*, or rite of initiation, in the Agni Purána, from the specification of formulæ comprising the mystic monosyllables of the Tantras in that and other similar compilations, and from the citation of some of them by name in different Pauranic works, we must conclude that some of the Tantras are prior to those authorities. * * * * * It may be inferred that the system originated at some period in the early centuries of Christianity, being founded in the previous worship of the female principle, and the practices of the *Yoga* with the *Mantras*, or mystical formulæ of the Vedas. It is equally certain that the observances of the Tantras have been carried to more exceptionable extremes in comparatively modern times ; and that many of the works themselves are of recent composition. They appear also to have been written chiefly in Bengal and the eastern districts, many of them being unknown in the west and south of India ; and the rites they teach having failed to set aside the ceremonies of the Vedas, although they are not without an important influence upon the belief and the practices of the people.

The Tantras are too numerous to admit in this place of their specifications, but the principal are the *Syáma Rahasya, Rudra, Yámala, Mantra Mahodadhi, Sárada Tilaka,* and *Kaliká Tantra ;* whilst the Kula Chúdámani, Kularnava, and similar works, are the chief authorities of one portion of the Sáktas ; the sect being

* Quarterly Review, July 1870.

divided into two leading branches, the Dakshinácháris and Vámácháris, or followers of the right-hand and left-hand ritual. *Works of H. H. Wilson, Vol., I, p.* 250.

Tapa-loka—The sphere or world of the seven Rishis.

Tapaniyas—Brahmans of a branch of the Yájush.

Tapas, Tapasya—The names of two of the months occurring in the Vedas, and belonging to a system now obsolete.

Tapaswin—One of the sons of the Manu Chákshusha.

Tapati—A daughter of the Sun ; the Taptí river.

Tapo-loka—The sphere of penance, inhabited by the deities called Vaibhrájas, who are unconsumable by fire.

Taptakhumba—One of the Narakas, that in which murder and incest are punished.

Taptaloka—The redhot iron Naraka, for jailers, horse-dealers and deserters.

Tara—The wife of Vrihaspati, the preceptor of the gods ; she was carried off by Soma, who refused to give her up even at the command of Brahmá. A fierce contest ensued, termed the Tárakamaya war. It was brought to a close by the interference of Brahmá who compelled Soma to restore Tárá to her husband. Her son Budha was born shortly after. See BUDHA. SOMA.

Tara—The wife of Báli, the elder brother of Sugríva. She attempted to diṣsuade Báli from fighting with his brother, but was unable to do so, and Báli was killed. When she was grieving for her loss, Ráma consoled her, and she was afterwards married to Sugríva, in conformity with the rude customs of a barbarous age.

Taraka—1, A Daitya of great prowess, the son of Hiranyaksha ; 2, A Danava son of Kaṣyapa by Danu.

Taraka—A female Rákshasí, the mother of Marícha. She lived in a dreadful jungle and ravaged the whole country round. The sage Visvámitra earnestly requested Ráma to kill her. Ráma promised to deprive her of her strength and power, but was unwilling to slay a woman. A terrific combat took place, and at the instigation of Visvámitra, Ráma at length killed the dreaded Rákshasí.

Tarapida—A prince, the son of Chandrávaloka, one of the rájas of Ayodhya before the great war.

Tejas—Light or fire, the element ; said to be produced from the rudiment of form or colour ; while itself is the producer of that of taste. V. P.

Tigma—A prince, the son of Mridu, of the race of Puru.

Tillotama—A celestial nymph or Apsarasa, of the Laukíka class.

Tillotamá is described as having been originally a Brahman female, who in consequence of being born in the month of Mágha, dwelt four thousand ages in Vaikuntha, and was then born as the Apsaras Tillotamá, for the purpose of causing the mutual destruction of Sunda and Upasunda, an incident taken from the Mahábháratu.—*Wilson's Works, Vol. III, p. 55.*

Timi—A daughter of Daksha, who was married to Kaṣyapa, and became the mother of fishes.

Tirtha—A holy shrine or sacred place ; in the Pádma Purána, persons are also considered as Tírthas, as a guru, a father, a wife, a son ; and in illustration of this, Vishṇu recited several stories to king Veṇa.

Tirthankara—A Jain saint of the present era, of whom twenty-four are enumerated.

1. Riṣhaba.
2. Ajita.
3. Sambhava.
4. Abhinandana.
5. Sumati.
6. Padmaprabhu.
7. Suparsva.
8. Chandraprabhu.
9. Pushpadhanta.
10. Sitála.
11. Sreyánsa.
12. Vasu pujya.
13. Vimala.
14. Ananta.
15. Dharma.
16. Tánti.
17. Kunthu.
18. Ara.
19. Malli.
20. Manisuvrata.
21. Nami.
22. Nemi.
23. Parsva.
24. Mahávíra or Vardhamanisvami.

Colossal statues of these Tírthankaras are often placed in the court yards of the Jain temples. There is a remarkably fine one at Sravana Bella Góla, near Chenraipatam, in Mysore. Its height is seventy feet three inches. The Duke of Wellington who visited the place in 1801, was of opinion that the rock had been cut until nothing but the image remained.*

Tiryaksrotas—The name given to the animal creation at their first "manifestation," from their nutriment following a winding course. V. P.

Titiksha—Patience ; a daughter of Daksha, married to Dharma ; one of the allegorical unions.

Titikshu—A prince, the son of Mahámanas, a descendant of Yayátí.

Tittiri—A pupil of Yaska, and a teacher of the Taithriya Yajush.

Transmigration—" Or the passing from one place, state, or condition into another, means, in the theological acceptation of the term, the supposed transition of the soul after death into another substance or body than that which it occupied before. The belief in such a transition is one of the most important phases in the religions of mankind. It was common to the most uncivilised and the most civilised nations of the earth, it was the object of fantastical superstition, as well as that of philosophical speculation, and it is the property of both ancient and modern times. Its basis being the assumption that the human soul does not perish together with the body, it could belong to those nations only which had already conceived an idea of the immortality of the soul ; but in proportion as such an idea is crude or developed, as it is founded merely on a vague fear of death, and a craving for material life, or on ethical grounds, and a supposed casual connection between this and a future life, the belief in transmigration assumes various forms, and influences more or less the actions of men.

At the time when in *India* the dogma of transmigration became an integral part of the Brahmanic religion, the Hindus believed

* BUCHANAN's Mysore, III, 410.

that the human souls emanated from a Supreme Being, which, as it were, in a state of bewilderment or forgetfulness, allowed them to become separate existences, and to be born on earth. The soul, thus severed from the real source of its life, is bound to return to it, or to become merged again into that divine substance with which it was originally one ; but as its nature becomes contaminated with sin through its earthly career, it must, so long as it remains in this world, endeavour to free itself from all guilt, and thus to become fit for its ultimate destiny. Religion teaches that this is done by the observance of religious rites, and a life in conformity with the precepts of the sacred books ; philosophy, that the soul will be re-united with Brahman, if it *understands* the true nature of the divine essence whence it comes. So long, therefore, as the soul has not attained this condition of purity, it must be born again, after the dissolution of the body to which it was allied ; and the degree of its impurity at one of these various deaths, determines the existence which it will assume in a subsequent life.

Since there can be no proof of the soul's migrations, the detail in which these are described in the religious works of the Hindus, is merely fantastical, and interesting only so far as it affords a kind of standard by which, at various epochs, and by different writers, the moral merit or demerit of human actions was measured in India. Thus, Manu (in the 12th book of his Code of Laws) teaches : 'The slayer of a Bráhmaṇa—according to the degree of his guilt —is reborn as a dog, a boar, an ass, a camel, a bull, a goat, a sheep, a stag, a bird, a Châṇdâla, or a Pukkaṣa. A Bráhmaṇa, who drinks spirituous liquor, will migrate into the bodies of a worm, an insect, a grasshopper, a fly feeding on ordure, or some mischievous animal. A twice-born who steals (the gold of a Bráhmaṇa,) will pass a thousand times into the bodies of spiders, snakes, and chameleons, of aquatic monsters, or of murderous blood-thirsty demons. He who violates the bed of his guru, will a hundred times migrate into the forms of grasses, of shrubs, and of creeping plants, of carnivorous animals and beasts with long teeth, or of cruel brutes. Those who inflict injury (on sentient beings,) become flesh-eaters ; and those who eat forbidden things, worms. Thieves become devourers of each other ; and those who embrace women of the lowest castes, become ghosts......If a man, through covetousness, has stolen gems, pearl, or coral, or whatever belongs to the precious substances, he is reborn in the tribe of goldsmiths ; if he has stolen grain, he becomes a rat ; if kánsya (a composition of zinc and copper,) a *hansa* bird ; if water, a diver ; if honey, a gadfly ; if milk, a crow ; if juice (of the sugar-cane or the like,) a dog ; if clarified butter, an ichneumon ; if flesh, a vulture ; if fat, a shag ; if oil, a cockroach ; if salt, a cricket ; if curds, the crane, called Valáká ;' &c. A more general doctrine of the migration of souls is based by Hindu philosophers on the assumption of the three cosmic qualities of *sattwa, i. e.*, purity or goodness ; *rajas, i. e.*, troubledness or passion ; and *tamas, i. e.*, darkness or sin, with which the human soul may become endued. And on this doctrine, again, Manu and other writers build an elaborate theory of the various births to which the soul may become subject. Manu, for instance, teaches that 'souls endued with the quality of *sattwa*, attain the condition of deities ; those having the quality of *rajas*, the condition of men ; and those having the quality of *tamas*, the condition of beasts.' Each of these conditions, he continues, is, according to the acts or knowledge of the soul, threefold : the lowest, the middle, and the highest. 'The lowest embodiment of the quality *tamas* is inanimate objects, worms, insects, fish, serpents, tortoises, tame and wild beasts ; the middle state, to which the same quality leads, is (the state of) an elephant, a horse, a Súdra, a Mlechchha or barbarian, a lion, a tiger, and a boar : the highest, that of a public performer, a bird, a cheat, a demon called Rakshas, and a vampire-demon. The lowest condition to which the soul imbued with the quality *rajas* arrives is that of a cudgel-player, a boxer, a public dancer, a man who lives on the use of weapons, and one addicted to gambling and drinking ; the middle condition, that of a king, a man of the Kshattriya or military caste, a house-priest of a king, and a man fond of learned controversy ; the highest, that of a Gandharva or musician in Indra's heaven, a Guhyaka or Yaksha (two kinds of attendants on the god of riches,) or another attendant on another god, or an Apsaras or heavenly nymph in Indra's heaven. The lowest state procured by the quality of *sattwa* is that of a Vánaprastha—or a hermit of the third order of life—a religious mendicant, a Bráhmaṇa, or one of the demigods travelling about in palace-like cars, one of (the genii presiding over) the lunar mansions, or an offspring of Diti. The middle state, procured by the same quality, is that of a sacrificer, a Rishi (q. v.), a god of the lower heaven (a deity personating one of the) Vedas, (a deity presiding over one of) the luminaries or years, one of the manes or progenitors of mankind, and of the demigods called Sádhya. The highest condition to which the quality of *sattwa* leads is that of the god Brahmá, that of a creator of the world (as *Maríchi,* or another patriarch of the same rank,) that of the genius of Dharma (virtue or right,) of *Mahat,* or the intellectual principle of creation, and of *Prakriti,* or matter.'

It is not necessary here to show that this detail regarding the migrations of the souls is more or less differently given by other authors at other periods of Hindu religion, according to the views which they entertained of right and wrong, of the value and rank of imaginary or created beings, and of the social conditions of men. For, since all orthodox Hindu writers agree in principle with Manu, the quotations alleged from his work suffice to illustrate the imaginary positiveness with which the doctrine of transmigration was propounded, and to establish the conclusion that this doctrine rested in India on ethical grounds.

It has been already pointed out that the belief in the soul's life after the death of the body must precede the doctrine of transmigration. As such a belief, however, may be traced in some hymns of the *Rig Veda,* it has been supposed that this doctrine, too, is as old as this Veda. But apart from the uncertainty which still exists regarding not only the age, but even the relative age at which the different hymns of the *Rig Veda* were composed, and setting aside the fallacy which therefore attaches to speaking of this Veda as a contemporaneous whole, it is necessary to observe that the only passage which has been adduced in proof of this important discovery does not bear it out. It is the 32nd verse of the hymn I, 164, and according to the translation of Professor Wilson (Vol. II, pp. 137, 138,) runs as follows: 'He who has made (this state of things) does not comprehend it; he who has beheld it, has it also verily hidden (from him); he, whilst yet enveloped in his mother's womb, *is subject to many births*, and has entered upon evil.' But the word of the text, *bahuprajáh*, rendered by Wilson, according to the commentator, 'is subject to many births,' may, according to the same commentator, also mean, 'has many offsprings,' or 'has many children;' and as the latter sense is the more literal and usual sense of the word, whereas the former is artificial, no conclusion whatever regarding the doctrine of transmigration can safely be founded on it.

The Buddhistic belief in transmigration is derived from that of the Brahmanic Hindus; it agrees with the latter in principle, though it differs from it in the imaginary detail inwhich it was worked out.

Like the Brahmanic Hindus, the Buddhists believe that all souls have existed from the beginning; like them, they believe in the unreality and sinfulness of the world in the necessity of the soul's freeing itself from the bondage of this world, and in the causal connection between the actions of man in this, and his condition in a subsequent, life. Like the Brahmanic Hindus, they hold, therefore, that sin is the cause of transmigration, and that by a total expiation of sin, the soul ceases to be reborn, and attains its final resting-place. But since this resting-place is to the Buddhists Nirvána (q. v.,) or Non-entity, whereas to Brahmanism it is Brahman, or the principle of Entity; since they reject the institution of caste, which is the social foundation of Brahmanic life; since they do not acknowledge the authority of the Vedas, and the codes based on it, and therefore consider as morally wrong much that the Brahmanic Śastras enjoin as morally right, the standard according to which the life of a Buddhist is regulated must differ in many respects from that which governs the conduct of a Brahmanic Hindu; and his ideas of reward and punishment, therefore, as reflected by his ideas of the mode of transmigration, likewise differ from those of the Brahmanic believer. To enlarge here on this difference is not necessary, for, after the illustrations already afforded from Manu, it is easy to conceive that the *detail* of the Buddhistic doctrine of transmigra-

81

tion is as fanciful as that of the Brahmanic doctrine; that it is therefore partly devoid of interest, and partly intelligible only if taken in connection with the detail of Buddhistic religion and literature. Yet it is not superfluous to point out one great difference which separates the notions of one class of Buddhists from those of the rest, as well as from those of the Brahmanic Hindus. According to the latter, and the great mass of Buddhists, it is always the same soul which ever from its first birth re-appears in its subsequent births, until it is finally liberated from transmigration. But among the southern Buddhists, another idea has also taken root. In their belief, the succession of existences of a being is also a succession of souls; and each such soul, though the result of its predecessor, is not identical with it. According to this view, the body dies, and with it the soul, too, is 'extinguished,' leaving behind only the good and bad acts which it has performed during its life. The result of these acts now becomes the seed of of a new life, and the soul of this new life is therefore the necessary product of the soul of the former life. Thus all the succeeding souls have to labour at the solution of the same problem, which began when their first ancestor entered this world, but no succeeding birth is animated by the same soul. This dogma is illustrated in their works by various similes. One lamp, they say, for instance, is kindled at another; the light of the former is not identical with that of the latter, but nevertheless, without this, the other light could not have originated. Or, a tree produces fruit; from the fruit, another tree arises, and so on; the last tree is therefore not the same as the first, though the fruit is the necessary cause of the last."—GOLDSTUCKER.

Trasadasyu—"The Terrifier of thieves." 1, A name given in the Bhágavata to Mándhátri; 2, The son of Prukutsa.

Trasarenu—A measure of time, consisting of three Anus.

Trayyaruna—1, The Vyása of the fifteenth Dwápara age; 2, A contributor to the Rig Veda, he was a prince, the son of Tridhanwan; 3, Another prince, the son of Urukshaya, a descendant of Bharata.

Treta—The Second Yuga or age, consisting of three thousand divine years.

Tridhaman—The Vyása of the tenth Dwápara age.

Tridhanwan—An ancient Rája of the solar line, the son of Sumanas.

Trijata—One of the Rákshasí women, who, when her companions wished to torture and devour Sítá, told them of a dream she had which betokened victory to Ráma and destruction to Rávaṇa ; they then left Sítá alone in the grove and returned to their own apartments.

Trikuta—A mountain ridge in the south of Meru.

Trimadhu—A class of Brahmans so denominated from the particular part of the Vedas they study and recite. Three Anuvákas of the Yajur Veda begin Madhuváta, &c.

Trimurti—"(From the Sanscrit *tri*, three, and *múrti*, form) is the name of the Hindu triad, or the gods *Brahman* (masculine,) Vishṇu, and Śiva, when thought of as an inseparable unity, though three in form. The *Padma-Purána*, which, being a Purána of the Vaishnava sect, assigns to Vishṇu the highest rank in the Trimúrti, defines its character in the following manner : 'In the beginning of creation, the great Vishṇu, desirous of creating the whole world, became threefold : creator, preserver, and destroyer. In order to create this world, the supreme spirit produced from the right side of his body himself as Brahman ; then, in order to preserve the world, he produced from the left side of his body Vishṇu ; and in order to destroy the world, he produced from the middle of his body the eternal Śiva. Some worship Brahman, others Vishṇu, others Śiva ; but Vishṇu, one, yet threefold, creates, preserves, and destroys ; therefore, let the pious make no difference between the three.' And the *Matsya-Púrana*, where speaking of *Mahat*, or the intellectual principle of the Sánkhya philosophy, says that 'Mahat becomes distinctly known as *three* gods, through the influence of the three qualities, goodness, passion, and sin ; being one person and three gods—viz., Brahman, Vishṇu, and Śiva.' Apart, therefore, from sectarian belief, which makes its own god the highest, and gives him the attributes also of the other gods, *Trimúrti* implies the unity of the three principles of creation, preservation, and destruction, and as such belongs more to the philosophical than the popular belief. When represented, the Trimúrti is one body with three heads: in the middle, that of Brahman; at its right, that of Vishṇu; and at its left, that of Śiva. The symbol of the Trimúrti is the mystical syllable *om*, when (*o* being equivalent to *a* + *u*) *a*, means Brahman; *u*, Vishṇu; and *m*, Śiva."—GOLDSTUCKER.

Trina—A prince, the son Uṣínnara, descendant of Yayáti.

Trinachiketa—A class of Brahmans so called from studying or reciting the Rathaka branch of the Yajur Veda, commencing with the term Trinachiketa.

Tinavindu—1, The Vyása of the twenty-third Dwápara age; 2, A prince, the son of Budha, of whom the celestial nymph Alambusha became enamoured.

Triprishtha—Mahávíra in one of his births was a Vásudeva, named Triprishtha, from having three back bones: his uncle and foe in a former life, Visabhánandi, was born as his Protagonist or Prativásudeva, named Aṣvagriva or Hayagriva, and was in the course of events destroyed by the Vásudeva, a palpable adaptation of the Pauranic legend of Vishṇu and Hayagriva. Triprishtha having put his chamberlain cruelly to death was condemned to hell, and again born as a lion.

Tripti—One of the Siddhis, or eight perfections of man. Tripti is the second and means mental satisfaction, or freedom from sensual desire.

Trisala—The wife of Siddhártha, king of Pavana, and mother of the celebrated Tirthankara Mahávíra.

Trisanku—A prince of the solar line, the son of Satyavrata. He was banished by his father for his bad conduct, and degraded t o the condition of a Cháṇḍála, or outcaste. But during a twelve years' famine be provided the flesh of deer for the nourishment of he wife and children of Visvámitra, suspending it on a tree on the Ganges, that he might not subject them to the indignity of receiving presents from an outcaste. On this account Visvámitra, being highly pleased with him, elevated him in his living body to heaven.

Trishna—"Greediness;" one of the children of Mritya, 'death.'

Trishtubh—The name of the metre, created along with the Yajur Veda, &c., from the southern mouth of Brahmá.

Trishyas—The designation of Sudras in Krauncha Dwipa.

Trisiras—1, The son of Tvashṭṛi, and sometimes called Viṣvarúpa; he is twice mentioned in the Rig Veda under this name. He is said to have had three heads and six eyes, and three mouths; one of his mouths was the soma drinker, the second the wine drinker, and the third was destined for consuming other things. Indra hated this Viṣvarupa and cut off his three heads.—*Muir, O. S. T., Vol. V., p.* 228-232.

2. One of the sons of the giant Rávaṇa who was killed at the siege of Lanka.

Trivrishan—The Vyása of the eleventh Dwápara age.

Trivrit—A collection of hymns created along with the Rig Veda from the eastern mouth of Brahmá.

Truti—A measure of time, consisting of three Tresarenus.

Tryambaka—One of the eleven Rudras.

Tulasi plant—A tree sacred to Krishṇa, said to have been produced at the churning of the ocean; but considered by Wilson to be a sectarial addition to the articles originally specified.

Tulyata—One of the Siddhis, the fourth, meaning similarity of life, form, and feature.

Tumburu—A Gandharba, who resides in the sun's car as one of its seven guardians in the month of Madha or Chaitra.

Tunda—A fierce demon mentioned in the Pádma Purána, which has a long narrative of the destruction of the demon by Nahusha the son of Áyus.

Tundikeras—One of the great divisions of the Haihaya tribe.

Tunga—The son of Atri, who having propitiated Náráyana by penance, obtained a son equal to Indra; this son was Veṇa, who was made by the Rishis the first king of the earth. [VENA.]

Tungaprastha—A mountain to the east of Ramghur.

Tuni—One of the Saineya princes, the son of Asanga.

Turvasu—One of the sons of Yayáti, to whom his father made over the south-east districts of his kingdom, to govern as viceroy under his younger brother Puru. Turvasu refused to take his father's infirmities on him, in consequence of which his line soon failed and became merged in that of Puru.

Tusharas—1, A people, called also Tukháras, probably the Tochari, or tribe of the Sakas, by whom Bactria was taken from the Greeks, and from whom Tocharistan derives the name it still bears; 2, A race of princes; the dynasty consisted of fourteen, and the Váyu Purána states that their united reigns lasted 500 years.

Tushitas—A class of deities of the second Manwantara; and who were called the Ádityas in the Manwantara of Vaivaswata. According to the Váyu the Tushitas were the sons of Kratu. The deities of each period are those to whom offerings of the soma juice, &c., are presented collectively.

Tushti—1, Resignation; a daughter of Daksha who became the wife of Dharma; 2, A daughter of Paurnamáṣa.

Tushtimat—One of the sons of Ugrasena and Devaka.

Tvashtri—This god, who in the later mythology is regarded as one of the Ádityas, but does not bear that character in the Rig Veda, is the Hephaistos or Vulcan, of the Indian Pantheon, the ideal artist, the divine artizan, the most skilful of workmen, who is versed in all wonderful and admirable contrivance. He sharpens the iron axe of Brahmaṇaspati, and forges the thunderbolts of Indra, which are described as golden, or of iron, with a thousand points and a hundred edges. He is styled the beautiful, or skilful-handed, the skilful worker, the omniform, or archetype of all forms, and *Savitri*, the vivifier. He imparts generative power and bestows offspring. He develops the seminal germ in the womb, and is the shaper of all forms, human and animal. He has produced and nourishes a great variety of creatures; all worlds (or beings) are his, and are known to him; he has given to heaven and earth and to all things their forms. He bestows long life. He puts speed into the legs of a horse. He is said to be skilled in all Sámatexts, and to have created Brahmaṇaspati above all creatures;

and is said, along with heaven and earth, the waters, and the Bhṛigus, to have generated Agni. He is master of the universe, a first-born protector and leader. He is a companion of the Angirases and knows the region of the gods. He is supplicated to nourish the worshipper and protect his sacrifice. He is the bestower of blessings and possessed of abundant wealth; and is asked, like other gods, to take pleasure in the hymns of his worshippers, and to grant them riches.

Tvashtri is in several passages connected with the Ribhus, who, like him, are celebrated as skilful workmen, and are called his pupils. An exhibition of their skill is mentioned; they are said to have made into four a single new sacrificial cup which Tvashtri had formed, and when he saw this alteration of his work, he is represented as becoming ashamed and hiding himself among the goddesses. In one place he is said to have resented this change in his own workmanship, while in another he is made to applaud their design and admire the superior products of their skill.

Tvashtri had twin children, (a daughter) Saraṇyú, and (a son) Triṣiras. He is represented as having for his most frequent attendants the wives of the gods; which Professor Roth considers to refer to the principal sphere of his creative action, as the bestower of offspring.

Indra sometimes appears to be in a state of hostility with Tvashtri and his son; and at last a quarrel occurs in which Indra slays him. In the Márkaṇḍeya Purána Tvashtri is identified with Visvakarman and Prajápati. See Muir's Orig. Sans. Texts, Vol. V, pp. 224–233, where the authorities are quoted for all the preceding statements.

Twisha--A daughter of Paurnamáṣa.

U

Uchchraissravas—The horse produced at the churning of the ocean, and taken by Indra. It is called the chief of horses.

Udaksena—A king of Hastinápura, the son of Viswaksena.

Udaradhi—The son of Pushti, and grandson of Dhruva.

Udavasu—A king of Mithila, the son of Janaka, (q. v.)

Udavraja—A country mentioned in the Rig Veda as one "into which the waters flow," the residence of the black-skinned aboriginal king Sambara, who possessed one hundred ancient impregnable cities.

Udayana—A prince, the son of Satánika ; of the race of Puru, "the race which gave origin to Brahmans and Kshatriyas, and which was purified by regal sages." V. P.

Udayaswa—A king of Magadha, the son of Dharbaka.

Udayin—One of the sons of Vasudeva, by his wife Devakí.

Uddalin—One of the fifteen teachers of the White Yájush.

Uddhava—A sage, versed in the Yoga doctrine, foreseeing the destruction of the Yádavas, applied to Krishṇa for advice, and was sent to Badarikaṣrama to practise penance and prepare for heaven.

Udgatri—The title of the priest who chaunts the prayers and hymns in the administration of sacrificial rites.

Udgitha—One of the kings of Bhárata Varsha, the son of Bhava.

Ugra, Ugraritas—Two of the eleven Rudras.

Ugradeva—The name of a deceased ancestor conceived of as still existing in another world, and invoked in one of the hymns of the Rig Veda, along with the souls of other deceased ancestors ; they are thus called on, "Let not the gods injure us here, nor our early Fathers who know the realms ! 'May the Fathers protect me in my invocation to the gods.'"

Ugrajit, Ugrampasya—Two Apsarases, who are invoked in the Atharva Veda, and asked to remit sins committed while gambling. There are many verses which show that the Apsarases were intimately connected with gambling. Dr. Muir translates the following :—"I invoke hither the skilfully-playing Apsaras who cuts up and conquers and gets gains in the game of dice. I invoke hither the skilfully-playing Apsaras who collects and scatters, and receives gains in the game of dice. May she who dances about with the dice, when she wins by gaming, grant gain to us, and obtain success through her skill. May she come to us with abundance of food. Let them not conquer this money of ours. I invoke hither the joyful and exulting Apsaras—those [goddesses] who delight in dice, and who cherish grief and anger. In another verse they are said to be "fond of dice," and soul-bewitching."

Ugrasena—1, The Rája of Mathura, who was deposed by his son Kansa and kept in confinement. The Rája Kansa was afterwards killed by Krishṇa in a severe contest. Krishṇa then restored Ugrasena to the throne, and sent to Indra for his royal hall Sudharman, which was conveyed from heaven by Váyu, and used by the Yádava chiefs. Ugrasena is then described as reigning wisely and well for a long period at Mathura; but when the death of Krishṇa took place, Ugrasena and his wives committed themselves to the flames ; 2, One of the sons of Paríkshit.

Ugrayudha—A Kaurava prince, the son of Krita ; by whose prowess the Nipa race of Kshatriyas was destroyed. Ugráyudha was slain by Bhíshma in consequence of demanding in marriage the widow of Sántana.

Uktha—1, The name of a portion of the Sáma Veda, created from the southern mouth of Brahmá ; 2, A prince, the son of Chhala, descendant of Kusa.

Ulmuka—One of the sons of Balabhadra by his wife Revatí.

Uluki—The parent of owls. V. P., 148.

Ulwana—One of the seven Rishis of the third Manwantara ; they were sons of Vasishtha.

Uma—The Harivansa gives the following history of Umá, which differs in some points from that of the Rámáyana, as it assigns three daughters to Himavat and Mená, among whom the Ganga is not included. 'Their (the Pitṛis') mental daughter was Mená, the eminent wife of the great mountain Himavat. The king of the mountains begot three daughters upon Mená,—viz., Aparṇá, Ekaparṇá, and Ekapáṭala. These three, performing very great austerity, such as could not be performed by gods or Danavas, distressed with alarm both the stationary and moving worlds. Ekaparṇá (one leaf) fed upon one leaf. Ekapáṭalá took only one páṭalá (Bignonia) for her food. One (Aparṇá) took no sustenance, but her mother, distressed through maternal affection, forbade her, dissuading her with the words, *u ma* (O don't). The beautiful goddess, performing arduous austerity, having been thus addressed by her mother on that occasion, became known in the three worlds as Umá. In this manner the contemplative goddess became renowned under that name. But this world shall remain distinguished by having these three maids...Umá was the eldest and most excellent among the three. Distinguished by the force derived from deep contemplation she obtained Mahadeva for her husband.—*O. S. T., Vol. IV, p.* 367.

The first work in which the name of Umá occurs is the Talavakára, or Kena Upanishad. In his remarks on a passage in this work, relating a victory gained by Brahmá for the gods, Weber supplies an ingenious contribution to the mythlogical history of Umá. He says : " The representation in Sections 3 and 4 indicates that the Kena Upanishad was produced at a time when,—in place of the three principal gods, Agni, Váyu, and Súrya, who had come to be regarded as the representatives of the divine principle on earth, in the atmosphere, and in heaven,— Agni, Váyu, and Indra were regarded as such. These are properly only two, since Indra is essentially identical with Váyu. Though I have found numerous examples of the first triad, especially in in the two Yajur-vedas, I have noticed only one other of the second triad, which is properly one a duad, viz., in the Rik-text of the Purusha Sukta (R. V., x. 99, 13). Nor am I able to give a satisfactory explanation of it. On the other hand, the totality of the divine was already comprehended in Brahmá (neuter), and it is the object of the legend here to make clear and to enforce the supremacy of Brahmá over all temporary divine manifestations, and even over the triad of such.

" But how shall we explain the position of Umá Haimavatí, who comes forward as mediatrix between the eternal Brahmá and the gods ? According to Sáukara, she is Vidyá (knowledge) who appears Umá rupiṇi (in the form of Uma) to Indra. The same explanation is found in Sāyana, who (on Taitt. Ar. x, 1, 150) when interpreting the word *soma*, cites this passage, and remarks : " Since Gauri, the daughter of Himavat, is the impersonation of divine knowledge, the word Umá, which denotes Gaurí, indicates divine knowledge. Hence in the Talavakára Upanishad, in the passage on the impersonation of divine knowledge, the impersonation of divine knowledge is introduced in these words : ' He said to the very resplendent Umá Haimavati.'

There are, however, some additional points which seem to place the original signification of Umá in quite a different light. First of all, why is she called Haimavatí ? What has she to do with Himavat ? Is it that the *brahmá-vidyá* (divine knowledge) came originally from the Himavat to the Aryans dwelling in Madhyadésa (the central region of Hindustan) ? We have learnt from the Haushítáki Bráhmana (Ind. Stud. i, 153) that the north of India was distinguished by greater purity of speech, and that students travelled thither to learn the language (*vácham sixitum*) and on their return thence enjoyed great consideration and authority. Now it would have been quite natural if this state of things had not been confined to language, but had become extended to speculation also, and if the knowledge of the one, eternal Brahmá, had been sooner attained in the peaceful valleys of the Himálaya, than was possible for men living in Madhyadéṣa, where their minds were more occupied by the practical concerns of life." Such a view of Umá Haimavatí appears to me, however, to be very hazardous.

For,—not to say that in our explanations of the ancient Indian deities we act wisely when we attach greater importance to the physical than to the speculative element,—we are by no means certain that Umá actually does signify divine knowledge (*brahmá vidyá*) ; and moreover, her subsequent position as Rudra's wife (in the Taitt. Ar.) would thus be quite inexplicable. Now there is among the epithets of this latter goddess a similar one, viz., Párvatí, which would lead us in interpreting the word Haimavatí, to place the emphasis not upon the *Himavat*, but upon the mountain (*parvata*) *:* and with this I might connect the epithets of Rudra which we have learnt from the Sátarudriya, *Girisa, Girisanta, Girisaya, Giritra,* in which we recognize the germ of the conception of Śiva's dwelling on Kailása. He is the tempest, which rages in the mountains, and his wife is therefore properly called Párvatí, Haimavatí, "the mountaineer," 'the daughter of Himavat.' At the same time, it is not clear what we have to understand by his wife ; and further she is perhaps, originally not his wife, but his sister, for Umá and Ambiká are at a later period evidently identical, and Ambiká is Rudra's sister (Ind. Stud. I, 183). Besides, this identification of Umá with Ambiká leads us to a new etymology of the former. For as Ambiká, 'mother,' appears to be merely an euphemistic and flattering epithet, employed to propitiate the cruel goddess, in the same way it appears that we must derive Umá from the root *u, av*, 'to protect.'*

As the consort of Śiva, the goddess has various names ; as Durga, Devi, Káli, Párvati, Bhavani, &c. Some of these names have in the Vedic writings a different import from those assigned in the later mythology, as Śiva was not a deity of the Vedic period, or not of the whole of it. "Though this double character of the consort of Śiva is not always discernible in the myths which are connected with special designations of hers, and though at a late period the popular creed looked upon her far more as the type of destruction than as that of divine wisdom, yet the works devoted to her praise never fail to extol her also as the personification of the highest knowledge." Various myths relating to this goddess are to

* Muir, O. S. T., Vol. IV, p. 360.

be found scattered over nearly the whole range of Hindu literature. Some of those have already been narrated in the articles given under her other names in this volume. In a previous existence she is said to have been Sati, the daughter of Daksha, who abandoned her mortal life because she was slighted by her father when he performed his great sacrifice and neglected to invite Śiva to partake of it. As Umá she was the mother of Ganeṣa and Karttikeya, (q. v.)

"According to the Harivansa she was, in another life, born as the daughter of Yaṣoda, and exchanged for Vishṇu, when in his incarnation as Krishṇa he was born as a son of Devaki. On that occasion she was killed by Kansa, but as soon as he had dashed her to the ground, she rose to the sky, leaving behind her corporeal frame, and became a divine virgin to whom the gods addressed their praises. Hence her names Kanyá, Kumari, &c., the virgin. This connection between the legendary history of Umá and Vishṇu, is also briefly referred to in the Devimahátmya, though this work is chiefly concerned in the narrative of the martial exploits of the goddess. The latter consisted in the destruction by her of two demons, Madhu and Kaiṭabha, who had endangered the existence of the god Brahmá ; and of the demon Mahisha or Mahishasura, who, having conquered all the gods, had expelled them from heaven, and who met Umá, assisted only by her lion, with a numberless host of demons ; moreover in her defeating the army of Cháṇḍa and Muṇḍa, two demon servants of Śumbha and Nisumbha ; in her killing the demon Rakavija, who had a sort of charmed life, each drop of his blood, when shed, producing hundreds of demons like himself; and ultimately in her destroying the demons Śumbha and Nisumbha themselves.

"In commemoration of her victory over Mahishásura, a festival called the Durgápúja is annually celebrated in Bengal. The goddess is there represented with ten arms trampling upon the demon, who is also attacked by her lion, and wounded in the chest by her spear. She has also laid hold of him by the hair, and is about to chop off his head."—GOLDSTUCKER.

Unmada—Insanity ; a form of Brahmá.

Unnati—Elevation ; one of the allegorical daughters of Daksha, married to Dharma.

Upadanavi—1, The daughter of Vrishaparvan the Daitya, and wife of Hiranyaksha.

Upadeva—1, One of the sons of Akrúra ; 2, A son of Devaka.

Upadeva—A daughter of Devaka.

Upagu—A king of Mithila, the son of Satyarathi.

Upamadgu—A prince, one of the sons of Swaphalka by Gandini.

Upananda, Upanidhi—Two sons of Vasudeva, by his wives Madira and Bhadrá respectively.

Upanishad—" Is the name of those Sanskrit works belonging to the Vedic literature which contain the mystical doctrine of the Hindus on the nature of a supreme being, its relation to the human soul, and the process of creation. The word (derived from the Sankrit prefixes *upa*, ' beneath' or ' near,' and *ni*, ' in,' combined with the radical *sad*, ' sit') is explained by the great theologian *Sankara* (q. v.), and others after him, as meaning the ' science of Brahmá,' or ' the understanding of the identity of Brahmá and the soul,' because ' in those devoted to it, this science *sets to rest* (or destroys) the world, together with (ignorance) its cause ;' or in other words, because it shows to them that the world has, besides Brahman, no reality. Grammatical commentators explain its etymology as implying that ' eternal bliss *reposes on it (upanishidati sreyo 'syam)* ;' and Professor Max Müller has surmised that the word ' Upanishad meant originally the act of sitting down near a teacher, of submissively listening to him,' whence it came to mean ' implicit faith, and at last truth or divine revelation.' But apart from the artificialness of all these interpretations, it deserves notice that the earliest sense of the word appears to be that of ' secret' or ' mystery' (literally, that which *sits* or rests *beneath*.') In this sense, it is mentioned by the grammarian Paṇini ; and as it is very probable that, in his time, the works bearing the name of Upanishads were not yet in existence, it may be assumed that these works derived their name from the mysteriousness of the doctrine contained in them ; and perhaps also from the mystical manner in which they propounded it.

In order to understand the origin and purport of the Upanishads, as well as the relation in which they stand to the Vedas, properly so called, it must be borne in mind that, though the Vedic hymns are based on the worship of the elementary powers, and the Bráhmaṇa portion connected with them is chiefly concerned in legendary and ritual matter relating to that worship, yet in both these portions of the Vedas, and especially in the Bráhmaṇas, the beginning of a period become already visible when the poets raised the questions as to the origin of the world and the true nature of the gods. A first attempt at a systematic answer to these questions was made in works which bear an intimate relation to the Bráhmaṇas ; and so great was the awe in which, on this account, these works were held, that they had to be read in the solitude, where the mind could ponder in perfect calmness over the mysterious problems in which they are engaged. These are the Áraṇyakas (from araṇya, a forest.) But as the style and contents of the Áraṇyakas are extremely obscure, and as, through the close alliance of these works to the Bráhmaṇas, of which some of them form part, the theological questions of which they treat are much overlaid with ritual and other matters which properly belong to the Bráhmaṇas, a further progress made in the same direction, led to the composition of works and treatises, the diction of which is somewhat clearer, and less entangled with subjects extraneous to the problems they intend to solve. Such works and treatises are the *Upanishads.* Their object, like that of the Áraṇyakas, is to impress the mind with the belief in one Supreme Spirit (*Brahmá,* as a neuter, and different, therefore, from the same word as a masculine, which is the name of the first god of the *Trimúrti,* q. v.,) to show that this Supreme Spirit is the creator of the world ; that the world has no reality if thought of besides Brahmá, and that the human soul is identical in nature with that same spirit whence it emanates. The reward the Upanishads hold out to the believer, who understands their doctrine, and firmly adheres to it, is freedom from Transmigration (q. v.,) and consequent eternal bliss. The object and aim of the Upanishads are therefore the same as those propounded in the philosophical systems ; and the Upanishads may therefore be looked upon as the forerunners of these systems themselves—those Upanishads, at least, which we may call the older Upanishads ; for as to the more recent ones, and those which bear the stamp of sectarian character, their claim to be ranked among the Vedic writings is extremely doubtful, if at all admissible.

Though agreeing in the main points of their doctrine, it is easily understood that works of this nature, ranging over different periods of Hindu religion, will also differ from one another both in the manner and detail in which they deliver their subject-matter, and in the degree of completeness with which they treat of it. Thus, in some, the legendary narrative, and even ritual detail, are still considerably blended with the theosophical speculation—and these stand nearest, therefore, the Áraṇyakas, probably also in time ; in others, more philosophical, the nature of Brahmá and the human soul is the only subject of inquiry ; in others, the process of creation is also enlarged upon, with detail which harmonises more or less either with the ulterior views of the Vedanta (q. v.) or those of the Śáṅkhya (q. v.) philosophy ; some Upanishads, again, especially emphasise the inefficiency, for the attainment of eternal bliss, of the performing religious acts and of worldly studies—the knowledge of Brahmá being the only means that leads to this end ; others, on the contrary, in conformity with the Yoga (q. v.) doctrine, assign a prominent place to the exterior means, by using which the soul would qualify itself for union with the Supreme Spirit ; while the sectarian Upanishads, which identify this spirit with Vishṇu and Śiva, have, besides, the tendency of reconciling the popular with the philosophical creed.

Of the older Upanishads, a typical instance is furnished in the Chhándogya Upanishad of the Sámaveda, the framework of which is legendary throughout, and its contents allegorical and mystical. Other shorter Upanishads, freer from narratives and allusions to the mysterious import of ritual acts, aim at a more intelligible exposition of the doctrine of the soul. Of their mode of treatment, the following passage from the Káṭhaka Upanishads will serve as an example : *Nachiketas*, the son of Vájaṣravas, having come to the abode of Yama, the judge of the dead, and obtained from him the grant of three boons, asks of him, for his third boon, an answer to the following question : 'There is this doubt: some say that (the soul) exists after the death of a man (in connection with another body than this) ; others say that it does not. This I should like to know, instructed by thee.' And Yama, after some hesitation, explains to him that the soul and Brahmá are one, but that a man attains immortality only by understanding this unity, and that, to arrive at this understanding, he must free his mind from sensual desires, and get a correct knowledge both of the nature of Brahmá and of the soul. 'Know the soul as the rider, and the body as the car ; know intellect as the charioteer, and *manas* (the organ of volition) as the rein. The senses, they say, are the horses, the objects (their) roads ; and the enjoyer (*i. e.*, the rider) is (the soul) endowed with body, senses, and manas. Thus say the wise. If he (the charioteer) is unwise, and his manas is always unbridled, his senses are uncontrolled like vicious horses ; but if he is wise, and his manas is always bridled, his senses are controlled like good horses. He who, always impure, is unwise, and whose manas is unbridled, does not attain *that* abode (of immortality,) but comes to the world (of birth and death) ; he, however, who, always pure, is wise, and whose manas is bridled, he attains *that* abode whence he is not born again. The man who has a wise charioteer, and whose manas is bridled, reaches the other shore of the road (of the world,) the highest abode of Vishṇu. Higher, (*i. e.*, subtler,) indeed, than the objects are the senses ; higher than the senses is manas ; higher than manas, intellect ; and higher than intellect, the great one, the soul. Higher than the great one is that which is unmanifested, and higher than the unmanifested is Purusha, the Supreme Spirit. But higher than Purusha there is nothing ; he is the goal, the highest resort. The highest spirit is the soul hidden in all created beings ; it is not manifest, but is beheld by those who can see what is subtle with an attentive, subtle intellect.' The coincidence between the allegory, in the foregoing passage, and that in Plato's *Phædrus*, imparts an additional interest to this Upanishad, which is valuable, moreover, on account of the evidence it affords as to points of agreement and difference between its views of the development of the world and those expounded in the Sánkhya (q. v.) The Muṇḍaka Upanishad is important for the relative position which it assigns to the teaching of the Vedas, and the doctrine of the Upanishads. 'Two sciences,' it says, the knowers of Brahmá tell us, 'must be known, the higher and the inferior. The inferior is (the knowledge of) the Rig Veda, the Yajurveda, the Sámaveda, and the Atharvaveda, the knowledge of pronunciation, the ritual, grammar, explanation of Vedic texts, prosody, and astronomy. But the higher knowledge is that by which that imperishable Brahmá is comprehended. That which is invisible, unseizable, without descent (or origin,) without either colour, eye, or ear, without hand or foot, eternal, manifold (in creation,) all-pervading, very subtle, undecaying—the wise behold it as the cause of created beings.' And in another place, the performers of the sacrificial rites ordained by the Veda are said to attain, indeed, to Indra's heaven in virtue of their pious work ; but this state of bliss is declared to be unstable and perishable, and these 'fools... drop (from their heaven) as soon as this heaven (the reward of their acts) has faded away. Fancying that pious acts, ordained by the Vedas and codes of law, are the highest (object of man,) these ignorant people do not know that there is something else which leads to eternal bliss. Having enjoyed (the reward of their deeds) on the happy summit of paradise, they enter again this world, or one that is (even) lower. Those, on the contrary, who practice penance and faith, and, with subdued desire, live in the forest, under the vow of a religious mendicant, they, free from sin, enter through the sun to that abode where resides that immortal spirit, that spirit, indeed, of undecaying nature.'

The *Talavakára*, or *Kena*, Upanishad, which, being one of the shortest, is in form one of the most philosophical treatises of this kind, puts in clearer language, perhaps, than any other Upanishad, the doctrine that the true knowledge of the Supreme Spirit consists in the consciousness which man acquires of his *incapacity* to understand it, since the human mind being capable only to comprehend finite objects, cannot have a knowledge of what is infinite.

The Upanishads are not supposed to have been revealed in the same manner as the Vedic hymns. Nevertheless, with the exception of a few confessedly modern Upanishads, they are not assigned to human authorship, but looked upon as inspired writings, to which the term Śruti (q. v.) applies. In several Upanishads, no special mention is made of their divine origin ; in some, however, this is done. Thus the *Chhándogya* Upanishad, in its concluding section, relates : ' This (knowledge of the soul) Brahmá (the god of the Trimúrti) imparted to Prajápati (a lord of creation—the patriarch Kaṣyapa, as Śankara explains) ; Prajápati imparted it to Manu, and Manu to mankind ;' the Brihadáraṇyaka Upanishad, which on three occasions gives long lists of teachers who handed it down to their pupils, always ascribes itself, in the last instance, to the authorship of ' the self-existent Brahmá (the Supreme Spirit) ;' and in a similar manner the Muṇḍaka Upanishad says that it was Brahmá (the god of the Trimúrti,) the creator of the universe, who first taught the science of the Supreme Spirit to his eldest son, Atharvan. As in the case of most ancient works of Sanskrit literature, the date of the Upanishads also still remains quite uncertain, and, wherever given, is purely conjectural. According to the native system, they are classified as belonging to one or the other of the four Vedas, with which they are held to stand in immediate connection. There are Upanishads, consequently, of the Rig-, Yajur-, Sáma-, and Atharva-veda. But this classification has no reference whatever to chronology."—*Chambers' Encyclopædia*.

Upa-puranas—Minor Puránas, of which there are said to be eighteen ; " but the names of only a few of these are specified in the least exceptionable authorities, and the greater number of the works is not procurable." (*Wilson.*) The Matsya enumerates but four, but the Devi Bhagavata specifies eighteen. The Revi Khanda has a different list but enumerates eighteen. " Of the Upa Puránas few are to be procured. Those in my possession are the Śiva, considered as distinct from the Váyu ; the Kálika, and perhaps one of the Naradíyas." *Wilson.*

Uparichara—A Vasu, who by command of Indra became king of Chedí. He had five sons, the eldest of whom Vrihadratha, was king of Magadha ; by another wife he had an Apsaras, condemned to the form of a fish, Matsya, a son, and Satyavati or Káli, a daughter ; the latter was the mother of Vyása.

Upasunda—A Daitya, the son of Nisunda, and father of Múka.

Upendra—The divinity who presides over the feet.

Urddhabahu—One of the seven pure sages, of the first and third Manwantara, the sons of *Vasishtha* by his wife Urjja.

Urddhabahus—"Personal privation and torture being of great efficacy in the creed of the Hindus, various individuals, some influenced by credulity, and some by knavery, have adopted modes of distorting their limbs, and forcing them out of their natural position, until they can no longer resume their ordinary directions.

The Uraddhabáhus extend one or both arms above their heads, till they remain of themselves thus elevated. They also close the fist, and the nails being necessarily suffered to grow make their way between the metacarpal bones, and completely perforate the hand. The *Urddhabáhus* are solitary medicants, as are all of this description, and never have any fixed abode : they subsist upon alms ; many of them go naked, but some wear a wrapper stained with ochre ; they usually assume the *Saiva* marks, and twist their hair so as to project from the forehead, in imitation of the Játá of Śiva.—***Wilson, Vol. I.***

Urja—1. One of the seven Rishis of the second Manwantara ; 2, An obsolete name of a month.

Urjja—Energy ; A daughter of Daksha who was married to Vasishtha.

Urjaswati—1. A daughter of Daksha who was married to Dharma ; 2, The daughter of Priyavrata.

Urjjavaha—A king of Mithila, the son of Suchi.

Uru—One of the ten noble sons of the Manu Chakshusha.

Uruashaya—A prince, the son of Mahavírya, a descendant of Bharata.

Urvasi—A celestial nymph, who having incurred the imprecation of Mitra and Varuna determined to take up her abode in the world of mortals; and descending accordingly behold Purúvaras. As she saw him she forgot all reserve, and disregarding the delights of Swarga became deeply enamoured of the prince. See PURURAVAS.

Usanas—1. The preceptor of the Daityas, one of the Brahmanical tribe of Bhárgavas, sons of Bhrigu; 2, The Vyása of the third Dwápara age; 3, A prince, the son of Támas, who celebrated a hundred sacrifices of the horse.

Usha—1. The wife of the Rudra Bhava; 2, The daughter of Báṇa, who saw Aniruddha in a dream and became enamoured of him. She related this to Chitrarikha, a female confidante, who advised the employment of a portrait painter to take likenesses of all the young princes in the neighbourhood. On seeing the portrait of Aniruddha, grandson of Krishṇa, Usha recognised the youth she had seen in her dream. The same confidante now offered her services; and by her means Aniruddha held clandestine meetings with Usha; and at length was secreted in her private apartments. Báṇa discovered this, and made Aniruddha a prisoner. Krishṇa then interfered, and after a terrible fight Aniruddha was released; both parents agreed to a marriage, which was publicly celebrated at Dwáraka. See ANIRUDDHA.

Ushas—The Dawn. The Aurora of Hindu mythology. "This goddess, who corresponds to the Ἠώς of the Greeks and to the Aurora of the Latins, is a favourite object of celebration with the poets of the Rig Veda, and the hymns addressed to her are among the most beautiful—if not the most beautiful—in the entire collection."*

Ushas is continually described as the daughter of the Sky. She is called the sister of Bhaga, and the kinswoman of Varuṇa. She is also the sister of Night, who is also the daughter of the Sky. Ushas is also frequently brought into connection with the Sun. He is called her lover and is said to follow her track; and she is

* MUIR, O. S. T., Vol. V, p. 181.

represented as leading on the beautiful white horse the Sun. She is declared to be the mistress of the world and the wife of the Sun. Ushas and Agni are also frequently brought into conjunction, fire being always kindled for sacrificial purposes at dawn. He is called her lover and is said to appear with or before the dawn. Ushas is also often connected with the Aṣvins, the time of whose manifestation is regarded by Yáska as being between midnight and sunrise. They are said to associate with her, and she is called their friend.* In one place the moon is said to be born again and again, ever new, and to go before Ushas as the herald of the day. Indra is said to have created, or lighted up, Ushas. He is however sometimes represented as assuming a hostile attitude towards her, and is said to have crushed her chariot with his thunderbolt.†

The Nighaṇṭu gives sixteen names of Ushas, which seem to be almost entirely epithets, viz., the 'resplendent,' the beautiful, the shining, the flowing, the possessor of brilliant riches, the white, the bringer of food, the giver of joy, the bright, the fair-coloured, the ruddy, the utterer of pleasant voices. Some of these epithets are of frequent occurrence in the hymns, and there are also many others to be found there, such as the magnificent, the righteous, the immortal, the gold-hued, &c., &c.‡

Ushas is borne onward on a shining chariot, of massive construction, richly decorated and spontaneously yoked, drawn by ruddy horses, or by cows or bulls of the same colour, traversing rapidly a distance of thirty yojanas. Like a beautiful young woman dressed by her mother, a richly-decked dancing girl, a gaily attired wife appearing before her husband, or a female rising resplendent out of the bath, smiling and confiding in the irresistible power of her attractions, she unveils her bosom to the gaze of the beholder. She dispels the darkness, disclosing the treasures it had concealed : she illuminates the world, revealing its most distant extremities. She is the life and breath of all things, causing the birds to fly forth from their nests, visiting every house, and like an active housewife arousing her household, awakening the five races of men, yea all creatures, as if from death, and sending men forth

* MUIR, O. S. T., Vol. V, p. 181. † *Ibid.* ‡ *Ibid.*

to the pursuit of their several occupations ; and rendering good service to the gods by causing all worshippers to awake, and the sacrificial fires to be kindled. She is however entreated to arouse only the devout and liberal worshipper, and to leave the ungodly niggard to sleep on in unconsciousness. She is young, being born anew every day, and yet she is old, nay immortal, and wears out the lives of successive generations, which disappear one after another, while she continues undecaying.*

The worshippers however sometimes venture to take the credit of being more alert than Ushas, and of awaking her instead of being awakened by her : and in one place she is solicited to make no delay that the sun may not scorch her as like a thief or an enemy. She is prayed to bring the gods to drink the libations of Soma. Agni and the gods generally are described as waking with Ushas.†

Dr. Muir gives the following metrical sketch of Ushas as represented in the hymns of the Ṛig Veda.

Hail, Ushas, daughter of the sky,
    Who, borne upon thy shining car
    By ruddy steeds from realms afar,
And ever lightening, drawest nigh :—

Thou sweetly smilest, goddess fair,
    Disclosing all thy youthful grace,
    Thy bosom bright, thy radiant face,
And lustre of thy golden hair :

(So shines a fond and winning bride,
    Who robes her form in brilliant guise,
    And to her lord's admiring eyes
Displays her charms with conscious pride :—

Or virgin by her mother decked,
    Who, glorying in her beauty, shows
    In every glance, her power she knows
All eyes to fix, all hearts subject :

---

* MUIR, O. S. T., Vol. V, p. 181.   † *Ibid.*

Or actress, who by skill in song
And dance, and graceful gestures light,
And many-coloured vestures bright,
Enchants the eager, gazing throng :—

Or maid who, wont her limbs to lave
In some cool stream among the woods,
Where never vulgar eye intrudes,
Emerges fairer from the wave) :—

But closely by the amorous sun
Pursued, and vanquished in the race,
Thou soon art locked in his embrace,
And with him blendest into one.

Fair Ushas, though through years untold
Thou hast lived on, yet thou art born
Anew on each succeeding morn,
And so thou art both young and old.

As in thy fated ceaseless course
Thou risest on us day by day,
Thou wearest all our lives away
With silent, ever-wasting, force.

Their round our generations run :
The old depart, and in their place
Springs ever up a younger race,
Whilst thou, immortal, lookest on.

All those who watched for thee of old
Are gone, and now 't is we who gaze
On thy approach ; in future days
Shall other men thy beams behold.

But 't is not thoughts so grave and sad
Alone that thou dost with thee bring,
A shadow o'er our hearts to fling ;—
Thy beams returning make us glad.

Thy sister, sad and sombre Night
    With stars that in the blue expanse
    Like sleepless eyes mysterious glance,
At thy approach is quenched in light :—

And earthly forms, till now concealed
    Behind her veil of dusky hue,
    Once more come sharply out to view,
By thine illuming glow revealed.

Thou art the life of all that lives,
    The breath of all that breathes ; the sight
    Of thee makes every countenance bright,
New strength to every spirit gives.

When thou dost pierce the musky gloom,
    Birds flutter forth from every brake,
    All sleepers as from death awake,
And men their myriad tasks resume.

Some prosperous, wake in listless mood,
    And others every nerve to strain
    The goal of power or wealth to gain,
Or what they deem the highest good.

But some to holier thoughts aspire,
    In hymns the race celestial praise,
    And light, on human hearths to blaze,
The heaven-born sacrificial fire.

And not alone do bard and priest
    Awake ;—the gods thy power confess
    By starting into consciousness
When thy first rays suffuse the east :

And hasting downward from the sky,
    They visit men devout and good,
    Consume their consecrated food,
And all their longings satisfy.

Bright goddess, let thy genial rays
To us bring stores of envied wealth
In kine and steeds, and sons, with health,
And joy of heart, and length of days.

Utkala—One of the sons of Sudyumna after his transformation.

Uttama—1, The son of Uttanápada and grandson of the Manu Swáyambhuva.

2. A Manu, the son of Priyavrata.

3. The Manu of the third Manwantara.

4. The Vyása of the twenty-first Dwápara age.

Uttanapada—The son of the Manu Swáyambhuva. The Vishṇu Purâna describes him as heroic and pious, but gives no particulars of his history.

Uttara-bhadrapada—A lunar mansion in Vaiswánari in the Southern Avashthána.

Uttarakuru—A varsha or country beyond the Sringi range of mountains, south of Meru.

Uttara-phalguni—A lunar mansion in Arshabhí, in the Central Avashthána.

Uttarashadha—A lunar mansion in Ajavithi, in the Southern Avashthana.

Uttatahya—A sage, the son of Angiras, and husband of Mamata.

V

Vach—1, The goddess of speech, who resides in the region intermediate between heaven and earth. In the later mythology Sarasvatí was identified with Vách, and became under different names the spouse of Brahmá and the goddess of wisdom and eloquence, and is invoked as a Muse. In the Mahábhárata she is called the mother of the Vedas, and the same is said of Vách in the Taitt. Br. ii, 8, where she is also said to be the wife of Indra, to contain within herself all worlds, and to have been sought after by the rishis who composed the Vedic hymns, as well as by the gods through austerity.—*O. S. T.*, *V*, 342.

Vách is represented as the wife of Prajápati, and as pervading all that exists. She is termed the mother of the Vedas. Vách is also designated as a cow. "Let a man worship the cow Vách. She has four udders, the formulæ, *svaha*, *vashat*, *hauta*, and *svadha*. The gods live upon her two udders, *svaha* and *vashat*; men upon *hauta*; and the fathers upon *svadha*. Breath is her bull; the mind, her calf."—*O. S. T.*, *II*, 256.

Vach—2, A daughter of Daksha, married to Kaṣyapa.

Vadhrimati—The wise female to whose invocation the Asvins listened and gave her a son called Hiranyahasta.—*O. S. T.*, *V*, 247.

Vahan—Sans., a vehicle. One is allotted to each of the gods. Brahmá has the Hamsa, a goose or swan. Vishṇu, Garuda, half man, half bird, but now, in Southern India, identified with the Haliætus Pondicherianus, or Brahmany-kite; Śiva, the bull; Indra, the elephant; Ganeṣa, a rat; Kartikeya, a peacock; Agni, a ram; Váyu, an antelope; Yama, a buffalo; Sani, Saturn, a vulture; Ráma, a monkey; Kamadeva, a parrot; Durga or Párvati, a lion and bull, and the other goddesses, the vahans of their respective lords. The vahan of Brahmá, Hamsa, or Hahns, sometimes Hahnsi, Major Moor tells us, is precisely the name that in Suffolk, is commonly given to the heron, that Saraswati rides on. The swan or goose, the eagle, and the bull, are the vehicles respectively allotted to the three great powers. The terrestrial sluggish nature of the first, is an apt type of matter, personified in the creative power, and a contrast to Vishṇu, or spirit, the preserving power, appropriately mounted on a buoyant eagle, the celestial Garuda. Śiva, the destructive energy of the Deity, is Time or Justice; and the Hindus, deem the bull also its type, and give it to Śiva as his vahan, or modė of conveyance. These vehicles are supposed by Mr. Paterson (As. Res. Vol. VII, p. 48,) to have allusion to Purity, Truth, and Justice: the first, he says, typified by the swan, which, clothed with unspotted whiteness, swims, amidst the waters, as it were, distinct from, and unsullied by, them; as the truly pure mind remains untainted amidst the surrounding temptations of the world. Garuda, brother to Aruna, is remarkable for strength and swiftness; and the latter is described as imperfect, and, on account of his defects, destined to act as charioteer to the Sun, he being the dawn, the twilight preceding the sun. Garuda is perfect light; the dazzling full blaze of day; the type of Truth; the celestial vahan of Vishṇu. Perhaps the Hindus may, like western observers, have noticed the strong optic nerves of the eagle tribe; and have heard of the fable of the parents destroying such of their brood as are unable to look steadily on the sun; the eagle in western poetry is called bird of the sun, as well as bird of Jove; in both of which characters Vishṇu particularly appears. Justice, typified in the sacred bull, is the vahan of Śiva: the bull, whose body is Paramesvara, and whose every joint is a virtue; whose three horns are the three Vedas; whose tail ends where ad'harma, or injustice, begins.—*Coleman, Moor.* " The creatures here named, alone suffice to indicate the northern origin of the people who believe in them, and the readiness with which they have accommodated themselves to change. There is no swan nor eagle in Southern India, so far as we know, nor is the buffalo or brahmany-kite known in the highlands of Central Asia."—BALFOUR.

Vahnijwala—One of the Narakas that for shepherds and potters.

Vaibhraja—A large forest in the west of Mount Meru.

Vaideha—" The son of the bodiless ;" a name of Rája Janaka, (q. v.)

Vaideyha—One of the fifteen teachers of the White Yajush.

Vaidurya—One of the principal mountain ridges which project from the base of Meru, on the western side.

Vaikanka—A similar ridge in the eastern side.

Vaikuntha—The heaven of Vishṇu. This is considered by Wilson to be a sectarial addition to the seven Lokas or spheres above the earth. Vaikuntha is also the name of an incarnation of Vishṇu in the seventh Manwantara.

Vaikunthas—A class of deities of the sixth Manwantara.

Vaikrita—Secondary or instrumental creation.

Vaimanikas—The deities who travel in Vimánas, 'heavenly cars,' or rather 'moving spheres.'

Vainahotra—One of the Rájas of Kási, the son of Dhrishtaketu.

Vairaja—1, Part of the Sama Veda created from the northern mouth of Brahmá ; 2, A name of the first Manu.

Vairajas—A class of deities who dwell in Tapoloka, the sphere of penance ; these deities are inconsumable by fire.

Vairupa—The name of a portion of the Sama Veda created from the western mouth of Brahmá.

Vaisakha—An obsolete name of one of the months.

Vaisakhi, Vaislai—Two of the wives of Vasudeva.

Vaisali—A city of considerable renown in Indian tradition, but its site is a subject of some uncertainty. It is celebrated among the Buddhists as a chief seat of the labours of Sákhya and his first disciples, and would thus be Prayága or Allahabad ; but the Rámáyana places it much lower down on the north bank of the Ganges.

Vaisampayana—The coadjutor of Vyása in arranging the Vedas. "It seems probable that the tradition is true that records the first establishment of a school, of which the Vyása was the head, and the other persons named were the teachers." Vaisampáyana was the teacher of the Yajur Veda. There is a legend that Rája Janamejaya killed a brahman and in order to expiate this dreadful crime he listened to a recitation of the whole of the Mahábhárata, which was performed by Vaisampáyana. Accordingly the Mahábhárata, which is said to have been originally composed by Vyása, is supposed to be written as it was recited by Vaisampáyana.

Vaiseshika—" Is the name of one of the two great divisions of the Nyáya (q. v.) school of Hindu philosophy, and probably a later development of the Nyáya itself, properly so called, with which it agrees in its analytical method of treating the subjects of human research, but from which it differs in the arrangement of its topics, and more especially by its doctrine of atomic individualities, or *vis'eshas*—whence its name is derived." The reputed founder of the Vaiseshika is Kanáda, of whose history or date, however, nothing is known.

Kanáda taught that the visible form of God was light; that when the desire of creation arose in the divine mind, he first gave existence to water, and then to innumerable worlds, floating on the waters like the mundane egg; that in these primæval eggs water was contained, on which lay Vishṇu, and from whose navel issued a lotus, in which Brahmá was born; that Brahmá, receiving instructions from God, created the world, first from his mind, and then with the primary atoms; that spirit and animal life were separate substances.

To him are attributed the *Vaiseshika-Sutras*, which contain about 550 aphorisms, or sentences. These relate to seven subjects *(padarthas,)* under the following distinct heads, viz. ;—1, *Things;* 2, *Qualities;* 3, *Actions;* 4, *Genus;* 5, *Spirits;* 6, The inseparable *Connection of Constituent Parts; and* 7, *Non-entity.*

After a long discussion of the different subjects included in this arrangement, Kanáda discourses on religion, riches, happiness, and final liberation. Having first explained the nature of religion, he then arranges the component parts of the universe, and, lastly, gives a discourse on the divine nature, which he divides into three heads: (1) that God is essentially possessed of wisdom (which, however, does not comprise the whole of his nature or character);

(2) that He is the ever blessed and supremely happy ; and (3) that in all His works and His will He is irresistible and omnipotent. Emancipation from matter he held to be inseparably connected with complete deliverance from sorrow, and the enjoyment of final bliss.

Several commentaries have been written, and are extant on the Sútras of Kanáda, of which the principal are a large one called the *Bháshya*, and a smaller one entitled the *Vaisesheka Sútrapushkara ;* but the only work now read in Bengal which has any relation to the Vaiseshika Philosophy is that of Visva Nátha Siddhánta, which merely treats of the logical terms of this system, and of the Nyáya school. In the Nyáya Colleges of Bengal the students read that part of this work which relates to the Vaiseshika system, and then proceed to study the Nyáya system itself.—GOLDSTUCKER, *in Chambers' Encyclopædia.*

Vaishnavas—Is the name of one of the great divisions of Hindu sects. The word, derived from Vishṇu (q. v.,) designates the worshippers of this deity, and comprises a great variety of sects ; but this variety itself differs according to the different periods of the medieval history of India, old divisions becoming extinct, and new ones taking their place. Thus, the account of the Vaishnavas, as given in a celebrated work of *Anandagiri*, the *Sankaradig-vijaya*, or the victory of the great theologian Śankara over his religious adversaries, would no longer apply in detail to the present condition of the Vaishnavas ; and even some of those varieties mentioned by the late Professor Wilson in his *Sketch of the Religious Sects of the Hindus*, written in 1832, would seem to have disappeared already in our days. The common link of all the sects comprised under the name of Vaishnavas, is their belief in the supremacy of Vishṇu over the other gods of the Trimúrti (q. v.) Their difference consists in the character which they assign to this supremacy, and to the god Vishṇu himself, in the religious and other practices founded on the nature of their belief, and in their sectarian marks. The following sects belonging to this category may especially be noticed here.

1. The *Rámánujas*, or *Sri Vaishnavas*, or *Sri-Sampradáyins.* They derive their origin from *Rámánuja*, a celebrated reformer,

who was born at Perumbur, in the south of India, about the middle of the twelfth century, and is considered by his followers as an incarnation of *Sesha* (q. v.,) the serpent of Vishṇu. He studied at Conjeveram, resided afterwards at Sríranga, and then travelled over different parts of India, where he was especially engaged in combating the professors of different creeds, particularly the Saivas. On his return to Sríranga, he was seized by the king Kerikála Chola, but effected his escape, and found refuge with the Jain king of Mysore, Vitála Deva, whom he converted to the Vaishṇava faith. For twelve years he then remained at Mysore; but at the death of the Chola king, returned to Sríranga, where he spent the remainder of his life in religious seclusion. The Rámánujas address their worship to Vishṇu and his consort, Lakshmí (q. v.,) and their respective incarnations, either singly or conjointly. Hence their sect consists of corresponding sub-divisions, according as Náráyaṇa or Lakshmí, or Lakshmí-Náráyaṇa, or Ráma, or Sítá or Sítá-Ráma, or any other incarnation of these deities, is the preferential object of the veneration of the votary. Their most striking peculiarity is the preparation and the scrupulous privacy of their meals; for should the meal during its preparation, or while they are eating, attract even the looks of a stranger, the operation is instantly stopped, and the viands buried in the ground. The marks by which they distinguish themselves from other sects are two perpendicular white lines, drawn with a white earth, *Gopíchandana*, from the root of the hair to the commencement of each eyebrow, and a transverse streak connecting them across the root of the nose; in the centre is a perpendicular streak of red, made with red sanders, or a preparation of turmeric and lime; other marks, representing several of the attributes of Vishṇu, they have either painted or impressed on the breast and each upper arm; and, besides, they wear a necklace of the wood of the Tulasí (holy basil,) and carry a rosary of the seeds of the same plant, or of the lotus. The sacred formula with which a member of this sect is initiated into it consists merely of the words *Om rámáya namah*, 'Om, salutation to Ráma.' Their principal religious tenet is the belief that Vishṇu is the cause and creator of all worlds; that he and the universe are one, though he is of a two-fold form: the supreme spirit or cause, and the gross one, the effect or matter. In distinction from the Vedánta, with which their doctrine has otherwise many points of contact, they regard their supreme deity as endowed with qualities, all of which are of course excellent; and teach that the universe consists of *chit*, thinking or spirit, *achit*, unthinking or matter, íṣwara, or god; the relation of which is that of enjoyer, the thing enjoyed, and the ruler of both. The deity, they assume, is or has been visibly present in five modifications: in the objects of worship, as images, &c.; in the incarnations; in certain forms called Vyúhas, viz., Vásudeva or Krishṇa; Balaráma, Pradyumna, and Aniruddha; and in the subtle form which comprises six qualities—absence of passion, immortality, exemption from pain or care, absence of natural wants, love, and practice of truth—and the human soul; all of which have to be worshipped seriatim, as the votary ascends in the scale of perfection. It is in the south that the followers of Rámánuja, and their temples and establishments, are still numerous; in the north of India, where they are better known as *Sri Vaishnavas*, they are not of frequent occurrence.

2. The *Rámánandas*, or *Rámávats*. They are by far the most numerous class of sectaries in Gangetic India: in the district of Agra, they alone constitute seven-tenths of the ascetic population. They belong chiefly to the poorer and inferior classes, with the exception of the Rajputs and military Brahmans. The founder of this sect was *Rámánanda*, who, by some, is considered to have been the immediate disciple of Rámánuja; by others, the fifth in descent from that teacher, when he would have lived about the end of the thirteenth century; but other more reliable accounts place him toward the end of the fourteenth, or the beginning of the fifteenth century. According to common tradition, Rámánanda seceded from the Rámánujas, to whom he originally belonged, because, having spent some time in travelling through various parts of India, and, in consequence, having been suspected by his fellow-disciples not to have conformed to the rule of the Rámánujas in taking his meals, he was condemned to feed in a place apart from the rest of them, but did not acquiesce in the affront thus offered him. His residence was at Benares, at the Pancha Gangá

Ghát, where a *Math*, or monastery, of his followers is said to have existed. The especial object of their worship is Vishṇu, in his incarnation as *Rámachandra*, and his consort *Sítá*, and, as amongst the Rámánujas, these deities either singly or jointly. Some members of this sect also pay adoration to other forms of Vishṇu ; and the religious mendicants of the sect consider all form of adoration superfluous, being content with the incessant invocation of Krishṇa and Ráma. Their practices are less precise than those of the Rámánujas ; but the most important difference between them consists in the fact, that Rámánanda abolished the distinction of caste amongst the religious orders, and taught that a *Vairágin*, or one who quitted the ties of nature and society, shook off at the same time all personal distinction. The initiatory formula of a Rámánanda is *Srí Ráma*, or 'blessed Ráma.' Their sectarian marks are the same as those of the Rámánujas ; except that the red perpendicular streak on the forehead is varied in shape and extent, and generally narrower than that of the Rámánujas. There are various sub-divisions of this sect, believed to have been founded by several eminent disciples of Rámánanda. Their doctrines vary often from that of the latter, but they maintain an amicable intercourse with the Rámánujas and with each other.

Besides these Vaishnava sects there are others of less importance who are sometimes included, on the ground of paying more respect to Vishṇu than to any other god of the Trimúrti, (q. v.) —*Chambers' Encyclopædia.*

Vaisravana—The eldest son of Pulastya, who deserted his father and went to Brahmá, who as a reward made him immortal, and appointed him the god of riches, with Lanka for his capital and the car Pushpaka for his vehicle. He was afterwards expelled from Lanka by his younger brother Rávaṇa, and retired to Gandhamádana.—[KUVERA.]

Vaiswadeva—A ceremony in the observance of a Śraddha, which comprehends offerings to both paternal and maternal ancestors, and to ancestors in general.

Vaiswanara—1, A Danava, the father of Puloma and Káliká ; 2, The Southern Avashtháṇa.

Vaiswanari—A division of the lunar mansions, comprising the last three in the Southern Avasthána.

Vaisyas—The third of the regenerate caste—said to have been born from the thighs of Brahmá. The occupations of commerce and agriculture, the feeding of flocks and herds, are the duties of the Vaisyas. No opposition seems ever to have arisen between the Vaisyas and the other two castes, like that which broke out between the Brahmans and the Kshatriyas. Indeed the wealth of the Vaisyas rendered them at a later period of considerable influence, inasmuch as they employed Brahmans to perform sacrifices, and took Kshatriyas into their pay as soldiers and guards.—(*Wheeler*.)

Vaitalika—A poetical watchman or crier or bell-man—one who announces in verse the change of the seasons and the hours of the day—when not retained for the purpose he is a public singer.—*Wilson.*

Vaitalaki—A teacher of the Rig Veda.

Vaitandya—The eldest son of the Vasu Apa.

Vaitarani—One of the Narakas, that for the punishment of the man who destroys a bee-hive or pillages a hamlet.

Vaitarani—A sacred river at Tripishtapa in the country of the Kalingas. It is connected with the worship of Śiva, and the act of bathing there and worshipping the god who wields the trident and whose ensign is the bull, (Mahádeva) is said to ensure purification from all sin and the attainment of the highest felicity. —*O. S. T., IV*, 241.

Vaivaswata—1, The son of the celestial luminary, (the Sun), and Manu of the seventh (or present) Manwantara ; 2, Also an appellation of one of the Rudras.

Vajasaneyi—A portion of the Yajur Veda.

Vajins—Students of the white Yajush ; this Veda was revealed by the sun in the form of a horse, (vaji) hence the name applied to the brahmans.

Vajra—The son of Aniruddha, who by order of Krishṇa was installed sovereign of the Yádavas at Indraprastha, and thus escaped the destruction which overwhelmed their kinsmen at Dwáraka. This, says Wilson, was a fortunate reservation for the tribes which in various parts of Hindustan, both in the Ganges and in the Dakhin, profess to derive their origin from the Yádavas.

Vajramitra—One of the ten Sunga princes, the son of Ghoshavasu.

Vajranabha—A prince, the son of Uktha, of the line of Kúsa.

Vaktrayodhi—An eminent Dánava, one of the sons of Viprachitti.

Valaka—A teacher of the Rig Veda, and disciple of Sákapurni.

Valakaswa—A prince, the son of Ajaka, descendant of Purúravas.

Vallabha—A celebrated Vaishnava teacher who lived in the sixteenth century.

Vallabhas—A people mentioned in the Puránas, and supposed to be inhabitants of Vallabhí in Rajputana. See *Tod's Rajasthan*.

Valmiki—The Vyása of the twenty-fourth Dwápara age, called also Reksha, a descendant of Bhrigu.

Valmiki—A sage and bard, famous as the author of the Rámáyana ; he lived at Chitra Kúta, a celebrated hill in Bundlekund, to the south of the river Jumna. He was surrounded by a band of Brahman disciples, who led the ideal life of austerity, sacrifice and devotion, so frequently described and recommended by Brahmanical writers. It was in this hill, that Ráma, with his wife and brother, took up their abode, when exiled from Ayodhya. According to the Rámáyana they spent some pleasant years there. The locality is said to have abounded in game, fruit, honey, and other products of the jungle which were suitable for food. Long after, when Ráma and Sítá had returned in triumph to Koṣala, and Sítá was about to become a mother, she was repudiated by Ráma, though she had passed the ordeal of fire and been declared innocent ; she was conveyed to the jungle by Lakshmana, who left her in a panic of surprise and fear, near the hill Chitra Kúta ; in this state she was found by Valmíkí, who had been the brahman preceptor of her father Janaka, he took her to his own house and placed her in charge of his wife and female servants. It was then that Sítá's two sons, were born ; Valmíkí gave them the names of Lava and Kúsa, and brought them up, and educated them with the greatest care. It is said he taught his poem, the Rámáyana, to them. There are however many chronological difficulties connected with the history of Valmíkí, though it seems certain he was a real person.

Vama—One of the eleven Rudras, according to the list in the Bhágavata.

Vamana—Vishṇu, at the request of the deities, was born as a dwarf, Vámana, the son of Adití by Kaṣyapa ; when Vámana applied to Rája Balí, the monarch of the Daityas, for alms, he was promised by the Rája whatever he might demand, notwithstanding Sukra, the preceptor of the Daityas, apprised him whom he had to deal with. The dwarf demanded as much space as he could step over at three steps ; and upon the assent of Bali, enlarged himself to such dimensions as to stride with one pace over the earth, with a second over the intermediate space (the atmosphere), and with a third over the sky, thus leaving for Bali only the subterranean regions, which he assigned him for his future abode. " The demons endeavoured to frustrate this result, after Vishṇu had taken his first two strides, but they were overcome by the followers of Vishṇu ; and Bali, when resigning himself to his fate, in reply to a reproach addressed to him by the dwarf for trying to break his promise, uttered—according to the Bhágavata-Puráṇa—the following words, which may serve as one of many instances to shew how sacred a promise was held by the Hindus when once given, and even though artfully obtained : 'If, renowned chief of the gods, you consider the word which I uttered to be deceitful, I now do what is sincere, and can be no deception—place your third step on my head. Fallen from my position, I fear not the infernal regions, or binding in bonds, or misfortune difficult to escape, or loss of wealth, or your restraint, so much as I am afflicted by a bad name.' (See J. Muir's *Original Sanscrit Texts*, Vol. IV, p. 128.) For his righteousness, he was then rewarded by Vishṇu with the promise, that after a temporary residence in one of the most delightful places of Pátáḷa (q. v.), he should be born as the Indra, in the reign of the eighth Manu. In this incarnation as dwarf, Vishṇu is considered to have been a son of the same Kaṣyapa who is also the father of Hiraṇyakaṣipu and Hiraṇyáksha ; but while their mother is Diti, the dwarf's mother is Aditi (space) ; and since she previously had brought forth Indra, Vishṇu is sometimes called Upendra, or the younger or later Indra. As a son of Aditi, Vishṇu becomes one of the Ádityas (see before).—The Vedic conception of the three strides of Vishṇu, is doubtless the basis of the idea whence this Avatára arose."—*Goldstücker.*

Vamana Purana—This contains an account of the dwarf incarnation of Vishṇu : Wilson thinks its contents scarcely establish its claim to the character of a Purána.

" There is little or no order in the subjects which this work recapitulates, and which arise out of replies made by Pulastya to questions put, abruptly and unconnectedly, by Nárada. The greater part of them relate to the worship of the Linga ; a rather strange topic for a Vaishṇava Purána, but engrossing the principal part of the compilation. They are, however, subservient to the object of illustrating the sanctity of certain holy places ; so that the Vámana Purána is little else than a succession of Máhátmyas. Thus, in the opening, almost, of the work, occurs the story of Daksha's sacrifice, the object of which is to send Śiva to Pápamochana Tírtha, at Benares, where he is released from the sin of Brahmanicide. Next comes the story of the burning of Kámadeva, for the purpose of illustrating the holiness of a Śiva-linga at Kedáreṣwara in the Himalaya, and of Badarikáṣrama. The larger part of the work consists of the Saro-máhátmya, or legendary exemplifications of the holiness of Stháṇu Tírtha ; that is, of the sanctity of various Lingas and certain pools, at Thanesar and Kurukhet, the country north-west from Delhi. There are some stories, also, relating to the holiness of the Godávarí river : but the general site of the legends is in Hindusthán. In the course of these accounts, we have a long narrative of the marriage of Śiva with Umá, and the birth of Kárttikeya. There are a few brief allusions to creation and the Manwantaras ; but they are merely incidental : and all the five characteristics of a Purána are deficient.

In noticing the Swárochisha Manwantara, towards the end of the book, the elevation of Bali as monarch of the Daityas, and his subjugation of the universe, the gods included, are described ; and this leads to the narration that gives its title to the Purána, the birth of Vishṇu as a dwarf, for the purpose of humiliating Bali by fraud, as he was invincible by force. The story is told as usual ; but the scene is laid at Kurukshetra.

A more minute examination of this work than that which has been given to it, might, perhaps, discover some hint from which to conjecture its date. It is of a more tolerant character than the Puránas, and divides its homage between Śiva and Vishṇu with tolerable impartiality. It is not connected, therefore, with any sectarial principles, and may have preceded their introduction. It has not, however, the air of any antiquity ; and its compilation may have amused the leisure of some Brahman of Benares three or four centuries ago."—*Wilson.*

Vanakapivat—The son of the patriarch Pulaka.

Vanaprastha—Hermit. The third stage of Brahmanical life. " When the householder, after performing the acts incumbent on his condition, arrives at the decline of life, let him consign his wife to the care of his sons, and go, himself, to the forests. Let him there subsist upon leaves, roots, and fruit ; and suffer his hair and beard to grow, and braid the former upon his brows ; and sleep upon the ground. His dress must be made of skin, or of Káṣa or Kuṣa grasses ; and he must bathe thrice a day ; and he must offer oblations to the gods and to fire, and treat all that come to him with hospitality. He must beg alms, and present food to all creatures ; he must anoint himself with such unguents as the woods afford ; and, in his devotional exercises, he must be endurant of heat and cold. The sage who diligently follows these rules, and leads the life of the hermit (or Vánaprastha,) consumes, like fire, all imperfections, and conquers, for himself, the mansions of eternity." V. P.

Vaneyu—One of the ten sons of Raudraṣwa, a descendant of Puru.

Vapra—The Vyása of the fourteenth Dwápara age.

Vapu—Body ; a daughter of Daksha, married to Dharma.

Vapushmat—One of the sons of Priyavrata and Kámya ; he was installed by his father in the sovereignty over the Dwípa of Salmali, (q. v.) He had seven sons, whose names gave designations to seven varshas or divisions.

Varaha—A boar. The Varáha Avatár is the third incarnation of Vishṇu in the shape of a boar. It is supposed to have taken place when, at the period of creation, the earth was immersed in water, and Vishṇu, in order to raise it up, assumed the form of a gigantic boar. The boar is said to be a type of the ritual of the Vedas. "The elevation of the earth from beneath the ocean, in this form, was therefore, probably, at first, an allegorical representation of the extrication of the world from a deluge of iniquity, by the rites of religion. Geologists may perhaps suspect, in the original and unmystified tradition, an allusion to a geological fact, or the existence of lacustrine mammalia in the early periods of the earth."—*Wilson.*

The boar is described as the sacrifice personified ; his feet being the Vedas ; his tusks the sacrificial posts to which the victim is tied ; his teeth, the sacrificial offerings ; his mouth, the altar ; his tongue, the fire ; his hairs, the sacrificial grass ; his eyes, day and night ; his head, the place of Brahmá ; his mane, the hymns of the Vedas ; his nostrils, all the oblations ; his snout, the ladle of oblation ; his voice, the chanting of the Sáma-veda ; his body, the hall of sacrifice ; his joints, the different ceremonies ; and his ears as having the properties of voluntary and obligatory rites.

According to a legend in the Bhágavata Purána, Jaya and Vijaya, two doorkeepers of Vishṇu, once offended some Munis who claimed admission to the paradise of Vishṇu, and in consequence were doomed to lose their position in heaven, and to be reborn on earth. They became thus the sons of Kaṣyapa and Diti, under the names of Hiraṇyakaṣipu and Hiranyáksha. The former subdued the three worlds, and the latter went straight to heaven to conquer the gods also. The gods implored the assistance of Vishṇu, who at that period was the mysterious boar and slew Hiranyáksha. A similar contest between Vishṇu and numerous demons, the progeny of Diti, always ending in the defeat of the latter, is also described, showing that the boar-avatara had gradually lost its original character, and assumed that common to the remaining avatars.

Varaha—One of the six minor Dwípas, peopled by Mlechchhas who worship Hindu deities.

Varahamihira—A celebrated astronomer and astrologer, born at Ujein A. D. 530 and died in 587. Dr. Kern observes that "he was in the awkward position of a man who has to reconcile the exigencies of science with the decrees, deemed infallible, of the Rishis;" for curious examples of which he refers to the Brihat-Sanhita, chapters v and ix.* With a strong taste for astrology, and falling into errors which Aryabhata had exposed, Varahamihira made some remarkable observations on the moon and on eclipses —thus

"One-half of the moon whose orbit lies between the sun and the earth, is always bright by the sun's rays; the other half is dark, by its own shadow; like the two sides of a pot standing in the sunshine."

After alluding to the popular notion of Ráhu as the demon that causes eclipse by devouring part of the sun or moon, he says

"The true explanation of the phenomena is this: in an eclipse of the moon he enters into the earth's shadow; in a solar eclipse the same things happen to the sun. Hence the commencement of a lunar eclipse does not take place from the west side, nor that of a solar eclipse from the east." Brihat Sanhita, quoted in A. and M. I., Vol. I, p. 371.

Varana—The ninth division in Bhárata Varsha.

Varanavata—The modern Allahabad, "the sacred city at the junction of the Ganges and Jumna, and one of the most famous places of pilgrimage in Hindustan. It is said to have been celebrated for gold and jewels. The visit of the Páṇḍava princes to

* A work which Dr. Kern edited and published at Calcutta in 1865, and is understood to be now translating into English.

this city as related in the Mahábhárata is considered by Mr. Wheeler to be a later interpolation for the sole purpose of associating the Páṇḍavas with the famous city of Váranávata.

Vararuchi—A celebrated brahman, the son of Somadatta, distinguished for a wonderful memory, which enabled him to recite perfectly any discourse he had once heard. He instructed Vyádi, and both of them were writers of note on philological topics. They were contemporaries of Nanda who reigned at Pátaliputra—a fact which Professor Wilson regards as of considerable interest in the literary history of the Hindus. Vararuchi is also called Katyáyana (q. v.) who is one of the earliest commentators of Pánini (q. v.) Nanda is the predecessor, or one of the predecessors of Chandragupta ; and consequently the chief institutes of Sanskrit Grammar are thus dated from the fourth century before the Christian era.—*Wilson, III,* 166.

Varchas—Light ; the son of Vasu Soma, and father of Varchaswi, Radiance.

Varenya——Most Excellent ; a name of Vishṇu ; said to be the same as supreme felicity.

Varhadrathas—A dynasty of kings of Magadha, who according to the Vishṇu Purána were to reign for a thousand years.

Varhaspatyas--Heretics ; followers of Vrihaspatti, who seem to have been numerous and bold at some period anterior to the fourteenth century.—*Wilson.*

Varishads—A class of Pitris, identified by some with the months. They are formless or incorporeal Pitris, sons of Atri, and Pitris of the demons.

Varishmati—The wife of Priyavrata, according to the Bhágavata, which states that she was the daughter of Visvakarman.

Variyas—One of the sons of the patriarch Pulaha, according to the Bhágavata.

Varman--This designation is said in the Vishṇu Purána to be an appropriate name for a Kshatriya.

Varnam—Colour—Caste.

Varshas—Countries ; a term applied to the divisions in Jambu Dwípa.

Varuna—The Neptune of Hindu mythology. The god of ocean, the god of rain and clouds. He is distinctly termed the god of Ocean in the Vishṇu Purána, and Wilson in noticing the circumstance that it was Varuṇa who supplied the sage Richíka with a thousand fleet horses, remarks that the agency of the god of ocean in procuring horses is a rather curious additional coincidence between Varuṇa and Neptune. The Vedic Áryans were evidently acquainted with the sea, for the hymns contain allusions to merchants, to sea voyages, and to ships with a hundred oars. Professor Max Müller in his History of Sanskrit Literature, has translated a beautiful hymn to Varuṇa in which this deity is addressed in the two-fold character of controlling tempests and punishing sin.

"The grandest cosmical functions are ascribed to Varuṇa. Possessed of illimitable resources (or knowledge), this divine being has meted out, (or fashioned), and upholds, heaven and earth ; he dwells in all worlds as sovereign ruler, indeed, the three worlds are embraced within him ; he made the golden and revolving sun to shine in the firmament. The wind which resounds through the atmosphere is his breath. He has opened boundless paths for the sun, and has hollowed out channels for the rivers, which flow by his command. By this wonderful contrivance the rivers pour their waters into the one ocean, but never fill it. His ordinances are fixed and unassailable. They rest on him, unshaken, as upon a mountain ; through their operation, the moon walks in brightness, and the stars which appear in the nightly sky mysteriously vanish in daylight. Neither the birds flying in the air, nor the rivers in their sleepless flow, can attain a knowledge of his power or his wrath. His messengers behold both worlds. He knows the flight of birds in the sky, the path of ships on the ocean, the course of the far-travelling wind, and beholds all the secret things that have been, or shall be done. No creature can even wink without him. He witnesses men's truth and falsehood. He instructs the rishi Vasishṭha in mysteries. But his secrets and those of Mitra are not to be revealed to the foolish."

In the sixteenth hymn of the fourth book of the Atharva-veda, his power and omniscience are thus celebrated :—

" 1, The great one who rules over these worlds beholds as if he were close at hand. When any man thinks he is doing aught by stealth, the gods know it all ; 2, (and they perceive) every one who stands, or walks, or glides along secretly, or withdraws into his house, or into any lurking-place. Whatever two persons, sitting together, devise, Varuṇa the king knows it, (being present there as) a third ; 3, This earth, too, belongs to the king Varuṇa, and that vast sky whose ends are so remote. The two oceans [the aerial and terrestrial] are Varuṇa's stomachs ; he resides in this small pool of water ; 4, He who should flee far beyond the sky, would not there escape from Varuṇa the king. His messengers, descending from heaven, traverse this world ; thousand-eyed, they look across the whole earth ; 5, King Varuṇa perceives all that exists within heaven and earth and all that is beyond. The winkings of men's eyes are all numbered by him. He handles (all) these (things) as a gamester throws his dice ; 6, May thy destructive nooses, O Varuṇa, which are cast seven-fold, and three-fold, ensnare the man who speaks lies, and pass by him who speaks truth."

> The mighty Lord on high, our deeds, as if at hand, espies :
> The gods know all men do, though men would fain their deeds disguise.
> Whoever stands, whoever moves, or steals from place to place,
> Or hides him in his secret cell,—the gods his movements trace,
> Wherever two together plot, and deem they are alone,
> King Varuna is there, a third, and all their schemes are known.
> This earth is his, to him belong those vast and boundless skies ;
> Both seas within him rest, and yet in that small pool he lies.
> Whoever far beyond the sky should think his way to wing,
> He could not there elude the grasp of Varuna the king.
> His spies descending from the skies glide all this world around,
> Their thousand eyes all-scanning sweep to earth's remotest bound.
> Whate'er exists in heaven and earth, whate'er beyond the skies,
> Before the eyes of Varuna, the king, unfolded lies.
> The ceaseless winkings all he counts of every mortal's eyes :
> He wields this universal frame, as gamester throws his dice.
> Those knotted nooses which thou fling'st, O god, the bad to snare,—
> All liars let them overtake, but all the truthful spare."

Varuṇa is represented as having unlimited control over the destinies of mankind. He is said to have a hundred, a thousand remedies, and is supplicated to shew his wide and deep benevolence, and drive away evil and sin ; to untie like a rope, and remove sin ; he is entreated not to steal away, but to prolong, life ; and to spare the supplicant who daily transgresses his laws. In many places mention is made of the bonds, or nooses, with which he seizes and punishes transgressors. Mitra and Varuṇa conjointly are spoken of in one passage as being barriers against falsehood, furnished with many nooses, which the hostile mortal cannot surmount ; and in another place Indra and Varuṇa are described as binding with bonds not formed of rope. On the other hand, Varuṇa is said to be gracious even to him who has committed sin. He is the wise guardian of immortality, and a hope is held out that he and Yama reigning in blessedness shall be beheld in the next world by the righteous.

"The attributes and functions ascribed to Varuṇa impart to his character a moral elevation and sanctity for surpassing that attributed to any other Vedic deity. This appears not only from the passages to which I have already referred, but also from the two hymns translated by Professor Müller in his *Anc. Sansk. Lit.*, *pp.* 540 *f.*, and *Chips, I,* 39 *ff.;* in which the rishi, who is said to be Vasishṭha, while palliating his sins, implores the god's forgiveness, and entreats that his life may be spared. I shall quote a part of the first and the whole of the second :

"Seeking to perceive that sin, O Varuṇa, I inquire ; I resort to the wise to ask. The sages all tell me the same ; it is Varuṇa who is angry with thee.

4. What great sin is it, Varuṇa, for which thou seekest to slay thy worshipper and friend ? Tell me, O unassailable and self-dependent god ; and, freed from sin, I shall speedily come to thee with adoration ; 5, Release us from the sins of our fathers, and from those which we have committed in our own persons. O king, release Vasishṭha like a robber who has fed upon cattle ; release him like a calf from its tether ; 6, It was not our will, Varuṇa, but some seduction, which led us astray,—wine, anger, dice, or thoughtlessness. The stronger perverts the weaker. Even sleep occasions sin."

"Let me not, O king Varuṇa, go to the house of earth. Be gracious, O mighty god, be gracious; 2, I go along, O thunderer, quivering like an inflated skin; be gracious, &c.; 3, O bright and mighty god, I have transgressed through want of power, be gracious, &c.

4. Thirst has overwhelmed thy worshipper when standing even in the midst of the waters; be gracious, &c.; 5, Whatever offence this be, O Varuṇa, that we mortals commit against the people of the sky (the gods): in whatever way we have broken thy laws by thoughtlessness, be gracious, O mighty god, be gracious."

In another place the same rishi alludes to his previous friendship with Varuṇa, and to the favours the god had formerly conferred upon him, and enquires why they had now ceased:

"Varuṇa placed Vasishṭha on his boat: by his power the wise and mighty deity made him a rishi to offer praise in an auspicious period of his life, that his days and dawns might be prolonged; 5, Where are those friendships of us two? Let us seek the harmony which (we enjoyed) of old. I have gone, O self-sustaining Varuṇa, to thy vast and spacious house with a thousand gates; 6, He who was thy friend, intimate, thine own, and beloved, has committed offences against thee. Let not us who are guilty reap the fruits of our sin. Do thou, a wise god, grant protection to him who praises thee."

The same or nearly the same functions and attributes as are ascribed to Varuṇa are also attributed to him and Mitra conjointly. They uphold and rule over the earth and sky, the shining and the terrestrial regions, and place the sun in the heavens.

In his paper on "the highest gods of the Arian races," Professor Roth has the following ingenious and interesting observations on Mitra and Varuṇa: "Within the circle of the Ádityas there subsists the closest connection between Mitra and Varuṇa, who are invoked more frequently together than Varuṇa is invoked singly. We find only one hymn in which Mitra is invoked by himself.

The essential character of the two gods, as distinguished from one another, is nowhere distinctly expressed in the hymns, and was in fact originally one which could not be defined with intellectual precision. But the stage of religious culture which lies before us in the Rig Veda, enables us to distinguish this difference as one already existing, viz., that Mitra is the celestial light in its manifestation by day, while Varuṇa, though the lord of light and of all time, yet rules especially over the nightly heaven. A hymn of Vasishṭha: 'One of you (Varuṇa) is the lord, and unassailable guide, and he who is called Mitra, (*i. e.*, the friend) calls men to activity.' Here so much at least is declared (and the same thing is expressed in nearly the same words in other places), that the light of day, which awakens life, and brings joy and activity into the world, is the narrower sphere of Mitra's power; though, however, Varuṇa is not thereby relegated to the night alone, for he continues to be the lord and the first.

"Though therefore such representations as are expressed in Indian exegesis, (as for instance, when Sáyaṇa says on R. V., vii. 87, 1, that Varuṇa is the setting sun), are far too narrow and one-sided, they still contain some truth; and we may guess by what process they are to be developed. If Varuṇa is, as his name shews, that one among the lucid Ádityas whose seat and sphere of authority is the bright heaven, in whose bosom is embraced all that lives, and therefore also the remotest boundary, beyond which human thought seeks nothing further, then is he also one who can scarcely be attained either by the eye or by the imagination. By day the power of vision cannot discover this remotest limit, the bright heaven presents to it no resting place. But at night this veil of the world, in which Varuṇa is enthroned, appears to approach nearer, and becomes perceptible, for the eye finds a limit. Varuṇa is closer to men. Besides, the other divine forms which, in the clouds, the atmosphere, the rays of light, filled the space between the earth and yonder immeasurable outermost sphere, have disappeared: no other god now stands between Varuṇa and the mortal who gazes at him."—*O. S. T., Vol. V, p.* 70.

Varuni—The goddess of wine, produced from the churning of the ocean. She was in the later mythology the wife of Varuṇa, and was sent by him to promote the enjoyments of Balaráma when he lived for two months at Vraja.

Vashatkara—Deified oblation ; one of the thirty-three divinities who are born again at the end of a thousand ages, according to their own pleasure.

Vashkala—A Daitya, the son of Sanhráda, or Prahláda, according to the Pádma Purána.

Vasishtha—One of the most celebrated Vedic Rishis, the author of several hymns of the Rig Veda, and a personage who played an important part in the early history of the Brahmanic or priestly caste of the Hindus. In the account given of him, historical events and mythological fictions are so much blended together that it is scarcely possible to gather more from it than that he was a sage of high reputation and a priest jealous of the privileges and the position of his caste, and ever ready to assist its superiority over the second or military and royal caste. In one of his Rig Veda hymns he claims to have been enlightened by the god Varuṇa, and in another he is called the son of Mitra and Varuṇa, born from the mind of Urvaśí.—[GOLDSTUCKER.]

Vasishṭha was the family priest of Nimi, son of Ikshváku, who was the son of Manu Vaivasvata, and the first prince of the solar race of kings ; and in a passage of the Mahábhárata, he is stated to have been the purohita of all the kings of that family. He is accordingly mentioned in the Vishṇu Purána, as the religious teacher of Sagara, the thirty-seventh in descent from Ikshváku ; and as conducting a sacrifice for Sandása or Mitrasaha, a descendant in the fifteenth generation of the same prince.

Vasishṭha is also spoken of in the Rámáyana, as the priest of Ráma, who appears from the Vishṇu Purána, to have been a descendant of Ikshváku in the sixty-first generation.

Vasishṭha, according to all these accounts, must have been possessed of a vitality altogether superhuman ; for it does not appear that any of the accounts, intend under the name of Vasishṭha to denote merely a person belonging to the family so called, but to represent the founder of the family himself as taking part in the transactions of many successive ages.

It is clear that Vasishṭha, although he is frequently designated in post-vedic writings as a Brahman, was, according to some other authorities, not really such in any proper sense of the word, as in the accounts which are there given of his birth he is declared to have been either a mind-born son of Brahmá, or the son of Mitra, Varuṇa, and the Apsaras Urvaśí, or to have had some other supernatural origin."

Vasishṭha was the preceptor of the Mahárája Dasaratha. He identified Ráma as an incarnation of Vishṇu, and educated him and his brothers. He invested him with the sacred thread, taught him the Gáyatri, and directed the preparations for his installation as Yuvarája. On the death of the Mahárája he directed the funeral ceremonies, and endeavoured to persuade Ráma to accept the Ráj. He also conducted the installation of Ráma after his return from exile. The seven sons of Vasishṭha were the sages of the first Manwantara; and were born again as Rishis in the third period. He was the Vyása of the eighth Dwápara age. Numerous legends are related of Vasishṭha, some of which have been given under the names to which they refer: See Kalmashápada, Nimi, &c. It is said he was changed to a starling by the curse of Visvámitra, who was himself transformed into a crane by the imprecation of Vasishṭha. In these forms they fought for a considerable time until Brahmá interposed and reconciled them. Wilson says if the tradition have any import it may refer to the ensigns of the contending parties; as banners with armorial devices were invariably borne by princes and leaders.—See VISVAMITRA.

Vasu—A celestial; a leader; a sort of demi-god. There are eight Vasus, so called because they are always present in light, or luminous radiation: or according to the Vishṇu Purána, because preceded by fire they abound in splendour and might. Their names are Apa, Dhruva, Soma, Dhava (fire,) Anila (wind,) Anala (fire,) Pratyusha (day break,) and Prabhasa (light.)

Vasu—1, A daughter of Daksha who was married to Dharma; 2, One of the sons of Kúsa.

Vacubhridyana—One of the sons of Vasishṭha, who was devoured by Rája Kalmashápada.

Vasudeva—1, One of the sons of Súra; at his birth the gods, to whom the future is manifest, foresaw that the Divine Being would take a human form in his family, and thereupon they sounded with joy the drums of heaven ; from this circumstance Vasudeva was also called Ánakadundubhi ; Vasudeva had seven wives ; by one of them Devakí, he had Balaráma and Krishṇa, the two divine incarnations. Vasudeva was imprisoned by Kansa, who also destroyed many of his children and attempted to kill Krishṇa too. Vasudeva lived to see the power and greatness of Krishṇa and Ráma, and at their death he and his wife committed themselves to the flames ; 2, The first prince of the Kanwa dynasty. V. P

Vasudeva—A name of Vishṇu : it means, says the Vishṇu Purána, that all beings abide in that supreme being, and that he abides in all beings. " The form or sensible type of Vásudeva is here considered to be the monosyllable Om, and which is one with the three mystical words Bhuh, Bhuvar, Swar, and with the Vedas : consequently the Vyáhritis and the Vedas are also forms of Vásudeva, diversified as to their typical character, but essentially one and the same."—*Wilson.*

Vasuki—One of the progeny of Kadru ; a powerful many-headed snake ; he was the snake king according to some authorities : but chiefly celebrated from having been used as a cord or rope, around Mount Mandara as a churn, when the gods and Asuras churned the ocean for the Amrita.

Vasumitra——One of the ten Sunga princes.

Vasava—Váyu, a name of the god of the winds.

Vata—Another name of Váyu or Pávana, the god of the wind.

Vata-tree—The Ficus Indica ; the enormous tree which is fabled to grow in the mountain Supárṣwa, to the south of Meru, and described as spreading over eleven hundred yojanas, is a Vata tree.

Vatapi—1, A celebrated demon, the son of Hláda ; 2, A powerful Danava, the son of Viprachitti ; 3, A cruel Rákshasa, a devourer of brahmans ; he lived in the forest near the Vindhya mountains, and was himself eaten, according to the Rámáyana, by the sage Agastya.

Vatsa—Child ; a name of Pratarddana, from his father's frequently calling him by that name.

Vatsabalaka—A son of Súra and brother of Vasudeva.

Vatsabhumi—A prince, the eighth in descent from Alarka.

Vatsapri—A celebrated prince of the solar race, the son of Bhalandana.

Vatsara—1, One of the sons of Dhruva ; 2, The fifth cyclic year.

Vatsavyuha—An ancient Rája of the solar race, the son of Vatsa.

Vatsya—1, A teacher of the Rig Veda ; 2, One of the fifteen teachers of the White Yajush.

Vavriddhas—A class of deities in the fourteenth Manwantara.

Vayu—The god of wind ; the Æolus of Hindu mythology, while the Maruts are the breezes who attended upon Indra. Váyu was the mythical father of Bhíma, and of Hanumán. It was Váyu who testified to the fidelity of Damayanti ; who conveyed the palace of Indra to the earth, &c.

In the Vedic mythology of the Hindus, Váyu is a deity who originally seems to have held an equal rank with Indra, but much more rarely occupies the imagination of the poets than this god, or Agni, or the Sun ; for though, according to Yâska, ancient commentators of the Vedas hold that there are only three great deities—viz., Agni, fire, whose place is on earth ; Surya, the sun, whose place is in heaven ; and Váyu, or Indra, whose place is in the intermediate sphere—only a few hymns, comparatively speaking, are dedicated to Váyu, whereas the other deities named are the subject of manifold praise. The description given by the Rig Veda of the greatness of Váyu nevertheless answers the position which those ancient commentators assign to him.

Váyu, is said to be the son-in-law of Tvashtri. He moves in a shining car, drawn by a pair of red or purple horses. His team is often said to consist of ninety-nine, of a hundred, or even of a thousand horses, yoked by his will. Váyu, like the other gods is a drinker of soma. In fact, he alone, or in conjunction with Indra, was, by the admission of the other gods, entitled to the first draught of this libation. It is remarkable that Váyu is but rarely connected with the Maruts or deities of the storm ; but in one place he is said to have begotten them from the rivers of heaven ; and in another place to be attended by Pushan, the Maruts and the Viṣva devas.

The following hymns are addressed to Váta (another name of the god of the wind). The imagery in the first is highly poetical.

"1, (I celebrate) the glory of Váta's chariot ; its noise comes rending and resounding. Touching the sky, he moves onward, making all things ruddy : and he comes propelling the dust of the earth ; 2, The gusts (?) of the air rush after him, and congregate in him as women in an assembly. Sitting along with them on the same car, the god, who is king of this universe, is borne along ; 3, Hasting forward, by paths in the atmosphere, he never rests on any day. Friend of the waters, first-born, holy, in what place was he born ? whence has he sprung ? 4, Soul of the gods, source of the universe, this deity moves as he lists. His sounds have been heard, but his form is not (seen) : this Váta let us worship with an oblation."

"1, Let Váta, the wind, waft to us healing, salutary, and auspicious, to our heart : may he prolong our lives ; 2, And, Váta, thou art our father, our brother, and our friend : cause us to live ; 3, From the treasure of immortality, which is deposited yonder in thy house, O Váta, give us to live."

Here the same property is ascribed to Váta which is elsewhere ascribed to Rudra, that of bringing healing.*

Vayu-Purana—The Váyu Purána is narrated, by Súta, to the Rishis at Naimisháraṇya, as it was formerly told, at the same place, to similar persons by Váyu ; a repetition of circumstances not uncharacteristic of the inartificial style of this Purána. It is divided into four Pádas, termed, severally, Prakriyá, Upodgháta, Anushanga, and Upasamhára ; a classification peculiar to this work. These are preceded by an index, or heads of chapters, in the manner of the Mahábhárata and Rámáyana—another peculiarity.

*Dr. Muir, O. S. T., Vol. V, p. 146.

The Prakriyá portion contains but a few chapters, and treats, chiefly, of elemental creation, and the first evolutions of beings, to the same purport as the Vishṇu, but in a more obscure and unmethodical style. The Upodgháta then continues the subject of creation, and describes the various Kalpas or periods during which the world has existed; a greater number of which is specified by the Saiva, than by the Vaishnáva Puránas. Thirty-three are here described, the last of which is the Śweta or 'white' Kalpa, from Śiva's being born in it, of a white complexion. The genealogies of the patriarchs, the description of the universe, and the incidents of the first six Manwantaras are all treated of in this part of the work; but they are intermixed with legends and praises of Śiva, as the sacrifice of Daksha, the Maheṣwara Máhátmya, the Nilakaṇṭha Stotra, and others. The genealogies, although, in the main, the same as those in the Vaishnáva Puránas, present some variations. A long account of the Pitris or progenitors is also peculiar to this Purána; as are stories of some of the most celebrated Rishis who were engaged in the distribution of the Vedas.

The third division commences with an account of the seven Rishis and their descendants, and describes the origin of the different classes of creatures from the daughters of Daksha, with as profuse copiousness of nomenclature, not found in any other Purána. With the exception of the greater minuteness of detail, the particulars agree with those of the Vishṇu Purána. A chapter then occurs on the worship of the Pitris; another, on Tírthas or places sacred to them; and several, on the performance of Śráddhas, constituting the Śráddha Kalpa. After this comes a full account of the solar and lunar dynasties, forming a parallel to that in the Vishṇu Purána, with this difference, that it is, throughout, in verse, whilst that of our text, as noticed in its place, is, chiefly, in prose. It is extended, also, by the insertion of detailed accounts of various incidents, briefly noticed in the Vishṇu, though derived, apparently, from a common original. The section terminates with similar accounts of future kings, and the same chronological calculations, that are found in the Vishṇu.

The last portion, the Upasamhára, describes briefly the future Manwantaras, the measures of space and time, the end of the world, the efficacy of Yoga, and the glories of Śivapura, or the dwelling of Śiva, with whom the Yogin is to be united. The manuscript concludes with a different history of the successive teachers of the Váyu Purána, tracing them from Brahmá to Váyu, from Váyu to Bṛihaspati, and from him, through various deities and sages, to Dwaipáyana and Súta.—WILSON.

Vayuna—A sage, one of the sons of Kriṣáṣwa ; the Rámáyana terms the sons of Kriṣáṣwa the Sastra devatas, or gods of the divine weapons.

Vedabahu—A son of the patriarch Pulastya.

Vedamitra—A teacher of the Rig Veda ; who divided his Sanhita into five, which he distributed to as many disciples.

Vedana—Fortune ; a daughter of Anrita (falsehood,) married to Naraka (hell).

Vedanga—From Veda and *anga*, limb ; hence, literally, 'the limb of (the body of) the Veda'—is the name of six Sanscrit works, the object of which is to teach how to read and understand correctly the Vedic texts, and how to apply them correctly to sacrificial purposes. Whether the number of these works was originally the same as it now is, and already was at the time of the Upanishads, may be doubtful. Tradition mentions the following Vedángas : 1, Śikshá, or the science of proper pronunciation. It is represented by a short treatise of 35, or, in another recension, of 59 verses, which explains the nature of letters, accent, and pronunciation, and is ascribed to Páṇini ; 2, *Chhandas*, or (a work on) metre, which is ascribed to *Pingala*; 3, Vyákarana, or grammar, by which native authorities understand the celebrated work of Páṇini ; but never those short books, especially concerned in Vedic peculiarities, called Prátiṣákhyas, the existing representatives of which, in all probability, are posterior to Páṇini ; 4, *Nirukta* ; 5, *Jyotisha*, or astronomy. 'Its chief object is to convey such knowledge of the heavenly bodies as is necessary for fixing the days and hours of the Vedic sacrifices ;' 6, *Kalpa*, or works on the Vedic ceremonial, which systematise the ritual taught by the Brahmana portion of the

Veda, omitting, however, all legendary or mystical detail. They are composed in the Sútra style. The Kalpa, or Śranta, Sútras belonging to the Rig Veda are the Aṣwaláyana-, *Sánkháyana*, and Saunaka *Sútras*; those relating to the Sámaveda, the Maṣaka-, *Látyáyana-*, and Dráhyáyaṇa Sútras ; those of the Black Yajurveda, the Apastamba-, *Baudháyana-*, Satyashádha-, Hiraṇyakeṣin-, *Mánava-*, *Bháradvája-*, *Vádhúna-*, Vaikhánasa-, *Laugákshi-*, *Maitra-*, Kaṭha-, and *Váráha Sútras*. The White Yajurveda has only one Kalpa, or Śranta, Sútras connected with it, the *Kátyáyana* Sútra, and the Atharvaveda likewise only one, the *Kusika Sútra*.— At a later period, these works were supplemented by a similar class of works, which, however, merely describe the domestic ceremonies, viz., 'the marriage rite, the rites to be performed at the conception of a child, at various periods before his birth, at the time of his birth, the ceremony of naming the child, of carrying him out to see the sun, of feeding him, of cutting his hair, and lastly, of investing him as a student, and handing him to a guru, under whose care he is to study the sacred writings.' Works of this kind are called Gṛihya-Sútras (from *griha*, house), and to these, again, were added the *Sámayáchárika-Sútras* (from *samayáchára*, conventional practice), which treat of customs sanctioned by the practice of pious men, but not enjoined or expressly stated in the Grihya-Sútras. The two last classes of Sútras, which are not comprised amongst the Kalpa works, then grew into the Dharmaṣástras, or law-books, of which that of Manu is the chief representative.—*Chambers' Encyclopædia.*

Vedanta—(From the Sanscrit *veda*, and *anta*, end ; hence, literally, "the end or ultimate aim of the Vedas") is the second great division of the Mimamsa school of Hindu philosophy. It is chiefly concerned in the investigation of *Brahman* (neuter) or the Supreme Spirit, and the relation in which the universe, and especially the human soul, stands to it ; and in contradistinction from the Púrvamímánsa, or the investigation (*mímánsá*) of the former (*púrva*) part of the Vedas—viz., the Sanhitá, and especially the Bráhmaṇas—which contain the *dharma*, or religious law, it is also called *Uttara-mímánsá*, or the investigation (*mímánsá*) of the latter (*uttara*) part of the Vedas—viz., Áraṇyakás and *Upanishads*, which treat of (the neuter) *Brahman*, or the Supreme Spirit [not to be confounded with (the masculine) *Brahman*, or the god of the mythological *Trimúrti*]. Sometimes, the name given to it is *Sáríraka-mímánsá*, or the investigation of the soul (Sáríraka). In its method, the Vedánta differs from the Nyáya by endeavouring to explain the universe as a successive development from one ultimate source or principle—whereas the Nyáya, in both its divisions, treats of the object of human knowledge of which the universe is composed, under different topics, unconcerned about their mutual relation of effect and cause ; and from the *Sánkhya*, it is distinct, inasmuch as that system is based on the assumption of a duality of principles whence the universe derives its origin.

The object-matter of the Vedánta is the proof that the universe emanates in a successive development from a Supreme Spirit or soul, which is called *Brahman*, or *paramátman ;* that the human soul is therefore identical in origin with Brahman ; that the worldly existence of the human soul is merely the result of its ignorance of this sameness between itself and the Supreme Spirit ; and that its final liberation or freedom from Transmigration is attained by a removal of this ignorance, that is, by a proper understanding of the truth of the Vedánta doctrine.

According to this doctrine, *Brahman* (neuter) is both the efficient and material cause of the world, creator and creation, doer and deed. It is one, self-existent, supreme, as truth, wisdom, intelligence, and happiness ; devoid of the three qualities, in the sense in which created beings possess them ; and at the consummation of all things, the whole universe is resolved or absorbed into it. From Brahman individual souls emanate, as innumerable sparks issue from a blazing fire. The soul, therefore, is neither born, nor does it die ; it is of divine substance, and as such, infinite, immortal, intelligent, sentient, true. Its separate existence, as distinct from Brahman, is the cause of its ignorance ; and this ignorance, which consists in regarding the world as a reality capable of subsisting without Brahman, has a double power—that of enveloping and projecting. By means of the former, it makes the soul liable to mundane vicissitudes, as to the sensations of pleasure, pain, &c. The projective power of ignorance, when encompassing the soul in its fourth condition, or that of pure intellect (its other conditions are : waking, dreaming, and dreamless sleep) produces out of the darkness which then prevails the five subtile elements—viz., *ether*, which is the substratum of the quality sound ; *air*, which arises from ether, the substratum of touch ; from air, *fire or light*, the substratum of colour ; from light, *water*, the substratum of savour ; and from water, *earth*, the substratum of smell. From these subtile elements are then produced seventeen subtile bodies and the five gross elements. The former, also called lingaṣaríra, because they are bodies (ṣaríra) which impart to existing beings their individual character (*linga*), are *the five organs of perception*—viz., the organs of hearing, touch, sight, taste, and smell, which arise severally from the *pure* or inactive particles of each of the subtile elements ; further, *two intellectual organs*, which are produced from the *mingled pure*, or inactive particles of the subtile elements—viz., *buddhi*, understanding, the function of which is to arrive at a certainty or conclusion, and *manas* (an organ of volition and imagination), the function of which consists in willing and doubting—thinking and referring the external objects to one's own self, being two functions common to both of them ; lastly, *the five organs of action*—viz., the voice, the hands, the feet, the organ of excretion and that of generation, which are severally produced from the *foul* or *active* particles of each of the subtile elements ; and *the five vital airs*, which are produced from the *mingled foul*, or *active* particles of the subtile elements—viz., the air breathed forth, which has its place in the fore-part of the nose ; the air breathed downwards, which has its place in the lower intestines ; the air which circulates through the whole body ; the ascending air, which has its place in the throat, and the descending air in the middle of the body, which causes assimilation and digestion of food, produces semen, excrements, &c. (Later Vedantists assume ten such vital airs—viz., besides the foregoing, the airs which severally cause retching, winking, hunger, yawning, and fattening.) The five *gross elements* are the five subtile elements, when, according to a theory derived from a scriptural text, they have become so divided and combined that each of them retains a preponderating portion of itself, and consequently of the quality of which it is the substratum as ether of sound, &c.—and besides smaller portions of the other subtile elements, and the qualities of which they are the substrata. From these gross elements then arise the various (mythological) worlds, and this world too, with bodies which are distinguished as viviparous, or those produced from a womb, as men, beasts, &c.; oviparous, or those produced from an egg, as birds, snakes, &c.; those generated by 'sweat' or hot moisture, as lice, gnats, &c.; and those germinating, as creepers, trees, &c. The soul, when existing in the body, is encased in a succession of 'sheaths.' The first or interior 'sheath' consists of *buddhi*, associated with the organs of perception; the second, of *manas*, associated with the organs of action; and the third, of the vital airs together with the organs of action. These three 'sheaths' constitute the subtile body of the soul, which attends the soul in its transmigrations; and the collective totality of such subtile bodies is the supreme soul, as regarded in its relation to the world; when it is also called 'the soul which is the thread,' or passes like the thread through the universe, or Hiraṇyagarbha, or life. The fourth and exterior 'sheath' of the soul is composed of the gross elements; and the collective aggregate of such gross bodies is the gross body of the deity. This whole development being the result of ignorance, the soul frees itself from its error by understanding that the different stages in which this development appears, do not represent real or absolute truth; and when its error has completely vanished, it ceases to be re-born, and becomes re-united with Brahman, whence it emanated. But since the means of arriving at a final deliverance can only be the complete mastery of the truths of the Vedánta, other means, such as the performance of sacrifices or other religious acts enjoined by the Vedas, or the practice of the Yoga, cannot lead to the same result. They may be meritorious, and are even recommended as such, but can effect only an apparent liberation. Of this, there are two kinds: one liberation which is effected in lifetime, and enables a man to perform supernatural actions or wonders, as the evocation of the shades of progenitors, going anywhere at will, and similar feats; and another which takes place after death, and enables the soul, not divested of its subtile body, to reside in heaven; but after a time its effect ceases, and the soul has to renew its mundane existence. In order to fit the mind for meditating on these truths, various moral duties are enjoined, and various practices are recommended, especially by later Vedánta writers. Thus, the student of the Vedánta is told not to hurt a sentient being, to speak the truth, not to steal, to practise continence, and not to accept gifts ; to remain pure and content, to do penance, and to study the Vedas ; also to remain in certain postures, to practise various modes of suppressing his breath, and the like. These injunctions, however, are extraneous to the doctrine itself, and appear to be a compromise with the old orthodox faith, which requires the performance of religious acts, and a later stage of it, which favours such austere practices as are especially known by the name of Yoga. The doctrine of *bhakti*, or faith, does not belong to the older Vedánta ; it is, however, an interesting feature of the later periods of this philosophy ; and the same observation applies to the doctrine of *Máyá*, or illusion, according to which the world has no reality whatever, but is merely the product of imagination ; for the older Vedánta, as will have been seen, merely teaches that the world is not *the truth*, but does not deny its material reality."* The late Dr. J. R. Ballantyne published an able Lecture on the Vedánta, embracing the Text of the Vedánta Sara. Allahabad, 1850. There is an excellent article on the Ontology of the Vedánta, in the Benares Magazine for December 1851, written by Dr. F. E. Hall.

Vedas--The Vedas are four in number : the eldest is the Rig-veda ; next stands the Yajur-veda ; the Sáma-veda, and the latest is the Atharva-veda. Each Veda is divided into two parts ; 1st, The hymns or Mantras, which express the wants and aspirations of the worshippers, and thereby throw some light on the social condition of the people ; 2nd, The Bráhmanas which belong to a Ritualistic age, and refer to rites and ceremonies of an unmeaning or artificial character.

" The Veda has a two-fold interest ; it belongs to the history of the world and to the history of India. In the history of the

* Goldstücker in Chambers's Encyclopædia.

world the Veda fills a gap which no literary work in any other language could fill. It carries us back to times of which we have no records anywhere, and gives us the very words of a generation of men of whom otherwise we could form but the vaguest estimate by means of conjectures and inferences.

" It is difficult no doubt to believe that the most ancient literary work of the Áryan race, a work more ancient than the Zendavesta and Homer, should, after a lapse of at least three thousand years, have been discovered, and for the first time published, in its entirety, not in one of the Parishads on the borders of the Ganges, but in one of the Colleges of an English University. It is difficult to believe that sufficient MSS. should have been preserved, in spite of the perishable nature of the material on which they are written, to enable an editor to publish the collection of the Vedic hymns in exactly that form in which they existed at least 800 years before the Christian era ; and, still more, that this collection, which was completed at the time of Lykurgos, should contain the poetical relics of a pre-Homeric age ; an age in which the names of the Greek gods and heroes had not yet lost their original sense, and in which the simple worship of the Divine powers of nature was not yet supplanted by a worship of personal gods. It is difficult to believe this and we have a right to be sceptical. But it is likewise our duty to inquire into the value of what has been preserved for us in so extraordinary a manner, and to extract from it those lessons which the study of mankind was intended to teach to man."*

" The religion of the Vedas, as far as we are acquainted with it, differs in many very material points, from that of the present day. The worship they prescribe is, with a few exceptions, domestic, consisting of oblations to fire, and invocations of the deities of fire, of the firmament, of the winds, the seasons, the moon, the sun ; who are invited by the sacrificer, if a brahman, or by his family priest if he is not a brahman, to be present and accept the offering, either oiled butter or the juice of the soma, a

* Max Müller, Hist. Sans. Lit.

species of asclepias, which are poured upon the sacrificial fire, in return for which they are supplicated to confer temporal blessings upon the worshipper, riches, life, posterity ; the short-sighted vanities of human desire, which constituted the sum of heathen prayer in all heathen countries.

" The titles and functions of the deities commonly addressed on these invocations give to the religion of the Vedas the character of the worship of the elements, and it is not unlikely that it was so in its earliest and rudest condition. It is declared in some texts that the deities are only three ; whose places are earth, the middle region between heaven and earth, and the heaven ; namely, fire, air, the sun. Upon this however seems to have been grafted some loftier speculation, and the elements came to be regarded as types and emblems of divine power, as there can be no doubt that the fundamental doctrine of the Vedas is monotheism.* " There is in truth," say repeated texts, " but one deity, the Supreme Spirit." " He from whom the universal world proceeds, who is Lord of the universe, and whose work is the universe, is the Supreme Being." Injunctions also repeatedly occur to worship Him, and Him only. " Adore God alone, know God alone, give up all other discourse ;" and the Vedant says, " it is found in the Vedas that none but the Supreme Being is to be worshipped, nothing excepting Him should be adored by a wise man."—*Wilson's Works, Vol. II, pp.* 50–52.

" The simple patriarchal life of the Áryans is indicated in the Vedic hymns, precisely as it is depicted in the main tradition of the Mahábhárata. They were a people partly pastoral and partly agricultural ; keeping cows for the sake of their milk, butter, and curds, and sowing the land with grain. They also seem to have had some acquaintance with the manufacture of weapons and coats of mail, and to have sometimes undertaken sea-voyages for the sake of gain. These people prayed to their gods, as such a people might be expected to pray, for plenty of rain, abundant harvests, and prolific cattle ; for bodily vigour, long life, numerous progeny,

* Colebrooke's Essays, I, p. 12 ; Max Müller, History of Ancient Sans. Lit., pp. 558—71.

and protection against all foes and robbers, such as the cattle-lifting aborigines. Their gods appear to have been mere abstractions; personifications of those powers of nature on whom they relied for good harvests. They wanted seasonable rain, warmth, and fresh breezes. Accordingly, they prayed to the god of rain, the god of fire and light, and the god of wind. But from the very first, there appears to have been some confusion in these personifications, which led both to a multiplicity of deities, and the confounding together of different deities. Thus the conception of the god of rain was Indra, and he was identified with the firmament as well as with the unseen power which smote the rain-cloud and brought down the waters; and so important was the acquisition of rain in due season, that Indra is regarded as the sovereign of the gods, and subsequently became a type of sovereignty. But rain and water are frequently different things, and thus there was another, and perchance an older, deity, named Varuṇa, who was particularly worshipped as the god of the waters, and deity of the ocean. Again, the conception of the god of fire was Agni, and Agni was not only the flame which burns upon the hearth or altar, but also the lightning which manifests itself in the clouds, and even the light of the sun, moon, and stars. Yet both the sun and moon appear as separate and individual deities, the latter under the name of Soma or Chandra. Again, there seems to have been a striking difference as regards wind. The god of wind, or air, was Váyu; but the different breezes which bring on or accompany the rain, are called Maruts, and are represented as the attendants of Indra. Thus, whilst there is a Pantheon of separate and individual deities, the conception of one deity frequently overlapped the conceptions of other deities; and whilst the more prominent powers of nature, such as water, fire, and wind, were separately individualized, a monotheistic tendency was always at work, ascribing the attributes of every deity to each one in turn. Of these deities, the following appear to be the most important:—

RAIN.

Indra, god of the firmament.
Varuṇa, god of the waters.

Fire.

Agni, god of fire.
Súrya, the sun.
Soma, or Chandra, the moon.

Air.

Váyu, the god of wind.
Maruts, the breezes who attended upon Indra.

To these must be added a god of death, or judge of the dead, who was known as Yama. The characteristics of Yama as a Vedic deity would open up a large field of inquiry; but the subject at present is vague and speculative. In the Epics, Yama appears distinctly as a judge of the dead; and men who are about to die are frequently said to be about to go to the mansions of Yama."

"In the Vedic period the Brahmans were scarcely known as a separate community; the caste system had not been introduced, and the gods who were worshipped were subsequently superseded by deities of other names and other forms."*

Vedasiras—A sage, the son of Márkáṇdya: he married Pívarí, and had many children, who constituted the family, or Brahmanical tribe, of Bhárgavas, sons of Bhrigu. The most celebrated of these was Uṣanas, the preceptor of the Daityas.

Vedavati—The vocal daughter of the Rishi Kuṣadhvaja, sprung from him during his constant study of the Veda. She was a damsel of brilliant beauty, but dressed in ascetic garb, and lived in forests on the Himálaya. It was there she was seen by the giant Rávaṇa, in the course of his progress through the world, and he at once became enamoured of her. He enquired who she was, and told her that such an austere life was unsuited to her youth and attractions. As a reason for leading such an ascetic existence she said the gods, gandharvas, &c., wished that she should choose a husband, but her father would give her to no one else than to Vishṇu, the lord of the world, whom he desired for his son-in-law. This resolution provoked Sambhu, king of the Daityas, who slew her father, Kuṣadhvaja, while sleeping, on which her mother

* Talboys Wheeler History of India, Vol. I, pp. 8—11.

(whose name is not given) after embracing his body, entered into the fire. Vedavati then proceeds "In order that I may fulfil this desire of my father in respect of Náráyana, I wed him with my heart. Having entered into this engagement, I practice great austerity. Náráyana, and no other than he, Purushottama, is my husband. From the desire of obtaining him, I resort to this severe observance." Rávaṇa's passion is not in the least diminished by this explanation, and he urges that it is the old alone who should seek to become distinguished by accumulating merit through austerity; prays that she who is so young and beautiful, shall become his bride; and boasts that he is superior to Vishṇu. She rejoins that no one but he would thus contemn that deity. On receiving this reply, he touches the hair of her head with the tip of his finger. She is greatly incensed, and forthwith cuts off her hair, and tells him that as he has so insulted her, she cannot continue to live, but will enter into the fire before his eyes. She goes on: "'Since I have been insulted in the forest by thee who art wicked-hearted, I shall be born again for thy destruction. For a man of evil design cannot be slain by a woman; and the merit of my austerity would be lost if I were to launch a curse against thee. But if I have performed, or bestowed, or sacrificed, aught, may I be born the virtuous daughter, not produced from the womb, of a righteous man.' Having thus spoken, she entered the blazing fire. Then a shower of celestial flowers fell from every part of the sky. It is she, lord, who (having seen Vedavati in the Kritá age, has been born in the Treta age) as the daughter of the king of the Janakas and [has become] thy bride; for thou art the eternal Vishṇu. The mountain-like enemy who was [virtually] destroyed before by her wrath, has now been slain by her, having recourse to thy superhuman energy." On this the commentator remarks: "By this it is signified that Sítá was the principal cause of Rávaṇa's death; but the function of destroying him is ascribed to Ráma." On the words "thou art Vishṇu," in the preceding verse the same commentator remarks "By this it is clearly affirmed that Sítá was Lakshmi. This is what Parásara says. In the god's life as Ráma, she became Sítá, and in his birth as Krishṇa [she became] Rukminí."—*O. S. T., IV.*, 392.

Veda-vyasas—Arrangers of the Vedas : "In every Dwápara (or third) age, Vishṇu, in the person of Vyása, in order to promote the good of mankind, divides the Veda, which is properly but one, into many portions : observing the limited perseverance, energy, and application of mortals, he makes the Veda fourfold, to adapt it to their capacities ; and the bodily form which he assumes in order to effect that classification, is known by the name of Veda-vyása."—*Vishnu Purâna.*

Veddah—A wild semi-savage race, residing in the interior of Ceylon. *The forest Veddahs* dwell in hollow trees or caves, subsist on game which they kill with rudely formed bows and arrows, wandering from jungle to jungle, as the game becomes scarce. They will not hold the slightest intercourse with any natives but those of their own tribe, and their language is said to be unintelligible to all others. The village Veddahs dwell in certain districts, hold but slight intercourse with the other inhabitants of the island, will not intermarry nor mix with them. They can make themselves understood to the Singhalese. Their sole clothing is a strip of cloth which hangs down in front, and is fastened by a coir cord, which passes round their loins. Their hair, beards and whiskers are never shorn or cleansed, but hang down in matted masses. The forest Veddahs are dexterous hunters, and especially skilful in snaring the wild elephants. The two tribes do not intermarry, as they mutually distrust each other. The Veddahs generally deposit their dead in the jungle to be devoured by wild animals. They seem to worship the planets ? evil spirits, and spirits of their deceased ancestors. They have their own headmen whom they elect and obey. They use bows and arrows and clubs of iron wood.—*Sirr's Ceylon, Vol. II, p.* 216. They occupy a district about 90 miles long and 45 broad in the south eastern side of Ceylon, lying between the sea and the base of the Badulla and Oovah hills. They are a remnant of the Yakkos, the aboriginal inhabitants of Ceylon, who, 2000 years ago, after the conquest of the island by Wijayo and his followers, returned into the wilds as the Kulis in Guzerat, the Bhíls in Malwa, the Putu in Cuttack, the Konds in Gondwana, and the Bedas in Mysore, retired before conquerors. The Bisadæ, or

Besadæ, which in mediæval Greek is called Vesadæ, are alluded to in the tract of Palladius de Moribus Brachmanorum, written about A. D. 400, and the same name is applied by Ptolemy to a similar race inhabiting northern India. A forest tribe of Mysore, known by the name of Vedas or Redas, formed part of the army of Tippu Sahib. The Veddahs live by hunting and use the bow, in drawing which they employ their hands and their feet. They are omniverous, and eat carrion and vermin, roots, grain, fruit, birds, bats, crows, owls, kites, but refuse the bear, elephant and buffalo. Their language is a dialect of Singhalese, free from Sanskrit or Pali, but the vocabulary is very limited and they have recourse to gestures and signs. They have no knowledge of God, nor of a future state, and have no temples, idols, altars, prayers or charms, but have a devil worship. They do not bury but cover their dead with leaves in the jungle. They are regarded by the Singhalese as of high descent.—*Sir J. E. Tennant.*

Vedha—A measure of time ; 100 Trutis.

Vedhaka—One of the Narakas ; that for the makers of arrows.

Vegavat—An ancient prince of the solar race ; the son of Bandhumat.

Vela—The daughter of Meru and wife of Samudra.

Vena—A Chakkra-vartti, or universal emperor ; the son of Anga or Tunga. When he was inaugurated by the Rishis monarch of the earth he caused it to be everywhere proclaimed that no worship should be performed, no oblations offered, no gifts bestowed upon the Brahmans. " I, the king ' said he' I am the lord of sacrifice ; for who but I, am entitled to the oblations." The Rishis remonstrated without effect ; and then says the Vishṇu Purána, " these pious Munis were filled with wrath, and said let this wicked wretch be slain : and they fell upon the king, and beat him with blades of holy grass, consecrated by prayer, and slew him who had first been destroyed by his impiety toward God."

According to the Pádma Purána, Veṇa commenced his reign auspiciously, but lapsing into the Jain heresy, the sages deposed him, and pummelled him until the Nisháda, or progenitor of the wild races, was extracted from his left thigh, and Prithu from his right arm. Being freed from sin by the birth of the Nisháda, Veṇa retired to the banks of the Narmadá, where he performed penance in honour of Vishṇu, who appeared to him and read him a lecture on the merit of gifts of various kinds, especially at different holy places or Tírthas. After this Vishṇu desired Veṇa to demand a boon, and he solicited that he might be incorporated with the deity; Vishṇu told him first to celebrate an Aṣwamedha, after which the king should become one with himself, and he then disappeared. Prithu enabled his father Veṇa to consummate the sacrifice by which he was united to Vishṇu, and this incident is said to illustrate the efficacy of a son considered as a Tírtha.—*Wilson's Works, III,* 38.

Venu—A Yádava prince, the son of Satajit.

Vibhishana—The younger brother of the giant Rávaṇa; when he and his brothers had practised rigid austerities for a long series of years, Brahmá appeared to offer them boons: Vibhíshaṇa asked that he might never meditate any unrighteousness. When his elder brother Vaisravana (Kuvera) was expelled from Lanka, Vibhíshaṇa followed him to Gandhamádana, where he is said to have dwelt with a white umbrella and white garlands, on the Śvebaparvata or white mountain, attended by his four counsellors, and apart from his disreputable brothers Kumbhakarṇa, &c., who, naked, with dishevelled hair and red garlands, frequented the south.

When Hanumán was taken before Rávaṇa, and announced himself as the ambassador of Sugríva, warning the ravisher of Sítá that nothing could save him from the vengeance of Ráma, Rávaṇa, infuriated, ordered him to be put to death; but Vibhíshaṇa reminded his brother that the life of ambassadors was sacred. On another occasion, after a long altercation, Rávaṇa was so enraged with Vibhíshaṇa for persisting in urging the restoration of Sítá, that he rose in a fury and kicked him from his seat. Smarting under this outrage, Vibhíshaṇa left Lanka and flew through the air to Kailása to the court of his brother Kuvera, where Śiva also at that time happened to be present. The latter made known to Vibhíshaṇa the divine character of Ráma, and directed him to desert Rávaṇa and join Ráma's standard, which

Vibhíshaṇa accordingly did. He was at first taken for a spy, but afterwards Ráma accepted him as an ally and embraced him. On the death of Rávaṇa, Vibhíshaṇa was installed as Rája of Lanka; he afterwards accompanied Ráma and Lakshmana to Ayodhya.—*I. E. P.*, 80–83.

Vibhratra—A king of Hastinápura, the son of Sukriti.

Vibhu—1, The Indra of the fifth Manwantara ; 2, A prince, the grandson of Alarka.

Vibudha—A king of Mithila, the son of Krita.

Vichitra-virya—A prince, the son of Śántanu, rája of Hastinápur : "he married Ambá and Ambalika, the daughter of the rája of Kásí ; and indulging too freely in connubial rites, fell into a consumption of which he died. (Vishṇu Purána.) See Śántanu. The legend as related in the Mahábhárata is slightly different. Vichitravirya's half brother Bhíshma is there said to have gone to Kásí for the purpose of seeing the Rája's daughters, and finding them very beautiful he did not wait for the day of the Swayamvara, but seizing the three damsels, placed them in his own chariot, and challenged every Rája present to do him battle. Thus did Bhíshma win the daughters of the Rája of Kásí and carry them away in triumph to the city of Hastinápur, that they might become the wives of Vichitra-vírya. The widows of Vichitra-virya were afterwards the mothers of Dhritaráshtra and Páṇḍu.—[Vidura.]

Vidarbha—1, The only son of Jyámagha and Saivya ; he was married to the damsel the father had brought home before his birth. See Jyámagha ; 2, The name of a city, the modern Berar.

Vidhatri—A son of the demi-god Bhrigu, married to Niryati.

Vidmisara—A king of Magadha, the son of Kshatranjas.

Vidura—The brother of Dhṛitaráshtra and Páṇḍu. "Soma, the moon, the progenitor of the lunar race, who reigned at Hastinápur, was the child of the Rishi Atri, and father of Budha, who married Ilá, or Iḍá, daughter of the solar prince Ikshváku, and had by her a son Aila or Purúravas. The latter had a son by Urvaṣi named Áyus, from whom came Nahusha, the father of Yayáti. The latter had two sons, Puru and Yadu, from whom proceeded the two branches of the lunar line. In the line of Yadu we need only mention the last three princes, Sura, Vasudeva, and Krishṇa, with his brother Balaráma. Fifteenth in the other line—that of Puru—came Dushyanta, father of the great Bharata. Ninth from Bharata came Kuru, and fourteenth from him Śántanu, this Śántanu had by his wife Satyavatí, a son named Vichitra-vírya. Bhíshma who renounced the right of succession and took the vow of perpetual celibacy, was the son of Śántanu by a former wife, the goddess Gangá, whence one of his names is Gángeya. Satyavati also had, before her marriage with Sántanu, borne Vyása to the sage Paráṣara ; so that Vichitra-vírya, Bhíshma and Vyása were half-brothers : and Vyása, though he retired into the wilderness to live a life of contemplation, promised his mother that he would place himself at her disposal whenever she required his services. Satyavatí had recourse to him when her son Vichtra-vírya died childless, and requested him to pay his addresses to Vichitra-vírya's two widows, named Ambiká and Ambáliká. He consented, and had by them respectively two children, Dhṛitaráshtra who was born blind, and Paṇḍu, who was born with a pale complexion. When Satavati begged Vyása to become the father of a third son (who should be without any defect) the elder wife, terrified by Vyása's austere appearance, sent him one of her slave girls, dressed in her own clothes ; and this girl was the mother of Vidura. Vyása was so much pleased with this slave-girl that he pronounced her free, and declared that her child Vidura should be eminently wise and good.

Dhṛitaráshtra, Páṇḍu and Vidura, were thus brothers, the sons of Vyása, the supposed author or compiler of the Mahábhárata. "Vidura is one of the best characters in the Mahábhárata, always ready with good advice both for the Páṇḍavas and for his brother Dhṛitaráshtra. His disposition leads him always to take the part of the Páṇḍu princes, and warn them of the evil designs of their cousins." Bhíshma promoted the marriage of Vidura with a beautiful slave girl belonging to king Devaka. *I. E. P.*

Viduratha—1, A prince ; the son of Bhajamána and father of Súra ; 2, The son of Suratha, a descendant of Kuru.

Vihanghamas—A class of deities of the eleventh Manwantara.

Vijaya—1, A prince, the son of Chunchu ; 2, A king of Mithila, the son of Jaya ; 3, The son of Sanjaya, of the race of Áyus ; 4, A son of Jayadratha ; 5, One of the Andhra princes.

Vijaya—A daughter of the patriarch Daksha, married to Kriaṣwa.

Vijitaswa—The eldest son of Prithu, called also Antarddhána, in consequence of having obtained from Indra the power of making himself invisible.

Vikala—A measure of time, six Práṇas.

Vikesi—The wife of the Rudra Sarva.

Vikranta—One of the Prajápatis.

Vikramaditya—A celebrated Hindu king of Malwa, whose reign began fifty-six years before the Christian era. The ancient city of Ujein was his capital. Vikramaditya had no estate assigned him by his father, and lived for a considerable time with his illegitimate brother Bhurtri at Ujein, of which Bhurtri was governor. A quarrel having occurred between the brothers Vikramaditya left Ujein and travelled in great poverty over Guzerat and other parts of India. On his return to Malwa he found that his brother had resigned all worldly concerns and become a religious mendicant ; he therefore assumed charge of the province, and from that period commenced a career which led to the establishment of his power over the greatest part of India. He is said to have restored the Hindu monarchy to that splendour which it had lost through a succession of weak sovereigns, whose character had encouraged the governors of distant provinces to rebel, and to form the territories committed to their charge into independent states.*

Vikramaditya is described as the greatest monarch of his age, of which there is the most satisfactory proof in the fact that his era is still current throughout Hindustan. He encouraged literature beyond all former example. He invited learned brahmans from every part of India, and rewarded them with magnificent presents ;

* Malcolm's Memoir of Central India, I, 24.

and they have repaid him by investing him with immortality. They have exhausted the resources of flattery in their attempt to describe the magnitude of his power, and have assured us that without his permission the loadstone had no power over iron, or amber on the chaff of the field. So exemplary was his temperance, that while in the enjoyment of supreme power, he constantly slept on a mat, which, with a water-pot replenished from the spring, formed the whole furniture of his chamber. It is stated that while he extended his patronage to the worship of the gods and goddesses then rising into popularity, he himself continued to profess the old creed, and adored the one infinite and invisible God.*

For the legend of Vikramaditya's birth, see the article SENA in the Appendix.

Vikriti—A king of Chedi, the son of Jímúta.

Vikukshi—One of the hundred sons of Ikshváku: The V. P. has the following legend of this prince:—On one of the days of Ashtaka, Ikshváku being desirous of celebrating ancestral obsequies, ordered Vikukshi to bring him flesh suitable for the offering. The prince accordingly went into the forest and killed many deer and other wild animals for the celebration. Being weary with the chase and hungry, he sat down and ate a hare; after which being refreshed, he carried the rest of the game to his father. Vasishtha, the family priest, was summoned to consecrate the food; but he declared that it was impure in consequence of Vikukshi's having eaten a hare from amongst it, (making it thus, as it were, the residue of his meal.) Vikukshi was therefore abandoned by his offended father, and the epithet Sasáda, hare-eater, was affixed to him by the Guru. But on the death of Ikshváku, the sovereignty of Ayodhya descended to Vikukshi. The Matsya Purána says that Indra was born as Vikukshi, and that Ikshváku had a hundred and fourteen other sons who were kings of the countries south of Meru; and as many who reigned north of that mountain. Wilson says that it seems very probable that by these sons of Ikshváku we are to understand colonies or settlers in various parts of India.

* Marshman's History of India, I, 20.

Viloman—A Yádava chief, the son of Kapotaroman.

Vimada—1, A Rishi mentioned in the Rig Veda as on very friendly terms with Indra ; 2, A young prince to whom the Aṣvins brought in a car a bride named Kamadyú, who seems to have been the beautiful wife of Purumitra.—*O. S. T., V.*, 244.

Vimala—One of the sons of Sudyumna after his transformation.

Vimohana—One of the Narakas ; the place of bewildering ; for the punishment of the thief and the contemner of prescribed observances.

Vinata—A daughter of Daksha, who was married to Kaṣyapa and became the mother of Garuda and Aruṇa. The Váyu adds the metres of the Vedas as the daughters of Vinatá.

Vinaya—Good behaviour ; a son of Dharma by Lajja, modesty, daughter of Daksha, obviously allegorical.

Vinda—One of the sons of Jayasena, king of Avanti.

Vindhya—The chain of mountains that stretches across Central India ; in the Purános it is often restricted to the Sathpura range.

Vindhyasakti—The chief of the Kailakila Yavana kings ; a warrior of a mixed race, sprung from a Brahman father and a Kshatriya mother. Kailakila was a city in the Mahratta country. Wilson is of opinion that the Purános refer to a time when the Greek princes, or their Indo-Scythic successors, following the course of the Indus, spread to the upper part of the western coast of the peninsula.

Vindhya-Vasini—An ancient and still celebrated shrine of Durgá, a short distance from Mirzapur.

Vindumati—The wife of the Rája Mándhátri.

Vindusara—The son and successor of Chandragupta.

Vinita—One of the sons of the sage Pulastya.

Vipaschit—The Indra of the second Manwantara.

Vipra—1, One of the sons of Dhruva ; 2, A king of Magadha, the son of Srutanjaya.

Viprachitti—The king of the Dánavas, he was the son of Kaṣyapa and Danu, and the hero of many legends. He was one of the leaders in the contest between the gods and demons that took place after the churning of the ocean.

Vipritha—A prince of the solar race, the son of Chitrika.

Vipula—A mountain in Ilávrita, forming the western buttress to Meru.

Virabhadra—A formidable being created from the mouth of Śiva, for the purpose of spoiling the sacrifice of Daksha. He is thus described in the Váyu Purána.

"A divine being, with a thousand heads, a thousand eyes, a thousand feet; wielding a thousand clubs, a thousand shafts; holding the shell, the discus, the mace, and bearing a blazing bow and battle-axe; fierce and terrific, shining with dreadful splendour, and decorated with the crescent moon; clothed in a tiger's skin dripping with blood, having a capacious stomach, and a vast mouth armed with formidable tusks. His ears were erect; his lips were pendulous; his tongue was lightning; his hand brandished the thunderbolt; flames streamed from his hair; a necklace of pearls wound round his neck; a garland of flame descended on his breast. Radiant with lustre, he looked like the final fire that consumes the world. Four tremendous tusks projected from a mouth which extended from ear to ear. He was of vast bulk, vast strength, a mighty male and lord, the destroyer of the universe, and like a large fig-tree in circumference; shining like a hundred moons at once; fierce as the fire of love; having four heads, sharp white teeth, and of mighty fierceness, vigour, activity, and courage; glowing with the blaze of a thousand fiery suns at the end of the world; like a thousand undimmed moons; in bulk, like Himádri, Kailása, or Sumeru, or Mandara, with all its gleaming herbs; bright as the sun of destruction at the end of ages; of irresistible prowess and beautiful aspect; irascible, with lowering eyes, and a countenance burning like fire; clothed in the hide of the elephant and lion, and girt round with snakes; wearing a turban on his head, a moon on his brow; sometimes savage, sometimes mild; having a chaplet of many flowers on his head, anointed with various unguents, adorned with different ornaments and many sorts of jewels, wearing a garland of heavenly Karṇikára flowers, and rolling his eyes with rage. Sometimes he danced ; sometimes he laughed aloud ; sometimes he stood wrapt in meditation ; sometimes he trampled upon the earth ; sometimes he sang ; sometimes he wept repeatedly. And he was endowed with the faculties of wisdom, dispassion, power, penance, truth, endurance, fortitude, dominion, and self-knowledge."

Viraj—A person of a mythical or mystical character. Manu says " Having divided his own substance, the mighty power of Brahmá became half male, half female : and from that female he produced Viráj. Know me to be that person whom the male Viráj produced by himself." The Linga and Váyu Purána describe the origin of Viráj and Satarúpá from Brahmá ; in the first instance, and in the second, with Manu, who is termed Vairája, is the son of Viráj. It is also explained allegorically ; Viráj being all male animals, Satarúpá all female animals.

Viraja—One of the Rájas of India in the Swayambhuva or first Manwantara : he was the son of Tvashtri.

Virajas—1, A son of the sage Paurnamása ; 2, A son of the sage Vasishtha.

Virana—1, A sage, the father of Viraní and Asikní ; 2, A teacher of the White Yajush.

Virani—The daughter of the above, and mother of the Manu Chákshusa.

Virat—1, One of the Rájas of India in the first Manwantara ; the son of Nará ; 2, The material universe—Brahmáṇda.

Virata—The fourth book of the Mahábharata is called Viráta-Parva, as it recounts the adventures of the Páṇḍavas, when, being obliged to live incognito, they journeyed to the court of king Viráta, and entered his service in various disguises. Viráta's capital was called Matsya, (or sometimes Upaplavya.) There, four months after the arrival of the Páṇḍavas, a great festival was held, at which a number of wrestlers exhibited their prowess. Bhíma then astonished Viráta by dashing to the ground and killing the strongest of the wrestlers named Jimúta.

When Suṣarman, king of Trigarta, made a raid into Viráta's territory for the sake of plunder and carried off his cattle, Viráta, accompanied by all the Páṇḍavas except Arjuna, invaded Trigarta to recover the property. A great battle was fought and Viráta was taken prisoner by Suṣarman. Bhíma, as usual, tore up a tree and prepared to rescue him ; but Yudhishthira advised him not to display his strength too conspicuously, lest he should be recognised. He then took a bow, pursued Suṣarman, defeated him, released Viráta, and recovered the cattle.

Virochana—A Daitya, the son of Prahláda.

Viruddhas—A class of deities in the tenth Mauwantara.

Virupa—An ancient rája who reigned somewhere on the banks of the Yamuná, he was the son of Ambarísha.

Virupaksha—One of the eleven Rudras.

Visakha—A sage, one of the sons of Kumára.

Visakha—A lunar mansion in Járadghavi, in the Central Avashthána.

Visakhayupa—A king of Magadha, the son of Pálaka.

Visala—The founder and king of the city of Vaisálí ; he was the son of Trinavinda, by the celestial nymph Alambusha.

Visasana—One of the Narakas, for the punishment of the maker of swords, lances and other weapons.

Visoka—One of the eight original properties or perfections of man, called Siddhis ; it means exemption alike from infirmity or grief.

Visravas—The son of the great sage Pulastya, and father of Kuvera, the deity of wealth.

Visrutavat—A distinguished prince of the family of Ikshváku ; he was the son of Mahaswat ; and took part in the great war.

Vishnapu—In the legends regarding various persons delivered or favoured by the Aṣvins, it is said " they restored Vishṇápú, like a lost animal, to the sight of Viṣvaka, son of Krishṇa, their worshipper. The names both of Viṣvaka and Vishṇápú occur in the Rig Veda."—*O. S. T., V., p.* 244.

Vishnu—The second person of the mythological Hindu triad, and now the most celebrated and popular of all the gods of India. But it appears from the Rig-Veda that Indra at that time was regarded as superior to Vishṇu, who is there classed with Varuṇa, the Maruts, Rudra, Váyu, the luminous deities called Ádityas, and, others. "There is no trace of Vishṇu, or anything relating to him in the Institutes of Manu, although the allusions to idolaters and the worship of inferior gods might possibly have some reference to him also." "In the Mahábhárata, Vishṇu is often identified with the supreme spirit; but while in some portions of this poem—the different parts of which belong to different epochs of Hindu antiquity—he is thus regarded as the most exalted deity; he is again, in others, represented as paying homage to Śiva (q. v.), the third person of the Trimúrti, and as acknowledging the superiority of this god over himself. Taking, therefore, the Mahábhárata as a whole, he does not occupy, in this epos, the exclusive supremacy which is assigned to him in the Rámáyana, and still more in those Puránas especially devoted to his praise.

"The large circle of myths relating to Vishṇu, in the epic poems and Puránas, is distinguished by a feature which, though not quite absent from the mythological history of Śiva, especially characterises that of Vishṇu. It arose from the idea, that whenever a great disorder, physical or moral, disturbed the world, Vishṇu descended 'in a small portion of his essence' to set it right, to restore the law, and thus to preserve creation. Such descents of the god are called his *Avatáras* (from *ava* and *tri*, descend); and they consist in Vishṇu's being supposed to have either assumed the form of some wonderful animal or superhuman being, or to have been born of human parents, in a human form, always, of course, possessed of miraculous properties. Some of these Avatáras are of an entirely cosmical character; others, however, are probably based on historical events, the leading personage of which was gradually endowed with divine attributes, until he was regarded as the incarnation of the deity itself. With the exception of the last, all these Avatáras belong to the past ; the last, however, is yet to come."*

"His ten avatáras are: '1, The Matsya, or fish. In this avatár, Vishṇu descended in the form of a fish to save the pious king Satyavrata, who with the seven Rishis and their wives had taken refuge in the ark to escape the deluge which then destroyed the earth ; 2, The Kúrma, or Tortoise. In this he descended in the form of a tortoise, for the purpose of restoring to man some of the comforts lost during the flood. To this end he stationed himself at the bottom of the ocean, and allowed the point of the great mountain Mandara to be placed upon his back, which served as a hard axis, whereon the gods and demons, with the serpent Vásuki twisted round the mountain for a rope, churned the waters for the recovery of the amrita or nectar, and fourteen other sacred things ; 3, The Varáha, or Boar. In this he descended in the form of a boar to rescue the earth from the power of a demon called 'golden-eyed,' Hiraṇyáksha. This demon had seized on the earth and carried it with him into the depths of the ocean. Vishṇu dived into the abyss, and after a contest of a thousand years slew the monster ; 4, The Narasinha, or Man-lion. In this monstrous shape of a creature half-man, half-lion, Vishṇu delivered the earth from the tyranny of an insolent demon called Hiraṇyakaśipu ; 5, Vámana, or Dwarf. This avatár happened in the second age of the Hindus or Tretáyug, the four preceding are said to have occurred in the first or Satyayug ; the object of this avatár was to trick Bali out of the dominion of the three worlds. Assuming the form of a wretched dwarf he appeared before the king and asked, as a boon, as much land as he could pace in three steps. This was granted ; and Vishṇu immediately expanding himself till he filled the world, deprived Báli at two steps of heaven and earth, but in consideration of some merit, left Pátáḷa still in his dominion ; 6, Parasuráma ; 7, Rámachandra ; 8, Krishṇa, or according to some Balaráma ; 9, Buddha. In this avatár, Vishṇu descended in the form of a sage for the purpose of making some reform in the religion of the Brahmans, and especially to reclaim them from their proneness to

* Chambers' Encyclopædia.

animal sacrifice. Many of the Hindus will not allow this to have been an incarnation of their favourite god ; 10, Kalki, or White Horse. This is yet to come. Vishṇu mounted on a white horse, with a drawn scimitar, blazing like a comet, will, according to prophecy, end this present age, viz., the fourth or Kaliyug, by destroying the world, and then renovating creation by an age of purity."*

"This number and enumeration of Avatáras, however, was not at all times the same. The Mahábhárata, though also mentioning ten, names successively the Hansa-, tortoise-, fish-, boar-, man-lion-, dwarf-, Paraṣu-Ráma-, Ráma-, Sátvata-, and Kalkin-Avatáras. The Bhágavata-Purána speaks of twenty-two Avatáras of Vishṇu, which, for instance, also comprise Prithu, (q. v.), Dhanvantari, the god of medicine ; and Kapila, the reputed founder of the Sánkhya (q. v.) philosophy. Other works have twenty-four Avatáras, or even call them numberless ; but the generally-received Avatáras, are those ten mentioned before."†

Vishnu-loka—Vaikuntha, the lofty world of Vishṇu.

Vishnu-Purana—"The Vishnu-Purána most closely conforms to the definition of a Pancha-lakshaṇa Purána, or one which treats of five specified topics. It comprehends them all ; and, although it has infused a portion of extraneous and sectarial matter, it has done so with sobriety and with judgment, and has not suffered the fervour of its religious zeal to transport it into very wide deviations from the prescribed path. The legendary tales which it has inserted are few, and are conveniently arranged, so that they do not distract the attention of the compiler from objects of more permanent interest and importance.

The first book of the six, into which the work is divided, is occupied chiefly with the details of creation, primary (Sarga) and secondary (Pratisarga) ; the first explaining how the universe proceeds from Prakṛiti or eternal crude matter ; the second, in what manner the forms of things are developed from the elementary substances previously evolved, or how they re-appear after their

* Williams' English Sanskrit Dictionary. † Chambers' Encyclopædia.

temporary destruction. Both these creations are periodical; but the termination of the first occurs only at the end of the life of Brahmá, when not only all the gods and all other forms are annihilated, but the elements are again merged into primary substance, besides which, one only spiritual being exists. The latter takes place at the end of every Kalpa or day of Brahmá, and affects only the forms of inferior creatures, and lower worlds; leaving the substance of the universe entire, and sages and gods unharmed. The explanation of these events involves a description of the periods of time upon which they depend, and which are, accordingly, detailed. Their character has been a source of very unnecessary perplexity to European writers; as they belong to a scheme of chronology wholly mythological, having no reference to any real or supposed history of the Hindus, but applicable, according to their system, to the infinite and eternal revolutions of the universe. In these notions, and in that of the co-eternity of spirit and matter, the theogony and cosmogony of the Purânas, as they appear in the Vishṇu Purána, belong to and illustrate systems of high antiquity, of which we have only fragmentary traces in the records of other nations.

The course of the elementary creation is, in the Vishṇu, as in other Puránas, taken from the Sánkhya philosophy; but the agency that operates upon passive matter is confusedly exhibited, in consequence of a partial adoption of the illusory theory of the Vedánta philosophy, and the prevalence of the Pauráṇik doctrine of pantheism. However incompatible with the independent existence of Pradhána or crude matter, and however incongruous with the separate condition of pure spirit or Purusha, it is declared, repeatedly, that Vishṇu, as one with the supreme being, is not only spirit, but crude matter, and not only the latter, but all visible substance, and Time. He is Purusha, 'spirit;' Pradhána, 'crude matter;' Vyakta, 'visible form;' and Kála, 'time.' This cannot but be regarded as a departure from the primitive dogmas of the Hindus, in which the distinctness of the Deity and his works was enunciated; in which, upon his willing the world to be, it was; and in which his interposition in creation, held to be inconsistent with the quiescence of perfection, was explained away by the personification of attributes in action, which afterwards came to be considered as real divinities, Brahmá, Vishṇu, and Śiva, charged, severally, for a given season, with the creation, preservation, and temporary annihilation of material forms. These divinities are declared to be no other than Vishṇu. In Śaiva Puránas, they are, in like manner, identified with Śiva; the Puránas thus displaying and explaining the seeming incompatibility, of which there are traces in other ancient mythologies, between three distinct hypostases of one superior deity, and the identification of one or other of those hypostases with their common and separate original.

After the world has been fitted for the reception of living creatures, it is peopled by the will-engendered sons of Brahmá, the Prajápatis or patriarchs, and their posterity. It would seem as if a primitive tradition of the descent of mankind from seven holy personages had at first prevailed, but that, in the course of time, it had been expanded into complicated, and not always consistent, amplification. How could these Rishis or patriarchs have posterity? It was necessary to provide them with wives. In order to account for their existence, the Manu Swáyambhuva and his wife Satarúpá were added to the scheme; or Brahmá becomes twofold, male and female; and daughters are then begotten, who are married to the Prajápatis. Upon this basis various legends of Brahmá's double nature, some, no doubt, as old as the Vedas, have been constructed. But, although they may have been derived, in some degree, from the authentic tradition of the origin of mankind from a single pair, yet the circumstances intended to give more interest and precision to the story are, evidently, of an allegorical or mystical description, and conduced, in apparently later times, to a coarseness of realization which was neither the letter nor spirit of the original legend. Swáyambhuva, the son of the self-born or uncreated, and his wife Satarúpá, the hundred-formed or multiform, are, themselves, allegories; and their female descendants, who become the wives of the Rishis, are Faith, Devotion, Content, Intelligence, Tradition, and the like; whilst, amongst their posterity, we have the different phases of the moon and the sacrificial fires. In another creation, the chief source of creatures is the patriarch Daksha (ability,) whose daughters—Virtues, or Passions, or Astronomical Phenomena—are the mothers of all existing things. These legends, perplexed as they appear to be, seem to admit of allowable solution, in the conjecture that the Prajápatis and Rishis were real personages, the authors of the Hindu system of social, moral, and religious obligations, and the first observers of the heavens, and teachers of astronomical science.

The regal personages of the Swáyambhuva Manwantara are but few; but they are described, in the outset, as governing the earth in the dawn of society, and as introducing agriculture and civilization. How much of their story rests upon a traditional remembrance of their actions, it would be useless to conjecture; although there is no extravagance in supposing that the legends relate to a period prior to the full establishment, in India, of the Brahmanical institutions. The legends of Dhruva and Prahláda, which are intermingled with these particulars, are, in all probability, ancient; but they are amplified, in a strain conformable to the Vaishṇava purport of this Purána, by doctrines and prayers asserting the identity of Vishṇu with the Supreme. It is clear that the stories do not originate with this Purána. In that of Prahláda, particularly, circumstances essential to the completeness of the story are only alluded to, not recounted; showing, indisputably, the writer's having availed himself of some prior authority for his narration.

The second book opens with a continuation of the kings of the first Manwantara; amongst whom, Bharata is said to have given a name to India, called, after him, Bhárata-varsha. This leads to a detail of the geographical system of the Puránas, with mount Meru, the seven circular continents, and their surrounding oceans, to the limits of the world; all of which are mythological fictions, in which there is little reason to imagine that any topographical truths are concealed. With regard to Bhárata or India, the case is different. The mountains and rivers which are named are readily verifiable; and the cities and nations that are particularized may, also, in many instances, be proved to have had a real existence. The list is not a very long one, in the Vishṇu Purána, and is, probably, abridged from some more ample detail, like that which the Mahábhárata affords, and which, in the hope of supplying information with respect to a subject yet imperfectly investigated, the ancient political condition of India, I have inserted and elucidated.

The description which this book also contains of the planetary and other spheres, is equally mythological, although occasionally presenting practical details and notions in which there is an approach to accuracy. The concluding legend of Bharata—in his former life, the king so named, but now a Brahman, who acquires true wisdom, and thereby attains liberation—is, palpably, an invention of the compiler, and is peculiar to this Purána.

The arrangement of the Vedas and other writings considered sacred by the Hindus,—being, in fact, the authorities of their religious rites and belief,—which is described in the beginning of the third book, is of much importance to the history of Hindu literature and of the Hindu religion. The sage Vyása is here represented, not as the author, but the arranger or compiler of the Vedas, the Itihásas, and Puránas. His name denotes his character, meaning the 'arranger' or 'distributor;' and the recurrence of many Vyásas, many individuals who new-modelled the Hindu scriptures, has nothing, in it, that is improbable, except the fabulous intervals by which their labours are separated. The re-arranging, the refashioning, of old materials is nothing more than the progress of time would be likely to render necessary. The last recognized compilation is that of Kṛishṇa Dwaipáyana, assisted by Brahmans who were already conversant with the subjects respectively assigned to them. They were the members of a college, or school, supposed, by the Hindus, to have flourished in a period more remote, no doubt, than the truth, but not at all unlikely to have been instituted at some time prior to the accounts of India which we owe to Greek writers, and in which we see enough of the system to justify our inferring that it was then entire. That there have been other Vyásas and other schools since that date, that Brahmans unknown to fame have remodelled some of the Hindu scriptures, and especially, the Puránas, cannot reasonably be contested, after dispassionately weighing the strong internal evidence, which all of them afford, of the intermixture of unauthorized and comparatively modern ingredients. But the same internal testimony furnishes proof, equally decisive, of the anterior existence of ancient materials ; and it is, therefore, as idle as it is irrational, to dispute the antiquity or authenticity of the greater portion of the contents of the Purânas, in the face of abundant positive and circumstantial evidence of the prevalence of the doctrines which they teach, the currency of the legends which they narrate, and the integrity of the institutions which they describe, at least three centuries before the Christian era. But the origin and development of their doctrines, traditions, and institutions were not the work of a day ; and the testimony that establishes their existence three centuries before Christianity, carries it back to a much more remote antiquity, to an antiquity that is, probably, not surpassed by any of the prevailing fictions, institutions, or beliefs, of the ancient world.

The remainder of the third book describes the leading institutions of the Hindus, the duties of castes, the obligations of different stages of life, and the celebration of obsequial rites, in a short but primitive strain, and in harmony with the laws of Manu. It is a distinguishing feature of the Vishṇu Purâna, and it is characteristic of its being the work of an earlier period than most of the Purânas, that it enjoins no sectarial or other acts of supererogation ; no Vratas, occasional self-imposed observances ; no holydays, no birthdays of Krishṇa, no nights dedicated to Lakshmí ; no sacrifices or modes of worship other than those conformable to the ritual of the Vedas. It contains no Máhâtmyas or golden legends, even of the temples in which Vishṇu is adored.

The fourth book contains all that the Hindus have of their ancient history. It is a tolerably comprehensive list of dynasties and individuals ; it is a barren record of events. It can scarcely be doubted, however, that much of it is a genuine chronicle of persons, if not of occurrences. That it is discredited by palpable absurdities in regard to the longevity of the princes of the earlier dynasties, must be granted ; and the particulars preserved of some of them are trivial and fabulous. Still, there is an inartificial simplicity and consistency in the succession of persons, and a possibility and probability in some of the transactions, which give to these traditions the semblance of authenticity, and render it likely, that they are not altogether without foundation. At any rate, in the absence of all other sources of information, the record, such as it is, deserves not to be altogether set aside. It is not essential to its credibility, or its usefulness, that any exact chronological adjustment of the different reigns should be attempted. Their distribution amongst the several Yugas, undertaken by Sir William Jones, or his Pandits, finds no countenance from the original texts, further than an incidental notice of the age in which a particular monarch ruled, or the general fact that the dynasties prior to Krishṇa precede the time of the Great War and the beginning of the Kálí age; both which events we are not obliged, with the Hindus, to place five thousand years ago. To that age the solar dynasty of princes offers ninety-three descents, the lunar, but forty-five; though they both commence at the same time. Some names may have been added to the former list, some omitted in the latter; and it seems most likely, that, notwithstanding their synchronous beginning, the princes of the lunar race were subsequent to those of the solar dynasty. They avowedly branched off from the solar line; and the legend of Sudyumna, that explains the connexion, has every appearance of having been contrived for the purpose of referring it to a period more remote than the truth. Deducting, however, from the larger number of princes a considerable proportion, there is nothing to shock probability in supposing, that the Hindu dynasties and their ramifications were spread through an interval of about twelve centuries anterior to the war of the Mahábhárata, and, conjecturing that event to have happened about fourteen centuries before Christianity, thus carrying the commencement of the regal dynasties of India to about two thousand six hundred years before that date. This may, or may not, be too remote; but it is sufficient, in a subject where precision is impossible, to be satisfied with the general impression, that, in the dynasties of kings detailed in the Purápas, we have a record which, although it cannot fail to have suffered detriment from age, and may have been injured by careless or injudicious compilation, preserves an account, not wholly undeserving of confidence, of the establishment and succession of regular monarchies, amongst the Hindus, from as early an era, and for as continuous a duration, as any in the credible annals of mankind.

After the date of the great war, the Vishṇu Purána, in common with those Puránas which contain similar lists, specifies kings and dynasties with greater precision, and offers political and chronological particulars to which, on the score of probability, there is nothing to object. In truth, their general accuracy has been incontrovertibly established. Inscriptions on columns of stone, on rocks, on coins, deciphered only of late years, through the extraordinary ingenuity and perseverance of Mr. James Prinsep, have verified the names of races and titles of princes—the Gupta and Andhra Rájas, mentioned in the Puránas—and have placed beyond dispute the identity of Chandragupta and Sandrocoptus ; thus giving us a fixed point from which to compute the date of other persons and events. Thus, the Vishṇu Purána specifies the interval between Chandragupta and the Great War to be eleven hundred years ; and the occurrence of the latter little more than fourteen centuries B. C., remarkably concurs with inferences of the like date from different premises. The historical notices that then follow are considerably confused ; but they probably afford an accurate picture of the political distractions of India at the time when they were written : and much of the perplexity arises from the corrupt state of the manuscripts, the obscure brevity of the record, and our total want of the means of collateral illustration.

The fifth book of the Vishṇu Purána is exclusively occupied with the life of Krishṇa. This is one of the distinguishing characteristics of the Purána, and is one argument against its antiquity. It is possible, though not yet proved, that Krishṇa, as an Avatára of Vishṇu, is mentioned in an indisputably genuine text of the Vedas. He is conspicuously prominent in the Mahábhárata, but very contradictorily described there. The part that he usually performs is that of a mere mortal ; although, the passages are numerous that attach divinity to his person. There are, however, no descriptions, in the Mahábhárata, of his juvenile frolics, of his sports in Vṛindávana, his pastimes with the cow-boys, or even his destruction of the Asuras sent to kill him. These stories have, all, a modern complexion ; they do not harmonize with the tone of the ancient legends, which is, generally, grave, and, sometimes, majestic. They are the creations of a puerile taste and grovelling imagination. These chapters of the Vishṇu Purána offer some difficulties as to their originality. They are the same as those on the same subject in the Brahmá Purána : they are not very dissimilar to those of the Bhágavata. The latter has some incidents which the Vishṇu has not, and may, therefore, be thought to have improved upon the prior narrative of the latter. On the other hand, abridgment is equally a proof of posteriority as amplification. The simpler style of the Vishṇu Purána is, however, in favour of its priority ; and the miscellaneous composition of the Brahmá Purána renders it likely to have borrowed these chapters from the Vishṇu. The life of Krishṇa in the Hari Vamṣa and the Brahmá Vaivarta are, indisputably, of later date.

The last book contains an account of the dissolution of the world, in both its major and minor cataclysms ; and, in the particulars of the end of all things by fire and water, as well as in the principle of their perpetual renovation, presents a faithful exhibition of opinions that were general in the ancient world. The metaphysical annihilation of the universe, by the release of the spirit from bodily existence, offers, as already remarked, other analogies to doctrines and practices taught by Pythagoras and Plato, and by the Platonic Christians of later days.

The Vishṇu Purána has kept very clear of particulars from which an approximation of its date may be conjectured. No place is described of which the sacredness has any known limit, nor any work cited of probable recent composition. The Vedas, the Puránas, other works forming the body of Sanskrit literature, are named ; and so is the Mahábhárata, to which, therefore, it is subsequent. Both Bauddhas and Jainas are adverted to. It was, therefore, written before the former had disappeared. But they existed, in some parts of India, as late as the twelfth century, at least ; and it is probable that the Purána was compiled before that period. The Gupta kings reigned in the seventh century. The historical record of the Purána which mentions them was, therefore, later ; and there seems little doubt that the same alludes to the first incursions of the Mohammedans, which took place in the eighth century; which brings it still lower. In describing the latter dynasties, some, if not all, of which were, no doubt, contemporary, they are described as reigning, altogether, one thousand seven hundred and ninety-six years. Why this duration should have been chosen does not appear; unless, in conjunction with the number of years which are said to have elapsed between the Great War and the last of the Andhra dynasty, which preceded these different races, and which amounted to two thousand three hundred and fifty, the compiler was influenced by the actual date at which he wrote. The aggregate of the two periods would be the Káli year 4146, equivalent to A. D. 1045. There are some variety and indistinctness in the énumeration of the periods which compose this total: but the date which results from it is not unlikely to be an approximation to that of the Vishṇu Purána."—*Wilson's Works, Vol. VI,* 102–112.

Visva—A daughter of the patriarch Daksha, who was married to Dharma and became the mother of the Visvadevas.

Visvabhavana—A name of Vishṇu, as creator of the universe; meaning one with crude nature.

Visvachi—One of the Daiviki Apsarasas, or divine nymphs who engage in the interruption of the penances of holy sages.

Visvadevas—A class of deities to whom sacrifices are daily offered. The worship of the Viṣvadevas forms a part of the general Sráddhas, and of the daily sacrifices of the householder. According to the Váyu this was a privilege conferred on them by Brahma and the Pitris, as a reward for religious austerities practised by them upon Himálaya. Their introduction as a specific class seems to have originated in the custom of sacrificing to the gods collectively, or to all the gods, as the name Viṣvadevas implies. They appear, however, as a distinct class in the Vedas, and their assumption of this character is therefore of ancient date. The daily offering to them is noticed by Manu.—*Wilson's Notes to Vishnu Purána.*

Visvagaswa—An ancient rája of the solar line—the son of Prithu.

Visvagjyotish—The eldest of the hundred sons of Satajit, who reigned in India in the first Manwantara.

Visvajit—1, A king of Hastinápura, the son of Jayadratha ; 2, A king of Magadha, the son of Satyajit.

Visvakarma—The celestial architect, the Indian Hephæstus, Mulciber, or Vulcan ; originally called Tvashtri (q. v.) The architect and artist of the gods. He was the son of the Vasu Prabhása and his wife, the lovely and virtuous Yogasiddha. He is said in the V. P. to be the author of a thousand arts, the mechanist of the gods, the fabricator of all ornaments, the chief of artists, the constructor of the self-moving chariots of the deities, and by whose skill men obtain subsistence. Sir W. Jones considers Visvakarma to be the Vulcan of the Greeks and Romans, being, like Vulcan, the forger of arms for the gods, and inventor of the agnyastra, or fire shaft, in the war between them and the Daityas or Titans.—*As. Res., Vol. I*, 264. See TVASHTRI.

Visvakarman, Visvakarya—Two of the seven principal solar rays.

Visvakena—1, The Manu of the fourteenth Manwantara according to the lists in the Matsya and Pádma Puránas ; 2, A king of Hastinápura, the son of Brahmadatta.

Visvamitra—A celebrated Rishi. According to the Rámáyana he had originally been a Kshatriya and a great warrior, but subsequently practised so may religious austerities in the Himálaya mountains that he ultimately became a brahman. His character is therefore somewhat anomalous. Max Müller considers that he opposed the ambition of the brahmans, and would not submit to their exclusive claims. He at length succeeded in gaining for himself and family the rights for which he struggled, and which the Brahmans had previously withheld from all but their own caste. Visvámitra, however, was reconciled as soon as he was allowed to share in the profits of the priestly power, and became a favourite hero in Brahmanical tradition.

When Mahárája Dasaratha was one day discussing with his Councillors the subject of his son Ráma's marriage, Visvámitra arrived at the gate of the palace, and desired the doorkeeper to go within and tell the Mahárája that Visvámitra the son of Gadhi, was there. The Mahárája on hearing the message rose up with his two priests and went out to meet the sage, whom he received with every honour, saying, " Your coming, O great sage, is as grateful to me as amrita, as the fall of rain in the proper season, as the birth of a son to a childless father, as the recovery of lost treasure, as the dawning of a great joy." Visvámitra then stated the object of his visit—that Ráma should accompany him back to his hermitage to destroy the Rákshasas ; an arrangement to which the Mahárája reluctantly consented. He then acted as Guru to Ráma and commanded him to slay Táraká ; removing his objections about killing a woman, and providing him with divine weapons and mantras. After the marriage of Ráma, Visvámitra retired to the Himálaya mountains. During a twelve years' famine, Triṣanku provided food for Visvámitra and his family, and the sage being highly pleased, elevated him in his living body to heaven. This legend Wilson thinks is astronomical, and alludes possibly to some reformation of the sphere by Visvámitra under the patronage of Triṣanku, and in opposition to a more ancient system advocated by the school of Vasishṭha, q. v. The fact of Visvámitra having been both a rishi and an officiating priest, is undoubted. If we look to the number of Vedic hymns ascribed to him and to his family, to the long devotion to sacerdotal functions which this fact implies, and to the apparent improbability that a person who had himself stood in the position of a king should afterwards have become a professional priest, we may find it difficult to believe that although (as he certainly was) a scion of royal stock, he had ever himself exercised royal functions.—*O. S. T., I,* 364.

" A kind of consecutive biography of Visvámitra is given in the first book of the Rámáyana, of which it forms one of the most interesting episodes. Its substance is as follows :—Once, when roaming over the earth with his armies, Visvámitra came to the hermitage of Vasishṭha, and was there received by the saint in the most sumptuous style. Vasishṭha could afford to entertain the king in this manner because he possessed a fabulous cow of plenty that yielded him everything he desired. Visvámitra becoming aware of the source of Vasishṭha's wealth, strongly wished to possess the cow, and asked Vasishṭha to sell her to him. The saint however refusing this offer, the king seized her, intending to carry her off by force. But the cow resisted and ultimately displayed her supernatural powers in producing from different parts of her body numerous peoples, and by them destroying the armies of Visvámitra. The king then had recourse to the magical weapons he possessed, but they were defeated by those of Vasishṭha, and to the humiliation thus inflicted on him he then gave vent in exclaiming: 'Contemptible is the might of a Kshatriya; a Brahman's might alone is might.' And reflecting what he should do in this emergency, he resolved to practise austerities in order to attain the rank of a Brahman. In consequence he went to the south, and performed severe penance during a thousand years; when at the end of this period the god Brahmá appeared to him, and announced that he had become a Rajarshi, or Royal Rishi. But Visvámitra was not satisfied with this degree of promotion, and continued his austerities for another such period. During that time, king Trisanku of Ayodhya, of the family of Ikshváku, had determined to perform a sacrifice that would enable him to proceed bodily to heaven, and solicited for this purpose the assistance of Vasishṭha, who was the family priest of "all the Ikshvákus." This saint, however, having declared the scheme of the king impossible, and his sons also having refused to act in their father's place, Trisanku told them he would resort to another priest. He applied to Visvámitra, who showed his power by performing the sacrifice so much desired by Trisanku, and accomplishing his object in spite of the resistance of Vasishṭha and his sons, and that of the gods themselves.

This event having caused a serious interruption in the austerities of Visvámitra, he proceeded to the forest Pushkara in the west, to remain undisturbed. It was then the tragic incident related under HARISCHANDRA occurred. It was in the forest that Sunaṣepha saw his uncle Visvámitra, and implored him to come to his rescue. Visvámitra first commanded fifty of his own sons to offer themselves up as a ransom for their cousin. And on their refusing to do so, cursed them to become outcastes: but afterwards taught Sunaṣepha two hymns, which if sung by him at the sacrifice would save his life. The liberation of Sunaṣepha having been effected, anḍ Visvámitra having continued his penance for another thousand years, Brahmá conferred on him the dignity of a Rishi. But not satisfied with this distinction he went on practising still fiercer austerities than ever. These the gods interrupted by sending a heavenly nymph Menaka, who excited his worldly passions; still in the end he attained the rank of a Maharshi, or great Rishi. And after two thousand years of still more rigorous penance which for a time was again interrupted by the allurements of a nymph Rambha, the gods headed by Brahmá, came to acknowledge that he had now become a Brahmarshi, or Brahman Rishi; and Vasishṭha himself was compelled to express acquiescence in the result he had achieved.

The above three paragraphs are abridged from Goldstücker's arṭicle in Chambers's Encyclopædia. Many other legends are given in Muir's O. S. T., Vol. I. Visvámitra's cruel treatment of Harischandra and his family has already been quoted. (See SAÍVYA). Various versions are given of the legend of Triṣanku; and of the conflicts between Vasishṭha and Visvámitra. Professor Lassen, who quotes the stories, makes the following remarks on their import:

"The legend of the struggle between Vasishṭha and Visvámitra embraces two distinct points; one is the contest between the priests and warriors for the highest rank; the other is the temporary alienation of the Ikshvákus from their family priests. Vasishṭha is represented as the exemplar of such a priest; and the story of Kalmáshapáda is related for the express purpose of showing by an example that the Ikshvákus, after they had retained him, were victorious; in his capacity of priest he continued to live on, and is the representative of his whole race. We may conclude from the legend that his descendants had acquired the position of family priests to the Ikshvákus, though neither he himself nor his son Śaktri belonged to their number. Triṣanku is the first prince who forsook them, and had recourse to Visvámitra. His successor Ambarísha received support from that personage, as well as from Richíka, one of the Bhrigus;—a family whose connection with the

Kuṣikas appears also in the story of Paruṣaráma. The hostility between the Ikshvákus and the family of Vasishṣṭha continued down to Kalmáshapáda. Visvámitra is represented as having intentionally fostered the alienation ; while Vasishṭha is represented as forbearing (though he had the power) to annihilate his rival.

The conflict between the two rivals, with its motives and machinery, is described in the forms peculiar to the fully-developed epos. To this style of poetry is to be referred the wonder-working cow, which supplies all objects of desire. There is no ground for believing in any actual war with weapons between the contending parties ; or in any participation of degraded Kshatriyas, or aboriginal tribes, in the contest ; for all these things are mere poetical creations. Besides, the proper victory of Vasishṭha was not gained by arms, but by his rod. The legend represents the superiority of the Brahmans as complete, since Visvámitra is forced to acknowledge the insufficiency of a warrior's power ; and acquires his position as a Brahman by purely Brahmanical methods.

From Visvámitra are derived many of the sacerdotal families which bear the common name of Kauṣika, and to which many rishis, famous in tradition belong. As there were also kings in this family, we have here an example of the fact that one of the old vedic races became divided, and in later times belonged to both of the two higher castes. It appears impossible that any of the aboriginal tribes should have been among the descendants of Visvámitra's sons, as the legend represents ; and the meaning of this account may therefore be that some of his sons and their descendants accepted the position of priests among these tribes, and are in consequence described as accursed."—*O. S. T., I*, 426.

Visvamitras—The Visvámitras are known as Kuṣikas or Kauṣikas ; that is, they came from Kush, to this day the name of a river near the Asia Palus, where M. Ferrier found the ruins of a large place called Kussan. The Kushan, he tells us, were a famous Scythian race, who held Balkh in remote antiquity. Sir H. Rawlinson found their bricks, with cuneiform Scythic legends at Susa and in the Persian Gulf. Kush is largely used in a local nomenclature in Central Asia. The Caspian Sea, Cashgar, Kashmere, Khas-Saks, (Sacæ or Cossaks) Caucas-as (Khas-mountain)

Cossæ or Cisü in Persia, the Bal-kash lake and the Kush, and these are but a mere sample, and it is supposed that the Scythians did not come to the Cushites, but that the Cushites colonized Mongolia as they colonized Arabia, Ethiopia and the N. coast of the Indian Ocean. Indra himself is called a son of Kuṣika. Fire and Indra-worship seem to have been introduced by the Visvamitras and to have supplanted a previous sun-worship of earlier immigrants.—*Calcutta Review.*

Visvarupa—1, A name of Vishṇu ; who is both Bhúteṣa, 'lord of created things ;' and Visvarúpa, 'universal substance ;' he is therefore as one with sensible things subject to his own control ; 2, A name of one of the Rudras.

Visvasaha—1, A king of Mithila, the son of Ilavila ; 2, Another king of Mithila, the son of Abhyutthi-taṣwa, descendant of Ráma.

Visvasphatika—A Rája of Magadha, who is said to have extirpated the Kshatryas and elevated fishermen, barbarians, Brahmans, and other castes, to power. His name is sometimes made Viṣwasphurtti.

Visvavasa—One of the sons of Purúravas.

Visvesa—A daughter of Daksha married to Dharma.

Vitahavya—A king of Mithila, the son of Sunaya.

Vitala—The second of the seven divisions of Pátáḷa ; whose soil is black.

Vitasta—A river, the modern Jhelum, but still called in Kashmere the Vitasta or Hydaspes.

Vitatha—Unprofitable ; a name given to Rája Bharatwája, who was a sage as well as king.

Vithi—A division of the planetary sphere.

Vitihotra—1, The ninth son of Priyavrata, according to the Bhágavata ; he is called Putra in the other Puranas, and adopted a religious life ; 2, The eldest son of Tálajaugha, a Yádava chief.

Vitihotras—A branch of the Haihaya tribe.

Vitunda—A demon, the son of Tuṇḍa; the Pádma Purána contains an account of its destruction by Bhágavati.

Vivaswat—1, A Prajápati; 2, One of the twelve Ádityas; 3, The Sun, and father of Vaivaswata Manu.

Vivinsati—A prince of the solar dynasty, the son of Vinsa.

Vraja—One of the sons of Havirdhána and uncle of the Prachetasas.

Vrata—An occasional self-imposed observance or ceremony.

Vrihadbala—A prince of the solar race, the son of Visrutavat; he was slain in the great war by Abhimanyu, the son of Arjuna.

Vrihadaswa—A Rája of Bhárata, the father of the celebrated Kuvalayaswa, q. v.

Vrihadbhanu—A Rája of Bhárata, the son of Vrihatkarman.

Vrihadisha—1, A king of Hastinápura, the son of Ajamídha; 2, One of the five sons of Haryyaṣwa, termed the Panchálas.

Vrihadratha—1, A Rája of Bhárata, the son of Bhadraratha; 2, A son of Uparichara the Vasu; 3, A son of Tigma of the race of Puru; 4, The last of the ten Mauryan kings of Magadha, the son of Sasadharman.

Vrihannaradiya Purana—A modern compilation, erroneously termed a Purána, containing panegyrical prayers addressed to Vishṇu, and injunctions to observe various rites and keep holy certain seasons in honour of him.

Vrihaspati—A sage, the son of Angiras, the priest and preceptor of the Devatas; a teacher of the science of government. He had a handsome wife named Tárá, who was carried off by Soma (the moon), which led to a fierce contest termed the Táraká war. The Daityas, Danavas, and other foes of the gods took part with Soma; whilst Indra and all the gods were the allies of Vrihaspati. Peace was not restored till Brahma interposed and compelled Soma to restore Tárá to her husband. Vrihaspati was Vyása of the fourth Manwantará.

Vrihaspati—The planet Jupiter; described in the V. P. as having a golden car drawn by eight pale-coloured horses.

Vrihatkarman—1, A prince, the son of the Rája of Bhárata, Bhadraratha ; 2, A king of Hastinápur, son of Vrihadvasu ; 3, A king of Magadha, son of Sukshatra.

Vrihatshana—A Rája of the solar race after the great war. His father Vrihadbala, was killed by Abhimanyu.

Vrihatkshatra—A prince of Bhárata, the son of Bhavanmanya.

Vrihat-sama—A portion of the Sáma Veda, created from the southern mouth of Brahma.

Vrijinivat—A Yádava prince, the son of Kroshtri.

Vrika—1, One of the sons of Prithu, according to the Bhágavata ; 2, The son of Rája Ruruka ; 3, A son of Krishṇa.

Vrikadeva—One of the daughters of Devaka, who was married to Vasudeva.

Vrikala, Vrikatejas—Two sons of Slishtí, and grandsons of Dhruva.

Vrisha—1, The Indra of the eleventh Manwantara ; 2, A Yádava chief, the son of Vítihotra.

Vrishadarbha—A Rája of the solar race, the son of Sivi.

Vrishakapi—An appellation of one of the eleven Rudras.

Vrishana—One of the hundred sons of the Mahárája Karttavirya.

Vrishaparvan—A powerful Dánava chief, the son of Kaṣyapa and Danu.

Vrishasena—One of the Anga kings, the son of Karṇa.

Vrishni—1, A Yádava chief, the eldest son of Madhu ; 2, Another Yádava chief, the son of Kunti or Kumbhi ; 3, A son of Satwata, a Rája of Mrittikavati ; 4, A cousin of the above, the son of Bhajamána.

Vrishnimat—A Rája of the solar race, the son of Chitraratha.

Vritra—The demon who personifies drought ; the cloud enemy of Indra, who imprisons the rain in the storm-cloud. He is represented as false and treacherous as he is malignant. He is termed the thief who hides away the rain-clouds. He constantly appears as the enemy of Indra, who is called Vritrahan, the Vritra-slayer, Vritra became a name applied to any enemy. "The Vrittra of the Vrittras denoted the most malignant of adversaries. So again Vrittra the thief is also called Ahi, the throttling snake, or dragon with three heads."*

"Who is that, without alarm,
Defies the might of Indra's arm;
That stands and sees without dismay
The approaching Maruts' dread array;
That does not shun in wild affright,
The terrors of the deadly fight?
'Tis Vrittra, he whose magic powers
From earth withhold the genial showers,
Of mortal men the foe malign,
And rival of the race divine
Whose demon hosts from age to age,
With Indra war unceasing wage,
Who, times unnumbered, crushed and slain,
Is ever newly born again,
And evermore renew the strife
In which again he forfeits life.
Perched on a steep aerial height,
Shone Vṛittra's stately fortress bright.
Upon the wall, in martial mood,
The bold gigantic demon stood,
Confiding in his magic arts,
And armed with store of fiery darts.
And then was seen a dreadful sight,
When god and demon met in fight.
His sharpest missiles Vṛittra shot,
His thunderbolts and lightnings hot
He hurled as thick as rain.
* * * * * *
And soon the knell of Vṛittra's doom
Was sounded by the clang and boom

* Cox, Mythology of the Aryan Nations.

Of Indra's iron shower ;
Pierced, cloven, crushed, with horrid yell,
The dying demon headlong fell
Down from his cloud-built tower."*

Vyadhi—Disease ; Represented as the son of Mritya, (Death.)

Vyadi—A brahman who stopped at the dwelling of Vararuchi on one occasion and solicited hospitality, as a stranger weary with long travel. He then became acquainted with Vararuchi's wonderful powers of memory—was instructed by him, and became a writer of note on philological topics.—*Wilson, III*, 165.

Vyahritis—The three mystical words, Bhúh, Bhuvar, Swar ; which, with the monosyllable Om, and the Vedas, are considered as forms of Vásudeva (Brahmá,) diversified as to their typical character, but essentially one and the same. The daily prayers of the Brahman commence with the formula, Om bhúh, bhuvar, swar ; Om earth, sky, heaven ; these three mystical terms called Vyáhritis, are scarcely of less sanctity than the Praṇava itself. Their efficacy, and the order of their repetition preceding the Gáyatri, are fully detailed in Manu, II, 76–81. In the Mitákshara they are directed to be twice repeated mentally, with Om prefixed to each ; Om bhúh, Om bhuvah, Om swar ; the breath being suppressed by closing the lips and nostrils.—*Wilson's Notes to Vishnu Purána.*

Vyakarana—Grammar ; an Anga of the Vedas. That a scientific study of Grammar was cultivated at a very early period of Hindu literature is borne out by the testimony of the oldest glossator on the Vedas, Yaska (q. v.) The oldest extant work, however, on Sanskrit Grammar is posterior to the work of Yaska ; it is the Grammar of Pánini (q. v.) which was criticised by Kátgáya, in the Várṭṭikas, these again being commented on and criticised by Patanjali in the *Mahábhásya*. (See PÁNINI, where some of the principal later works connected with his system are mentioned.)—GOLDSTUCKER.

Vyakta—Visible substance ; a form of Vishnu.

* MUIR, O. S. T., V, 133—5.

Vyansa—A powerful Dánava, the eldest son of Viprachitti.

Vyapti—Universal ; the inherent and essential presence of any one thing or property in another, as the deity in the universe, &c. In the Nyáya system of Gautama a Vyápti means a pervading rule. It is thus explained by Professor Max Müller : knowledge is a quality of the Self, in the same manner as colour is of light. It is inseparably connected with it, and is explained as the cause of every conception that is expressed in language. Knowledge is either remembrance or perception. Perception is two-fold, right or wrong. Right perception represents the thing such as it is, silver as silver. Wrong perception represents the thing as the thing is not, mother o'pearl as silver. Right perception is four-fold, sensuous, conclusive, comparative, and authoritative. It is produced by the senses, by inferring, by comparing, and by revealed authority.

The different kinds of sensuous perception arise from the different ways in which the organs of sense are brought into contact with their objects, which objects may be either substantial matter, or qualities and actions, as inherent in substance, or the Genus as inherent in substances, qualities and actions.

After sensuous knowledge comes conclusive knowledge, which is gained by means of inferring. Conclusive knowledge is for instance. " This mountain is a volcano," whereas our sensuous perception is only that the mountain smokes. In order to arrive from this at the conclusion that it is a volcano, we must be in possession of what is called a pervading rule or a Vyápti. This smoke is inseparably connected with fire, or as the Hindu calls it, that smokiness is pervaded by fieriness, that wherever there is smoke there is fire. If we possess this Vyápti, which we may remember by such instances as a culinary hearth, &c., then in order to arrive at conclusive knowledge we only require consideration, (parámarsa) in order to find out in any sensuous impressiop something which can be pervaded, something which can make the mountain the member of a Vyápti, this something being in our case the smoke. If we know that the smoke which we perceive is qualified to become part of a Vyápti (this Vyápti being ' wherever there is smoke there is fire'), then we know conclusively that this mountain is fiery because it smokes.

The conditions under which it is allowed to form a Vyápti, that is to say to form Universals, have occupied the attention of Hindu philosophers more than any other point in Logic. They distinctly exclude the mere accumulation of observations. For things they say may be together a hundred times and may still not be mutually inherent. They make exceptions for practical purposes. Their repeated observations may be turned into a general rule, but not in philosophical discussions. Volumes after volumes have been written on this subject, and though I do not believe they will throw new light on the question of the origin of Universals, yet they would furnish a curious parallel to the history of the European intellect.*

Vyasa—A great brahman sage who lived in the forest, and by a long course of religious penances had become emaciated and hideous in appearance. He is described as the son of Paráṣara and a fish girl named Matsya, who was employed as a ferry woman in one of the many small rivers which intersect eastern Bengal, and flow into the Brahmaputra. His original name was Krishṇa Dwaipáyana, but having become famous as the compiler of the Mahábhárata, and the Vedas, he is generally known by the name of Vyása, or "the arranger." Among all the Brahman sages of antiquity famous for their learning, their austerities, and their miracles few can be compared with the Rishi Vyása. The following legend is related to show that he was the direct ancestor of the Kauravas and Páṇḍavas who fought in the great war; but is considered by Mr. Wheeler to be open to the gravest suspicion. After the death of Rája Vichitra Vírya (q. v.) his widows were filled with sorrow, because they had no son to perpetuate the race of Bharata. The custom was that when a man died without issue, his brother or near kinsman should marry his widows. The Ráni Saṭyavati therefore applied to Bhíshma, who refused on account of his vow. She then requested the sage Vyása to take his place. He proceeded to the palace of Hastinápur and fulfilled the wishes of the Ráni; but his presence filled the widows with terror. The first shut her eyes when she beheld him, and she gave birth to a

* Indian Logic. Outline of the necessary Laws of Thought, by Archbishop of York. 286-90.

son who was blind, and who was named Dhritaráshtra ; and the second widow was so white with fear that she gave birth to a son who was pale, and who was named Páṇḍu. Then Satyavati requested Vyása to become the father of a third son who should be without blemish ; and the first widow would not go to him, but arrayed her maid servant in garments of her own, and sent her to the sage in her stead ; and the servant gave birth to a third son who was named Vidura. Thus were born three sons to the royal house at Hastinápur ; viz :—

Dhritaráshtra the blind ; Páṇḍu, the pale ; and Vidura, the slave-born.

Vyasas—Arrangers of the Vedas in every Dwápara age ; twenty-eight are enumerated : The following is the list contained in Vishṇu Purána :—

" Twenty-eight times have the Vedas been arranged by the great Rishis, in the Vaivaswata Manwantara in the Dwápara age ; and, consequently, eight and twenty Vyásas have passed away ; by whom, in their respective periods, the Veda has been divided into four. In the first Dwápara age, the distribution was made by Swayambhú (Brahmá) himself ; in the second, the arranger of the Veda (Vedavyása) was Prajápati (or Manu) ; in the third, Uṣanas ; in the fourth, Brihaspati ; in the fifth, Savitṛi ; in the sixth, Mrityu (Death, or Yama) ; in the seventh, Indra ; in the eighth, Vasishṭha ; in the ninth, Saraswata ; in the tenth, Tridháman ; in the eleventh, Trivrishan ; in the twelfth, Bharadwája ; in the thirteenth, Antariksha ; in the fourteenth, Vaprívan ; in the fifteenth, Trayyáruṇa ; in the sixteenth, Dhananjaya ; in the seventeenth, Kritanjaya ; in the eighteenth, Riṇajaya ; in the nineteenth, Bharadwája ; in the twentieth, Gautama ; in the twenty-first, Uttama, also called Haryátman ; in the twenty-second, Vena, who is likewise named Rájaṣravas ; in the twenty-third, Saumaṣushmáyaṇa, also Tṛiṇabindu ; in the twenty-fourth, Riksha, the descendant of Bhrigu, who is known also by the name Válmiki ; in the twenty-fifth, my father, Sakti, was the Vyása ; I was the Vyása of the twenty-sixth Dwápara, and was succeeded by Játúkarna ; the Vyása of the twenty-eighth, who followed him, was Krishṇa Dwaipayana. These are the twenty-eight elder Vyásas, by whom, in the preceding Dwápara ages, the Veda has been divided into four. In the next Dwápara, Drauṇi (the son of Droṇa) will be the Vyása, when my son, the Muni Krishṇa Dwaipáyana, who is the actual Vyása, shall cease to be (in that character)."

"A similar list is given in the Kúrma and Váyu Puránas. Many of the individuals appear as authors of different hymns and prayers in the Vedas; and it is very possible that the greater portion, if not all of them, had a real existence, being the framers or teachers of the religion of the Hindus before a complete ritual was compiled."—*Wilson's Notes to V. P.*

Vyavasaya—Perseverance. One of the allegorical sons of Dharma.

Vyaya—A name of Pradhána—meaning "that which may be expended."

Vyoman—A Rája of the solar race, the son of Dasárha.

Vyushta—A name of Day: night is called Usha, and the interval between them, Sandhya.

Y

Yadavas—The descendants of Yadu, the eldest son of Yayáti and Devayáni. A nomade race who grazed cattle and made butter, and occasionally migrated to different places accompanied by their cows and waggons. The time and circumstances under which they first entered Hindustan are alike unknown. At the birth of Krishṇa they appear to have settled in the neighbourhood of the city of Mathurá, the modern Muttra, on the banks of the river Jumna, and about a hundred and twenty miles to the south of the site of the ancient city of Hastinápur. They dwelt on both sides of the river, in the village of Vrindávana on the western bank, and in the country of Gokula on the opposite shore. They afterwards migrated to Dwáraka, on the western coast of the peninsula of Guzerat, above seven hundred miles from Hastinápur.

Krishṇa belonged to this tribe; and many mythical details seem to have been connected with its history for the purpose of exalting the tribe from which the favourite deity sprung. It is plain that great violence and disorder prevailed wherever the Yádavas settled. They were induced by Krishṇa to renounce the worship of Indra and substitute the mountain Govarddhana in his place; an incident which Mr. Wheeler thinks seems to imply a conflict between a low Fetische worship, and the worship of the Vedic deities.

The Puránas describe the destruction of the whole tribe in a drunken affray at Prabhása. The Mahábhárata says that all the Yádavas were slaughtered by the curse of the three Rishis, and all the sons and grandsons of Krishṇa were among the slain.

"The Rájas of Vijayanagur, who in the 15th century of the Christian era maintained a supremacy over the whole of the country south of the Krishṇa river, and thus possessed the last great Hindu empire which was established in India, claimed to be descendants of the Yádava tribe; and it is a curious fact that it was from one of the decayed chieftains of this fallen dynasty that the East India Company obtained, in the first half of the 17th century, the grant of land on the coast of Coromandel on which stands the modern city of Madras. The original grant on a gold plate appears to have been preserved for more than a century; but was finally lost in 1746 when Madras was captured by the French under Labourdonnais."—*Wheeler.*

Yadu—The eldest son of Yayáti, and ancestor of the Yádavas. When Yayáti ceased to reign he installed his youngest son Puru in the sovereignty, and consigned the southern districts of the kingdom to Yadu.

Yajna—Sacrifice; the character of Brahmanical sacrifice is thus expressed by Dr. Haug, in the Introduction to the Aitareya Brahmana.* "The sacrifice is regarded as the means for obtaining power over this and the other world, over visible as well as invisible beings, animate as well as inanimate creatures. Who knows its proper application, and has it duly performed, is in fact looked upon as the real master of the world: for any desire he may entertain, even if it be the most ambitious, can be gratified; any object he has in view can be obtained by means of it. The *Yajna* taken as a whole is conceived to be a kind of machinery, in which every piece must tally with the other; or a sort of large chain in which no link is allowed to be wanting; or a staircase by which one may ascend to heaven; or as a personage, endowed with all the characteristics of the human body. It exists from eternity and proceeded from the Supreme Being, (Prajápati or Brahmá *neuter*) along with the *Traividya, i. e.*, the three-fold science. The creation of the world was even regarded as the fruit of a sacrifice performed by the Supreme Being. The Yajna exists as an invisible thing at all times. It is like the latent power of electricity in an electrifying machine, requiring only the

* Vol. I, p. 73.

operation of a suitable apparatus in order to be elicited. It is supposed to extend, when unrolled from the Áhavaníya or sacrificial fire, (into which all oblations are thrown,) to heaven, forming thus a bridge or ladder, by means of which the sacrifice can communicate with the world of gods and spirits, and even ascend when alone to their abodes."

Yajna—Sacrifice; an allegorical son of the patriarch Ruchi, said to have been married to his sister Dakshina, "donation" to brahmans. At the spoiling of Daksha's sacrifice Yajna was decapitated, and afterwards became the constellation Mrigasiras, being elevated to the planetary region by Brahmá.

Yajnabahu—The name of one of the sons of Priyavrata, as given in the Bhágavata. See AGNIBÁHU.

Yajnas—Five are enumerated, which are translated great sacrifices, or great obligations: 1, Brahmayajna, sacred study; Pitriyajna, libations to the manes; Devayajna, burnt offerings to the gods; Baliyajna, offerings to all creatures; Nriyajna, hospitality.

The Prajápatiyajna, propagation of offspring, and Satyayajna, observance of truth, are apparently later additions.—*Wilson's Notes to V. P.*

Yajnasri—One of the Andhrabhritya rájas: the son of Swaskandha.

Yajnawalka—A teacher of the Rig Veda.

Yajnawalkya—A celebrated ascetic, the pupil of Vaisampáyana who adored the sun until the luminary in the form of a horse, appeared to him, and imparted to him the text of the Yájush called Ayátayáma (unstudied,) which were unknown to Vaisampáyana. It was Yajnawalkya who officiated as one of the Hotris, and cooked the sacrifice at the great Rájasuya of Yudhishthira. Professor Max Müller observes "that it would be a mistake to call Yajnawalkya the author, in our sense of the word of the Vájasaneya Sanhita and the Satapatha Brahmana. But we have no reason to doubt that it was Yájnawalkya who brought the ancient Mantras and Brahmanas into their present form." A. S. L.

"Yajnawalkya Vajasaneya was evidently a man of great influence, a leader of public opinion in his day; and one longs to know when he lived. But this is a subject still requiring much elucidation, as may be seen in the Introduction to Professor Goldstücker's Pánini."—*Mrs. Manning, A. & M. I.*

Yajur Veda—See Appendix.

Yajush—The Yajur Veda.

Yaksha—The son of Khasá and parent of the Yakshas, as his brother Rákshas was of the Rákshasas.

Yakshas—Minor deities; inferior divinities. Demi-gods especially attendant on Kuvera, and employed by him on the care of his garden and treasures.

Yama—1, One of the minor Dwípas; 2, A watch of the day or night.

Yama—The monarch of the Pitris and judge of the dead—the Pluto of Hindu mythology. He is represented to be the son of the Sun.

"Yama is the son of Vivasvat, and of Saraṇyú, the immortal daughter of Tvashtri. He is elsewhere said to have been one of the original pair of human beings, and to have sprung from the Gandharva, a deity of the atmosphere, and his wife. In the same hymn he is said to have resisted the solicitations of his twin sister Yamí to form a sexual union with her for the continuation of the species. He was the first of mortals who died, and discovered the way to the other world; he guides other men thither, and assembles them in a home which is secured to them for ever. In one place he is represented as carousing with the gods under a leafy tree. He is a king and dwells in celestial light, in the innermost sanctuary of heaven, where the departed behold him associated in blessedness with Varuṇa. He grants luminous abodes in heaven to the pious, who dwell with him in festive enjoyment.

"In the Rig Veda Yama is nowhere represented (as he is in the later Indian Mythology,) as having anything to do with the punishment of the wicked. Nevertheless, Yama is still, to some extent, an object of terror. He is represented as having two insatiable dogs, with four eyes and wide nostrils, which guard the road to his abode, and which the departed are advised to hurry past with all possible speed. These dogs are said to wander about among men as his messengers, for the purpose of summoning men to the presence of their master, who is in another place identified with death, and is described as sending a bird as the herald of doom. Again, death is said to be the messenger of Yama, who conveys the spirits of men to the abode of their forefathers.

"To great king Yama homage pay,
Who was the first of men that died,
That crossed the mighty gulf, and spied
For mortals out the heavenly way.

No power can ever close the road
Which he to us laid open then,
By which in long succession, men
Ascend to his sublime abode.

By it our fathers all have passed;
And that same path we too shall trace,
And every new succeeding race
Of mortal men, while time shall last.

The god assembles round his throne
A growing throng, the good and wise
All those whom, scanned with searching eyes,
He recognizes as his own.

Departed mortal, speed from earth
By those old ways thy sires have trod;
Ascend, behold the expectant god,
Who calls thee to a higher birth.

First must each several element
That joined to form thy living frame
Flit to the region whence it came,
And with its parent source be blent.

Thine eye shall seek the solar orb,
Thy life-breath to the wind shall fly,
Thy part ethereal to the sky;
Thine earthy part shall earth absorb.

Thine unborn part shall Agni bright
With his benignest rays illume;
And guide it through the trackless gloom
To yonder sphere of life and light.

All imperfections leave behind;
Assume thine ancient form once more,
Each limb and sense thou hadst before,
From every earthly taint refined.

And now with heavenly glory bright,
With life intenser, nobler, blest,
With large capacity to taste
A fuller measure of delight.

Thou there once more each well known face
Shalt see of those thou lovedst here;
Thy parents, wife, and children dear,
With rapture shalt thou soon embrace.

The good which thou on earth hast wrought,
Each sacrifice, each pious deed,
Shall there receive its ample meed;
No worthy act shall be forgot.

In those fair realms of cloudless day
Where Yama every joy supplies,
And every longing satisfies
Thy bliss shall never know decay."

Muir, O. S. T., V, 329.

Yama—The first of the eight stages of Yóga, being self-government, of which five kinds are specified :—

1—Freedom from any wish to injure others.

2—Truth in reference to words and thoughts.

3—Freedom from appropriation of others' property in thought, word or deed.

4—The subjection of one's members in order to overcome desire.

5—Renunciation of all indulgence of pleasure.

Yama-gita—The song of Yama; a name given to the seventh chapter of the third book of the Vishṇu Purána.

Yamas—Moral duties; five acts of restraint: absence of cruelty or violence, (Ahinsa), honesty (Asteya), truth (Satya), chastity (Bramácháryya), disinterestedness (Aparigraha).

Yamas—Twelve deities, sons of Yajna and Dakshiṇa.

Yami—1, A daughter of Daksha and wife of Dharma; 2, A daughter of the sun, the twin sister of Yama; she became the Yamuna river.

Yamuna—A celebrated river, described in the Puránas as the daughter of the sun. There is a legend that Balaráma compelled the river to change its course and follow him in his wanderings; which Wilson thinks may allude to the construction of canals from the Jumna, for the purposes of irrigation.

Yasaś—A son of Dharma.

Yaska—A predecessor of Páṇini (q. v.) and author of Nirukta, explaining different Vedic words. Yáska was also the author of a Commentary which bears the name of Nirukta. "Besides the great importance which Yáksha's Nirukta possesses for a proper understanding of the Vedic texts; it is valuable also on account of several discussions which it raises on grammatical and other questions; and on account of the insight it affords us into the the scientific and religious condition of its time."—GOLDSTUCKER.

Yasoda—1, The daughter of king Samoravira, who was married to Varddhamána, who afterwards became the twenty-fourth Tirthankara of the Jains, Mahávira.

Yasoda—2, The nurse of Krishṇa; who was conveyed at his birth to the bed of Yaṣodá, by his father Vasudeva, and her own new born infant Yoganidrá, removed to the bed of Devakí, and destroyed by Kansa.

Yasodhara—The wife of Sahishnu and mother of Kámadeva.

Yati—One of the sons of Nahusha and brother of Yayáti.

Yavanas—Ionians or Greeks. The term Yavanas, though in later times applied to the Mohammedans, designated formerly the Greeks. They are placed by the V. P. in the west of Bhárata.

Yavinara--A king of Hastinápura, the son of Dwinudha and grandson of Hastin.

Yaudheya—The wife of Yudhishthira and mother of Devaka.

Yayati—The son of Rája Nahusha. He had two wives, Devayání, the daughter of Uṣanas, and Sarmiṣhthá, the daughter of Vṛishaparvan; of whom this genealogical verse is recited: "Devayání bore two sons, Yadu and Turvasu. Sarmiṣhthá, the daughter of Vṛishaparvan, had three sons, Druhyu, Anu, and Púru." Through the curse of Uṣanas, Yayáti became old and infirm before his time; but, having appeased his father-in-law, he obtained permission to transfer his decrepitude to any one who would consent to take it. He first applied to his eldest son, Yadu, and said: "Your maternal grandfather has brought this premature decay upon me. By his permission, however, I may transfer it to you for a thousand years. I am not yet satiate with worldly enjoyments, and wish to partake of them through the means of your youth. Do not refuse compliance with my request." Yadu, however, was not willing to take upon him his father's decay; on which, his father denounced an imprecation upon him, and said: "Your posterity shall not possess dominion." He then applied, successively, to Druhyu, Turvasu, and Anu, and demanded of them their juvenile vigour. They all refused, and were, in consequence, cursed by the king. Lastly, he made the same request of Sarmishthá's youngest son Púru, who bowed to his father, and readily consented to give him his youth, and receive, in exchange, Yayáti's infirmities, saying that his father had conferred upon him a great favour.

The king Yayáti being, thus, endowed with renovated youth,

conducted the affairs of State for the good of his people, enjoying such pleasures as were suited to his age and strength, and were not incompatible with virtue. He formed a connexion with the celestial nymph Viṣwáchí, and was wholly attached to her, and conceived no end to his desires. The more they were gratified, the more ardent they became; as it is said in this verse: "Desire is not appeased by enjoyment: fire fed with sacrificial oil becomes but the more intense. No one has ever more than enough of rice, or barley, or gold, or cattle, or women. Abandon, therefore, inordinate desire. When a mind finds neither good nor ill in all objects, but looks on all with an equal eye, then everything yields it pleasure. The wise man is filled with happiness, who escapes from desire, which the feeble-minded can with difficulty relinquish, and which grows not old with the aged. The hair becomes grey, the teeth fall out, as man advances in years; but the love of wealth, the love of life, are not impaired by age." "A thousand years have passed," reflected Yayáti, "and my mind is still devoted to pleasure: every day my desires are awakened by new objects. I will, therefore, now renounce all sensual enjoyment, and fix my mind upon spiritual truth. Unaffected by the alternatives of pleasure and pain, and having nothing I may call my own, I will, henceforth, roam the forests with the deer."

Having made this determination, Yayáti restored his youth to Púru, resumed his own decrepitude, installed his youngest son in the sovereignty, and departed to the wood of penance (Tapovana). To Turvasu he consigned the south-east districts of his kingdom; the west, to Druhyu; the south, to Yadu; and the north, to Anu; to govern, as viceroys, under their younger brother Púru, whom he appointed supreme monarch of the earth." V. P.

A different account is given in the Pádma Purána. It is there said that Yayáti was invited by Indra to heaven, and conveyed on the way thither by Mátali, Indra's charioteer. For the conversation that took place between them, see Mátali; the result was that Yayáti returned to earth, where, by his virtuous administration he rendered all his subjects exempt from passion and decay: Yama complained that men had ceased to die, and Indra sent Kámadeva and his daughter Asruvindumati to endeavour to excite passion in the breast of Yayáti ; they succeeded, and it was then the aged king asked his sons to give him their youth in exchange for his decrepitude. As related above they all refused except Púru, the youngest. Not long after Yayáti proceeded with his subjects to Indra and ultimately to the abode of Vishṇu.—*Wilson, III*, 37.

Yedillian—The wife of Ladurlad. It was on the latter that Southey makes the terrible curse of Kehama to rest. Ladurlad was at this time a widower, but his beloved daughter Kaliyal was miraculously preserved to him, and afforded him some solace amidst his wanderings and sufferings, so well depicted in Southey's poem. When at length by the descent of the Ganges to the earth the father and daughter are enabled to escape to Mount Meru and find a place of rest beyond the influence of Kehama's Curse, and then the long-lost Yedillian returns to him in this bower of bliss to complete his happiness. The scene is so affectingly described that the whole passage may be quoted :

Three happy beings are there here,
The Sire, the Maid, the Glendoveer ;
A fourth approaches, ... who is this
That enters in the Bower of Bliss ?
No form so fair might painter find
Among the daughters of mankind ;
For death her beauties hath refined,
And unto her a form hath given
Framed of the elements of Heaven ;
Pure dwelling place for perfect mind.
She stood and gazed on Sire and Child ;
Her tongue not yet had power to speak,
The tears were streaming down her cheek ;
And when those tears her sight beguiled,
And still her faltering accents fail'd,
The Spirit, mute and motionless,
Spread out her arms for the caress.
Made still and silent with excess
Of love and painful happiness.

The Maid that lovely form survey'd ;
Wistful she gazed, and knew her not,
But Nature to her heart convey'd
A sudden thrill, a startling thought,
A feeling many a year forgot,
Now like a dream anew recurring,
As if again in every vein
Her mother's milk was stirring.
With straining neck and earnest eye
She stretched her hands imploringly,
As if she fain would have her nigh,
Yet fear'd to meet the wish'd embrace,
At once with love and awe opprest.
Not so Ladurlad ; he could trace,
Though brighten'd with angelic grace,
His own Yedillian's earthly face ;
He ran and held her to his breast !
Oh joy above all joys of Heaven,
By Death alone to others given,
This moment hath to him restored
The early-lost, the long-deplored.

They sin who tell us Love can die,
With life all other passions fly,
All others are but vanity.
In Heaven Ambition cannot dwell,
Nor Avarice in the vaults of Hell ;
Earthly these passions of the Earth,
They perish where they have their birth ;
But Love is indestructible.
Its holy flame for ever burneth,
From Heaven it came, to Heaven returneth ;
Too oft on Earth a troubled guest,
At times deceived, at times opprest,
It here is tried and purified,
Then hath in Heaven its perfect rest :
It soweth here with toil and care,
But the harvest time of Love is there.

Oh ! when a Mother meets on high
The Babe she lost in infancy,
Hath she not then, for pains and fears,
The day of woe, the watchful night,
For all her sorrow, all her tears,
An over-payment of delight ?

Yoga—Union, junction ; in a spiritual sense it denotes union of separated with universal soul ; and with some latitude of expression it comes to signify the means by which such union is effected. In the Bhágavat Gítá it is variously applied, but ordinarily denotes the performance of religious ceremonies as a duty, and not for interested purposes. The word has accordingly been rendered 'devotion' by Wilkins [and by Mr. J. C. Thomson] and 'devotio' by Schlegel, in their translations of the Gítá. In the Vishṇu Purána it is used in a less general sense, and signifies reunion with spirit, through the exercises necessary to perfect abstraction as they are taught and practised by the followers of Patanjali.

Yoganidra—Personified delusion : the great illusory energy of Vishṇu, by whom, as utter ignorance, the whole world is beguiled. Yoganidrá is the sleep of devotion or abstraction, the active principle of illusion, personified, and also termed Máya and Mahamáyá, also Avidya or ignorance. In the Markáṇḍeya Purána she appears as Devi or Durgá, the Sakti or bride of Śiva ; but in the Vishṇu Purána as Vaishṇavi, or the Sakti of Vishṇu.

Yogasiddha—The lovely and virtuous daughter of Váchaspati who pervades the whole world without being devoted to it, was the wife of Prabhása, the eighth of the Vasus, and bore to him the patriarch Visvakarma, the architect and mechanist of the gods.

Yogi-Yogin—A devotee seeking the attainment of Yóga ; he has to pass through four principal stages :

1.—He learns the rules of Yóga.

2.—He acquires perfect knowledge.

3.—He employs this knowledge practically and overcomes the material influence of the primary elements.

4.—He destroys all consciousness of personality and individuality, (*ahankára*); and the soul thus becomes free from matter.

Thus by the prescribed methods, he has attained the state termed Yóga, the union of the living with the supreme soul; the identity of the living with the supreme spirit; of the Jívátma, with Brahmá; the identity of the contemplator with the object contemplated.

Yudamushti—One of the sons of the Yádava chief Ugrasena.

Yudhajit—1, A prince, the son of Asvapati, rája of Kekaya, and uncle of Bharata.

Then Bharat for the road prepared,
And with Satrughna forth he fared.
First to his sire he bade adieu,
Brave Ráma, and his mothers too.
Lord Yudhájit with joyful pride
Went forth, the brothers by his side,
And reached the city where he dwelt:
And mighty joy his father felt.

2, A prince, the second son of Vrishni, rája of Mrittikávati.

Yudhishthira—The eldest of the Páṇḍu princes. "The characters of the five brothers in the Mahábhárata are drawn with an individuality which is very unusual in Oriental poetry. They each have their distinguishing traits, which are often painted with much discrimination and even delicacy of touch in the lighter shades; and yet there evidently runs a family likeness through them all. To the European reader, Arjuna, the third brother is the most interesting, and approaches the nearest to our ideal of chivalry; many of his exploits remind us of Arthur's knights, or Charlemagne's paladins; and it is he who wins Draupadi as his wife in a tournament, where her father had offered her hand as the conqueror's prize. With the Hindus, however, Yudhishthira, the eldest, is the favourite; his cold passionless heroism is with them the *beau ideal* of humanity; and he moves through the poem in a calm majesty of self-possession, as if far above all the weaknesses of man, while the sorrows and joys which chequer his life.

'Viennent tonjours glisser sur son étre insensible,
Commes de gouttes déau sur un marbre poli.'*

Yudhishthira, as we have already seen, [PANDAVAS] was taught the use of the spear by Droṇa, but became more distinguished by wisdom and goodness than for military exploits. His uncle the Mahárája Dhritaráshtra decided that Yudhishthira had the best right to succeed him, and he was installed as Yuvarája. This excited the jealousy of his cousin Duryodhana, who expostulated with the old Mahárája until he agreed to divide the kingdom between them, when Yudhishthira and his brethren took leave of the Mahárája, and of all their kinsmen, and departed with their mother Kunti to the city of Váranávati. Before their departure they were cautioned by their uncle Vidura to beware of fire; and soon after their arrival they discovered a wicked plot that had been devised by Duryodhana and his friends for their destruction. A trusty retainer of Duryodhana's, named Purochana, had been sent on to prepare a handsome house in the city of Váranávati for the sons of Páṇḍu: and Purochana had built the walls of the house with lac or resin, mingled with hemp; so that some night when the Páṇḍavas were asleep, the doors might be fastened in the outside and the house set on fire, and all within it be consumed in the flames. Accordingly Purochana heartily welcomed the Páṇḍavas; and after having conducted them to the college of devotees, he led them to the house prepared for their reception, and set before them a collation of fruit, &c. Shortly after a man came from their uncle saying, "Vidura has sent me to dig an underground passage from your house, to deliver you from it, should it be set on fire." When the passage was completed Bhíma resolved that Purochana should fall into the snare he had laid for them. One day Kunti invited all the poor people of the city and gave them a feast; among her guests were a Bhíl woman and her five sons, who according to the practice of their tribe drank a large quantity of strong liquor, and then lay down and slept heavily. The same night a violent wind arose, and Bhíma stole out through the passage, and

* Westminster Review, Vol. I, p. 53.

strongly barricaded the house of Purochaa and set it on fire ; and the flames speedily destroyed the building and reached the house of the Páṇḍavas ; then Bhíma conducted his mother and brethren through the passage underground and hurried them away into the jungle. Next morning the people of the city saw that both houses were destroyed by fire, and believed that all the inmates had perished; for they discovered the blackened remains of Purochana and his servants, and also those of the Bhíl woman and her five sons, whom they took to be those of Kunti and the Páṇḍavas. The tidings now reached the city of Hastinápur, and the Kauravas greatly rejoiced at the supposed death of their enemies the Páṇḍavas ; but Bhíshma, Droṇa, and Dritaráshtra were affected even unto tears.

The Páṇḍavas having escaped into the jungle met with many adventures there. Once when the party, overcome with fatigue were all asleep except Bhíma, who stood by to guard them, an Asúra named Hidimba attacked him, but after a severe fight, Bhíma slew the cannibal. The sister of the Asúra then set up a terrible cry, but afterwards followed Bhíma and his party. She was ultimately married to him. They all afterwards dwelt in the city of Ekachakra, (q. v.). The next event of importance was the marriage of the five brothers to Draupadí, the beautiful daughter of Drupada, the Rája of Pánchála. At her Swayamvara the Kauravas and many distinguished Rájas assembled ; but all failed to bend the bow, when Arjuna disguised as a brahman, accomplished the feat, and shot the arrow in the eye of the golden fish, having first gone through the whirling Chakra below the fish. Draupadi then threw the garland round Arjuna's neck and accompanied him to the house of his mother. Afterwards by the advice of the sage Vyása she was married to all the five brothers. They then returned to Hastinápur on the invitation of Bhíshma, and were given the sovereignty of Khaṇḍava-prastha, as their half of the Ráj.

When the Páṇḍavas were settled in this new country, they built at first at Indra-prastha, cleared the jungle of Khaṇḍava, and drove out the Scythian tribe known as the Nágas. When they had thus established a supremacy over every bordering enemy, and proved to the satisfaction of their new subjects that they could protect cattle and harvests, they invited all their kinsmen and neighbours to a Rájasúya, and in the presence of all the people solemnly inaugurated their elder brother Yudhishthira as Rája of Khándaprastha. The ceremonies performed at the sacrifice were these: a number of priests marked out the spot, and strewed the place with the sacred kusa grass, kindled the sacrificial fire and chanted the Vedic hymns. The so-called Rájas who attended, were probably a rude company of half-naked warriors who feasted boisterously beneath the shade of trees.*

The Rájasúya excited the jealous anger of Duryodhana, who arranged for his cousin's visit to a great gambling match at Hastinápur. Yudhishthira reluctantly consented to go from a sense of obligation to obey the Mahárája, and accept a challenge. Through the fraudulent contrivances of Duryodhana he lost the whole of the Ráj; staked his brothers as slaves and lost them; lost himself; then Draupadí; then went into exile.

After thirteen years of exile in which they had many adventures, negotiations were opened for the return of the Páṇḍavas. These all-failing, preparations were made for the great war which forms the chief event in the Mahábhárata, q. v. See also PANDAVAS, &c.

The closing scene of the Mahábhárata, describing the last days of Yudhishthira, is considered the very finest specimen of the heroic poetry of India. "We know of no episode even in the Homeric poems, which can surpass its mournful grandeur, or raise a more solemn dirge over the desolation of the fallen heart of man! Yudhishthira has won the throne, and his enemies are all fallen; and an inferior poet would have concluded the story with a pæan upon his happiness. But the Hindu bard had a far deeper insight into man's nature, and his genius would not content itself with any such commonplace catastrophe; he knew well that the human soul was born for the infinite, and that no finite line could fathom the depths of its longings! It was no idle fiction in Grecian mythology, that Ulysses after his return to Ithaca, wandered forth again with his hungry heart into the world.

* Wheeler, I, 167.

'For all experience is an arch, where thro'
Gleams that untraversed land, whose margin fades,
For ever and for ever as we move.'

"And Ulysses had found that the Ithaca, which had lured him on through ten years of war, and ten more of wandering, changed, upon his arrival, into a bleak barren rock, and his restless soul stretched out her hands once more towards the untrodden beyond. Just in the same way, and with the same deep significance, Yudhishthira learns, after his victory, that the throne for which he had suffered so much leaves him unsatisfied and hungry as before. The friends of his youth are fallen, and the excitement of contest is over; and he learns in sorrow that kings are but men, and that the Fall has overshadowed the throne as much as the poorest cottage! In gloomy disappointment Yudhishthira resigns his crown, and he and his brothers and Draupadí set out in a forlorn journey to Mount Meru, where Indra's heaven lies amongst the wilds of the Himálayas,* there to find that rest which seemed denied to their search upon earth. We present a literal prose version of their pilgrimage and with it close our extracts.

I.

Having heard Yudhishthira's resolve, and seen the destruction of Krishna,
The five brothers set forth, and Draupadi, and the seventh was a dog that followed them,
Yudhishthira himself was the last that quitted Hastinápura;
And all the citizens and the court followed them on their way,
But none felt able to say unto him 'return;'
And at length they all went back unto the city,
Then the high-souled sons of Pándu, and far-famed Draupadi,
Pursued their way, fasting, and with their faces turned towards the east,
Resolved upon separation from earth, and longing for release from its laws;
They roamed onward over many regions, and to many a river and sea.
Yudhishthira went before, and Bhima followed next behind him,
And Arjuna came after him, and then the twin sons of Madri,
And sixth, after them, came Draupadi, with her fair face and lotus eyes.
And last of all followed the dog, as they wandered on till they came to the ocean.

---

* This is in fact a precise counterpart to the legend of Ulysses, as Tennyson describes it in his poem,—the most epicean fragment since Milton's days.

For my purpose holds
'"To sail unto the West until I die.
It may be that the gulfs will wash us down,
It may be we shall reach the blessed isles;
And see the great Achilles whom we knew.'"

But Arjuna left not hold of his heavenly bow,
Lured by the splendour of its gems, nor of those two heavenly arrows ;
And suddenly they saw Agni* standing like a mountain before them,
Standing in gigantic form and stopping up their path ;
And thus to them spoke the god,—'O sons of Pándu, do you know me not?'
O Yudhishthira, mighty hero, knowest thou not my voice?
I am Agni, who gave that bow unto Arjuna ;
Let him leave it here and go, for none other is worthy to bear it ;
For Arjuna's sake I stole that bow of Varuna, the ocean god,
Let Gandhiva, that best of bows, be given back to ocean again !'
Then the brothers all besought Arjuna to obey,
And he flung the bow into the sea, and he flung those immortal arrows ;
And lo ! as they fell into the sea, Agni vanished before them.
And once more the sons of Pándu set forth, with their faces turned to the south.
And then by the upper shore of the briny sea,
They turned toward the south-west, and went on their way ;
And as they journeyed onwards, and came unto the west,
There they beheld the old city of Krishna, now washed over by the ocean tide,
Again they turned to the north, and still they went on in their way,
Circumambulating round the continent to find separation from earth.

II.

Then with their senses subdued, the heroes having reached the north,
Beheld, with their heaven-desiring eyes, the lofty mountain Himavat,
And having crossed its height they beheld the sea of sand,
And next they saw rocky Meru, the king of mountains.
But while they were thus faring onwards, in eager search for separation,
Draupadi lost hold of her hope, and fell on the face of the earth ;
And Bhíma the mighty having beheld her fall,
Spoke to the king of justice,† looking back to her as there she lay,
'No act of evil hath she done, that faultless daughter of a king.
Wherefore then, O conqueror, hath she fallen thus low on the ground?'
And thus to him answered Yudhishthira 'too great was her love for Arjuna,'
And the fruit thereof, Oh Bhíma, hath she gathered here this day.
Thus speaking, Bharata's glorious descendant, went onwards, not looking back,
Gathering up his soul in himself in his unstooping wisdom and justice.
Next the fair Sahadeva fell upon the face of the earth,
And Bhíma, beholding him fall, thus spake to the king ;
'Oh Yudhishthira, *he* the greatest, the least froward and wilful of us all,
He the son of fair Madri,—wherefore hath he fallen on the ground?'
And him thus answered Yudhishthira, 'He esteemed none equal to himself,
This was his fault, and therefore hath the prince fallen this day.'
Thus speaking, he left Sahadeva, and went on ;
Yudhishthira, king of justice, and his brothers, and the dog.
But when Nakula saw the fall of Draupadi and his brother,
The hero, full of love for his kindred, in his grief fell down like them to the earth.
And when Nakula, the fair-faced, had thus fallen like the others,
Once more, in his wonder, spoke Bhíma unto the king :—
'What ! *he* the undeviating in virtue, ever true to his honour and faith,

* The god of Fire from whom Arjuna had obtained the bow Gandhiva.
† The usual title of Yudhishthira.

Unequalled for beauty in the world, hath he too fallen on the ground?'
And him thus answered Yudhishthira, 'Ever was the thought in his heart,
There is none equal in beauty to me, and I am superior unto all!'
Therefore hath Nakula fallen; come Bhíma, and follow my steps;
'Whatsoever each hath done, assuredly he eateth thereof.'
And when Arjuna beheld them thus fallen behind him,
He too, the great conqueror, fell, with his soul pierced through with sorrow:
And when he, the lion-hearted, was fallen, like Indra himself in majesty,
When he, the invincible, was dead, once more Bhíma spoke unto the king:
'No act of evil do I remember in all that Arjuna hath done;
Wherefore then is this change, and why hath he too fallen on the ground?'
And him thus answered Yudhishthira, 'In one day I could destroy all my enemies.'
Such was Arjuna's boast, and he falls, for he fulfilled it not!
And he ever despised all warriors beside himself,
This he ought not to have done, and therefore hath he fallen to-day.
Thus speaking, the king went on, and then Bhíma himself next fell to the earth.
And, as he fell, he cried with a loud voice unto Yudhishthira,
'Oh king of justice look back, I—I thy dear brother am fallen,
What is the cause of my fall, Oh tell it to me if thou knowest!'
Once more him answered Yudhishthira, 'When thou gazed'st on thy foe,
Thou hast cursed him with thy breath, therefore thou too fallest to-day!'
Thus having spoken, the mighty king, not looking back, went on,
And still, as ever, behind him, went following that dog alone!

III.

'Lo! suddenly, with a sound that ran through heaven and earth
Indra came riding on his chariot, and he cried to the king 'ascend.'
Then indeed did the lord of justice look back to his fallen brothers,
And thus unto Indra he spoke with a sorrowful heart,
'Let my brothers who yonder lie fallen, go with me,
Not even into thy heaven would I enter if they were not there;
And yon fair-faced daughter of a king, Draupadi, the all-deserving;
Let her too enter with us? Oh Indra, approve my prayer!'

INDRA.

In heaven thou shalt find thy brothers, they are already there before thee,
There are they all with Draupadi; weep not then, Oh son of Bharata!
Thither are they entered, prince, having thrown away their mortal weeds,
But thou alone shalt enter, still wearing thy body of flesh.

YUDHISHTHIRA.

Oh Indra and what of this dog? It hath faithfully followed me through;
Let it go with me into heaven, for my soul is full of compassion.

INDRA.

Immortality and fellowship with me, and the height of joy and felicity,
All these hast thou reached to-day; leave then the dog behind thee.

YUDHISHTHIRA.

The good may oft act an evil part, but never a part like this;
Away then with that felicity, whose price is to abandon the faithful.

INDRA.

My heaven hath no place for dogs; they steal away our offerings on earth,
Leave then thy dog behind thee, nor think in thy heart that it is cruel.

YUDHISHTHIRA.

To abandon the faithful and devoted is an endless crime, like the murder of a Brahman,
Never therefore, come weal or woe, will I abandon yon faithful dog,
Yon poor creature, in fear and distress, hath trusted in my power to save it;
Not therefore, for even life itself, will I break my plighted word.

INDRA.

If a dog but beholds a sacrifice, men esteem it unholy and void;
Forsake then the dog, O hero, and heaven is thine own as a reward.
Already thou hast borne to forsake thy fondly-loved brothers and Draupadi,
Why then forsakest thou not the dog? wherefore now fails thy heart?

YUDHISHTHIRA.

Mortals, when they are dead, are dead to love or hate, so runs the world's belief,
I could not bring them back to life, but while they lived I never left them;
To oppress the suppliant, to kill a wife, to spoil a Brahman, and to betray one's friends,
These are the four great crimes; and to forsake a dependent, I count equal unto them.

Yudhishthira then enters heaven; but one more trial awaits him. He finds there Duryodhana and the other sons of Dhritaráshtrá, but he looks in vain for his own brothers. He refuses to stay in the Swerga without them, and a messenger is sent to bring him where they are. He descends to the Indian hell and finds them there; and he proudly resolves to stay with them and share their sorrows, rather than dwell in heaven without them. But the whole scene was only a *máyá* or illusion, to prove his virtue; the sorrows suddenly vanish, the surrounding hell changes into heaven, where Yudhishthira and his brothers dwell with Indra in full content of heart for ever.

Thus closes the Mahábhárata, the new mythic world, which a modern Columbus has opened."*

Yudhishthira is also called Dharmarája, Dharmaputra and sometimes simply Rájan.

Yuga--A cycle of five years. The years are called severally Samvatsara, Parivatsara, Idvatsara, Anuvatsara, and Vatsara. There are four kinds of months: 1, the Saura, or Solar-sidereal, consisting of the sun's passage through a sign of the zodiac; 2, the Saumya or Cháṇḍra or lunar month, comprehending thirty lunations or Tithis, and reckoned most usually from new moon to new moon, though sometimes from full moon to full moon; 3, the Savana, or solar month, containing thirty days of sunrise and

* Westminster Review, Vol. L, p. 61.

sunset; and 4, the Nakshatra or lunar asterismal month, which is the moon's revolution through the twenty-eight lunar mansions. The five years forming the Yuga differ only in denomination, being composed of the months just described, with such Malamásas or intercalary months, as may be necessary to complete the period, according to Vriddha Garga. The cycle comprehends therefore sixty solar-sidereal months of 1,800 days: sixty-one solar months or 1,830 days; sixty-two lunar months, or 1,860 lunations; and sixty-seven lunar-asterismal months, or 1,809 such days.

Yugas—There are four Yugas or ages; the Kṛita, the Tretá, the Dwápara, and the Kálí. To estimate the length of each it is necessary to remember that six months form an Ayana (the period of the sun's progress north or south of the ecliptic); and two Ayạnas compose a year. The southern Ayana is a night, and the northern a day, of the gods. Twelve thousand divine years, each composed of three hundred and sixty such days, constitute the period of the four Yugas or ages. They are thus distributed: the Kṛita age has four thousand divine years; the Tretá, three thousand; the Dwápara, two thousand; and the Kálí age, one thousand. The period that precedes a Yuga is called a Sandhya, and it is of as many hundred years as there are thousands in the Yuga; and the period that follows a Yuga, termed the Sandhyásana, is of similar duration.

Thus Kṛita Yuga	4,000	
Sandhya	400	
Sandhyásana	400	
		4,800
— Tretá Yuga	3,000	
Sandhya	300	
Sandhyásana	300	
		3,600
— Dwápara Yuga	2,000	
Sandhya	200	
Sandhyásana	200	
		2,400
Carried over		10,800

	Brought over...	10,800
— Kálí Yuga	1,000	
Sandhya	100	
Sandhyásana	100	
		1,200
		12,000

—See V. P. and Notes.

Yuvanaswa—1, A prince, the son of Ardra ; 2, the son of Prasenajit, and father of Mandhatra, q. v. ; 3, the son of Ambarísha.

Yuyudhana—The son of Satyaka, and grandson of Siní.

Yuyutsu—The youngest son of Dhritaráshtra, by a woman of the Vaisya caste, making altogether a hundred and two children.

APPENDIX.

A

Adityas—[Page 10]—The sons of Aditi. They were first reckoned as seven or eight. In the later Indian literature they are always said to be twelve. Contradictory accounts of them are cited by Dr. Muir (IV, 104). In texts from the Mahábhárata the Ádityas, though their names are not always uniformly given, are stated to be twelve in number, except in one case where only eleven are specified. Vishṇu is always named as one of them, and as by the time when these works were written, his dignity had become enhanced in general estimation, he is declared to be the greatest of the twelve. In the V. P. and Harivamsha it is stated that those who formerly, in the Chakshusha Manwantara, were called the Tushitas, are known as the twelve Ádityas in the Vaivasvata Manwantara.

Professor Roth, (in the Journal of the Germ. Or. Soc. VI, 68) has the following observations on the Ádityas. There (in the highest heaven) dwell and reign those gods who bear in common the name of Ádityas. We must, however, if we would discover their earliest character, abandon the conceptions which in a later age, and even in that of the heroic poems, were entertained regarding these deities. According to this conception they were twelve sun-gods, bearing evident reference to the twelve months. But for the most ancient period we must hold fast the primary signification of their name. They are the inviolable, imperishable, eternal beings. Aditi, eternity, or the eternal, is the element which sustains them, and is sustained by them. The eternal and inviolable element in which the Ádityas dwell, and which forms their essence, is the celestial light. The Ádityas, the gods of this light, do not therefore by any means coincide with any of the forms in which light is manifested in the universe. They are neither sun, nor moon, nor stars, nor dawn, but the eternal sustainers of this luminous life, which exists, as it were, behind all these phenomena.—*O. S. T.*, *V*, 56.

Ahi—A name of Vrittra, the demon who personifies drought, and is also called Sushṇa.

Ajobhaga—The unborn part of man. After death and the cremation of the body, Agni is supplicated to kindle the unborn part with his heat and flame, and, assuming his most auspicious form, to convey it to the world of the righteous. Before, however, this unborn part can complete its course from earth to the third heaven, it has to traverse a vast gulf of darkness. Leaving behind on earth all that is evil and imperfect, and proceeding by the paths which the fathers trod, the spirit, invested with a lustre like that of the gods, soars to the realms of eternal light, &c.—*O. S. T.*, *Vol. V*, *p.* 303.

Akampana—A king who lived in the Kṛita Yuga, but who was so far from enjoying the tranquillity generally predicated of that happy time, that he was overcome by his enemies in a battle, in which he lost his son, and suffered in consequence severe affliction.—*O. S. T.*, *Vol. I*, *p.* 505.

Anakadundubhi—A name of Vasudeva, q. v.

Aranyani—The goddess of forest solitude. Several hymns in the Rig- and Átharva-vedas are addressed to this goddess. See O. S. T., V, 423.

Arhat—A perfect saint, amongst the Jains or Buddhists ; one in whom evil desire is entirely destroyed ; one entitled to the homage of gods and men.

Aruna—The ruddy. The son of the patriarch Kaṣyapa and his wife Vinata ; the younger brother of Garuda, the bird vehicle of Vishṇu. This deity has in the classical period taken the place of Ushas, the personification of dawn in the Vedic creed.

Arushi—The daughter of Manu and wife of the great sage Chyavana.—*O. S. T.*, *Vol. I*, *p.* 124.

Arvalan—The son and heir of Rája Kehama, who offered violence to Kaliyal, the beautiful daughter of a peasant in the neighbourhood of the palace, and was felled to the earth and slain by the avenging arm of her father.

Aryabhata—At page 48 this name was spelt after Colebrooke as *Aryabhatta;* but in old Sanskrit works recently discovered it is written almost invariably with one *t* Aryabhata; and this is therefore the spelling now adopted. It is ascertained on his own authority that he was born at Kusumapura, near the modern Patna. The date which he assigns for his birth corresponds with A. D. 476. Aryabhata was evidently a great man and is recognised as such by all Orientalists. Lassen calls him 'the founder of mathematical and astronomical science in India.' His chief work is the Arabhatíya Sútra, which includes two other works, the Dasagíti Sútra, and the Aryashtasata.—*Mrs. Manning, A. & M. I., Vol. I, p.* 365–6.

Asruvindumati—The daughter of Kámadeva, who was sent by Indra, along with her father, to endeavour to excite passion in the breast of Yayáti. In this they succeeded, and in order to become a fit husband for his young bride, the aged king applied to his sons to give him their youth in exchange for his decrepitude. As elsewhere related they all refused, except Púru, the youngest. After a time, however, Yayáti was prevailed upon by the persuasion of his young bride, at the instigation of Indra, to go to heaven, on which he restored his youth to Púru, and proceeded with his subjects to Indra, who sent them to Śiva, and he directed them to Vishṇu, in whose sphere they obtained a final abode.—*Wilson's Works, III*, 37.

Atikaya—One of the sons of the giant Rávaṇa, who was killed at the siege of Lanka.

Atit—From *Atita,* passed away; a religious mendicant liberated from worldly cares and feelings.

Atyarati—The unwise man mentioned in the Aitareya Brahmana, who by means of a Rajasuya sacrifice or religious ceremony, subdued the whole earth; but when the brahman who had officiated asked for his reward, Atyaráti replied: "When I conquer

Uttara Kuru, thou shalt be king of the earth, holy man, and I will be merely thy general." The brahman replied: "Uttara Kuru is the land of the gods ; no mortal can conquer it. Thou hast cheated me, therefore I take all from thee. And Atyaráti, thus deprived of vigour, was slain by king Sushimna. For Atyaráti had not kept his oath.—*A. & M. I., Vol. I, p.* 104.

B

Badarikasrama—The part of the Himálaya known as Badarínáth. It is a shrine of ancient celebrity.—*Wilson.*

Bahu—A king of Ayodhya, the seventh in descent from Hariṣchandra. He was overcome by the Haihayas and Tálajangas, and compelled to fly with his queens to the forest, where he died. After his death one of his wives gave birth to a son, who received the name of Sagara (q. v.) When he had grown up the youth learnt from his mother all that had befallen his father, and vowed to exterminate the enemies who had conquered his paternal kingdom. He acquired great celebrity, and takes a conspicuous place in Hindu history.

Bahusalin—A name of Bhíma.

Bhima—Page 95. "Bhíma is the Hercules or Orlando of the mythological poetry of the Hindus ; his uncommon strength was a supernatural endowment. In his youth he was the great plague of the Kuru princes, beating them in every sport and contest. They therefore plotted to get rid of him, and at a juvenile party at one of the water palaces of the king, administered a poisonous drug to him, and took advantage of his slumber to push him into the Ganges. He fell into the region of the sub-terrene snakes, by whom he was bitten ; one poison was the antidote of the other, and Bhíma, recovering from his sleep, soon beat off his antagonists ; they fled to their king Vásuki who was induced by their report to see the wonderful boy, and went to meet him. In his train was Aryaka, the maternal great great grandfather of Bhíma, who recognised, and welcomed his descendant. Aryaka being a great favourite with the king of the Nágas, Vásuki offered to give his relation any treasure or gems he could desire, but Aryaka asked permission for him to quaff the invigorating beverage, of which one bowl contained the strength of a thousand Nágas ; permission being granted, Bhíma drained this bowl eight times at as many draughts, and then went quietly to sleep for eight days : on his waking he was feasted by the Nágas and then restored to his sorrowing mother and brethren. From this period, dates his miraculous strength. Many of these incidents find parallels in Western Romance. The lady of the Lake inhabits the depths of the water, and is called by Merlin the "white serpent ;" the Fata Morgana resided beneath a lake while caressing one of her lovers as a serpent. She is also styled the Fairy of Riches : her treasures were spread over a plain to which Orlando arrived by falling in a conflict with Arridano to the bottom of an enchanted lake : Manto, the protecting fairy of Mantua [Orl. Fur. 43, 74.] being saved by Adonis when pursued in the form of a snake, proffers him anything he may desire. The account she gives of herself makes her to be a regular Nága Kanyá, or Ophite Maiden. The feat of Bhíma may be paralleled by a similar one of Orlando, and many others of the preux chevaliers of chivalry."—WILSON'S WORKS, III, 337.

Bhimasena—A name of Bhíma.

Bhujyu—The son of Tugra, who was abandoned by his malevolent companions in the middle of the sea, and rescued by the Aṣvins, who are said to have conveyed Bhujyu out of the liquid ocean with their headlong flying horses. Another account states "Tugra abandoned Bhujyu on the water-cloud, as any dead man leaves his property. Ye, Aṣvins, bore him in animated water-tight ships, which traversed the air. Three nights and three days did ye convey him in three flying cars, with a hundred feet and six horses, which crossed over to the dry land beyond the liquid ocean." —*O. S. T., V, p.* 244.

Bibhatsu—A name of Arjuna.

Bindumati—The daughter of Śasabindu, who was married to the celebrated king Mándhatṛi, and became the mother of three sons and fifty daughters.

Brahmaketu—A prince, the son of Visvaketu, king of Drávida, who was doomed to die in his sixteenth year, but who, by advice of Angiras, went to Benares, and lay down in the path of Yama, when on a visit to Śiva. Yama who never deviates from a straight path, and even an equal step, and could therefore neither walk round Brahmaketu nor stride over him, at last, to induce him to rise, promised to allow him to live a century, which accordingly happened. There is an underplot of Brahmaketu's marrying the daughter of the king of Kámpilya, in lieu of the hunchbacked son of the king of Kekaya, which has some resemblance to a story in the Arabian Nights.—WILSON'S WORKS, III, 44.

Bura Pennou—The deity worshipped by the Khonds; he is called the god of light and source of good; while his consort Tari-Pennou is the source of evil in the world.

Byroba—A demi-god of the herdsmen; worshipped wherever a few of the pastoral tribes are settled.

C

Chanda—A demon servant of the demon chief Śumbha, who was killed by the goddess Umá, who ultimately slew his master also. The Kálipúja festival is in commemoration of the victory of Umá over Cháṇḍa and Muṇḍa.

Chandrakanta—The moon-gem, which is supposed to absorb the rays of the moon, and emit them again in the form of pure and cool moisture.

Cobra—"Next to the Rakshasas the Cobra, or deadly-hooded snake, plays the most important part in the legends, as a supernatural personage. This is only one of the many traces still extant of that serpent-worship formerly so general in western India....... Serpent-worship, as it still exists is something more active than a mere popular superstition. The Cobra, unless disturbed, rarely goes far from home, and is supposed to watch jealously over a hidden treasure. He is, in the estimation of the lower classes, invested with supernatural powers, and according to the treatment he receives, he builds up or destroys the fortunes of the house to which he belongs. No native will willingly kill him if he can get rid of him in any other way ; and the poorer classes always after he is killed, give him all the honours of a regular cremation, assuring him, with many protestations, as the pile burns, 'that they are guiltless of his blood ; that they slew him by order of their master ;' or 'that they had no other way to prevent his biting the children or the chickens.' " Sir *B. Frere.**

D

Dadhicha—One of the nineteen Bhrigus, composers of hymns. — *O. S. T., Vol. I, p* 279.

Dadhyauch—One of the ancient great sages, the son of Atharvan.

Damins—The name of brahmans in Kusa-dwípa.

Danayja—A name of Arjuna.

Dasagriva—A name of the giant Rávaṇa.

Devadatta—One of the five sons of a brahman named Govindadatta who lived on the banks of the Ganges. The sons were of goodly persons, but rude manners and uncultivated minds. A brahman of great learning having on one occasion, when the father was abroad, demanded the rites of hospitality, was treated with disrespect by the youths, and was about to depart in wrath when the father arrived. The severity with which he rebuked the lads pacified the brahman and he was induced to remain. The anger of his parent produced a favourable impression on Devadatta, who, repenting of his idle habits, set off to Badarikáṣrama to propitiate Śiva. The rigour of his austerities engaged the approbation of the god. Śiva appeared to him and promised that he should become possessed of learning, for which purpose he directed him to go to Pátaliputra, and study under Vedakhumba. He afterwards repaired to Pratishṭhána, where he studied with diligence and success under another teacher of repute.

* Introduction to Old Deccan Days.

He there beheld the daughter of the king Suṣarma at a balcony of the palace. She also noticed him, and the attraction was mutual. After they had interchanged glances she beckoned to him to approach. He obeyed ; on which she took a flower, and having touched her teeth with it, threw it to him, and then disappeared. Devadatta taking the flower returned home. The flame that preyed on his heart soon betrayed itself to the experience of his preceptor, and he quickly drew from him the secret of his passion. He explained the story of the flower to signify an assignation on the part of the princess to meet Devadatta at a temple called Pushpa, (a flower.) The youth was charmed with this explanation, and set off to the temple to await the coming of the princess. On her arrival in due course she enquired how he had so readily apprehended her meaning ; but when he confessed he was indebted to his preceptor's sagacity, rather than to his own, she was highly offended with his lack of discernment and left him in displeasure.

Devadatta was now more wretched than ever, when Śambhu, commisserating his condition, sent one of his attendants, Panchisikha, to console and assist him. Panchisikha made the youth put on a female garb, whilst he assumed the appearance of an aged brahman. Thus changed, they repaired to the palace, when the supposed brahman thus addressed the monarch : "King, I am an old man, without connections in your capital. I sent my only son on family affairs some time ago to a distant country, and he does not return. I am weary of expecting him, and fear some evil may have befallen him. I will therefore go forth in quest of him ; but how can I dispose of my daughter-in-law in the mean time ? I leave her, king, as a sacred deposit in your charge." The monarch, afraid of the brahman's malediction, reluctantly accepted the trust, and the supposed brahman departed. The daughter was transferred to the interior of the palace, where, revealing himself to the princess, Devadatta succeeded in pacifying her indignation, and recovering her regard. She listened to his suit with complacency, and they pledged their troth to each other by the ritual that unites in wedlock the inferior spirits of heaven.

When it became no longer possible to conceal their secret intercourse, the friendly spirit was summoned by a wish to their assistance—he appeared, and conveyed Devadatta out of the palace by night. The next morning he made the youth discard his female habiliments, and accompany him, again metamorphosed to a venerable brahman, to the palace, in the character of the son of whom he had been in search. He came, he said, to claim his daughter-in-law, and the king ordered her to be sent for; but all parties were struck with real, or seeming consternation, when it was announced that she was nowhere to be found. The king, at a loss to comprehend the possibility of her evasion, and recollecting old legends, suspected that the brahman was not what he seemed to be, and, apprehensive of incurring his displeasure, professed himself willing to submit to any conditions he should impose. These were readily arranged, and the princess was given to the brahman's supposed son, in exchange for the bride that he pretended to have lost. The princess bore a son, who was named Mahídhara. When the king was advanced in years, he retired to the forests, resigning his sovereignty to his grandson; and after witnessing the glory of Mahídhara, his parents also withdrew from the world to the silence of the hermitage: devoting all their thoughts to Śambhu, they obtained his favour; and when released from this mortal coil, they were elevated to the rank of spirits, attendant on the god and his celestial consort, as Pushpadanta and his wife Jayá, the same whose indiscreet curiosity had lately been punished by their temporary return to the infirmities of human nature.—WILSON'S WORKS, III, 185.

Devantaka—One of the sons of the giant Rávaṇa, who was killed at the siege of Lanka.

Dhananjaya—"The conqueror of wealth;" a name of Arjuna, the third of the Páṇḍava princes, eminent for his valour, and the particular friend of Krishṇa.

Dhanyas—The designation of Vaisyas in Krauncha Dwípa.

Dhumraksha—One of Rávaṇa's generals who was killed at the siege of Lanka.

Dipakarni—An ancient monarch, whose wife, named Śaktimati, more dear to him than his existence, whilst reposing in a bower in the garden, was bitten by a snake, and died. The king, overcome with grief for her loss, made a vow to observe perpetual continence—a vow to which he rigidly adhered, although the want of a son to succeed him in the kingdom was a subject of profound affliction to him. Whilst thus distressed, he was directed by Śiva, in a dream, in what manner to obtain a son and successor, without violating his faith to his departed wife. For the remainder of the legend, see SÁTAVÁHANA.

Dyutirnan—The king of Krauncha Dwípa.

E

Ekashtaka—The mother of Indra. Ekáshṭaká, practising austere fervour, bore as a child the glorious Indra. In the next verse Ekáshṭaká is called the mother of Soma as well as of Indra, and the daughter of Prajápati."—*O. S. T., Vol. V, p.* 80.

Ereenia—The benevolent Glendoveer (Gandharba) in Southey's poem "the curse of Kehama."

G

Garuda—[Page 224]—A wundervogul, or wonderful bird, is the property of all people; and the Garuda of the Hindus is represented by the Eorosh of the Zend, Simoorgh of the Persians, the Anka of the Arabs, the Kerkes of the Turks, the Kirni of the Japanese, the sacred dragon of the Chinese, the Griffin of Chivalry, the Phœnix of classical fable, the wise and ancient bird that sits upon the ash Yggdrasit of the Edda, and according to Faber, in common with all the rest, is a misrepresentation of the holy cherubim that guarded the gate of paradise. Some writers have even traced the twelve knights of the round Table to the twelve Rocs of Persian story.—WILSON'S WORKS, III, 193.

Gonika—The mother of Patanjali the grammarian.

Govindadatta—A brahman who lived on the banks of the Ganges; he had five sons, one of whom was Devadatta, (q. v.) whose subsequent celebrity conferred distinction on the father.

Gritsamada—A name given by Indra to the Muni Śaunahotra, because he delighted in praising. His hymn was termed *Indrasya indriyam*, the might of Indra. He was born again as Śaunaka, in the race of Bhṛigu, and saw the second Mandala of the Rig Veda as it was revealed to him together with the hymn Śajaníya, &c.—*A. S. L.*, 231.

Gudakesa—A name of Arjuna.

Gunadhya—The human name of Mályaván, when he was condemned to return to the infirmities of human nature. He was born at Pratishṭhána, the capital of Sáliváhana, supposed to be the same as Pattan or Pyetan on the Godáveri.—WILSON.

I

Ida—The wife of Manu, and mother of the human race after the deluge.

Indrasena—The charioteer of Yudhishthira.

J

Jrimbhaka—A celestial or magical weapon, which causes drowsiness. These weapons are of a very unintelligible character. Some of them are occasionally wielded as missiles, but in general they appear to be mystical powers exercised by the individual; such as those of paralysing an enemy, or locking his senses fast in sleep, or bringing down storm and rain and fire from heaven. There is a list of one hunderd of these weapons given in the first book of the Rámáyana.—WILSON, XI, 297.

K

Kaliyal—The beautiful daughter of the peasant Ladurlad whose violation was attempted by Arvalan, the son of Rája Kehama. Arvalan was slain in consequence by Ladurlad, upon whom was afterwards pronounced the doom which gives the title to Southey's poem. Kaliyal afterwards joined her father, and often soothed him under the withering effects of Kehama's curse, and Ladurlad is often able to extricate his daughter from great dangers of fire and flood.

Kamadhenu—The sacred cow of the Muni Jamadagni, which was stolen by Rája Kártavírya, and afterwards recovered by the Muni's son Paraṣaráma, who slew the robber king.

Kamalasna—A name of Brahmá, as the soul of the universe, contained in the Egg of the world.

Kanakhala—A place of pilgrimage celebrated in Hindu fiction ; it is near Gangadwára, the modern Haridwár.

Katyayana—A name of great celebrity in the literary history of India. It belongs in all probability, to several personages renowned for their contributions to the grammatical and ritual literature of the Brahmanical Hindus ; but it is met with also amongst the names of the chief disciples of the Buddha, Sakyamuni. The most celebrated personage of this name, however, is Kátyáyana, the critic of the great grammarian Pánini ; and he is most likely the same with the Kátyáyana who wrote the grammatical treatise called the Prátiṣákhya of the white Yajurveda, (q. v.) Professor Goldstücker, in his Pánini, &c., *his Place in Sanscrit Literature* (London, 1861,) has shewn that he cannot have been a contemporary of Pánini, as was generally assumed ; and in a paper recently read by him before the Royal Asiatic Society (February, 1863,) he has proved that this Kátyáyana lived at the same time as the great grammarian Pátanjali, whose date he had previously fixed between 140 and 120 before the Christian era. See PATANJALI.—*Chambers' Encyclopædia.*

Kehama—The name of the mythical Rája who is the principal figure in Southey's poem "The Curse of Kehama." By a long course of penances and austerities he acquired supreme power over the world, and caused the gods themselves to tremble for their independence. His son Arvalan, the heir apparent to all his power and wickedness, was slain with a stake by a peasant whose daughter he was attempting to violate. The incensed Rája pronounced on the peasant, Ladurlad, the doom which gives name to the poem.

Kuhu—The goddess of the day, when the moon is in the first and second quarters.

Kundoba—A deified hero of the shepherds, who, amongst the pastoral tribes supersedes all other popular idols.

Kunjara—An old parrot mentioned in the Pádma Purána. When the sage Chyavana was wandering over the world in pilgrimage, he came to the south bank of the Narmadá, where a linga called Omkára was erected; and having worshipped it, he sat under an Indian fig tree where he overheard a conversation between Kunjara and his four sons, in which the latter related to the former what they had beheld in their flight during the day. Several stories were related the moral of which was the same, the good effects of venerating holy men, and meditating upon Vishṇu. Kunjara then related to Chyavana an account of the preceding births of his sons and himself.—WILSON's *Works, Vol. III, p.* 37.

Kusadhvaja—A rishi, the father of Vedavati. He was slain by Sambhu, king of the Daityas.

L

Ladurlad—The name of the peasant in Southey's poem, on whom the curse of Kehama is pronounced. See YEDILLIAN, KEHAMA, &c.

M

Mada—A demon, created by the sage Chyavana, intoxication personified; in terror of whom and of the power of the saint, the gods acceded to the participation of the Asvini Kumáras in divine honours. Mada was afterwards divided, and distributed amongst dice, women, and wine.—WILSON, XI, 263.

Mahatmya—A legendary and local description of the greatness or holiness of particular temples, or individual divinities. A chapter taken from some Purána, descriptive of the virtues of some place or person, is termed a Mahátmya.—WILSON.

Mahidhara—The son of Devadatta, (q. v.)

Mandakini—A river near the hill Chitrakuta in Bundelkund; regarded as a sort of sacred stream on account of Ráma, Lakshmana, and Síta, having resided in its neighbourhood, Ráma thus points out to Síta, some of the beauties of the river.

" My life in fair Ayodhya's town
Was not so sweet to me,
As gazing on this lovely flood,
That glorious hill and thee.

Bathe in the gentle stream, to her
With friendly love repair,
And pluck her lilies in thy play,
And twine them in thy hair.

This mount, with all its savage life,
Ayodhya's city deem,
And on this beauteous river look
As our own Sarju's stream.

O Síta, I am wild with joy,
So rare a lot is mine,
Cheered by a duteous brother's care,
And loved with love like thine."

GRIFFITH. *Scenes from the Rámáyana.*

Maruty—A name of Hanumán, the offspring of Marut, a name of Pávana or Váyu, all meaning wind.

Mrigavati—The wife of Sahasráníka, (q. v.)

Munda—A demon servant of the demon ruler Niṣumbha, who was killed by Umá. The goddess ultimately slew his master also. The Kálipúja festival in Bengal is held annually in commemoration of the victory of Umá over Cháṇḍa and Muṇḍa.

N

Namuchi—One of the demons who personify drought; they are represented in the Rig Veda as hostile powers in the atmosphere, who malevolently shut up the watery treasures in the clouds.

Nandaka—One of the hundred sons of Dhritaráshtra. Duryodhana was the eldest, but as the legend of their birth was not given in the article under his name, it may be recited here. One day the sage Vyása was hospitably entertained by the queen Gándhári, and in return he granted her a boon. She choose to be the mother of a hundred sons, and soon afterwards became pregnant. After two years gestation she produced a mass of flesh which was divided by Vyása into a hundred and one pieces, (as big as the joint of a thumb) and placed in jars. In due time the eldest son Duryodhana was born, but not till after the birth of Pritha's son Yudhishthira. In another month the remaining ninety-nine sons were born from the remaining jars, and one daughter, called Duhṣalá (afterwards married to Jayadratha.) The hundred names are all given in the Mahábhárata ; it will be sufficient here to mention the principal ones :—Duryodhana, Durvishaha, Durmukha, Dushpradarṣana, Vivinṣati, Vikarna, Duhṣaṣana, Virochana, Kundaka, Nandaka, &c. —Williams. I. E. P.

Nishada—The progenitor of the wild races, extracted from the left thigh of king Veṇa.—Wilson.

Nisumbha—A demon ruler of prodigious strength and power who was destroyed by the goddess Umá. The Devimahátmya narrates this as one of her chief martial exploits.

P

Panchasikha—One of Śiva's attendants who was sent down to earth to console and assist Devadatta, when his course of true love did not seem likely to run smooth.

Paramarthika—Being, in its highest sense.

Pataliputra—The famous and much disputed city of Palibothra ; an ancient place of great sanctity, being the favoured shrine of Lakshmi and Sarasvati. Its origin is thus narrated. A Brahman from the south, whilst engaged on a pilgrimage to Kanakhala, near Gangádwára, died, and left three sons. They subsequently repaired to Rájagriha for instruction, and thence removed to

Chinchiní, a city on the seashore, south from the shrine of Kumára Swámi. They were kindly entertained by Bhojika, a Brahman, who gave them his three daughters in marriage. After a time, the country was afflicted by famine; and the three husbands, deserting their wives, set off to seek their fortunes elsewhere. Talents and relationship touch not the hearts of the wicked. The wife of the second brother proved pregnant, and was delivered of a son, whose helpless situation attracted the pity, and propitiated the guardian care of Deví and Śiva. The first effect of this powerful patronage was the discovery, by the women, of an immense treasure, which being judiciously expended, elevated the boy to princely possessions. By the advice of his grandfather's friend, and his own guardian Yajnadatta, Putraka, as the lad had been named, distributed publicly splendid gifts, at various seasons, to the Brahmans, in the hope of attracting and discovering his father. The scheme succeeded, and the three brothers returned to claim their wives, and interest in the young Rája. The claim was joyfully recognized; but the evil propensities of the fraternity prevailing over natural affection, they conspired the death of the prince, and his own father led him into a temple, where he left him to be murdered by assassins, covertly stationed for the purpose. The murderers were, however, induced, by the intreaties and presents of Putraka, to let him escape, and he fled into the forests. His father and uncles met the fate that ever attends the ungrateful: the officers of the young Rája accused them of having killed him, and falling upon the culprits, sacrificed them to his memory.

In the meantime, Putraka, whilst wandering in the woods, beheld two men struggling with each other. He enquired who they were. They replied, that they were the sons of Mayásur, and were contending for a magic cup, staff, and pair of slippers: the first of which yielded inexhaustible viands, the second generated any object which it delineated, and the third transported a person through the air. The strongest of the two was to possess these articles. Putraka then observed to them, that violence was a very improper mode of settling their pretensions, and that it would be better they should adjust the dispute by less objectionable means. He therefore proposed that they should run a race for the contested articles, and the fleetest win them. They agreed, and set off. They were no sooner at a little distance, than Putraka, putting his feet into the sleepers, and seizing the cup and staff, mounted into the air, and left the racers to lament in vain their being outwitted.

Putraka alighted at a city called Ákarshiká, and took up his residence with an old woman, from whom he received accounts of the beauty of the king's daughter, whose name was Páṭali. Having in consequence formed an intimacy with the princess, he carried her off, and alighted on the bank of the Ganges, where tracing the walls and buildings of a city with his staff, a stately town immediately arose. The people attracted to this place he maintained by the stores of his cup; and the place named after his bride and himself Páṭaliputraka, became the capital of a mighty empire.—WILSON, III, 165.

Patanjali—Is the name of two celebrated authors of ancient India, who are generally looked upon as the same personage, but apparently for no other reason than that they bear the same name. The one is the author of the system of philosophy called Yoga, the other the great critic of Kátyáyana and Páṇini. Of the former nothing is known beyond his work—see YOGA. The few historical facts relating to the latter, as at present ascertained, may be gathered from his great work the Mahábháshya, or the great Commentary. The name of his mother was Goṇika; his birthplace was Gonarda, situated in the east of India, and he resided temporarily in Kashmír, where his work was especially patronised. From circumstantial evidence Professor Goldstücker has, moreover, proved that he wrote between 140 and 120 B. C. (*Pánini, his place in Sanskrit Literature.*) The Mahábháshya of Patanjali is not a full commentary on Páṇini, but with a few exceptions, only a commentary on the Várttikas, or critical remarks of Kátyáyana on Páṇini. Patanjali being the third of the grammatical triad of India, and his work therefore having the advantage of profiting by the scholarship of his predecessors, he is looked upon as a paramount authority in all matters relating to classical Sanskrit Grammar; and very justly so, for as to learning, ingenuity, and conscientiousness, there is no grammatical author of India who can be held superior to him.—*Chambers' Encyclopædia*.

Pavana—The god of the wind, Váyu, (q. v.)

Pitamaha--A name of Brahmá.

Pratibhasika—Being, merely seeming—that belonging to what presents itself in dreams, &c., illusions rather than realities.

Pururavas—See pages 486–90. In a recent paper read before the Philological Society, " On Nomina Numina in its Two Phases." Professor Goldstücker said its object was to illustrate the influence which in ancient times, the mistaken etymology of words exercised on the formation of religious ideas and myths, and in modern times the mistaken interpretation of myths on the formation of wrong etymologies. In adverting to Max Müller's view of the supposed original import of Daphne in Greek, and of Urvaṣí in Hindu mythology, Professor Goldstücker observed that the common feature of the Greek and Hindu legends of Daphne and Urvaṣí, was the transformation of these beings—of Urvaṣí into a bird or vine, and of Daphne into a laurel tree. Moreover in the Hindu legend, Urvaṣí disappears in the lightning of the Gandharbas who steal her rams, and Purúravas establishes a new ceremony, which consists in producing fire by means of the attrition of two pieces of wood. And finally in all legendary accounts Urvaṣí is represented as an Apsarasas, or as the name indicates (from *ap* water, and *saras*, arising,) from a water-born being ; while Daphne as we are told by the Greek mythonomists, is the daughter of a river. Not any one of these *essential* features of the legend receives any light from the assumption that Daphne or Urvaṣí is the Dawn. Professor Goldstücker therefore proposed to read the legend thus : the sky is clouded (the ram being the symbol of the cloud) and the atmosphere charged with electricity. Lightning flashing through the cloud disperses them (the Gandharbas,) under lightning, steal the rams of Urvaṣí ; the sun comes forth and absorbs the vapours which had enveloped the scene, when the objects hidden until then become visible. Again the effect of the tropical sun may be a conflagration of the dry forest wood ; or as the legend says, Purúravas is the institution of the ceremony by which fire is produced through natural heat.

Pushpotkata—One of the wives of the patriarch Pulastya and the mother of the great giant Rávaṇa.

Putraka—The founder and sovereign of Páṭaliputra; his history will be found under that heading.

R

Raktavija—A powerful demon possessed of a charmed life, each drop of his blood when shed producing hundreds of demons like himself; he was slain by Umá, and his destruction is regarded as one of the great martial feats of the goddess.

Rudra—In the Vedic period, Rudra was the god of the tempest. The Maruts are called the sons of Rudra. As their father he is very often mentioned; as a divinity with independent attributes he is of much rarer occurrence; hymns addressed to him alone are but few. He is, as might be expected, a terrible god: he carries a great bow from which he hurls a sharp missile at the earth; he is called the slayer of men; his wrath is deprecated, and he is besought not to harm his worshipper; if not in the Rik, at least in the Atharva and Bráhmanas, he is styled 'lord of the animals,' as the unhoused beasts of the field are especially at the mercy of the pitiless storm. At the same time, he is to propitiate him, addressed as master of a thousand remedies, best of physicians, protector from harm; this may have its ground, too, partly in the beneficial effects of the tempest in freshening the atmosphere of that sultry clime. Rudra's chief interest consists in the circumstance that he forms the point of connection between the Vedic religion and the later Śiva worship. Śiva is a god unknown to the Vedas; his name is a word of not unfrequent occurrence in the hymns, but means simply propitious; not even in the Atharva is it the epithet of a particular divinity, or distinguished by its usage from any other adjective. As given to him, whose title it has since become, it seems one of those euphemisms so frequent in the Indian religion, applied as a soothing and flattering address to the most terrible god in the whole pantheon. The precise relation between Śiva and Rudra is not yet satisfactorily traced out. The introduction of an entirely new divinity from the mountains of the north has been supposed, who was grafted in upon the ancient religion by being identified with Rudra; or again, a blending of some of Agni's attributes with those of Rudra to originate a new development: perhaps neither of these may be necessary: Śiva may be a local form of Rudra, arisen under the influence of peculiar climatic relations in the districts from which he made his way into Hindustan proper; introduced among, and readily accepted by, a people which, as the Atharva shows, was strongly tending towards a terrorism in its religion."—*Professor Whitney, as quoted in O. S. T., IV*, 337.

S

Sabhika—A person who presides at houses where assemblies are held for purposes of gambling, and who provides the dice and all other materials.

Saganka—"Fawn-spotted," a name of the god Soma or Chándra. He is also called *Sasin;* from a fancied resemblance of the spots of the moon to a leveret.

Sahasranika—The son of Śatáníka, (q. v.) The fate of his father naturally interested Indra for the young prince, and he not unfrequently conveyed him to visit the regions of the skies. On one of these occasions he incurred the displeasure of Tilottamá, a nymph of paradise, and she denounced an imprecation on his future fortune, sentencing him to the pangs of separation from his beloved. Sahasráníka was married to Mṛigávatí, daughter of Kṛipavarmá, king of Oude. During her pregnancy she was seized with a strange fancy, inspired, in fact, by the influence of the imprecation, to bathe in human blood. When the king found compliance with her longing was unavoidable, he deceived her by substituting an infusion of the lac-dye, in which the queen contentedly performed her ablutions. The crimson tint left upon her person by the effect of the immersion, deceived one of the gigantic brood of Garuḍa, as he pursued his flight through the air. Thinking her to be a lump of flesh, he pounced upon the queen, and carried her off to the mountain Udya, where, finding her alive, he abandoned her to her destiny, having thus been the unconscious instrument of separating Śahaṣráuíka from his bride.

In this helpless condition the queen, overcome with terror and affliction, sought alone for death to terminate her distress. With this view she threw herself in the way of the wild elephants and the vast serpents, with which the thickets were peopled; but in vain—an unseen spirit of the air protected her, and guided her unharmed amidst the ferocious monsters of the forest, until she was encountered by a holy hermit, Jamadagni, who resided on the mountain, and who led her to his cell, where he consoled her with assurances, that she would in time be re-united to her lord. Mṛigávatí was here delivered of a son, whom, in allusion to the place of his nativity, she named Udáyana, and who was trained in letters and arms, and in the duties of his regal birth, by his venerable guardian.—WILSON, III, 192. [VATSA.]

Salivahana—A Hindu king who reigned in Magadha. He instituted an era which bears his name and is still commonly used in the Deckan. It commenced when 3179 years of the Kali-Yuga, or the present mundane age, had expired; that is 78 years after the beginning of the Christian era. This era is called Sáliváhana Śáka, or simply Śáka. Thus 1871 of the Christian era would be tantamount to 1793 of the Śáka era. The Śáka year is the same as and begins with the common solar year.

Sambhu—A name of Śiva.

Thy journey next o'er Kanakhala bends,
Where Jahnu's daughter from the hills descends;
Whose sacred waters to Bhagírath given,
Conveyed the sons of Sagara to heaven.

She who with smiling waves disportive strayed
Through Śambha's locks, and with his tresses played;
Unheeding, as she flowed delighted down,
The gathering storm of Gauri's jealous frown.

Sambhu—2, The king of the Daityas, who slew the rishi Kusadhvaja, the father of Vedavati.

Sammada—The name of the fish that lived in the pond where the sage Saubhari was immersed for twelve years.

Sanmukha—A name of Kartikeya, the war-god.

Satabali—One of the generals of the monkey king Sugríva.

Satanika—The son of Janamejaya and grandson of Paríkshit. He was killed in battle with the Titans, having gone to the assistance of Indra, and was succeeded in his throne by Śahaṣráníka.

Satva-devi—1, A name of Párvati ; 2, The name of a nurse to the children of the giant Rávaṇa.

Satavahana—The son and successor of Dípakarní, (q. v.) Dípakarní, in obedience to Śiva's commands, repaired to a certain forest to hunt ; and whilst thus employed, met, as he had been forewarned, a lovely boy riding upon a monstrous lion. Still acting as he had been enjoined, the king aimed an arrow at the beast, and he fell as dead. Immediately, however, up rose from the carcase a celestial form, who thus addressed the astonished monarch. 'Dismiss your apprehension ; I am a Yaksha, Sáta by name. It was my chance to see and love the beautiful daughter of a holy sage ; my passion was returned ; and this boy whom you behold, is our son. When the secret of our union was discovered, the angry sire condemned us both to wear the forms of brutes during the remainder of our earthly career. My bride was liberated from the effects of the curse in giving birth to her son ; and your shaft has rendered me the same kind office. I am now at liberty ; but ere I depart to the region of the gods, I bequeath to you this child, to be cherished by you as your own.' So saying, he vanished, leaving the boy with the king, who gladly received him, and gave him the name Sátaváhana, in reference to the appellation of his father and the váhana, or vehicle, on which the king had first beheld the infant mounted. Upon the death of his adoptive father Sátaváhana succeeded to the throne and became a mighty monarch.—WILSON'S WORKS, III, 183.

Satyavama—One of the wives of Krishṇa. She is also known as one of the wives of Vishṇu ; in his avatar of Krishṇa she was with him, and Lakshmi is said to have been also incarnate as Rukminí.

Satyavrata—The original name of Trisanku, (q. v.)

Savitri—One of the twelve Ádityas. Súrya and Saviṭri are exact personifications of the sun. It is under these two different appellations that the sun is chiefly celebrated in the Rig Veda. Saviṭri is permanently the golden deity ; being hiraṇyáksha, golden-eyed ; *hiranya-hasta*, golden-handed, &c. Luminous in his aspect, he ascends a golden car, drawn by radiant, brown, white-footed horses ; and beholding all creatures he pursues an ascending and descending path. Surrounded by a golden lustre, he illuminates the atmosphere and all the regions of the earth. His robust and golden arms, which he stretches out to bless, and infuse energy into all creatures, reach to the utmost ends of heaven. In one place, however, he is called *ayohanu*, the iron-jawed, though even there the commentator says that *ayas*, which ordinarily means iron, is to be rendered by gold. His ancient paths in the sky are said to be free from dust. He is called (like Varuṇa and others of the gods) *asura*, a divine spirit. His will and independent authority cannot be resisted by Indra, Varuṇa, Mitra, Aryaman, Rudra, or by any other being. The other gods follow his lead. The waters and the wind obey his ordinance. His praises are celebrated by the Vasus, by Aditi, by the royal Varuṇa, by Mitra, and by Aryaman. He is lord of all desirable things, and sends blessings from the sky, from the atmosphere, and from the earth. He impels the car of the Aṣvins before the dawn. He is *Prajápati*, the lord of all creatures, the supporter of the sky and of the world, and is supplicated to hasten to his worshippers with the same eagerness as cattle to a village, as warriors to their horses, as a cow to give milk to a calf, as a husband to his wife. He is called viṣvadeva, " in all attributes a god." He measured (or fashioned) the terrestrial regions. He bestows immortality on the gods, as he did on the Ribhus, who by the greatness of their merits attained to his abode. He is prayed to convey the departed spirit to the abode of the righteous. He is supplicated to deliver his worshippers from sin.

Saviṭri is sometimes called *apam napat*, son of the waters, an epithet which is more commonly applied to Agni.

The word Savitri is not always a proper name ; but is sometimes used as an epithet.—*O. S. T., V*, 164.

Sena or Sein—Sometimes written Gandharba-Sena, or Gundrusein, a Gandharba who was condemned for an affront to Indra, to be born on earth in the shape of an ass, but on entreaty the sentence was mitigated, and he was allowed at night to re-assume the form and functions of a man. This incarnation took place at Ujein, in the reign of Rája Sundersein, whose daughter was demanded in marriage by the ass ; and his consent was obtained on learning the divine origin of his intended son-in-law, confirmed, as he witnessed, by certain prodigies. All day he lived in the stables like an ass ; at night, secretly slipping out of his skin, and assuming the appearance of a handsome and accomplished young prince, he repaired to the palace and enjoyed the conversation of his beauteous bride.

In due time the princess became pregnant ; and her chastity being suspected, she revealed to her father the mystery of her husband's happy nocturnal metamorphosis ; which the Rája, being conveniently concealed, himself beheld ; and unwilling that his son should return to his uncouth disguise, set fire to, and consumed, the vacant ass's skin.

Although rejoiced at his release, the Gandharba foresaw the resentment of Indra, disappointed of his vengeance ; and warned his wife to quit the city, about to be overwhelmed with a shower of earth. She fled to a village at a safe distance, and brought forth a son, the celebrated *Vikramaditya ;* and a shower of cold earth, poured down by Indra, buried the city and its inhabitants. —*As. Res., Vol. VI.* [Ujein.]

This legend gives a date to the catastrophe ; for the prince, so renowned in his origin and birth, was not less so as a monarch and an astronomer ; and his name marks an era much used all over India, commencing fifty-six years before our era.—*Moor, H. P., p.* 262.

This story is supposed to be the original form of the 'Golden Ass' of Apuleius, which is in fact the story of Beauty and the Beast.

Sramanaka—A Buddhist mendicant.

T

Tunda—A powerful demon, that was destroyed by Nahusha, the son of Ayus ; the Pádma Purána contains a long narrative of the event.

U

Ujein—The ancient Avanti ; a city of great antiquity, that is considered the first meridian by Hindu geographers and astronomers. The ancient city was about a mile further south, and now lies buried in the earth, to the depth of from fifteen to eighteen feet : on digging, its walls are said to be found entire, pillars unbroken, &c. Whatever may have been the real cause of this catastrophe, Hindu fancy has attributed it to the intervention of the gods, and dressed it up in a mythological allegory which is believed to be the original form of the "Golden Ass of APULEIUS." See SENA.

Upakosa—The wife of Vararuchi, (q. v.) During her husband's absence she attracted the notice and desires of several suitors, whom she succeeded in exposing and punishing in a very ludicrous manner. See Wilson's Works, III, 170.

Upayaja—A brahman of eminent learning and sanctity, to whom king Drupada applied in his anxiety to procure a son, promising a million of cows if he enabled him to obtain the son he desired. Upayája however declined the task, and referred him to his elder brother Yája, (q. v.)

V

Vaitalika—A sort of poetical warder or bard, who announces fixed periods of the day, as dawn and evening, &c., in measured lines, and occasionally pours forth strains arising from any incidental occurrence.—*Wilson, XI,* 209.

Vatsa—A celebrated character in Hindu fiction. He was the son of Sahasráṇika, (q, v.) and king of Kausambi. Vatsa was named Udáyana, from being educated on the Udya mountain, by the sage Jamadagni. When arrived at maturity he was decoyed into captivity by the king of Ujein. On his escape he carried off Vasavadatta, the daughter of his captor. Vatsa is the hero of the Ratnávali.—See *Wilson, XII,* 264.

Vigneswara—A name of Gaṇeṣa, (q. v.)

Vina—The Hindu lute; an instrument of much sweetness and compass, but little power.

Vittora—The name of Vishṇu in one of his minor Avatars, as related in some of the Puránas. He is represented as retaining on his breast an indelible mark of Bhrigu's foot, with which the following legend is connected. In a divine assembly Bhrigu was asked who, of the gods, was the most mighty; he said he would proceed to inquire, and first went to Brahmá, in approaching whom it was usual to pay very respectful obeisance, which on this occasion, Bhrigu purposely omitted, and experienced in consequence severe reprehension, including copious abuse, (for the Hindu gods, like Homer's, are very abusive,) from Brahmá, who however became pacified by seasonable apologies. Bhrigu next proceeded to Śiva, and omitted, as before, the usual tokens of adoration on entering the divine presence; Śiva was still more enraged than Brahmá, but was in like manner pacified by Bhrigu's apologies. He then repaired to Vaikuntha, the celestial residence of Vishṇu, whom he found asleep, with Lakshmi shampooing his feet. Bhrigu knew that the mere omission of respect would not be sufficient to move the gentle god to anger, and to make a trial of his temper he boldly gave the recumbent deity a severe kick on his breast. Vishṇu awoke, and seeing Bhrigu arose, and in place of anger, expressed apprehensions that he must have hurt his foot by striking it against his (Vishṇu's) breast, and proceeded to lament it and to rub and chafe Bhrigu's foot to remove any consequent pain. 'This, said Bhrigu, is the mightiest god; he overpowers by the most potent of all arms, affability and generosity?' See Moor's Hindu Pantheon, p. 418.—This is a favourite story amongst the Brahmans of the south.

Vithoba—A deified sage, very popular, and extensively worshipped in the Poona Deccan.

Vetal—The demon-god of the outcaste helot races ; the circle of large stones, which may be observed outside almost every village, is sacred to this god ; the superstition has for ages held, and still holds, its ground against all Brahmanical innovations. The stones remind the traveller of the Druid circles of the northern nations. Sir B. FRERE.*

Y

Yaja—A brahman of distinguished attainments to whom king Drupada was referred when he was seeking to obtain a son. The king promised Yája ten million of kine ; and with much reluctance Yája undertook to direct a sacrificial ceremony by which the king should obtain offspring and called his younger brother to his assistance. When the rite had reached the proper period, the queen was invited to partake of it, but she had not completed her toilet and begged the brahmans to delay the ceremony. It was too late, and the sacrifice proceeding without her, the children were born independent of her participation.—WILSON, III, 326.

Yajur Veda—" The history of the Yajur Veda differs in so far from that of the other Vedas, as it is marked by a dissension between its own schools, far more important than the differences which separated the schools of each other Veda. It is known by the distinction between a Yajur Veda, called the *Black-*, and another, called the *White-Yajur Veda.* Tradition, especially that of the Puránas, records a legend to account for it. Vaiṣampáyana, it says, the disciple of Vyàsa, who had received from him the Yajur Veda, once having committed an offence, desired his disciples to assist him in the performing of some expiatory act. One of these, however, *Yájnavalkya*, proposed that he should alone perform the whole rite ; upon which, Vaiṣampáyana, enraged at what he considered to be the arrogance of Yájnavalkya, uttered a curse on him, the effect of which was, that Yájnavalkya disgorged all the Yajus texts he had learned from Vaiṣampáyana. The other

* Introduction to Old Deccan Days.

disciples, having meanwhile been transformed into partridges (tittiri), picked up these tainted texts, and retained them. Hence these texts are called *Taittiríyas*. But Yájnavalkya, desirous of obtaining other Yajus texts, devoutly prayed to the Sun, and had granted to him his wish—' to possess such texts as were not known to his teacher.' And because the Sun on that occasion appeared to Yájnavalkya in the shape of a horse (*vája*), those who studied these texts were called *Vájins*. That part of this legend was invented merely to account for the name of the *Taittiríyas*, after whom a Sanhitá and Bráhmaṇa of the Black Yajur Veda, and for that of the *Vájasaneyins*, after whom the Sanhitá of the White Yajur Veda is named, is clear enough. Nor is greater faith to be placed on it when it implies that the origin of this dissension ascended to the very oldest period of the Yajur Veda ; for there is strong reason to assume that the division took place even after the time of the grammarian Páṇiní, (q. v.). But so much in it is consistent with truth—that the Black Yajur Veda is the older of the two ; that the White Yajur Veda contains texts which are not in the Black ; and that, compared to the motley character of the former, it looks ' white,' or orderly. This motley character of the Black Yajur Veda, however, arises from the circumstance, that the distinction between a Mantra and Bráhmaṇa portion, is not so clearly established in it as the other Vedas ; hymns and matter properly belonging to the Bráhmaṇas there being intermixed. This defect is remedied in the White Yajur Veda ; and it points, therefore, to a period when the material of the old Yajus was brought into a system consonant with prevalent theories, literary and ritual.

The contents of both divisions of the Yajur Veda are similar in many respects. Two of the principal sacrifices of which they treat are the Darṣapúrṇamása, or the sacrifice to be performed at new and full moon, and the Aṣwamedha, or the horse-sacrifice, at the performance of which 609 animals of various descriptions, domestic and wild, were tied to 21 sacrificial posts. A *Purusha-medha*, or man-sacrifice, unknown to the other Vedas, is also mentioned in it ; its character, however, is symbolical.

The text of the Black Yajur Veda is extant in the recension of two schools—that of *Apastamba,* to which the *Taittiríya Sanhitá* belongs, and that of *Charaka.* The former, which is in course of publication—the first volume and part of the second having been already published, with the commentary of Mádhaváchárya (Sáyaṇa), by Dr. E. Roer and E. B. Cowell in the *Bibliotheca Indica* (Calcutta, 1860—1864)—consists of seven Káṇḍa, or books, which comprise 44 Prapáṭhaka, or chapters sub-divided into 651 Anuváka, or sections, and containing 2,198 Káṇḍikás, or portions.

The *Vájasaneyi-Sanhitá,* or the Sanhitá of the White Yajur Veda, exists in the recension of the *Mádhyandina* and Káṇva school. In the former—the text of which, apparently also with the commentary of *Mahídkara,* has been edited by Professor A. Weber (Berlin, 1852)—this Sanhitá has 40 *Adhyáyas,* or books, sub-divided into 303 *Anuvákas,* with 1,975 Káṇḍikás.

The principal Bráhmaṇa of the Black Yajur Veda is the *Taittiríya*-Bráhmaṇa, which, with the commentary of (Mádhava) Sáyaṇa, is in the course of publication by Baboo Rajendralála Mitra—the first volume and part of the second having already appeared in print (Calcutta, 1860—1865) in the *Bibliotheca Indica.* That of the White Yajur Veda is the Śatapatha-Bráhmaṇa, the most complete and systematic of all Bráhmaṇas. Its text, with a semblance of the commentary of Sáyaṇa, has been edited by Professor A. Weber (Berlin, 1855).—*Chambers' Encyclopædia, Vol. IX, p.* 727.

FINIS.